Also by Tom Peters

In Search of Excellence
(with Robert H. Waterman, Jr.)

A Passion for Excellence
(with Nancy Austin)

Thriving on Chaos

LIBERATION MANAGEMENT

Necessary Disorganization
for the Nanosecond Nineties

LIBERATION MANAGEMENT

Necessary Disorganization
for the Nanosecond Nineties

Tom Peters

Alfred A. Knopf
New York
1992

THIS IS A BORZOI BOOK
PUBLISHED BY ALFRED A. KNOPF, INC.

Copyright © 1992 by Excel/, A California Limited Partnership

All rights reserved under International and Pan-American Copyright Conventions. Published in the United States by Alfred A. Knopf, Inc., New York, and simultaneously in Canada by Random House of Canada Limited, Toronto. Distributed by Random House, Inc., New York.

Owing to limitations of space, all acknowledgments of permission to reprint previously published material will be found following the index.

Library of Congress Cataloging-in-Publication Data

Peters, Thomas J.
    Liberation management: necessary disorganization for the
nanosecond nineties / Tom Peters. — 1st ed.
      p. cm.
    Includes index.
    ISBN 0-394-55999-1
    1. Organizational change. 2. Organizational effectiveness.
3. Work groups. 4. Information technology. I. Title.
    HD58.8.P478   1992
    658.4′063—dc20   90-53071
                                     CIP

Manufactured in the United States of America

First Edition

For:

Percy Barnevik, who abhors bureaucracy

F. A. Hayek, who loved markets

Warden Dennis Luther, who respects prisoners

Hans Beck, who knows quality when he sees it

Tom Strange and Joe Tilli, Teamsters who've become world-beating
  salesmen

Anita Roddick, who believes joy has a place in business

Mike Walsh, who has a lot of nerve

Ted Turner, who's nuts

With the advent of fast personal computers, digital television and high bandwidth cable and radio-frequency networks, so-called post-industrial societies stand ready for a yet deeper voyage into the "permanently ephemeral."

MICHAEL BENEDIKT
Cyberspace: First Steps

Recently I was talking to one of Japan's best foreign-exchange dealers, and I asked him to name the factors he considered in buying and selling. He said, "Many factors, sometimes very short-term, and some medium, and some long-term." I became very interested when he said he considered the long term and asked him what he meant by that time frame. He paused a few seconds and replied with genuine seriousness. "Probably ten minutes." That is the way the market is moving these days.

TOYOO GYOHTEN
Former vice-minister
Japanese Ministry of Finance
Changing Fortunes (with Paul Volcker)

The Fortune 500 is over.

PETER DRUCKER
Fortune 500 issue
Fortune, April 20, 1992

Contents

VI FASHION!   631

Preface

Liberation Management appears ten years, almost to the day, after the publication of *In Search of Excellence*. Many readers of that book claimed it vindicated American management practice (at a time when Japanese approaches were the rage). I think that's wrong. *Search* was an out-and-out attack on the excesses of the "rational model" and the "business strategy paradigm" that had come to dominate Western management thinking. What it counseled instead was a return to first principles: attention to customers ("close to the customer"), an abiding concern for people ("productivity through people"), and the celebration of trial and error ("a bias for action").

But whether or not Bob Waterman and I were on management's case or on its side, there are more important fish to fry. To wit, an enormous error that resided between the lines: While *Search* condemned the excesses of dispassionate "modern management practice," it nonetheless celebrated big manufacturing businesses. With the exaltation of IBM and more than one nod to GM, we implicitly endorsed the humongous American technocratic enterprise in general—the institutions that economist John Kenneth Galbraith and business historian Alfred Chandler had not so long before declared almost perfect instruments for achieving America's economic manifest destiny. Make no mistake, Bob Waterman and I, who came of age in the '50s and '60s, were Galbraith and Chandler's offspring!

Five years later I declared that "there are no excellent companies" (*Thriving on Chaos*, first page of text), and suggested—as others had pointedly suggested to me—that time, and quite a short time at that, had not treated some of *Search*'s almost perfect instruments very well. So in 1987, chastened, I proposed *flexibility* as the watchword for the '90s.

I'll give myself a nanosecond pat on the back. It was a start. But the road left untraveled was much longer and more serpentine than I had imagined. Though the word "revolution" *(Handbook for a Management Revolution)* appeared in the subtitle of *Thriving on Chaos*, in retrospect I don't think it was a revolutionary book. (Many readers did. Everything, of course, must be seen in context: The modest close-to-the-customer plea of *In Search of Excellence* was perceived as "revolutionary" in 1982.) I hope *Liberation Management* is revolutionary.

The new definition of revolution? In the introductory section of this book, titled "Necessary Disorganization," we'll meet Percy Barnevik, who, upon merging Asea (Sweden) with Brown Boveri (Switzerland) to create ABB Asea Brown Boveri, quickly cut the latter's corporate staff from 4,000 to 200 (he'd done the same thing at Asea a few years earlier). Could 38 of every 40 "staffers" really have been excess baggage? Yup!

"Organization structure" comes first in this book, customers last. And that *is* quite a switch from *In Search of Excellence, A Passion for Excellence,* and *Thriving on Chaos* ("structure" issues accounted for about 2 percent of those books, but take up over 50 percent of this one). Does that mean customers have slipped off my radar screen?

Hardly. The close-to-the-customer message was right-on as far as it went. Still, I need to offer a mea culpa: If you've done all the close-to-the-customer things that I begged you to do in my first three books ("to-do" lists that, combined, contain hundreds of items), I'm not sure you'll be any "closer" five years from now than you are today. Not, that is, unless, like Barnevik, you have also demolished the corporate superstructure. Not unless, like former Union Pacific Railroad chief Mike Walsh (Chapter 7), you've torn a 30,000-person organization apart—*fast* (Walsh did it in about 100 days). The fact is, that earlier message was the cart put miles before the horse—the horse being the enormous structural impedance that made a mockery of the most profound close-to-the-customer "culture change" efforts undertaken by nine out of ten progressive companies in the 1980s. So, do what these bold souls have done first—and then get on with all that "close-to-the-customer stuff."

Get on with it, yes . . . and no. Because there's a sense in which, now, I would counsel *not* listening to customers at times, and therein lies the *real* revolution. This book is animated by a single word: fashion. Life cycles of computers and microprocessors have shrunk from years to months. Some 300 new grocery and drugstore products grace the shelves of American retailers each *week*. Even the materials and chemicals and pharmaceutical industries have gone high-fashion—with a rash of "products" spewing forth, each aimed at customers' ever-shifting, ever narrower-gauge needs.

All this means that we must engage far more intimately with customers (and large numbers of other temporary "network" partners) than I had imagined 10 years ago—"symbiosis" is the preferred word, a word you'll see again and again in these pages. That's one form of more than "close to" the customer. But to stand out from the crowd also calls for communing with your own muse and that of quirky partners from around the globe to create startling products and services which respond to needs customers hadn't dreamed they had (and which are completely impermeable to even the cleverest "market research").

The idea of fashion, as we'll soon see, unnerves traditional managers. It demands liberation, everyone exhibiting flair and bravura, pursuing breathtaking failure as assiduously as success. We're *all* in Milan's haute couture business and Hollywood's movie business (thus organizations such as CNN are prominently featured in this book, intended as exemplars for the likes of Du Pont or GM).

Fashion also connotes liberation in another sense. To offer a barrage of customized solutions to fleeting customer problems requires quick-change artistry within our product lines, and calls forth the pirate and the gambler in us all. It cries out for the wholesale exercise of the human imagination. In short, as the service sector grows and the service component of manufacturing comes to dominate, every one of us is in the "brainware business."

Among others, *Liberation Management* is dedicated to Tom Strange and Joe Tilli. They are a pair of "line workers" in heavy manufacturing, and Teamsters to boot. But they are something else. Their employer, the high-tech hose maker Titeflex (Chapter 5), has cut order-cycle time from about 10 weeks to a couple of days by busting a 500-person business into a half-dozen-or-so 80-person bits and, like ABB, decimating the central staff ranks. The ultimate expression of the new Titeflex is its Rapid Deployment Team—that is, Strange and Tilli. They can turn out a crash job for, say, Boeing or GE, from customer query to loading dock, in three to four hours. Tom and Joe may hoist a hose or two along the way, but the truth is that they're adding value through "brainware." As I see it, they're not much—any?—different from the McKinsey & Co. consulting teams I was part of 15 years ago. They're not really two "pairs of hands"; they are, instead, a full-blown professional service delivery team!

Strange and Tilli are, in a way, our new paradigm, model, metaphor (lots more on metaphors to come—carnivals, spiderwebs, etc.). They are liberated as hell *(Liberation Management)* by old standards, including those of *Thriving on Chaos,* and also part of a company that by yesterday's lights is highly *disorganized (Necessary Disorganization for the Nanosecond Nineties).* They are brainworkers as much as Microsoft's programmers, and as independent and wholly responsible/accountable as EDS's 5,000 or so teams of 10 in the information-systems business (Chapter 2).

Brain-based companies have an ethereal character compared to yesterday's (1982's!) outfits, and that's putting it mildly. Time clocks certainly have no place. And headquarters intrusions had best be rare. Strange and Tilli—like their counterparts at Microsoft, EDS, CNN, and my teammates in developing this book at Knopf/Random House—will go where they have to go to add value and do what they have to do to get the job done quickly. Barking orders is out. Curiosity, initiative, and the exercise of imagination are in.

For a quarter of a century I've hung my professional hat in Silicon Valley. It's arguably the most fertile 1,300 square miles in the world economy. It is also a carnival. I've had all of my assumptions about "organization" ripped asunder as I've watched the Valley thrive. It has elbowed its way into the planet's consciousness, largely courtesy of failure after failure after failure (and, along the way, many more than its fair share of successes—mostly by-products of the most exciting failures). It's instructive to think about how Silicon Valley pulled off its coup: It provides many people with a heavy dose of liberation, and, god knows, it's disorganized. By living in its midst, I've been forced to acknowledge that it's time to shed—make that shred—the old images. When I worked on *In Search of Excellence,* from 1978 to 1982, my eyes still mostly turned eastward (Detroit, etc.), toward yesterday's big manufacturers. Now my gaze has shifted, and that shift has allowed me to look at CNN, at Britain's crazy "imagineers" (of the "marketing"—you'll see why it's in quotes soon enough—firm Imagination), and at a whole series of wild and woolly endeavors that are now creating most of the economic value in developed economies.

Writing this book has been agony. I've finally shaken off the vestiges of 30 years of traditional thinking. And it has been ecstasy. I've allowed myself the unalloyed pleasure of enjoying the mess of market economies, powered by lunatics and dreamers, by failure far more than success. If this book lives up to its title, and is as liberating for you to read as it was for me to write, then I shall feel my labors to have been more than worthwhile.

Welcome aboard. I pray we have a bumpy ride in the pages ahead.

TOM PETERS
Palo Alto, California
October 1992

I

Necessary
Disorganization:
The New Exemplars

1

Toward Fashion, Fickle, Ephemeral

First came Nike's Air Shoe. Then came Reebok's Pump. And now there's Puma's Disc System Sneaker. Forget about shoelaces and a tongue. The Disc System instead features a "closure unit" that is turned like the dial on a ski boot, an "anatomically pre-molded compression unit" that replaces the tongue, and "lateral stabilizing elements" that tighten the sides for a better fit. All for just $125 a pair.

> JOSEPH PEREIRA
> *The Wall Street Journal*
> October 31, 1991

You in the West think of [consumer electronics] products as consumer *durables*, things which last. For you consumption is an act which you undertake in bursts, periodically. Japanese consumption is a continuous cycle of new products replacing old products, everything is in a process of change, nothing endures. We do not seek permanence.

> MASATOSHI NAITO
> Chief of Design, Matsushita
> *Financial Times*
> September 3, 1991

We are trying to sell more and more intellect and less and less materials.

GEORGE HEGG
Vice President for Strategic Planning, 3M
The Economist, November 30, 1991

Microsoft's only factory asset is the human imagination.

FRED MOODY
The New York Times Magazine,
August 25, 1991,
profiling Microsoft founder Bill Gates

In the mid-1980s, Sony chairman Akio Morita rounded on Americans at every opportunity, accusing us of neglecting manufacturing, hollowing our corporations. He had a point. But perhaps the message of this book is best symbolized by the *new* Mr. Morita. In March 1991, Sony, manufacturers of electronic hardware par excellence, signed a deal that could pay out a billion dollars—to American rock star Michael Jackson. Talk about going soft! (This, of course, was hardly Sony's first soft step. In 1988, it spent $2 billion on CBS Records. In 1989, it shelled out $3.4 billion for Columbia Pictures. Sony's extravagance was soon topped by that of another Japanese hardware company gone soft, Matsushita, which in late 1990 spent almost $7 billion acquiring MCA/Universal. As McKinsey & Co.'s Bill Pade said, commenting on that merger, "There's a lot more money to be made in a large-scale software business than in their traditional hardware businesses.")

YO, FASHION!

The headline read, "Calvin Klein to Start Announcing Its Fall Line." No surprise there—except I made it up. The headline, in the September 3, 1991, *Wall Street Journal, did* read: "IBM to Start Announcing Its Fall Line." Fashion. What else can you call it?

● New food products, *The New York Times* reported in September 1991, are being described as "software for the microwave."

● Over the past 10 years, economist Taichi Sakaiya reported in *The Knowledge-Value Revolution* in 1991, "the number of types of containers in which beer is sold [in Japan] has shot up from eight to over 130."

- Go to the local pharmacist's—and you may find all *41* varieties of Tylenol! An article in the October 1, 1991, *San Jose Mercury News* is titled "Designer Mice"; it reports on, among other things, the development of new, "specialized" breeds of mice for use in drug research, and in general describes the increased fashionization, customization, and specificity of the process of searching for and developing drugs to treat more and more precisely defined conditions. Welcome to the biotechnology revolution.

- "Even" materials are being reinvented. Consider this account from *Time* (November 26, 1990) of a "new class of souped-up substances called advanced materials. These novel building blocks are basically futuristic versions of present-day metals, glasses, plastics, and ceramics. But unlike conventional counterparts, the materials are made with extra ingredients that greatly enhance their performance or give them new features. By blending in stiff carbon fibers, for example, modern-day alchemists have developed plastics that are up to 10 times as strong as conventional plastics. And by mixing copper with zinc and aluminum, scientists have produced a metal with a 'memory': the stuff returns to its original shape after being bent or twisted. The materials are usually designed on computers, which can analyze exactly how the molecules of different substances will fit together. As a result complex compounds can be made to order for specific tasks. . . . Such potential has made the materials business one of the most hotly contested high-tech fields."

- In the March 1992 issue of *Mobile Office*—a lengthy monthly magazine designed for today's on-the-go executive or professional—page 19 featured a rather sexist ad. About 90 percent of the page was covered with a photo, from shoulder to thigh, of a very slim, curvaceous woman in a bright magenta swim suit. The tag line on the ad: "To Get a Body This Slim, Call Audiovox." It was an advertisement for a *very* slim (and *very* curvaceous) cellular phone.

- Grid Systems, which brought highly portable computers to the front lines of the Gulf War, "rolled out its first 'wearable' pen-based computer, called the PalmPad," *The Wall Street Journal* reported on March 20, 1992. It includes a "wrist strip allowing a user to carry the computer on his arm," and "was introduced at a 'fashion show' in New York." Yikes! Innovation expert Michael Schrage put it this way in a 1991 newspaper column: "Beyond a certain point, personal media such as telephones, computers and planners aren't just functional objects anymore—they're fashionable accessories."

THE SHIFT TO SOFT

When the government looks at Basler Electric Co., it sees a maker of voltage regulators and transformers. But when Basler vice president Herb Roach looks around the main plant in Highland, Illinois, he sees bins of components anyone can buy—and dozens of computer and electrical engineers who add unique value to resistors and semiconductors. The company "is more and more moving into a software role," Roach says.

Newsweek
June 8, 1992

In sum, the definition of every product and service is changing. Going soft, softer, softest. Going fickle, ephemeral, fashion. An explosion of new competitors, a rising standard of living in the developed world, and the ever-present (but still in early adolescence) new technologies are leading the way.

No corner of the world is exempt from the frenzy. My local paper featured this headline: "Only the Food Tells You It's a Supermarket." The story of Draeger's, a Menlo Park, California, grocery store, followed. After a $10-million renovation, the "store" is now a cross between Disneyland and Tiffany's—and the food for sale is almost incidental to the "event" of "Draegering." And, ho hum, 10 days later, the same paper featured a story on local bookstores titled "Bookstores Turn Over a New Leaf," about the value-adding "services"—readings by renowned authors, coffee bars, art exhibits—the stores must offer to compete. Uh, what about the books?

Top this: California's raisin crop is touted by a promotional group called the California Raisins. In 1989, the Raisins garnered more revenue from personal appearances and license fees for T-shirts and other accessories than the raisin farmers did from selling their "hard" product—raisins, that is. (Well, of course you can top it. On Sunday, October 6, 1991, Liz Taylor got married for the eighth time. It was said that anyone who could get in under the tent—literally—and get a photo of the ceremony might be able to earn a million dollars for his or her trouble. In the bizarrely competitive world of the tabloids, the *Globe* went further than most. "At our command post overlooking the historic Foxen Vineyard, *Globe* will have two helicopters, a refueling truck and ground crew, a motor home for on-site photo processing, cellular phones, and walkie-talkies and a hospitality tent," said Mary Ann Norbom, the rag's Los Angeles bureau chief.)

The shift attacks you. You can't hide. While preparing for a lengthy seminar, I happened across three stories in two different magazines that arrived in my mailbox the same day. From *The Economist* of September 14, 1991: "Coca-Cola has stumbled while Pepsi . . . has stolen the limelight. Now Coke is banking on a Hollywood talent agency to help it regain center stage. . . . Creative Artists Agency, which represents many of the world's biggest film stars, will serve as global media advisor to Coca-Cola." From *Time*, September 23, 1991: "Jeans genius [Calvin] Klein pumps lots of cash and controversy—but not many jeans—into a [116-page] magazine supplement." And *Time* again: September 23, 1991: "California Dreamin' . . . Ideas for the world's autos now come from design studios clustered around (where else?) trend-setting L.A."

So Coca-Cola has decided that the multibillion-dollar battle for share of consumer minds hinges on signing up more movie stars faster. Calvin Klein shells out megabucks to provide 116 pages of sexy pictures, few of which even bother to feature jeans. And the battle for dominance in the still huge auto market now mostly takes place in design studios nestled in the hills above Santa Monica, California. California Dreamin' brought us the Lexus and Infiniti, among other gems. (Ironically—and depressingly—Japanese auto firms started doing serious design work in L.A. before Detroit did.)

And lest you think I've succumbed to California Dreamin' myself—consider the lead article in the July–August 1991 issue of the *Harvard Business Review*. "The Computerless Computer Company," by computer industry guru Andy Rappaport and his colleague Shmuel Halevi, heralds the dominance of fickle, ephemeral software over solid hardware. "By the year 2000," the authors write, "the most successful computer companies will be those that buy computers rather than build them. The leaders will leverage fabulously cheap and powerful hardware to create and deliver new applications, pioneer and control new computing paradigms, and assemble distribution and integration expertise that creates enduring influence with customers. . . . The strategic goal of U.S. companies should not be to build computers. It should be to create persistent value in computing"—which, the authors make clear, comes from software.

"Soft" is what makes the new fashion world go round. It includes the tools for creating the "fashionable" end product itself (computer-aided design, computer-aided manufacturing, computer-aided engineering, computer-aided software engineering, computer-integrated manufacturing, and so forth); it includes the instantaneous linkages between producers and suppliers and distributors, called electronic data interchange (EDI), which compresses, dramatically, the time required to do everything—and makes fashion possible. It is the intelligence "embedded" in products—or, rather, embedded in the microprocessors that are in almost everything these days, from the toilet to the shopping cart to the oven to the house. "Soft" is the emphasis on industrial design and user-friendliness, and the new methods of target marketing by means of relational databases abetted by expert systems (which allow Nintendo, for instance, to directly track millions upon millions of customers and cater to their individual needs), and it is the "entertainizing" of everything—those California Raisins, your local grocery store as the palace at Versailles. Sure, there will still be a "hard" product. But as Taichi Sakaiya puts it, "The significance of material goods [will be] as containers or vehicles for knowledge-value."

Grasping all this is damned tough—soul-wrenching—for traditional managers. And I put myself in that league. I was trained as a civil engineer. I cotton to bridges, dams, and other *very* lumpy objects. I went on to business training—where the hard, cold numbers, Joe Friday's "just the facts, ma'am" attitude, prevailed. But now we live in an environment where it is barely a stretch to say, as one executive summed it up, "If you can touch it, it's not real."

To drive the point home: The fabled Dow Jones average is based on the performance of 30 bellwether stocks, taken to represent the economy as a whole. In May 1991, USX (U.S. Steel, until it decided to "soften" its image), on the list since day one, dropped out. So did Primerica (the softened name for American Can), also on the list since the start. Guess what firms replaced those two? Disney and J. P. Morgan. Get the drift?

A commercial world where everything has "gone soft," "gone fickle," "gone fashion"—a world where Disney and J. P. Morgan (entertainment and financial services) have replaced USX and Primerica (steel and cans) on Dow Jones's list—is to most of us a world gone bonkers. How do you deal with a bonkers world other than with bonkers organizations, peopled with bonkers folk? My answer, in short: You can't!

BONKERS ORGANIZATIONS

Competition is now a "war of movement" in which success depends on anticipation of market trends and quick response to changing customer needs. Successful competitors move quickly in and out of products, markets, and sometimes even entire businesses—a process more akin to an interactive video game than to chess. In such an environment, the essence of strategy is *not* the structure of a company's products and markets, but the dynamics of its behavior.

GEORGE STALK, PHILIP EVANS, and
LAWRENCE E. SHULMAN
"Competing on Capabilities:
The New Rules of Corporate Strategy"
Harvard Business Review, March–April 1992

People think the president has to be the main organizer. No, the president is the main *dis*-organizer. Everybody "manages" quite well; whenever anything goes wrong, they take immedi-

ate action to make sure nothing'll go wrong again. The problem is, nothing new will ever happen, either.

HARRY QUADRACCI
CEO, Quad/Graphics

Employees who try to keep a tight hold on their job miss the
point and fail to comprehend the reason why they were hired
in the first place: to contribute to the molecular activity at the
magazine and add a new layer of complexity to the ongoing
drama.

VÉRONIQUE VIENNE, on the corporate
culture of Condé Nast
"Make It Right . . . Then Toss It Away"
Columbia Journalism Review,
July–August 1991

Later in this section, we'll examine $28.9 billion (1991 revenue),
Zurich-based ABB Asea Brown Boveri. No other huge manufacturing firm has
been so bold in owning up to tomorrow's challenges. One indication: Almost
overnight the enterprise cut corporate staffing by 95 percent—it now manages
with a 150-person contingent (squished into a nondescript building across
from a train station in west Zurich). Britain's successful BTR oversees a
$12-billion operation made up of 500 profit centers (from BAE, a baggage-
handling equipment company, to Pretty Polly, in hosiery) with a spartan
headquarters staff of 47. Chairman Richard Branson runs billion-dollar-plus
Virgin Group (entertainment, real estate, an airline) with no headquarters and
a "central staff," if you stretch the definition of staff, numbering five. From the
likes of these examples, I've developed what I call "the rule of five": no more
than five central staffers per billion dollars in revenue booked! Funny thing,
I'm serious. Only a fickle, decentralized operation will survive in a fickle,
decentralized global economy. One essential element of decentralization is the
demise of central staffs. In fact, it's arrogant to suggest that you can "manage"
at all from the center in a fickle economy. The best you can do is unleash the
power of subordinate units with distinct personalities of their own, induce
subordinate units to keep spinning out new units—and then pray that the law
of large numbers will "guide" you into the way of new market opportunities.

Magic Numbers

To deal with a fashionized environment—even in the heaviest industries imaginable—ABB has "de-organized" 215,000 people into 5,000 largely independent profit centers that average only 50 people each. In fact, small-scale,

independent units—even "units" of one—will play the lead role in responding to a fickle marketplace. Thence what I call the "new numerology." Here, for example, are some of the key "numbers" that will emerge from more than 50 case studies in this book.

One. I call this "everyone-a-businessperson," the "entrepreneur-on-the-huge-firm-payroll," the "informated" individual ("informated" courtesy of Harvard professor Shoshana Zuboff's *In the Age of the Smart Machine*). The new-look employee is empowered—a topic I and others have discussed ad nauseam—and also has access, via information technology among other things, to *all* the firm's information. Today's Union Pacific Railroad conductor (case to come), with a computer terminal in his caboose, can independently deliver the full power of the railroad to any customer transaction.

Two to Four. I call these "micro-enterprises." There's no better example than the "care pairs" at Florida's Lakeland Regional Medical Center. A nurse and a lab technician, thoroughly cross-trained, can perform for a patient about 80 percent of all necessary services (services which used to require several dozen people). In addition, thanks to a computer terminal in the patient's room, the same "care pair" can coordinate, schedule, and manage the remaining patient activities. The surprisingly versatile duo amounts to a "microhospital" within an 897-bed monster operation.

Seven to Ten. Hail the self-contained work group! Johnsonville Foods' sausage-making teams do *everything*—hiring and firing, performance evaluation, accounting, engineering, capital budget proposals, even strategy analysis. The key new word is "self-contained": We're talking about moving far beyond the grouping of seven people doing roughly the same thing, called a "self-managing team" (and still an idea whose time has not yet come to many firms).

Three to Twelve. This is the all-important "project team." Fundamental to at least beginning to understand how to cope with a fickle/ephemeral environment has been our extensive analysis of largely unstudied professional service firms—starting with 72,000-person EDS (later in this section). Almost all of tomorrow's work will be done in project configurations. Functional staffs will all but disappear, and maybe not "all but." The professional service firm is the best possible model for future survival.

Twelve to Twenty. I call this the "mini-enterprise." In the "Learning to Hustle" section of this book, we'll examine the Business Development Teams at high-tech hose maker Titeflex. Titeflex's BDTs are de facto small businesses that can take orders from inception to delivery in no time flat.

Forty to Two Hundred. Remember that sea of 50-person "organizations"—the independent profit centers—at giant ABB? I believe there's something special—for today's fickle world—about the number 50 (more or less). We'll examine a half-dozen examples from a variety of industries. In each case, the modest-size grouping turns out to be amazingly effective (both efficient and flexible), and capable of competing with anyone.

The emphasis on small, self-contained elements, even, at times, in big collections (e.g., EDS, ABB), is the essence of necessary disorganization. Constructing and then perpetually reconstructing networks of such self-contained elements / units / "businesses" ("interactive video," per the epigraph from Stalk et al.) is the *only* plausible response to today's cockamamie marketplace.

Professional Service Firms as Model "Organizations"

Though I'd worked at the big consulting company McKinsey, revelation came while doing research at CNN, then reviewing research that colleagues had done at Denmark's Oticon (the world's market share leader in hearing aids—see Chapter 13): *All firms are becoming professional service firms.*

I try to remind myself not to use the word *organization* without quotes around it—i.e., "organization." For the brainware / software / professional service firm is not an organization as you and I and our grandfathers have known it. Tomorrow' s effective "organization" will be conjured up anew each day. At Oticon, for example, after a quick scan of the on-line project listings, employees decide what to work on, whom to work with, and what desk to take their personal cart to for the day! At CNN, a 30-minute, 8:00 a.m., 9-bureau, on-line "meeting" invents the network for the coming day—until everything changes, which it usually does in short order. Such odd procedures will become / are becoming as commonplace in "hardware" companies as in "software" firms; Oticon, after all, makes hearing aids.

The starting point for most books like this (including mine in the past) is examining the exciting, important—*very* exciting, *very* important—transformation of a factory, then exclaiming at how interesting it all is. Well, it *is* interesting. But not interesting *enough* for the newly fashionized, fickle world. The wonderful news: Professional service firms have long been organized in a different manner, to deal with their historically more fickle environment of shifting, temporary assignments.

Typically we thought of these "service" firms as on the periphery, or worse—as parasites living off the "real" producers (of steel, cars, etc.). No more. Such firms are pure "knowledge plays," as an oil man might put it, and *all* economic organization is fast becoming "knowledge plays." Hey, it's not an issue of whether or not "manufacturing matters"—*manufacturing has itself become an almost pure knowledge play.* Today 75 to 95 percent of a typical manufacturer's payroll is "service sector" / knowledge employees—information systems experts, designers, engineers, accountants, marketers, trainers. Brainware / knowledgeware / software / "informated individuals" / "scattered brains" (Charles Handy, see below) are the awkward terms that best describe the successful manufacturing firm as well as such "softies" as EDS, CNN, Chiat / Day / Mojo (the ad agency), Random House, The Gap—or Microsoft, which in mid-1992 had a total market value exceeding that of General Motors. Even the few nominally left in the factory spend most of their days staring at computer terminals, keeping statistical track of progress, working on project teams developing new products or improving old ones, and can be found routinely visiting customers, distributors, and vendors.

When Imagination Fails

Review the epigraph on p. 4 about Microsoft: "[Its] only factory asset is the human imagination." Fine. But how do you *manage*, if that's the right word (and it's not), "human imagination"? Answer: Ask CNN and Walt Disney, not GM or Ford, or IBM.

The consequences of getting it wrong are enormous. The all-purpose global ad agency Saatchi and Saatchi went on a buying binge in the late 1980s. A lot of the organizations it purchased went very sour. Commenting on one of the failures, a financial analyst told Britain's *Management Week*, "The Saatchis bought crap which doesn't really exist today. They spent $500 million on nothing."

That's undoubtedly an exaggeration. But not, perhaps, by much. In the "soft" world, where the human imagination is all (and 90 percent of stock market value), even a huge corporation (with a billion-dollar price tag) can literally turn to "nothing" almost overnight. How much would Microsoft be worth if something happened to founder Bill Gates? Several *billion* dollars less than yesterday.

Add It Up

"When a friend joined Digital [Equipment], he was told a good news-bad news story," Charles Savage reports in *Fifth Generation Management*. "The good news was that he had 120,000 people working for him. The bad news was that they did not know it. It was up to him to figure out how he could best network himself and build working alliances." This quotation captures, from the perspective of the employee in the company, the brave new world that's unfolding. Those who would survive, managers and nonmanagers alike, will simply "have to make their own firm," create their own projects.

Yes, you damned well better put organization—"organization," that is— in quotation marks. Most work will be done by project teams. The "average" team will consist of various people from various "organizations" with various skills. Networks of bits and pieces of companies will come together to exploit a market opportunity, perhaps stay together for a couple of years (though changing shape, dramatically, several times in the process), then dissolve never to exist again in the same form. That's tough to swallow, tougher to "manage." So what? What's the alternative in a fickle, fashionized world?

The Case for Structure

At a 1990 meeting with Motorola communication sector execs, I was asked, "What importance would you assign to structure, human resources, and top management decision making/strategy setting in the coming years?" Given the thrust of my prior books, I suspect my answer surprised the questioner. First, I named one additional category, "systems"—in particular, "horizontal systems" (call it multifunctional projectization, if you must), which will determine how most of *any* corporation's future business gets done. (Oops, there I go again! I said "corporation's business." Such language is dangerous and wrongheaded: Business, yes, but it'll get done by networks and alliances; corporation without quotation marks—it should be "corporation"—is as bad as naked organization.) Then I assigned some numbers: 55 percent for structure, 30 percent for systems, 15 percent for people (I despise the term "human resources," because I don't see myself as one—and prefer the simpler "people"), and nought for top management decision making and strategy setting.

That's right: I don't believe top management should be in the business of strategy setting at all, except as creators of a general business mission. Strategies must be set from below. (No, not "from" below. Set "in" below—i.e., by the autonomous business units, for the autonomous business units. And "below" is all wrong, too . . . damnable words!)

For those of you who've read my previous books, there's another surprise in my response to the Motorola executive: I only assigned 15 percent to people. Have I changed my view about them? In fact, no. People are everything, have no doubt—though many firms still don't act that way. But I've come to realize that, in this madcap world, turned-on and theoretically empowered people (not to mention genius management strategy makers, even if strategy making did make sense) will never amount to a hill of beans in the vertically oriented, staff-driven, thick-headquarters corporate structures that still do most of the world's business. Empower until you're blue in the face. Call in the best consultants and create the best strategies. It'll make no difference unless the arteries are unclogged (the "structure" part), then radically rewired (the "systems" part).

MARKETS, BY DAMN! (AND TRIES)

If you want a really dynamic, effective economy, the only damn thing you can do is pursue the market logic completely. Whole hog, not halfway.

MICHAEL MANLEY
Vice President of the Socialist
International and former prime
minister of Jamaica
New Perspectives Quarterly,
Summer 1992

Fashion demands bonkers organizations ("organizations"!). And it demands continuous innovation. Appropriately paced innovation, in turn, leads us toward one end: *blasting the violent winds of the marketplace into every nook and cranny in the firm.* (See the section Markets and Innovation—note that "Markets" comes first.) This is precisely what ABB is doing, via both its small, fleet-of-foot, close-to-the-market profit centers and its decimation of central staff operations (which ipso facto allows the profit centers great freedom).

Why markets? Because only markets, as I see it, can "deal with" a fickle environment. Summarizing 30 years in Hollywood, and describing the ability of studio chiefs to pick winning movies, screenwriter William Goldman commented: "Nobody knows anything!" Long before, Oliver Cromwell may have put it even better: "No one rises so high as he who knows not whither he is going." Why?

F. A. Hayek insisted that the global market—in times past, let alone tomorrow—is the most complicated phenomenon on earth, and therefore totally unpredictable. "Unintended consequences," he wrote in *The Fatal Conceit* (edited by W.W. Bartley III), "are paramount." (The fatal conceit is the presumption that one can move forward via central plans.)

The innovation issue is learning that in a fashionized world we *must* create organizations that attempt, at least, to survive by getting close to the market, putting zanies in charge, and staying small enough to shift focus fast. "Ignorance of the present, ignorance of the future—these are pardonable," the historian Arthur Schlesinger, Jr., wrote in *The New York Times* in late 1990. "But ignorance of how ignorant we are is unpardonable." CNN is a superb role model for Du Pont precisely because it's the rare firm that is aware of its ignorance, and is structured accordingly. CNN thrives on ignorance—a willingness to acknowledge its own. Its chief skill is doing things, fast; permitting the market to tell it whether or not it's on target; and killing off, fast, what the market rejects.

It adds up to "how to destroy your company before a competitor does," as one exec puts it. And he's right—a troubling, not to say terrifying, prospect for those of us who are comfortable with the old ways, and that's most of us. But in a bonkers world, there's no other choice than violent market-injection strategies; voluntary dismemberment (raiding yourself before the raider calls); perestroika inside the firm (most of us are Adam Smith's children until we get to the front door of our own business, when we become devoted advocates of centralized planning); inundation by "outsiders" of all sorts (almost all teams should include customers, distributors, and vendors, for instance); headquarters/staff destruction (corporate decapitation); "de-verticalization" (ending any semblance of vertical integration); subcontracting most anything and at least a substantial part of everything; and, as I said in the Preface, not listening to customers. (It's a complicated story, and we'll get to it. Listening to customers is all-important—but relying on intuition, taking a chance with new products that customers can't imagine, is also "all-important" in a fashionized world. What customer could have told you he cottoned to Disc System sneakers until they actually arrived?)

The root cause for pushing so hard at marketization: Only a passel of fully empowered, coherent, close-to-the-market units will try enough stuff to up the odds of overall success. "Anything worth doing is worth doing poorly!"—that's what Johnsonville Foods CEO Ralph Stayer (with a tip of the hat to G. K. Chesterton) says is his key to success. He reminds us that we'd not sign up for a cross-country flight on the Wright brothers' first plane. It was nothing to write home about. Neither was the first phone. But no Wright brothers, no Boeing 747s. No A. Bell, no extra-slim Audiovox cellular phone. Again, in a fashionized world, doing something, anything, getting it out there, trying it in the real world is the chief imperative. Examine the picture on the next page. It's the first Apple computer. Nothing to brag about, that's for sure. But without it, no $8-billion Apple Computer company. And Apple Computer's latter-day problems are largely due to the fact that lots of new people are building ugly—but *very* interesting—little boxes, and giving Apple fits.

Getting employees to think like "barbarians, not bureaucrats" is Borland Software chief Philippe Kahn's top job, he told *Upside* in September 1991. "I always tell our people to think small, think start-up, think how you'd do it if you were in a garage. Don't try to do it [like] a $300 million dollar software company [Borland in 1991] would do it." Kahn went on to offer Microsoft's Bill Gates some advice: "Split [the] company into two pieces. . . . Put them in two different locations." I don't know Microsoft's situation in detail, and Kahn's remarks are clearly self-serving. Nonetheless, I tend automatically to take his side. If I were IBM chairman John Akers, I know exactly what I'd do—split the company up into a half-dozen or more pieces, then sell over 50 percent of each to the public. Same thing if I were running General Motors. It's not that tiny is beautiful (after all, one-sixth of IBM would be over $10 billion); it's that inflexible is very, very ugly—and getting uglier with each passing day. Traditional scale economies? Mostly joke. We need to turn our full attention to scale *dis*-economies.

THE QUEST FOR METAPHORS I: CARNIVAL

Add up fickle and fashion, the need for bonkers "organizations," lots of tries and the matchless power of markets, and what do you have? Among other things, a clarion call for a new imagery.

In short, today's organizational images stink. Not just those that derive from the military ("Kick ass and take names") and "pyramids" (heavy, steep, immobile), but even the new "network," "spiderweb," "Calder mobile." These modern notions are a mighty step forward, but they still miss the core idea of tomorrow's surviving corporation: dynamism.

How about company-as-carnival? Consider these attributes of carnivals:

• Parts and wholes. "The State Fair's next week." "The circus is coming to town." An image forms of the day with the kids at the Big Apple Circus last

The first Apple computer. (Photo courtesy of Apple Computer, Inc.)

August, or of a trip to Disneyland. That overall image (the whole) is central to our "purchase decision," yet we largely experience parts—a ride, a concert, a horse show, the booth where you hurl baseballs at wooden milk bottles to win the tacky Kewpie doll.

● The booth. As carnival organizer, you must think booth. The booth is the pearl. Excellence is the booth. (Or not.) A booth requires a champion, an architect, a contractor—and all-important front-line people who staff it for low pay, or as volunteers. Just as one spunky flight attendant can change the entire character of a flight, an energetic person in the booth makes all the difference.

● The "underpark." Carnivals are about excitement and festivity. But we'll think twice about coming back if the portable toilets are dirty (or scarce), or if the parking is far away and overpriced. The "underpark" at Disney is the well-oiled, no-nonsense, unheralded, unseen mechanism that permits the surface frenzy to proceed without a glitch.

● Microeconomy. A carnival is the ultimate marketplace. Fickle/"cruel" customers make hundreds of choices each hour: to stop at this booth or event, to skip that one. Carnival chiefs track booth/event attendance as carefully as retailers now track the hour-to-hour sales of each item off the shelf. They engage in a constant process of creation and destruction: removing a booth or act that can't draw a crowd, refreshing an old favorite, pursuing exciting acts and new ideas.

• Same/different. The carnival boss, like the corporate boss, must address a prickly issue: Customers want "their" carnival the same, *and* they want it different. They want those clean toilets and their favorite rides/booths from last year. But they won't keep coming back unless they are regularly surprised by new offerings.

• A moving target. The excitement and frustration of creating/managing/maintaining a carnival is that it won't stay put. Carnivals have a completely different character from one day to the next. Or one hour to the next—due to weather, different crowds in the afternoon (mostly kids) and evening (mostly grown-ups), etc. Moreover, a carnival's personality changes when it moves from city to city and, of course, from year to year.

• Low overhead, multi-entrepreneurial. A bare-bones staff of four (a chief, an accountant, a computer ace, an administrative specialist), working out of a dingy, 200-square-foot, low-rent space, may oversee a traveling carnival with 100 booths, 30 rides, 20 special events (which change from town to town), and an annual attendance in the millions. The carnival is the ultimate in "networked" or subcontracted events: Tents, toilets, and acts/booths are the work of entrepreneurs. Yet it all must add up, quirky day after quirky day, to a coherent whole.

• The customer *creates* his or her own carnival (I call it "customerizing"—see Chapter 47). The carnival is a set of opportunities, a canvas on which the customer paints his or her own customized experience. If there are 5,000 customers tonight, they are painting 5,000 substantially different pictures.

• Dynamism. Say "carnival" and you think energy, surprise, buzz, fun. The mark of the carnival—and what makes it most different from a day at most offices—is its dynamism. Dynamism is its signature, the reason we go back. To create and maintain a carnival is never to get an inch away from dynamic imagery. As chief, you must feel the dynamics in your fingertips, be guided by them in *every* decision.

Economics is fun! Real economics, that is, not the standard classroom variety. Real economics is about entrepreneurs, births and deaths of products and companies, oddball reasons that a product/service takes off—now, ever, or never. The essence of real economics is dynamics, though we teach economics as a static discipline—hence, its "dismal science" moniker.

Today's global economic dance is no Strauss waltz. It's break dancing accompanied by street rap. The effective firm is much more like Carnival in Rio than a pyramid along the Nile. The practical point for the firm's leaders: Constantly using dynamic imagery, thinking of yourself as running a carnival, and stomping out all forms of static thinking and imagery will help point you toward the right structure and strategy for these woozy times.

TOWARD ZANY

When the sea was calm
  All ships alike
Showed mastership in floating.

WILLIAM SHAKESPEARE

German chemical and automobile companies for a long time thrived in a tidy, oligopolistic market context. So, too, American automakers. Maybe even American computer makers, as IBM allowed the "others" (the seven sorry sisters, or whatever) to fit comfortably under its umbrella—as long as they weren't too noisy. But the sea—it's *the* reason for this book—is decidedly uncalm now. Not many ships, especially big ones, are showing mastership in sailing anymore. Another way of putting it: Dull leaders for dull times. Zany leaders for zany times.

To wit: If you don't feel crazy, you're not in touch with the times! The point is vital. These are nutty times. Nutty organizations, nutty people, capable of dealing with the fast, fleeting, fickle, are a requisite for survival. A requisite for survival at EDS and CNN and Condé Nast Publications. A requisite for survival at GM, IBM, Du Pont, and Sears Roebuck. No one can escape the clutches of fashionization—of radically altered technologies, a completely turned-upside-down competitive context. And yet—and I realize I repeat, as I will again and again—most of our organizations and their leaders are far from zany.

I like the word "ephemeral" almost as much as "fashion" or "fickle." In fact, I'm fond of speaking of "the four ephemerals": ephemeral "organizations" . . . joined in ephemeral combinations . . . producing ephemeral products . . . for ephemeral markets . . . FAST.

The point is obvious. It's so obvious that it is going to take a ton of pages to come even close to perhaps convincing you, a little bit, of what I'm saying. If the marketplace has "turned ephemeral" on us—all of us—then we must turn ephemeral, too. "The chump-to-champ-to-chump cycle used to be three generations," the late MCI chairman Bill McGowan told me. "Now it's about five years." Oh, so true. Several "unassailable" superstars of *In Search of Excellence*—none comes to mind more poignantly than IBM—have been deconstructed by competitors. Numerous firms touted in this book will doubtless go kaplooie in a couple of years, 10 years maybe, who knows.

I will only guarantee that each one we examined is trying to do something interesting. And trying to do something interesting—pursuing the four ephemerals, if you will—is so much more important than sitting on your duff, experimenting a little here and a little there. Bold times call for bold leaders. Bold times call for bold experiments. The time for incrementalism has passed. ("The Fortune 500 is over"—Peter Drucker.) It's true, to be sure, that the march into the future will take place one step at a time. But those steps had better be in pursuit of a zany, bold—and yes ephemeral—future. Period.

No Port in *This* Storm

In a speech to a thousand or so people in Orange County, California, I talked about the need for dramatic change, the degree to which our sizable companies seem to have turned, almost overnight, into dinosaurs. A letter arrived at my Palo Alto office a couple of days later. One paragraph read: "Your description of a Dinosaur Company that resists change fits [my company] perfectly. Changing the corporation is probably next to impossible." The letter came from a vice president of a huge Japanese firm. I can't give you his name or his company's name. However, if you bring to mind the half-dozen household-word Japanese companies, I'm sure that this one will be on the list for most of you.

Learn from the best in Japan. In Germany. In Sweden. In Switzerland. In Korea. In Taiwan. In Brazil. In Britain. It would be stupid not to. But let's not allow the case for change to be clouded by any absurd notion that the Japanese, the Germans, the Americans, or anyone else have a patent on the future. No one does.

2

EDS, the World's Largest Project Organization in the World's Zaniest Industry: 72,000 Smart People in Bands of 10 Equals $7.1 Billion in Revenue

Electronic Data Systems, or EDS as it prefers, is, quite simply, 72,000 smart people who make, um . . . uh. They make . . . well. . . .

The company is a "systems integrator," at the heart of the information systems business—i.e., part of the biggest industry in the world (information, electronics, telecommunications, etc.). Once, EDS helped others perform mundane chores like automating payroll processing. Today the firm wants to be the prime mover in shaping its clients' strategies—creating information processing schemes which help define and exploit fast-changing markets. In 1991, the Dallas-based corporation tallied $548 million in profit on revenues of $7.1 billion; its 72,000 employees toiled in 28 countries for some 7,000 customers. In 1984, when the company became a wholly owned subsidiary of General Motors (while retaining almost total autonomy), revenues were $950 million, profits $71 million.

WHY EDS?

Why begin the "meat" of this book with EDS?

• EDS is in the knowledge extraction, integration, and application business—which is becoming the world's business. EDS is a pure "knowledge play." Moreover, its current work reflects the dramatic shift between the first and second eras of the computer revolution. The first was the "DP," or data processing, era. Old organization schemes remained intact ("vertical," functional structures), and "DP" amounted to automating mindless white-collar tasks *within* these functions—e.g., accounts receivable.

The task of the unfolding second era—systems integration, "solutions to enterprise needs" (EDS's term, see below), etc.—is to marry technology, new organization structures (mostly "horizontal"), and new strategies to create whole new ways of doing business (e.g., EDS's humongous "C4" project for GM, also outlined below). The second era is driven by the growing but still inchoate awareness that knowledge per se, appropriately integrated within and beyond the firm and rapidly applied, is the source of almost all economic value.

• EDS is beyond traditional hierarchy. The professional service firm is necessarily a wholly projectized operation. EDS is probably the world's biggest professional service firm, and also one of the best. (*All* professional service firms are pure knowledge plays—and their time has come, or at least the time for their form/structure has come.)

• But EDS is struggling like everyone else—albeit with the "right" issues. On the one hand, the traditional professional service firm "model" is better positioned to exploit tomorrow's flibbertigibbet economy than most. On the other hand, such firms typically do a rotten job of leveraging the enormous amount of knowledge they contain, gained as it is in dispersed, autonomous project activities. EDS (and a few enlightened others in professional services and beyond—see the analysis below of ABB Asea Brown Boveri) is struggling to learn how to learn—and help its clients do so at the same time. Recall the words of 3M's strategic planner, George Hegg: "We are trying to sell more and more intellect and less and less material"; no issue is more pressing for EDS, 3M, or business in general.

WHO IS EDS?

EDS makes nothing. It offers information systems consulting, information systems development, information systems integration, and even total information systems management for clients. Its growth mirrors the growth of applications and complexity in the world of information technology in general. For example, an average health-care claim—for an appendectomy, say—used to generate about 250 bits of data. Today, typically, some 50,000 bits are generated, including the surgeon's track record of charges for appendectomies, or whatever the procedure is.

Giant EDS is divided into 38 profit-responsible Strategic Business Units (SBUs), including 32 "vertical" industry units, such as communications, energy and chemicals, finance, manufacturing, transportation, retailing, health benefits; and a half-dozen "horizontal" SBUs, which provide specific, across-the-board information system capabilities in such areas as artificial intelligence.

Consider the communications industry SBU. About 3,000 people work on 200 accounts. AT&T is its biggest customer, absorbing about 1000 people at work on several dozen separate accounts. The head of EDS's AT&T operations lives close to the customer in New Jersey, recruits and trains in New Jersey, and conducts business development activities in New Jersey. Characteristically, EDS's affair with AT&T started as a small project. In 1982, Tom Bockholt (now a vice president and "affinity group" leader, with responsibility for the communications and energy and chemical SBUs—see below) went from Dallas to New Jersey on an ambiguous 60-day assignment to "figure out how to add some business." Following his initial success, the account grew by fits and starts to its imposing size today.

One Year in the Life of

A glance at EDS's 1990 annual report indicates the direction of the information technology industry, and the company's role in it. For example, EDS signed a 10-year systems management agreement with Cummins Cash and Information Services, Inc. That's right—the *information services division* of the maker of truck engines will work with EDS on electronic funds transfers, fuel purchase programs, and temporary truck permit services, among other things. Such "soft" services are increasingly the prime source of "value added" and the clincher of deals for "hardware" companies like Cummins.

In 1990, EDS also signed one of its largest government contracts ever, worth $712 million, with the Army, Navy, and Defense Logistics Agency for a "small multiuser computer" project. The eight-year effort will provide hardware, software, integration services, local area networks, and maintenance for 450 different products from 59 different vendors supporting various small (1 to 16 people) scientific, engineering, management, administrative, and business groups. A more modest government project will help the Chicago Parking Authority deal with 23 million overdue parking tickets (a one-year backlog). Parking enforcement agents in the windy city will now travel about with handheld wands (the sort Federal Express drivers carry), the data from which will be downloaded to a central system at the end of each day.

EDS will also work with American International Health Care, Inc. (a subsidiary of the insurance giant American International Group) to develop—and then market to customers throughout the industry—a managed-care information system. And EDS's contract with Apple Computer was extended to provide a Macintosh-based Document Management and Control System for Apple operations in California, Ireland, France, and Singapore; a substantial reduction in Apple's product development cycle time is the objective.

This short list illustrates both the range of EDS's activities—and the range of new information systems products and services that are transforming commerce worldwide.

Philosophy

CEO Les Alberthal believes that tomorrow is EDS's oyster. In the 1960s, he says, the "box [the computer hardware] was the thing." You were supposed to "buy the box," and all your information technology problems would go away; so you "bought the box, but in the end you still had the problems." In the '70s, packaged applications software was the rage; it was "buy the box, buy the package, and all your problems will go away." The result per Alberthal: "You bought the box, you bought the package, but the problems remained." The '80s added consulting to the mix, and saw the emergence of powerful new competitors for EDS such as Arthur Andersen's consultants. But the end result was the same: "Buy the box, buy the package, buy the consulting—and the problems are still there."

Information systems in the '90s, Alberthal concludes, will require "systems integration"; it's not, he and other EDS executives insist, primarily a technology issue. "Solutions to enterprise needs" is the buzz phrase reverberating throughout the Dallas headquarters. EDS says, with at least a little justification, that it invented "systems integration"—beginning with federal government work in the late 1970s that included systems training, systems maintenance, software development, and overall integration all in one package.

Not all would agree with Alberthal's proposition. Andersen staffers argue that the 1980s was the decade of the failed promise of systems integration. The 1990s, they say, will be the years of "business enterprise solutions," in which—surprise—Andersen's consultants specialize! Though each claims special expertise in filling the gap, the fact is that EDS's version of systems integration ("solutions to enterprise needs") and Andersen's ("business enterprise solutions") are remarkably similar. Both companies—and lots of others, including IBM—are trying to position themselves as nothing less than co-architects of their clients' corporate strategies.

In fact, most of the grand strategy debate dissolves when you look at EDS's historic strength and day-to-day existence—a direct legacy of founder Ross Perot. From the start, EDS avoided proffering the elegant solutions to problems so beloved of technocrats. Instead, EDSers are known for rolling up their sleeves and working directly with customers on the nitty-gritty practical solutions to the customers' practical problems. Call it opportunism if you like: EDS eyes a small project as an entryway; the aim is to become intimately engaged with the client. Witness the AT&T progression described above—a 60-day date has become an almost 1000-person marriage. EDSers admit they specialize in "trauma"—helping companies react to major shifts in their market, such as industry-wide deregulation or sudden spurts of growth. Though they do some pure research and development (in network management, for instance, at the company's Plano Information Management Center), they normally take a more action-oriented/action-research approach. The firm declares an area to be of interest—pharmaceuticals, say—and seeks out a top-rank client to work with on a modest-size project. Then EDS and the client experiment their way toward greater understanding of the potential of information systems.

That's not to say that such on-the-run opportunism doesn't aim at grand goals. Consider pharmaceuticals again. "The point is not to cut a [pharmaceutical] company's data processing bill from, say, two hundred million dollars a year to fifty million a year," one EDS executive sniffs. "That's like striking out the pitcher." Instead, he insists, EDS's objective would be to shrink the 110 months it takes the typical drug company to win the approval of the Food and Drug Administration to market a new drug. Industry-best Merck, thanks in part to unique data management and systems integration skills, gains the FDA's nod, on average, in just 65 months. Paring even 10 months from the 110-month norm could be worth billions to a company!

The objective of EDS's work with owner GM is no less than a radical transformation. The first goal is to help the company develop cars much faster. For example, the monster C4 project will integrate computer-aided design, computer-aided manufacturing, computer-integrated manufacturing, and computer-aided engineering (CAD, CAM, CIM, CAE, the four "Cs") throughout the $125-billion corporation. And there's the new GM Pulsat Network, aimed at putting a satellite dish at each of GM's 10,000 U.S. dealerships. Also among EDS's audacious plans: electronic shop manuals, invoicing, and vehicle diagnostics as well as links to GM's overall manufacturing system, so that when you order a car, manufacturing will begin at approximately the same time. Altering GM's "overall business practice," not working on narrow technology issues, is the object.

But how do you *do* all this?

DOING BUSINESS: THE PROJECT

Boil down any SBU and you'll find projects. *In fact, EDS is one big collection of project teams.*

The number of people on a project can vary greatly throughout its life.

The norm is 8 to 12 EDSers, working together for a period of 9 to 18 months. More often than not, the team will also include full-time customer people. The chief, or project manager, will usually have 4 to 8 years of experience. (An account—one of many at AT&T, say—usually consists of several discrete projects.)

Though the project's product/result is buttoned down, the formal structure of the project team is murky. (You need to get used to this paradox in discussions with EDSers—and professional service firm denizens in general.) "We report to each other," one performance-oriented senior EDS exec nonchalantly puts it. Who reports to whom is not critical. Getting the job done is.

You can, however, loosely discern three "ranks": individual performer (who spends most of her or his time coding), sub-project team leader ("a role more than a detailed job title"), and project manager, a formal designation. It's normal for an individual performer to become a sub-project team leader for a while because of a particular, needed skill, then return to being an individual performer. Two or three such alternations will take place before the designation as a more or less "official" team leader. Formal project manager status usually comes along after "the individual performer starts to display project management skills"—a typically imprecise but clear (to the speaker) EDS locution.

Despite the size of the institution, which would seem to cry out for more "structure," the process of advancing at EDS is quite informal. There's a long "twilight zone," execs declare, when an EDSer operates in leadership positions of some sort without formal designation. A sub-project team leader, for example, may—or may not—have administrative responsibility for team members. But make no mistake: Despite the ambiguity, that team leader will have clear and unmistakable project/subproject accountability. She or he understands this. EDS understands it. The customer understands it. The ball, when it comes to on-time, on-budget results, is clearly in that leader's court, formal designation or not.

Keeping Communications Open

EDS still operates mostly by word of mouth. Though there are drawbacks when it comes to leverage and learning systematically from across-the-board experience (see below), this means you can talk with whomever you want to generate the connections necessary to help get any job done. If you're staffing a critical job, for instance, and your network intelligence surfaces a particularly good candidate—well, you go after that candidate, regardless of location or SBU or your "rank." Civility suggests that you call the prospect's boss to tell him or her what you're up to, but that's all.

EDS executives admit that "some bosses hoard resources." Most, however, help out—because they understand that "he who gives is likely to receive," as Tom Bockholt puts it. That is, "the network" can be "worked" to your advantage only if you yourself are forthcoming when called upon for help. There's also the matter of pride: satisfaction that "your guy, the fellow you developed, will be working on a critical, creative, and important project in another area," says marketing head and longtime technologist Barry Sullivan. Bockholt emphasizes that most people remember that "their own opportunity was created by someone who once gave them up when it wasn't easy to do. I remember that. Sure, it leaves a hole in a team. Eight people have to do the work of nine or ten. But people fill in. In fact, that's what creates the opportunities."

EDS has cobbled together some more or less formal structures to help get people attached to appropriate projects. There is a "skills inventory" and a "fast-track" scheme; neither works very well. "Mostly assignment is via conversation, the network," Sullivan asserts. "It's still the best way."

Loose, Flexible—and Disciplined

EDS is "loose and flexible," per one exec—but damned disciplined. Accountability is unmistakable. If you're assigned a job, you're expected to get it done, even if nothing is written down, even if "your 'authority' doesn't come close to matching your 'responsibility,'" Sullivan told us. In fact, such "mismatches" are common. But the EDS ethic admits no exceptions. "If you don't have the authority," Sullivan snapped, "find it!" It's assumed, another EDSer chimed in, that you'll "figure out what you have to do to succeed, then do it."

Those who flounder in such settings have limited futures at EDS. Sullivan remembers when he was first given a potential team-leadership assignment: "I went out and recruited five people. My boss came back later with a list of five candidates. 'Too late,' I told him, 'I've already got my team.'" It's precisely this sort of initiative that's expected at EDS from the git-go—*if* you plan to get ahead. And, it's expected as much in the early '90s, with a cast of tens of thousands, as it was in the early '60s, when the cast numbered only in the tens.

A Day in the Life of

On any given day, five out of six EDS people are closer than "close to the customer"—most actually on the customer's premises, the rest at "systems engineer" sites nearby.

"Indoctrination"—as much the right word today as in Perot's time—in this "indistinguishable-from-the-customer" imperative centers around the systems engineer development process, which takes about three years. The experience of systems engineer manager Gwen Phillips, a liberal arts grad, was typical: Her entire first eighteen months were spent on customer location. At EDS you learn on the job—begin by getting a feel for the real world of the customer. At the company's birth in 1962, its "close-to-the-customer-from-the-start" philosophy set EDS apart. And though it might seem readily copiable, apparently it's not. On this all-important score, EDS is almost as special today as it was three decades ago.

After that first year or so, it's off to school in Plano, joining 20 others in an intense 10-week "boot camp." Though you've picked up some programming skill already, programming dominates the curriculum—along with more of the "EDS way." After school, it's most likely back to a customer operation. At the end of roughly three years, you "graduate" and get a certificate. By then, the most effective have already become team leaders.

That initial period spent living with the customer leaves in most EDSers (and all who are successful) an indelible idea: The customer comes first. Almost everyone, EDS executives point out, has a ton of "customer war stories" to tell—about going the extra mile, beyond reason at times, to serve the customer better.

Every strength can become a weakness, and obsessive customer contact is no exception. EDS's ultra-closeness "means we can start to look too much like our customers," Sullivan told us. That is, EDSers risk becoming too much like insiders, not pushing hard enough for innovative ideas that will upset the apple cart but in the end offer the customer the highest leverage. On the other hand, the still-infant information systems industry has most often sinned by pursuing cleverness for its own sake, and failing to attend to the humdrum of life on the customer's premises that EDS takes to so instinctively.

INTEGRATION, LEARNING, AND LEVERAGE

Though most of EDS's Strategic Business Units are "vertical" (those industry and geographic units), CEO Alberthal insists that EDS's future is "horizontal"—learning how to leverage its skills and its dispersed-but-rich knowledge base. To get there from here, EDS first has to figure out what those skills are, then learn to extract knowledge from around the fragmented institution and efficiently bring it to bear on several thousand active customer projects.

Horizontal SBUs

Part of EDS's answer is the six "horizontal SBUs," which encompass across-the-board (non-industry-specific) skills such as payment processing, telecommunications management, and artificial intelligence. The horizontal SBUs should not, however, be confused with "staff groups." Each one is charged, like the vertical/industry SBUs, with generating its own projects, seeking its own clients, *and* making money—from day one.

But there's much more to EDS's "horizontal" potential. Industry- and geographically based SBUs naturally pick up expertise in the course of doing business—a high share of which *could* be leveraged across the giant firm, *if* an efficient system to capture and share experience could be forged. Top that off with the awesome total of systems development knowledge rumbling around in 10s of thousands of individual heads and the possibilities seem limitless.

Centers of Service

Enter the new idea of "Centers of Service." For example, in 1991 Barry Sullivan initiated a two-year Center of Service in imaging capabilities. The objective: to implant general imaging capability into every SBU. The diagrams opposite illustrate the path being followed: The boxes in the top row of Figure A represent "vertical"/industry SBUs. The second row represents leverageable skill areas (more or less "horizontal"). Right now, imaging occupies a single box in row two. It's *not* a formal horizontal SBU, but a less formal Center of Service with a finite life. The idea, shown in Figure B, is to get imaging capability "out of" row two and "into" every box/SBU in row one.

The "horizontalizing" trick, in ever-pragmatic EDS, will be the ability of the Center of Service leader (full-time, but not under the gun to turn a profit) to wheedle her or his way into the hearts of busy vertical/industry SBU people. For example, early on in the imaging project, the leader stumbled across an energy-industry project for which he felt his technology provided a better answer than the one the vertical SBU was proposing. He tried the idea out, and got no sale. "You win some, you lose some," Sullivan said and shrugged. On the other hand, Sullivan told us that the Center's imaging schemes were being diffused into projects involving several health-care clients. The imaging project manager's objective is to provide direct, immediate help to the health-care SBU's clients; the bigger objective, of course, is to diffuse imaging skills and enthusiasm for imaging throughout the health-care SBU.

The fact that EDS is conceptualizing its concerns about knowledge transfer, knowledge management, and systemwide leveraging takes it a big step beyond most companies. But note: EDS sees "row two" activities in terms of "how do we transfer one hundred percent of this skill to line units, then fold up the tent?" No consideration has been given to creating a ponderous "functional staff unit" (for imaging, say) that would then foist itself on unsuspecting SBU chiefs as a direct or indirect (per head) cost item. When a "horizontal" area is deemed worthy of permanence—like those six horizontal SBUs—it will be established as a full-blown profit center, charged with making a buck in the same way a "line" (industry) unit does.

Affinity Groups and More

Other knowledge-diffusion mechanisms aim to move EDS beyond dependence upon "word of mouth." For example, there's a Corporate Capability Directory, built on a relational database. (It's currently of limited value, some say, because it has too much information.) Then there's the "affinity group" concept, which loosely ties a few SBUs together under an executive who runs an

EDS Centers of Service

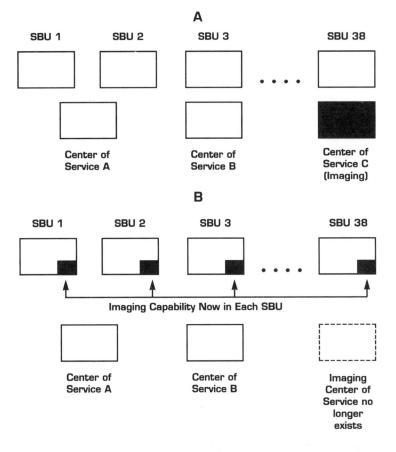

SBU but acts as group coordinator, cheerleader, and prod—aiming to push knowledge gained in one arena into others. But note: Affinity groups shouldn't be confused with traditional, big-company "sector organizations." For one (major) thing, the affinity group leader doubles as an SBU boss and has no staff; affinity groups are chatting-up mechanisms, not a back-door way of adding on a new level of management.

Though EDS has long been an effective, close-knit "network," this overall effort to achieve leverage across SBUs nonetheless requires major culture change. The key, in an institution that cut its teeth on the idea of autonomy and independence, is teaching people "how to get things done when you don't control all the assets," one EDS executive observes. How will that be accomplished? Mostly by informal oversight at the top. Kudos will go to SBU heads who cooperate with one another, execs say. Promotions will go—are going— to managers who finesse the formal structure and create leverageable, "horizontal" opportunities. The next generation of top leaders, CEO Alberthal vows, will be determined "horizontalists"—those who have pursued leverage most vigorously. When we talked with him, though, he put the "problem of tunnel vision, looking beyond the vertical orientation" at the top of his list of concerns.

IT CAN BE DONE!

You *can* organize a giant firm as a collection of 10-person, highly accountable teams—ever shifting and seldom at home. Moreover, word of mouth still can—and does—work as the chief "organizing" device. Subjective evaluation is also possible—those who behave well (e.g., support horizontal efforts, help out peers by giving up a precious resource/person) are "taken care of," EDS execs confidently proclaim. Readers who work in traditional manufacturing operations may find all this hard to believe. For those like me, who've grown up in sizable professional service firms, it seems as natural as breathing.

A host of subtle forces makes the unimaginable doable. EDS today owes a huge debt to its founder—the ideas of unmistakable accountability to teammates and customers, of getting the job done regardless of the official resources at your beck and call, are Ross Perot to the core. So are starting a career, no matter what, on the customer's premises and learning that the customer "comes first, second, third, fourth . . . and there ain't no fifth."

Nonetheless, a 72,000-person firm is not a 10,000-person firm, let alone a 300-person firm. Future EDS growth must come, somehow or other, from that word Alberthal uses so much—"leverage." In particular, leverage born of mastering the management of knowledge and inducing the multitudinous parts of the giant, spread out, diversely skilled company to behave "horizontally" and learn from one another—quickly, efficiently, effectively.

3

Cable News Network:
Information as Fashion,
Corporation as Carnival

Usually one of the first questions Mr. Baker got from all these
Central Asian leaders was: "How do I get CNN?" . . . Having
CNN, they explained, was . . . a real membership card in the
club of Western states.

> *The New York Times*
> February 20, 1992

Our philosophy is live, live and *more* live.

> REESE SCHONFELD, first
> president, Cable News Network

When the Cable News Network went on the air on June 1, 1980,
it had secured access to about 1.7 million cable subscribers, far short of the 7.5
million "minimum" founder Ted Turner needed to cover 50 percent of operating costs. By 1992, the number had grown to almost 60 million in the U.S.
alone. Profits have accompanied increased reach. Through 1984, founder
Turner had lost $77 million pursuing his dream of CNN as a full-scale net-
work. In 1985, black ink appeared for the first time, with the network earning
$13 million on $123 million in revenue. In 1991, profits of $167 million were
recorded on $479 million in revenue.

NEWS ON DEMAND

CNN's core concept is "delivering news on demand." By my lights, the world of weekly or monthly magazines, newspapers, radio, and TV is heroic to begin with. Take the newspaper: It must arrive at my driveway with a new set of stories at 5:00 a.m. each day—that's almost unthinkable for those of us who conceive most tasks in terms of weeks, months, or years. Yet CNN performs on an entirely different plane. Newspapers, and the older TV networks, deliver at *their* convenience. That newspaper gets to the driveway at 5:00 a.m.—regardless of what's happening in the world. With the exception of a very special event, like the first few days of the Gulf War or the Challenger explosion, the TV networks give you the news, need it or not, at 6:30 or 7:00 p.m. (And if you live west of Chicago, they feed you regurgitated news—one, two, or three hours delayed.) That's that. Like it or lump it. Their convenience, not yours.

But the world seems to be spinning faster these days. And CNN's offering is matching, mimicking—and leading—a world gone mad for instant everything. We are no longer a nine-to-five society, for one thing. Most U.S. families today have two people who work, often in shifts that don't exactly (or even nearly) coincide. The family that sits around the dinner table, quietly eating and then reading aloud from Shakespeare or the Bible—or tuning in to the evening news—is the exception. And for the new majority, on the fly, CNN is made to order.

TURNER'S NUTTINESS

CNN was created in 374 days! On May 21, 1979, Ted Turner held a press conference at the National Cable Television Association in Las Vegas. He bravely (foolishly, most said) announced that his all-news network would go on the air on June 1, 1980. It did.

Turner had some useful experience. His small Atlanta station, WTCG (now WTBS), had begun widely distributing programs by satellite in December 1976. His "superstation" logic was that the world wanted to watch every game played by his beloved Atlanta Braves (at the bottom of the league, often as not, before 1991). An absurd idea! Or so said the cognoscenti from Manhattan, Chicago, and Los Angeles. But to the baseball-hungry throughout most of the nation, the Braves would do just fine when they were the only major-league option on TV.

Considering the success of WTCG, new technology, and cable's ever wider reach, Turner began to ponder a 24-hour-a-day all-news television network. Late in December 1978, according to Hank Whittemore in *CNN: The Inside Story,* he tried the notion out on cable system owners at the Western Cable

Show. They shrugged their collective shoulders, and then he put his plans aside. Six months later, he revived them, for keeps this time. Why? Only Turner knows the answer, but I can guess. He probably figured—knew in his bones?—that common sense just doesn't make sense in a world gone bonkers!

The Luck Factor

The network seemed blessed, starting in its very first half hour. At 6:00 p.m. on June 1, when CNN went on the air, President Jimmy Carter was at the hospital bedside of Vernon Jordan in Fort Wayne, Indiana, after an assassination attempt on the civil rights leader. At 6:22 p.m., Whittemore reports, CNN scored its first scoop by covering Mr. Carter—live—coming out of Jordan's hospital room. (CNN paid for a satellite link to Fort Wayne only until 6:30. If Carter had popped out eight minutes later, CNN would have been out of luck.) Also in the early days, the fire at the MGM Grand Hotel in Las Vegas, the attempted assassinations of Ronald Reagan and Pope John Paul II (while CNN was, by coincidence, on the air doing a brief live report from Rome), and the collapse of the walkway at the Kansas City Hyatt Hotel demonstrated the value of this oddball 24-hour TV news notion.

ALL IN A DAY'S WORK

The idea behind CNN was completely different from that of the Big Three networks. There was a "role in the process for our viewers," CNN's first president, Reese Schonfeld, said, according to Whittemore. That is, ragged edges would be on display—the way real news stories evolve. "Avoid slickness at all costs" was another of Schonfeld's guiding dictums. The idea of "real"/raggedness has been CNN's strength, and at the same time a continuing target for its critics. A reporter from *Home Video* magazine asked Ted Turner about detractors who pointed out CNN's lack of focus. "Wait just a goddamned minute!" Turner snapped. "You think it lacks focus—what is focus, anyway? If you're live, all the time, how can you have focus? Focus means that you know where you're going! You can't focus in on somethin' unless you know what it is you're focusing on! Focus is something a newspaper has, because there is a day to think about it. Or with a magazine there's a month. Whoever said that was a yo-yo!"

On demand. Live. Ragged. But how do you *run* the darn thing? Ed Turner (no relation to Ted), part of CNN from the start, is executive vice president for news gathering. He ordinarily arrives at the CNN center in Atlanta at about 6:00 a.m. and begins by checking the domestic and international desks to see what's gone on in the course of the night. From then on, he told me, his work is mostly 50 to 75 or so phone conversations and quick, stand-up meetings. Turner doesn't attend committee meetings. There are no committees to have meetings! Moreover, he insists it never takes more than three or four folks, all located within a few yards of one another, to make any decision—which they do, with no fuss, on the spot, and often on the run. Chairs, too, it seems, are for yo-yos.

During one visit, I followed current CNN president Tom Johnson around during a breaking event in the Gulf crisis. I watched him make a half-dozen critical decisions—including one that committed millions of dollars—in the space of a minute or two each, while standing toe to toe with three or four key people. (Key meaning those closest to the action, senior or junior.) Ed Turner observes from long pre-CNN experience that decisions which would take others (the major networks, newspapers) hours or more are routinely accomplished in seconds at CNN. Johnson, who came to CNN from *The Los Angeles Times* and the Times-Mirror Corporation, agrees: "What it used to take us twelve hours to do, you can do here in twelve minutes."

Add another piece to the CNN puzzle and consider the world of Earl Casey, vice-president and managing editor, domestic. Casey also tends to come in about 6:00 a.m., to "read in" (the wires, newspapers, etc.). Then at 8:00 a.m., he and a couple dozen others (some in person, some by phone link) sit down for the only affair approaching a regular meeting.

People arrive, hurriedly (not because of a request to be on time, but because "hurry" is the normal style at CNN), with no formality whatsoever (some don't show at all for one reason or another), and a document 30 or so pages long is passed out. It's only a minor exaggeration to say that the document *is* the network. It's more or less the day's schedule—still warm copies of computer printout, hastily thrown together, consisting of a couple of pages (or more in the case of Washington) from each of CNN's nine U.S. bureaus. The headings on each page are, in order: Story, Location, Reporter, ETA (estimated time on the air), Contents. That's it.

I sat in on the November 15, 1990, meeting. It began on time at 8:00*; the "date" on the scheduling document was 7:45—fifteen minutes before. The first Story, on page one, was "shuttle payload." Location, "Atlanta." Reporter, "Mintier." ETA, "possible 4-??? pending launch conditions." Contents: "Another 'almost' secret mission. Atlantis will most likely be carrying another spy SAT. This one capable of providing intelligence on the Persian Gulf . . ." Another note on this two-inch entry about the story says, "This package will be revised for 8:00 p.m. to include launch." (See the top sheet, opposite, of the November 15 document.)

In the course of about 30 minutes, these busy executives hustled through those 30 pages, skipping from here to there. During the meeting, which was nominally chaired by Ed Turner, most were simultaneously reading newspapers. Side conversations were rife. The chatter was open, free and easy—

---

*Let me be clear: "Began on time" doesn't mean it was called to order, or anything of the sort. Somebody just started talking and away they went.

CNN "Schedule," Nov. 15, 1990, p. 1

baker, c Thu Nov 15 07:45 page 1

SLUG	WRITER	DAY/DATE/TIME	REV. BY	ON	STATUS TIME
SHUTTLE ATLANTIS	broadman	Tue Nov 13 15:58	broadman	Nov 15 06:45	HOLD 1:12

THE ATLANTIS MISSION IS MILITARY. THIS MEANS THAT WE WON'T HAVE ANY INFORMATION AND/OR NASA
SELECT DURING THE MISSION.
WE WILL GET PRE-LAUNCH AND LAUNCH COVERAGE LIVE. THEN NASA WILL GOODNIGHT THE BIRD.
MISSION IS EXPECTED TO LAST 3 DAYS, 23 HOURS, 5 MINUTES

NASA SELECT: COMES UP AT 1PM AND GOES DOWN SOMEWHERE AFTER SEPARATION
             REC TBA

COVERAGE PLAN: ZARRELLA WILL START LIVE COVERAGE FROM THE CAPE AT 2PM.
                   HE'LL BE JOINED BY TOM MINTIER WHO'LL ANCHOR LAUNCH
                   COVERAGE IN ATLANTA AT 4PM. WE'LL CONTINUE OUR LIVE
                   COVERAGE THRU LAUNCH.

FEEDS: 210P-225P   REC 12 EAST COAST IFB
              350P-415P   REC 12 EAST COAST IFB
           ING550P-615P
              615P-7P>   REC 11 EAST COAST IFB

STORY	LOCATION	REPORTER	ETA	CONTENTS
SHUTTLE PAYLOAD	ATLANTA	MINTIER	POSS 4P PENDING LAUNCH CONDITIONS	ANOTHER "ALMOST" SECRET MISSION. ATLANTIS WILL MOST LIKELY BE CARRYING ANOTHER SPY SAT. THIS

    THIS PKG WILL BE REVISED FOR 8PM TO   ONE CAPABLE OF PROVIDING
    INCLUDE LAUNCH   INTELLIGENCE ON THE
                                                        PERSIAN GULF. WE DO A
                                                        TIC TOC ON SOME OF THE
                                                        LATEST SPY BIRDS

LAUNCH PREPS	KSC	ZARRELLA	LIVE	

                                        2P . . . . UPDATE WEATHER
                                                   WITH DONUT . .
    MINTIER BEGINS ANCHORING FROM   4P . . . . LAST MINUTE PREPS
    ATLANTA AT 4PM   6P . . . . FINAL COUNTDOWN
                           LAUNCH: BEST GUESS 6:46P
                                               WINDOW: 630P-1030P

LAUNCH WRAP	KSC	ZARRELLA	2 HRS AFTER LAUNCH

baker, c Thu Nov 15 07:45 page 1

BUREAU	DAY	DATE	WRITER	REV BY	ON	STATUS TIME
WX STORIES	THURSDAY	11/15/90		baker,c	Nov 15 07:44 READY 1:51	

SLUG	LOCATION	REPORTER	ETA FEED	CONTENTS
WHITE HOUSE REPORTER: OLSON SESNO				COVER EVENTS AT WHITE HOUSE: 8A- INTELLIGENCE BRFG 815A- NATL SECURITY BRFG

consistent with the overriding emphasis on action, action. Perhaps a dozen "decisions" were made; nothing major, just whether to move this from here to there, whether to put that on ice while waiting for the other to unfold. A couple of people were criticized rather openly (though with very little sting). A couple of screwups from the day before were laughed at by all. It was a far cry from an executive committee session at Ford or GM (or . . . or . . .)!

How does this document get put together? There's no pat answer. It sort of comes into being. Earl Casey's predecessor, Cissy Baker, would sit down late in the day—typically between four and six—with people at her "Futures Desk." They'd chat a while (though they had chatted a dozen times during the day) about the next day; their contribution to the document would emerge more or less out of that.

The document is a "plan"—but one whose details "dribble away in a matter of hours," as Baker put it. Nonetheless, it is a useful base line, no matter how unstable the nature of its contents. In fact, it's a marvelous example of that ugly-sounding idea from *In Search of Excellence*—"simultaneous loose-tight controls." On the one hand, there *is* a document—a master set of sheets that describes what's going to happen, as things now stand. On the other hand, it is *always*—and by definition—a very rough draft, subject to instant, no-sweat modification, whether the day's an "average" one (actually, there are no average days at CNN) or one in the middle of a Gulf-like crisis.

While CNN had no TV role models in 1979, it could and did look to 24-hour, all-news radio, born a few years before. The key to 24-hour news radio (and more or less to CNN), Hank Whittemore claims, is the idea of "the ever revolving news wheel," and "twenty-two new minutes each hour." In the course of moving from one hour to the next (unless the likes of "Larry King Live" is on), about 22 minutes will be changed. A new story might be added. An old story might drop out. The preceding hour's lead story might be updated (a minute added, a minute subtracted, a minute modified). In any event, the relentless "news wheel" keeps on spinning. You can say it revolves "beneath" the operation of the network.

Of course, going live is the "wild card" that upsets everything, and gives CNN its special signature at the same time. But even though "live" regularly intrudes, the image of the spinning wheel underneath is crucial: It's the gyroscope that must never falter—though no day in fact bears much resemblance to the day as "planned" at the morning meeting.

CNN LIVE

Ah, that wild card—CNN *live*. Bob Furnad is executive vice president and senior executive producer. On January 10, 1990, I watched him direct an hour of very live news, in the midst of the Gulf crisis: the supposedly last-ditch try for peace—the meeting in Geneva between Secretary of State

James Baker and Iraqi Foreign Minister Tariq Aziz. Furnad was in control—and out of control—at all times. It's important to understand both aspects, for it is this being simultaneously in control and out of control that is the key to "making it work" at CNN—and at EDS and all *other* organizations trying to deal with today's frenzied environment.

In the control room, Furnad was in perpetual motion, balanced like a ship captain at the tiller in the midst of a Force 5 hurricane. Four phones and a fax machine were within reach. Several people sat one "row" down from Furnad (about eight feet away), actually creating—live—a news program. They worked at terminals in front of dozens upon dozens of TV monitors. (Other nearby screens displayed—within Furnad's view—the Big Three networks, among other things. His observations of their coverage, out of the corner of his eye, got factored into his decision making.)

Though CNN is awash in high technology, with computer terminals covering almost every available surface, Furnad's tools were paper and pencil. He kept track, on an 8½-by-14 legal sheet, of who (reporter, expert, etc.) was available from where to tell him what next about whatever from wherever. He'd simultaneously listen, bark orders, and draw arrows from here to there indicating what report would come before or after what other, scratch bits out as they occurred or became (instantly) passé, add bits as someone whispered in his ear or after a glance at a two-line note waved furiously in front of his face.

The "show" that ensued was far from TV's norm, if you're used to looking at CBS, NBC, or ABC. There were, to be sure, a pair of late-afternoon "anchors" sitting at a rather traditional anchor desk on the other side of the glass wall of the control room. (And so they sat, utterly silent, for 60 minutes—see the "no star" discussion below. Dan Rather need not apply.) But Furnad decided not to use them this hour. Ralph Begleiter, a highly articulate reporter in Geneva with Secretary Baker, was Furnad's de facto "anchor" for this story. Begleiter had a receiver in his ear and, with Furnad's direction (from 3,000 miles away in the Atlanta control room), was asking questions of other reporters (at the UN, in Israel, in Washington, etc.) passing one reporter's question on to another, and so on.

It's fair to say that Furnad, in the course of an hour, made several dozen—hundred is more like it—decisions. They shaped CNN's presentation to the world for that wild, frantic period of time. Beyond the immediate story, some of these instant decisions may have had lasting impact. For example, CNN tried to get spot feedback from Capitol Hill. Though most legislators were skittish, a reporter managed to entice Virginia senator John Warner into CNN's Washington studio. But Warner didn't fit into Furnad's unfolding scheme, so the senator was left sitting. That was unlikely to help CNN's future relationship with Warner—and Furnad, of course, knew that and had to take it into account, as one of hundreds of variables he "routinely" (CNN-style) juggles during an hour like this.

TO LOVE CNN IS TO LOVE FRENZY

CNN is not a "star network." CNN executives, from the start, liked to say "the news is the star," says Hank Whittemore. But if not a star network, then what? Try the "VJ" (video journalist)-and-assignment-desk-quarterback network. (See the extended discussion of new-fangled "informated workers," "case workers," etc., in chapter 15; the VJ and assignment-desk person fit the specs exactly.)

"Video journalist" is a new category of generalist reporter invented by CNN, and VJs do a lot more than their traditional network counterparts. The man or woman reporting for CBS or NBC will sally forth with a fairly massive supporting cast. (I was once the subject of a pair of three-minute "packages" for the *CBS Evening News*. The armada that put the story together included several directors with large crews, and a passel of New York-based functionaries of one sort or another.) The VJ from CNN will often as not go out with just a cameraman and perhaps a soundman. She or he does most of the writing, directs "the show," may do the sound—whatever it takes. The VJ is a nonspecialist by design, a jack of all trades—"multiskilled," to use the new management lingo.

The person at the assignment desk is the other central, multiskilled, front-line actor at CNN—and another who is less honored, by contrast, at the news arms of the other big networks. "The assignment desks run the network," Ed Turner said flatly. At the older networks, where the news show is focused on a relatively small number of stories, the ball for a "package" typically gets rolling when an order is issued by an Executive Producer—and don't forget to capitalize the "E" and "P"—in New York. At CNN, the assignment desk usually surfaces a story idea, working alone or with one of the bureaus. The assignment desk person "checks with" Earl Casey or Ed Turner (no memo, just a 90-second stand-up chat on the control-room floor, or a head stuck into Turner's or Casey's tiny office). After tentative signoff, the assignment desk calls the lead bureau, talks directly with the reporter (VJ) who will do the story, then asks the ultimate question—"Can you get it in twenty-four hours?"

What kind of person does CNN hire? Who can—and can't—handle this frantic existence? CNN seeks reporters desperate to tell their stories, Cissy Baker told me. A reporter at CNN will typically do two or three packages a day that air, versus one (max!) for a typical CBS counterpart. Moreover, it's not uncommon for a CNN reporter to go live for a half-dozen hours running, when a big story breaks on her or his turf.

Baker said she hired people mostly on the basis of their enthusiasm for and love of the news. "We can teach the technical part," she added. A successful candidate must also be judged capable of dealing with extraordinary ambiguity. In fact, Whittemore claims that people from the traditional networks have had difficulty adjusting to CNN. Those with wire service or all-news radio backgrounds, having lived with more chaos, cope better with perpetual frenzy, CNN-style.

Burt Reinhardt, CNN's second president and now vice-chairman, said it best. " 'Doing it' means figuring out how to do it yourself," he told Whittemore. "If your way works most of the time, you'll get promoted." CNN, like EDS, insists that people at every level take the initiative from the moment they come aboard. You can become whatever you want to become. (There's a raft of evidence supporting this assertion.) Nobody is going to tell you what to do. It's up to you to figure out what to do, then do it. Always take the proactive path. Ask for advice, sure, but don't sit on your hands waiting for an order. And P.S., there are no "quality circles" here: It's just part and parcel of everyone's job to do her or his "it" a bit better each day.

RUNNING CNN, REAL-TIME, AS A BUSINESS

CNN works. It has fulfilled its imposing vision and made its mark. Its impact is enormous. It also makes a ton of money. How? In short, CNN does much, much more for much, much less.

Ed Turner looked back to explain the difference between CNN and the older network news shows. As he sees it, "they had money." During a 60- to 70-year history (since the start of the radio networks), the old-timers gathered a lot of bureaucratic barnacles and an insatiable appetite for lavish expenditures. CNN started lean and has managed to keep it that way—as Cissy Baker put it, "good, cheap, and flexible." Though it spends whatever it must and then some on technology, it otherwise exudes "no frills" from every pore.

CNN seems as if it would absorb a ton of dough—it's on the air 24 hours a day, and prides itself on live coverage. Yet, as Baker pointed out, in her 10 years at the network CNN hired no more than a dozen charter aircraft to get people somewhere in a hurry. CNN's "fleet" of airplanes, she said, laughing, "is Delta's scheduled flights out of the Atlanta hub"—at coach rates. CNN also eschews "beauty shots"—beautiful background cinematography that absorbs megabucks per minute on the air. "That's not why we're here," Ed Turner said simply.

(CNN is about as different from CBS as Wal-Mart is from Sears. Sears was born no-nonsense, became everyman's store, then got spoiled by success. Despite its shaky financial condition and deteriorating consumer franchises, a visit to the Sears Tower is a visit to the lap of luxury. A visit to Wal-Mart's non-tower HQ ain't! Yet aggressively chintzy Wal-Mart, like CNN, spends lavishly on technology. More on those all-important accidents of birth in Chapter 40.)

Everyone a Businessperson

CNN has a master budget, of course. But more important, everyone at CNN—starting with the VJs and other field people—knows what things cost. That's an apparently innocuous statement, but it has major consequences. In large measure, the company is in control financially because each person has a sense of managing the whole, not just his or her bit.

Anyone in the field, Baker told us, knows exactly what it costs to rent a satellite uplink from Tokyo, or a land line from Los Angeles to Atlanta. People have a "feel" for budgets, a "feel" for what's excessive, what's not. Much of CNN's ability to make instant, big decisions, Turner explained, is embodied in that feel. To illustrate, he pointed to what happened after CNN spent an unplanned $100,000 to cover an unexpected overseas trip by President Bush. Turner, with no "plan" but a clear sense of every nickel of cost, made up most or all of the $100,000 shortfall—by saving a few thousand bucks here, a few thousand bucks there—milking this story a little longer (the investment in it was already made), delaying that one a day or two. (CNN does know the value of a dollar! Per diem in the U.S. for reporters in 1992 ran $35 a day. Overseas, it was $45.)

In Control, Out of Control, Self-Control

CNN is a superb example of radical centralization *and* radical decentralization—at once. Activities are centralized in Atlanta. Senior decision makers are a few yards apart. The ability to make decisions fast is enhanced by that physical centralization, and by the familiarity top decision makers have with one another. (The leanness of staffing at the highest levels also helps in other ways—for example, by making traditional big-firm politics mostly impossible. There's no time for it.) At the same time, the network pushes decentralization at every turn: the primary role of the video journalist and the prominence of the assignment desk, the insistence that everyone take the initiative as she or he sees fit, and the concomitant tolerance for errors (with little or no re-hashing after one occurs, a huge difference from the three bigger nets). People on or close to the firing line have extraordinary autonomy, yet they must buy into the vision and understand how their piece fits into the larger puzzle.

CNN is cost-conscious, clearly under control—but not via the tentacles of huge accounting departments or massive, intrusive control documents. Above all, the culture induces an astonishing degree of self-control. It's hard to explain to managers with traditional backgrounds. However, it's easy to "feel" when you get up close. CNN is a zoo. But a damned disciplined one!

The contradictions that underpin—and vitalize—the CNN culture are largely direct by-products of Ted Turner's vision, personality, and way of doing business. Turner doesn't believe in failure. (Sounds like a line from

Norman Vincent Peale or Dale Carnegie. But in Turner's case, it's no exaggeration.) He does believe in taking the initiative. His visions are unfailingly grand. He is very unstructured, but very determined. Turner's approach, Whittemore claims, can be captured by two words—"Do it."

Above all (and this is mirrored all the way to the "bottom" of CNN), Turner believes in finding terrific people, then getting out of their way. During the frenetic 374-day period when CNN was invented, Turner was mostly away from Atlanta preparing his 1980 defense of the America's Cup. He was around in spirit, but seldom a physical presence. Reese Schonfeld and others got the job done. (To be sure, Hank Whittemore reported, Turner appeared, at flank speed, at crucial moments: to deal with RCA and the FCC over the availability of satellite transponders, to cajole skeptical cable system owners to come aboard.)

CNN Planet

Where does CNN go from here? "We've only begun," president Tom Johnson told me in earnest. He and Ted Turner are determined to create nothing less than the first truly "global information company" (their term); to be the "global network of record"—seen in every nation on the planet (in mid-1992, they were on the air in 137 countries); to broadcast in most major languages; to focus on non-U.S. journalists; to become world citizens who just happen to be based in the United States.

CNN AS CARNIVAL

CNN redefined an entire industry by learning how to reinvent itself each day. Of equal or greater significance, and strange as its world may seem to most of us (starting with me), CNN is a generic model for tomorrow's successful organization.

What's the right metaphor for CNN? Is Bob Furnad, for example, a "symphony conductor" (a favored "new-age management" metaphor)? Not on your life! His activity may look like that of a symphony conductor, but there's one big twist: He not only conducts his version of Beethoven's Ninth, but scores it as he goes along. Is CNN a "basketball game" (another new-management favorite), where you know the location of the goals, but not exactly how to get there? To some extent. But the locations of the goals shift too often for the basketball metaphor to really hold up.

Thinking at all in a fixed way about CNN—other than looking at that underlying document that lays out the network for the day—is dangerous. (I should come clean: CNNers don't make a to-do about that document. *I* was the one who needed something tangible to grasp.) Perhaps, then, CNN more than any other organization in this book *is* a carnival: a well-oiled underpark below, madness on the surface—and always dynamic.

Jump In with Both Feet

Despite my importunings to the contrary, many managers I talk with respond to the above with "But that's television." Suppose I grant you the point (for a moment): Confirmation for CNN's zany ways of "decision making" (in quotes, because it has so little to do with conventional ideas of approaching decisions) comes from a prizewinning *California Management Review* article by Stanford professor Kathleen Eisenhardt. Titled "Speed and Strategic Choice: How Managers Accelerate Decision-making," the article reports on Eisenhardt's study (with University of Virginia colleague Jay Bourgeois) of decision makers at 12 microcomputer firms. The slowpokes took 12 to 18 months to do what the quick set pulled off in 2 to 4.

Eisenhardt discovered five major distinctions between the two sorts. To begin with, the speedos swam in a deep, turbulent sea of real-time information, while the slugabeds relied on "planning and futuristic information." The hustlers obsessively tracked a few key operating measures such as bookings, backlog, cash, and engineering milestones, often updating them daily. And they typically scheduled as many as three weekly, must-attend, top-team meetings to chew over "what's happening," as Eisenhardt put it. Constant e-mail chatter and face-to-face meetings almost completely superseded the ubiquitous memos, lengthy reports, and ponderous get-togethers that marked the languorous firms.

Perversely, Eisenhardt notes, slow decision makers considered fewer alternatives than their speedy kin! They minutely dissected each possibility, while the greased-lightning gang considered a batch of options—all at once. The bunch-at-once approach had wonderful side benefits. "Comparative analysis sharpens preferences," Eisenhardt says. Looking at lots of choices also built confidence and provided fallback positions, which are frequently needed in today's zany marketplace.

The one-at-a-timers mulled and mulled—and mulled and mulled—often until opportunity passed them by. When the much-belabored option died, they were left with nothing, and had to fire up the cumbersome process once again.

Slow deciders, Eisenhardt says, were "stymied by conflict. They [wait as for consensus and delay] in hopes that uncertainty will magically become certain." The quicksters, by contrast, thrived on conflict, which they saw as "natural, valuable, and almost always inevitable." At some point, the senior decision maker, when he's certain that disagreement wouldn't evaporate, cut off debate and made the call.

Speedy chiefs relied on "an older and more experienced" mentor, Eisenhardt claims, while slow decision makers rarely had such advisers. She speculates that the counselors, often 10 to 20 years the boss's senior, "boost the confidence of decision makers to decide"—which is essential, she says, given that "one of the highest barriers to fast decision making is anxiety."

Finally, in yet another example of "all at once" behavior, the fast decision makers thoroughly integrated strategies and tactics. They juggled budgets, schedules, and organization options simultaneously. Sluggish blokes examined strategic decisions in a vacuum, delaying grubby operational considerations until the "big choices" were made; as a result, despite their painstakingly big-picture analyses, they were more likely to trip over details of implementation.

The five differences can be summarized with one word that also stood out at CNN: *immersion.* Eisenhardt's speedy decision makers thrived on the fray itself. They were anything but detached. "The carefully conducted industry analysis or broad-ranging strategic plan is no longer a guarantee of success," Eisenhardt concludes. "The premium now is on moving fast and keeping pace."

4

ABB Asea Brown Boveri: Giant Industrial Company, Small Businesses, Lean Staff, Big Leverage through Knowledge Dissemination

People are not dumb. They know that if their company is not competitive, there is no job security.

PERCY BARNEVIK
Fortune, June 29, 1992

In his "Doom Speech," ABB Asea Brown Boveri CEO Percy Barnevik insists that two-thirds of Europe's giant companies will fail in the wake of European economic integration. He's determined that ABB will not be among them.

In 1991, ABB booked $28.9 billion in revenue in 140 countries ($6 billion in North America). ABB competes in eight business segments: Power Plants, Power Transmission, Power Distribution, "Industry" (e.g., Metallurgy, Process Automation), Transportation, Environmental Control, Financial Services, and "Various Activities" (e.g., robotics, superchargers). It is a classic heavy-industrial behemoth. Or was, at least, until Barnevik began to concoct what may be the most novel industrial-firm structure since Alfred Sloan built "modern" GM in the 1920s.

FIVE THOUSAND FEISTY PROFIT CENTERS

At the top, ABB is broken into those eight major business segments. Next come 65 Business Areas, then 1,300 independently incorporated companies, and some 5,000 autonomous profit centers. At the "bottom," the profit centers are beginning to reorganize into 10-person, multifunction High-Performance Teams. ABB employs about 215,000 people, so a company averages 200 people, a profit center about 50.

Often as not, ABB is the biggest competitor in a business segment. However, that bigness frequently emerges from a combination of relatively small operations. (A "small" ABB transformer operation may be big in a different sense—i.e., the largest "firm" making a specialized component for certain kinds of transformers.)

The spotlight belongs first on the 5,000 profit centers. During a conversation in 1991, Barnevik told us that if it were not for the blizzard of legal paperwork it would generate, he'd consider incorporating each one. Why? Mostly to heighten the sense of ownership among each center's employees. As it is, almost all the centers have their own profit-and-loss statements and a balance sheet; they own assets; and they serve external customers directly. Each of these elements is important, but none more than the last. "Everything changes when there's a real customer yelling at you from the other end of the phone connection," Barnevik said. Direct attachment to customers transforms the little unit into a "real business."

The average profit center is led by a "management team" of five—a chief and four colleagues—or, as Barnevik put it, the centers are run collectively by "5,000 profit-responsible individuals with teams of three or four." Suddenly, vast ABB seems a lot more "manageable"—which is precisely the point. (Barnevik was born in rural Uddevalla near Sweden's west coast, where his father ran a small print shop. Barnevik often contends that his operating philosophy is no more than a large-scale extension of print-shop logic: Consider the 5,000 profit centers as 5,000 print shops.)

Barnevik is the most insistent enemy of bureaucracy I've met. Partial proof: The gargantuan operation, he explained, typically has just *three* layers of management! A 13-member executive committee (including Barnevik) based in Zurich runs the show. Below it come 250 senior executives, including 100 country managers and most of the Business Area chiefs, then the 5,000 profit center managers with their management teams. That's it—only *two* layers ordinarily between the big chiefs and the High-Performance Team members on the shop floor.

HOLDING ABB TOGETHER

Barnevik calls ABB a "multidomestic" corporation. Translation, still abstract: ABB's structure is designed to "leverage core technologies and economies of scale without eroding local market presence." Further translation: ABB is a matrix structure, with countries and industries as the two dimensions.

Individual profit centers, plants, and companies within a "country structure" constitute one dimension of the matrix. Business Areas (e.g., Hydropower Plants, Electric Metering, Complete Rail Systems, Leasing and Financing) make up the other. Sixty-five Business Area chiefs "have responsibility for" the overall, global strategy of "their" businesses; they also ensure that "their" businesses stick by agreed-upon budgets. In practice, Business Area chiefs and their small staffs are roving itinerant preachers—cajoling, comparing unit and competitor results, arranging job shifts for key people so as to transfer—and leverage—knowledge gained from here to there.

A Business Area boss is very powerful—and not so powerful. Suppose, for example, his analyses suggest a "rationalization"—reducing the number of factories producing similar components from five to two. Suppose those five factories are under the "command" of five different, equally powerful country presidents. It's up to the Business Area chief and the country bosses to sort out the economic and sociopolitical considerations and come to a decision.

To be sure, there is a formal mechanism for conflict resolution. Each Business Area manager reports to one of the 13 members of the Executive Committee. So does each country manager. (Ordinarily they report to different Executive Committee members.) In instances of lingering impasse, the Business Area chief and country heads will buck their cases up to their Executive Committee members. But Barnevik made it clear that this should occur only rarely. If country managers and Business Area chiefs come repeatedly to Executive Committee members to resolve disputes, he told us, "We'll fire both of them."

The Business Area concept is purposefully fluid. Consider process automation. The Business Area was originally headed by the president of one of ABB's process automation companies; the rest of his team consisted of the other four process automation company presidents. The Business Area was "headquartered" in Sweden—because the chief and his company were there. Later on, the "headquarters" moved to Germany, then to the United States (after ABB acquired America's Combustion Engineering, the Executive Committee decided that the most significant process automation opportunities were in the U.S.—hence the move). The current Business Area leader does not double as a company president; he performs the Business Area task full-time and is supported by a local, expert staff of seven.*

*The staff lives in the Combustion Engineering headquarters. But that's only because ABB can't unload the building in a lousy New England real estate market. Otherwise, there is no general expectation that a Business Area team would "live with" one of its companies.

Business Area teams range in size from one (or less, a part-time company president) to 10 or 15. Business Area chiefs occasionally complement their professional staffs with senior officers from various Business Area companies, gathered on short-lived project teams to assess a strategic issue (quality improvement, a new technology, etc.). Overall, though, it's no exaggeration to say that Barnevik is obsessed—a word he regularly uses—with keeping Business Area staffs tiny and responsive to their units.

A Matrix That's Mostly Not

I've railed against the matrix organization structure for years. Matrices become hopelessly complex bureaucracies and gut the emotional energy and "ownership" of those closest to the marketplace. I still believe that. Yet Barnevik's unique format passes my high-energy/accountability test, though I'm not confident that an ABB without Barnevik wouldn't deteriorate—his abiding hatred of bureaucracy is critical to making the ABB structure work. But as it stands today, ABB's Business Area idea in practice differs dramatically from the traditional matrix. For example:

—Staffs are tiny. Business Area teams are purposefully kept very small. Period.

—They live "where it makes sense," and move when it makes sense. In the traditional matrix, Business Area equivalents are typically berthed at mecca—i.e., corporate headquarters—and often win debates by mere proximity to top execs. There are no Business Area heads/teams at the Zurich headquarters, and neither grass nor excessive self-esteem grows readily under the feet or between the ears of Business Area staff members.

—Local profit center managers are accountable. Goals are agreed upon, and that's that—local managers are not beholden to numerous bosses, as in the traditional matrix. (The ABB ethos of accountability almost matches that of EDS.)

—ABB's avowed approach is for top management "to be an insider, not an invader." That is, the company has the utmost respect for local country operations. Business Area staffs do not promiscuously move production workers around in pursuit of short-term advantage—again, in sharp contrast to the silly shenanigans of many 1970s-style, headquarters-based matrix managers.

—Business Area chiefs live by persuasion. They are on the road and away from the political center almost all the time. They earn their spurs by being helpful and only seek higher-level conflict resolution assistance at their peril.

Rationalize but Don't Kill Competition

Despite Barnevik's drive for decentralization, ABB does openly seek some "old-fashioned" manufacturing scale economies. This seeming contradiction can mostly be explained by the atomized structure of European commerce. Upon putting the ABB pieces together, mostly by merger, Barnevik frequently ended up with a dozen plants in one industry producing the same low-volume, highly specialized component—each generating minuscule revenues. He attacked this massive overlap directly; today, instead of 10 plants performing the same small task, you'll find 2 or 3. Moreover, any one plant (a $15- to $30-million operation) will be producing many fewer products than before.

The Low-Voltage Apparatus Business Area is typical. The diagram opposite shows major products and plants. Three of nine key products (such as low-voltage breakers) are made at only one plant; two are made at two plants; two at three plants; and two at four plants. Looked at another way, each low-voltage apparatus factory makes between two and six products. Before rationalization, almost every box on the chart would have been filled. On the other hand, despite the significant rationalization, there is still internal competition in most cases.

Changes in the modest-size Power Semiconductor Business Area (which provides components for several other ABB businesses) illuminate Barnevik's thinking about scale and internal competition. In 1991, ABB closed a 200-person power semiconductor factory in Sweden, concentrating all production at the site of ABB's 150-person operation in Switzerland. Two full-blown factories for such a modest-size business made no sense, Barnevik insists. Despite closing the factory, however, ABB left Sweden's power semiconductor *design group* intact. The Swedish designers had some special skills, and Barnevik didn't want to lose their energy or independence. Retaining the two design groups (which could "economically" have been folded into one) induces all-important "brain competition," Barnevik claims.

Internal competition in ABB is hot. The central information system makes timely information on the details of every operation's performance widely available. Furthermore, Business Area managers are always on the trail of efficiencies. Suppose a Swedish plant is one of three ABB operations building a particular component, and as a result of a new management approach, like the "T50" program described below, it dramatically outperforms the other two. In time, the Business Area manager may decide to move some—or all—of the other plants' business to Sweden. But if the Swedish plant doesn't directly win business away from its sister plants, it will almost certainly be chosen as home for the Business Area's next generation of products (and product development).

Overall, Barnevik works at keeping enough operations going in parallel

ABB Business Area (Low-Voltage Apparatus)

Production Facilities	LV Breakers	MCCB	Switches	Disconnectors	Contactors	Overload Relays	Starters	Monitors	Pushbuttons
Heidelberg Germany					X	X	X	X	
Pelercem France					X		X		
SACE Italy	X	X							
NEBB Norway			X	X					
Dist/D Sweden			X		X	X	X	X	X
Strömberg Finland			X	X	X	X	X		

production to maintain superheated internal competition—yet he's effectively countered the extreme fragmentation that is the heritage of the European industrial past.

LEAN STAFF

Percy Barnevik arrived as CEO at Sweden's Asea in 1980, having just concluded a highly successful tour as chief of the U.S. arm of Sweden's Sandvik (carbide cutting tools, etc.). He discovered a central staff of 2,000, gasped, and reduced it to 200. Barnevik flatly told HQ staffers that they had three months to find a job in one of the company's line operating units. "You can't postpone tough decisions by studying them to death," Barnevik said in an interview in the *Harvard Business Review*. "You can't permit a 'honeymoon' of small changes over a year or two. A long series of small changes just prolongs the pain. . . . [Y]ou have to accept a fair share of mistakes, [but] I'd rather be roughly right and fast than exactly right and slow. We apply these principles wherever we go."

Indeed he has. When ABB acquired Finland's premier industrial firm, Stromberg, a headquarters of 880 greeted him. A couple of years later that number was 25! At the German ABB headquarters in Mannheim, Barnevik found a staff of 1,600 people in 1988. Now there are 100. (How do you get from 1,600 down to 100? About 400 got the boot. But most went to nearby profit centers, since the Mannheim headquarters was surrounded by numerous small ABB factories.)

Barnevik has gotten the business of reducing central staff down to a near-science. He insists the head count in any headquarters activity can be cut by 90 percent the first year: About 30 percent disappear through attrition and other layoffs; another 30 percent go to one of the 50-person profit centers; and 30 percent become members of freestanding service centers (often new companies) that perform real work on a competitive basis and bill operating units for it at market prices (e.g., ABB Marketing Services manages ad campaigns for subsidiaries, but also has outside clients and is expected to turn a profit); about 10 percent remain at the corporate center.

But that's just the start. By year three or four, Barnevik declares, the 30 percent in the freestanding service centers can be reduced by half; the 30 percent in the profit centers can be cut by a third; and the 10 percent in the corporate center should be further slashed by half. Add it up, and about 30 percent of the staff is eliminated in the first year, another 30 percent by year three or four—and after the second round of cuts, only 5 percent will remain in the corporate center. That is precisely what happened when Asea merged with Brown Boveri in 1987. Asea, of course, had already reduced its center to rubble; now Brown Boveri absorbed the sledgehammer's bitter blow—a rapid cut of its pre-merger 4,000-person central complement to 200 (95 percent!). To run the newly combined entity, Barnevik created a headquarters with a complement of 100 professionals and a clerical support team of 50. Among them, for example, there's a single human resources executive, Arne Olson, supported by a secretary and three other junior staffers. (Olson, *Fortune* reported in June 1992, spends most of his time on the road, giving seminars on management development to ABB subsidiaries.)

LEVERAGING KNOWLEDGE

Staffs are lean (no intrusive bureaucrats). Local units (profit centers) are empowered and substantially autonomous. And the Business Areas' evangelists are out and about preaching an overall scheme for "their" units. But there's still more to ABB; part of that "more" amounts to a whole new way of conceiving "global" and "scale."

It turns out that most Business Area teams *are* pursuing economies of scale, but mostly *learning* scale, not production scale. Consider the Power Transformers Business Area (part of the Power Transmission segment). With $1 billion in revenue, it's four times the size of its next-largest competitor. Led by a Swede, Sune Karlsson, the business is headquartered in Mannheim, Germany, but "owns" 25 factories in 16 countries.

"We are not a global business," Karlsson told *Harvard Business Review* writer William Taylor. "We are a collection of local businesses with intense global coordination. This makes us unique." He added that he wants "local companies to think small, to worry about their home market and a handful of [assigned] export markets, and to learn to make money on smaller volumes." It's been tough, he noted, convincing "local managers that they can run small operations more efficiently [than large ones], meet customer needs more flexibly—and make money." Karlsson's factories, small by industry standards, run from $10 million to $150 million in volume, and at least two-thirds of a typical factory's output goes to local markets. To be competitive, Karlsson has emphasized slashing delivery time, maximizing design and production flexibility, and focusing on domestic customers—rather than attempting to achieve volume efficiencies.

So what is the advantage in combining the 25 factories in one "Business Area," or, for that matter, belonging to ABB? Karlsson dismisses "hard" advantages, such as the ability to make efficient purchases, that theoretically come from overall size. It's the "soft" stuff, emanating from effective global coordination, that makes the difference:

> Our most important strength is that we have 25 factories around the world, each with its own president, design manager, marketing manager, and production manager. These people are working on the same problems and opportunities day after day, year after year, and learning a tremendous amount. We want to create a process of continuous expertise transfer. If we do, that's a source of advantage none of our rivals can match.

But learning to learn effectively in a dispersed organization, many of whose members came from acquired companies (and different national cultures), is not easy. On the one hand, Taylor reports that Karlsson stirs internal competition by providing detailed monthly information on the performance of all 25 units. But Karlsson is also aware that such competition must be constructive; he insists, says Taylor, that the key task is creating a "culture of trust and exchange."

Taylor describes several mechanisms, or "forums for exchange," that Karlsson has created to foster learning. A Business Area management board, for example, meets four to six times a year to chart global strategies. Then there's the Business Area staff—five veterans with special responsibility for areas such as R&D and purchasing, who travel constantly, confer with the managements of local units, and push the overall learning and coordination agenda forward. Functional coordination teams, made up of expert members from various operations, meet a couple of times a year to work on production, quality, marketing, and other issues.

While the formal gatherings are important, most of the value comes, Taylor observes, from "creating information exchange throughout the year. The system works when the quality manager in Sweden feels compelled to telephone or fax the quality manager in Brazil with a problem or an idea." "Sharing of expertise does not happen automatically," Karlsson admitted. "People need to spend time together, to get to know and understand each other. . . . People must also see a payoff for themselves. I never expect our operations to coordinate unless all sides get real benefits. We have to demonstrate that sharing pays—that contributing one idea gets you twenty-four in return."

Creating value through the accumulation of knowledge across diverse, mainly locally focused businesses has other twists as well. Take Finland's ABB Stromberg. When ABB acquired Stromberg, it was—typical of small-country European firms—trying to be all things to all people. Though Stromberg remains in many businesses today, it is capitalizing on its special talent in electronic drives, where the company has long been a technology and manufacturing leader. Officially, Taylor reports, ABB Stromberg has been designated a Center of Excellence for Electronic Drives, with coordination responsibility in that specialty for the rest of the ABB family. Such Centers of Excellence are springing up all over ABB. (The idea—and language—is strikingly similar to EDS's "Centers of Service.")

T50: THE NEXT STEP

But there's more afoot. In fact, ABB Sweden's T50 program may be the most dramatic learning spearhead of all. The Swedish arm of ABB has 46,000 employees in 150 independent companies in 200 locations; in 1990 it booked about $8 billion in revenues—and its T50 program is shaking the company to its roots. In short, ABB Sweden intends to cut total cycle time (order, design, engineering, manufacturing, shipping) for everything it produces by 50 percent by the end of 1993. If successful, T50 promises to add about half a billion dollars to ABB Sweden's bottom line!

T50 emerged from a 1989 corporate (Zurich) task force. The president of ABB Sweden, Bert-Olof Svaholm, chose to pick up the ball and run hard with it. Today ABB Sweden's executive vice president Kenneth Synnersten (who characteristically doubles as a Business Area head for Materials) spends about half of his time on the project; he works with an ABB Sweden steering group and is supported by four staffers (who also, characteristically, are de facto "salesmen"—on the road touting the program's early successes to fence-sitters and laggards).

The average ABB company in Sweden has 200 to 400 people. Many are still structured the traditional way, with functional departments—sales, design, production, distribution. The structural objective of T50 is to completely flip the primary axis of doing business, getting almost everyone—representing all functions—out of the specialist departments and into "horizontal" product divisions numbering 30 to 100 people. This is possible, Synnersten insists, even though most of the businesses are "heavy industrial." The final step is to further decompose those 30- to 100-person product divisions into the 10-person, multifunction High-Performance Teams mentioned at the outset of this analysis.

In the new structure, there may still be a "head of sales" reporting to the company president to provide sales advice. But in this advisory role, the sales chief will have *no* supporting functional staff. Moreover, the odds are high that he or she will double as general manager of one of the small, largely self-contained product divisions. Synnersten estimates that in a 200-person company, at least 160 people can be assigned to product division units, leaving no more than 40 in functional slots.

ABB Controls, which reorganized on January 1, 1992, is a case in point. First, the 500-person company split into four units/divisions of 125 people each. (For example, the central 60-person design unit was split into four bits, each with a "local" office.) The outfit was further subdivided into about 50 High-Performance Teams. Approximately 25 staffers still have some central duties; but each one of them also has a line role in one of the four divisions.

Singing the new tune of "time-based competition" experts (see the Learning to Hustle section), Synnersten claims that rejiggering manufacturing per se is a minor issue; it's already a "superhighway"—all sorts of clever techniques have been applied to make it efficient, so much so that, as the diagram on the next page shows, it absorbs only 3 percent of total sales-to-delivery cycle time. On the other hand, very little emphasis had previously been placed on the integration of the "other" functions (sales, order entry, order coding, engineering, specification development, planning, delivery) into a well-oiled whole. Focusing on these "other activities"—performing work holistically/horizontally/in parallel—offers the lion's share of T50's huge performance enhancement opportunity.

After little more than a year (at the time of my visit), Sweden's T50 gang could point to several extraordinary successes. Consider new product development in one part of ABB Distribution. A new-look, multifunctional product development team was formed in June 1990, just as the T50 process kicked off. The Eurocenter Switchgear Cabinet, incorporating new technologies and a computerized support system for generating customized specifications (to be hooked up to PCs all over Europe), was introduced almost 10 months to the day after project launch; ordinarily, such an effort would have eaten up 4 years.

Then there's the 10-person High-Performance Team in the $5-million safety switch business. The newfangled "horizontal" group began work in

ABB Sweden:
Functions as a Percentage of
Total Sales-to-Delivery Cycle Time

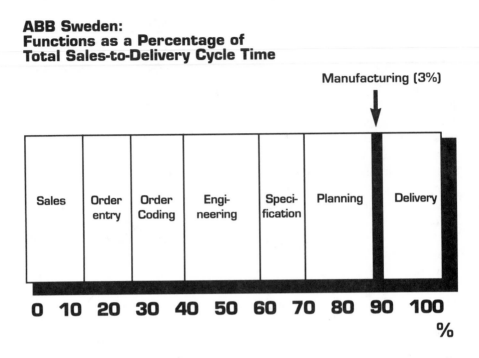

Manufacturing (3%)

| Sales | Order entry | Order Coding | Engineering | Specification | Planning | Delivery |

0 10 20 30 40 50 60 70 80 90 100
%

early 1991. In eight months, total cycle time (order to delivery) was reduced from between 15 and 33 days to 5 days. On-time deliveries shot up from 50 percent in January 1991 to 96 percent in September 1991. Switches produced per person per day (an overall productivity measure) increased by about 20 percent, from 144 in January 1991 to 169 in September. Absenteeism, a strategic problem for Sweden as whole, dropped from 20 percent to 8 percent. The team does its own planning, scheduling, purchasing, and overall customer satisfaction management. Some engineering tasks are still performed by a residual central staff, though many of these may be delegated to the teams as T50 progresses.

Synnersten has established a bare-bones T50 guidance "structure" for ABB Sweden as a whole: Each company has one member of senior management designated "T50 Responsible." These managers oversee progress in their own units and serve as liaisons with Synnersten's central T50 team; the "T50 responsibles" meet one day each quarter and swap experiences. Furthermore, T50 must be part of each Swedish company's strategic plan and annual budget. It's also permanently "on the agenda" at individual company board meetings.

Synnersten expects that by the end of 1993, about two-thirds of ABB Sweden's home-country employees will be actively involved in a T50 project. (In fact the overall steering group has set precise quantitative goals for its march to 50 percent overall cycle-time reduction.) There's no doubt that Synnersten's impatient. At the same time, however, he stresses the need for patience. "Project managers," Synnersten told us, "must allow individuals to buy into the process at their own rate. They must be willing to let people 'reinvent the wheel' in order to get buy-in."

Synnersten's real cudgel is a growing catalog of success stories. Almost everyone was skeptical at first, he said. Only true believers were willing to join the T50 crusade. But now Synnersten can send skeptics to see for themselves the hard evidence. "Bragging—and peer pressure—are the key motivations," he concluded with a smile.

T50: More Than Speed

As usual, it's murky out. Raw speed is only part of the "speed issue." It begs the "speed for what" question. Fashion means getting new products out the door faster. But it also means more clever products, and intertwining with customers in ever more intimate ways. So going faster, lots faster, and eliminating functional barriers are as much efforts to get dramatically closer to customers as they are to churn out orders or new products at a frantic pace. Any way you define it, though, ABB Sweden does not intend to be caught napping—and ABB chairman Barnevik does not intend for his enterprise to be one of the doomed giants of post-1992 Europe.

II

Learning to Hustle

PROLOGUE: THE QUICK AND THE DEAD

Since 1979, when Sony Corp. invented the Walkman, the company has developed 227 different models, or about one every three weeks.

Steven Brull
*International Herald
Tribune*
March 26, 1992

Intel's R&D costs are especially high because the company pays for work on two generations of products at a time so it can introduce products at a more rapid rate.

San Jose Mercury News
February 11, 1992

The nineties will be a decade in a hurry, a nanosecond culture. There'll be only two kinds of managers: the quick and the dead.

David Vice
Vice-Chairman
Northern Telecom

Competing Against Time: How Time-Based Competition is Reshaping Global Markets, by Boston Consulting Group senior partners George Stalk, Jr., and Thomas M. Hout, has become the bible of the new hustlers' movement. Stalk and Hout begin with the "H-Y War"—the early 1980s donnybrook between the motorcycle manufacturing arms of Honda and Yamaha, which anticipated today's marketplace turmoil. In 1981, Yamaha started work on a new factory that would, by definition, make it Japan's number one producer of motorcycles, assuming that demand for all its output could be secured. Honda responded to the challenge with speed. At the time, Honda produced some 60 motorcycle models. In the next 18 months, the company shattered all precedent and flooded the market with 113 new models, turning motorcycle design, say Stalk and Hout, into "a matter of fashion." Yamaha was unable to match Honda's pace, and, remarkably in face-conscious Japan, publicly announced its "surrender" to Honda.

Why aren't others up to the Sony, Intel, or Honda standard? The short answer is organizations designed (misdesigned) to soak up time like a sponge. Stalk and Hout coin a number of rules, based on meticulous research. None is more "impressive"—frightening!—than "the 0.05 to 5 rule." It goes like this: "Most products and many services are actually receiving value for only .05 to 5 percent of the time they are in the value delivery systems of their companies." Reverse those figures and you have the phenomenon of 95 to 99.95 percent lost time. On average!

Ouch! Or wow? On the one hand, such findings offer the glimmer of a golden opportunity (organize right, get swift, get rich—see our CNN analysis). On the other, there's an enormous threat: If your competitor does "it" to you (95 percent time compression) and you're unable to respond, Katy bar the door.

The idea of—and necessity for—doing everything faster is hard to challenge. The problem, as we saw at the end of the ABB case, is that cycle time compression means much more than running faster. That's why we've chosen hustle, rather than speed per se, as the main thrust of this section. To become one with the customer (beyond "get close to"—see the chapter on EDS), to work in ever-changing networks with ever-changing partners to develop and market revolutionary products (fast), calls for an encompassing culture of hustle. The cases that follow describe firms learning to hustle; they are purposefully chosen from corners of the economy where we would not expect to see fashion driving change: high-tech industrial hose (workers entwined with customers—and moving fast—add up to stunning success), power tools (user-friendliness—and speed—redefine a piece of an industry), and, get this, the railroad (where slow decision making and useless information destroyed faith in a bedrock industry—and almost destroyed the industry).

Don't Let the Morning Slip By

Even the most timely industry newsletter is usually at least a week old before it gets to readers. Not *The White House Bulletin.* It reaches paid subscribers *18 minutes* after leaving the editor's desk, by fax. The service carries a premium: As of mid-1992, several hundred Washington, D.C., political insiders were paying from $980 (for a small law firm) to nearly $4,500 (the White House itself) to read about daily White House activities.

Profitable after only six months of publication, the *Bulletin* summarizes what's happened since the morning papers hit the streets and gives quick analyses and inside information about the day's policy and personnel moves. When major news breaks late in the day, the editors fax readers a special update.

"We're an outlet for a different type of information, because we come out right after people have read the morning papers," Publisher Paul Roellig told us. "We can report the immediate reactions of the people involved. . . . This town operates on information, and if you have it before someone else, you have an advantage."

5

Titeflex: Unplug the Computer, Unleash the Teamsters, and "Just Do It"

It is time to stop paving the cow paths. Instead of imbedding outdated processes in silicon and software, we should obliterate them and start over.

MICHAEL HAMMER
"Re-engineering Work: Don't
Automate, Obliterate"
Harvard Business Review
July–August 1990

The idea was to rebuild the company, a "blank page" approach. The key thing was flowcharting all the processes. At each step, you ask about 10 times, "Is that adding value for the customers?"

JON SIMPSON
Former president, Titeflex

In 1777, George Washington and his chief of artillery, Henry Knox, chose Springfield, Massachusetts, as the site of the first U.S. arsenal. Springfield's place in history was assured during the next 100 years. The British may well deserve credit for inventing many of the elements that went into mass, or standardized, production. But it was the Americans who perfected them. (Witness the stream of British visitors to America in the mid-19th century, aiming to learn the ins and outs of mass production.) Much of that perfecting took place at the Springfield Arsenal.

The idea for identical gun stocks—the first, tentative step toward mass production, according to historians—sprang from the mind of Thomas Blanchard in 1819. From the start the emphasis was on specialization. Job breadth was narrowed, then narrowed again. "Craft" disappeared. "Head work" all but disappeared. For a long time it paid off. Springfield's success was America's success. But now the old practices are in tatters—and a second American manufacturing revolution is taking place within Springfield's city limits. It's occurring at a company named Titeflex, manufacturer of fluid and gas holding systems—hoses to you and me. There some 500 U.S. employees, in industrial products and aerospace divisions, are creating a brand-new way of doing business.

TITEFLEX, CIRCA 1988

Take a glimpse at Titeflex in late 1988 (per the diagram on the next page). A new order would be entered in the MRP I (Materials Requirements Planning) computer wonder system. "It" (MRP I) would "create" paperwork for purchasing, production schedulers, the storeroom, and the quality-assurance department. Engineering reviews and cost reviews—more paper jumbles—would also be initiated.

According to Jon Simpson, Titeflex president from late 1988 to early 1992,* all this required (generated?) umpteen meetings—"morning meetings," "afternoon meetings," "engineering review meetings." Not to mention "quality review meetings," "make-buy meetings," and "purchasing meetings." Typical elapsed time for order entry alone: *three to five weeks.*

On to the factory floor, where the next set of convoluted processes would begin. Part of the order went to the basic hose manufacturing line, along with the paperwork ginned up by the various reviews. ("It amounted to a book," one worker told us.) That factory-floor group, in turn, started out by creating more paperwork to fuel the voracious "system." Another part of the order went to a factory group responsible for fittings for the basic hose. (Five different departments usually got in on the act of making such fittings.) After the hoses and associated components were built, they went to another department to be cleaned; then through at least three more departments for final assembly; then to the 50-person quality-assurance department; and, finally, to the shipping department.

*Titeflex (formerly a part of the Bundy Corp.) is a wholly owned subsidiary of Britain's TI Group. As a result of his success at Titeflex, Simpson was promoted to vice president of marketing, TI United States Ltd.

Old (Complicated) Titeflex System

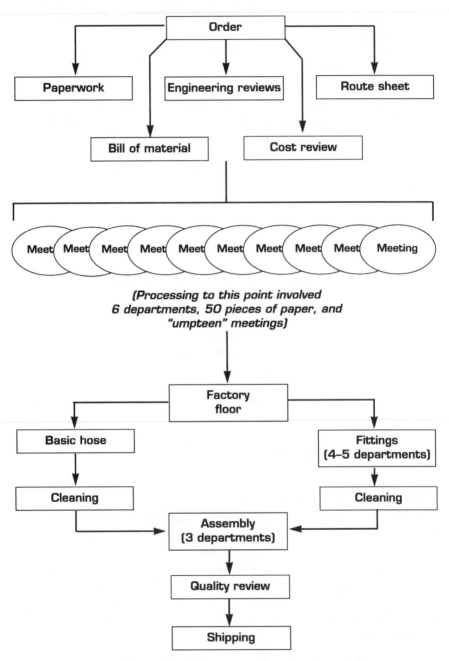

(Processing to this point involved
6 departments, 50 pieces of paper, and
"umpteen" meetings)

(elapsed time on floor, approximately 6 weeks)

Factory-floor "management" was overseen by a big production control planning unit. Its plate was always full, since bits and pieces of orders were continually stuck in this or that corner of the plant. A typical order-in-progress went through the stockroom, labeled Spaghetti Junction on the master flow-chart, no less than six times, as part of a three-quarter-mile voyage from initial order to shipping dock!

Production controllers were also forced to invent six "expedite lists." They were necessary to override the formal systems. There was a Hot List (angry customers), a Luke-Hot list (moderately angry customers), an End-of-the-Month List (to assist in getting stuck orders out the door, so that they could be recorded for accounting purposes), and so on.

Altogether, manufacturing absorbed at least 6 weeks, on top of the 3 to 5 weeks for order entry—for a grand total of 9 to 11 weeks, *if*, Simpson underscored, everything went smoothly.

TITEFLEX TODAY

Things have changed! The bureaucratic jungle has been slashed and burned. Layers of management rooted out. Processes trashed, then completely reinvented. Old computer systems disconnected.

Now: New orders feed into an "administrative cell," called a Genesis Team, consisting of five people with their desks arranged in a tight circle. Among the players are (1) a contracts administrator, the voice of Titeflex to the outside customer (discussing price, delivery dates, etc., and setting up "master contracts" with in-house "small businesses"); (2) applications engineers, who immediately review each order from an engineering standpoint; (3) a quality engineer, who checks that quality requirements are being met; (4) a draftsman, who draws up new designs if necessary; and (5) a clerical support person.

In place of those endless preliminary meetings, Genesis Team members simply pass stuff back and forth, talk to one another informally; they handle all the details themselves—supported marginally by the vestiges of that old MRP I system (which they say is now no more than a "helpful calculator"). Paperwork is minimal (often no more than a page for a complex order), and the whole process can consume as few as 10 minutes for something routine, no more than two to five days for a truly novel and intricate request.

The rest of the operation (the factory) has been organized into de facto "small businesses" (focused, self-sufficient "manufacturing cells") of 6 to 10 people each. For example, Business Development Teams (BDTs) are in-house small units/cells in several flavors which "sell" complete hose-and-fitting sets to the Genesis Team. Final Assembly Teams are cells that handle ultimate construction.

Before an order is even released to the factory, the Genesis Team has been in touch with a Business Development Team. Immediately after order release, the Business Development Team begins manufacture. (In fact, it frequently begins before official order release.) When the BDT finishes building components, its output goes to the stockroom—the *only* trip to the stockroom these days!—and from there to one of the Final Assembly Teams.

Total manufacturing time now typically varies from two days to one week. Crash orders go to a special, lightning-fast Rapid Deployment Team, which can handle the whole shebang, from order entry to the shipping dock, in as little as three or four hours. (See the discussion of Tom Strange and Joe Tilli—the RDT—in the Preface.) The diagram opposite illustrates the new approach.

In the reorganization, functional genocide was the order of the day: The entire production control planning operation disappeared. (Today 10 of the 30 controllers remain, but as line members of Business Development Teams.) The pricing department evaporated, too. So did that big quality-control operation. A small finance department still exists to perform end-of-the-month consolidations and overview analyses, but most of the bean counters were folded into the line teams. Of course, the expedite lists vanished, since virtually all the work is out the door within a few days.

"JUST DO IT"

Titeflex was an early adopter of the touted MRP I computer/ software system. Unfortunately, as was true for so many pioneer MRP I users in the '80s, the system was superimposed directly upon antiquated processes. We "automated chaos," Simpson told me. "The computer governed our lives." But that didn't last for long in the new regime. Simpson, on a business trip to Boston right after he came aboard, called back to the office and was informed that the computer was down. Customer orders could not be shipped. He recalls commanding one of his senior managers to "Go down to the local five-and-dime and get a box of crayons, then write the customer's address on the box and ship the product." The manager did. It worked. MRP I, R.I.P. The revolution was on!

The computer was essentially removed from the loop. Business processes were then executed "by hand." In August 1988, 23 percent of Industrial Products Division orders were going out on time. (This story has any number of twists and turns: Even coming up with that number was a big step forward, since before the revolution there were no measures of time or timeliness.) Only 120 days later, in December, the on-time rate had soared to 65 percent—by "brute force," said Simpson. By March 1989, with fewer people and nary a penny of new capital spending, it had hit 90 percent.

There were a host of "management variables" associated with the turn-around: the Genesis Team for order entry, the Business Development Teams,

New (Streamlined) Titeflex System

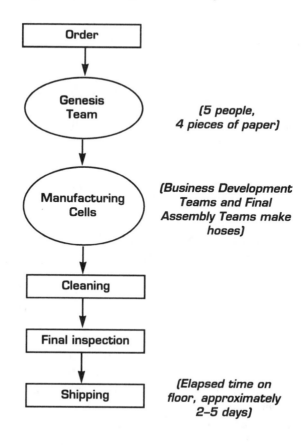

Order

↓

Genesis Team — *(5 people, 4 pieces of paper)*

↓

Manufacturing Cells — *(Business Development Teams and Final Assembly Teams make hoses)*

↓

Cleaning

↓

Final inspection

↓

Shipping — *(Elapsed time on floor, approximately 2–5 days)*

and so on. But in some respects, they're the icing on the cake. Something more important underpinned the process: Simpson got out on the floor. Listened to the people who do the work. Responded to their long-standing frustrations. Fundamental to what happened at Titeflex—dollars or technology, or even the revolution in "management" structures—was a change of "culture," the introduction of "a sense of urgency," as Simpson put it.

When Simpson debuted at Titeflex, people from key functions, such as accounting, engineering, and manufacturing, didn't talk much to one another—and it would have been a cold day in hell when an engineer was seen on the shop floor, seeking workers' advice. The average person on the front line was foiled at every turn.

Simpson's answer was a song from the EDS (or CNN) hymnal: Just let people know, unmistakably, that it is up to them to do whatever is necessary—and that they shouldn't bother checking with higher-ups before acting. And Simpson himself set the tone: Whenever he or his mostly new top team came across an expression of desire to do something that went beyond the "rules," the reply almost always was, "O.K., go do it."

For example, during Simpson's first weeks on the job frustrated teams of customers poured into the factory, usually furious about some order delayed for months (in some cases "even years"). Simpson would take the angry group down to the shop floor (unusual in itself), turn them over to the Titeflex workers, tell the two groups "to work it out," then walk away. "They did," he said with a smile. Business development manager Kevin Roberts put it unequivocally: "We gave them unlimited authority to do whatever is necessary to support the customer."

THE WEEKEND THAT WAS

We believed in our vision, so we decided to do it all over a weekend, trusting that the operators . . . would pick up the pieces and run with them.

ROBERT CONDON
Quality Assurance Director
Titeflex

Simpson delayered and debureaucratized. He reduced management levels by one to three in every function—for example, from five to three layers in operations. (There were no cuts, however, among front-line operators.) Then he established those self-managing cells/teams. Many aspects of the change were not as hard as the textbooks suggest, Simpson asserted. Why? "Workers were hungry for change."

How fast can big change be accomplished if workers are "hungry"? The answer, astonishingly, is virtually overnight. Out of 35 first-line supervisors, 20 vanished in the course of a single weekend. (Some left. Some took on engineering jobs.) The first self-managed cell was created by the workers themselves between Friday afternoon and Monday morning. In less than a month, the entire Industrial Products Division was converted.

"Seventy percent of the people wanted to kill each other," Simpson admitted of the first few weeks after teams were installed. One line worker I talked to agreed. "None of us thought it would work," she said. "We thought it was a joke." But chaos did not ensue. Frayed nerves or not, "performance improved on Monday morning," Simpson bluntly asserted. The numbers back him up.

Titeflex is a longtime Teamsters shop. Shooting straight with the union and building respect were at the top of Simpson's early—and continuing—agenda. The approach consisted of talking, one on one, with workers; regularly visiting people on each of the three shifts; learning everyone's name (minor as that may sound compared to some of the other moves, any number of workers pointed it out as a dramatic symbol of Simpson's commitment); and providing unlimited access to accounting information. "Our books are completely open," Kevin Roberts told us.

There are no limits to worker involvement. Upon developing a $5-million capital proposal in 1990, top management took it before a group of machinists and asked them to look at it through bankers' beady eyes: "Would you approve it?" "Where are the holes?" The exchange was invaluable to moving the project forward, Simpson reports.

The story Simpson tells was repeated chapter and verse at the front line. "The changes really aren't that hard [for us] to accept. It's something we've always asked for," a Teamster with twenty years' seniority told me. "Middle management had the biggest problem." One of his colleagues stunned me, insisting that the changes, which seemed monumental and quick to me, "aren't coming fast enough." So much for the time-honored rot about workers having difficulty adjusting!

The Accompanying Relationship Revolution

Relationships between functions were revolutionized. Those engineers, who had never been seen on the shop floor in "the old regime," are now constantly out and about, checking out the feasibility of doing this or that, seeking workers' advice as a matter of course. (I'd ask workers, "You said 'never,' right?" "That's right, *never*," was the reply.) Furthermore, workers who'd never left the shop before on Titeflex business now routinely travel to visit with customers. For example, a band of operators voyaged to General Electric's big aircraft engine operation in Evandale, Ohio. After much shuffling, they gained a "five-minute audience," Simpson reported, with the operation's big boss. He was so taken with their account of speed and worker involvement that he questioned them for four hours. Later, wandering the line with GE counterparts, Titeflex workers commented on the presence of a competitor's hoses. A Teamster line-worker-cum-super-super-salesperson asked: "Can we have this business?" The reply from GE was yes.

Customers also routinely visit Springfield to work with Titeflex employees. One result of working together: New-product development cycle time has been reduced by more than 50 percent.

Achieving such dramatic reductions in order-to-delivery cycle time requires cooperation—"partnership" is the preferred word in Springfield—with suppliers as well as customers. So teams from Du Pont, whose powdered Teflon is the basic ingredient in a Titeflex hose, visit with Titeflex teams quarterly to discuss product and process improvement. Titeflex operators also head out regularly to Du Pont. Neither firm would likely have allowed the other intimate access to its processes and operations a couple of years ago, Simpson claimed.

VELOCITY!

Simpson stressed the V-word—"velocity"—again and again. He remembered a GE aerospace customer arriving at Springfield in desperate pursuit of a special order that would have taken six weeks, at best, in the past. The customer left, customized part in hand, at 1 p.m. the same day. Given his description of the complexity of that product, I questioned Simpson about the amount of prior wasted time his report revealed. "Yes, Tom," he solemnly intoned, "there *was* that much waste." And he reiterated the point that the hurry-up demonstrated by the GE story was *not* the result of capital-intensive technical improvements (even though, by this point, the company had begun to add some capital goods as a result of newfound profitability). What made the whole difference, he insisted, was a new attitude, and tearing out bureaucratic constraints that got in the way of people doing what they had known how to do (and wanted to do) all along.

Titeflex is now taking business from competitors and charging healthy premiums for its swiftness and ability to customize its products. But as efficiency increases, I asked workers on the front line, aren't jobs threatened? (In some cases, increases in output have been phenomenal: from 300 or 400 pieces a month to 9,000 or 10,000 pieces a month in the underground tank hose business, for example.) To my surprise (again), workers responded like enlightened economists. "The better we get, the more business we create," was the reply of one. In fact, the front line is now putting pressure on marketing and salespeople to bring in more work.

Paradoxes are rife. It would seem to be "obvious" that the intense, speedy pace of work at the new Titeflex would be daunting for the average human being. Yet a line worker told me that it was "more relaxing [and] fun. Cooperation [among formerly sparring groups] leads to less tension, less wasted effort."

I can't overstate the importance of this last point. Star car dealer Carl Sewell's mechanics do 50 percent more jobs than the industry standard. Yet their lives are less stressful than those of their counterparts. Why? For one thing, parts they routinely use are stored at their meticulously designed workstations, rather than in some distant parts department. (Small thing? Not if you have to go get parts 15 times in an eight-hour day.) In fact, the whole Sewell "back room" operation is designed to make the mechanics' jobs proceed smoothly. At Sewell Cadillac or Titeflex or ABB Sweden, these accounts of radical increases in hustle are not Chaplinesque tales about "rats running faster in the maze."

The Titeflex gang is my favorite "stuff it in your face" example. When I discuss these odd ideas—e.g., turning all work into projects—I'm repeatedly confronted with, "Well, *sure*, at CNN, or EDS. But what about the *real* world?" Titeflex's hose-making Teamsters are as "real" as they come.

Fashion's Common Denominator

Two key organizational ideas which surface in the Titeflex story are central to this book. First, projects. It's not much of a stretch to say that Titeflex has become almost totally "projectized." It looks far more like EDS than EDS's parent, GM. The *average* Titeflex worker is calling on customers, working directly with vendors, seeking constant improvement. Moreover, functional "barriers" have been *removed*, not just "*bashed*." A day, a week, at Titeflex is now a series of novel projects—for virtually everyone.

Pondering Titeflex's dramatic changes also led me to a definition, what I call Fashion's Common Denominator. To wit:

> *Coherent, self-contained, multifunction, fully accountable, self-managed cells/clusters/teams/"businesses" of 2 to 35—supported, real-time, by all the organization's (and appropriate outsiders') information and expert resources, on-call as needed; and fully empowered to do whatever it takes to serve/respond to the customer/other members of the value-adding chain.*

Yes, it's a cumbersome definition! Yet I think—and I've tested this with thousands of seminar participants by now—it captures a lot of the essence of operations at EDS and CNN—and, as they begin to acquire the hustle that fashion requires, ABB Sweden and Titeflex (which are almost there). Each word and phrase is critical, but none more than "coherent, self-contained." Units like Titeflex's Business Development Teams are "businesses." Their workers are "businesspersons." That idea is essential to all that follows.

6

Ingersoll-Rand: Barbecues, Drag Tests, Medieval Warriors; and Slowing Down to Speed Things Up

Athens, Pennsylvania, is another most unlikely setting for a renaissance. But one has occurred there, in a factory first occupied by the fledgling Ingersoll-Rand (IR) organization in 1905. Now the facility is part of the $200-million (1991 revenue) Power Tool Division of the $3.5-billion industrial products conglomerate.

Athens today is home to a hot, industry-leading product—the Cyclone Grinder, an air-powered hand tool used for material removal and fine finishing (grinding metal burrs off everything from aircraft engine turbine blades and auto engine blocks to bar stool legs—customers like Boeing and Caterpillar buy them by the thousand).

In 1987 IR's air-powered grinder ranked third in the industry. It had been reconceived four times in the preceding dozen years—with each round of "innovation" less creative, more expensive, and more time-consuming than the round before, according to grinder line product manager Brian McNeill.

But that all changed. The four years it had taken to develop the last grinder was squeezed to one year. And along the way, a "commodity" was transformed into a zippy, value-added product. (It would take a bucket to hold all the design awards the Cyclone has bagged.) Margins, sales, and market share soared. Competitors were, and so far have stayed, befuddled.

The story has some unsurprising elements. Today's favorite innovation buzz phrase is "simultaneous product development," popularized in the U.S. in the early 1980s by Ford's launch of the Taurus. The trick is putting all the key players (e.g., marketing, manufacturing, engineering) on a team from the start. That contrasts with the traditional "sequential product development" approach: Engineering does its bit first, then passes the thing over a Himalaya-high functional wall to manufacturing; and so on. "Put 'em all in one place" is part of it. But there's much more—a host of subtleties that make a mockery of the pop one-line formulas which I must myself admit to having proffered in the past.

TWENTY-ONE STEPS TO RENAISSANCE: A CHRONOLOGY

To take even partial measure of the all-important nuances, a chronology is a must.

1. November 1987. Brian McNeill's cohort, Jim Stryker, marketing manager, business and industry development, was "invited" to dinner by Dick Poore, sales and marketing vice president of the IR Power Tool Division. (Poore is now division general manager, in part owing to the success of the Cyclone Grinder.) Stryker told us Poore picked up the tab for a good French meal, and waited for the dessert plates to be cleared before issuing his curt order concerning the sagging IR grinder: "Do something, fast."

Project Lightning (the name came later) was thus conceived—and a path-breaking product ensued. Today, in addition to basking in the project's commercial and artistic glory, Stryker trots around the world telling his tale. The centerfold—literally—of his presentation is a fold-up, three-foot chart laying out the new, quick development process in detail. The chart is impressive. Oohs, ahhs, and "so that's the secret" are common reactions to it. But the chart is *not* the point. At the inception of the project, Stryker hurriedly sketched a 12-by-25-inch rough draft. There was no reference to time or time compression. The chart was a help, still is a help. But the story that unfolded—engineers and MBAs take note—was far more complex than can be shown by the bubbles and lines on any diagram.

2. December 1987. Right after Poore issued his edict, a session in Athens provided a portent of what was to come. Major players from the Athens plant (divisional manufacturers and product engineers) and a contingent from IR's New Jersey headquarters (divisional marketing and sales people) gathered. There Stryker, de facto project manager at that point, made it clear that manufacturers, engineers, and marketers would have to bury their oft-used hatchets and, as one, bury their noses in engineering issues from the start. (IR had previously followed the traditional "sequential" product development

path I just described. King Engineer would set the pace, untroubled by the concerns of Grubby Manufacturing or Imperious Purchasing.) Those present were asked to pull together, to act "as a team," whatever that meant.

Getting people from several functions together had been done before at IR, but, Stryker says, such sessions were typically "formal dog and pony shows," preceded and followed by a blizzard of memos in which one group would blame the others (and vice versa) for faults and delays in prior development efforts. This time Stryker and McNeill decided "to lock everybody in a room" and thrash out the issues.

3. February 1988. An "all hands" meeting was called at the factory. Near the end of a drawn-out discussion about the new product reformulation effort, Poore asked all those present to stand up. Then he said, "Everyone willing to support a one-year product development cycle, sit down." They sat. But wait. Suddenly Poore realized that one lone soul was still standing (despite keen group pressure)—the head of engineering at Athens, unquestionably the person most important to shortening the process. Some start!

4. March 1988. Despite the chief engineer's skepticism, the new five-person product development team (now called Project Lightning) was officially formed. It consisted of representatives from marketing, engineering, manufacturing, sales, and purchasing. Members were assigned to the team full-time, in order to cleanly snip traditional functional ties; and the team was given its own physical space in the engineering area of the plant.

Team manufacturing expert Jim Holton, for example, moved out of the cubicle in manufacturing he'd occupied for over a decade and set up shop in the engineering area. Though he had only been a couple of minutes away before, this formal move was an early sign that the new group was "for real," according to both Stryker and Holton. "It wasn't easy," Holton told me in 1990, with a grimace. Family pictures, mugs, and reference books were all transported into alien country. Such "small steps" are at the heart of this case. Physical location, for instance, is seldom given the credit it's due in creating group and project cohesion. But it made a profound difference here. (See Chapter 27 for a more encompassing discussion of this issue.)

5. While March winds still blasted Pennsylvania, the new team trooped down to Atlanta to spend a day with 4 of IR's top 10 grinder distributors. Once again, it's difficult to portray the full drama of this event. For example, several veteran team members had never before traveled on IR business!

The group convened in a cramped hotel room, and the distributors were solemnly anointed as "team members." Such language was another departure—though none of the tough old distributors, Stryker admitted to us, believed a word of it at the time. IR, like its industry counterparts, had a tradition of lip-service distributor involvement in new-product development. Only many more meetings like this one would give credibility to any "partners" spiel by one of the "suits from Jersey."

Despite these departures from tradition, however, big change was still not the ticket. Get a new version of the grinder out there, quickly, and stop market-share erosion. That was the point. In fact, the group in Atlanta rapidly concluded that the new product should be exactly like the current leader's offering, only cheaper. At this point, Stryker pulled up short (the first of many such strategic "slow downs" on the way to "hurry up") and asked the group to go through a "walking in the competitor's shoes" exercise.

After some initial embarrassment—"playacting" didn't come naturally to most—it became clear that if IR simply introduced a cheap copy of what was now tops, its chief competitor would react by cutting its own price. IR, the group realized, would have to consider doing more. By the end of the daylong meeting, the distributors, Stryker recalled, were beginning to get "turned on" about pursuing some unspecified fundamental innovation.

Though the goal was still murky, this group learning process was monumentally important. The painstaking development of shared concerns—outsiders/insiders/marketers/engineers/manufacturing/purchasing—defines this new approach.

6. April 12, 1988—"the barbecue at JD Ranch." It's once again difficult to appropriately dramatize this "little" event. The previously stay-at-home team members trekked from Athens again, and visited Stryker at his home ("JD Ranch," as it's now nicknamed, in Clinton, New Jersey). Bonding and team-building—never a focus before—took place on a grand scale. (In presenting this case at seminars, I've argued that "barbecues are the name of the game." Despite unmistakable audience skepticism of the "Oh, come on" sort, I mean it.)

Substantive change occurred, too. Traditionally, new-product activities began with last things first: Engineering would kick off the process by working on specifications for the motor, for example—before anyone knew what the overall point was (except that the product would be a "better" grinder). This time, the group as a whole began by spending a couple of days scribbling on butcher paper, talking about the general objectives for the project. It was yet another crucial part of team development. People from different functions started to move onto the same wavelength; intellectual (and social) boundaries began to erode.

7. While the palaver that followed the barbecue didn't produce much agreement on objectives, the team made one crucial decision: to make visits to a half-dozen end users. Typically, when a new product was being considered at IR, sales (and occasionally marketing) people would talk to a few customer purchasing agents, and, via those purchasing agents, to some shop foremen. Engineers and manufacturers had *never* visited customers. ("Never?" I asked once more. "Never," the chorus of voices intoned as one. "Never." "Never"— shades of Titeflex.)

Conventional wisdom supposes that getting past purchasing agents to the end user is next to impossible. IR's salespeople, however, found that purchasing agents were generally amenable to setting up the meetings. It's all so dratted sensible in hindsight: Sure, a purchasing guy is not all that keen on a salesperson going directly to a factory hand; such a visit smells like a trick to bypass purchasing. But that purchasing guy may not be as parochial as you think. When the same salesperson makes a case for engineers and manufacturers speaking directly to the factory hand, hey, why not?

The findings that resulted from these visits sound almost trivial in retrospect. In fact, they were "revolutionary" by normal standards. Team members visiting Sikorsky Aircraft observed, for one thing, that many workers wrapped mounds of tape around the business end of the grinder, to prevent their hands from sliding into the dangerous spinning grinding pad. Subsequently, working with an industrial designer (see below), the creators of the new tool incorporated a simple guard piece which prevents the hand from slipping. This "insignificant" feature was completely new to the industry.

Stryker and McNeill, both sophisticated marketers, sound at times like adolescents just discovering the opposite sex when they talk about the team's end-user visits. "We got to see how they actually used the tool," Stryker excitedly exclaimed during our interview. "We were finally exposed to the idea that people used these tools to earn a living, eight hours a day. They depend on the productivity and comfort of that tool." Stryker reverently described the ultimate user of the air-powered grinding tool as a "medieval warrior," wearing a heavy helmet and shin guards, working in dungeon-like surroundings, laboring with tool in hand, hour after hour. Designing the tool "around the operator," as McNeill put it, was an "industry first."

As is true with so many attributes of this process, the end-user visits had other, subtle, but equally important effects. For the first time, for example, user needs (gathered, at best, secondhand in the past) did not subsequently have to be translated by "untrustworthy" salespeople for the engineers, manufacturers, and purchasers. And when arguments came up later about necessary design compromises, resolution was far easier than before, since those forced to make the compromises had actually watched, with eight or ten eyes at once, the tool in use.

8. Late April. The die was cast. Sales boss Poore launched the annual distributors' meeting by bluntly promising that something big would be ready for the next annual meeting. The distributors were openly skeptical.

9. Mid-May. Top management signed off on the project. Now the team began to crisscross the country in earnest, going "belly to belly" with customers. As the pace increased, the entire process became infused with "passion." The word is McNeill's, not mine. But you can't have genuine transformation without it.

10. Late May. The team reconvened for a critical meeting. The "outside of the tool," the interface between the tool and its ultimate user, had now

become the project's "number one priority," according to Stryker. Normally, engineers would have wound up the "real work" on motor speeds and such before an industrial designer, with little room left to play, was called in—to mop up and fiddle with what was disparagingly called "the wrapper." Now, as a consequence of those end-user visits, the wrapper had become all-important.

Group Four, a respected industrial design firm, had been hired in April. Its staffers had made extensive customer visits. At the May meeting, Group Four reported its results to the Project Lightning team, then calmly announced plans to develop 20 or 30 design concepts within two weeks. The Athens group was stunned. (Again, note a subtle, unexpected effect: The sense of urgency that spread to the IR team as a result of Group Four's speed was as important as the design work Group Four did.)

11. Early June. Group Four delivered on schedule. Then, while IR's engineers fretted about "getting boxed in" by an exterior design they couldn't live with, Group Four committed to quickly producing Styrofoam models of the five preferred designs. Energy and momentum were building.

12. June 1988. The five Styrofoam models were presented, and, after heated debate, two "finalists" were selected. At this point, following normal rituals, marketing would have "made the call," Stryker said, ordering the group to proceed in one direction or the other. But Stryker decided *not* to decide. Speed was of the essence, but he sensed it wasn't time to choose. Customer buy-in—inside IR and out—was a must, and it hadn't occurred yet. So Stryker waffled. The team would follow up on a not very exciting "insurance" design, as well as a revolutionary design. The latter would feature housing made of a lightweight composite (glass-filled polymer). Both to the group and to outsiders, the proposed shift from metal to plastics was a "terrifying" departure from industry norms.

It's impossible to overestimate the *strategic* importance of Stryker's decision not to decide. The passion and energy and commitment necessary to creating something new (the essence of fashion) just don't happen when someone "outside" or "upstairs" makes the crucial decisions.

13. June 1988. The composite material was discussed by a doubtful top management at a June meeting in New Jersey. The tide was turned when a Project Lightning engineer produced a bunch of what looked like grinder housings dangling on the ends of strings—offering them as proof that the lightweight composite was every bit as durable as the traditional metal. The team had conducted a unique durability test. They had gathered some metal and composite cylinders shaped like the grinder's housing. Then, for hours (some say until the police came), one of the team members dragged the set of mock housings behind his car, round and round in a nearby hotel parking lot. The composite cylinders had stood up just fine—and the down-home demo overcame doubts that no engineering analysis had been able to squelch.

Of equal import, a handful of oft-recounted events like that "drag test" became part and parcel of the team's lore—essential to sustaining its members through the trying times ahead.

14. July 1988. The second meeting with the four distributors began with another barbecue. Then Stryker and McNeill quietly broached the idea of the composite material. To their surprise, the distributors, who were beginning to see the tool as more than a commodity, didn't dismiss it out of hand. In fact, one said it might be "fun to sell." Another was heard to utter the word "wow." (Stryker has officially enshrined "the 'wow' reaction" on his list of necessary new-product goals for any subsequent projects.)

Despite the "wow," however, distributors were not yet ready to commit. The IR team urged them to "bear with us," promising that the radical design would be scrapped at the prototype stage if the distributors weren't enthusiastic about it.

15. To develop the composite, Philips Plastics Corp., a critical supplier, was brought on board—all the way on board. The approach was tradition-shattering once more. In the past, complete specifications for, say, housing material would have been sent out at the last minute to a bevy of suppliers for bids. Price would have been the decisive factor in selection. Supplier creativity was definitely not encouraged. But now Philips was treated as a "partner," another full-blown member of the development team. Via CAD terminals, drawings and specifications were exchanged real-time; visits between Philips and IR team members became routine.

Other "outsiders" also became insiders at this relatively early stage. 3M makes most of the "razor blades" for IR's razor—that is, the abrasive grinding pads that go on the spinning end of the tool. Normally, IR folks might have made a single trip to St. Paul to tell 3M what they were going to do. In this case, contact was intense (monthly visits), aimed at getting 3M to focus attention on the potentially exciting product.

Consider one result of the interchange with 3M. It's important, for safety reasons among others, that the grinder rotate at the speed the grinding tip is designed for. (If the abrasive tip is "rated" for 12,000 revolutions per minute, say, and the tool's business end spins at 35,000 RPM, injury can result.) In the past, this base had supposedly been covered by stamping the tool's speed rating on its casing; the backs of 3M's abrasive pads would be stamped as well. This fell short, however, given the gloomy work spaces where grinders are typically used. Now, working together, 3M and IR came up with a simple color-coding scheme. Thus, IR's new 35,000-RPM grinder has a very visible red marking, the 12,000-RPM tool has a tan code, and so on; 3M similarly and boldly color-coded the rubber backings of the abrasive tips. Though it's "not exactly rocket science," as Stryker said with a grin, the feature has proved to be a major selling point.

16. Late summer. The project began to move toward manufacture. It's one thing to have engineers and manufacturers, in small numbers, working to-

gether as full-time members of something like the Project Lightning design team. It's another matter to integrate and motivate the whole cast of characters responsible for implementation. In the past, team-to-factory transfer had usually and generated the longest delays. This time, a lot of potential snafus were headed off by having manufacturing and purchasing represented on the team from the start. Still, increasing the number of people involved was a critical, uncharted move for the fragile new process.

Once more, numerous path-breaking steps marked the way. For example, after the 1981–83 recession, the Power Tool Division had begun implementing a radical new factory configuration at Athens. As Project Lightning geared up, plant manager Mark Amlot was in the midst of shifting to cellular manufacturing of the sort described at Titeflex. Now, to hasten the in-plant revolution and tie it to Project Lightning's bold goals, Stryker, McNeill, and Amlot put together a two-day "design-for-manufacture" (DFM) seminar for members of the core team and the others, including line workers, who would be responsible for final production. As usual (per the new way of doing things), a pizza party got things started. Past problems in moving from prototype to full-scale production were openly discussed in a convivial setting. Subsequently, a substantially altered "assembly index" flowed from the DFM exercise: Ease of manufacture was greatly improved—for one thing, the number of parts in the tool was dramatically reduced.

Athens workers informed me in no uncertain terms that this was a big deal. For the first time, "management started using the experience we had. They asked us what we thought," said line worker Bob Johnson. "We felt like we were part of it." "They had [previously] overlooked the people they had." In fact, workers reported—and management confirmed—that most of the Cyclone's numerous "engineering breakthroughs," which equaled the more visible changes in exterior design, were ideas that had been lying about for decades in front-line workers' heads.

17. November 1988. As the core team's dependence on others (who had not been through the team-building process or the experiences with distributors and users) increased, numerous coordination problems arose. Sensing a crisis in morale, the engineering manager—the stubborn soul who hadn't shown "solidarity" some nine months before—broke with his past and joined the pizza and barbecue brigade. At his suggestion, about 30 members of the "extended factory family" went to dinner at the Guthrie Inn, across from the Athens plant. Stryker and McNeill rushed down from New Jersey, bearing T-shirts and athletic-gear bags with Project Lightning labels, to reinforce the sense of teamwork, momentum, camaraderie, and energy.

18. Late fall 1988. The top managers were increasingly worried about their shaky product position and imagined disaster lurking around every bend. They wanted to "help." Discerning the emotional fragility of the overall process, Stryker spent many an early-winter hour and risked his career keeping the honchos at bay. Hard-won "ownership" on the team and at Athens was

all too likely to be gutted by orders "issued from the top." The team and its extended family, Stryker told us, were always on tenterhooks, waiting to be zapped by top management as they had been in the past.

19. December 1988. Distributors joined the team for a third session, and the composite prototypes were subjected to the "stall test." While surveying end users, Stryker and McNeill had noticed that customer foremen would take any new air-powered grinder, hand it to the biggest worker around, and order him to push up against it with all his might in an effort to stall it. Now the distributors were invited to try and stall the prototypes. The new tool passed the test, and energetic dealer support for the radical composite design began to blossom.

20. February 1989. A large number of prototypes were placed with key customers. While prototypes had been tested by customers before, the extensiveness of these trials once again broke new ground.

Caterpillar Tractor was test site for several prototypes. One end user, during a follow-up visit by an IR salesman, described the new tool as "okay." He added in passing, "My hands don't hurt anymore." Upon hearing those words, the Project Lightning team knew it had, as McNeill put it, "struck the mother lode."

There were other stories. McNeill, visiting a Boeing supplier in Everett, Washington, noticed that the hands of one young woman, who was using a competitor's aluminum-cased tool, were blue with cold. "Doesn't that bother you?" he asked her. "She didn't seem to understand my question," he told me. "She assumed it was normal to have ice-cold hands." McNeill gave her a prototype. Two weeks later, when the IR salesperson came back to collect it, she had hidden it, and refused to give it up.

21. April 1989. Finally, the distributors' conference in Scottsdale, Arizona. Once again, the "stall test" would be decisive. Stryker demonstrated the new tool in a breakout room. He placed a five-dollar bill on a table, daring any distributor to stall the grinder. Several took up his challenge, and he'd begun to relax as the last fellow stepped up. To Stryker's dismay, the tool stalled. As he dejectedly picked up the five-dollar bill and started to hand it over, the old pro admitted he'd resorted to a time-honored trick: stepping on the line from the air compressor to cut off power to the tool.

GETTING BEYOND THE OBVIOUS

There's much more to this story, of course. I've shortchanged a hundred other variables—particularly those dealing with the extraordinary level of involvement by Athens shop-floor workers (for the first time) with manufacturing design and, today, constant product improvement. But one thing is clear: Success has been stunning. As noted, sales and market share have taken off. At least as important, a product declared a commodity by one and all has not been discounted—which is unheard of. Better still, say both Stryker and McNeill, IR sales force confidence is sky-high, and distributors, for once, are beaming.

As we have seen, the IR process had all the garden-variety elements associated with the modern-day transition from "sequential" to "simultaneous" product development: (1) all key functions (marketing, manufacturing, purchasing, engineering, etc.) were represented on the team from the start; (2) there were dedicated team facilities; (3) there was early and continuing customer (distributor, end user) involvement; (4) there was early and continuing vendor involvement; and (5) there was continuous shop-floor involvement.

But, as important as these elements are—and they are still not in place at most companies—they only scratch the surface. The subtle imperatives, or "orchestration variables," as I call them, include:

• Let customers *shape* the project, going beyond customer involvement to customer leadership. Customer visits at the start, for example, were essential to creating overall project goals.

• Get everyone—often in groups—visiting customers. The fact that purchasers, marketers, engineers, etc., saw the same customer at the same time was important to developing a "shared language," so helpful down the pike when hard choices had to be made.

• Find the *right* customer. Getting past the purchasing agent and shop foreman to the hardened end user was crucial.

• Visit customers again and again. Intense customer involvement continued with no letup throughout the project. Stryker flatly contends that this constant, intimate customer involvement was the single most important factor in creating, and then sustaining, team enthusiasm.

• Begin with dialogue and goal development, not details. Normally engineers would have gone to work on detailed specifications for the new tool's innards, following perfunctory discussions with sales and marketing. With the Cyclone, the team—including outsiders—spent "forever" working toward overall product objectives, taking care not to jump too quickly to the fine print.

• Imbue the process with both urgency *and* patience. One of Stryker's many shrewd moves was keeping toes to the fire (one year or bust) while allowing slack at critical moments (e.g., allowing lots of time to talk with customers). I call it dealing with the "hurry up–slow down" paradox.

To Hurry Up, Slow Down

"From time to time, [the] tribe [gathered] in a circle. They just talked and talked and talked, apparently to no purpose. They made no decisions. There was no leader. And everybody could participate. There may have been wise men or wise women who were listened to a bit more—the older ones—but everybody could talk. The meeting went on, until it finally seemed to stop for no reason at all and the group dispersed. Yet after that, everybody seemed to know what to do, because they understood each other so well. Then they could get together in smaller groups and do something or decide things."

—DAVID BOHM, quantum mechanics pioneer,
On Dialogue

• Take advantage of offbeat outsiders. Group Four, the industrial designers, led the way in keeping everyone focused on the end user's perspective. Moreover, the little outfit's boldness and speed (performing tasks in days that normally took months) pushed tradition-bound IR team members to keep up.

• Make "vendor partnerships" real. Regular contact with and design involvement by the likes of Philips (and 3M) took the word "partnership" miles beyond lip service.

• Get the plant involved—also beyond lip service. "New look" product-development teams often perform an initial miracle, then blow it when they try to pass their efforts back to the plant for final implementation. But Stryker and Athens plant manager Mark Amlot handled the transition artfully (though it looked messy at the time). From the start, the Project Lightning team worked frequently with members of its eventual extended family.

• Keep the barbecue pit stoked! Stryker's first "Barbecue at JD Ranch" set the tone. Recall that team members from Athens had never traveled on company business before. Similar precedent-shattering social activities—several involving distributors, then the full implementation team at the plant—were essential to success.

• Master project psychology. Stryker's deftest moves were least visible—deciding not to decide between the routine and revolutionary designs until the whole team and key outsiders (e.g., distributors) were ready to commit to one or the other. Recall also that he kept divisional top management from parachuting in to "save the day."

• Work at getting lucky. Memorable serendipitous events, like the parking lot "drag test," were essential to building team cohesiveness—and maintaining it through the trying times that are part and parcel of such a process. (I include "work at getting lucky" on my list of orchestration variables because I believe project leaders can be on the lookout for these "events," and foster an atmosphere that urges them into existence, even if none can be planned. See the story of Union Pacific's Mike Walsh and the Louisiana meeting in Chapter 7.)

Stryker insists that the Cyclone Grinder process is replicable. Those involved agree. Core team member Jim Holton, for example, calls Project Lightning "the highlight of my life," and adds that he'd sign up in a flash to do it again. Workers on the line remain turned on about their involvement, too.

I concur up to a point. The palpable excitement associated with hanging out with end users, distributors, and vendors can be copied. Putting the key players from key functions together from the start can certainly be repeated—as can any number of other activities.

Yet I remain somewhat apprehensive. So many "little things" were handled so skillfully—luckily at times?—in this process. (How do you repeat the high that comes from first-time travel on company business?) Stryker and I did agree wholeheartedly that the subtleties of generating commitment and maintaining momentum were the most important discriminators between success and failure.

In any case, Stryker won the replicability debate in the end. "What's the option?" he said. As fashion comes even to grinding tools used in dark places, firms of all stripes must simply learn to shrink new-product development cycle times as dramatically as Ingersoll-Rand did—*and* inject more creativity along the way. So Stryker's right. There is no option—even if it does require, as I contend, Ph.D.-level expertise in clinical psychology, a heavy dose of artistic flair among "the suits" . . . and a little bit (or more) of luck.

Translating "Listening" into Strategic Advantage

MIT professor Eric von Hippel makes his living studying the sources of innovation. He says that sophisticated early adopters of new products, whom he labels "lead users," can be worth their weight in gold to manufacturers. The trick is finding those who are disposed toward pioneering and engaging them in the next round of product development.

Von Hippel developed his ideas with scientists and engineers in the chemical and computer industries. Now he's taken a big step toward universalizing his principles. With Cornelius Herstatt of the Swiss Federal Institute of Technology, von Hippel published in 1991 "An Implementation of the Lead User Market Research Method in a 'Low-Tech' Product Area: Pipe Hangers." Working with Hilti AG, a leading European manufacturer of fastening-related products, von Hippel and Herstatt validate the "lead user" concept in an unlikely nook of the economy and present a step-by-step methodology for getting customers in on the act.

1. Survey of specialists. The researchers and Hilti examined the industry and determined that the specialists who plan, specify, and purchase pipe networks were likely their best sources of what's up (or ought to be) in the

field. Eight specialists from Switzerland, Germany, and Austria were systematically polled for characteristics that should mark the next generation of pipe-hanging hardware—e.g., easy to put together (no need for instruction books); fewer components; lightweight (plastic instead of steel).

2. Survey of lead users. Demonstrated unease with current products marks a customer as a lead user. So 120 randomly sampled Hilti customers were asked: "Do you/did you ever build and install pipe-hanging hardware of your own design?" "Do you/did you ever modify commercially available pipe-hanging hardware to better suit your needs?" Seventy-four front-line practitioners ("tradesmen who actually installed pipe hangers") were subsequently interviewed in depth, and 22 were determined to be true pacesetters.

3. Concept development workshop. Based on judgments about personal interest in new-product development, the 22 "finalists" were further winnowed to 12. Joined by two of the eight industry "specialists" and a marketing manager, product manager, and three design engineers from Hilti, they participated in a three-day "product-concept generation workshop."

The first day, participants reviewed the specialists' findings, then broke into five subgroups to consider various design and installation issues. They spent half the second day in their groups, then did generic creativity exercises. The third day, groups presented their solutions, which the entire workshop evaluated on originality, feasibility, and comprehensiveness. Then they formed new groups to explore the most promising concepts (even producing informal engineering drawings to be examined by their peers). In the end, all hands converged on a single product concept.

4. Validity testing. But were these pacesetters too far ahead of the industry? To find out, Hilti tested the workshop's idea on a dozen "routine" users—regular customers, not at the leading edge. Ten preferred the new "product" to current offerings and said they'd pay up to 20 percent more for it.

Hilti claims that a recent, analogous development project required 16 months and cost $100,000. It had followed the time-consuming sequential product development approach: Marketers had spent five months, on their own, doing surveys. Then marketers and engineers had spent the next two months together developing tentative product specifications. Next, engineers, on their own, had eaten up another four months developing a new set of technical approaches. Then the engineers and marketers spent three months adjusting the various designs, and a final two months writing up formal specifications.

The lead-user technique cost about half as much money ($51,000) and took about half as much time (nine months): survey of experts (two months); customer telephone survey (two weeks); lead-user workshop (three days—and half the total expense); Hilti's evaluation of lead-user concept (three months); concept test with routine users (two months); write-up of formal product specifications (two months).

It's significant, von Hippel and Herstatt argue, that the approach works with users "not characterized by advanced technical training." They add that the joint-development process had numerous unanticipated spinoffs: Morale among Hilti's engineers and marketers, working together from the start for the first time, rose; both groups came to share a greater sense of urgency and common language; and the translation of user needs between marketers and engineers was smoother than in the past.

Even pipe hangers can become fashion goods!

7

The Union Pacific Railroad: Decimate the Middle Ranks, Liberate the Conductors, and Launch a Counterattack against the Truckers

The information component of our service package is growing bigger and bigger. It's not just enough to deliver products. Customers want information. Where their products will be consolidated and deconsolidated, what time each item will be where, prices, customs information, and much more. We are an information-driven business.

ALEX MANDL, an executive
in the transportation company
CSX, quoted in *Power Shift*, by
ALVIN TOFFLER

Railroads in the fashion and customization business? You bet. Or rather, they'd better be. Truckers have clobbered the railroaders of late. (From 1980 to 1989, truckers picked up all but $2 billion of the $60-billion increase in intercity ground freight transportation revenue.) Why? The truckers—like CNN's "on demand" news compared to the big networks' "7:00 p.m., take it or leave it"—pick up and deliver at the customer's, not the shipper's, convenience.

In fact, the railroads' main problem vis-à-vis the trucks has not been raw speed (Hustle I). Railroads may be slower than trucks, but they have an enormous cost advantage (see p. 98)—and they've thrown it away through sheer arrogance and unreliability. So this turns out to be mostly a story about Hustle II: quick, effective decision making that improves reliability and customer confidence. After all, research consistently shows that the chief issues driving customer satisfaction and retention are reliability, some mix of keeping the customer informed, quick and forthcoming responses to concerns—and trust.

THE UPRR OWNS UP TO ITS SHORTCOMINGS

We used to change the customer's service [to try and save money] and wonder if he'd figure it out. The idea was to see how much we could get away with. Furthermore, we didn't know how to say "no." A customer would ask for something, we would say "sure." But we didn't have the faintest idea as to whether or not we could do the job.

BILL HILLEBRANDT
Vice President for Customer Service
Union Pacific Railroad

The Union Pacific takes in over $5 billion in annual revenue. At any given moment, it must contend with 180,000 cars on the rails. So much for the dry statistics. What's the *story*? You've just heard Hillebrandt (epigraph). Lifer Chuck Dettman, now assistant vice president in charge of the Service Reliability Action Team, added that the UPRR in 1985 was "totally unreliable. We got the car there when we got the car there. The customer could take it or leave it."

Despite such rot, the Union Pacific was the pick of railroading's litter in 1980. But starting in the mid-'80s, the company has attempted, with astonishing success, to become world-class by any industry's standard. A lot of the credit goes to former UPRR chief executive officer Mike Walsh, who arrived at the railroad's Omaha headquarters in 1986 from Cummins Engine.*

The UPRR was stiff, hyper-formal, bureaucratic, stodgy, sluggish, militaristic. Everyone "stayed in his little box," as Walsh put it. Everything was

---

*Walsh was CEO when we conducted our research in 1990–91; in August 1991, he took the helm of troubled Tenneco. (As a result of Walsh's move, others with whom we talked have changed jobs and titles.)

"done through channels." Open exchange "was anathema." Informal functional integration was nil: "If you were talking about a marketing plan or strategic plan, there was a lot of attention given to who was going to see it before it could be moved up the line." At one outpost, Walsh discovered a manager responsible for business totaling $22 million, but "he didn't have the authority to spend more than two thousand dollars without the written approval of Omaha. And it took eight weeks for that!"

Walsh began by meeting with front-line railroaders. He quickly came across a raft of examples of Byzantine bureaucracy. "I went down to the Jenks Shop, a big locomotive repair operation in Arkansas," he recalled. "Two weeks before, I had written a memorandum telling everybody I was coming, asking them to submit questions in writing so I'd know what was on their minds. When I got there, I noticed a piece of paper on the bulletin board, dated the day before, telling people I was coming. I asked, 'What happened?' Well, even though it came directly from me, the manager of the shop—he's not with us anymore—didn't feel he had the authority to act on it. This is the honest-to-God truth: First he sent it up to the general manager in Texas. That guy sent it back—noting that while the shop *was* in the Texas region, this was really a matter for the mechanical department to decide. So the shop boss sent it back to Omaha, to the head of the mechanical department. After it sat in his office for a couple of days, he okayed it and sent it back to the shop. In the meantime, nothing happened."

CLEANING OUT THE RAT'S NEST

The Jenks fiasco was characteristic of the UPRR's approach to decision making. Ponder this typical operational example. Suppose a customer was having difficulty getting a bead on a railcar—it was either not the right one, or wasn't where the customer needed it for loading or unloading. The customer would go to his UPRR sales representative—who "went up" to the district traffic manager, who in turn "went up" to the regional traffic manager. The regional boss passed the problem from his sales and marketing organization, across a chasm psychologically wider than the Grand Canyon, to the operations department's general manager. The general manager then "went down" to the superintendent, who "went down" to the train master to find out what had gone wrong.

After which the whole cumbersome mechanism shifted into reverse. The information meandered up the operations hierarchy, then down the sales and marketing hierarchy. All this could easily absorb several days, as the daisy chain of bureaucrats played telephone tag with one another. "People tried to figure out how to cover their ass so they wouldn't get into trouble," one employee told us. "The issue wasn't whether you won or lost," said another, "it was where you placed the blame."

Today, a customer with the same problem goes directly to the crew foreman on the scene—who resolves the quandary on the spot, thanks to a revised procedure worked out by a Union Pacific Customer Action Team (UPCAT). Such UPCATs, according to VP Bill Hillebrandt, develop processes for "getting people together at the ground level and giving them responsibility and the control necessary to solve the problem."

Consider the consequences of that revised decision-making scheme and 1,000 others like it. From 1985 through 1990, the UPRR's on-time delivery improved from about 40 percent to about 70 percent. For selected, big customers the UPRR arrives on schedule 85 percent to 95 percent of the time. In fact, audacious targets such as 99.9 percent on-time—"Just-in-Time" in modern parlance—are being hit regularly for the likes of Toyota. (A few years ago, railroad veterans would have laughed aloud "at even the *idea* of a JIT railroad," Walsh told us.) Volume has gone up 18 percent, revenue about 25 percent; the number of employees has been reduced from 45,000 to about 30,000. Productivity per employee—25 percent more revenue with 25 percent fewer people—has nearly doubled.

Failure cost (so called "poor-quality cost") has also been reduced, from 20 percent of gross revenue to 15 percent—representing a 5-year savings of almost $750 million. For example: Locomotive down-time has been reduced from 13 percent to 8 percent, which is the equivalent of saving $150 million (eliminating the need to purchase 125 new locomotives). Derailment costs have also nose-dived. Most important, by 1990 the railroad's parent holding company (the Union Pacific Corporation) had reclassified the UPRR as an "invest and grow" operation; previously it had been a "harvest" (divestiture) candidate, with excess cash generated by the railroad going back to the parent for acquisitions: e.g., billions for the purchase of *trucking* companies. Now that cash stays at home.

Many of the performance figures just cited weren't even tracked when Walsh arrived at the UPRR. Or were mistracked. Take the amusing—tragic? —matter of timeliness. "I'd be told our delivery [for a given customer] was eighty-five percent or ninety percent on time," Walsh remembered. "I'd talk to the customer and I wouldn't get that sense at all. So I'd ask where the numbers came from. They were the actual time against standard transit time— once the shipment got under way. Suppose the train left two days late. The move should take twelve hours, but once it got going it took eleven and a half hours. Our data would show the shipment getting to the customer half an hour *early*." The railroad, Walsh added unnecessarily, was "focused internally, on how to run the trains efficiently rather than how to serve the customer's needs. That meant longer trains and heavier weights; if you only had fifty cars today, you just waited until tomorrow or the next day when you had a hundred. It built up tonnage and it saved fuel, but it drove our customers up the wall."

WALSH PUSHES THE NEEDLE ALL THE WAY OVER

Upon arriving at the UPRR, Walsh visited 10,000 employees at about 100 sessions, which came to be called Town Meetings. "What came through above everything else," he told us, "was a sense of frustration. People knew what to do, but they weren't being allowed to do it."

Against the advice of the railroad's former chairman and damned near everyone else, Walsh determined to "push the needle all the way over" and go for radical change. "Organizations are capable of taking on more than most of their leaders give them credit for," he insisted to us. "The risk was stopping way too early, more so than thinking you've pushed past the breaking point." Forget the last 130 years, Walsh told his small cadre of planners: Create "a brand-new railroad." Begin with "a blank sheet of paper." (Exactly the language of Titeflex's Simpson.)

The first step was a massive reorganization of the 30,000-person operations bureaucracy. Figure A opposite shows the department's organization scheme when Walsh arrived, with nine layers of management between the operations chief and the folks at the front line who do the day-to-day work of the railroad. But it was far worse than it looked, Walsh explained. Each level had come to mirror the one above it. To cope with the blizzard of paper coming down from above, it would duplicate the departmental structure of that next-higher level; some field bureaucracies were exact replicas of headquarters, with local staffs of 100 or more people. The simplest decisions were being fully staffed a half-dozen times.

In just 90 days, Walsh stripped out five layers—and 800 attendant middle managers—from the operations hierarchy. What was left is shown in Figure B. Both centralization and decentralization were increased. Certain activities, such as dispatching and customer service, were centralized. On the other hand, "running the railroad"—taking care of day-to-day customer needs—was radically decentralized.

New "Top Guns" in Business

Power was devolved to 30 local superintendents of transportation services, whom Walsh dubbed "Top Guns." How did the number 30 emerge? What's the industrial-engineering optimization algorithm that the UPRR's master planners used to spec these critical units?

People were the key. Walsh insisted that units be sized so the Top Gun could know all members of the unit by name, and know all the unit's major customers and their requirements intimately. Translation: Create 30 "businesses," as Walsh called them, each with 400 to 600 people overseeing 800 to 1,600 miles of track. Human scale at the worker and customer end, then, was the defining logic.

UPRR Operations Hierarchy

Figure A	Figure B
Prior to 1987 Reorganization	**1990**
Executive VP Operations | VP Operations | General Manager | Asst. General Manager | Regional Transportation Superintendent Division Superintendent | Division Superintendent Transportation | Trainmaster/Terminal Superintendent | Asst. Trainmaster/ Terminal Trainmaster | Yardmaster | *Railroaders*	*Executive VP Operations* | VP Field Operations | Superintendent Transportation Services Manager Train Operations | Yardmaster | *Railroaders*

Use of the term "business" is important. (It pops up time and again in the Beyond Hierarchy section, as it has in this section—recall the discussion of "fashion's common denominator" on p. 71.) Before the reorganization, sales and marketing at the UPRR focused on revenue and the customer; operations focused on costs and "playing trains," as one cynical observer put it. And rarely the twain did meet. A cornerstone of Walsh's overall strategy was inducing "business sense"—a passion for revenue and cost and profit and service—at the working level in every function. For example, the new, stream-lined finance department shifted focus from internal ("closing the books") to external (conducting formal "outreach programs" to support the line in sales, marketing, and operations).

The overall objective was plain: Drive decisions affecting the customer closer to the action. "Reliability is the watchword for the nineties," said Chuck

Dettman. To get there, decisions that "took weeks or months" would now be handled in "days or hours"—or else.

Walsh explained the new way of doing business by describing a project with a major customer, Boise-Cascade. The local transportation superintendent (Top Gun) knows the ins and outs of Boise. He and the customer routinely work together to plan transportation requirements for the coming year. (Unheard of before.) He knows the facts, real-time—and the facts are accurate. (Unheard of before.) The Top Gun routinely crosses that former chasm between operations and sales and marketing. (Unheard of before.) He has daily contact with a UPRR national account manager—a new position, sales's Top Gun equivalent. And he works with a cross-functional National Account Team for Boise, which includes railroaders from operations, marketing, financing, car scheduling, and billing accuracy. (Unheard of before.) Who works for whom? While Walsh insisted that accountability is higher than ever, he added that "everyone reports to each other." The result of it all, unthinkable in the past: Walsh claimed that the UPRR, at the time of our research, was on time with Boise-Cascade, to the minute, 100 percent of the time, at all Boise locations! The special Boise-UPRR program is an unabashed effort to demonstrate to everyone that "JIT" and "railroad" are not antonyms.

DEMOLISHING FUNCTIONAL BARRIERS

The Union Pacific revolution is awash in contradictions. On the one hand, Walsh oversaw a radical program of decentralization, stripping out over half of the layers of operations management. At the same time, he substantially centralized any number of things. But the centralization itself is paradoxical: Walsh centralized in large measure to enhance the effectiveness of information collection—so that he could turn around and hand back information, real-time, to those closest to the action to use as the basis for quick decisions to serve the customer better.

Another contradiction: Walsh gave people close to the front much more authority. That's traditionally associated with autonomy in a "vertical" organizational sense—as in, "I 'own' my box on the org chart." Yet at the same time he stripped away some of that just-granted autonomy by insisting that a chief goal for the railroad was learning how to cooperate and operate "horizontally"—across functional borders.

Before Walsh, the most trivial decisions would bounce up the full half-dozen or more layers of a "functional stovepipe" (e.g., the operations hierarchy). Integration across functions took place, Walsh swore to us, only in the chairman's office. Now, as the new approach to Boise-Cascade suggests, the idea is to get all the functions working as one—at the customer level, in the field, real-time, with no second-guessing from above. This translates into major alterations in technology (e.g., an ongoing effort to put computers in each train), training (e.g., for conductors—local Top Guns in their own right), increased spending authority (VP Dettman claimed that field operatives can now commit huge sums to support a customer), compensation and performance evaluation (to explicitly emphasize close-to-the-customer and cross-functional objectives), and so on.

The Herculean effort to integrate historically defiant, autonomous functions began with formation of a Supply/Demand Committee. Walsh brought together the heads of finance, sales and marketing, and operations to oversee day-to-day operation of the railroad—matching customer needs (demand) with train capability (supply). For the first time in the railroad's history, the functional barons were given responsibility—and a mandate—for getting things done together. The results of cooperating (or not) are unmistakably reflected in their performance ratings and compensation.

Getting the high-level team to mesh was no piece of cake. At a meeting of Union Pacific and Stanford University executives, Walsh described a defining moment, when the supply/demand team learned to live in a world where the chairman doesn't make all the tough calls:

> While they were screwing around, trying to decide how to balance all the considerations [involved in a major movement of agricultural goods mandated by national policy], I'm getting calls from United States senators, governors, customers raising hell about the fact that we can't move the grain. So I got the supply/demand team together and asked them what the hell was holding them up. And the answer was, "We are going through a lot of calculation to determine whether or not we can get the grain cars fixed in time to actually move the grain so that we can get the revenue to offset the cost." It was taking time to do the analysis—people didn't agree, etc. This was a nasty but liberating experience for the supply/demand group. For the first time, they realized that *they* had the ball, and that *they* had to orchestrate a correct resolution, fast.

The team survived its baptism by fire, and eventually the process began to diffuse downward. Four or five subsidiary teams formed to pick up cross-functional supply/demand activities below the senior-level committee. According to one UPRR exec, the new lower-level teams now resolve 99 percent of coordination issues, bumping only the thorniest stuff to the parent committee.

While Walsh was adamant about forcing the entire railroad to work "horizontally," he was also well aware of the pitfalls—new outcroppings of bureaucracy. For example, he made it clear that the supply/demand "organization" should not develop any permanent staff: "You've got to have a leadership that is willing to delegate," he declared, but "you've got to resist the temptation to create a separate organization. That never works. The trick is to make the damn thing work horizontally *without* new bureaucracy."

(Walsh and ABB's Barnevik are soulmates in this regard. Both tout matrix-like approaches to running a complex enterprise, but are rabidly vigilant against the stultifying effects of the old-style staff-heavy matrix structures. Both are fanatically dedicated to keeping "horizontal" efforts—Business Area structures at ABB, the likes of the Supply/Demand Committee at the UPRR—from growing bureaucratic barnacles of any sort.)

CENTRALIZING IN OMAHA AND ST. LOUIS— TO BETTER DECENTRALIZE

On July 5, 1988, the innards of the old UPRR freight house in Omaha were demolished. Nine months and $50 million later, the high-tech Harriman Dispatch Center opened up inside the old shell. Part of the operations organization, it oversees the composition of trains and keeps tabs on 20,000 miles of rail and the 180,000 cars that are on them at any time. When Walsh took over, plans were afoot to pare 10 warring regional dispatch centers to 3. But after his "clean sheet of paper" edict and careful analysis, the decision was made to go to one. The dysfunctional competition between regional centers ("running ten separate railroads," as one manager put it) would ipso facto stop. Harriman would do it all. But, and it's *the* big but, those 30 Top Guns (and any number of special groups, such as that Boise-Cascade team) would be given demonstrably increased authority to meet changing, local, day-to-day customer needs. While these local variations affect only a small percentage of railroad movements, they account for the lion's share of the customer's *perception* of railroad responsiveness—or nonresponsiveness.

Ditto at St. Louis, home to the National Customer Service Center (NCSC), the part of the sales and marketing organization that handles customers' orders and other requests. What was an 80-site (in 1986) service operation—"eighty sites, eighty railroads," I was told—was also trimmed to one, located at the old headquarters of the Missouri-Pacific Railroad (which merged with the Union Pacific in 1982). Establishing the NCSC, which handles 24,000 phone calls, 8,000 faxes, and 15,000 electronic data interchange (EDI) messages each day, chewed up another $37 million in capital.

The NCSC logic—again—is centralization *and* decentralization. On the one hand, the NCSC (like Harriman) makes thousands of decisions each day that aim to optimize the use of a mass of frightfully expensive assets. On the other hand, the center makes all information—now accurate and timely—available to those closest to the front line, so that they can deal with the thousands of customer perturbations that necessarily crop up each day.

Teams

Look closely at the NCSC, and the autonomy/cross-function contradictions become more transparent. The big organization consists largely of self-managing teams that mimic, on a small scale, the Top Gun operations set up in the field. Consider, for example, the Northern California NCSC day-shift team—a hearty three-person band I spoke with. These three "manage" 3,000 customers, including giants such as Del Monte, Toyota, and Mitsui, the huge Japanese trading company.

Being based—centralized—in St. Louis means they are supported by a state-of-the-art computer and telecommunications system, which knows no peer in railroading and few anywhere else. The system, which team members said gives them "instant access to the whole railroad," handles virtually all the routine work. The team is left with "problem solving to support the customer," team leader Catherine McIntosh told me.

Despite the centralization, however, team members are on the go. McIntosh had just returned from a spur-of-the-moment visit to California, to work with a multifunction Union Pacific team—and customers—on what's called a Major Account Action Plan. Customer-UPRR supply/demand requirements for the coming year were reviewed. Such a conference, which now borders on the commonplace, would never have taken place in the past.

The peripatetic NCSC employee also set aside a day during her California visit to "ride the rails." The objective was subtle but vital: getting to know the conductors and engineers who run the local trains. In fact, she took photos of her operations counterparts; they now adorn the team's work-space wall in St. Louis, and, she says, "add a face-to-face dimension to our phone relationships." Northern California team members have also been encouraged to make pals at the Harriman center (another departure). It's one more brick in the real-time, cross-functional problem-solving edifice.

Add up all the elements of the St. Louis NCSC (or Harriman Dispatch Center) story and you've got revolution. The hallways and team-area walls are a mass of charts and graphs of everything imaginable. Performance and performance measurement are obsessions. Teams have all the numbers at their fingertips (everyone does), and, in several cases, photos of field counterparts on the wall. Members visit customers and conductors, routinely work on cross-functional teams. Creative problem solving and project work have mostly replaced rote work. The barriers, built in the course of 125 years, have begun to crumble. Each talks to each. All talk to all. A two-minute walk across the room—or a computer-terminal entry—solves a problem for a customer or a colleague in another function that would have taken months to work out before. Centralization is high. Decentralization is higher. Information—accurate and timely—is abundant; and all, including outsiders (shippers and customers), share it. Cooperation is routine, and team performance goals are emphasized as much as or more than individual performance goals. It is indeed "a brand-new railroad." In fact, those NCSC teams look a lot like the bands at EDS—we'll return to the theme of railroad (etc.)-as-professional-service-firm in Chapter 15.

. . . And More Teams

A major new quality-team thrust tops off these evolving, formal and informal cross-functional activities. The Quality Improvement Team (QIT) process at St. Louis began in 1989. Finding volunteers for the first team took three weeks, NCSC chief Bill Hillebrandt recalled. When I visited in 1990 there were 50 teams in place and a waiting list of 60 volunteers who wanted to be part of the team process. Skeptical career railroaders were starting to believe that the resolve to work together is genuine.

The NCSC's first QIT worked on the "trivial" task of improving the internal telephone call transfer process. Part of the answer was technical, a better system for getting the calls to the right person. But there was also an essential human dimension: adding to front-line workers' skills. The technical fix minimized misdirected calls, but the increase in skills means that whoever gets the call can more likely handle it, and won't have to transfer it to someone else.

Often as not, the new team efforts aim to simplify overly complex processes. For example, one time-consuming, 20-step process (both physical movement of assets and paperwork) was reduced to 6 steps. The result, Hillebrandt told us, is "less confusion, less bad information, less missing information—and speed."

There are, then, new teams, new projects, and new technologies—all aimed at demolishing old walls. But beneath it all lies something more fundamental, the basic idea of "learning how to work together," as Hillebrandt put it. Considering some of the activities that contained so many time-consuming, error-ridden, unnecessary steps, he allowed as how it was "simple to unwire it and rewire it if you flowchart all the connections." But, he quickly added, "it just had not been done before."

Why? Those damn layers and functional barriers—which so successfully impeded informal chatter, problem solving, and timely information flow. Despite the major technology investments at Harriman and St. Louis, most of the simplification had "little to do with technology," Hillebrandt vowed, and everything to do with "priority setting and meshing data from several sources."

Hillebrandt pooh-poohed the idea of any conflict between the emergent cross-functional orientation and the equally strong, new emphasis on individual accountability. The cross-functional activity, he said, is "personal to all of us. Hard cross-functional targets must be met in everyone's performance objectives."

Rewiring with a Vengeance

Meticulously rewiring processes is close to the top of the Union Pacific's agenda. In fact, some are calling process "reengineering" (the term comes courtesy of consultant Michael Hammer) as important as the quality movement to improving overall competitiveness. Motorola is leading the way. This detailed example, reported in the February 25, 1991 issue of *Fortune*, gives another dramatic demonstration of the potential for speeding things up—by making life simpler and by getting "customers," "producers," and "suppliers" directly involved with one another:

> The essence of Motorola's approach is a concept known as process management. . . . Take corporate auditing, an arcane activity performed by highly trained professionals who produce a very limited number of "products" each year—150 audits of Motorola plants around the world. Three years ago it took an average of *seven weeks* from the time a field auditor first penned a report to the time the final version was delivered to top management. The auditor would visit a plant to vet its books, return to headquarters in Schaumburg, Illinois, write his report in longhand, give it to a typist, revise it, send it to his supervisor, revise it again, have it retyped, send it to his audit manager, have it revised again, send it to the auditee for comment, incorporate changes, and then type up a final version. Each twist and turn of the process affords new opportunities for delay and error.
>
> To speed things up, the company sequestered four auditors and two managers in a conference room for two weeks. Their charge: to identify and eliminate those tasks that were not essential to producing quality products for the "customers," Motorola's top management and the members of the corporate board's audit committee. The task force recommended radical changes in procedures and a judiciously expanded use of information technology.
>
> As a result, an auditor now writes his report in the field on a personal computer (equipped with a spell-checking program), shows it to the auditee on the spot, and incorporates his comments and those of an auditing department manager in the field. Back in Schaumburg, a secretary does a quick clean-up of the copy on the disk, then prints it out. Another auditor scores it for quality, using a 36-point questionnaire that takes about one hour to complete. (Later, the department uses the quality rating sheets in determining how to improve procedures.) The whole process, from the time the auditor returns to his office to the time his report reaches the customer, now takes just five days, a tenfold improvement in cycle time.

The bottom line on the audit department: While Motorola's revenues have doubled in the past five years, it hasn't had to hire any more auditors. The department has reduced its supervisory and support staff by a third. Thanks to the improvement in quality and timeliness, Motorola now saves $1.8 million a year in external audit fees.

THE SERVICE RELIABILITY TEAM

Walsh claimed that Chuck Dettman's new Service Reliability Action Team, which started as a "skunk works," is the mainspring of the next stage of the UPRR revolution. Its top priority is working to redefine the way business is done with key customers. For example, the railroad has made a $27-million commitment to Ford to build a special receiving facility in Southern California. It's also made other "concessions" (an "old" word) to Ford, such as slowing down railcar connection speed and shifting entirely to closed cars to reduce vehicle damage. Under the Service Reliability Action Team's spur, the UPRR has also been able to win—from trucks—the contract to deliver Chrysler components from Detroit to Mexican assembly plants.

Part of the redefinition involves the UPRR's newfound reliability. Another part involves raw speed. In the case of Chrysler, a highly variable 11-to-14-day Detroit to Mexico City transit time was reduced to a for-certain 5 days. For Toyota, the UPRR has transformed a Portland, Oregon, to Kansas City, Missouri, run from a vague 5-to-8 days to a guaranteed 4 days, 95 percent of the time. For the chemical firm Rohm & Haas, an iffy 4-to-7-day "promise" is now guaranteed 3d-morning, on-the-dot delivery.

In fact, Dettman explained, railroads have an enormous opportunity *if* they can increase speed a bit and reliability dramatically. Suppose a truck can promise (with truckers' typical 90 percent reliability) a 48-hour transit time for a load going from North Carolina to Los Angeles. For this level of service, the trucker is likely to charge $300 to $500 more than the railroad. Dettman figured that a truckload of goods runs the average customer about $75 in inventory carrying costs per day. If the trains can only promise a vague 4-to-6-day delivery, the cost advantage of rail is lost. That is, the difference between the truck's guaranteed 2 days and rail's worst case of 6 days is 4 days, which costs the customer $300—4 days times $75 per day. In such circumstances, the customer would prefer to pay the price difference to the trucker—because he can (almost always) count on the result. But if the railroad can promise 3 to 4 days, *with high reliability*, then the differential becomes 1 or 2 days. That costs the customer at most $150 in carrying charges, and amounts to a significant saving compared to the trucker's price premium.

Dettman and his team also are now overseeing the ultimate "horizontalization" effort—the identification, management, dewiring, and rewiring of 106 discrete cross-functional processes that add up to "how the UP does business." Gaining control over these processes is as important as the first big reorganization, and will move the UPRR to an entirely new level of performance, according to former CEO Walsh. In effect, those 106 horizontal/cross-functional processes *are* the UPRR.

THE "SOFT STUFF"

So far I've emphasized the mechanics and shortchanged the atmospherics—especially Walsh's extraordinary effort to induce openness and trust. The battle for the UPRR's corporate soul—and a structural, cultural reorganization on this scale is nothing less—was no easy fight to win.

"Do what you're told." That, Chuck Dettman said to us, was "railroad culture," at the UPRR and elsewhere. "We never gave [front-line employees] credit for having sense," he added almost wistfully. "They've wanted to do this all their lives and we've prevented them from doing it." But to get people to show initiative and take responsibility you have to let them know you trust them—and they have to trust you. To improve the sad state of affairs at the UPRR, so long in the making, Walsh went out of his way to look for opportunities that would allow him to underscore the new culture.

Managers Don't Melt in the Rain

"When I'd been here about three or four months, I heard that we had made a drug raid down in a parish in Louisiana. We'd called people together, maintenance and way workers, under the guise of a safety meeting. When they got there, we'd flattened them on the ground and used dogs to sniff for marijuana and cocaine. We didn't find anything. I was outraged.

"I said to our people, 'OK, I am personally getting on an airplane and so are you, Mr. Head of Operations, and so are you, Mr. Head of Engineering. And we're going down there. We're going to meet with those people, and we're going to apologize publicly to them for what we did. We're going to tell them that we don't tolerate drugs in this railroad, but we don't tolerate this kind of management behavior either.'

"Everybody was aghast, and said, 'You can't do that.' And I said, 'Why the hell can't I? Furthermore, *I'm* not going to do it. You're going with me.'

"We went down and met with those men. It was fantastic. They accepted our apology in about ten minutes. Then it was kind of interesting. I said, 'You got anything else on your mind?' A fellow raised his hand and said, 'Yeah, you talk a lot about safety. Have you ever seen the bunk cars where we live?' I said, 'No.' And he said, 'You don't have adequate safety precautions. The steps are a mess. If we have to get up in the middle of the night and go to the bathroom, we're going to get hurt.'

"One of our managers stood up and said, 'Well, Mike, I can handle this question.' And he started to tell this man how much money we spend on the maintenance of bunk cars every year. I said, 'Look, that's got nothing to do with this guy's question. He said the bunk cars where he lives are unsafe.' I said to the man, 'How far away are they?' He said, 'About three blocks.' It was pouring rain outside. I said, 'Let's go look at them.' 'But it's pouring down rain,' he said. 'We don't melt, you know,' I said. We went over to the bunk cars and they were exactly like this guy described. They were unsafe and they were embarrassing.

"Going down there said a lot to our people. It said we are not going to tolerate the sort of behavior that was reflected in the drug raid. And it doesn't make any difference how much we spend every year—if somebody tells us that something is unsafe, we want to respond to that guy, We don't want to give him a lecture."

—MIKE WALSH

The cultural revolution at the UPRR featured continuous work with the unions. UPRR management must deal with 85 chief labor officers and 500 local chairmen. Walsh started early, by presenting his rationale for change to union leadership. He shot straight about the possibility of the UPRR's staying (or not staying) in business, the low opinion of the railroad held by the parent company, the Union Pacific Corporation. Union leaders were impressed enough by the new openness to urge Walsh to take his case directly to their members. They couldn't do it for him, the leaders said, but could give him their quiet support for what became the Town Meetings. (Walsh gleefully reminds anyone who will listen that the crucial Town Meeting idea did not come from corporate communications or anyone else in management, but directly from the supposedly intractable unions.)

Walsh also initiated a highly articulated "labor management process." It features a pair of three-day labor briefings each year, at which the UPRR's senior officers make presentations to the chief labor officers and a few others from the ranks and the national organization. The chief labor officers have gotten more and more involved over time; for example, they now create the agenda for the meetings. Management picks up the tab.

The universal dissemination—all the way down the line—of reliable data is another essential element in transforming the UPRR culture. "Data are visible," Walsh said, and "that is probably the single most important thing in fostering credibility and good working relationships." He insisted that if the data are visible, accurate, trusted, and available to *all*, real-time—well, then, the intelligent people who work on the railroad will in fact solve problems effectively, based on those data.

KISS CONVENTIONAL WISDOM GOODBYE

In a 1990 speech to securities analysts, Walsh suggested that the change at the UPRR to date countered most conventional management wisdom. To begin with, he said, it demonstrated that "all at once" change was possible. Second, massive change can occur in a very tough union environment. Third, you can keep people spirited and motivated, while at the same time undertaking massive job cuts. Fourth, you can do it in a stodgy and traditional organization, without cleaning house in top management. (Some couldn't adapt to the new regime and did leave. But a surprisingly high share took a real shine to the liberating new way.) Fifth, such change can be accomplished in a semiregulated environment. And finally, conventional wisdom supposes that major change must be accompanied by a temporary decrement in financial performance. Union Pacific Corporation chairman Drew Lewis had no intention of permitting such a negative blip (since divestiture was on his mind to begin with), and Walsh deftly avoided it.

The battle was far from won when Walsh left the company in late 1991, but enormous strides have been made. While truckers aren't yet quaking in their boots, the UPRR today at least knows the meaning of the term "on time": speed plus reliability. Can customized (fashionized) service across the board be far behind?

HUSTLE'S ROOTS

Several basic "must believes" form the roots of the rather astonishing tales we've just reviewed:

• First, you must believe that we *do* exist in an environment with 95 to 99.95 percent waste time (Stalk and Hout's "0.05 to 5 rule"). "Yes, there *is* that much waste," Titeflex's Simpson told me in what was one of the most unsettling moments in this entire research program. I repeat these stories in many corporate settings. I provide the *facts*—a Titeflex reduces delivery time from several months to a few hours (or at most a week). I don't believe that those who listen think I'm lying. And yet I intuit—when I look into their eyes—that down deep they don't buy it, don't get in the gut the notion that *they* are 95 percent (or even 75 percent) wasteful. If you don't believe it, then you won't dare do what Walsh, Simpson, et al. did.

• Second, you must believe that people can "handle all that change." I have misspoken. It's not that people can handle the change. It's that most people *want* the opportunity. Remember Chuck Dettman at the UPRR: This is what railroaders have wanted to do all along. Remember the "revolution" in the innards of IR's Cyclone Grinder; the engineering innovations came from tuning in to workers' pent-up ideas. Recall the Teamster at Titeflex: Having just absorbed what any management text would call revolutionary change, he commented only that the pace was still too slow for his taste.

I think we've been fundamentally misguided by our popular "change models," working as they do (and as I have done) to teach "them" how to "love change." It's *not* "change"; it's doing what the conductor has known all along that it makes sense to do (e.g., talk with the customer before the pimple becomes a boil), the underlying logic of the industrial revolution notwithstanding. Yes, there *is* a change problem all right—on the part of management: middle management, one Titeflex Teamster insisted vociferously.

But let's not take the easy way out and lay it all on middle management, either. As I see it, the principal problem is a failure of nerve on the part of top management. "Push the needle all the way over" and quit "underestimating people"—that's what Mike Walsh told us. I think he's on the money. He stripped out five layers of management in 100 days at the Union Pacific. Self-managing work teams were established in a flash at Titeflex.

• Third, we must come to grips with the nauseating possibility that most managers have added negative value to our corporations. Go back and review the story of the Jenks Shop (p. 88), or the travails of the customer in pursuit of information about a shipment. In the past, queries at the UPRR were bucked up a half-dozen layers, then over a functional gap, then down another half-dozen layers in another bureaucracy. The front-line railroader was humiliated (or simply turned off) and the customer tuned out. What, then, was the "value-added" by those intervening layers—that is, by the likes of you and me? Answer: none at best—negative, in fact. But if you don't buy that, agonizing as it may be, then you don't get the point of this section (or this book)!

• Finally, you must believe that systems need more than "alteration," even "major alteration." Remember reengineering guru Michael Hammer's term—"obliterate." Hammer and all three cases in this section suggest destruction, obliteration. If "clean sheet of paper" seems too radical for you—well, whoops.

On the Other Hand...

While unmercifully sluggish bureaucracies need their comeuppance, it is also important to add that there's more to life than speed—even in a fashion-driven commercial environment. To wit, the case of Steve Chen. He left Cray Research in 1987 to found Supercomputer Systems. With backing from IBM, he's been quietly working away ever since. He surfaced in June 1992, only to announce that he didn't know when his product would be ready—then he disappeared again.

Then there's a friend at CBS who talks admiringly about a former colleague who drove top management crazy. He'd get an idea for a documentary, she says, then take it to his bosses—who'd usually approve. He'd return to his office, sit quietly and mull. And mull. Days would pass. Weeks would pass. Often as not, months would pass. "When in the hell is he going to go out on the road and shoot?" the hierarchs wanted to know. One day his office would be empty, and a few weeks later he'd return with a bag of tapes. Did he start editing? Fat chance. Back to the office. Feet up. Mull. Massive accumulations of pipe ash. Eventually, he'd head for the editing room, and from it would emerge a near-perfect show. This whole sequence was repeated time and again, and the results were invariably so good that CBS's muckety-mucks had little choice but to put up with his aberrant behavior.

George Leonard, author of the 1991 book *Mastery*, would doubtless smile at these stories. Real mastery of anything, he says, means eschewing the normal American bias toward "bottom line" thinking (we're rushing too much as it is, according to Leonard). The path to mastery is predictable: (1) practice, practice; (2) a brief spurt of progress; (3) a slight decline in performance; then (4) achievement of a new plateau, usually somewhat higher than the plateau preceding it. And so on. The problem, per Leonard, is that most of us live for those spurts of progress and consider the plateaus a sort of "purgatory." Yet the key to mastering anything is "loving the plateaus" (one of the book's chapter titles). "How do you best move toward mastery?" Leonard writes. "You practice diligently for the sake of practice itself. . . . You learn to appreciate and enjoy [the plateaus] just as much as the upward surges." Leonard honed his ideas learning aikido; he says he experienced little sustainable progress until he changed his ideas of progress and accepted the notion of making practice his bliss.

Does this word of caution mean that Procter & Gamble ought to extend its already lengthy product-development cycle? Don't be silly. Cleaning up bureaucratic snake pits is a must, as I hope I've already demonstrated. Still, I would say P&G—and CBS and IBM—would be wise to have a few folks on the payroll who march to a different drummer. (In a way, IBM's long-lasting, deep-pocket support for a Steve Chen amounts to such a strategy.) Will such oddballs consistently hit home runs? Of course not. (Chen has more than a few detractors.) But without a few Steve Chens who go to ground for five or ten years, the low odds of home runs get far lower.

We're beset by a paradox. The metabolism of commerce *has* speeded up dramatically, from information technology to spaghetti sauce (we were honored with 64 new varieties of the latter in 1991). On the other hand, the increased pace of everything makes genuine standouts all the more rare and valuable—which amounts to a case for pipe smokers who sit for ages, musing on grandiose schemes.

A friend in a huge consultancy says his firm desperately needs a few big ideas, championed by highly visible advocates who amass global reputations. "The problem is that [top management] doesn't understand it takes ten years to really establish a position of authority in any important field," he told me in 1991. "We think a year is a long time, three years an eternity." Once again, I can see George Leonard smiling.

III

Information Technology: More, and Less, than Promised

8

Computer Nerds, as Far as the Eye Can See

By 2020, 80 percent of business profits and market value will come from that part of the enterprise that is built around info-businesses.

STAN DAVIS and
BILL DAVIDSON
2020 Vision

Life on the farm will never be the same! Take it from Tom Urban, CEO of Pioneer Hi-Bred International, the world's largest producer of hybrid seed corn, located in Des Moines, Iowa. In mid-1991, he told *Enterprise* magazine, a Digital Equipment Corporation publication:

We're beginning to think horizontally rather than vertically. . . . A research decision has an enormous impact on a production decision, which has an enormous impact on sales and availability. It's collapsing that thinking process—and putting together teams with members of historically discrete components—that allows you to make more efficient decisions.

Information systems are the way to talk to each other. You can only talk by sharing applicable data. . . . We're going to save about four million dollars or five million dollars this year in parent corn. Parent corn is the generation between research and production. When we diagrammed the decision-making process from research to parent production to hybrid production to sales, we found that everybody was fudging numbers. . . . So we ended up with about twice as much parent corn as we really needed.

... [All of us have] now started to understand what [our] real role is and what information [we] can depend on. We've begun to make more intelligent decisions, cutting parent seed inventory by about 30 percent. . . .

In research we used to collect data in the fall on yield. It would take us almost until planting time the next spring to make decisions about what to plant. We are now, in some cases, turning those data around in 24 hours. So we can do winter production. We can make decisions about what to plant in Chile or Hawaii or Florida. We get a whole extra generation—we have doubled our productivity. We've reduced product development time from about 12 years to six years. . . . I can breed plants without a computer, but I can't compete worldwide without one. . . .

Our strategy is to divide the market into finer and finer targets, and to become more efficient in reaching those targets. The question is, How do you communicate with 500,000 farmers? . . . We started a communication business, satellite-based, now a joint venture between ourselves, Farmland Industries, and the Illinois Farm Bureau. . . . It allows us to talk to even a single farmer. . . . We'll be able to talk to one or 50,000, profile those 50,000, and then identify red-headed, right-handed, blue-eyed, alfalfa farmers, and send them a message on their tube. That is neat stuff—and highly efficient.

From the Union Pacific railyard to the farm to the factory to Wall Street, information technology is altering everything. It's causing the most significant change in the way we organize, live, make war, and do politics in a thousand years. The world has been turned upside down, and the computer, along with telecommunications networks, is the engine of the revolution.

It's easy to get mesmerized by the information technology "thing." And dangerous *not* to. Information technology, as broadly defined below, hovers around the edge—and often the center—of almost every page in this book. It even caught up with us in Germany, where manufacturing is still king and apprentices still devote most of a year to hand-filing metal. Yet at the premier machine-tool maker Trumpf, we discovered that about one third of the research staff are now software engineers. Even Trumpf has become a thinly disguised computer company!

INFORMATION IS EVERYTHING

One of my alma maters, Stanford University, celebrated its centennial in 1991. It's unquestionably one of a handful of leading educational institutions in the world. But its founder, Leland Stanford, was a *failure*. He went West seeking gold but didn't find any. So Stanford opened a store to sell supplies to gold miners. That was the real gold mine. The late Sam Walton also found his family's $20 billion worth of gold in retailing (Wal-Mart). Others on the short list of U.S. billionaires are fellow retailer Les Wexner (The Limited), Microsoft's youthful Bill Gates, and EDS's founder, Ross Perot. Walton, Wexner, Gates, and Perot, like Stanford, never "made" a thing. They were information organizers.

Long before Leland Stanford came on the scene, the creators of medieval marketplaces were Information Age harbingers, reshaping all of Western society and pulling us out of the Dark Ages. A physical marketplace (the crossroads of a medieval town or Stanford's store) or a computer-based trading system (e.g., the London Stock Exchange, which replaced its trading floor with an electronic network that links it to the world in 1989) simply brings together—efficiently—information to aid buyers and sellers. The denser the information, the more customers will benefit; they get the best value possible from nearly "perfect information," as the economists call it, about the market.

Information per se—the ultimate intangible—is playing an increasingly important role in world commerce. But we are uncomfortable with the shift to information dominance and view. So what's new? In Leland Stanford's time, *real* men tilled the soil; others were looked down upon. Just a few decades ago, we denigrated "college boys" at work—*real* men were supposed to spend their first 10 working years shoving iron ingots into red-hot blast furnaces. Harvard political economist Robert Reich won plaudits a few years ago when he assaulted money manipulators, labeling them "paper entrepreneurs." The term captured the disgust many felt over America's best and brightest going into such professions as investment banking.

The public's lingering suspicion of "head work" is especially worrisome as the U.S. becomes, like all developed countries, an almost totally brain-based economy, where information manipulation per se is the basis for advantage in every job and industry, old or new. The fact is, until the computer came along and its dramatic impact became clear, we seldom talked much about information processing. That was always a mistake. After all, it's not much of a stretch to suggest that the human body, the corporation, and the economy are "nothing but" information-processing machines. In some sense, information has been "everything" since long before William Shockley invented the transistor or Steve Jobs and Steve Wozniak emerged from Jobs's garage with the Apple I.

One of the hottest software topics is "fuzzy logic." What is it? An effort—one of the latest, hardly the first, and surely not the last—to capture in software the fuzzy way human beings think and process information. For example, at the most trivial level, "fuzzy logic devices" are being incorporated into automobile cruise controls. Consider your cruise control, if you have one: If it's like mine, it's pretty choppy. The variation in speed can run seven or eight miles an hour, depending on whether you're heading uphill or down. "Fuzzy logic" software will anticipate and smooth out the control process—eliminating that chop. (In other words, the cruise controller's "product"—

"managed speed"—will now more closely mimic the human driver's ability to anticipate tiny changes.)

Move from the brain's processes to the corporation. Organizations are pure information processing machines—nothing less, nothing more: Organizational structures, including hierarchies, capture, massage, and channel information—period. The first giant, modern corporations were America's railroads. As railroads grew to span several time zones, middle management had to be "invented" to sort out the newfound complexity. In fact, the most important of all the inventions that made the railroad work were arguably not those which had to do with steam engines or laying rail, but those concerned with information processing. For example, standard time. It was impossible to have complex schedules—and avoid head-on collisions (which were common in railroading's early days)—until time became uniform from community to community. The bill of lading was another major "information invention." Suddenly the number of daily transactions exploded. How to keep up? With the bill of lading, naturally—or naturally we say now. (Today, giant retailer Wal-Mart has set the new pace by demanding that all vendors, of any size, do business with it computer-to-computer—via electronic data interchange. Wal-Mart's encompassing use of EDI is "nothing more than" an extension of the railroads' introduction of standard time and bills of lading 130 years ago.) The railroads even "invented" modern Wall Street, an "information trading room" extending several blocks north and south on lower Manhattan Island. Railroads were the first to need huge capital infusions; investment banking emerged to tap numerous, dis-integrated sources of money in an effort to supply the rails' insatiable need for cash.

All of economics is information processing. You like green running shoes with air bubbles showing? Fine. I like blue ones, no bubbles. Figuring out who likes what—information!—and serving those specialized needs more quickly than the next person are what "steer" the firm, innovation, and the overall marketplace. Like it or not, the farmer gets no more than a penny or two from the 50 cents or so that a can of tomato soup brings the retailer. Only a little of the rest is absorbed by processing and canning. Distribution, logistics, advertising, wholesaling, and retailing claim the big bucks. That is, information processing—creating connections between the product (the tomato with a little water and a few chemical additives) and the consumer. Bankers, financiers, and merchants have never been loved. That causes special problems today, because more and more of us are, in effect, bankers and financiers and merchants—i.e., full-time information masticators.

Over the last few years, Nintendo's database has grown to encompass information on millions of users in the U.S. alone (see Chapter 45). Nintendo is, in effect, a modern-day banker. Though it provides a terminal and software that come in boxes, the "real" Nintendo product, and what makes Nintendo so special, is that database and the way Nintendo cleverly adds to it, and exercises it. (Ditto Pioneer Hi-Bred and the 500,000 farmers it can communicate with individually, right?) The big difference today, then, is that the role of information is becoming more visible. The information element of businesses is suddenly becoming transparent—and dominant.

How Many Zeroes in a Trillion?

In 1980, computers were able to perform 330,000 calculations per second. The current battle rages over what firm will be first to create a *teraflop* machine—which will make *one trillion calculations per second.* Bolt, Beranek and Newman, Cray Research, IBM, Intel, NCube, Parsytec, Thinking Machines, and Tera Computer are the major combatants. In fact, NCube brashly announced in June 1992 that its machine, due in 1994, will be able to execute 6.5 trillion calculations per second! (Not all are sure that the right battle is being fought. "We'd be in the race, too, if we could find a customer to build such a machine for," IBM's Abraham Peled told *The New York Times* on June 10, 1992.)

THE NEW INFRASTRUCTURE

No nation can operate a 21st-century economy without a 21st-century electronic infrastructure, embracing computers, data communications, and the other new media. This requires a population as familiar with this informational infrastructure as it is with cars, roads, highways, trains, and the transportation infrastructure of the smokestack period.

ALVIN TOFFLER, *Power Shift*

The computer is the locomotive of the Information Age. But the highways over which computers will exercise their combined power are just as important (like standard time). One of the biggest policy issues facing the U.S. in the 1990s is the construction of "data highways." It's largely unsung, but vital to international competitiveness. Congress has been considering a largely publicly-financed interstate highway equivalent, called NREN, or National Research and Education Network. A private-sector alternative is called Advanced Network Services, a product of the imaginations of IBM, MCI, and the State of Michigan. The private initiative would be analogous to the predominantly private ownership of railroads that marked the first couple of decades of the railroading age (which, to be sure, were followed by decades of massive public support).

"Highways of the Mind," the lead article in the Spring 1991 issue of the *Whole Earth Review,* begins like this:

> A quiet but crucial debate now underway in Congress, in corporate boardrooms, and in universities has the potential to shape American life in the twenty-first century and beyond. The outcome may determine where you live, how well your children are educated, who will blossom and who will wither in a society in which national competitiveness and personal prosperity will likely depend on access to information.
>
> This battle is about who will build, own, use and pay for the high-speed information networks of the future and whether their content will be censored. These data highways, capable of transporting entire libraries coast-to-coast in a few seconds, joining millions of people into communities of interest, or sending crucial CAT scans from remote villages to urban specialists, could be linked in a vast network of "highways of the mind."

Nothing has been of greater historical importance to relative economic development, in the U.S. and elsewhere, than the growth of networks: canals, railroads, highways, phones. The former Soviet Union feared famine in the winter of 1992. It was not the farmers' failure, despite the disastrous 50-year experiment in collectivized agriculture. Underdeveloped networks were the enemy. Over half the fall 1991 harvest was lost because of lousy roads and the absence of a distribution infrastructure. The development of information networks, within firms and nations as a whole, will have as great an impact on relative economic health in the 21st century as rail and highway systems did in the 19th and 20th centuries.

STUFF

OK, information is everything. Information networks will be decisive to relative future competitiveness. But that's maddeningly vague. Just what is this information technology stuff? Well . . . My 1992 Bass Pro Shops catalog features the EZ6600 ($549.88) on page 275. It's a sonar system. But instead of seeking Russian nuclear subs, Tom Clancy-style, it helps anglers hunt for fish. Stored in its computerized memory bank are the acoustic characteristics of trout, muskie, walleye, bass, panfish, stripers, and salmon. Scroll to the selected fish, scroll to "lake," "river," or "ice"—and your EZ6600 (which also features split-screen displays, zooms, and cross-hair target cursors) will show you what's going on as far as 600 feet beneath your keel.

And more:

- Consultant Stan Davis and University of Southern California professor Bill Davidson report in *2020 Vision*: "Otis Elevator Company created Otis-Line service so that if anything starts to go wrong in one of its boxes, it is diagnosed and, if possible, self-corrected within the box. Otherwise, a message is sent to the servicing office about what parts, labor and maintenance are needed. The building owner is covered by the service contract, where [Otis's] real profit lies."

- *Business Week*, October 1991: "In the future, U.S. apparel factories will need automated sewing equipment to remain competitive with overseas producers. But one question that raises is quality control. Now, researchers at the Georgia Institute of Technology in Atlanta have designed electronic 'ears' that enable sewing machines to supervise their own work and check for mistakes. The sensors detect wear or breakage in the sewing-machine needles before they can damage apparel. . . . Broken or worn needles have a distinctive sound, or acoustic signature. Computer analyses of those signatures reveals that the amplitudes increase in proportion to how badly the needle is worn. When the sewing-machine ears hear this, they trigger a flashing light that notifies a human operator that maintenance or adjustments are necessary."

- Davis and Davidson again: "Cattle were sold in stockyards in the industrial economy, but video auctions on an electronic network could mean that stockyards would go the way of the old-fashioned cattle drive. Superior Livestock Auction of Fort Worth uses satellite transmission, television cameras and computerized buying networks to auction steers that never leave the ranch until they are sold."

- *Business Week*, July 1991: "Want to turn your stodgy car into a hot rod? Adaptive Technologies, a Port Hueneme (California) company, has designed a system that lets you select the computer chip controlling your engine. Until now, speed freaks who wanted to tweak their engines had to crawl under the dash to swap the carmaker's engine computer for one that boosts power by altering the air-fuel ratio and the spark timing. The new system, which costs $219, fits most General Motors Corporation cars and trucks built since 1984 and holds up to four different engine-controller chips. . . . You can choose a chip that gives you more power when you want it—or one that provides better fuel economy. Another can be a security chip that foils thieves by disabling your car's fuel and electric systems. You can even choose one that limits engine power and then remove the key, so that kids can't get too wild on the way to the store." (It's a long way from gapping the spark plugs by hand, which my dad taught me how to do. Hey, do cars even *have* spark plugs anymore?)

- The Toronto *Globe and Mail* of May 26, 1992, lets us in on the secret of Coors beer's talking cans, of which some 30,000 were to be found among Coors Light 12-packs in a summer 1992 promotion: "A microchip inside a container nestled within a can of Coors Light enables it to 'talk.' When exposed to light, it is supposed to say, 'You win!,' and then describe the prize, items like stereos and compact discs, valued in excess of $1 million."

● *Mobile Office*, August 1991: "When one of the nation's largest manufacturers of supermarket goods recently introduced a new, three-flavored product, the account executive was able to sell the wholesaler only two flavors; the third was refused. An aggravating situation to be sure, but the account exec hoped that once the promotional package hit, strong sales for the first two flavors would sell the third. Normally, he would have waited 30 to 45 days for that sales information. But all *this* account executive had to do was key his laptop into the company mainframe the next week, and there on the screen [was] all the information he needed. . . . He went to his buyer with the latest out-of-stock reports, a list of stores that were out of stock and the percentage summaries for different areas. He was even able to compare in detail his products' performance to those of his competitors during the same period. On the basis of this information, he persuaded his client to buy the third flavor.

"How innovative [is this system]? Well that's something Pillsbury, Lipton, R. J. Reynolds, Gerber and others would rather you didn't know. In fact, the success of this technology can best be measured by their reluctance to talk about it. . . . In an industry where a new product can have as few as 90 days to prove itself, information is at a premium. And because of the scope of its distribution, this highly competitive industry has nearly always suffered from slow information turnaround. The Sales Information System (SIS), which these companies are now implementing, represents the first effective response to this problem."

This hardly constitutes a full-scale review. It does offer a sense of the reach, from the sublime to the ridiculous, of information technology's tentacles. Suddenly, Davis and Davidson's claim that 80 percent of economic value will stem from information technology by 2020 doesn't seem so farfetched after all.

INFORMATION TECHNOLOGY AND CHANGING "PRODUCTS"/INDUSTRIES

Information processing equipment accounted for 51 percent of all the durable equipment bought by [U.S.] private enterprises in 1989. That compares to only 11 percent in 1970.

CIO Magazine, March 1992

Information technology is an enormous industry in its own right. It's also having an extraordinary effect on virtually every product—new or "old." (There really *are* no old products—to wit: the "smartening" of needles in commercial sewing machines.) To top it off, information technology is revolutionizing every aspect of product development, marketing, delivery, and service. Information technology, then, encompasses:

- <u>Pure, new info-related products.</u> This includes the giant, powerful computer, computer chip, peripherals, telecommunications, consumer electronics, and software business. Estimated total revenues in 1991: close to a trillion dollars, or maybe twice that.

If you don't believe this market is dynamic, consider that just 10 years ago about three-quarters of all computing power was on mainframes. Now that number is somewhere between 1 and 5 percent. PC industry (hardware/software) sales alone grew to $82 billion in 1990 from just $2 billion in 1981.

- <u>The design of new products—chemicals, materials, automobiles, and bathroom scales.</u> Computer-aided design has dramatically changed the look, shape, and method of developing products. Invention processes per se are also colored by the use of e-mail networks: A Digital Equipment engineer stumped with a problem can send out an instant query to several thousand fellow DEC engineers. Advanced teleconferencing techniques are leading to global brainstorming among members of an "organization" (don't forget those quotation marks!), its suppliers and distributors, and an ever-expanding array of outsiders (e.g., professors from a dozen universities on four continents). And don't forget Pioneer Hi-Bred and the seed business—tight global communications links cut *six years* from its product development cycle!

Network Collaboration = Competitive Advantage

"In a move that could pose a formidable threat to Europe's Airbus Industrie, Boeing Co. and its five Japanese partners in the B-777 aircraft development project will build a ¥150 billion transpacific telecommunications system to link their design operations.

"The system . . . is also likely to draw the Japanese firms further into the Boeing network, making it difficult for them to link up with other foreign aircraft manufacturers. . . . [It] will include more than 500 engineering workstations on both sides of the Pacific, running on computer-aided design, manufacturing and engineering (CAD/CAM/CAE) software developed by France's Dassault. . . . In addition to linking design operations, the system will . . . manage materials, parts supply and production processes for the project."

The Nikkei Weekly
October 26, 1991

- <u>The construction of prototypes.</u> Do your design of some intricate part at a CAD terminal, and the physical prototype will be automatically constructed in plastic—real-time—a block, a mile, or a continent away, as you wish.

- <u>The invention of new products via powerful computational schemes.</u> The biotechnology industry is arguably more the product of the computer revolution than the of discovery of DNA's structure. Computer simulation and modeling forms the bedrock, for example, of the massive, controversial human genome project, aimed at mapping our entire genetic structure. The chemical industry is being reinvented as well; chemical compounds now are often highly specialized molecules, tailor-made for highly specialized uses. Thanks to "virtual reality" devices and software, drug researchers are now routinely climbing around inside molecules (figuratively) to check connections between one atom and another.

- <u>The smartening of everything.</u> "Smart" commercial knitting needles. "Smart" cars. "Smart" shopping carts. "Smart" sensors embedded in materials. "Smart" self-diagnosis (elevators, auto engines, copiers). "Smart" stoves. "Smart" machine tools. *And* "smart" buildings.

Consider this description of "smart homes" from *The Wall Street Journal*, October 21, 1991:

> The ultimate vision for home electronics is the electronic home. One of the most advanced abodes is just a ten-minute walk from the center of Tokyo. Approach the TRON Pilot Intelligent House, and the lights turn on. Inside, you can drop your briefcase in a bin in the closet; the briefcase is photographed and whisked to the basement. (Later, you turn on a video monitor and scroll through the pictures of as many as ten bins. When you see the one you want, you select it, and the briefcase is whisked back to the closet.)
>
> The bath is already drawn; you set the time by phone before leaving the office. To cook a Chinese meal, punch a couple of buttons on the combination oven/VCR. A video shows you how to prepare the dish of your choice, while the oven turns on at the appropriate moment. Don't worry about watering the plants; sprinklers turn on by themselves. If it starts to rain, the windows close.
>
> Then there's the toilet: a remote control unit adjusts the strength, direction, and temperature of the water spewing from the bidet, while an attached computer conducts a detailed urinalysis and blood-pressure test. Sensors cut the need for the disease-spreading human touch by flushing the bowl automatically as well as turning the sink on and off. [Over 5 million smart toilets, though not all are *this* smart, have already been sold in Japan.]
>
> The two-story home—which isn't available for occupancy but does

take occasional guests—is controlled by wires, cameras, and sensors running through the walls and ceilings leading to an underground central computer. Eighteen Japanese companies, including Nippon Telegraph & Telephone Corp., Mitsubishi Electric Corp., and Seibu Department Store Ltd., cooperated to complete the home in December 1989.

Not to mention *buying* a home. *The Wall Street Journal* again:

Japanese home buyers are using computer-intelligence to design their houses. In April [1991], a Matsushita subsidiary set up a test showroom where prospective shoppers can "walk through" a three-dimensional computer blueprint of their kitchen.

The exercise relies on an emerging technology called "virtual reality." The user puts on headgear made up of two small television sets and a pair of stereo speakers, as well as a glove with fiber-optic sensors. A computer detects a person's hand and head movements from the sensors, then sends images and sounds to give the sensation of movement. A [prospective] home buyer, for instance, can "walk" through the kitchen, turning on the sink and opening cupboards.

Is all this available for the average consumer? No. Will it be available in 1995? No. Should you ponder it when considering today's business strategy? You bet.

• <u>The building of new products.</u> Computer-aided manufacturing (CAM) and computer-integrated manufacturing (CIM) are radically shifting the way products are moved from the design "board" (the computer terminal's screen!) to and through manufacture. Among other things, this results in "mass customization," as some call it: A graduation-weekend visit to a pair of campus souvenir shops at Cornell University revealed no fewer than 350 varieties of logo-emblazoned sweatshirts, sweatpants, and so on, including a few for "Mom/Dad of the Cornell Class of 1991 Grad"—i.e., "mass" products (sweatshirts, etc.), "customized" to take advantage of a narrow (one school, three-day graduation weekend!) market window.

Speaking of three days, consider this extract from *Manufacturing 21 Report: The Future of Japanese Manufacturing,* which summarizes a five-year study sponsored by the Japan Machinery Federation and the System Science Institute of Waseda University.

The success of the concept depends upon cultivating the automotive prosumer. ["Prosumers"—the term was coined by futurist Alvin Toffler in *The Third Wave*—are ordinary customers who actively engage in the product design process.] The prosumer participates in the design of his vehicle at a work station at the dealership. Using the car company's

CAD/CAM software, the prosumer can first select the combination of body structures, drive train components, and suspension components. . . . Many features of the car can be custom-designed depending on how much the customer wants to pay. . . . The seat contour can be fitted to the customer, the car's lighting system designed as the customer likes, the instrument panel layout modified to suit personal preferences. . . . Within limits, prosumers can create the shape of body panels, design their own trim, and "imagineer" sound systems to their own tastes. . . . The production system is triggered as soon as the feasible order, with all the CAD/CAM data generated, is entered at the dealership. *The lead time to delivery: three days.*

When will all this be ready? Perhaps by the turn of the century, perhaps earlier. It's no fantasy.

Go Cardinal!

At 4 p.m. on Saturday, November 23, 1991, the Stanford Cardinal football team unexpectedly beat the sixth-ranked University of California at Berkeley Bears. At 2:00 p.m. on Monday, November 25, 1991, I bought a sweatshirt commemorating the game at a shopping center in Palo Alto. It didn't say "Upset Win" or anything that could have been proposed in advance. Instead, it featured six boxes, each with a detailed sketch and description of a key play in the 38–21 contest. Talk about customization. Talk about narrow market windows. Talk about fashion.

- The re-creation of old *industries.* Philadelphia's Rosenbluth Travel has grown from bookings of a few million to a billion and a half dollars in just a decade—thanks largely to proprietary software packages introduced at the rate of about one every 30 days. Rosenbluth saves companies like Motorola, for which it manages corporate travel, millions—e.g., by selecting optimal travel arrangements at the best prices, while also taking full account of individual preferences ("mass customization" again).

But no industry has been—or will be—more affected by information technology than financial services. Banking, for example, used to be a cozy, regulated game. Banks were all things to all people. Profits were pretty much assured. Then came deregulation in the early 1980s. Next, new technologies. Computer power and data storage in banking are growing at over 25 percent a year; the "systems side" of the banking business, McKinsey consultants Tom Steiner and Diogo Teixeira reported in *Technology in Banking* in 1990, is reshaping the industry.

In retrospect, banking is the obvious place to look today for manifestations of 21st-century information technology. "[All] banking products," Steiner and Teixeira point out, "are simply information combined in new ways, so with hundredfold increases in the amount of information available, it is not surprising that there are a lot of new products."

Banks are farming out more and more, focusing on only those things which they believe make them distinct. First Wachovia of Winston-Salem, North Carolina, for example, became the country's second-largest processor of student loans. "Student lending," Steiner and Teixeira tell us, "is extremely complex, because each state has different rules for each type of student. A medical education loan is different from a liberal arts education loan, which is different from a truck driving school loan. . . . First Wachovia has developed proprietary software to track student loans and deliver the required servicing. The software is, of course, unique and serves as a substantial entry barrier [to would-be competitors]."

Or consider State Street Boston Corporation, which the authors declared is not a bank anymore, but "a computerized record keeping and accounting business." The giant institution sold or closed 90 percent of its branches and then chiefly aimed to capture the "custodial" business, performing intricate and highly regulated record-keeping activities for the securities industry. In 1989, State Street handled 10 percent of all the globe's securities transactions ($625 billion), collaring a 36 percent return on equity in the process.

Banking's saga is every industry's saga. Financial services are just 10 years further along because of the central role information plays, by definition, in the industry. Yet even here, only the tip of the iceberg is in view: By 1990, barely 10 percent of the industry's transactions were automated.

• <u>New connections equal new companies.</u> Companies that thrive on connectivity, such as MCI, Federal Express, Rosenbluth Travel, The Limited, Pioneer Hi-Bred, and Wal-Mart are coming to the fore. The power and competitive advantage lie in the connectivity per se.

Take the accountants Coopers & Lybrand. *CIO* magazine reported in 1991 that they've built a "global network to make it easier to share information and expertise across disciplines as well as geographies. . . . [The firm's] network allows a partner in the United Kingdom who is proposing a tax audit and consulting services to a global airline reservation company to get input from American partners who may have more experience with such companies." Coopers & Lybrand *is* its connections!

• <u>The rise of the solo entrepreneur.</u> Telecommuting is becoming a way of life for millions of Americans and others. Micro-entrepreneurial specialties, located anywhere as long as there's a phone—fax, modem—connection within reach, are absorbing more and more of the ever-"smarter," ever more connected work force.

Add all this up and three familiar words come to mind: *fashion, speed, intangibles.* The "soft" or "knowledge-intense" part of any "product" (this term, too, must be used in quotes, since product has so little to do with its old, hard, lumpy manifestation) is growing by leaps and bounds.

From Palm to Planet

Relational database whiz Oracle Corp. has figured out how to link giant information utilities to Sharp's Wizard handheld computers, *Computerworld* reported in early 1992:

> The Wizard—usually sold in department stores for $250 to $400—joins computers as diverse as IBM mainframes, Digital Equipment Corp. VAXs and Unix workstations that can access Oracle databases.
> Oracle's new Palmlink application interface would enable developers to build applications to link the 500,000 Wizards on the market with databases residing on desktop IBM Personal Computers or Apple Computer, Inc. Macintoshes. All users would need is a $129 cable kit to connect the Wizard with the PC's backplane, a $299 copy of Palmlink and the $299 Oracle Card application tool kit. . . . Data entered on a Wizard can update an Oracle database or be sent to another Oracle user via Oracle*Mail electronic mail, said Bill Ford, director of marketing at Oracle's New Technology Division.

9

Information Technology and Organizing

The quality and quantity of information comprehended per unit of time may now determine who wins or loses a sales order or a war.

MEL PHELPS, venture
capitalist, writing
in *Upside*, June 1991

The largest section of this book, Beyond Hierarchy, is—*and isn't*—a product of the new world of information technology. Listening harder to employees, getting them involved in improvement processes, turning the organization into a collection of projects—all these things *could* be done before the advent of the Information Age. And, of course, some firms did such things to varying degrees. On the other hand, information technology—appropriately used—can clearly transform these activities. Hence information technology's stunning organizational implications:

- The "insiderization" of outsiders and the "informating" of all employees. There's no option! Outsiders *must* become privy to virtually all of the firm's information—this includes suppliers, suppliers' suppliers, distributors, franchisees and other middle persons, customers, and customers' customers. So must *all* the people on the company's own payroll. (Yes, you've heard this before . . . but most companies have yet to take it to heart.) Sharing information on a virtual real-time basis and encouraging, via the likes of relational databases and expert systems, access to information in friendly forms that are helpful to many different users are essential. Functional barriers are effectively penetrated only when information about what's going on in other functions is made instantly available to people throughout the organization—this is the cornerstone, for example, of Pioneer Hi-Bred's remarkable strategy.

Bits of the changing nature of "organizational" relationships include (1) demonstrating trust (a willingness to share virtually *everything* with *everybody*, inside and out); (2) creating on-line databases that can be used across functional boundaries (to the extent that old functions will even exist anymore); (3) installing an "e-mail ethos," where informal communication across remaining levels and functions becomes normal; (4) hooking into on-line databases and electronic bulletin boards external to the firm; and (5) using electronic data interchange (EDI) extensively to routinize and automate transactions with "outsiders." (Again: Information technology is a major *enabler*. But there's lots, lots more to the story—as we shall see in the next section.)

- The creation of electronic highway systems. Access to a huge number of on-line, external databases and the like is possible via the proprietary or public electronic networks and bulletin boards springing up all over. Thinking about "electronic highway systems" is imperative for creating tomorrow's organization.

- "Extended family" project management. Effectively using e-mail and various other direct electronic links enables project teams to include many who are far from "home"—e.g., Boeing and its Japanese partners designing aircraft together. A project/network can readily include, real-time: members of the firm throughout the world, suppliers, distributors, customers, and special resources (at universities and think tanks, for instance). Through the use of various groupware and other problem-solving tools, the project management/brainstorming/idea generation/social integration process is changed forever. Dramatic accounting changes are central to the new decentralized/projectized/information technology-enhanced environment. Above all, we need to know costs that are associated with micro-bits of the work that goes into the total "product" delivery cycle—a surprisingly new idea! Moreover, accounting information must be available more readily—updated daily, hourly, or more frequently—for even the smallest unit (e.g., the project team).

- New scale I: Smaller is better. Plausible minimum, coherent unit size is going down, down, down. (See both the Beyond Hierarchy and the Markets and Innovation section.) In manufacturing, for example, smart industrial tools frequently permit maximum "scale economies" to be achieved in 1,000-square-*foot* rather than 10,000-square-*yard* facilities.

- New scale II: "Network size." Abetted by information technology, the "network organization"—utilizing temporary collections of contractors of all sizes, from all over, to accomplish specified tasks—brings new meaning to the words "big," "small," "scale," and "power." Scale used to be associated with vertical integration—what you owned. Today, scale and power are associated with your ability to quickly bring to bear the talents of people and bits of organizations dispersed around the globe.

- Organizations as knowledge-based societies. Organizations that have learned how to learn, that are engaged by electronic bulletin board with outsider organizations to which they are just slightly related, that are hooked into universities and other learning centers—they alone will thrive. The "knowledge component" of every "product" and every "service" and every producing network is shooting up (toward Davis and Davidson's 80 percent—or beyond). The ability to rope in knowledge, learn from what other parts of the organization/network are doing, and reinvent the organization/network in a flash becomes, arguably, the principal source of future value-added—for corporations and nations alike.

KNOWLEDGE-BASED SOCIETIES

One day, the electronics industry may be recognized in history books for having helped link planet earth with networks of knowledge before ignorance destroyed the world. Openness-or-perish alternatives are forcing computer and communication industries to cooperate or disintegrate on a global scale. National barriers are tumbling as knowledge reaches the formerly uninformed citizenry, which is no longer willing to sit idly by and let the government do what's "best" for them.

MEL PHELPS
Upside, June 1991

Information technology can be incorrectly applied to "organizations." It usually has been. On the other hand, information technology's ability to influence every aspect of organization is clear. "The best gross indicator of competitiveness," Davis and Davidson claim, "may be simply the amount of resources committed to information infrastructure." This applies to the individual, the company, and, Davis and Davidson insist, nations as a whole.

In a working paper titled "Electronic Organization and Expert Networks: Beyond Electronic Mail and Computer Conferencing," MIT's Chandler Harrison Stevens writes:

Expert networks represent a new dimension, an electronic societal and organizational dimension, that did not exist prior to the development of Computer-Aided Communication. . . . An example of expert networks was developed in the late 1970s when science advisors to state legislators joined together with technical professional societies, federal labs and public interest research groups to form Legitech Network. . . . [Using the network], for example, one frost-belt state posed the question: "What are alternatives to road salt for dealing with icy highways without polluting water supplies?" Another state, having recently dealt with the problem, responded, as did associations and labs that knew of relevant research on the topic. Other frost-belt states joined the topic to get the benefit of inquiry responses that might help their states as well as the inquiring state. . . .

Electronic organization and expert networks are more powerful than familiar [computer-aided communication] forms, such as electronic mail and computer conferencing. . . . [Computer-aided communication] is less formal than most other writing and in fact seems more like talking. . . . The medium is more interrogative than declarative. Interacting more than expounding becomes the norm. Questions are often asked. The best answers frequently come from surprising sources. An unknown peer with irrelevant experience can sometimes provide better help than the more famous expert, who may be less accessible or less articulate. . . . . The store-and-forward nature of most forms of [computer-aided communication] allows for a . . . type of mulling over that is not possible in more traditional types of synchronous, face-to-face interaction. . . . More and more work is being done by less organization-dependent professionals. They earn their pay based upon their expertise, which has to be renewed mainly through networking with their peers.

In 1992, Stevens's world is still the exception, hardly the rule. Yet as projects become the standard approach to doing most of the work of the organization (from CNN to grinding-tool design at Ingersoll-Rand), and networks including a passel of those we previously called "outsiders" become an average way of getting things done, his vision of the future moves ever closer to the norm. In any event, it's not to be taken lightly.

PARADOX

Deere [& Co.] discovered, after much reflection, that it had simply computerized and automated operations as they existed in a manual mode. After much soul searching, Deere realized that it had computerized the contradictions, confusion, and inconsistencies of its existing operations. Reflecting upon this experience, Jim Lardner, a Deere vice-president, recommends that companies simplify existing operations before introducing heavy computerization.

CHARLES SAVAGE
Fifth Generation Management

Despite years of impressive technological improvements and investment, there is not yet any evidence that information technology is improving productivity or other measures of business performance on a large scale—or, more importantly, significantly enhancing U.S. economic performance. . . . The fundamental blame rests with organizations. Information technology holds great potential, but companies have failed to provide structures and processes that facilitate the use of information technology in ways that create significant net value.

GARY LOVEMAN
Computerworld
November 25, 1991

Those carried away by the promise of information technology in the last 50 years are members of an enormous club. (Some will recall those early-1950s books about the work-force decimation that automation would quickly cause.) On the one hand, it's fair to say that it is highly dangerous *not* to be carried away. On the other, it is equally dangerous to *be* carried away. Recall Titeflex. The MRP I pioneer automated and computerized most everything—and almost brought the company to its knees. Titeflex's path to salvation began with *de*computerizing. Then it completely reorganized. Only then did it recomputerize, consistent with a brand-new model of organization. The story is a garden-variety tale of the late '80s. Hard evidence: Half of all "CIOs" (chief information officers) have had their job status reduced in the last few years. As the info-revolution has bloomed, its chief corporate spokespersons have been demoted—the price for having promised much too much, much too early.

There are numerous other paradoxes associated with information technology:

● <u>It's happening fast, yet it's less than promised.</u> The promise of information technology seems almost infinite. Former Citicorp chairman Walter Wriston, economics commentator George Gilder, and others have predicted the overnight democratizing of the planet, courtesy of information technology. Indeed, information technology played an important role in the achievement of Eastern European freedom. (When Ted Turner, not Boris Yeltsin, became *Time*'s Man of the Year for 1991, the choice certified the shift in relative power between modern information brokers and modern political performers. In part, Yeltsin is Turner's creation.) On the other hand, as the Gulf War and numerous other conflicts demonstrate daily, we're hardly one big happy global family.

The computer revolution—the growing numbers of PCs, the multiplication of networks and electronic bulletin boards, and the gross increases in computer power per se—is breathtaking. These few pages give but the slightest hint of what's to come. Yet probably 95 percent of those who've pioneered have made fools of themselves, as is typical of pioneers in general. It's important, as Davis and Davidson assert again and again in *2020 Vision,* to think through business implications before concocting organizational responses. To move too quickly with information technology is disastrous. To move too slowly is equally disastrous. Tough!

● It's a world of high tech, but still a world of high touch. Recall the Union Pacific Railroad case. On the one hand, astonishing sums of money were spent on information technology. On the other hand, the greatest change in relationships came when bureaucrats were removed and line workers empowered to converse—across formerly impenetrable functional barriers, and with customers. (Remember NCSC team member Catherine McIntosh riding the rails and taking snapshots home to the St. Louis computer center.) Furthermore, the UPRR's success in the end was less a matter of raw speed than of keeping customers informed—that's "high touch," as futurist John Naisbitt called it. But hold on! *Effective* "high touch" could not have taken place without the high tech—the huge investment in the space-age Harriman Dispatch Center and the National Customer Service Center. And around and around we go.

● It's about centralization, and about decentralization—simultaneously. CNN is centralized from an information technology standpoint. So, too, is Union Pacific. On the other hand, the objective of the centralization is to foster more and more *de*centralization. That's a glib statement. It's easy to say. It works in these two cases. Often as not—frankly, much more often than not—it doesn't work, and the centralizers win out over the decentralizers. In a "fashionized" world, that amounts to a quick ticket to the economy's dustbin.

● It's about destruction and creation (obliterate, then automate). This is the Titeflex story. (And the nub of the Savage epigraph on Deere and Company.) Automating hundred-year-old systems, so commonplace in the 1960s, '70s, '80s, and even today, is a losing proposition—and the chief reason that so many information technology installations have created more problems than they've solved. You've got to take a "clean sheet of paper" to the organization first—then think technology. (In fact, it's interactive. The scribbler on the clean sheet will be greatly influenced by the ability of advanced information technology to support the wildly altered forms of "organizational" relationships she or he can conjure up.)

● It's about mass, and about customization. The new tools allow us to customize—for a large mass of people. That's what database management means at Nintendo, for example. Not to mention the near-future opportunity to, de facto, design your own car—then pick it up three days later. Production for the masses isn't dead. It has just been changed dramatically to encompass tailoring at blinding speeds.

- It means slowing down in order to hurry up. At Ingersoll-Rand, the objective was cutting product development from four years to one. But for that to happen, more attention had to be paid to relationships—and that takes time. Return to MIT's Stevens: The new technology permits all manner of rapid chatter to take place. On the other hand, the technology must be designed "loose," so that *informality* can reign. The best e-mail systems are typically "inefficient"—loaded with all kinds of extraneous chatter. Those that fail are usually formal and stilted—and mimic the stuffed-shirt organizations that spawned them.

"Necessary disorganization," this book's title proclaims. And "liberation." Fashion's stringent demands—in railroads (UPRR), hose-making (Titeflex), and transformer production (ABB)—can only be met if small, itinerant bands are set loose on the marketplace. But those wee bands can only serve their demanding customers effectively if they have access to global networks of peers—connecting, disconnecting, then reconnecting at will. It's information technology's promise. Yet the path from here to there is laid with an almost unimaginable array of booby traps. We'll look in more depth at both the promise and the perils in the next section.

IV

Beyond Hierarchy

10

Unglued Organizations

"Battleship I.B.M." is trying to become a fleet of nimble "destroyers."

The New York Times,
November 27, 1991

On November 26, 1991, sagging IBM—after looking in the mirror and studying the likes of ABB—announced an historic increase in subunit autonomy. Despite the announcement of a $3-billion charge that accompanied the restucturing, the stock market instantly signaled its delight by boosting the firm's share price by $2.75.

Getting *very* close to the customer. A dandy idea in general, an immediate necessity in a marketplace where fashion has become the name of every company's game. So how do you do it? I've offered a ton of advice in my three prior books. Measure customer satisfaction. Empower the front line. Etc. Etc. Etc.

But, as I said in the Preface, I blew it, if the truth be known. IBM defined "close to the customer" for years—per all the tricks of the trade (many of which it invented). As the customer changed, though, IBM didn't. Why? In a word, an enormous, numbing, top-heavy organization structure. Destroy that structure or else. That's the message. A jillion smart, energetic people submitting to the "right" incentives won't get you a micrometer closer to the customer unless the dead weight of a vertical hierarchy is lifted—almost entirely—off their backs. There's no liberation when much more than a semblance of the superstructures remains.

"Reduce layers"? "Flatten the pyramid"? No. Go to your local stationer's. Buy that clean sheet of paper we talked about in the Learning to Hustle section. And, then, rip. R-I-P. Rip, shred, tear, mutilate, destroy that hierarchy. That's the Percy Barnevik story (ABB). The Jon Simpson story (Titeflex).

The Mike Walsh story (Union Pacific). But hold on, you say. What *is* hierarchy? *Why* hierarchy in the first place? And how do you get "beyond" hierarchy without committing to anarchy?

Forget academic definitions. This section will be unabashedly *inductive*. Cases will tell our tale. And the best way to begin is as far away as possible from theory. What in the hell is it like to live without formal hierarchy, anyway? I know someone who can answer that from experience. Me.

I'll lead off, then, with an intimate tale, a personal reflection (with all the bias that implies) on what it's like to function in a big, but fluid and thoroughly atomized, organization—McKinsey & Company, the management consultants. McKinsey, where I hung my hat for seven years, trades in ideas, nothing else. "Soft" as that may seem, it's the coming way of everyone's world.

Think project organization, and unless NASA comes to mind, you probably think on a fairly modest scale—a half-dozen people squirreled away in a corner somewhere, working on a narrow-gauge task of finite duration. That's a perfect description of McKinsey (and EDS). And a lousy one. Most of McKinsey's work-for-pay *is* accomplished by teams of half a dozen (or less), with a customer or two as full-time members. And they *are* usually squirreled away in a corner somewhere—an unused cranny in the client's operation, a 20-by-20-foot "project room" with a dime-store table, battered coffee machine, phone, PC, and copier. On the other hand, these little squirrels' nests add up to a $1-billion company that doubled in size between 1986 and 1991.

THE FLUID LIFE

To have created a product that basically is an empty box that then goes out and figures what to do each time: That's pretty spectacular when you think about it.

RICHARD BETTIS,
Southern Methodist University,
on McKinsey & Co.

No doubt there is a good deal of cover-my-behind in bringing in consultants, especially consultants with an almost legendary name like McKinsey. . . . But you don't get the kind of reputation McKinsey has by providing alibis for temporizing managements. . . . If McKinsey is a legend, it is a legend with considerable substance supporting it.

Forbes, cover story,
October 19, 1987

McKinsey. Say the name and otherwise sensible persons genuflect. Adviser to GE, Fujitsu, BASF, and thousands of other blue-chip clients around the globe. Consultants were a footnote to commerce, years ago. No longer. In a commercial context where knowledge is king, knowledge merchants are, by definition, the new elite. McKinsey is a knowledge merchant with few peers.

It's axiomatic. Anyplace we see close up resembles a zoo. McKinsey was no exception. In fact, it's taken me 10 years to realize that these oddly organized knowledge merchants, managed so "poorly" by conventional standards (e.g., no job descriptions, no organization charts, no annual objectives, an unfathomable performance evaluation scheme), have now—in the age of "value-added through knowledge"—become premier role models for almost everyone else. Their ugly (if you're a traditionalist) way of doing things is looking more attractive every day.

Signing On, Heading Out

I arrived at McKinsey at 9:00 a.m., December 2, 1974. Got my credit cards. Got my keys. All that was wrapped up by about 9:30. None of the "team" I'd been assigned to was in the San Francisco office. The three other members were in Oklahoma, Iowa, and New York City, or at least that's what people guessed. I'd be working on a $150-million investment proposal for an ammonia-plant extension for the Skelly Oil Company. I was advised to hop on a plane to New York later that afternoon, to talk fertilizer with a McKinsey microeconomics expert, consultant to the team of consultants. He was a vital part of the project head's "informal network" (certainly not the term we used then!) and had been called in to deal with some thorny supply and demand issues. I'd spend the next day in New York, then head to the customer's plant in Clinton, Iowa.

By the time I arrived in Clinton, now a two-day McKinsey veteran, my teammate who'd been there had scooted off to Tulsa (Skelly headquarters). So there I was, at the customer site for the first time, commanding a hefty daily fee, with virtually no guidance. But it never occurred to me that what I was doing wasn't "normal."

A couple of days later, still not having met my team leader, I was off to Calgary, by myself, to work on a key piece of the puzzle—assessing Canadian supply and demand for agrichemicals over the next 20 years. *(Where's Calgary? What are agrichemicals?)* About a day after I arrived, I determined that I needed help—that is, the consultant desperately needed a consultant. Without advice or consent from my team leader (*Who is he? Where is he?*), I hired a two-person firm that I had determined knew the ins and outs of the Canadian agrichemical industry to undertake a weeklong study.

Just doing what came naturally. Yikes!

The Project Is *Everything*

From literally hour number one of day number one at McKinsey, I was part of a project team. And I was part of some project team from then until the last day of my career there. Before one project was over, if you were a valued employee, the next project had already started. Life, then, was a succession of small-team activities.

The project team was "it" at McKinsey. It was the source of revenue. The source of reputation. The source of challenge. Organizational experts have long written about "task orientation" as one of the principal bases for structuring any outfit. (Most traditional firms fail to emphasize the integrated task dimension and overemphasize de-integrated, narrow functional specialties.) "Task orientation"—that project—was the beginning, the middle, the end at McKinsey. Even family life revolved around it. Yet nothing about it was formal. It worked, and worked well. But there was, for example, not a moment devoted to "team training."

The description I just gave of my first few days begged many a question. Why, for instance, was the San Francisco office handling a Tulsa-based client—Skelly—when there were a Chicago office and a Dallas office closer at hand? Simple: During an earlier stint in Los Angeles, Getty Oil (headquartered there) had become the client of McKinsey partner Jon Katzenbach; when I joined up, Katzenbach was in San Francisco; and Skelly Oil had become a subsidiary of Getty (which has now been subsumed by Texaco—*tempus fugit*). Katzenbach kept Getty as a client when he moved from Los Angeles to San Francisco. He negotiated "my" project with Skelly as part of his ongoing service to Getty.

But the team didn't just include San Franciscans. To be sure, senior partner Katzenbach had made San Francisco's Allen Puckett partner-in-charge of the project; the day-to-day project manager ("engagement manager") was another San Franciscan, Jim Crownover, while I was the sole full-time "associate," as we junior consultants were called. But because of the nature of the assignment, we also had that New York-based economics "expert" working for us quarter-time: New York partner Jerry Hillman tended to flit from project to project, exporting his special talent rather than managing client relationships and projects. By dint of personality and intelligence, he'd created his own role and network by generating personal demand. McKinsey approved of such a setup—as long as Hillman was bringing in the bucks and his "network" sang his praises. But McKinsey also felt slightly uncomfortable with such behavior. After all, Hillman's wasn't straight project work. (Ironically, McKinsey feels as awkward about "normal" functional activity of the Hillman sort as most "traditional" firms do about project work.)

Such multi-office teams were common at McKinsey—and generally by design. In fact, I don't recall a single team I was on that consisted entirely of locals. In later years, I never worked on a team where all of us were from the same country. Moreover, and talk about nutty by conventional standards, in seven years I never worked twice with exactly the same team.

So . . . I never went to a formal training course at McKinsey. And I was on the road just hours after signing on. But "somehow" it became instantly clear that THE PROJECT WAS EVERYTHING. I picked up those credit cards, the front-door key, and plane tickets—and I was off, a full-fledged member of a temporary task team, off to The War Zone, The Front Line, The Engagement (which was what McKinsey called projects), The Client. And quick as a wink, I'd be on the verge of our team's first Progress Review.

Ah, yes, Progress Reviews, the presentation of interim findings, the moment you formally strutted your stuff before the senior members of the client outfit. A project team's life was organized around those inevitable Progress Reviews. They were the punctuation marks, the playoff games of the consultants' existence. Family and schedules and sanity went out the window around Progress Review time, which "happened" every six to eight weeks. During those six weeks, we pulled out all the stops.

Who Crawled into the Bed Next to Me?

It was about 2:00 a.m., in the then Amfac Hotel at the Dallas-Fort Worth Airport, in 1976. There was a light knock on the door, and somebody came in and climbed into the double bed next to me. It made me damned uncomfortable, but it wasn't all that weird. After all, this was McKinsey.

My unexpected bedmate happened to be a young guy from Britain who was assigned to my project team (working on Getty Oil–Skelly Oil post-merger issues). When he got to the hotel, there were no rooms available. Being a clever sort, he talked the night manager into giving him a key to my room, came on up, and, climbed in. He promptly went to sleep. His name was Tom Kellock; he was a witty man and a fine consultant. Neither of us had a preference for people of the same sex. The fact is that such stuff is rather typical of project team camaraderie. (It's a bit different now, I suppose, with a large number of women in the firm's consulting ranks. Such things would be frowned upon, though doubtless not unheard of.)

The point? The project "thing" was a *very* intense, *very* personal experience. For a period of three to nine months, you were in pursuit of a hopelessly complex goal—"solving" (you sort of thought you were doing that, though you knew it was not really possible) an ambiguous problem a client had confronted you with. You and a handful of colleagues would plunge into businesses and technologies you barely understood, hang out in places you couldn't have found on a map the week before, and work with people you'd never met. In a period of a few months you were to master all of the above, including the political machinations of the client firm, which had to be doped out if there was to be any possibility of implementing the solutions you proposed. It was you against the world. It was frequently frustrating, always exhausting (the burnout rate was high)—and almost always exhilarating. This was what working for McKinsey was all about—and precisely why no formal hierarchy was necessary. And also why, oddly enough, team-building training wasn't necessary. The task was so daunting that you *had* to get down to it posthaste, had to depend upon your teammates. Since there was no option, it worked.

"Getting" the Culture

> [The] sense of dedication is more than just show. Behind McKinsey's imposing mahogany doors on Manhattan's East 52nd Street are people who unabashedly think of themselves as secular versions of the Jesuits, gifted intellectuals uplifting the world of commerce with their vision. Newcomers quickly learn that McKinsey is not engaged in a "business" but a "profession." McKinsey does not work "for" clients, it works "with" them. McKinsey consultants do not go out on "jobs," they go out on "engagements."
>
> *Forbes*, October 1987

McKinsey's values are not taught by paper documents. To this day (18 years after starting work at McKinsey), I have no idea whether or not the company even *has* a written policy manual—which may help explain why I have such a tough time with people who keep asking, in effect, "How do you know what's going on unless there's something written down?" At McKinsey there are a few more or less mandatory training courses, but they're secondary to on-the-job training.

You're on the road a lot, which means that you eat dinner (and lunch and breakfast) with your teammates. You're working on those Progress Reviews every six weeks—they are clear indicators of firm values about how to approach problems (and problem-solving, after all, is what McKinsey does for a living). What McKinsey is, and what's important to it—the quality and thoroughness of analysis, the way you work with clients, the way you work with teammates—is something you eat, sleep, and breathe.

"The Movie Stars of the Business World"

Jim Crownover, my first project manager and now a senior office manager, called us "the movie stars of the business world." It's an important point that has a bearing on the hierarchy—yes or no—debate. McKinsey was an astonishingly proud organization (not infrequently to the point of arrogance). As a result, you didn't want to let down the side. You were wearing the Yankee pinstripes! You were heir to a fabled tradition of business problem-solving! The self-imposed pressure was unrelenting.

To be sure, I remember some consultants who didn't get it. At their separation interviews, those who flunked sometimes said they'd "never gotten any feedback." I think it was mostly their fault. I've never been anywhere that provides more regular feedback—daily, if you're at all alert to your surroundings. People were always nosing around in others' work. And while almost none of the feedback was written or formal, that surely didn't mean it wasn't there. (I recall only one formal feedback document, a one-page summary assessment filled out by the engagement manager, and initialed by the principal-in-charge, at the end of each project. It was of marginal value to the promotion process. Low marks were important bad signs, though it's inconceivable that any "grade" on such a sheet could come as a surprise. I suppose these reports did amount to some kind of ongoing transcript, but getting promoted to partner had little to do with them. Performance at McKinsey was a word-of-mouth, not a print-media, issue.)

It's Lonely Sitting Here Unused

Some professional service firms are batty about "utilization"—the exact percentage of the time you're "billed out" to clients (and hence, by subtraction, the percentage of time you're sitting "on the beach," bringing in no fees). McKinsey didn't worry about that at the micro level. Obviously, if there were a lot of people and no work, there'd be a problem for the office or for the firm as a whole, but there was little or no pressure put on the consultant per se to be "billed out" at a certain level.

Instead, consultants put pressure on themselves. You desperately wanted to be on a "good team." But you didn't think of it in terms of "percentage of time spent with the client." It was simple: If you had a solid or great reputation, good senior people were waiting in line for you. If you had a lousy or equivocal reputation, nobody was waiting in line for you. If nobody waited in line for you, you had a tough time getting assignments. You'd find yourself sitting in your office.

McKinsey seldom had to fire junior consultants outright, though unloved ones did often seem to hang on month after month. But at some stage of the game, the consultant and the office leadership would decide that enough was enough. After a farewell party, the unmentionable one would disappear, and all—junior to senior—would breathe a collective sigh of relief.

(It was a fairly gentle process. McKinsey nurtures its alumni network constantly and masterfully—a feat that is all the more impressive when you realize that "alumni" consist mainly of those who have in fact been canned. The key is turning the dumpees, ditched for the first time in their typically stain-free careers, into loyal allies rather than angry rejects. That process begins with an enormous investment on the part of the office manager in helping them get great jobs, perhaps in client organizations that had admired their work in the past.)

Building Supporters Away from Home

Performing on today's task team was the alpha and the omega for the newly arrived associate. But at about the 18-month mark, some stirring of concern for your position in the McKinsey universe began. If you were doing well at that juncture, you were then within a year of becoming an "engagement manager"—and that was the intervening step to the holy land called partnership.

In short, to pursue your place among the mighty of the Firm ("F" *always* capitalized) meant thinking about constructing a network. Again, I don't know how I "learned" that, probably over endless beers during endless nights away from home while a project was under way. But nonetheless, you *did* learn. You learned that making connections, mostly nonlocal, was your long-term task, that when the moment came for consideration for higher office, you'd best have a sizable set of allies from hither, thither, and yon championing your cause.

Part of "network-building" was finding new partners to work for, even though you might be very comfortable—and successful—with your current "boss." You needed to work successfully for a half-dozen or so senior people. Several in this set, in turn, had to be perceived as "powerful" in McKinsey's world. Several had to be from outside your home office. One or two ought to be from outside your country.

The onus was on you, not on "them," to get the ball rolling. Those who saw it that way tended to succeed. Those who left it to someone else, assumed that "the structure" would take care of it for them, tended quickly to fall behind. (Shades of EDS and CNN.)

How, precisely, did you go about building that network? "Word gets around" is probably the best description. Some consultants were considered "hot," others "dogs." Via the mysterious (and largely accurate) grapevine, the "hot" bunch were avidly pursued, sometimes from two continents away. The "dogs" were left to beg at their empty bowls.

The Nitty-gritty of Networking without Hierarchy

Here's how the process of signing up clients—on somebody else's turf—worked when I was a partner at McKinsey. Suppose I attend a local electronics convention in Silicon Valley, and end up spending most of an evening with an executive vice president of a big Swiss company. We get on well and agree to exchange notes.

When I go back to the office and put together a letter and material for him, I send a copy to the head of McKinsey's Zurich office. The Swiss company chief responds to me with a phone call—and is enthusiastic enough to say,

"Drop in the next time you're nearby. I'd like to have you talk to our management team."

When my next European trip is scheduled, I add my newfound Swiss pal to the agenda. Meanwhile, I've had several conversations with the head of the Zurich office, or a friend who's a partner in Zurich. (They've had some low-level contacts with the client company before, and have it on their informal "like to do work with" list.)

When I sort out the final details with the Swiss prospect, I mention that I'll be bringing along a couple of my Zurich-office McKinsey friends. (It would be unheard of for him to demur.)

Suppose the subsequent meeting generates a new-business nibble—in fact a foot-in-the-door project materializes in about six months. The Swiss client will unofficially be "my" client—officially all clients are "the Firm's." To use the McKinsey jargon from my days, I'll be the "director of client services." As the project begins to shape up, I work with the Zurich chief and tap a local partner to head day-to-day work. A couple of "associates" will be required for the legwork—perhaps one will be a specialist in the electronics area from God knows where, the other a valued youngster from the Zurich office.

At the end of the year, the total billings from "my" client will be tallied under my name. They'll also be tallied under the names of any Zurich partners who headed projects for the client. Obviously, "utilization" of specific Zurich personnel will be higher because we used Swiss youngsters to do the bulk of the project work.

In short, it's no big deal! The more it comes close to looking like a big deal, the less it probably is. Suppose the Zurich office head has been on the verge of negotiating a study with the client. The odds are, he'll be tickled pink that I've put yet another hook into that client. If we both start projects at the same time, it's standard procedure for him to be the director of client services (he's closer), but he'll doubtless encourage me to do as much as I want with "his" client—it will redound to his advantage over the long haul. In fact, the only person whose nose might be bent partially out of joint is the head of the San Francisco office. My Swiss distraction will dilute the effort I direct to the home front.

"STRUCTURE"

There are some "sorta" ranks at McKinsey: junior associate, senior associate, junior engagement manager, senior engagement manager, junior partner (principal), senior partner (director). The first steps up are accomplished within the context of the local office structure. Promotions to principal and director are firm-wide.

Getting Promoted

You somehow metamorphose from junior associate to senior associate, which essentially means that you have survived your first couple of assignments. You also metamorphose into an engagement manager. At some point someone says, "You're going to run the next project." Most likely, on the project before that, your engagement manager was working on some side tasks; you probably more or less ran that project for him.

Upon becoming an engagement manager, you start for the first time to think about "client development." That's a euphemism for cadging more work from today's client—doing so well on project A, and becoming so indispensable, that projects B and C come along as a matter of course.

McKinsey really doesn't have set criteria associated with becoming a partner. (No professional service firm does, to my knowledge.) A savvy senior partner described it best to me: "You get officially promoted [to partner] once you've been acting like a partner for a year or so." That is, there are certain things junior partners do that are mainly associated with quality control and client and junior consultant development. Once you "sorta" fall into the habit of doing those things and execute them with some skill—*and* if your network is extensive enough and supportive enough—well, then, you're ready to be initiated into the secret rites.

There is, to be sure, a superstructure, called the Principal Candidate Evaluation Committee (PCEC), which oversees the process of promotion to principal. Since newly anointed partners are the lifeblood of any professional service firm, their selection is a task of the utmost importance. Only top partners are assigned to the PCEC. And despite its members' "local" responsibility for generating substantial client revenue, by design the committee absorbs an extraordinary slug of time. For one thing, members spend about four weeks reviewing a dozen "candidates" from offices other than their own (a PCEC member based in San Francisco, for example, might be responsible for assessing candidates from Melbourne, Amsterdam, and Houston).

Consultants by and large give the murky process high marks. Why? You know that respected senior people have put in one hell of a lot of time on your behalf! Prior to meeting as a group, they've spent weeks doing evaluations (the chief issue is figuring out how much and how deep support is for a candidate); then they've spent more weeks of 16-hour days sorting it all out.

If all this sounds vague, it is. If it sounds imprecise, it isn't. The promotion process is one of McKinsey's strengths. The strength is in both breadth (the requirement that you have widespread support, and that your own office not be decisive) and depth (the extensive amount of time the best and most talented people in the firm invest in the process).

The Slow Consensus-Building Process

> Like [then Managing Director] Daniel, his successor in McKinsey's peculiarly collegial culture will more closely resemble a shepherd guiding a flock than a chief executive barking orders at subordinates. If the managing partner is too brusque with fellow partners, he will not be reelected. This was the case more than a decade ago with Daniel's predecessor, Alonzo MacDonald, who shortly thereafter left the firm and became Jimmy Carter's chief of staff in Washington.
>
> Says Daniel, "This place is literally democratic. The managing partner serves with the consent of the governed. If partners don't trust him, he's dead. If they do, he can get away with a lot."
>
> *Forbes*, October 1987

How is McKinsey governed? In part—which is revealing—the answer is "Beats me." I wasn't around long enough to become a key committee member. I did hang out at headquarters a lot, but most of us never thought much about governance. You were so busy doing your own (team) thing and worrying about client development that there wasn't time to think much about politics and governance. What follows is based mainly on rumor and barroom/airplane chatter.

To begin with, there's that firm managing director, a skeletal administrative staff, and some critical committees involved in personnel processes (e.g., the PCEC) and overall direction (the Shareholders Committee* is the chief vehicle for the latter). With such a consensual form of governance, McKinsey changes direction s-l-o-w-l-y. The managing director of the firm is first among equals, but barely. He (or she, perhaps someday) exercises his power by patiently gaining support, one prestigious (and proudly independent) senior partner at a time, for any new policy. In fact, I can't remember any new "policies," of the textbook variety, instituted from the top. We never changed "strategy." Part of the reason is that McKinsey has always been pretty clear on its core values—and successful precisely because of them. Started in 1926 by James O. McKinsey, a University of Chicago professor of accounting, the firm became what it is today under Marvin Bower, who guided it from 1939 until 1967, and who at 88 has a space in the New York office from which he still provides rigorous spiritual guidance.

---

*When you become a principal you automatically buy "shares" (usually with a mortgage-sized loan); among other things, the Shareholders Committee sets share value each year.

Bower patterned McKinsey after "professional" (a word he loves) law firm partnerships—he'd previously been a partner in a Cleveland law firm. At the top of his list of values (ahead of family and self, and perhaps God) was Living for the Client. And though the firm has faced some stiff challenges from competitors with strong "technologies," such as the Boston Consulting Group, it has never wavered in its all-out devotion to client services. This "intangible" has turned out to be an almost unassailable and very sustainable competitive advantage. Why? Because most, to their detriment, don't take such a "soft" strategic edge very seriously! (EDS did and does. And you'll come across more who do in the forthcoming reports on, for example, David Kelley Design and Chiat/Day/Mojo.)

The relationship of all this to governance is that the McKinsey governors really don't have much of a traditional "strategic" task to perform. Maintaining what has been useful in the past—people first, customer focus—and not allowing the outfit to become inflexible or bureaucratic in the face of phenomenal growth have been their challenge.

I suppose we consultants were subconsciously glad that there was a head office somewhere, that there was someone worrying some about the firm's overall position. But it wasn't a big deal. The fact is that the consultant, though part of a proud and effective institution, really managed—and created—his or her own "firm within a firm." Even as a principal, you mostly worried about developing your own clients and developing the people close to you. And that was mainly that, unless, much later, the bug to play firm politics bit.

The Second-Class Citizens

So far, I've discussed "consultants." Yet the majority of McKinsey employees are *not* consultants. They are "support staff," who work on research, presentation preparation, accounting, and so on, chiefly to assist those customer-centered project teams. (If there is internal work involving office management to be done, it is almost always set aside whenever a project team, only 24 hours away from a Progress Review for a client, needs help.) Sad to say, they are distinctly second-class citizens.

There is a pecking order among the support staff—"near consultants" (researchers) and "others" (finance people, report preparation people, etc.), and in the years since my departure, there's been a noticeable effort to upgrade the status of the researchers especially, as research and information networks become increasingly important to client problem-solving (see Chapter 26). Nonetheless, a yawning gap still exists. The most junior consultant "outranks" (sociologically) the most senior support staff member. Yet support staff often make a career of McKinsey. The pay is good, the quality of colleagues is high, and the discrimination is usually not overt.

The Squeaky Wheel Doesn't Get Oiled

As to consultants, however, whatever their "rank," near-egalitarianism is the norm. Obviously this varies from office to office—there is lots more informal "rank consciousness" in Düsseldorf than in San Francisco—but surprisingly few personalities stick way out. This is important. A few—Kenichi Ohmae, McKinsey's superstar in Japan, and for a while the likes of Bob Waterman and me, thanks to *In Search of Excellence*—do stick out. It's more or less okay for Ohmae, because he is 9,000 miles away from the head office and has created an independent power base in Japan to boot. (Though I understand he's had almost as many downs as ups in dealing with "New York.") It was less all right for Waterman and me. McKinsey had a tough time tolerating us, and eventually both of us left on the basis of a very mutual desire to part ways. In short, the squeaky wheel at McKinsey usually gets discarded, not oiled.

McKinsey nurtures the important (for its own self-governance) myth of partner interchangeability. Partners tend to be very bright and very aggressive—and certainly have distinct personalities. But, in fact, the firm does maintain an exceptional sense of partner/shareholder equality, up to and including the managing director of the firm. The fabric has seldom been rent by wild and woolly personalities, and this, for better (mostly) or for worse (a little), is more or less necessary to keep such a big place with so little formality from being shredded by partner politics (e.g., the sort of enmity between consultants and accountants that looked, for a while, as if it would destroy Arthur Andersen).

There are, however, costs—chiefly lost creativity. As the economic times demand more creativity, McKinsey is responding, but not as aggressively as it might. On the other hand, the benefits seem to have outweighed the costs over the years.

I *Still* Can't Find the Hierarchy

McKinsey is a huge company. Customers respect it. It's also the prototypical multi-domestic firm (and was so long before ABB's Barnevik coined the term), with offices in 25 countries, some with enormous local clout.

But there's no traditional hierarchy. There are no organization charts. No job descriptions. No policy manuals. No rules about managing client engagements. No rules about setting budgets for such engagements (which could easily run to millions of dollars). No guidelines that tell you how to get promoted or how to go about firing somebody. No set procedures for the all-important recruiting process. And yet all these things are well understood—make no mistake, McKinsey is not out of control!

It's not that it lives in a placid environment. McKinsey is a one-to-one reflection of the business environment. At times the business environment has been boring, and McKinsey has been as boring as that environment. On the other hand, in the volatile business environment of today, McKinsey looks different than it did years ago (even when I left). Non-placid times require new ideas. McKinsey people are much more engaged now in researching and writing for publication, for example—and then testing what they come up with in their clients' businesses.

But the point is, McKinsey works. It's worked for over half a century. It shows few signs of diminishing power—and yet it bears little if any structural resemblance to Sears, General Motors, Kodak, IBM, or any other older, hierarchical firm.

Hierarchies and Pecking Orders

> Human beings were held accountable long before there were corporate bureaucracies. If the knight didn't deliver, the king cut off his head.
>
> ALVIN TOFFLER
> *Across the Board*
> May 1991

McKinsey does not, by and large, have a hierarchy. But let's not mince words. McKinsey has a pecking order. There's a big difference.

Families have pecking orders. During my "formative years," when it came to child-rearing, Mom was queen of the roost. When it came to financial affairs, Dad was king. (If you must, Dad "reported to" Mom for "matters associated with child-rearing." Mom "reported to" Dad for "financial affairs." It was true in my family.)

Put five McKinsey people in a room, and they'll sort themselves out from top to bottom in short order—and be able to sort out all the people they know in common as well. In the same vein, a seminar participant cornered one of my colleagues, Reuben Harris, late one night and forced him to draw an organization chart for our org-chartless little company, The Tom Peters Group. Indeed, Harris was able to "rank" the entire group, from 1 to 25. We all had a good chuckle: Our 25-person company has 25 "layers" of management.

That is precisely true. And precisely false. Pecking order—yes. "Layers"—no way!

What's the difference? Everything. Despite the pecking order, anybody can talk to anybody else, and by and large people don't worry about organizational barriers even though we are divided into five companies (separate legal entities, incorporated as different firms in the state of

California). Getting things done is mostly unimpeded by a sense of up and down, over and around—the sorts of fiddling that slow down more sizable, traditional companies. There's certainly no need for anyone to get permission from anyone else to talk to any third party about anything.

"Social comparison," as the psychologists call it, is one of the most pervasive forces in the world. Whether the matter at hand is beauty, cello-playing skills, three-point basket shooting, engineering, or running a numerical control machine—people *will* compare themselves with others, sort themselves out. But to acknowledge this is not to yield to the perniciousness of traditional, overly specialized, overly elaborated hierarchies.

McKinsey and EDS are astonishingly fluid "organizations" when you consider their size—or even if you forget their size! That fluidity is a function of the (relative) absence of hierarchy. But pecking orders? You bet. Not a soul I know in either organization denies it.

A CONSISTENT MESSAGE FOR ALL WORKERS: THE AGE OF UNSTRUCTURE LOOMS

McKinsey—and EDS, CNN, and the new-look Titeflex—are fast becoming the norm. The impact of the demise of conventional hierarchy on millions upon millions of workers is enormous.

There was a time not long ago when people came to work after high school or college, pursued a career for life, slowly climbed a narrow (and precisely specified) functional ladder, and were pretty much assured of steady employment and a 5 percent raise each year. No more. When I spoke "on camera" (for a PBS TV show) with Harvard professor Rosabeth Moss Kanter in 1989, she flatly declared that tomorrow's winning firms will have "almost no middle managers." The era of "linear careers" has ended, she added. Survivors—managers *and* workers—will be "oriented toward projects" and will only succeed if they "find ways, company-supported or not, to invest in learning and development, lead change efforts, and somehow add value. You're dead if you don't do such things."

Dick Liebhaber, head of operations at upstart MCI when we talked to him in conjunction with the same TV show, seems to agree. "We don't shoot people who make mistakes," he told me. "We shoot people who don't take risks." MCI, now an almost $10-billion firm, has little respect for hierarchy. Everyone, no exceptions, Liebhaber claims, is responsible for creating projects that directly add value for the customer. "We don't coddle," he adds. "People who are uncomfortable in an unstructured world don't make it."

MCI employees confirm the boss's view. One young manager describes MCI as a "sink-or-swim environment. It's better to make a decision, right or wrong. Do something. Inaction will kill you." Another junior manager explained that you're "rarely *told* to do anything. No one hands down decisions." Instead, you're supposed to collect the facts, find the appropriate people to counsel with, then act on your own. "The responsibility for success or failure," she concluded, "lies within yourself."

Harry Quadracci, CEO of Quad/Graphics (the stellar $500-million Wisconsin printing company) echoes his counterparts. "We eat change for breakfast," he said during a conversation soon after my interviews at MCI. "Our employees look at change and learning as job security." Quadracci's "think small" concept pushes everyone to change "something, anything each day. Just start it, do *something*."

"I could tell the difference in the first five minutes," a new Quad employee told me. "They always want to teach you something. Within two months, I was teaching someone else! I take as many courses as I can. It's a matter of survival." But as at MCI, workers concede that Quad is "not for everyone." You take the initiative—or else. The "or else" is probably getting the boot, administered by your teammates, not the personnel department. (There is none at Quad.)

The message sounds scary. Coddling is out. Lean-and-mean structures, continuous education, self-generated projects, and ambiguity are in. The bad news: Brand-new definitions of careers and new shapes of organizations make the downside—organizations and individuals—onerous for those who don't get it.

THE QUEST FOR METAPHORS II

If there's a single theme—from the worker's perspective—that emerges in analyzing McKinsey (and EDS, CNN, Titeflex, UPRR, MCI, and Quad/Graphics), it's the idea of "create your own firm." It's up to you to take the initiative, start projects, seek out customers, build your own network. The marketplace has gone bonkers. Firms therefore must go bonkers to keep up. And so must you. Street rap replaces rigid marches to John Philip Sousa's predictable beat.

Checkerboards, Kaleidoscopes, Jazz Combos

The scramble for new imagery is on. And those messed-up new relationships are the cause. I began with my own two cents' worth—carnivals—at the start of this book. But I'm not alone. Alvin Toffler, in *Power Shift,* offers "checkerboard organization," "pulsating organization," and "two-faced organization," among other things. Take the "pulsating organization." It's simply a unit that "changes in size and organization from time to time," Toffler declares. A colleague speaks of "kaleidoscopic organizations"—the idea once more is to be fluid, ever shifting in size, shape, and arrangement.

Fluidity! In 1989 Rosabeth Moss Kanter published *When Giants Learn to Dance*—and dance imagery pervades its pages. (Book titles openly reveal our confusion. British consultant Charles Handy's 1989 offering was *The Age of Unreason*. And in 1992, consultants Bob Kriegel and Louis Patler gave us *If It Ain't Broke . . . BREAK IT!*)

In *Fifth Generation Management*, Charles Savage takes a shine to "jazz combos." University of Michigan professor of organization Karl Weick chooses "improvisational theater." Organization design, viewed from "the perspective of improvisation," Weick writes, "is more emergent, is more continuous, more filled with surprise, more difficult to control . . . than are designs implied by architecture." (Weick also alludes to organization designs that are "continuously reconstructed.")

Investment banker Richard Crawford (*In the Era of Human Capital*) opts for "the collapsible corporation":

> In the knowledge economy, bureaucracy will increasingly be replaced by *adhocracy*, a holding company that coordinates the work of numerous temporary work units, each phasing in and out of existence according to the rate of change in the environment surrounding the organization. The adhocracies of tomorrow will be staffed by employees who are capable of rapid learning (in order to comprehend novel circumstances and problems) and imaginative thinking (in order to invent new solutions). These men and women will participate in small teams, cross-disciplinary teams, partnerships, and quality circles.

At times, you may think I'm belaboring the issue: "You promised cases, now you're sending me to dancing class. What gives?" I'm merely following the advice of my Swedish colleague Gunnar Hedlund. In tumultuous times, metaphor and imagery are vitally important, he asserts. Few of us are aware of how often we use imagery. And as long as football remains our favorite model, we're in trouble!

Shape? or Shapeless?

> I no longer believe top down works at all. . . . We have measures everywhere. . . . Now people measure their own stuff. They used to have no idea what the schedule was. Now they set it. . . . It has been stressful, but I have eliminated ALL the layers of management. I have all 67 manufacturing people reporting to me (18 months ago we had *four* layers between

my position and the floor). . . . If you want to learn about empowering people, make it so you have way too many people to manage! . . . They will figure out how to make it work. . . . Cross training is a way of life. EVERYBODY is doing it. We went from 54 position descriptions to six. We are teaching our departments to run themselves as businesses . . . to think about EVERYTHING. . . . Everyone is asking to move to the shop floor (I did a few months ago), including cost accounting and planning.

Manufacturing executive,
small computer company,
in a letter to the author

"We need a litmus test, that is, a way of divining whether a company has begun the process of overall change," Harvard professor Quinn Mills wrote in *Rebirth of the Corporation* in 1991. "The test is at hand. To make the new systems work, there has to be a dramatic change in the structure of the organization. [For] it is in a firm's structure that traditional managerial practices are most reflected."

In *Strategy and Structure*, a book that influenced two generations of managers, Harvard business historian Alfred Chandler argued that organizational structure should take its form from a firm's chosen strategy. I understand Chandler's reasoning, but I think he got it exactly wrong. For it is the structure of the organization that determines, over time, the choices that it makes about the markets it attacks. Give me a vertically integrated, hierarchically steep organization and perhaps, even today, I can do a few things well. But one thing is certain: I can't shift course very rapidly! A McKinsey or EDS or CNN chooses to do what it does—i.e., continually reinvent itself, with apparent ease—because of its "structural" shape much more than its chosen strategy.

"Shape"? Part of the problem is that shape carries old-imagery baggage. Shapeless, by yesterday's standards, is more like it. Information systems expert Peter Keen offers this explication of the problem:

The traditional concept of an "organization" is no longer useful to managers or students of organizations. It is dominated by models of structure and physical identity at a time when telecommunications has eroded the boundaries between firms and changed the nature of coordination across geographic locations.

The traditional view of the organization as a structure with clearly stated goals and a clearly defined industry in which it competes . . . does not easily mesh with the emergence of electronic links. These links serve as the base for managing businesses and coordinating activities across time zones and within global marketplaces where the limits on trading are set by technology, not organizational structures and procedures.

Clearly, the resulting electronically linked "organization" cannot be defined by its formal hierarchy with a clear physical identity or boundary that separates it from other organizations. Nor is the organization a unitary "actor," defined by its goal, mission or strategy.

With that description, Keen knocks 200 years of industrial organization and a hundred years of "modern" management thinking into a cocked hat. The very idea of organizational borders with the "outside world" becomes passé, or worse—dangerous. Thinking of the organization as an entity standing on its own is dysfunctional in today's strange, fast-moving, interlinked world.

Another longtime student of organization, former University of California at Berkeley business school dean Ray Miles, chimes in with the "dynamic network" organization. He laid it out in the Winter 1989 *California Management Review*:

One example . . . provides a mental picture: A piece of ice hockey equipment, designed in Scandinavia, engineered in the U.S. to meet the requirements of the large U.S. and Canadian market, manufactured in Korea and distributed through a multinational market network with initial distribution from Japan. *The question is: Where is, what is the organization?* Instead of a single organization with design, engineering, manufacturing, distribution and sales under one corporate roof, the example shows several organizations hooked together for perhaps only one product "event." . . .

Overall . . . the brokering, connecting, "networking" role is becoming increasingly important in a fast-moving company. Whether locating materials, putting designers in contact with available plant space, or arranging temporary workforces, the frequently computer-based competence to bring people and things together quickly and efficiently is a key factor in organizational flexibility. . . .

Obviously, not all firms will move toward the highly decoupled and dynamic forms described here. Nevertheless, each day across the economy there are more examples of firms finding ways to fully utilize their core competence by renting, leasing, buying, or otherwise contracting for resources on a one-time or limited-run basis. The reason is straightforward—holding a full range of resources requires the ability to forecast and plan beyond the time horizons many firms are facing. . . .

Today it appears the more "networks" are used, the more developed they become, and the more use they get. Firms are obviously finding them of major benefit as a means of expanding, contracting, and maneuvering through the demands for product and service shifts and innovations. Of course, networks are not new. Relatively stable networks of suppliers, producers and distributors have existed for years in many industries. What *is* new is the expansion of this model into areas where vertical integration previously dominated and the speed with which today's networks can be put together, distributed and reassembled. . . .

Charles Handy's Shamrock

The chimney "may have caused more social change than any war," British consultant Charles Handy asserts in *The Age of Unreason*. "Without a chimney everyone had to huddle together in one central place around a fire with a hole in the roof above. The chimney, with its separate flues, made it possible in one dwelling to heat a variety of rooms." Taken to the extreme, the chimney led to the dismantling of the medieval economic structure (dominated by individual workshops) and to the eventual emergence of giant factories. A classic example, which I visited a while back, is the 65,000-person Ludwigshafen complex run by BASF, the German chemical giant.

But the age of the chimney—and immobile, 65,000-person plants—is past. "It is often the little things in life which change things the most and last the longest," Handy writes. "The telephone line has been and will be the modern-day equivalent of the chimney. . . . I saw a man sitting in his car in the parking place I coveted. 'Are you about to move?' I asked. 'Not for a couple of hours yet,' he replied. It was then I saw the portable computer on the seat beside him and the fax connected to his car telephone line. He was using his car as a mobile office. . . . The telephone and its attachments make it possible today for people to work together without being together in one place. The *scattered organization* is now a reality."

Organizations today "are more and more places for brains, not muscles," Handy adds. "Organizations used to be perceived as gigantic pieces of engineering, with largely interchangeable human parts. We talked of their structures and their systems, of inputs and outputs, of control devices and of managing them, as if the whole was one large factory. Today the language is not that of engineering but of politics, with talk of cultures and networks, of teams and coalitions, of influence or power rather than control, of leadership not management."

Thence Handy's "shamrock" idea: The first leaf "represents the core workers, what I prefer to call the professional core. . . . They own the organizational knowledge which distinguishes that organization from its counterparts. Lose them and you lose some of yourself. . . . If the core is smaller, who then does the work? Increasingly, it is contracted out [to the second leaf, a network of subcontractors]. The third leaf . . . is the flexible labor force, all those part-time workers and temporary workers who are the fastest-growing part of the employment scene.

"The three-leaved work force has always existed in embryo. What is different today is the scale. *Each* of the leaves is now significant. . . . Life in the core of more and more organizations is going to resemble that of consultancy firms, advertising agencies, and professional partnerships. The organizations are flat, seldom with more than four layers of rank, the top one being the assembly of partners, professors or directors. Promotion through the ranks comes quickly if you are any good. . . . Promotion, therefore, soon becomes an inadequate way of rewarding and recognizing people; success for those in the top rank can only mean doing the same job better and, presumably, for more money. . . . No organization can any longer guarantee that this year's pay rise can be next year's base line, not in a time of discontinuity. . . . [The professionals at the core] are paid for results, not for time, in fees, not wages."

Brian Quinn's Mind Trip: Companies as "Packages of Services"

Writing in the Winter 1990 issue of *Sloan Management Review*, Dartmouth's James Brian Quinn, with Penny Paquette and Braxton Associates' Thomas Doorley, provides us with a new conception of the firm as a package of service activities. The unconventional view emerges just by scanning a few of the article's subheads.

— "Infinitely Flat" Organizations
— "Spider's Web" Organizations
— Destruction of Bureaucracies
— The "Intellectual Holding Company"
— Service Technologies Smash Overhead through Outsourcing
— Learning to Love the "Hollow Corporation"
— Avoiding Vertical Integration
— Manufacturing Industries Become "Service Networks"

Services, not manufacturing activities, provide the major source of value to customers, the authors claim. "Most companies primarily produce a chain of services and integrate these into a form most useful to certain customers. As manufacturing becomes more universally automated, the major value added to the process increasingly moves away from the point where raw materials are converted into useful form (i.e., steel into an auto body in white) . . . and toward the styling features, perceived quality . . . and marketing presentation that service activities provide."

As service activities assume greater *strategic* importance, they, like manufacturing activities before them, become candidates for outsourcing. The straightforward advice of Quinn et al.: Pursue the best providers of any service and sign them up—before your competitors do. "One needs to ask," they write, "activity by activity, 'Are we really competing with the world's best, here? If not, can intelligent outsourcing improve our long-term posture?' Competitive analyses of service activities should not consider just the company's own industry but should benchmark each service against 'best in class' performance among all service providers . . . in the United States and abroad."

The authors tag such de-integration "learning to love the hollow corporation." But with so much outsourced, what's left of the firm? Answer: A lot. But something new. Company chiefs become "managers of intellectual systems," moving away from "functional" management and toward "coordination and conceptual" management. At Apple, which the authors label an "intellectual holding company," managers learn to focus their efforts on "dominating those services crucial to [their] strategy"—e.g., design and marketing.

The authors' "spider's web organization" is a nonhierarchical network featuring "a lightly structured quality of . . . interconnections." Consider Merrill Lynch. Its 500 domestic brokerage offices

> connect directly with their parents' central information offices for routine needs, yet can bypass the electronic system for personal access to individual experts in headquarters. In effect, technology permits the company to function in a coordinated fashion with the full power of a major financial enterprise, yet allows local brokers to manage their own small units independently. . . . [Such] network technologies allow front-line personnel to call forth and cross-matrix whatever details their customers' specific needs may require. . . . The result is to provide the most extensive possible local responsiveness and customization for the company's dispersed customer base.

The superstructure, in old-fashioned terms, for such organizations *is* light. Federal Express, another favorite of Quinn and his colleagues, has only 2.1 staff people per million dollars in sales—one-fifth the service industry average. Front-line span of control at FedEx runs 50:1. The firm's DADS and COSMOS computer systems allow employees total access to data—eliminating the need for middle management: "There is no inherent reason that organizations cannot be made 'infinitely flat'—in other words, with innumerable outposts guided by one central . . . 'computer controlled inquiry' system. In designing service company systems, instead of thinking about traditional 'spans of control,' our study suggests that the terms 'spans of effective cooperation,' 'communication spans,' or 'support spans' may have more meaning."

ABB learned that 95 percent or so of a manufacturer's sales-to-delivery cycle time is "eaten up" by nonmanufacturing activities. This is the sort of observation that really animates Quinn and company's strange tale. Manufacturing companies, like service companies, are turning out to be sets of perishable services. The problem is, we haven't looked at such firms—or managed them—accordingly.

ORGANIZING PROPOSITIONS: TOWARD NEW "STRUCTURES"

[Silicon Valley] is no respector of grey hairs. It is a meritocracy in which everyone has a chance to succeed. It matters little where you come from, or what you have achieved in the past, only what you can contribute today. . . .

Mr. Andy Grove, chairman of Intel, the world's largest maker of microprocessors, compares it to the theater business in New York which has an itinerant workforce of actors, directors, writers and technicians, as well as experienced financial backers. By tapping into this network you can quickly put a production together. It might be a smash hit, like *42nd Street*, or it might be panned by the critics. Inevitably the number of long-running plays is small, but new creative ideas keep bubbling up.

GEOFFREY OWEN and LOUISE KEHOE
"A Hotbed of High-Tech"
Financial Times, June 28, 1992

Intel. Broadway. You name it. The point of the story that unfolds in the pages ahead (and which has been foreshadowed in the analyses of McKinsey, EDS, ABB, et al.) is to translate all these jabs at hierarchy and glimmers of new images and models into practical terms. But, it's said, there's nothing so practical as a good theory. The 27 "organizing propositions" that follow amount to an outline of a new theory of organizing, and a glimpse of the "structures" that are requisite for survival in the 1990s.

1. Most *value-added*, from products and services of any sort, will come from head work/knowledge work.

2. Most *work*, in firms of any sort, will be head work/knowledge work.

3. Every business process must be erased, then revived. "Horizontal" business processes, which weld *all* former functional activities into seamless wholes, will be the main basis for doing business—and adding value.

4. Middle management has not added value to most firms in recent times. Middle management layers are worse than useless: They destroy value.

5. Most of tomorrow's work will be done in *project teams*.

6. Project teams will neither quash individualism nor blunt specialization. To the contrary, individual contributions will be more important than ever. Becoming expert—and enhancing your expertise—will be imperative for almost all of us.

7. Though expertise and specialization are more important than ever, developing "peripheral vision," a feel for the whole task, is essential. You will be forced, routinely, to work/learn any job on the team. Though you will be constantly investing in your own area of expertise, learning multiple jobs and understanding the entire function of the team—*and* its relation to the enterprise—will be imperative.

8. Traditional functional staff units will all but disappear—and will disappear entirely in many cases. As a result, almost all work (which becomes project team work) will encompass the major "functional" disciplines.

9. A project team is not a committee. The chief difference between a team and a committee is *dependence*. Teammates have to depend upon each other. Committee members are there to "represent a point of view" and retain their functional department's veto right.

10. Trust is essential! Given project autonomy, mutual dependence, contact with outsiders, and work away from "home," an atmosphere of trust is an absolute must—and more of a stumbling block to future organization success than, say, getting the information technology scheme right.

11. The goal is more than "winning *this* game." Developing a world-class team with world-class members may result in victory—but in the knowledge economy, developing stellar talent per se is more important than any single victory.

12. The lifespan of a project team can be life (very unlikely), or just a few hours (not so unlikely). Dynamic, short-lived project configurations will be commonplace. It will not be unusual to work on four or five project teams in a year, or a couple of teams at one time—but you may never work twice with the exact same configuration of colleagues, even in a 20-year "career."

13. The average project team will have at least a 75 percent chance of including "outsiders"—a vendor, a distributor, a customer, all of the above. Workers will spend at least half their time on teams that include people from the payrolls of others.

14. Who reports to whom will change over time, and you will routinely report to a person for one task who reports to you for another. Despite the muddle of "who reports to whom," accountability for a goal will be far higher than in traditional organizations.

15. If you "don't know where your people are today," that's probably a good sign (à la EDS, McKinsey, CNN, even the Union Pacific and Titeflex). It means they're working beyond functional walls, and are calling on customers, etc.

16. Feedback loops will be short. The presence of customers, in particular, will provide rapid feedback as to whether or not the project team is getting anywhere.

17. "Not letting down the side" and constant customer (outsider/market) presence will surpass "adhering to the boss's requirements" as the principal motivation for the project team.

18. New evaluation schemes are critical. Peer evaluation will be as important as/more important than boss evaluation. Subjective evaluation will be standard—focusing on your ability to be a team player as well as your ability to get the job done, and grow in your distinct skill. In fact, the *average* team member will be evaluated on: (a) team play, (b) external relationship management, (c) the ability to apply unique expertise, (e) a commitment to learning and improving that expertise, and (f) becoming a teacher, passing lessons learned on to teammates and the broader network.

19. There will be constant reorganization, in the sense of perpetual reconfiguration of project team structures and network structures. Perpetual reorganization will be "manageable" because of: (a) shared values at the team, corporate, and network levels; (b) performance evaluation schemes that emphasize the shared values and teamwork as well as task results; (c) strong performance rewards for managers who give up their best people so that those people can pursue better opportunities; and (d) an evaluation and compensation process considered to be fair and equitable over time.

20. Much of the value added over the medium to long term will come from special learning/teaching/communication devices. These learning/teaching/communication devices—from independent, profit-generating strategic business units to tiny staffs of itinerant experts—will have overall responsibility for guiding the organizational knowledge development process.

21. Organizational learning will be highly rewarded. Contributing to the knowledge development process of the organization as a whole will be one of the primary dimensions upon which performance and compensation are judged, particularly over the long haul.

22. Information technology is everything. *And* nothing. Utilizing the new technologies is essential to success. Applying the new technologies to outmoded organizations is a design for disaster.

23. Real-time access to *all* information, including information from "outsiders," is a must for *everyone* in the organization. Phenomenal amounts of time and money must be spent on communication required to hold slippery,

temporary networks together. That includes information technology—and face-to-face meetings and big travel budgets.

24. The "project manager" and "network manager" are the star players of tomorrow! *Everyone* will routinely fill project management/network management roles, directly or indirectly. Attention to these skills, and training in these skills, will be vital. Promotion will go to those who are particularly adept at exercising such skills.

25. The impermanent network will be used to execute almost every major task (e.g., developing and marketing a new product). It will be peppered with "supersubs"—super-subcontractors that are uniquely good at performing a very specialized task, *any* task. Using supersubs is *not* a way of "subcontracting out problems," but a method for adding value, particularly innovativeness. Furthermore, working with shifting arrays of "supersubs" allows you to stay lean, agile, and ready to respond with a new set of partners to unforeseen opportunities.

26. Three principal sorts of "firms" will be engaged in executing commercial projects: (a) *systems integrators*, which principally construct and manage networks; (b) *specialists* (e.g., supersubs), which have unique competence which they feed into various networks; and (c) *independent talents*, who may act alone or be part of a "talent-bank."

27. "Marketplace power" will be a function of the power of the array of networks of which various parts of your organization are a part at any time, not the amount of resources owned outright (as measured by degree of vertical integration); in fact, marketplace power may be inversely proportional to vertical integration.

The Quest for Metaphors III: The Movies

Robert X. Cringely's *Accidental Empires: How the Boys of Silicon Valley Make Their Millions, Battle Foreign Competition, and Still Can't Get a Date* is a readable, acerbic, funny tale of America's most important "industry": microprocessors, software, and personal computers. Few survive unscathed—even the index, with entries such as "IBM, demise of," packs a wallop.

Cringely concludes by addressing "the greatest threat" to our computing future. "Forget about the Japanese," he tells us; the real worry is the "loss of intellectual vigor." Cringely's intriguing answer is "the software studio." He likens today's software giants to movie studios of the 1930s. "They finance, produce, and distribute their own products," he writes. "Unfortunately, it's hard to do all those things well." Contrast that with today's movie studio. "It is just a place where directors, producers and talent come and go—only the infrastructure stays," he says.

Most start-up business teams, according to Cringely, "don't really want to . . . create a large organization. [They] end up functioning in roles they think they are supposed to like, but most of them really don't." But in his model, such bands could stay independent and vital by working with a movie studio equivalent, an umbrella organization which includes "central finance, administration, manufacturing and distribution."

Cringely hits the nail on the head, not only for the computer industry, but for everything from chemicals to food to pharmaceuticals. Consider a possible universal "movie" model:

—Infrastructure Inc./Integrator Inc. The main tasks of these "mother companies" are (1) deal conception and financing, (2) systems integration, (3) marketing, (4) sales, (5) logistics and distribution, and (6) service. Big movie studios already work this way. Publishers such as Random House and Simon & Schuster and telecommunications companies like MCI come close. Computer companies are learning: Apple farms out a great deal of almost everything. EDS *is* a systems integrator; for example, in early 1992 it was tapped by NCR, AT&T's computer hardware-making arm, to become one of eight specialist "integrators" through which NCR plans to pass 80 or 90 percent of its sales. Even automakers are cozying up to such ideas, appointing certain master suppliers as integrators for major automotive subsystems; these integrators manage dozens of suppliers in their own right.

—Independent infrastructure providers. Manufacturing, service, maintenance, training, and information systems "products" are increasingly offered by independent infrastructure subspecialists. Via its new Contract Financial Management service, Arthur Andersen, for example, will perform turnkey bookkeeping operations—and even provide a chief financial officer (see page 331).

—Talent Packager I. In Hollywood independent producers come to the integrator's "studio" with a total deal (story, stars on contract, director), maybe even financing. This role in high-tech industries is sometimes played, de facto or de jure, by venture capitalists.

—Talent Packager II. Michael Ovitz, head of Beverly Hills' Creative Artists Agency, is often called the most powerful person in the movie industry. He controls a huge talent bank and manages his stars' exposure. Superagents in sports and book publishing play similar mighty roles. Why not such talent banks in semiconductors, software, or biotech?

—Independent smart people. One-person bands with eye-popping backgrounds now number in the millions. Their schtick is gravitating from exciting task to exciting task, never tied to *anyone's* payroll.

Of course, it's not quite so easy as it sounds. In "Outsourcing and Industrial Decline" (*Academy of Management Executive*, February 1992), professors Richard Bettis, Stephen Bradley, and Gary Hamel write that a "series of incremental outsourcing decisions, taken individually, may make economic sense, but collectively they may also represent the surrender of the business's capability to compete." The de-integration notion, all-important for revitalizing moribund firms in fashionized markets, can go too far. How do Walt Disney, Paramount, Random House, MCI, and Apple retain their uniqueness? While exemplary network integrators combine clout and distinction with the energy of numerous independent entrepreneurs and superstars, they can quickly become hollow to the point of meaninglessness. Achieving the right mix is no mean feat.

11

Projects and Professional Service Firms I: Cases in Pursuit of a Common Denominator

Unlike Detroit, there's no caste system here. Our people don't think about which executive they work for, just which project they are working on.

RICK LEPLEY
Senior Vice President
Mitsubishi (U.S.A.)
The New York Times
March 3, 1992

Value-added in the economy—and for the corporation—will come from knowledge, knowledge accumulated from in-house skills and from all of one's network partners (organizations of all sizes around the globe). Bringing such knowledge to bear—to create a show at CNN, a new ride at Disney, a new approach to transportation worked out between UPRR and Ford, or to complete an information systems project for AT&T at EDS—will be "the world's work." In fact, there won't be an iota's worth of difference between tomorrow's factory and traditional professional service firm practice. What, after all, is Ingersoll-Rand's Project Lightning Team, if not a "temporary professional service firm"?

And as you read this, what's that Rapid Deployment Team doing at Titeflex? As I said in the Preface, Teamsters Tom Strange and Joe Tilli might be hoisting hoses at this instant—but they're working on a discrete *project* for (and with) a customer; *thinking* their way through a unique opportunity to add value. When the order's shipped, chances are that Strange and Tilli will sit down and decide how they could have done it better, how they *will* do it better tomorrow. What have I just described? A professional service firm! One Titeflex manufacturing cell member brought a camcorder to work. Team members taped each other. Another team member took the tape home, analyzed it as an NFL coach might analyze the film of Sunday's game, and came up with some improvement ideas. She subsequently worked them through with her teammates—and a 90 percent reduction in setup time ensued. How would you classify all that? I'd call it the commonplace doings of a "professional service firm."

The problem, as I've encountered it at dozens of seminars, is getting the average manager to feel comfortable with the apparently disconnected style of such firms. The thought of putting on Les Alberthal's shoes and being "in charge" of 5,000 or so wildly dispersed, 10-person EDS teams is intimidating. But try we *all* must—for there is no other option. So, for better or worse, it's Yo, EDS. Yo, McKinsey. Yo, CNN. And now three more, to round out our perspective.

IMAGINATION

"One day soon after British Airways and British Caledonian had merged after lengthy and tough negotiations, Lord King [chairman] and Sir Colin Marshall [managing director] popped by," Imagination founder Gary Withers told us when we visited in April 1991. "Everyone was happy with the merger except the line employees, who seemed very down and lackluster. They asked me what to do. We went down and interviewed some of their people and came to the conclusion that all they had to do was say, 'Thank you!' King and Marshall came back and I told them, 'Just say thanks.' They looked at each other and they said, 'That's it! How?' We decided to give a massive party for all forty thousand of the staff, running every night for two weeks. To pull it off, we turned an unused aircraft hanger into a nightclub—doing about six months work in two weeks, according to the facility manager. Sir Colin and Lord King came to every party and said a short piece at the start of the dinner; then everyone had a good time."

In its April 1990 issue, Britain's *PR Week* said, "Nowhere else under one roof are you likely to find architects, writers, film and video producers, graphic designers, theater and lighting technicians, engineers, photographers, composers and production managers." That's Imagination! The $80-million (1991 revenues), 200-strong company is growing fast—and is very special.

The "Product"

Asked what, exactly, Imagination *does*, managing director Brian Shepherd said (with a straight face) that it "offers a full range of creative services." Withers, called Britain's Walt Disney by some wags, said it's in the business of creating "theater." Indeed, the breadth of skills and tools found under Imagination's umbrella is extraordinary. There are sound studios, a graphics department, a film and video department, a lighting department, and a photography department. And there are world-renowned architects, interior designers, computer-aided design specialists, model builders, public relations gurus, artists, and graphics superstars. Imagination is broken down, more or less officially, into 4 profit centers with some 15 subordinate units. Which is tantamount to nothing. Because Imagination brings together whoever's needed, wherever, whenever, blithely ignoring any functional designations, to create something special for customers.

The firm has orchestrated numerous new-product launches for Ford throughout Europe. (Ford, an early customer, accounts for 20 percent of billings.) Imagination helped relaunch British Airways' stalled first-class service and is designing an airport in Macao. It has worked repeatedly with British Telecom on various internal and external product and culture change issues. "We set out to give them a more consistent image," Withers said, "and to present them less as a supplier of hardware than as an innovative service company." British Telecom and others, he added, see Imagination "as in the business of change."

Entertainment, theater, creating an image—the *Financial Times* quoted Withers as saying those ideas are "the way forward in the battle to send sales soaring." Imagination has time and again overcome initial skepticism, and pepped up some of the biggest outfits in Britain, and at times the United States (where clients include CBS, Sony, and Disney). It managed British Steel's "road show," which launched that firm's initial stock offering, a cornerstone of then-Prime Minister Margaret Thatcher's privatization efforts: Imagination crafted—including speechwriting for the chairman—34 presentations in 30 European and North American cities in just two weeks.

One of Imagination's guiding principles is not to do work unless you can have fun with it, learn from it, make it special. "If a brief comes in that's run-of-the-mill," said Withers, "we either won't touch it or we change it." Growth, Shepherd insisted, "cannot mean producing more of the same."

"Organization"

But what's the place *like*—a company that can pull together, at (almost literally) the drop of a hat, a party for 40,000 people? And bring so many different disciplines and, presumably, so many large egos to bear so quickly, so smoothly?

Part of the trick is tension—and total flexibility. "We meet impossible deadlines all the time," said a board member. "The only way we can do that is by being very flexible. If it needs doing, you do it, whether you're the cleaner or the project manager." And that's the result of what Shepherd called Imagination's "amoeba-like structure. It's a chameleon, always changing shape, color, depending on where we are." There's no grand design, he insisted, other than seeking out fascinating engagements that will allow people to push their collective limits. And in fact, every executive we talked with said it's imperative that the firm never be caught repeating itself. Topping itself, time and again, is Imagination's strategy and brand image.

Sometimes the Imagination approach is a tough sell to hidebound companies. "They can't understand the absence of job descriptions and the like," Shepherd told us. "We try to tell them that our people know what they're doing, know how to do it, go about it with dispatch, but we purposefully don't force-fit anyone into a tiny pigeonhole."

There's no personnel department at Imagination. Team leaders are, by and large, responsible for recruiting. The point, per Shepherd, is seeking out people "who want to join a vision." He added that "each new person must bring new, unique qualities." Candidates meet lots of people, not a recruiter. Interviewers, one executive said, look for "energy, creativity, enthusiasm, an ability to work with others." Paper credentials, Withers insisted, are not important.

It's not unusual for Imagination to hire people when no job is available. "It may take six months for them to find the right role, but we'll hire a good person anyway." Withers told us. With 50 percent annual growth since 1986, opportunities tend to pop up quickly.

A career at Imagination means anything but climbing a ladder. Horizontal movement is the norm, fluidity the key. "One of our best video guys came on board as a bookkeeper," Shepherd explained. "Gary [Withers] came across him one night working on his own in the editing suite. The fellow was petrified that he'd been caught. But Gary said, 'Let me see what you're up to.' The next day Gary told the finance head that the bookkeeper was now working on video."

With a smile, Shepherd admitted "that the first six months at Imagination are a nightmare for most people." Dealing with the exceptional level of ambiguity, pressure, and required creativity is no piece of cake. In short, you're on your own—regardless of the job. It's up to you to make a difference. "If you want to change something," said one new Imagineer (as they call themselves), "open your mouth." A secretary interested in information technology, for example, is voluntarily helping teams when computer expertise is needed. She's well on her way to creating a full-time, self-designed slot.

Projects!

When prospective work comes in, a "brainstorm team" quickly gathers. Headed by one of seven board members, it typically includes a "writer" (one of those little-used functional designations) and two others—a lighting person, a graphics person, whatever. If the job is won, a project team is cobbled together. But its shape is hardly set in concrete. It will evolve and change as the project unfolds.

The team is it! (Again.) Executing 200 or so client tasks each year, Imagination is simply a collection of projects. (Again.) Project teams consist of appropriate specialists. But once the team has formed, Imagineers assert, each person is expected to be involved in every element of the task. "Politics" and second-guessing are minimal, mostly because people are so stretched they don't have time to be catty. But that doesn't keep everyone from nosing around in everyone else's project. The constant kibbitzing is part and parcel of the creative brew.

Project teams decide how to organize themselves. "Who joins the team, how they report to each other, how the work gets done is up to them," Shepherd said. Project leaders nominally report to a senior officer who doubles as a department head (e.g., graphics). Their responsibility includes financial management. (Among other things, project chiefs can get, via their desktop computer, expenditure reports that are updated daily.)

Permanent Flexibility

Decision making at Imagination, Shepherd claimed, is "permanently flexible." He added that "no one is afraid to change a decision the day after it's made, if some new piece of information comes to light, no matter how small." Withers helps out by leading an incessant crusade against bureaucracy in the growing firm. At one point, time sheets were amended to include an employee number. Withers found out and went ballistic. Charging around the building, he ran into a coffee trolley. Dripping with coffee, he kept at it until he'd collected all the new time sheets. He raced directly down to the yard behind the building and set them ablaze. Most of the staff came to the windows and loudly cheered him on.

But make no mistake, the Imagination culture is tough. "People are as good as their last project," was the way Mark Winters, director of production management, put it. Another senior Imagineer added, "If someone starts promoting themselves rather than the team, we'd spot it a mile off"—and, he implied, the self-promoter would soon be on the street.

Imagination is 200 creative individuals "each fulfilling their entrepreneurial ambition," Shepherd said. He added, "It's typical to find, on any given morning, a half-dozen people in a studio who've been up all night working on a client project. The intensity of commitment, from clerical to senior creative, is enormous. It's the challenge that's the thing." Pay is a bit above average, but one board member admitted that "the 'package' of rewards is not outstanding." Yet the cleverest Imagineers stay on. One of the best, Paul MacKay, told us he can act as if he were running his own business, yet deliver much more than he could in a tiny, personally led firm.

"Managing"

Customers, said Shepherd, "routinely ask, 'How in the hell do you manage?' " Shepherd sees senior managers as "fitness coaches," preparing their junior colleagues to deal with the next zany opportunity. He's "senior fitness coach." He's also involved in the initial scoping of jobs with prospective clients and helps fill project slots as necessary—though the "resource allocation process," like most everything else at Imagination, is "pretty much organic" (i.e., word of mouth, as at EDS, McKinsey, and CNN).

There are those critical team leader slots to be filled. How? "If you're the right leader for the project, then you lead it," Shepherd said nonchalantly. "You don't need any certain number of years of experience." Moreover, project leadership may change from time to time as a task progresses, according to the team's wishes. (There is a project scheduler who updates a master resource allocation document every two weeks; it simply lists who's working on what for approximately how long. The output is available to everyone via desktop computer. But, Shepherd said with a shrug, "It's always out of date.")

Withers's style has shifted over the years. He drew a little sketch (opposite) to illustrate. At the beginning, he saw himself atop a small pyramid. Then, as the second frame suggests, he upended the pyramid and put himself at the bottom, working like Atlas to hold up his growing enterprise. Today's organization is modeled after Withers's understanding of Walt Disney's management approach. Disney, he learned, acted like "a bumblebee, floating around, pollinating ideas, providing the creative spark, but with no line responsibility as such." At Imagination, line responsibility has by and large been delegated to Shepherd. So what does Withers-as-bumblebee *do*? He described his day: "I come in around seven a.m. and the first hour is for *me*; to catch up on mail and to get letters out, etc. From eight o'clock to nine o'clock I take breakfast in the [company's] restaurant. People know where to find me that way and that there is a chance to get any discussion, comments, or decisions they need from me. The rest of the day I spend in the building wandering around. One of our guys might ring up during a presentation or meeting at a client's and say, 'It's going okay, but their architect is giving me a very hard time.' I'll say, 'I'll come down.' I'll jump in a taxi and be there for the afternoon session, backing my guy up."

The company restaurant, in a spacious, sun-lit atrium, is the firm's com-

Gary Withers's Changing Role

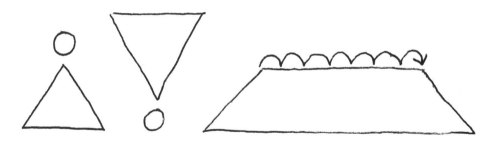

"At the beginning, with me at the top of a small hierarchy."

"When things started to take off, a bigger company with me working from 6:00 am to 12:00 midnight!"

"Today's Imagination, a three-layer, elongate (flat) company. I read a book on Disney somewhere where they described his role as that of a bumblebee: floating around pollinating ideas—providing the creative spark, but with no line responsibility as such."

munication hub, Withers said. Clients are there, Imagineers are there. All the time. People chat freely with one another. Withers insisted, again and again, that the Imagination process, and what it's trying to do for its clients, is pure theater. So the building must be theater, too. Every feature promotes energetic exchange. There's a "unique buzz," which Withers "manages" (in his own fashion). He, of course, is the model: always talking at high speed, sketching, racing around, ideas bursting forth.

Sit with Gary Withers for a couple of hours and you'll begin to believe in his oft-reported dictum, "Nothing is impossible." (You'll also be exhausted by the machine-gun-like pace at which he spits out ideas.) His style is to test, nudge, "work hard to fail," as he put it. "We always push the limits, sometimes beyond," he said. "The system starts to crack. Then others race in to support someone who gets in too deep. A chef, for example, will volunteer to fly a proposal to Italy—why not!"

Some years ago a fire destroyed Imagination's facilities. It happened on a weekend, and a major presentation to a client was scheduled the following Wednesday. Withers found new space within hours, the decorator showed up immediately, and the company was up and running, full-speed, in two and a half days. The presentation took place on schedule. It's this kinetic energy— along with, yes, imagination—that the firm succeeds so well in transmitting to its clients.

Project Models Are Accountability Models

> The pressure is self-induced. . . . You never think it's ever good enough. You're always left wondering, what have I done for them lately? Because there's a saying: "You're only as good as your last ad."
>
> ALFRED LINK
> Advertising copywriter
> Goldberg Moser O'Neill
> *Image*, July 7, 1991

Project models seem untidy—and they are to a degree. (Which is why we need them: untidy organizations for untidy markets, etc.) Moreover, there are lots of ways to do "the project thing" wrong—we'll discuss some of them below. But done right, à la EDS, McKinsey, CNN, or Imagination, project models are the ultimate accountability models.

• To begin with, done right, all projects/project teams have customers, sometimes internal but mostly external if you work at it (even at Titeflex, the UPRR). Real customers, top practitioners agree, breed high accountability almost automatically.

• Equally important, project teams held responsible for results (and always "understaffed by design," per EDS, McKinsey, CNN, Imagination) also develop internal accountability, one member to another, and among teams. All for one and one for all—it really works that way. Effective teams, though they consist of uniquely skilled members, are marked by dependence: Each needs the others' skills to serve the customer and get the job done. Thus the commonplace finding among top professional service firms: People under intense pressure to get a task done are the most likely to volunteer to help others out. Why? They know that the shoe will be on the other foot soon enough! (High pressure for task performance also tends to blunt carping—no time for it—and call forth what social psychologists call "the norm of reciprocity.")

• Project configurations also induce self-accountability. If life is a constant shuffle from project to project—again: EDS, McKinsey, CNN. Imagination—then it's imperative that you mind your own growth, so that you'll be high on lots of project managers' "desirables" list. "Create your own firm" is the motto of the wise.

Add it up—customer-driven accountability, dependence-based reciprocal accountability, self-accountability—and you have a potent combination. The fact is, none of these three "accountabilities" shows its face very often in normal hierarchies.

DAVID KELLEY DESIGN

Fail sometimes, be Left-handed, get Out there, be Sloppy, be Stupid.

DAVID KELLEY, the "FLOSS approach to design"

When we have some wacko problem, chances are that someone at [David Kelley Design] has the skills to take care of it.

STEVE JOBS, founder of
Apple and founder and chairman of NeXT
ID, September/October 1987

About 60 people, most electrical or mechanical engineers, half of them graduates of Stanford University's unique product design program, labored for David Kelley Design when I visited in early 1991. The main office is in Palo Alto, the heart of Silicon Valley. There are also tiny satellites in Chicago and Boston.*

The Work

So what is David Kelley Design? Equally important, what *isn't* it? "Prettying things up" is not its gig. Aesthetics are important at DKD. But other factors, such as manufacturability, get equal or better billing. The firm fits no standard mold, which is just the way founder David Kelley wants it.

Industrial design operations with staffs of 40 or 50 are playing a larger role in industry with each passing day. Some take on aesthetic issues exclusively. Some work only on manufacturability. Some are on board from day one of a client's new-product project. Some come on board when a client project is well under way, but having problems. Some work with the whole product. Some work with just a couple of components.

*In June 1991, after my interviews, David Kelley Design merged with the firms Matrix Product Design and ID2 to form IDEO. David Kelley heads the new 130-person firm. ID2 specialized in human-factor issues, employing numerous clinical psychologists. "We realized that companies needed to break down the barriers between marketing, engineering and manufacturing people," Kelley told the *San Francisco Examiner*. "They want people who can go from concept to customer." IDEO intends to do just that. Within the new organization, as of summer 1992, the old David Kelley Design operation remains mostly intact in the same locations; it's now called IDEO Product Development.

DKD will join a project at any stage, from very early to very late, and do anything from overall concept development (design, engineering, manufacturability, financial feasibility) to a very minor piece of technical work. There have been times—for example, the early days at Steve Jobs's NeXT Computer—when DKD served, de facto, as the corporate mechanical engineering department. Sometimes the firm has been so effective that clients have gotten rid of their mechanical engineering departments, deciding to rely exclusively upon Kelley.

The *San Jose Mercury News* describes a typical DKD project, engineering an aluminum can recycling device for start-up sjöberg Industries:

> For the same price, [sjöberg] could have hired three engineers and outfitted each with sophisticated computer-aided design systems. But they would have taken a year to get the product to market—four months longer than the David Kelley route. Don Massaro, sjöberg's chief executive, adds that it makes more sense to do internally only what truly improves a company's competitive edge. "You're better off strengthening internal resources in the areas where you can really add significant value."

Kelley clients include numerous Silicon Valley start-ups, such as sjöberg and pen-based computer maker Go. But Du Pont, Procter & Gamble, Steelcase (the furniture maker), and the medical instruments divisions of several pharmaceutical houses are also on DKD's client list.

The Process: High Kinetic Energy

David Kelley Design continually surprises clients. The "office" is a mirror of its work, and might best be described as a scene of moderately controlled frenzy. There's a sense of animation, of playfulness. Objects are scattered about. It's colorful. Fun things (models of special effects for a movie) sit comfortably next to serious things (bits and pieces of new computers DKD is at work on). Zany personal design projects—a bizarre lamp that can see around corners—will lie next to a half-finished model of a blood analyzer. In a minute, you can feel the spirit. People are constantly making things, talking about things, collaborating on things. There's a bit of the look of a kindergarten classroom, with materials lying about just waiting to be put together in some surprising fashion.

David Kelley won't—perhaps can't—sit behind his desk and lecture. He insists on showing you around, insists that you've got to see it and touch it and try it to understand it. His concept of collaboration, crazily juxtaposing multiple talents and ideas, is transparently obvious. As at Imagination, the look and smell of DKD also turns out to be a dandy marketing tool. "If we can get a customer to come in and take a tour, then they almost always sign up," Kelley told us.

The Process: Collaboration

America West Airlines Magazine labeled Kelley a "self-proclaimed 'horizontal engineer.' That means getting everybody together, from the start, to talk about the project—the whole project." *ID* added that while working as an employee at Boeing, "Kelley learned that product design, especially in new areas of technology, should not be approached serially, with each function, from engineering to design to marketing, handled separately. This, he believes, alienates creative workers from the overall project, and induces misunderstandings and negative competitiveness. Instead, when a new project comes into DKD, *everyone* is called in to a brainstorming session, where objectives are aired, and fresh ideas circulate." For instance, in a collaboration with Matrix Product Design on the Metaphor computer workstation, the first brainstorming session focused on what happens to a computer when it's not in use; out of that came the idea of using infrared input devices to avoid the usual cables and wires that connect the computer's parts.

"We get everyone in the same room, yelling at each other," Kelley told *Newsweek*. "Some of our clients don't even know how to ask the right questions." He described the development of a low-cost chair—the key was molding the tilting mechanism from a single piece of rubber. "They just didn't know you could do that with rubber," Kelley said.

The Kelley world is frenzied, chaotic, energetic, playful, intuitive—and structured. Kelley can go on for hours about the creative process. Brainstorming sessions—"brainstormers," as Kelley calls them—are a constant, and the centerpiece of the DKD approach. Anyone in the Kelley organization can "call a brainstormer" at any time. Others, no matter how busy they are, pretty much drop what they're doing and attend. Why? They know that others will do it for them tomorrow.

Over the years, DKD has developed a number of twists on the brainstorming idea, such as "back-to-back brainstormers." A half-dozen DKD staffers swap ideas with a client for a couple of hours. Then the first Kelley group leaves and is replaced—immediately—by another DKD sextet. A fresh working-over ensues. Kelley uses the approach to "work on the whole problem all at once." Though he claims that "speed is everything," he also adds that "premature closure" is enemy number one. "You pay later," he told us, "if there's not enough customer input, not enough time spent brainstorming." (Shades of Ingersoll-Rand: to hurry up, slow down.)

The Process: Multidisciplinary

The firm benefits from a special relationship with its next-door neighbor, Stanford University. Kelley worked through his approach there, and today is the rare tenured Stanford faculty member without a Ph.D. He's joined by about a half dozen other DKD staffers who teach part-time—a matchless source of renewal. (Several other DKDers also practice self-renewal by teaching, at such institutions as the San Francisco Art Institute.)

Stanford's elite product design program is nestled within the mechanical engineering department. Technically trained students hone their engineering skills and also develop an artistic appreciation and a head for business. Classes at the business school, at the engineering school, and in the art department are included in the curriculum, and make the program unique.

With its combination of disciplines, the Stanford program mirrors DKD. In particular, DKD staffers are expected to understand, in the end, the business consequences of their ideas (e.g., can their aesthetically appealing, mechanically clever gizmos be made at a cost which will turn a profit for the client). Kelley blasts industrial design schools—and industrial designers—for their overemphasis on art, deemphasis of the technical, and almost complete disregard for commercial considerations.

The Process: Model It!

Making something, fast, is essential to Kelley's approach. Turning ideas into action—instant prototypes—is gospel. Throughout the office, you'll find a blizzard of paper prototypes, cardboard prototypes with mechanical features, wood prototypes, Styrofoam prototypes. Full-scale mechanical prototypes are also sprinkled here and there. And DKD has a shop a few blocks away where a half-dozen-person gang translates commands from the main office's CAD system into instant prototypes. (The bent for prototyping is instilled from the start, courtesy of the Stanford program, where students are compelled to churn out an invention a week. A quick follow-up model allows them to develop a feel for what they've conjured up.)

Brownian Motion: The DKD "Organization"

All work at David Kelley Design is project team work. A tiny project absorbs 1 or 2 people; 12 to 15 people staff a huge one. A typical project has 4 or 5, with a couple of "principals" (design experts) and 2 or 3 support people (CAD experts, tooling experts). Short projects might last a couple of weeks. Long ones can run a year or more. The size of a project team often goes up and down like a yo-yo, from 1 to 12, then back down to 1 again.

There is a formal project leader/project manager designation. The leader may be more or less full-time on a single project for a year. (Like everyone else, though, that dedicated project manager will also be intensely engaged in the general hallway chatter and in those everyday "brainstormers.")

Most staffers want to lead a project. If they do it well, they usually want to lead a bigger project. In general, and this is a key to Kelley's success, the average professional staff member is eager to change his or her work venue, to increase his or her breadth, to get into a new industry or technology via the next project. (Any number of staffers claim that variety is DKD's principal attraction.) It's barely an exaggeration to say that DKDers refuse to do the same thing twice—with Kelley himself the most resolute.

Like Imagination's Withers, Kelley says he won't accept a new project unless he and the firm can learn from it. He insists that DKD's strength comes from the diversity of industries the small outfit serves—computers, medical equipment, toys, movie special effects, furniture, and so on. As people routinely—and obsessively—shift from one area to another, ideas from one context likewise pop up in another. For example, a ball-joint mechanism for a beach chair was originally designed for a computer-industry project. This Brownian motion is the way the firm learns, translates lessons, and broadens its skills over time. The "learning environment" that management gurus talk wistfully about these days? David Kelley Design is a learning lab—period.

(Talking with Kelley staffers is a joy. Most are caught up completely in their work. The project manager for an angioplasty device boasts electrical and mechanical engineering degrees—plus that DKD flair for aesthetics, manufacturability, and business. It's obvious she could talk all day and all night about her project—I was ready to sign on! "A year ago she probably couldn't even spell 'angioplasty'," Kelley commented. "Now I suspect she's one of the top two or three experts in the world.")

Kelley is adamant that cross-fertilization is *the* key to creativity, though he sometimes has trouble getting prospective clients, especially established firms, to buy in. Mighty Steelcase was dumbstruck when he insisted that they should hire him *because* he'd never designed a chair before! But Kelley is persuasive. After initial skepticism, he got the job.

DKDers are given free rein. Some want to go off and build their own stuff. Kelley helps them find financing to do so. In many respects, each of the 50 DKD designers (among a total of 60 employees) is an entrepreneur—with ready access to the world's best materials vendors, clients, CAD systems, and colleagues. As at EDS, McKinsey, and Imagination, project assignment is invariably via word of mouth. Would-be project leaders, needing people, scrounge to find them. They mostly know who's available and who's not. There is an "engineering manager" who, if necessary, can help sort out scheduling hassles. He keeps a spreadsheet that more or less tracks what people are up to. In practice, he's rarely called upon.

"Reporting relationships" are no big deal, I was told repeatedly. (Ho hum?!) It's normal for a project manager to be working for one of his "subordinate" team members who's leading another project. Who works for whom is mostly unclear, mostly irrelevant, as DKDers see it. "My boss is my subordinate is my boss," one Kelley designer told me with a shrug. That's "organization" for you.

CHIAT/DAY/MOJO

Other ad agencies don't want to make any mistakes, and that's a mistake.

TOM MIGNANELLI, President
Nissan Motor USA
on Chiat/Day/Mojo

While professional service firms in general may be the best models for tomorrow's organization, that doesn't mean there aren't good ones and bad ones, energetic ones and stodgy ones. We tend to think of ad agencies as zippy. Yet many mature ad firms have developed the same symptoms of advanced bureaucracy—grotesque overspecialization, wars between the tribes (the creative side, account executives), title-itis, and so on—that mark dying industrial outfits.

As is true in any industry you can name these days, upstarts have often surprised the elders of the ad market. None more so than Chiat/Day/Mojo, *Advertising Age*'s 1980s "Agency of the Decade." In mid-1992, C/D/M's worldwide billings stood at $1.1 billion. The privately held, 1,000-person firm was founded as Chiat Day in 1968 in Los Angeles, opened a New York office in 1980, and acquired Mojo of Australia in 1988. Its client list includes Nissan Motor USA, Nutrasweet, Toshiba America Information Systems, Reebok, and Shearson Lehman Brothers. Chiat may be best known for producing the controversial Apple ad for the 1985 Super Bowl, featuring martinet IBMers marching over a cliff. (How prescient, it turns out!)

Creativity Means Everyone

Creativity is C/D/M's hallmark. Everything and everyone serves that idea. It begins with "organization" structure—an absence of rigid boxes. C/D/Mers aren't tagged for narrow slots. Business cards have no titles. "I've been here two years and I've never seen a job description," account executive Sean Hardwick told us in 1989.

Founder Jay Chiat insists that a great idea can come from anywhere, that people should move forward according to their energies and interests. In fact, many of the firm's most creative people started in entry-level jobs. Take Amy Moorman. She started as a receptionist, but hoped to be a copywriter. After only three weeks on the job, she learned of an opening in the creative area for an assistant. She voluntarily took on the task (in addition to her regular duties), and has been inventing projects for herself ever since. She volunteered, for instance, to coordinate a special 10-week course for junior creative staff members. To be accepted into the program, you have to present your portfolio of prior work. Amy, of course, had no such portfolio—but the firm allowed her to sit in and audit the course anyway. She was on her way.

In general, C/D/Mers get unusually broad exposure. At traditional agencies, for example, assistant account executives are stuck with procedural matters—watching over the budget, scheduling. But at C/D/M, they can—and are more or less expected to—participate in client strategy meetings and develop client relationships on their own.

The abiding emphasis on creativity dramatically reduces traditional ad agency friction between "account people" and "creative people." Characteristically cautious account types are urged to emphasize the importance of creative ads to their client. *Advertising Age,* explaining its choice of C/D/M as the 1980s' best, pointed to the special relationship:

> The agency has long demanded creativity from its account management staff. . . . For example, it was an account supervisor who thought up the idea of using mythical "Artesians" to promote Olympia Beer in early 1981. Selling the creative concept also calls for Chiat fighting for what the agency's creative department believes in. "Most agencies don't have the balls to support a good idea . . .," [C/D/M Executive Creative Director Lee] Clow said. "They might . . . take it out to the client once in a while. But as soon as it gets killed by someone in authority, they don't have the rapport with their client to say, 'Now wait. We know this is risky, but here's why you should do it.' Most [account people] would go back to the office and say, 'Sorry guys. We gave it a try. Now this is what the client wants.' "

Loose but Tough (Again)

In return for "sky's the limit" opportunity, C/D/M demands a lot—almost everything. During hiring interviews, recruiters make it clear that Chiat must become the applicant's raison d'être. "If it's not the most important thing to you, we don't want you here," said vice president Sharon Stanley. "Life's too short not to do the things you really love. The job shouldn't be work."

Shades of Imagination. Account planner Ginny Kollewe went on to underscore the need for flexibility. "Everyone, even switchboard operators and accountants, is asked to do the strangest things. If you don't like it, you won't be here very long." "A lot of people," Laurie Coots, vice president and director of administration, told us, "do want to work here, but it's not for everyone." She emphasized that "if you don't have the self-confidence to take the initiative or are scared, or are waiting for your boss to say it's okay to try something, you're in trouble."

New hires are thrown at the work. "It's baptism by fire," said account executive Laura Gonzalez. "You have to bring yourself up to speed." A lack of structure can be "confusing for a new employee," says admin assistant Sally

Walsh, "but the openness and lack of job descriptions make you *want* to take on more."

Don't get the idea there's anarchy, though. "Our job functions are deliberately ambiguous," said Sharon Stanley. "But one thing is perfectly clear: the company mission." Executive producer Elaine Hinton added that "freedom doesn't mean that you don't have to be cost-conscious, that you don't have to pay attention to detail. You won't be led by the hand here. If you don't know something, you have to get up and ask. It's your responsibility to keep abreast of your job, and if you know something, you have the obligation to tell people involved. You have to be industrious, to investigate, to ask questions." As is true throughout most effective professional service firms, such ambiguous talk is well understood by the natives. Performance reviews? C/D/M mirrors McKinsey. "We have no closed-door mystique about performance reviews," said Sally Walsh. "You can talk to people at any time and find out how they think you're doing."

Planned Nosiness

Everyone we interviewed emphasized communications. There's nothing more frustrating, especially given C/D/M's growth, than managing by word of mouth. "Informal communication can be misunderstood, and you might not know it," as one respondent put it. On the other hand, Elaine Hinton quickly added, "The open structure forces you to build relationships. Besides, you can ask or discuss anything with anyone here. You don't have to wait forty-eight hours to talk with the upper echelon."

"Nosiness feeds creative energy," we were told by Michael Smith, a creative department staffer. "You can pop in and out of offices and exchange ideas, look at storyboards or ads. By being close together, creatives can bounce more ideas off each other. Our physical structure encourages communications. And our philosophy demands not hiding things." Another creative recalled that in the big New York agency he used to work for, "I could go an entire week without talking to *anyone*. No one would know what I was doing. Here, you're part of it, there's more personal involvement."

Every bit of the work space emphasizes openness and creativity. "Main Street," the main hallway in the L.A. office, is lined with partitioned offices. Not even Jay Chiat has a private office. (He shares a cubicle with his secretary.) VP Laurie Coots observed that "Jay will do anything to prevent complacency. If you get too comfortable, he'll move you. Every three months, in fact, we move around. This place is like a revolving gallery in which the paintings and sculptures change." Everyone is also kept informed about how things are going in general, via, among other things, frequent "tree meetings"—gatherings of the entire company around a "tree" on Main Street.

Client Involvement

Chiat/Day/Mojo's performance hinges on an apparent contradiction. Its brash push for creativity is paramount. On the other hand, C/D/M also stands just as far ahead of the pack by involving clients in the advertising process from the start. "[C/D/M] won't accept an account if the client refuses to get involved," *Business Month* reported. "A case in point is *Vogue* magazine, an advertiser that is not big in billings but is big in visibility. Says [Jay] Chiat: 'I asked the publisher, how does the advertising get approved? He said, Mr. Newhouse approves it all. [S. I. Newhouse, Jr., is chairman of Condé Nast Publications, *Vogue*'s parent.] I said, do we ever get to talk to Mr. Newhouse or present the work to him? He said, No. You give the work to me and I show it to Mr. Newhouse. And I said, Well, I don't think we can work for you because we would never understand what Mr. Newhouse wants.' "

Business Month also pointed out another special aspect of C/D/M's attention to the customer—the ultimate customer, consumers of whatever's being advertised:

> Chiat . . . helped introduce the English practice of *account planning* to the United States. Basically, an account planner is the agency person who represents the consumer in the process of creating an ad campaign. He or she goes out into the field and conducts countless interviews, either one-on-one or in focus groups. When the account and creative people sit down with their calculators and tissue paper, the account planner presents the consumer's perception of the product, and later makes sure that the same consumers understand the ads before they are produced. In the case of Nissan, the account planner "probably talked to thousands of car owners through focus groups," says Jane Newman, general manager of C/D/M's New York office.

Interviews we conducted with both suppliers and customers underscored the open, engaged atmosphere at Chiat. Mark Coppos is an outsider film director for some of C/D/M's ads. "When I go [to C/D/M], I'm going to visit people—it doesn't feel like going to a job, but to an enjoyable place," he said. "There's no nervousness or animosity or secrecy." As to other agencies, "They're not fun places to be. There's a feeling of high anxiety at all times, a requirement to act a certain way. They [often] see suppliers as spies and have all these things stamped confidential, and give you lots of disclaimers to sign. I'm not saying Chiat doesn't ask you to sign disclaimers, because they do and have to, but it's like, 'Here, you have to sign this for legal,' not 'Sign this or that's it.' They're cautious, but they're human. You'd *never* disclose any confidential information because that would be like screwing over a friend."

Tom Mignanelli, president of Nissan Motor Corp. in the USA, waxed euphoric to us about C/D/M's high-involvement strategy:

> Chiat has a step-by-step, detailed process for involving you right from the start. When you work with Chiat, you're involved with them every step of the way, and that's good, because there are no surprises. It's a technique that Jay Chiat believes in, to avoid wasted time and money and frustration, and rushing to meet deadlines. With other agencies, there was very much a feeling of "client" versus "agency." With Chiat, we all feel like one entity.
>
> The word "teamwork" gets thrown around a lot, and not many people really understand it. Chiat espouses teamwork more than any other company [I've worked with], because they understand that the team isn't just a collection of people with talent, it's a collection of people with the right attitude. And that attitude is that everyone can contribute ideas. It's an easy atmosphere to work in, because people aren't inhibited by rank.
>
> With other agencies, strategy is the opinion of the highest-ranking person in the room. Not at Chiat. There's an irreverence toward rank. We brought them into our product cycle plans, sharing proprietary information with them, because they're part of it. There's a high level of trust and mutual respect that allows this kind of relationship.
>
> What stands out in my mind as the best piece of advertising they did was called "Road to Rio"—which chronicled, over six to seven commercials, the journey of a four-wheel-drive Pathfinder from Chicago to Rio. That's as unique an approach as you'll see. It was created through joint sessions with Nissan and Chiat. The crazier the idea, the harder they pushed. They were doing something unique and encouraged us to take the risk. That's Chiat's way. Take risks, not in a reckless way, but in a business way, to go a bit beyond.

C/D/M pushes—and pushes—for creative risks. And pushes—and pushes—for intensive involvement. (Ditto Imagination and David Kelley Design.) But the seeming contradiction is readily resolved. The messy (by normal standards) process of early client involvement turns out to be an ideal "softening-up" tool. If clients are drawn into the initial rough and raucous discussions, they become engaged, partners in a joint crusade. As a result, they're far more receptive down the pike to more daring departures. In fact, the clients themselves frequently become champions of bold initiatives!

Alternatively, if you're not part of the early, unfocused dialogue, there's virtually no chance that you'll ever buy into anything dramatic. By definition, a willingness to take risks is the result of time-consuming dialogue, to-ing and fro-ing, accepting and rejecting—and inching out into the unknown over time. It's hardly a wonder when a client who hasn't shared the formative experiences is squeamish about taking a big risk with an ad campaign—even if that client "demanded highly creative results" in the project negotiation process. Intense dialogue paves the way for risk-taking—period.

CLIENT ENGAGEMENT REFLECTS INNER STRUCTURE

The professional service firm's characteristic small-team approach automatically induces intense customer contact—that's one major reason the model is so appropriate to the times. On the other hand, all five such firms we've examined—EDS, McKinsey, Imagination, David Kelley Design, and Chiat/Day/Mojo—broke substantial new ground in terms of deep, continuous client interaction. It's no exaggeration to say that Ross Perot (EDS), Marvin Bower (McKinsey), Gary Withers (Imagination), David Kelley, and Jay Chiat have a fetish about client involvement. (Once more, I'd point out that it is precisely this sort of involvement that is becoming the hallmark of Ingersoll-Rand, the Union Pacific Railroad, ABB, and Titeflex—hence my suggestion that each is becoming, de facto, a knowledge-added, risk-seeking professional service firm in its own right.)

Furthermore, this seamless, feisty client interchange is—and must be—a direct reflection of the internal "structure" (structurelessness is more accurate) of those firms, especially Imagination, DKD, and C/D/M. The trio's fluidity, nosiness, and buzz rub off on the client. The absence of such a "culture" in most such firms (let alone non-professional service firms) closes the damper on the sort of forthright, daring client engagement Nissan Motor USA experiences with C/D/M, and Steve Jobs experiences with David Kelley. Consciousness of rank *within* a firm, for example, is invariably magnified in its *outward dealings* with clients (and vendors, like C/D/M's contract film director, Mark Coppos).

A SYSTEMATIC LOOK AT PROFESSIONAL SERVICE FIRMS: THE CASE OF INVESTMENT BANKS

Harvard Business School professors Bob Eccles and Dwight Crane examined 17 investment banks in the late 1980s. The result, *Doing Deals*, faithfully portrays the industry's idiosyncrasies, but, more to the point, constitutes a peerless systematic study of management practice at professional service firms.*

Here are Eccles, Crane, and some of their respondents on key issues, with my own commentary interspersed from time to time.

*Since the research, any number of investment banks have paid the price for pursuing the "opportunities" of the '80s too vigorously. Eccles and Crane, for example, examined Drexel, Burnham and Salomon Bros. The experience of those organizations makes it clear that professional service firms can reel out of control (ditto Saatchi and Saatchi in advertising and public relations), particularly when they pursue growth for growth's sake and, unlike McKinsey, allow too many wild ducks to go their own way, unsupervised. All that said, the observations in this study are invaluable to understanding professional service firm "structure."

Idea Flow

Phil Purcell, CEO at Dean Witter (a Sears subsidiary): "Strategies are developed in the middle of the organization. Some of them result in business you really get good at and they start to define you. . . . We had three different key products in four years, so what is strategy? You simply get great people and back them. And even they can't tell you what they'll be doing next year."

Joe Perella, First Boston: "[We have] a breadth of culture that enables a lot of people to thrive. We get a lot of things percolating—the hot house concept. Sometimes you get strange things growing. There are product areas that exploded from a junior person who was given lots of room."

Eccles and Crane: If top management were to attempt to set strategy, "the unavoidable delays this would introduce or the deterioration in the quality of the decision would inhibit the firm's competitive effectiveness."

Another exec: "We have a 'reverse funnel effect' in the flow of ideas. We let ideas percolate up and most get discarded. There also must be hundreds of ideas that we never hear about. But the great ideas continue to sift up and withstand the test of time. Things that get sifted out prematurely get started again. . . . Sometimes ideas even start with senior management. We have to plant them in the middle of the firm, since we need the organization behind them."

Goldman, Sachs exec: "The basic issue is whether you have established structures and systems so that gadflies can challenge you and get lateral thinking. . . . You need a mechanism to push these ideas upstairs, since the best ones come from the trenches."

<u>Commentary:</u> Characteristics of the effective professional service firm captured here include:

— lots of "little starts"; success is a numbers game ("hot house concept"/ "percolate up");

— little starts come from anywhere, but most are begotten close to the action;

— competitive context too fluid to wait for top management to methodically set strategy; top management's role is to stand beside/behind energetic midlevel "opportunists" and give a boost at the appropriate moment;

— toleration of "strange things"/"gadflies" in strange (typical today) environments; it's tough to tell what will jell;

— organic process prevails; the best ideas grow and move up, and may end up defining/redefining the firm. Also, some ideas bounce up and down for an extended period of time, which is dandy—they may eventually pay off;

—a business opportunity *is* a turned-on person;

—annual strategic shifts not unusual.

Self-Design of Organizations

Eccles/Crane: "A distinctive characteristic of the firms in our study was the extent to which people throughout the organization could affect the organizational design. . . . In a self-designing organization, individuals bear most of the responsibility for establishing ties of the appropriate strengths with those they need help from or should give help to."

<u>Commentary:</u> Professional service firms are fluid networks; they are constantly redesigning themselves as their members, largely on their own initiative, form new alliances, flock to "winners" (people, ideas, products, clients), desert "losers." Organization design, like strategy formulation, is more organic and bottom-up than structured and top-down.

Specialization I

Eccles/Crane: "Specialization creates an external perception by customers that the firm has special expertise in doing certain types of deals or serving particular market segments [which] is an important competitive advantage. [For example,] by creating a specialized unit that focuses on serving all the needs of the thrift industry including mortgage securities, equity and mergers and acquisitions, the potential is created for maximizing the firm's penetration of these accounts. The price . . . will be a failure to fully exploit mortgage opportunities in nonthrift institutions, such as commercial banks and insurance companies."

<u>Commentary:</u> In a highly competitive context, you must be perceived as unique, or close to it, in areas of importance. To be so perceived means narrowness, and—*c'est la vie*—narrowness has costs. Nonetheless, in crowded marketplaces like today's, "all things to all people" competitors are usually doomed.

There is a larger point here. Though professional service firms are marked by fluidity and the absence of fixed staff departments, the requirement for expertise is not diminished. To the contrary, exceptional expertise is demanded of everyone—it's just that there's no "functional stovepipe" (the engineering or finance department in a typical manufacturing outfit, for example) charged with maintaining competence. The turbulence of the market, in investment banking or any other field, simply will not permit such rigid, slow, functional baronies.

Specialization II

Eccles/Crane: "If the [investment bank's client] relationship manager is a product specialist: [He] may not devote enough time and attention to identifying other opportunities for other specialists and to helping them develop ties with a customer. . . . The product specialist will have an especially strong tie with only the subset of individuals in the [customer] company who purchase his or her product. . . .

"Relationship managers who are not specialists: Without a product specialty, the relationship manager may have difficulty getting access to the customer and establishing credibility [in the first place]. . . . There are potential costs to a high degree of control [exercised by a non-specialist relationship manager]. Funnelling communication through the relationship manager . . . may slow communications down so much that deals are lost because of delays. It may also prove frustrating to the customer and the product specialist alike when the relationship manager's contribution is minor. There is also the risk that the relationship manager will avoid discussions about products he or she is less comfortable with."

Commentary: There's no free lunch! In traditional manufacturing businesses, there is no solution to "product/product family focus" versus "market/market segment/customer focus." In professional service firms, the story is the same. Focus on the product (specialist) dimension, and you will be narrowly perceived by the customer and lose lots of opportunities. Focus on the client relationship angle, and you will blunt the specialists' value, or never be special enough to get your foot in the door in the first place. Most important: Don't deny the problem: You cannot have (all) your cake and eat it (all) too.

Network Structure

Eccles/Crane: "The network structures of investment banks are flexible, flat, complex and rife with conflict. . . . Flexibility is required because . . . it is impossible to anticipate the deals a firm will do and what combination of resources will be needed. . . . Flatness is important because communications that must go up and down many hierarchical levels do so too slowly for the firm to respond in the short time that characterizes the market in investment banking. . . . [There is a] need for everybody to talk to everybody else, [for] a web of ties that goes in all directions."

Merrill Lynch exec: "We had to build a structure where everybody reported to everybody else."

Eccles/Crane: "[An individual frequently reports] to managers who are at different levels in the organization hierarchy, such as his boss and his boss' boss. . . . [The hierarchy can be flattened] by inverting management responsibilities between levels. This often occurs when the manager of the department is heavily involved in customer relationships. In order to preserve his time for this important activity, lower-level managers take on the responsibility for both planning and day-to-day operating management."

Commentary: This analysis reveals the oddball doings that go on naturally in big professional service firms—which can appear bizarre to traditionally trained managers:

— Flat is a must, not an option. If communication has to go up and down the hierarchy, business is lost, and the firm gets an irredeemable reputation for unresponsiveness in an industry where responsiveness is almost everything. (All industries will soon mimic investment banking on this score.)

— Everyone has to be able to talk with, work with, everyone else, unimpeded—or else. The web of relations *is* the firm: Survivors/stars are network virtuosos; losers/dropouts never come to appreciate the worth of major investment in network-building and relationship development.

— Forget the rules: "My boss is my subordinate is my boss," depending upon the task and situation. So what? (Which is not to say it's easy to deal with. Neat freaks need not apply.)

Constant Reorganization

Eccles/Crane: "A firm's structure influences the information it collects from its environment and how it combines and processes this information to generate future strategies. Changes in structure [automatically] result in changes in information flow, which in turn result in changes in the strategic opportunities that are considered and pursued. Changes also help to dissolve power bases that can interfere with necessary changes in strategy in an attempt to protect vested interests."

Commentary: Information *is* organization. Change the organization, and you change the information flow. What's wrong with constant reorganization? Nothing, say top professional service firm managers. (As long as underlying values are clear—see below.)

Structure Follows the Person

Goldman, Sachs exec: "I try not to develop too many dogmatic rules, but one iron-clad rule is that the structure should follow the person."

Commentary: You heard him!

Incentives

Eccles/Crane: "Attempts to measure revenues by departments or other units in the firm [are typically] complicated because many deals involve a number of departments. . . . None of the investment banks in our study went to any extraordinary effort to carefully allocate deal revenues to departments in proportion to their contribution. . . . The most common way of measuring each department's contribution to a deal was simply to let each one involved book total revenues of the deal. . . . Doing so sends a very clear signal about the importance of departments working together for the firm as a whole. . . .

"Top management addresses the problem of too much concentration on individual performance by basing bonuses on aggregate performance measures rather than on the performance of individual units in the firm. . . . To address the short-term orientation problem, senior managers use subjective judgment in determining how funds from aggregate bonus pools should be allocated to individuals. . . .

"Procedures used to determine an individual's bonus were similar among firms. The typical procedure begins with a memorandum submitted by the person describing his or her contributions to the firm over the past year. This was called a 'puff sheet' at Merrill Lynch and a 'brag sheet' at several other firms. . . .

"[A] more subtle reason for spending a substantial amount of time on the bonus determination process, and for making sure people know what a large commitment top management has to it, is to shape the perceptions people being evaluated have of this process. Because the stakes are so high, the reputation of the process will be enhanced if it is judged to be carefully done. One way of accomplishing this is to allocate a great deal of the precious resource of top-management time to it."

<u>Commentary:</u> So far, the Eccles/Crane analysis has mostly lauded opportunism, bottom-up strategy setting, fluidity, and the primacy of personalities/gadflies. But the flywheel is evaluation and compensation schemes that share these characteristics:

— Double, triple, quadruple booking of revenues that encourages cooperation and avoids time-consuming dogfights over the allocation of "credit" for revenues garnered.
— Bonus pools largely based on overall firm performance.
— Bonus pool/bonus determination that is overwhelmingly subjective.
— Since evaluation is mainly subjective: (1) those being evaluated must have their say and (2) top management must make an enormous real/perceived investment in the evaluation process so that it is believed to be fair.

Note: Some investment-bank flywheels, at Salomon Bros. and Drexel, Burnham, for example, turned out to be too loose. Opportunism clearly outran controls. Nonetheless, as the marketplace in general more and more mimics the zaniness of investment banking, all firms must step up to the need for lightly guided opportunism—while acknowledging the problems it brings along as baggage.

General

Eccles/Crane: "Management in investment banking means managing networks. . . . The firm must have the capability of bringing to bear whatever resources are needed, regardless of where they are located in the firm, and often at a moment's notice. The impossibility of predicting what deals will be done and what resources each will require means that the internal network must be complex and flexible. The management practices of investment banks have been developed to manage flexible and continuously changing networks of external and internal ties."

<u>Commentary:</u> Amen!

Professional Service Firm Conundrums

During a recent discussion about the approaches that professional service firms take to organizing, seminar participants voiced several concerns:

- <u>Customers lose confidence when team members are switched around.</u> Customers watch junior people slide in and out of projects at McKinsey or EDS, and feel some irritation at "spending our precious time—and money—training them." (Recall that EDS sends new members directly to customer sites with no training.) On the other hand, professional service firms trade only in ideas, and must continually refresh themselves. New members bring new perspectives from different disciplines and past projects. David Kelley sees this churn as his company's number one success factor.

However, professional service firms must provide the *sense* of continuity. While project-team membership—and leadership—may change, wise firms maintain stability in client relationship management. At McKinsey, for example, different people head different projects—but the chief relationship manager will likely stay in place for years. Which can cause problems! McKinsey's client service directors, like many ad agency account directors, come to depend on a single client for most of their billings and become too conservative—the kiss of death in the idea trade. (Recall Chiat's efforts to counter this by insisting that account chiefs stick up for the creatives.)

- <u>There's a lack of perceived control (accounting, performance, etc.).</u> Traditionalists blanch at the dispersed nature of project teams and the skimpy written policy guidance most professional service firms provide. And, yes, there certainly are instances of professional service firms having lost control—qualitative and financial. (Ironically, however, most failures of professional service firms result from a breakdown of partnership and trust, not disdain for accepted accounting procedures.)

In all the cases we reviewed, however, control (accountability, self-responsibility) outstripped that found in traditional bureaucracies. Reasons:

— project structures aim members at tasks and keep deadline pressure high

— team orientation provides strong motivation not to let down your mates (there are usually only a handful of you, and sloppy work sticks out like a sore thumb)

— initial socialization makes it clear that you must take the initiative

— customers (real "end users") are usually close at hand

— feedback lurks round every corner

— the "kibbitzing" mode of Chiat, Kelly, Imagination, McKinsey motivates you to "have something to brag about"

— subjective evaluation schemes direct your attention to qualitative issues (client relations, help given to colleagues)

• <u>Resource (people) allocation is nightmarish</u>. I've found no professional service firm that has a "good"—i.e., systematic—human-resource allocation technique. They've all tried formal schemes, but backed off. The alternative, word of mouth, *is* messy, but it can work. Effective project managers develop an extensive network over the years—it's a distinguishing success trait. When the first scent of an interesting new project is in the air, the savvy project manager heads for the phone and spends spare hours checking on people's availability, making deals with peers (cashing in chips), trying to concoct a potential team. Such recruitment moxie is among the project manager's most precious skills.

The process is self-regulating. Since team success depends on the ability to recruit first-rate talent, project managers who would succeed take network-building in general very seriously. (And they learn to pony up when it hurts—for reasons of unmitigated self-interest.) Moreover, given the ever-stretched nature of the typical professional service firm team, there's little room for sentimentality. Project managers with bum reps (lousy analysts, "people killers," etc.) don't get good recruits. First-line talents with bum reps don't get recruited for good jobs. An effective natural selection process results.

• <u>"Creative" time is scarce, given crushing project-deadline pressure</u>. Professional service firm apologists would answer that originality associated with the stream of new projects per se injects requisite creativity. While that overstates, each project is at least a fresh start. But some firms go much further than others. David Kelley Design and Imagination, for example, won't accept a project unless it can lead them someplace new. Both firms also have a cultural norm which pushes staff toward new classes of problems—and doesn't force people to milk the last ounce from the special knowledge they've just picked up. Both further believe such practices help them attract and then retain spicy people.

Despite such natural pressures pushing toward creativity, many professional service firms do have more in common with more traditional firms than they would like to admit. There's surely a routinized "McKinsey way of thinking," "EDS way of thinking." Sadly, it's the unusual McKinsey consultant who will admit it. Most professional service firms assume that the constant flow of new projects "takes care of" the creativity issue. Not so.

CHARACTERISTICS OF PROFESSIONAL SERVICE "ORGANIZATIONS"

From these cases—EDS, McKinsey, Imagination, David Kelly Design, Chiat/Day/Mojo, and Eccles and Crane's investment banking firms—I've extracted several guiding tenets:

- <u>Project/deal/"horizontal" axis dominates.</u> The reason is straightforward: speed of change in the marketplace. Professional service firms are organized as they are for one simple reason: There is no alternative.

- <u>Adhocracy is the norm.</u> Changing shape, perpetual fluidity in response to market demand (albeit maintaining core, largely invariant values underneath), is, once more, an *average* response to the *average*, unsettled marketplace.

- <u>Follow personal interests/strategy percolates up and changes opportunistically/weed the portfolio from time to time/same idea pops up again and again.</u> Professional service firms, though some are more loath to acknowledge it than others, are organized according to the personal interests of key players. When an exciting person comes along with a particular taste—banking strategy in a consulting firm, for example—then, over time, people gravitate to her or him, and the business which she or he builds. Professional service firms consider this perfectly normal, though most go out of their way to ensure that large egos are regularly brought down to size.

Top management oversight in these sorts of firms is the antithesis of the directive style that has marked "normal" firms. (*Hint*: There are no "normal" firms anymore.) The idea, as in gardening, is to create the context for luxuriant growth. Professional service firm chiefs attend to seed selection (recruiting) and fertilization and watering (encouraging all sorts of individual and small-group initiatives). Occasionally, they must weed out discordant growth—though they must take care in doing so, in the understanding that the unexpected wildflowers may well become the most beautiful in the garden—and in fact, over time, dominate and change the character of the garden.

• Reorganize. Shifting business opportunities naturally lead to reorganization as necessary, without much muss or fuss (partly because senior officers tend not to be measured by the number of bodies reporting to them). New relations with clients, especially big clients, are reason enough for a major reorganization—de facto or de jure.

• "All report to all." Though there are committees involved in performance appraisal, project leaders for any given project, and perhaps department heads, the notion of "report to" is more or less alien in the professional service firm. You seek out whomever you need for appropriate help/expertise. Today's boss is tomorrow's subordinate, and vice versa. And if you want help from "the extended network" tomorrow, you'd better offer help to the extended network today.

• Specialization is critical. Though hierarchy disappears and functional staffs are nonexistent, the need for expertise is not diminshed. To the contrary, for moderate-size teams to attack and conquer markets, expertise on the part of all team members, and towering expertise on the part of those who lead the team, are more important, not less important, than in traditional settings. However, it is "new specialization"—(1) specialization around a coherent task/niche-market opportunity, not specialization at a trivial part of a huge task; and (2) specialization driven by members acquiring expertise, not by specialist functional business.

• Relationship management is essential, but difficult to orchestrate. Professional service firms usually have a disproportionate share of business with a moderate number of clients. (The well-traveled 80–20 rule holds here as elsewhere.) There is a special skill called "relationship management," and nurturing relationships, especially with major clients, is imperative. On the other hand, the relationship, in fact, consists of a series of "products"—investment banking products, specialist consulting projects, ad campaigns—sold to the customer. To execute those projects—*with flair*—necessitates specialists having across-the-board, unfettered access to the client.

Relationship managers, by definition, want to control "off-the-wall" (as they see it) specialists, such as the ad agencies' creatives. Specialists, on the other hand, are perpetually frustrated by the relationship manager's reluctance to let them express themselves freely in front of the client. Both parties are right. Both parties are wrong. Never the twain shall meet! Moreover, there are no easy "combination" answers. When a specialist is the relationship manager, his specialty tends to be the focus of attention—not always bad, but not always good. When a non-specialist relationship manager is in charge, audacity of any flavor is unusual.

- The client is king. Figuring out how to organize to deal with the client means owning up to trade-offs. The answers a firm chooses make a big difference—Chiat/Day/Mojo's deferral to its creatives, for example. But make no mistake, compared to the average non-professional service firm, these are all quibbles about how to best achieve symbiosis with the customer (also see Chapter 45). "Relationship management" became a hot marketing topic, from bankers to high-tech wizards, in the '80s. McKinsey had been practicing it with aplomb since the '30s. The EDS, McKinsey, DKD, C/D/M, and Imagination approaches differ—but in degree, not kind: The fact is, all first-rank professional service firms, and even most also-rans, are organized in small groups around the customer.

- Evaluation based on the firm as a whole/no formula/double counting/high subjective component/highly variable. Eccles and Crane found that internecine warfare quickly got out of hand when objective, formulaic approaches were used in investment banking firms. Thus, though the individual financial stakes could be enormous, the best investment banking firms, without exception, relied upon subjective evaluation. Let as many people as possible take credit for what transpired. Moreover, performance for individuals was largely tied to performance for a large group (a big department) or the firm as a whole—thus strongly encouraging cooperation in an environment where bloodthirsty competitiveness would be the norm unless clearly quashed.

I have paraded this material before thousands of executives. While bits and pieces may seem downright strange, and most of it somewhat discomforting, the evaluation issue repeatedly turns out to be the showstopper—in particular, the apparent contradiction between exceedingly high levels of autonomy/accountability *and* subjective evaluation schemes.

I suggest you talk to a senior university professor. A small number of university evaluation decisions at the highest level—life tenure!—*define* the university. Universities are collections of strongly independent, entrepreneurial individuals. Yet even the biggest and most powerful departments in a given field have a dozen or fewer tenured faculty members (and only two or three when you look at sub-subspecialties, often the basis for evaluation). As a result, universities have the largest stake of any institution imaginable in the evaluation process.

The result is predictable. Lots of very senior, very busy people devote an inordinate amount of time to the tenure decision process. Collecting recommendations is a major chore. Moreover, the extended community shares the understanding of the importance of the process—distant colleagues at other universities will spend hours working up a recommendation. The norm of reciprocity is at play: They expect the same meticulous, thoughtful treatment in return. Evaluation committees usually include outsiders to the institution and outsiders to the department. But above all, the common denominators are *time* and *thoroughness*.

It is precisely this set of attributes which Eccles and Crane discovered at the investment banks. It is precisely this set of attributes which marked my McKinsey experience. Lots of smart, thoughtful, powerful people and (one hopes) a few gadflies must simply spend hour after hour, day after day, together working on these decisions. They are—obviously in retrospect—the lifeblood of the professional service firm. (And *all* firms, I repeat, in a knowledge economy.)

● <u>Methodology is philosophy.</u> Professional service firms do have core technologies—namely, distinct approaches to problem solving. Show me a nameless client consulting report, and I'll tell you in a flash whether it came from McKinsey, Boston Consulting Group, Bain & Co., or Booz Allen. David Kelley goes on at length about his methodology. In a world where value comes from knowledge, knowledge-application "technology" is by definition a most precious metal. Obviously such methodologies, just like a machine tool, can become outdated and hinder rather than spur progress. (More on those dangers in the Markets and Innovation section.)

12

Projects and Professional Service Firms II: The Fleeting "Organization"

For denizens of auto plants and steel mills, the goings-on at Imagination, Chiat/Day/Mojo, McKinsey, and EDS must sound borderline absurd. Constant reconfiguration. Never work with the same team twice in a longish career. But how about an "organization" that defies every rule? (Remember those quotation marks—see Chapter 1. We're a long way from stone pyramids here.) An "organization" of 30-odd people from 30-odd "organizations" from all over the country, who fly, drive, and bicycle to a place. They arrive 10 hours before a critical job is to be done, come together, perform a world-class task with imagination, and then, within an hour and a half of completion, disperse. Before coming together, many of the participants have never met one another. After the event, many will never work together again. Yet even though the future won't bring all in contact with all, the "network" to which members belong is vital to each one's future. Confusing? Read on.

THE BIRTH, LIFE, AND DEATH OF THE "DALLAS ORGANIZATION"

January 10, 1991. The Grand Kempinski Hotel, Dallas, Texas. 9:00 a.m. "Crew call." About 35 people gather. Some are local. Some flew in overnight from here or there. Some drove in. The 35 encompass almost that many different technical disciplines.

Many are meeting each other for the first time. Ten and one-half hours from now they will tape a two-hour lecture (given by the author), which will become the centerpiece of an hour-long public television show. They'll tape it again the next day. Then they'll disperse, never again to work together in the same configuration.

Who Says Perpetuity's a Must?

Just what *is* an organization? Professor Harold Leavitt's classic business school text *Managerial Psychology* says an organization consists of tasks, structure, information and control, people, and an outside environment. I was part of a group at McKinsey in the mid-1970s that developed the so-called 7-S Framework. Strategy, structure, systems, style, staff, skills, and a superordinate goal add up to "organization," we declared.

Neither definition, nor a hundred like them, includes anything about longevity. That is, organizations do not have to exist "in perpetuity" (despite the governing myth of permanence that marks American corporate law). It's perfectly fair to speak of an "organization," even if it only "lives" for a day or so. (There are lots of cellular and molecular "organizations" that are born, perform artfully, and die in a fraction of the time it took you to read this sentence.)

THE LARGER NETWORK FORMS

Over the years, I've helped develop a dozen TV shows for PBS. I and my company, The Tom Peters Group, have principally worked with Video Publishing House of Schaumburg, Illinois. Along the way, we hooked up with Federal Express, which funded parts of several programs.

In mid-1989, FedEx inquired about Video Publishing House's interest in creating a show based on corporate America's emerging concern with speed. VPH contacted my colleagues at TPG Communications (the book, audio, and TV company that is one of the five in The Tom Peters Group) and also got in touch with another perennial partner, Pat Perini, executive producer for national programming at public television station KERA-TV in Dallas. (You need a local "sponsor" station, within the decentralized PBS family, to give you access to the airwaves and to champion your cause with the national PBS apparatus which coordinates overall schedules.)

In several of our "documentary" programs (featuring on-camera interviews at three or four companies), we'd used footage from a "lecture" I'd given to tie the cases together. We decided to include such a lecture in the new show, too. Though the various activities involved in creating the show went on from November 1989 to March 1991, the two-day lecture/"shoot" in Dallas constituted a stand-alone event—the coming together of a one-of-a-kind "organization" to perform a specific task.

Numerous "organizations" contributed to what I'll call the Dallas Organization. Bits of very large outfits (Federal Express) and dozens of "freelancers" (from the local film-production "community") joined together. The "quarterback"—"leader"? "boss"?— was independent producer Ed Fouhy, who heads the tiny Concord Communications Group, based in Washington, D.C. He's been, among other things, a senior executive at CBS News, senior producer for the *CBS Evening News*, and CBS News Saigon bureau chief.

The organization Fouhy "commanded" in Dallas turned out a superb "product." That it did so defies *all* traditional managerial wisdom. Though everyone had some word-of-mouth connection with someone else, most people did not know many of the others who descended upon Dallas. No one knew everyone. Yet "they" put together a well-oiled production—with only two tries to get it right, and with lots of Video Publishing House's reputation, as well as capital (about $125,000 for the event) on the line.

In short, superb quality—emanating from a highly complex, sophisticated "organization"—can be created on the spur of the moment. (True, months of intermittent planning were involved, but the team did not meet until less than half a day before the Super Bowl). The reason for this chapter's gory details: Such ways of gathering people/bits of organizations together to get something done are becoming more and more commonplace—in the world of automobiles, computers, software, chemicals, and air-powered grinding tools, as well as films and recordings.

Language

As you'll see—and, indeed, as we are all quickly coming to see—words I've used like "quarterback," "boss," and "command" are very slippery indeed (and, like "organization," need those quotation marks). Video Publishing House production manager Steve Fanizza and I "worked for" Fouhy in Dallas. Fouhy called the shots. Yet he is under contract to Video Publishing House—he clearly (?) "works for" them. And The Tom Peters Group has final say on most matters connected with "our" "products," should it ever come to a shoving match. (It has on rare occasions.) "Who's in charge" and "who reports to whom," then, (1) depends on the occasion and (2) is a meaningless, even destructive, idea—since working as equal partners is the only way that the talent of experts can be corralled to create more than the sum of the parts. Oy vey!

THE "CAST"

In the end, forget all the "variables" except one: An organization is people. We all agree. The "people dimension" is always supreme. But it's more so here, if that's possible. Strangers from all over must show up at the exact moment; go directly to their battle stations; get on with their affairs with no muss or fuss (there's no slack time); and then perform as competent, individual professionals *and* as members of a well-oiled whole, or team. That's a tall order under any set of circumstances. It's a several-times-taller order when the players have no experience with one another, and less than a dozen hours to jell after first handshakes.

Who were the "personnel," or cast, of this two-performance drama in Dallas? And how were they connected?

Video Publishing House. As executive producers for the overall show, VPH is responsible for a variety of activities: conceiving the show; creating and overseeing the "network organization," which includes lining up appropriate personnel beyond their limited, on-board resources; arranging financing; and taking care of marketing and sales. Chief executive officer Von Polk was in Dallas to observe, cheerlead—and on several occasions make vital technical and content contributions. John Teegarden, director of programming from April 1990 through January of 1991, was responsible for day-to-day oversight of the show. In Dallas, production manager/stage manager Steve Fanizza worked in an unofficial/official capacity as "colleague" to Dallas Organization director Joe Cortina.

The Tom Peters Group. Peters (me) had been "intrigued" by the idea of time-based competition for quite a while, and jumped at Video Publishing House's suggestion that we do a "time show" together. Alison Peterson heads TPG Communications and was on the scene in Dallas.

KERA-TV. As the third member of the unofficial producing consortium, the Dallas PBS TV station's executive producer, Pat Perini, had overall responsibility for the show, and was present behind the scenes in Dallas. (Though full-time at KERA, she happens to live in Northern California—strange world, eh?) For the Dallas event, Perini was assisted by Barbara Sullivan, special events coordinator at the TV station.

Ed Fouhy, Concord Communications. Producer Fouhy was honcho in Dallas. VPH works with Ted Koppel's production company, Koppel Communications, on corporate films. Fouhy was recommended to VPH by Susan Mercandetti, a former ABC colleague of Fouhy's who's now with Koppel. (This is typical of the word-of-mouth tangle that marks every node in this organization.)

Joe Cortina. Based in Northern Virginia, free-lancer Cortina had worked as an assistant director for Fouhy in 1986 and spent most of the '80s at NBC. Fouhy tapped Joe Cortina to direct the taping of the lecture. (He was not otherwise involved with the show.)

The Green Line Group. The Boston, Massachusetts, firm is master of an odd specialty called "crew brokerage services"—i.e., pulling together members of television production's free-lance community. Green Line, under contract to Video Publishing House, hired the lion's share of the Dallas show players. The twisted connection: Peggy Rohlfing, a former VPH producer, had come across Green Line in 1988 and later hired it to do "crew brokerage" for a videotaped lecture I gave in Boston. (A Boston-based firm is considered best at tapping into the Dallas "network"? Go figure.)

Jon Epstein. The Durham, New Hampshire, free-lancer was technical director for the lecture. Epstein, after working for public television and NBC, started free-lancing in 1987. Third "in command" on-site (after Fouhy and Cortina), he had not known any other crew members prior to January 10. None of the Dallas Organization's big cheeses—Fouhy, Cortina, Epstein— had known any of the "workers" before this make-or-break event.

Bob Selby. Lighting director Selby, heads Fiat Lux, a Fort Worth, Texas, company. His specialty is lighting for multi-camera shoots. A 35-year industry veteran, he is a "living legend" according to several other crew members; his presence, we were told, certified this event as a "big deal." Selby had worked "with" ("for"?—language again) the Green Line Group from time to time since 1987.

Producers Mobile Service. "The truck," which contains several million dollars' worth of the high-tech "brains" required to coordinate a live, multi-camera shoot, came from Producers Mobile Service, Inc.—of St. Louis, Missouri. Producers Mobile's Don Geist was operations manager for the Dallas shoot; Green Line got word of him through a control-truck broker in King of Prussia, Pennsylvania. Mike Copeland, working out of Nashville, Tennessee, was tagged by Geist as Engineer in charge of the truck. Free-lancer John Fekas, audio-video engineer, also worked with Producers Mobile Service on this event. (He lives in Lawrence, Kansas.)

The Dallas Free-lance Community. The rest of the gang were from the Dallas area. Eric Norberg ran Camera No. 1. He'd never worked with Fouhy or Cortina, but knew the rest of the crew, who spoke highly of his fairness and ability to pull effective crews together. Among the other local players: Dave Elendt ran Camera No. 2; he worked for ABC and other organizations before moving to Dallas in 1984. Elendt knew almost everyone on the shoot. Chris Childs, who came to Dallas in 1989 and runs a camera for a local TV station's evening newscast, handled Camera No. 3; he knew most of the local crew members. Scott Maynard was honcho of Camera No. 4; he free-lances for CBS and ESPN. Maynard knew most of the locals. David McGill, Camera No. 5, works primarily on films (*Robocop I, Steel Magnolias, Dances with Wolves*) and knew few members of the crew. He had come to Green Line's attention through an equipment rental company. McGill's assistant for the Dallas affair, dolly grip Dan Clear, was another local free-lancer whose name Green Line got from the equipment rental company. (None of the cameramen had ever worked with Fouhy, Cortina, or Epstein.)

Kevin Spivey was in charge of audio. He works 200 shoots per year, mainly in sports, and manages Reunion Production Company. Spivey knew everyone except Fouhy, Cortina, and one or two others. Colin Deford was Spivey's assistant for the event; he's new to the business, and his mentors in the Dallas area include Spivey and first cameraman Eric Norberg. Randy Patrick was video operator; he's been in the business for 22 years and has run his own consulting and engineering company since 1984. Jay Hamlin was videotape operator. Steve Tennison, a colleague of Hamlin's, also operated a videotape machine; he usually works as a slo-mo replay operator on live sporting events for CBS. Brian Harbert and Pat Hawks, "cable pullers" for Scott Maynard and David McGill, respectively, are another pair of Dallas free-lancers. Dallas-based makeup artist Elaine Lauber has plied her trade for 15 years.

THE EVENT TAKES SHAPE

Work on the overall show got under way in early June 1990 when Fouhy signed a contract with Video Publishing House. In mid-August 1990, the dates for the lecture, January 10 and 11, 1991, were locked in. In October, Fouhy hired Joe Cortina to direct it. Fouhy and KERA's Sullivan visited three possible sites in Dallas, and chose the Grand Kempinski Hotel. Sullivan also was at work peddling hundreds of tickets for the event—which would take place before a "live" audience.

On November 20 (seven weeks before the event), Video Publishing House hired Green Line to make arrangements for the technical director, lighting director and lighting crew, mobile unit, and camera crews. The next day, Green Line reserved a Producers Mobile truck (and Don Geist) and invited Jon Epstein to be technical director and Bob Selby to be lighting director. (Green Line also asked Selby to start assembling the lighting crew.) On December 11, Video Publishing House's Teegarden flew to Dallas from Chicago and met with Cortina and lighting director Selby. Overall requirements were locked in—number of cameras, type of cameras, etc.

As Christmas approached, Cortina wrapped up set design. Teegarden worked with Green Line on set logistics—getting the right kind of drapes, carpeting, podium, and the like. Don Geist of Producers Mobile worked with the hotel on security, blocking off parking areas for the truck and coping with power-supply needs. He also sent a detailed description of the truck's interior to director Cortina, since this would be Cortina's never-seen-before control room for the affair. Green Line also began final crew assembly, depending upon Dallas cameraman Eric Norberg for most local contacts. (Norberg assembled the crew around the first of the year—with the last recruit signing up on January 4, six days before D-Day.)

NOW YOU SEE IT, NOW YOU DON'T

On Thursday, January 9, with 24 hours until "showtime," the members of the Dallas Organization began to gather. The 48-foot-long Producers Mobile truck raced to Dallas after finishing a live basketball game for ESPN in Norman, Oklahoma. At 10:00 a.m. Video Publishing House's Fanizza arrived from Chicago. Later that afternoon, Cortina showed up (his second visit, following the original site check). Fouhy and I, after finishing the last documentary shooting at CNN, got in at 9:00 p.m.

But the crew was still not "organized" by textbook standards. Technical director Jon Epstein would be working on the night of the ninth as technical director for a Celtics game—in *Boston*. Dolly grip Dan Clear and makeup artist Elaine Lauber were finishing a seven-day shoot for an Italian/French television miniseries. Videotape operator Steve Tennison and camera operators Dave Elendt and Scott Maynard were actually at the Grand Kempinski, completing a five-day industrial video production for BeautiControl Cosmetics. Camera operator (and crew assembler) Eric Norberg was also working with BeautiControl—though on the evening of January 9 he shunted off to act as technical director for the live televising of a Southern Methodist University basketball game. Camera operator Chris Childs ran a handheld camera for the same SMU game; utility Brian Herbert and videotape operator Jay Hamlin also worked the game. Videotape operator Randy Patrick was video operator for the five-camera shoot of the Dallas Mavericks' basketball game on the evening of the ninth.

On schedule, at 8:30 a.m. on January 10, Freeman Decorating Company appeared at the Kempinski's Malachite Room and began installing the special drapes, carpeting, and podium. Crew Call was 9:00 a.m. Now, for the first time ever, and next-to-last time ever, the "organization" became an Organization—capitalized, without quotes. Fouhy, Cortina, Fanizza, and most of the others set to work in earnest. (Did any one person have even a single sheet of paper with the phone numbers of all the players who had to be there? I doubt it. Yet the expectation was that everyone would show up—and they did.)

Cortina walked the group through the next 24 hours, and members went to their tasks as experienced, independent professionals. There was no time for fooling around, and, in the words of one crew member, "no room for prima donnas. . . . Everyone does a full share of dirty work"—as well as getting ready to do the professional/artistic part of his or her job.

At 9:45, Dan Clear arrived with his dolly and 40-foot track and began setting it up and leveling it. Selby and his crew began configuring the lighting. At noon, KERA's Sullivan arrived and began making final audience arrangements. Technical director Jon Epstein finally arrived at 1:30 p.m. (His 6:30 a.m. flight from Boston had been delayed due to a substitution of aircraft, a DC-9 for a DC-10, which necessitated a refueling stop in Virginia; the DC-10 had been pulled off the line and remanded to the government to fly troops to Saudi Arabia.) At 4:00 p.m. on the 10th, I arrived at the Kempinski for the first, last, and only rehearsal (not a full run-through, but a 25-minute walk around to set camera angles, test audio equipment, etc.). At 4:30, makeup artist Elaine Lauber appeared as scheduled and began to set up.

At 7:30, the shoot began. The Dallas Organization was in place, each of the professionals doing his or her bit. The filming was live, with no halts or retakes (other than the single repeat performance the next morning). Problems had to be dealt with "real-time." There were a couple: A live band began playing directly above the Malachite Room at one point. Calming it down became a big deal, with the Grand Kempinski's manager caught squarely in the middle between two customers. Also, the air-conditioning broke down—the "talent" (yours truly) quickly became drenched with unattractive sweat and the audience started getting antsy.

The all-clear sounded at 10:00 p.m. The crew tidied up. KERA's vice president of marketing and corporate development, Don Boswell, hosted a "thank you" reception for the show's underwriters in the hotel. Then several of us met with Fouhy to discuss what had gone on, and what needed to be revised for the next morning. (Which meant a 3:00 a.m. wake-up call for me—to start adjusting material to fill holes, etc. Video Publishing House's Polk had "commanded" a rather major revision.)

Crew call for round two, on January 11th, was at 7:00 a.m. At 9:45 a.m., the second performance began. It was all over at noon. No more Dallas Organization! Several members raced off for a 1:00 p.m. crew call at the Reunion Arena in Dallas, to begin setting up for that evening's Dallas Mavericks game. The Producers Mobile truck hustled off to Jackson, Mississippi, to cover a Saturday night basketball game for Black Entertainment Television. Fouhy and Cortina immediately headed home. So did Jon Epstein—or rather, he tried. His flight to Boston was canceled because of snow, which put him in a panic since he was scheduled to act as technical director for a basketball game there on Saturday morning. (Fortunately for him, the snow also scotched the game.)

CONCLUSION: A FULL-FLEDGED, ACCOUNTABLE ENTERPRISE

The Dallas Organization had a clear task and a clear goal—which it accomplished with élan. It had a clear organizational structure, despite the absence of "charts and boxes" on any piece of paper. And there was a scheme: Fouhy and Epstein were effusive in their praise for Cortina's meticulous planning of camera locations, angles, etc. The Dallas Organization also had a "culture"—as much as IBM or Procter & Gamble does. That culture (of "excellence"? "professionalism"?) largely grew from direct or indirect word-of-mouth reputations—each of which would be added to or subtracted from in the course of the 36 hours of the organization's existence.

To underscore the "reality" of the Dallas Organization, I've evaluated it according to McKinsey's 7-S Framework, mentioned above. The results (see next page) simply reveal that this apparently ephemeral "organization" was, in its own fashion, as robust as that found on any Navy aircraft carrier.

There's no doubt that the leaders made a difference. Researcher Shirley Robson talked to virtually all of the participants after the fact, bit players and stars. Several commended the absence of "Monday morning quarterbacking." There was also esprit de corps and recognition. One crew member recalled "a lot of 'atta boys!' from Cortina in the headsets." Cameraman Scott Maynard observed that "Ed Fouhy came out and shook my hand. He told me I did a good job and mentioned specific shots. That sort of thing really helps." Lighting director Selby said director Cortina "had a really good sense of humor. He puts everyone in a good mood." Audio chief Kevin Spivey summed it up: "The producer and director jelled well with the crew. They knew what they were doing. They knew what they wanted. It was a professional production."

Any number of "intangibles" were also important. "I like to use 'sporting' guys on multi-camera shoots," head camera operator Eric Norberg commented. "They're used to flying without a net, used to doing it right the first time." Furthermore, everyone saw how his/her job contributed in an important way to a first-class product—as much as "lifetime" line workers do at Honda.

We shouldn't neglect the uncertainties and difficulties—e.g., the plane switch that nearly kept the technical director from getting to the site; little irritants such as too much shine on a brass bar that ran around the walls of the room; the band pounding away overhead during the first go-around. A bushel of similar "problems" had to be sorted out in short order, with no time to debate whose dignity the fix was above or beneath. Moreover, the chiefs had to create a full-blown, highly coordinated team in a flash—there was no second chance other than that second shoot. They had to initiate, foster, and nurture an "organization culture" within 10½ hours of crew call on the 10th.

Here, more systematically, are a few of the features that made the Dallas Organization work:

- An extensive word-of-mouth network. Each player was well known to somebody(s), even though few, especially the "bosses," had known many others before the event.

- A commitment to professionalism and excellence on everyone's part.

- Enough people who had known one other to make this far from a random get-together. The Dallas-based free lancers had, in various combinations, worked together before. (A number had worked on my shows before—not a small point, since I am an animated lecturer and difficult to "cover.")

7-S Analysis of the Dallas Organization

7-S Variable	Dallas Manifestation
Superordinate Goal	Technically and artistically "perfect" production (Video Publishing House–Fouhy as drivers). Also: "It has to work because there's no second chance."
Strategy	Fouhy, Cortina, and Teegarden had clear plans (largely unwritten), and Fouhy knew precisely how Dallas event fit into the overall scheme.
Structure	Fouhy and Cortina were the ship's cocaptains. There was no formal organization chart, but in the Japanese sense, everyone knew his or her place—exactly.
Systems	Nothing was written or formal. Yet everyone understood exactly how his or her bit fit with the rest—though first-rate quarterbacks were needed to add cohesiveness (*see* superordinate goal, strategy, and style).
Skills	All the players—star or bit—knew what they were about; the "networkers" had made certain that individual skills were superb.
Staff	The recruiting process was critical—though hardly reducible to rules. "Word-of-mouth" was everything. Accountability was sky-high.
Style	"Professionalism" marked every aspect of the operation. "Loose-yet-tight" was crucial—that is, loose camaraderie and personal innovativeness were blended with buttoned-down, no-nonsense purposefulness.

- <u>Effective leadership</u>. Fouhy and Cortina had worked together and knew each other's style—and provided an overall "style" (supportive yet professional) which helped the group mesh instantly.

- <u>Leader reputation</u>. This group was motivated in part by the renown of its leaders, even though few of the players had previously met them.

- <u>Simultaneous centralization and decentralization</u>. A theme from CNN and UPRR is repeated here: Cortina and Fouhy were clearly "in charge," and the product was an "orchestral whole." Yet each team member was highly autonomous—there were no backups—and had no one breathing over his or her shoulder.

- <u>Experience with ambiguity</u>. Each member of the crew had been through this sort of coming together hundreds of times. (There is such a thing as "experience with ambiguity." Recall, at CNN, that new hires from big-network TV often fail, while all-news radio and wire-service veterans tend to handle the messiness with ease.) You wouldn't dare try and pull something like this off with a group whose life's work had been at General Motors!

- <u>An appreciation for everyone else's job</u>. There were no minor roles, though some jobs were certainly "more important" than others. Everyone had to do his or her task in a first-class fashion—this is the classic illustration of the weakest brick's ability to bring down the entire edifice. An understanding of the "whole," not normally found on the front line in industrial America, also meant that all pitched in automatically to support or cover for one another. (Shades of Imagination.)

- <u>Sky-high accountability</u>. Though no formal "performance evalua-tions" were issued, there was instant/constant feedback. These pros know whether things are going well or not, and why. Moreover, each member was being "evaluated" by every other member informally—as a reliable or less-than-reliable "member of the community." The quality of the bread on tomor-row's table would be determined by maintenance, enhancement, or degradation of the reputation of people whose economic life depends exclu-sively upon word of mouth. (Can you imagine the cost to reputation of not showing up at crew call, or even showing up 15 minutes late?)

- <u>The motivation of no second chance</u>. Such "brittle systems," as I call them, work in part because they have to. There's little backbiting, for example, because there's no time for it.

- <u>A "learning organization."</u> Since this "organization" lived so briefly, it sounds absurd to speak about "learning." Think again: Each member of the organization is an independent professional, perpetually hot to make himself or herself stand out a little more in a very competitive environment. There's a lot of motivation to learn! And an opportunity: Each such event brings a novel configuration together and adds up to exposure to new blood, new ideas, and new techniques. For example, I heard several crew members buzzing

about the way audio man Kevin Spivey attached a pair of wireless micro-
phones to my suit and shirt, to allow me maximum mobility. Others picked up
tips from Shelby, Geist, and Cortina. The overall "network's" learning—and
thence market value—increased in part precisely because of the transient
nature of the affair. (I'm no exception. The one-shot nature of the Dallas
lecture forced me to digest an enormous amount of material in short order—
which spurred me to write the Learning to Hustle section of this book.)

13

Projects and Professional
Service Firms III: Transformation

Aha! Members of the Dallas Organization have "experience with ambiguity." You'd dare not try such shenanigans with GM vets, I just cautioned. So, is transformation to these freewheeling ways possible?

CNN did it from the start. So too David Kelley, EDS, et al. True, the Union Pacific and, especially, Titeflex have taken some pretty long strides toward "projectizing"; but they're still a long way from CNN's world.

Enter Oticon! Founded in 1904, the Danish hearing-aid manufacturer Oticon was No. 1 in the world in 1979. However, though widely admired, the company "had become self-satisfied and lost its flexibility," according to president Lars Kolind. Market share plummeted, and by 1987 Oticon was losing money.

Coming aboard in 1988, Kolind hacked away, in a manner reminiscent of Mike Walsh's first years at Union Pacific. By the end of 1989, the company was solidly in the black. Still, as Kolind saw it, Oticon was far from energetic enough to regain its premier position.

KOLIND TRIES SPAGHETTI

"On New Year's Day 1990," Kolind told us, "I sat down and tried to think the unthinkable: a vision for the company of tomorrow"—a tomorrow that would require dramatically improving all aspects of marketing, getting more creative, and doing things faster.

His solution: a complete overhaul of the organization, aimed at "shaping jobs to fit the person instead of the other way around. Each person would be given more functions and a 'job' would be developed by the individual's accumulating a portfolio of functions." A research and development engineer, for example, "should be able to do sales or even answer the phones. He gets a total view of what's going on, and ends up designing better microprocessors if he knows the big picture."

To get there from here meant going from a "command structure" to a "problem-solving structure." In short, functional departments were abolished, and a project-based free-for-all took their place. Kolind tagged it a "spaghetti organization." In late 1991, when we talked with him, it covered all 130 people at headquarters and included administrative activities, R&D, sales, and marketing; some overtures had been made in manufacturing (see below).

The greatest transformation has taken place in R&D, which has quickly shifted from a "new products for the sake of new products" attitude to a much stronger market orientation—Kolind's chief aim all along. With no R&D department, Kolind reported to us, former staffers are now much more willing to take an expanded view of their role.

The basic idea: Everyone is responsible for filling his or her own days with useful projects. "If people don't have anything to do," Kolind said, "they need to find something—or we don't need them." Self-responsibility, then, is the new name of the new game. "The understanding is that you must complete projects you have accepted," said Kolind. "Initially we thought we'd have a complex computer system to keep track of everything, but it was going to cost so much money that we decided to muddle through. Now we can see that we probably don't need it. The individual employee keeps track of his projects himself. If you want to know what he's involved in, ask him." (It has been easier to projectize some jobs than others. "The receptionist still really just answers the telephone," Kolind admitted. "We haven't worked that one out yet.")

Roller Derbies and Shredder Wars

Physical changes were of great importance. The "traditional structures limited communication," Kolind asserted. "The offices and long corridors created emotional barriers. We took down the walls and liberated everyone from having to sit in the same space day in and day out." Now all members of the headquarters contingent gather where they wish to work with whomever on their self-selected projects. "The 'mobile office' means that the R&D engineer who likes marketing can join the marketers, and the same for the administration person interested in sales," Kolind said. "You can't get the process started if the employee can't move to see how things work in other groups."

Each workstation (desk!) in the giant, undivided space is identical. No workstations are assigned. Instead, employees roll their personal "caddies" to the spot where they'll work for the day. These mobile carts contain 10 or so files pertinent to their current project and whatever else they can squeeze in—a picture of the children, the dog, etc. If you're away on a long business trip, you stow your caddy in a storage area.

The paperwork setup was also radically revised to support the new structure. In the mailroom, for example, all incoming material is scanned each morning by an expensive new system, especially created for Oticon by Hewlett-Packard. The originals go to pigeonholes from which the addressees can retrieve them. After something is read it's thrown away—the contents are already stored in the computer's memory.

Employees stand at counters—by design, there are no nearby chairs—to go through their mail. There's also an obtrusive paper-shredding machine at the entrance to the mailroom. It's connected to a transparent chute which passes through the company cafeteria directly below. Each morning, a snowfall of paper can be seen floating past.

Behind the antipaper campaign is the idea that the more paper you accumulate, the harder it is to move around, and the less open you are to taking on new projects. Kolind estimated that the new scheme has reduced circulating paper by 80 percent. Wastepaper baskets are objects non gratae—using the shredder is "in."

Kolind added that his own style has changed dramatically. Communication is much faster. There are no bosses' secretaries to slow things down. (Secretaries, like everyone else, choose projects to support—see below.) Kolind estimated that he has "two to five times as many conversations per day as before." But, he quickly added, "I seldom tell anyone to do anything. People take action themselves. If someone comes to me with a problem or an idea, I ask him what he wants to do. Usually I tell him, 'Decide for yourself.' "

THE PROJECT PROCESS

There is a formal "computer job offer board." Switch on any terminal (each workstation has one) and use the "Jobs" icon to scroll through different projects "on offer." You'll also find the project leader's name, a description of the job with a list of some of the tasks the leader thinks will be involved, and the project's expected duration. Usually, though, project leaders informally search out key people for their tasks. And vice versa: If a "secretary," for example, wants to tackle a marketing project, then she or he is wisest to informally chat up the appropriate project leader. Theoretically, a person could write an application, but, said Kolind, "It's so much easier just to walk across the room and ask."

Some projects are initiated by a member of top management, who then appoints a project leader. But any employee can propose a project. If the proposal gets a green light from one of five members of top management (orally, no paper), then that employee may become project chief and organize the task.

Anyone can be a project leader. In fact, Kolind insisted that he doesn't know how many project leaders there are. The most dynamic staff members wear many hats, he said—at the same time heading one project, acting as sub-project leader on another, working as a team member on a third.

Project leadership also tends to shift over time. A technical leader may be more active in the initial stages of a new-product effort; later a marketing or sales member may come to the fore.

Project leaders have official decision-making authority, but rarely use it. Confrontation, especially in the consensually oriented Danish culture, is rare. Project leaders also have financial responsibility for their jobs, and spending authorities are liberal. Individuals make their own assessments of what makes sense. Some project leaders we talked with are comfortable making expenditures of, say, 10,000 Danish krones, while secretaries seemed at ease spending only a few hundred krones. If a project leader feels like it, he can clear an expenditure with Kolind or another member of top management.

Manufacturing is physically separate from the rest of Oticon. Nonetheless, production boss Svenning Thomsen is enthusiastic about the projectization of the head office—and is moving toward a somewhat similar structure in manufacturing. While there was no formal project scheme in manufacturing when we talked, all production activities had been molded around nine-person groups. Members routinely move from one group to another—monthly shifts are common. The aim (consistent with a fast-changing market) is to keep "production as flexible as possible," Thomsen told us, adding that employee transfers from team to team are voluntary and, contrary to conventional wisdom, "very few choose to stay in the same team for a long time."

A DAY IN THE LIFE OF INGE CHRISTOPHERSEN

Consider 37-year-old Inge Christophersen, who's been a secretary at Oticon for 15 years. "I used to say I was a secretary," she told us, "but now I suppose I'm more like an 'octopus.'" (The Danish colloquialism roughly translates as "jill-of-all-trades.") Christophersen said she "used to work for fixed people, doing only a limited number of things. Now I work for a lot of people." She added that she has "more responsibility. I take care of more things. When I worked for one boss, I only saw certain types of documents. Now I work for a project leader in the legal department, for example. That can be exciting. I do 'investigative' jobs for him, not just typing." She's also begun to teach advanced word processing—on her own initiative.

Christophersen admitted that when the new scheme was introduced a year and a half ago, "it was a shock. Some people thought 'Not on your life.' About half were scared of using computers. But there's no way back now, and no one would want to go back to the old way."

In fact, the adjustment hasn't been all that traumatic. Asked how she works with multiple bosses, Christophersen nonchalantly replied, "They tell me when they need the job done and I tell them whether I can manage it. It's my obligation to keep the jobs organized, and get done what I promised on time.

"People talk much more to each other," Christophersen went on, explaining benefits of the new system. "Different groups get to know each other better." And surprisingly, more "talk" has been accompanied by less "gossip." Greater openness and quicker communication mean less sniping, less office politics.

If problems do arise in this departmentless society, there is a scheme to sort them out. Each employee has an officially designated leader "who looks after you," Christophersen told us. "You may not work under him normally, but you can go to him if you have an office or personal problem."

Is the sky the limit? To listen to Christophersen, you'd think so. Asked if she planned to try other activities, she immediately replied, "I'd like to do something in advertising. In fact, I'm looking out for a project I can join."

The shift to projects has also changed the structure of Christophersen's typical day. Part of this was due to the introduction of flex-time when the organization structure was revised. But that's not all. Formal coffee breaks have disappeared, Christophersen told us. People take breaks now "when it makes sense." So, too, lunch: "You take your lunch when you finish a piece of work. Before, you'd fit work around lunch." She added that most people tend to go to lunch with project groups now, rather than with those of "the same rank or from the same [former] department."

When she gets a free moment, Christophersen usually works on new tasks which she hopes eventually will become project assignments. At the end of the day, everything on her desk-for-the-day goes into her personal file caddy. Wastepaper is tossed into the mail-room shredder on the way out. (To be sure, there are still "unprojectized" chores that are less than scintillating. The 12-person secretarial contingent does the new scheme's mail scanning on a rotational basis. Christophersen said that it's "boring work" which eats up an entire morning when her turn comes.)

A DAY IN THE LIFE OF SOREN HOLST

Thirty-year-old Soren Holst, trained as an economist, specialized in logistics during his first three years at Oticon. He bubbled about an expanded view of life in the spaghetti organization. "Logistics planning is still my main current project," he told us, "but I'm also a sub-project leader on an engineering part of a large R&D project aimed at developing a new product for a narrow customer segment. I've always been interested in mechanical engineering, but I ended up as an economist. So I'm really excited by this chance to get close to the subject again. I don't know as much as the engineers, but I look at a problem and ask, 'Why can't we do it this way?' because I don't know any better. And the engineers in my group say, 'Well . . . ' but then they think about it again. I'm the one who asks the stupid questions!"

As to the business of cobbling project teams together, Holst acknowledged that there is "competition among project leaders for the best staff. I know who I want for a particular project, and I go out and try to get them interested when the time is right." And it can cause problems. "The original staff at Oticon were not recruited for this type organization," Holst said, "so there are people who have trouble with project management skills." Overall, though, he added, "the pulse has quickened. People talk with each other more now. When a customer has a question, we get the right answer faster."

All in all, the transition at Oticon to a radically new form of organization has been smoother than almost anyone would have imagined. People have taken a shine to this crazy organization—economist, engineer, manufacturer, and secretary alike. The whole report card isn't in by any means at this writing, but first signs are encouraging indeed. Oticon, which de facto reinvents itself each morning, comes a lot closer to CNN or the Dallas Organization model than I would have thought possible.

14

Projects and Professional Service Firms IV: On the Way to Projects for All

Some firms, like EDS, CNN, and Imagination, were born to projects for all. Some, like Oticon, have almost completed the transformation to projects. And some, like Ingersoll-Rand and the Union Pacific Railroad, are just gearing up.

In fact, even the latter two are far ahead of the pack. And from the likes of them, in the midst of the shift, we can learn some "musts" for everyone who has the nerve to embark on such a journey.

— You *must* understand the difference between projects and committees.

— You *must* understand the importance of effective project management and effective project managers.

— You *must* get the accounting right.

— You *must* get started now.

— You *must* reconsider the course of a "career."

DON'T LET PROJECT TEAMS BECOME COMMITTEES

Project structures aren't new. "Task forces" were the rage for a while. The matrix structure was an effort to create more fluid, responsive enterprises—but committee-itis and a lack of accountability caused it to misfire. The project structure's key success variables turn out to be *outward focus, autonomy/accountability*, and *dependence*. The McKinsey project team, with just three people, is *focused on the customer;* it's *unmistakably accountable*; and, thanks to the nature and intensity of the work, *each team member depends upon the others* for personal and company success. That's no committee!

Here are a baker's dozen of must-do's to keep you on the straight and narrow:

● Set goals/deadlines for key subsystem tests. Committees *deliberate*. Project teams *do*. Successful project teams are characterized by a clear goal—though the path from here to there is not specified, to induce creativity. Also, the most effective teams set three or four inescapable due dates for subsystem technical tests/market tests/experiments and adhere to them religiously—e.g., McKinsey's "progress reviews" with senior client personnel.

● Keep team members' destiny in the hands of the project leader. The project boss, rather than a functional boss (if there is one), has primary responsibility for evaluating team members—*period*.

● Aim for full-time assignment to the team. Highly committed members are the hallmark of effective project teams. High commitment doesn't come in fifths or thirds. Therefore, assignment of key members must be full-time for anything but the most routine projects. That's the Project Lightning story from Ingersoll-Rand, and McKinsey's story on all projects. (Though the Union Pacific and Oticon violate this rule regularly, I would argue that they should use full-time member assignment more and more as time goes on.)

● Give members authority to commit their functions. Assuming that the remnants of a functional structure still exist (I hope an increasingly bad assumption), members must be able to commit substantial resources from their function without second-guessing from higher-ups. Top management must establish—and enforce—this "rule" from the start. If the ability to commit your home function is conditional, then you've got a committee. (This doesn't mean that the team's functional member from engineering, say, shouldn't take counsel with his colleagues in engineering. It does mean that if he does commit engineering's support, no chief in engineering should—or should be able to—countermand him the next day.)

● Allot space so that team members can "live" together. The most effective project teams are sequestered away from headquarters. Team camaraderie and commitment are to a surprising extent a function of hanging out together—away from the everyday affairs. At the very least, facilities should be flexibly configured, à la Oticon, so that all project teams—minor as well as major—can work in the same place (much more on this—see Chapter 27).

- <u>Remember the social element</u>. High spirits within a project team are not accidental. Successful team leaders facilitate what psychologists call "bonding": "signing up" ceremonies upon joining the team, frequent (at least weekly) milestone celebrations, humorous awards for successes and setbacks alike. (Remember the barbecue factor at Ingersoll-Rand.)

- <u>Allow outsiders in</u>. Make that: *Beg* outsiders to join up early. Product development teams, for instance, are useless unless outsiders participate wholeheartedly. Principal vendors, distributors, and "lead" (future test-site) customers should be full-blown members—from the start. Outsiders not only contribute directly, but also add authenticity and enhance the team's sense of distinctiveness, urgency, and task commitment.

- <u>Construct self-contained systems</u>. The engaged team needs its own workstations, local area network, database, etc. This may mean duplication of equipment or support, and if you go too far down this path excessive isolation creates problems and when the project has to be integrated back into the rest of the firm. But first and foremost, you're trying to create an "it's up to us and we've got the wherewithal" context for the team.

- <u>Let teams pick their own leaders</u>. A self-designated champion, blessed by management, may get things under way. But the most successful project teams often select—and shift—their own leaders, or even choose to be officially leaderless. You should expect leadership changes over the course of a project, as one role and then another dominates a particular stage (in the case of new products: engineering now, manufacturing later, distribution later still).

- <u>Let teams spend/approve their own travel, etc</u>. Spending authority need not be limitless (though McKinsey and EDS do just fine without strict rules), but team members must, for example, be able to visit a key customer, dealer, or competitor at the drop of a hat, or buy a new workstation, or outfit a small lab on their own authority. (Inability to approve a few hundred bucks is far more annoying—and enervating—than inability to approve millions, which no sensible person expects.)

- <u>Honor project leadership skills</u>. Projects become "the way we get things done around here." Horizontal (multifunction) project leadership skills therefore become the most cherished in the firm, rewarded by applause, dollars, and promotion.

- <u>Honor project membership skills</u>. Good team-member skills (e.g., how well you support teammates), for junior participants, are also cherished and rewarded.

• Make careers a string of projects. A career in the "project-minded company" is a string of multifunction tasks—i.e., projects. Success equals project success, no more, no less.

The list as a whole is daunting. Can you realistically leap all 13 hurdles? Review the professional service firm cases. Each one comes close to a "straight A" report card. That, in fact, is one reason I've spent so much time on the professional service firm model. These traits are musts, not just nice-to-do's. Professional service firms, which live or die by project effectiveness, understand that. The rest of us must learn.

Just How "Far Out" Is the New Way?

Q: Name something that involves an understanding of geometry, spatial relations, algebra, manual dexterity, strategic planning, and allotment of resources.

A: Making a dress.

Q: Name something that involves many chemical processes, arithmetic, timing, aeration, biology, and behavior of materials.

A: Following a recipe.

Q: Name something that involves politics, economics, kinesiology, game strategy, psychology, and sociology.

A: Baseball.

RICHARD SAUL WURMAN
Follow the Yellow Brick Road

Self-managed teams. Scheduling. Budgeting. Quality control. Projects. These are the new worker's daily fare. But such activities have long been the almost exclusive province of the senior and middle ranks. It's hardly surprising, then, that many execs are asking: *Is the worker up to the challenge?* To understand why in 9 cases out of 10—as at Titeflex and UPRR—the answer is a resounding "yes," just look at life *off* the job. "Managing" day-to-day affairs encompasses most big-business challenges.

• Long-term view. Corporate chiefs, not workers, are the ones who have a problem here. The chief may be a slave to the next quarter's earnings, but the average "real person" understands investment. For instance, workers routinely turn their wallets inside out to buy a house—and often undertake steep, 20-year tuition savings programs for their toddlers. (On the job, the story is the same. For example, workers usually comprehend better than their bosses the value of buying high-quality goods—rather than the cheapest goods—from vendors.)

- <u>Complex trade-offs</u>. Family life inevitably involves trade-offs. Take that $250 bonus to the store and buy some new clothes? Put the bucks aside for a long-desired vacation? Or toward a new car? The conflicting demands confronting self-managed work teams are surely no more complicated than such constant personal choices.

- <u>Self-management</u>. Experts say the shift to self-managed teams takes years of training and preparation. Really? What's a family but a "self-managed team"? Complex, "flex-time scheduling algorithms" for a seven-person work team pale beside the logistics of a family with two working adults (holding three jobs between them) and a pair of teenagers.

- <u>No job descriptions</u>. Some bosses doubt their employees can get through the day without job descriptions and a policy manual. So tell me, how many families have job descriptions and manuals? I'm all for "to do" lists, at work and at home. But face it, we juggle lots of balls and handle ambiguity and surprises at home (and in our community activities) without resorting to written guidance.

- <u>Budgets</u>. Some companies handle budgets well. Some don't. The same is true for self-managed teams. *And families*. But there's nothing alien about budgeting to the average 26-year-old worker, let alone the 36-year-old. The budget high-wire act is about the same for families and work groups. (If budgets are more complex at work, it's usually because accountants have obscured the obvious in a blizzard of technobabble aimed at enhancing their own status!)

- <u>Relationship management</u>. The bowling team is tied for first and you're the anchor. The showdown's Saturday, at the same time your 13-year-old starts his first youth soccer league game. *What's your call?*

"Investing in relationship development" is essential in fluid organizational configurations. Professional trainers insist it's an arcane art that only they can fathom. Hogwash! It's true that lots of people make lousy decisions about managing relationships (hence the high divorce rate), but nothing about the process requires a Ph.D. in clinical psychology.

- <u>Network management</u>. Yet another "complex," new-age, self-management must. But *new*? Many workers lead fund-raising drives for their club or children's school; chair First Presbyterian's building and grounds committee; coach Little League; lead a Brownie troop. That is, they can pass the basic test—and the advanced course—in "working in networks with 'outsiders' " who participate, not upon command, but only if they're motivated.

● <u>Dealing with vendors and customers</u>. Suppliers and customers are part of many modern work teams. And, ho hum, "special skills" must be acquired to handle the new setup. Huh? The average adult routinely works with numerous "outside vendors"—plumbers, dry cleaners, orthodontists, and occasionally realtors, contractors, and car dealers.

● <u>Projects</u>. Projects, rather than repetitive tasks, are now the basis for most value-added in business. But there's nothing mysterious about projects—except bosses' longstanding belief that workers can't deal with them. Consider a typical weekend: Blue-collar Sam and Sally do their fall planting, attack a complex home improvement project, and log several hours of community work as part of a team of volunteers spiffing up a local playground. See my point?

Add it up, and the ability of those Titeflex Teamsters to adapt to dramatic change in the course of one weekend is a lot more understandable.

UNDERSTANDING PROJECT MANAGEMENT

As "project," "network," "horizontal," and "organization" (in quotes) become the norm, "Who's in charge?" becomes a wrongheaded question. We will need to learn to work "in" teams "with" multiple, independent experts, often from multiple, independent companies. (Note the words: *in, with*.) Shades of the Dallas Organization—each will be dependent upon all others voluntarily giving their best.

Yet this does point to a paramount player in the future—the "project manager." Project management prowess is hardly an original idea. The stars at huge contracting firms such as Fluor or Bechtel are their several hundred project managers. Directors are movieland's real kings and queens. Or think back to your high school days: Remember that skinny kid with thick glasses who was a master at putting together proms and other major events? He or she was a project manager in the making.

Project management turns out mostly to be about mastering paradox:

● <u>Total ego/no ego</u>. Project managers must have phenomenal ego involvement. They are faced with a most daunting and complex task. To succeed, they must be consumed by it; the best "become" their projects, for 90 days or even a couple of years. But project managers must have no ego at all. They deal with numerous outsiders and insiders, whom they can hardly "command." (They neither have formal authority over them nor understand the details of the expertise these specialists provide.) Moreover, all "subordinates" must also have high ego involvement—which means the project manager must be expert at letting them take complete credit for what they've done *and* take a disproportionate share of the credit for the overall organization's success, no matter how "tiny" their bits.

• Autocrat/delegator. When the chips are down, the commander in chief (project manager) has got to issue the orders, fast—when the lights go out in the conference center as 5,000 people stream in. On the other hand, the project manager-as-superb-delegator will have turned "ownership" over to the lighting expert long ago—she or he will have gone to the battle station and made the fix before the chief ever hears about the problem.

• Leader/manager. Project managers, more than in traditional organizational settings, are as good as the commitment and energy of others whom they don't directly boss. That is, they must be "leaders"—visionaries, spark plugs, masters at transferring passion to others. On the other hand, "management," which seems to have been denigrated of late, implies being on top of the boring details. In fact, effective project bosses must match their passion for inspiring others (leading) with a passion for the grubby nuts and bolts of doing the job (managing).

• Ambiguity/perfection. The essence of any complex project (running the Olympics, developing a new product, putting on a high school prom) is ambiguity. "It" is always unfolding. The only "for sure" is the unexpected. The effective project manager must be able to handle almost complete ambiguity and uncertainty with élan—and a sense of humor. But she or he must have an equal zeal for perfection. Taking one last look—and then another *really* last look—to make sure the setup for tomorrow's filming is just right is a must.

• Oral/written. Most people are either "oral freaks" or "written freaks." Ho hum: Good project managers must be both. On the one hand, they're off base to insist upon an "audit trail" of memos to document every this, that, and the other. Dealing orally and on the run comes easily to effective project managers. But they must also be masters of the detailed plan and the daily checklist.

• Complexity/K.I.S.S. Nothing is more complex than dealing with a sophisticated, multiorganization project. The effective project manager must juggle, sometimes for years, hundreds of balls—of differing (and ever-changing) shapes, sizes, and colors. On the other hand, she or he must be a fanatic for the Keep It Simple, Stupid dogma, making sure that a few essential rules and values dominate the project—e.g., *nobody misses the 7:00 a.m. Monday meeting!*

• Big/small. Project managers must appreciate forests and trees equally. "Big picture" project managers will come a cropper over details. "God is in the details" project managers may miss the main game. Project managers must be able to see the relationship of the small to the big, the big to the small—and do so at every moment, simultaneously.

• <u>Impatient/patient</u>. On the one hand, project managers must be "action fanatics": Get on with it, try it, forget about yesterday's boo-boos and move on to tomorrow—those must be their watchwords. But at the same time, they're "running" a network and often dealing with hundreds of fragile (by definition) egos, cultures, and relationships at once. In fact, they're not "running" that network at all. The project manager is, at most, primus inter pares, or first among equals. In the 10-person, multifunction team (even if all are from the same corporation), the project manager (unlike the supervisor of 10 people all doing the same thing) is wholly dependent upon each player's unique skill and passion for improvement. Smart, dependent "leaders" spend lots and lots—and lots—of time on relationship-building and "networking"; it's exactly as important as perpetually pushing for action.

It's not clear that Mother Teresa could pass the test of all eight requirements laid out above! Yet there's no doubt that project management is the "coming" premier skill, and that something like this list of paradoxes lies at the heart of project management effectiveness. So how can firms start to emphasize the role of effective project management?

• <u>Train</u>. Project management is often a "taken for granted" skill, not even subject to special training. (McKinsey and EDS's "sink or swim" approach, marked by little or no formal training, only works if "the institution" has been living with nothing but projects for decades.)

• <u>Feature project management skills per se in all managerial performance evaluations</u>. (And emphasize project member skills in *everyone's* evaluation.)

• <u>Get junior people working on project teams, and "commanding" bits of such teams, as soon as possible</u>—e.g., from about day one, as EDS does.

• <u>Recruit with an eye toward project management skills</u>. The good news: Would-be project managers leave unmistakable footprints—in short, previous success at project management. When prospecting among college grads, the key is a history of putting together high school proms, a prizewinning yearbook, starting and sustaining a new association. Tomorrow's best project managers, by and large, were yesterday's best project managers.

"Heavyweight" Project Managers Bring Home the Bacon

Quantitative research on the importance of effective project management is skimpy, but there is some. In *Design Management Journal*'s Spring 1991 issue, Takahiro Fujimoto of the University of Tokyo describes a study of project management in the global automotive industry. His article, "Product Integrity and the Role of Designer-as-Integrator," reflects on 21 automotive product development organizations (17 from "volume producers," 4 from "high-end specialists"). He compares "modes of organization" that run from a strong functional orientation to a "heavyweight PM" (powerful, autonomous product/project manager). Success is measured in terms of a "total product quality index." In sum, Fujimoto found that "dependence on heavyweight product managers tended to result in higher total product quality index scores."

Heavyweight product/project managers by and large shared these traits: (1) responsibility from concept to market; (2) responsibility for coordination *and* concept creation/concept championing ("They go beyond being just neutral referees or passive conflict managers, sometimes aggressively advocating a particular approach"); (3) responsibility for costing and technical details, as well as design; (4) direct contact with customers, performance of independent market research "as a counterpoint" to research undertaken by formal, central market-research groups in the corporation; (5) one-on-one communication favored over "doing paperwork and convening formal meetings."

Fujimoto's research took place in the mid-1980s, when product quality, the study's principal dimension for evaluation, was considered *the* crucial variable in industry competitiveness. His follow-up research reveals that the "heavyweight PM" is just as important, perhaps more so, in coping with today's consuming time-to-market issue.

GETTING THE ACCOUNTING RIGHT

To stay on top of projects, you have to know what things cost at a very disaggregated level. Obvious? Yes! But for that to happen, traditional industrial costing systems, designed for functional organization structures, must undergo radical surgery.

Suppose, for example, your tooling center racks up costs of $1,000 in an accounting period; its work is divided equally ($500 each) between two products. Suppose Product A sells 200 units during the reporting period; Product B, 50 units. When it comes time to figure product profitability, tooling costs are clear: Product A (200 units) should get tagged with its $500 in tooling, which works out to $2.50 per unit. Product B (50 units) should absorb the other $500 (which works out to $10 per unit).

But that's probably not the answer your accounting system will spit out. Sad to say, most traditional systems would compute "250 total units, $1,000 in tooling charges, $4 per unit." Then when you assess product performance, these costing schemes end up assigning $800 in tooling costs to Product A (200 units times $4 per unit), and $200 to Product B (50 units, $4 per unit) instead of the "obvious" $500 each.

Such silliness is one of the hundreds of cases consultant-practitioner Peter Turney examines in his book, *Common Cents: The ABC Performance Breakthrough*. The "ABC," now being put to work in numerous firms, is activity-based costing. The revolutionary premise: Assign costs to "stuff" ("activities") according to what's actually done!

The pressing need for something like ABC arises partly from the tendency of ordinary accounting systems to spread all indirect costs across products based on the direct-labor hours the product requires. That was satisfactory in a bygone era, when mass production was the norm and direct labor was a firm's biggest expense. But now, direct labor seldom amounts to more than 15 percent of total costs. Typically undifferentiated "overhead"—order entry, design, marketing, inspection, tooling—now comprises the bulk of expenses.

Consider another of Turney's cases: Each batch (100 units) of Product C requires four direct-labor hours and needs to be inspected once. A batch of Product D (also 100 units) uses two direct-labor hours, but must be inspected twice. Suppose the cost of one inspection is $50. Product C clearly should get tagged with an inspection cost of $50 per batch of 100 units. Product D, with two inspections, has an inspection cost of $100 for every 100-unit batch. Don't bet on it.

Let's say you produce one batch of each product. You therefore incur $150 in inspection costs (3 inspections, one for Product C, 2 for Product D) and consume six direct-labor hours in all (4 for Product C, 2 for Product D). Conventional systems would usually calculate inspection costs at $25 per direct-labor hour used, and would end up assigning inspection costs of $100 to Product C (four direct-labor hours times $25 per hour) and $50 to Product D (two hours times $25). That is, Product C's unit cost of inspection, assigned on the basis of direct-labor hours, will be double, not half, Product D's. Reality be damned!

Turney leads us through true tales much more horrific than this. One situation involved a 25,000 percent costing error: A product with a calculated cost of $2 had a true cost of $500! To put it mildly, such a state of affairs will torpedo any wholesale shift to a project-based organization.

GETTING STARTED ON BECOMING A PROJECT MANIAC, NOW

Forget loyalty and conformity. We can't afford narrow-skill people. Go over the boss's head, find allies, find a corporate sponsor. . . . You've no future unless you add value, create projects.

ROSABETH MOSS KANTER
Interview with the author
May 1989

Suppose you're a midlevel accounting manager in a $100-million division of a bigger firm (one that, unlike ABB or Oticon, hasn't yet decimated the accounting department!). In the past your job description was narrow: Keep the books accurately and bird-dog those who are late or incomplete with their reports. Stay in your office, on call to answer instantly any queries from higher-ups.

Yes, you were—and will be—responsible for the accuracy and timeliness of vital financial numbers. Yet the task was inherently negative. It meant saying "no" more than "yes," being a cop more than a coach, destroying more than building. But no more—if you want to survive.

Imagine that your division has three factories, two distribution centers, a couple of sizable engineering groups, a marketing operation, and four sales branches. Your survival strategy begins with a wandering jag. Sally forth and meet with the leaders (or their deputies) in each of these dozen groups. Make an appointment or just drop by. Find out what's on their minds in general, and relative to your accounting group and financial reporting in particular. Your posture should be that of a humble servant: How can you and your gang help them? What new techniques being developed in your field might give them a leg up in theirs?

You'll likely spark the enthusiasm of one or two of the dozen or so other middle managers with whom you meet. Schedule a half-day briefing session with each, on his or her turf, and give them a pitch on "the revolution in activity-based accounting," or some such subject.

Visit with and talk to a half-dozen people before each session. That is, do your homework. Act like a consultant. Instead of playing cop or all-knowing expert, listen and learn what you can about the group; then tie it in to your expertise and your group's. On the day of presentation, give your spiel quickly. Reserve 75 percent of your time to answer questions and discuss cooperative efforts. Volunteer one of your staff (or perhaps yourself) to work part- or even full-time for a while on an experimental project—e.g., a major modification to a costing system to accompany the group's next product launch.

Your objective is to get to the point where you've got five or so pilot projects at various stages (assuming, say, that your staff numbers 15). Each of your people should be working on at least one project; and 10 percent of your people should be out on full-time pilot-project assignment. (So how do you get today's work done? Surely you won't pretend that you can't free up a fifth of your resources for special assignment. My experience suggests that your staff will lap up such assignments, effortlessly churning out the "real" work in what amounts to their spare time.)

How do you "sell" this concept "up" to your bosses? Don't! Not only should you not advertise, but when progress on a pilot project is worthy of note, let the "customer" (your new line partner) do the reporting to his or her boss or the executive committee. If that sounds too self-effacing in a dog-eat-dog world, realize that word gets around (to your benefit); and, anyway, that line operator is a better salesperson for you and your gang than you are.

Continuing to proceed like a consultant, you might eventually propose to sell your service to people outside the division—i.e., to other corporate operations. Such an "outside" sales strategy, if successful, not only makes you and your team more valuable, but it also serves as valuable preparation for a possible next step: selling your group's expert services outside the corporation, for a profit. If you're good, there's no reason to bet against you. (See Chapter 22 for more on these notions.)

What does such a scenario add up to? You guessed it: Transforming your unit, de facto, into a full-blown professional service firm.

Think Résumé or You're Not Thinking

Before the inevitable next round of white-collar layoffs (recession or not, they will keep coming), visit an imaginary outplacement counselor. That is, anticipate the advice any outplacement counselor would give you—start working on your résumé. Doing so will not only help you if the grim day does arrive, but, happily, substantially reduce the odds of that day coming by making you a more valued employee now.

A résumé, obviously, captures work experience. But what is "work" these days? With the lion's share of "manufacturing" employees performing nonmanufacturing tasks—engineering, accounting, purchasing, marketing, sales, distribution, information systems, personnel—just about everyone in service or manufacturing is a professional service provider. Put in slightly different terms, we're almost all "consultants" in one guise or another. That's the essential idea behind the knowledge society—the society of Titeflex and the Union Pacific Railroad as well as EDS and Arthur Andersen.

But there's a big difference between Andersen's professionals and the professionals on most companies' payrolls. Andersen employees peddle their "service" for a profit. As a consequence, they must be able to explain to clients what they do: "We do thus and such, for $100 an hour. This project will take 300 hours. Check my references. Have we got a deal?" As with any business proposal, it had better add up.

Now suppose you're in purchasing or personnel or accounting on someone's payroll. Ask yourself:

—What the hell is it that I *do?*

—What have I actually *done?*

—How do I *know* I've really done it?

—Who among my "customers" will *confirm* it?

—What's the evidence that my *skills are state-of-the-art?*

I know what you *think* you've done: You've been a "good staffer" in the XYZ Corp. tradition, you've done what you've been told, minded the store, helped out when needed, been generally of good cheer, and kept your boss off your case most of the time. And it's not good enough, for the imaginary outplacement counselor or for a real one.

On the other hand, an Andersen consultant, asked to account for her year, could probably (1) enumerate a handful of specific projects; (2) describe in detail the benefits she'd delivered to clients; and (3) offer an impressive list of "witnesses" (clients) who'll attest to it all. She could also (4) explain what she's learned during the year and how, therefore, she'll (5) be a more valuable ("marketable") member of the firm next year. She could, in effect, provide an updated 1993 "résumé" better than her 1992 version. Could you?

Let's get down to brass tacks. The real reason for these relentless white-collar layoffs of recent years is that most middle managers and professional staffers have not done much! Frightfully few can claim convincingly that they've provided clear-cut value for their "clients."

What, then, should you aim to do? What should your "ideal," year-end 1993 résumé look like? It must clearly demonstrate that you have, in fact, completed a couple of discrete project-type tasks with significant results—e.g., created a novel costing system that helped your division come in 24 percent under budget on an important project (if you're in accounting); developed and installed a purchasing scheme that takes into account the lifetime value of goods, rather than just initial price (if you're in purchasing). Focus on (1) content, (2) implementation, and (3) impact. The résumé should read like a continuing value-added odyssey which adds up to: "The firm is better off because of the projects I performed, and I can prove it in no uncertain terms." The projects are you, your signature, your professional reason for being.

I could offer a million bits of "practical advice." But they'd all boil down to one thing: Think résumé! "Résumé development" is selfish and selfless: selfish, in that each year (if you're wise) you are aiming to enhance demonstrably your reputation within and beyond the company; selfless, since your employer's competitive strength is the grand total of the service projects that white-collar professionals like you execute.

RECONSIDERING "CAREERS"

Looking at the longer haul, what about a "career" as a succession of projects? It's a valuable idea. Careers need not be specifiable "paths" that are governed, somehow, from on high by an organization where we hope to spend our life. Increasingly, and not just in the likes of Silicon Valley, sensible people—those close to the front line, as well as engineers, industrial designers, and executives—are looking at the world as a checkerboard upon which to play a project-based game called "my career." The most thoughtful companies are being more than accommodating: They see the checkerboard career as creating an advantage for them, as well as for the individual. They'd rather have the energized individual on the make (in the best sense of that word) on their square for two or three exciting years (exciting for both parties) rather than 25 dull years. In *Odyssey*, Apple Computer chief John Sculley puts it this way:

> You are asked to pour a part of yourself into the success of the company. . . . The individual is asked for a greater commitment than in the days when he or she was simply a cog in the wheel of a systematized corporation. In return, you should get an experience that sharpens your instincts, teaches you the newest lessons, shows you how to become self-engaged in your work, gives you new ways of looking at the world. . . . I'm not asking for open-ended loyalty . . . I am asking people who are at Apple to buy into the vision of the company while they are here.

Sculley is not alone. In a 1990 issue of *Management Review* magazine, Tom Horton, then chief executive of the American Management Association, struck a similar chord: "Tomorrow's typical career will be neither linear nor continuous, nor will it always be upward. Instead, one's work life will take more of a zigzag course. Those who prepare themselves for change and growth will have the highest probability of success." Likewise, Charles Handy writes in *The Age of Unreason* that "changing has to become a part of our life." He urges us to imagine careers as "portfolios" of different jobs and disciplines and, even while on the job, of different activities. (He proposes, for instance, that "homework" or "study work" become a large part of *everyone's* life.) Even *Business Week* has gotten the word, with a cover story (October 7, 1991) titled "I'm Worried about My Job!" and explaining "The New Career Path" in a series of subheads: "Starting Big" (in a big company), "Broadening Skills," "Branching Out" (shifting to a start-up), "Taking a Break," "Temping." Also featured was a "Career Survival Kit," proffering this advice: "(1) Build skills . . . (2) Moonlight . . . (3) Learn . . . (4) Choose your assignments . . . (5) Stay nimble . . . (6) Network now . . . (7) Know your headhunter . . . (8) Take responsibility . . . (9) Have an escape hatch."

Some, such as Harvard's Bob Reich in *The Work of Nations*, concur with the Handy view, but insist that the inevitable by-product is an ever-widening gap between "haves" and "have-nots"—those who are able to follow a project course and those doomed to a work-life at the margin. While Handy is no Pollyanna, he would tend to disagree. Me too. The "project focus" is as vital to—and plausible for—the front-line worker as it is for the engineer who graduated from the University of California at Berkeley 10 years ago, and whose disciplinary half-life is now running about 5 years. That is, the *secretary* who would thrive in a rapidly changing, global labor market must be determined to perpetually educate/reeducate herself or himself—and learn more than the next person. (Remember Oticon's Inge Christophersen.) "Homework" will be as common an idea tomorrow for the 43-year-old secretary as for the 10th-grader. Handy, for example, observes that certain professional service firms in London are subcontracting their typing to Taipei, thanks to modern telecommunications. Typists in London, then, must understand they're in direct competition with lower-wage counterparts 9,000 miles away. The relatively high-paid Londoner's only defense is to offer a better and improving skill package—e.g., to know more word processing or file management software than their "competitors."

Organizations such as Apple Computer, CNN, MCI, Quad/Graphics, and most professional service firms are, in effect, organized to abet such personal odysseys. They are "universities." If you're not interested in learning more as junior printer at Quad/Graphics, then the company isn't interested in keeping you around—neither are your pressed-to-grow teammates/peers, who, recall, will be the ones to give you the unceremonious boot if you don't improve and keep on improving. The idea of perpetual growth and perpetual education can be applied to 100 percent of those on any payroll. (To be sure, government could help those making the transition to a context where perpetual skill enhancement is necessary and job-hopping the norm—see the Afterword.)

The Personal Projects Enterprise Strategy

Few write more eloquently about "career projects" than Ed Freeman and Daniel Gilbert. In *Corporate Strategy and the Search for Ethics*, the authors propose "the personal projects enterprise strategy." They say their theory "will allow us to see persons and their organizations in a consistent, liberty-enhancing way. We seek a concept of the corporation that is empowering for individuals, . . . that is liberating rather than oppressive and coercive." Most see the organization's projects as taking precedence over the individual's projects. "Nothing could be farther from our minds," Freeman and Gilbert state flatly in rebuttal. "Corporations are human institutions," they add. ". . . . Our view of the corporation is fairly simple. It is a means to facilitate the realization of the projects of certain persons called 'corporate members.' A corporation is simply one way that we achieve our projects. Stated somewhat differently, persons are only passing through corporations on the way to their respective ends. . . . In our view, if a corporation fails to help person X with project P, then X will search for an alternative and withdraw support from the corporation. Other corporate members do not try to coerce X into staying, nor do they try to prevent other corporations from satisfying X's projects. . . . Corporations are fictions . . . that stand for *the interests of the members.* . . . Corporations can be thought of as sets of agreements among the members to achieve their projects."

Pie-in-the-sky thinking? Maybe in 1946, certainly in 1906. But it cannot be today! This apparently "idealistic" notion turns out to be consistent with competitive necessity. Conquering markets is no longer a "forever proposition"—as it was, de facto, for GM, IBM, or Sears in bygone days. Markets cannot be conquered. We live amid perpetual economic quicksand. Projects that bring together multiple people from multiple disciplines from multiple firms will "conquer" a market for a moment at most. "Actors" (people whom we used to call "workers"—or "hands") will all more or less be part of an improvisational theater troupe of ever-learning resources. Their projects (à la Freeman/Gilbert) will coincide with a given corporation/network for a bit, then evaporate.

TOWARD PROJECTS FOR ALL

Arguably, project work was the norm before the industrial revolution. Most activities took place in small, independent shops, and craft and craftsmen were the economy's centerpiece. The industrial revolution changed all that. Skills and tasks were narrowed. And narrowed again. Thousands of people went to work under the same roof. Now, thanks to new competitive pressures, new distributive information technologies and the like, we are, arguably, returning to the craft tradition. *The essence of craft is the project.* It may turn out that the 150 years from the time of Dickens to 1980 will have been the anomaly. What's normal, on the job or off, will end up being craft, learning, adding value—i.e., the project.

Véronique Vienne

At first blush, it doesn't sound like a recipe for success: seven jobs in 10 years, including at least one firing and countless blowups with the boss. But Véronique Vienne is philosophical about a "career" path that has zigzagged through several high-profile magazines and landed her, as of October 1991, in the tony New York offices of Yves Saint Laurent Parfums. The French-born "teal-collar" worker has gone from magazine art director to high-fashion marketer and successful free-lance writer. It sounds exotic, but make no mistake, the networking skills and steely attitudes essential to her world will become tools of the trade to survivors of all stripes in the new economy.

The marble and teak-trimmed offices of Yves Saint Laurent were quiet on a cold morning in December 1991 when my colleague Paul Cohen visited. Vienne, 49, hired as director of business development just two months earlier, was a little on edge. Most of the senior staff were either in Paris or San Francisco for the relaunch of YSL's original fragrance, and she was waiting for word. Also, Judith Harrison, president of YSL Parfums, had just been fired.

This was nothing new to Vienne, though. Eight years ago, as art director of *San Francisco* magazine, she saw the editor who'd hired her get fired—and ended up getting his job. (She later followed him to another post as art director of the *San Jose Mercury News* Sunday magazine.) It was her first brush with what Vienne calls "betrayal of the boss."

"You ask yourself if it's wrong to stay when your friend and protector leaves, or whether it's wrong to leave those who brought you on. It's painful, because loyalty and integrity are what keep you alive. The boss hires you, and it's like a marriage—you fall in love, and when you have to disengage yourself it isn't pretty. You're loyal while you're there. But you know that sometimes you leave them and sometimes they leave you."

Inevitably, said Vienne, the volatility of the workplace, the power of your reputation, and the strength of your Rolodex determine your career path. She sees herself firmly in control of the last two elements of that list, and views every job as an opportunity to enhance both her professional skill and her personal network. "My only career strategy is to plan what I can learn, specifically, from each job," she said. "I try to very clearly define two or three things I can accomplish while I'm there."

For example, in the course of four years working at three different Sunday magazines in the San Francisco Bay Area, she set out first to learn how to meet impossible deadlines and to work with illustrators; then to work with photographers; then to master the fine points of a particular style of graphic design.

The "what-can-I-learn-next" principle applies whether she's initiating a move or contemplating an unexpected offer. For example, when Condé Nast offered her a high-profile job at *Self* magazine, she jumped at the chance—but first defined her objectives (to "understand the mind" of Alexander Liberman, Condé Nast's commanding editorial director; to work with then-editor Anthea Disney; to experience the world of fashion).

During her eight years in San Francisco, Vienne had hosted dinner parties for visiting magazine mavens, stayed visible in graphic design circles, and frequently traveled to New York—all of which involved a genuine love of her work, and a lot of hours in the kitchen. "People underestimate the importance of food in networking," she remarked.

Life at Condé Nast, however, was no picnic. Her editor at *Self* was fired the day Vienne's furniture arrived from San Francisco, and after two tumultuous years Vienne was cast out in a bruising dismissal by Liberman. "Condé Nast hires people they don't want to see working for the competition," she said. "They throw you out and know that no one else will take you, that you're damaged goods."

Still, her design and networking experience helped Vienne position herself in the job market. Currently, she said, "I've been niched as a French person, the frog who speaks English." After Condé Nast, she worked as creative director of an international design consulting firm, then landed at YSL by way of a free-lance writing assignment for their marketing department. Her days are now marked by calls to and from Paris and negotiations with product managers, attorneys, and senior executives involving advertising copy for the U.S. market, product positioning, and contact with vendors and distributors.

Lunch represents another networking opportunity. On the day of Cohen's visit Vienne dined with a distressed friend and mentor at Hearst magazines who was retiring in the midst of layoffs and upheaval. She wanted to bring him a gift and drop off her rewrite of a story on lingerie for *Town & Country*. "I don't know why they [*Town & Country* editors] give me these assignments," she laughed.

Admitting to being "self-centered and egoistic" in some of her career moves, she keeps her perspective. "I've made mistakes. Editors liked me as an art director, but they liked me better when I wasn't working for them anymore. They'd dread the lectures I'd give them. And that worked against me, because I was a pain in the ass."

Susan Brennerman of the *Los Angeles Times Sunday Magazine*, who worked with Vienne at the *San Francisco Examiner*, vouched for that—but doesn't think she's all bad: "Véronique is a challenge, because she has strong feelings and high standards and speaks her mind. She makes people uncomfortable. But I consider that to be a plus. We often disagreed, but many of her ideas were good."

Late that afternoon, Vienne took one last call—from a headhunter who smelled blood after the change in regime at YSL. Vienne was skeptical about making any immediate moves, but admitted that once she learns the bottom-line lessons of the business world, she'd eventually like to return to publishing.

Does her persistent wandering count against her in the job market? "I'm not proud of having moved so much," she confessed, "but it's never been an issue in getting work. My reputation is not that I'm somebody who moves around. I think my reputation is that I'm somebody who knows what she's doing." Brennerman and others confirmed that assessment.

The chaos of life in the '90s seems natural to Vienne. "My attitude comes out of World War Two and the tumult of Europe. Growing up without the expectation of stability has served me well, because the world is not a stable place."

Sheryl Spanier, an outplacement consultant with Lee Hecht Harrison who counseled Vienne when she left Condé Nast, concurred. "There's no longer any assurance of a clear, steady career path, no rules you can use to get your meal ticket punched," she told us. "The key is doing interesting, challenging things professionally, developing a uniqueness and expanding your skills as opposed to fitting yourself into opportunities that present themselves."

Ultimately, said Vienne, job strategy is a small part of the story. "The hard thing in life isn't being a good businessperson. The hard thing is learning to cope with your strengths and weaknesses. It's learning to become a good human being."

15

Basic Organizational Building Blocks I: Every Person a Businessperson

We want every person to be a businessperson.

RALPH STAYER
CEO, Johnsonville Foods
Inc., November 1990

In the *Harvard Business Review* of July–August 1990, systems reengineering expert Michael Hammer describes a revolutionary change at a giant insurance company:

> The long, multi-step process [of handling applications] involved credit checking, quoting, rating, underwriting and so on. An application would have to go through as many as 30 discrete steps, spanning five departments and involving 19 people. . . . . [After the organizational redesign] existing job descriptions and departmental boundaries [were replaced by] a new position called a case manager. Case managers have total responsibility for an application from the time it is received to the time a policy is issued. Unlike clerks, who perform a fixed task repeatedly under the watchful gaze of a supervisor, case managers work autonomously. No more hand-offs of files and responsibility, no more shuffling of customer inquiries. Case managers are able to perform all the tasks associated with an insurance application. . . . In particularly tough cases, the case manager [can call upon] a senior underwriter or physician, but these specialists work only as consultants and advisors to the case manager, who never relinquishes control.

One result of the above: Turnaround time for applications was slashed from 5 to 25 days down to a couple of days, or a few hours in a crunch. "Case managers" also started handling, with ease, more than twice the volume of new applications than were processed under the old regime.

EACH EMPLOYEE A BUSINESSPERSON

Think about your corner grocer. Think about a line worker, or even a middle manager, in a big, traditional firm. The former is a businessperson, no mistake. The latter "fills a job slot." What a difference!

The most fundamental building block of the new organization is the "businessperson," or "informated individual," "case worker," "care pair," "mass customizer." Emerging organizational forms will permit—and the market will demand—that each employee be, per Ralph Stayer's epigraph, turned into a businessperson. Yes, it means being empowered. It also means having all the organization's information at your fingertips—make that *everyone's* fingertips. And much more.

Return to the Union Pacific Railroad. First, Mike Walsh stripped out several layers of bureaucracy and created 30 mini-railroads, 600 strong, each under a Top Gun (authorized to do and spend as necessary to run his business). Then he encouraged thousands of people closest to the front line to make whatever decisions were necessary to serve the customer better. A veteran track inspector previously had to go "up" *seven* layers of operations management, then down *four* layers in the sales and marketing group before he could (indirectly) connect with his customer. Now that inspector calls the customer straight away and even the thorniest problems are resolved on the spot 99 percent of the time (literally).

But the UPRR is going further than that—putting computers for conductors in cabooses, for instance. Recall that Harvard's Shoshana Zuboff gave us the ugly but potent term "informated" in her *In the Age of the Smart Machine.* That is, the front-line person is not only empowered (the track inspector who can/is expected to talk to the customer with no intervening layers of bureaucracy getting in the way), but also has all the institution's information/knowledge at his fingertips. Back to the new-look conductor with the computer in his caboose: He's *allowed* to get on with serving the customer as he sees fit (empowered). And he *can* get on with serving the customer, because he has access to all the railroad's financial and customer service data (informated). Empowered *and* informated, he becomes a "businessperson." And, in fact, it's not much of a stretch to call him a "one-man company" or even an "entrepreneur." (In *2020 Vision*, Stan Davis and Bill Davidson support this idea, suggesting that the "design limit" in tomorrow's organization is "each employee becomes a business.")

Stick with the UPRR and move up a notch, from one person to three people: Reconsider the National Customer Service Center team responsible for Northern California. It de facto "manages" and "quarterbacks" customer satisfaction—acting like the insurance company "case manager" for its several thousand customers. Members travel to customers' sites to do advance transportation and logistics planning; though nominally in the sales organization, they ride the rails to make pals with engineers and conductors on the operations side, with whom they deal regularly; and at the St. Louis NCSC they have full access to the railroad's information (and what's not at St. Louis, they get from their "informated" buddies at Omaha's Harriman Dispatch Center). They're also routinely engaged, on teams with outsiders and multiple functions from the railroad, in project work—work targeted at making the UPRR's "horizontal" processes mesh better with their customers' "horizontal" processes. For example, they aim to make all the relevant UPRR information (from many departments and locations) about an order-in-progress transparent to numerous parts of the customer organization. The trio, formerly powerless, isolated ciphers in a bureaucratic morass, are, then (1) empowered to do whatever is necessary to serve the customer, including the spending of significant sums; (2) encouraged to cross any and all functional borders at will, and without prior clearance from anyone; (3) routinely at work in multifunction service and process-improvement teams; (4) routinely working *inter*organizationally; (5) fully informed; (6) at the center of a very flat "spiderweb organization"; (7) and very *pro*active (e.g., they are urged to take the initiative before a problem arises).

NCSC teams are the new UPRR equivalents of the corner grocery. They're expected to take a holistic view—act as a *railroad,* rather than as members of a functional organization—and they have the wherewithal to do so. I further contend that such teams are micro professional service firms. Their new world of work looks more like that of McKinsey's consultants or EDS's information specialists than that of front-line clerical railroad employees circa 1885—or 1985.

And what about CNN's video journalists? Titeflex's Rapid Deployment Team? Ingersoll-Rand's now peripatetic, multifunction product development bands? Businesspersons all. See my point?

Such folks are also "mass customizers," to get back to the universal drift toward fashion. "Mass customization" is precisely what the new-flavor UPRR conductors and insurance company case managers are doing. They personalize (customize) service for large numbers of clients (mass). Highly informated, they do most of the work themselves, then oversee the rest of what needs to be done (remember Michael Hammer's insurance company case managers— they may call upon higher-ranking "specialists" for help, but they *never* relinquish control).

REVERSING HYPERSPECIALIZATION: "CARE PAIRS," "CARE TRIOS," AND THE "PATIENT-FOCUSED HOSPITAL"

For every dollar hospitals spend directly on patient care, Booz, Allen & Hamilton consultant J. Philip Lathrop calculates, they spend another "three to four dollars waiting for it to happen, arranging to do it, and writing it down." In the July/August 1991 issue of *Healthcare Forum Journal*, Lathrop slams service delivery practices in today's hospitals—and offers a stunning solution, which he and his colleagues call "the patient-focused hospital."

First, Lathrop's indictment. "It's no one's fault," he writes. "There was no conspiracy involved. . . . We in the health care industry have made thousands and thousands of basically sound decisions over the past 30 years. Unfortunately, they now add up to a mess that makes no sense:

—"A system within which we have convinced ourselves (and patients!) that a one- or two-hour odyssey for a routine X-ray exam is 'good service.'

—"A system that is so out of touch with its customers' needs that more than half of all basic lab tests are ordered 'stat' [emergency basis].

—"A preoccupation with specialization that results in: (1) five-minute EKGs requiring nearly an hour's worth of scheduling, documentation, and transportation—all to 'optimize' the time of a high-school graduate with two weeks of [specialized] education; (2) the presence of specialists and technicians whom we wouldn't dream of asking to do anything but their own narrow, and often self-defined, duties, even if it means they are idle much of the time; (3) separate job classifications for housekeepers who clean tile and housekeepers who clean carpets; (4) an average of fewer than five incumbents per job classification. . . .

—"An infrastructure nightmare where clerks and secretaries outnumber the inpatients in a large hospital.

—"Department-head meetings at large hospitals that typically have 60 to 100 people in attendance."

Hyperspecialization is public health enemy No. 1, as Lathrop sees it. At Indianapolis's 1,041-bed St. Vincent Hospital, for example, there are 598 separate job classifications, over half with just a single incumbent. The alternative model Lathrop and his colleagues advocate (based upon three years of research) takes dead aim at the centralization of routine activities—i.e., most of the services provided to a typical patient. The new approach features largely self-contained, modest-size service delivery units:

—"Caregivers are cross-trained to provide 80 to 90 percent of the services their patients need—including traditional bedside nursing, basic X-ray films, routine lab work, respiratory care, and EKGs. Appropriate X-ray and lab equipment is redeployed to the unit. As a result, patients seldom leave the unit and almost never require scheduling . . . [or] major transportation. . . .

—"Caregivers truly 'own' their patients. Continuity is maintained across shifts and across days of stay. Caregivers admit their own patients and perform medical record coding and abstraction. They perform even the mundane tasks of linen changing, tray passing, and phlebotomy. . . . Three-day-stay patients no longer interact with 55 employees; they interact with fewer than 15. . . .

—"Routine ancillary services are performed for the convenience of patients and doctors, not as dictated by central departments. Turnaround times outperform current 'stat' levels. . . .

—"Documentation now consumes less than 30 minutes per caregiver per day. Medical records can now be measured in millimeters, not inches.

—"Quality is more transparent. We no longer need to be satisfied with merely auditing 'the process of care.'

—"Long-term, sustainable reductions in personnel on the order of 15 to 20 percent are possible."

Lakeland's Self-sufficient "Care Pairs"

Journalist David O. Weber examined six hospitals following the patient-focused path, including a 40-bed pilot unit that opened in August 1989 within the 897-bed Lakeland Regional Medical Center in Lakeland, Florida. "[The] self-contained surgical service [includes a] mini-lab, diagnostic radiology rooms, supply stockrooms and administrative records/clerical area," Weber reported. But the crucial innovation was organizing bedside care around teams of "multi-skilled practitioners," made up of a " 'care pair'—a registered nurse and a cross-trained technician—backed by a unit-based pharmacist, a unit clerk, and a unit support aide." Each care pair handles up to 90 percent of the pre- and postsurgical needs for four to seven patients!

The pioneer unit's nurses and technicians took a six-week, full-time course encompassing dozens of therapeutic and diagnostic procedures previously spread among myriad specialists. "Between them," Weber writes, "the care-pair team [is] competent to shoulder the full range of direct patient care, records processing, and hotel functions—from admitting, charting, charging, tray passing, transportation, and room cleanup to care planning, assessment, therapeutic intervention, diagnostic test administration, and outcome evaluation." Special software ("Carelink") and a computer terminal in each patient's room further aid the team in coordinating/quarterbacking all the patients' activities, including the 10 percent or so that can't be performed directly by the dynamic duo.

At first, the shift caused fear and consternation on the part of virtually all the hospital's 2,300 employees. Many specialists were alarmed by the prospect of performing mundane tasks. But vice president of nursing Phyllis Watson told Weber that the doubts have mostly evaporated. The unit's nurses "say they'd rather pass trays than spend an hour on the phone," she said.

Among the dramatic results of Lakeland's pilot effort:

—Turnaround time for routine tests dropped from 157 minutes to 48 minutes, on average, Weber reports. (For example, diagnostic radiology procedures which used to take 40 steps now take 8, and what consumed 140 minutes now takes only 28.)

—Care pairs more than doubled the time they spend with patients—from 21 percent under the old system to 53 percent now.

—Fewer patient falls occurred in the patient-focused unit, and the medication error rate was the lowest in the hospital.

—The average patient encountered just 13 hospital personnel in the special unit, compared with 27 nurses, 10 food service workers, six ancillary service workers, and five central-transport workers in the normal scheme.

—Satisfaction levels soared. The unit's turnover in registered nurses became the lowest in the hospital. And physicians, Weber writes, "unanimously hailed the improvements in test result turnaround times, reduced paperwork, and efficiency in making rounds." Patient perceptions of quality, responsiveness, and empathy were far above average. "Direct bedside costs" also fell noticeably.

Though most problems are on their way to resolution, it hasn't been all smooth sailing. For example, designing a compensation and career advancement program that would "suitably reward and motivate multi-skilled practitioners" was difficult, Weber reports. A new, two-part basic pay scale considers skills (up to 600 points, determined by competency testing) and education (400 points). Incentive pay is based on an annual evaluation of the year's achievements in leadership (counting for 45 percent), cross-training (35 percent), and professional development (20 percent).

The clincher: A second pilot unit opened in 1990 and a third in 1992, and Lakeland expects to shift entirely to patient-focused mini-hospitals within five years. "As radical and significant as all this is," CEO Jack Stephens told Weber, "I believe we're only scratching the surface."

(Weber also examined changes at St. Vincent—the hospital that sports those 598 specialties overall. In January 1990, a 44-bed "general surgery/ subspecialties" pilot unit was organized around "care trios." The trio consists of a cross-trained RN and two other cross-trained, technically skilled employees. The patient-focused unit has just five job classifications: "care team member," "clinical manager," "unit representative," "pharmacist," and "unit support assistant." With stunning results in hand, St. Vincent opened a second 44-bed patient-focused unit in March 1991, this one in medicine. "This is probably the most exciting venture I've been associated with in my five years as CEO and twenty-year career with St. Vincent," CEO Bain Farris told Weber.)

Think about the Lakeland concept as three concentric circles: The care pair (the inner circle) are the patient's private, surprisingly self-contained customized micro-hospital. (Once more: Isn't it also fair to call the care pair a de facto "micro professional service firm" dealing with four to seven "clients" at any time?) The 40-bed unit is a mini-hospital. Then the corporate center (the rest of the hospital) provides the super-specialized and expensive resources like CAT scanners, which meet the remaining 10 percent or so of the patient's needs; the center also tends the overall network. Finally, note the almost eerie parallel between Lakeland and the insurance company vignette that opened this chapter. Newly designated case managers there do most of the processing of applications on their own; fully informated, they can access the rest of the institution (e.g., senior underwriters, physicians) for specialist help as needed while remaining in control.

EVERY ACCOUNT OFFICER "PRESIDENT OF THE BANK": THE CASE OF SILICON VALLEY BANK

At most banks, the bigger the staff, the harder it is for clients to get service. But Silicon Valley Bank (assets of $869 million at the end of 1991) is finding a way around the pitfalls of dramatic growth. "As soon as the bank gets large, it's my job to break it up," President Roger Smith told us. "My ideal work unit would be about eight people. Some banks are so huge we joke that we can fit our whole bank in their president's office."

Smith has aggressively broken up every functional department in the bank. "Each unit is its own bank with its own performance goals," said Bob Gionfriddo, head of Silicon Valley's commercial division. His group, which serves corporate clients, has four two-member teams—and all eight team members sit on the bank's top loan committee. The small-team strategy gives clients greater continuity, and helps attract new accounts because it "lets clients know they'll be serviced," Gionfriddo told us.

In 1991, for instance, one duo/team that serves high-tech clients opened its own small office in Palo Alto. "We let these people out on their own, and it's worked well," Smith noted. "Ownership increases because having the team apart increases dependence. When team leaders sit in the same area as top execs, their ownership is lessened by the physical presence of someone else." All told, the bank's technology division broke a group of 17 people into two- and three-member teams in three offices. The pairs consist of a leader—a senior banker—and a junior partner. Teams are matched for compatibility, and portfolios are built according to the expertise each client requires. "We try to be sensitive to personalities and see where people can benefit and relate well together," said Harry Kellogg, executive vice president and manager of the technical group. "We found there's more learning and ownership if there are fewer people involved," Kellogg added. "One of the challenges as we get larger is to keep units flat. We feel we can be successful using that idea." It's gone well so far—the bank's profit per employee ($69,153 in 1991) is among the highest in the industry.

"Any way you measure us, we have fewer people for our size than any bank in the U.S.," Smith asserted. "We want people to grow their [client] portfolio and their team's portfolio, rather than the number of people under them. We want people who like working together as 'partners'—we don't like a lot of 'assistants' running around. Clients don't want to deal with 'assistants.' Rather than 'promote' people into some title, we like to leave them in place, pay them more, and give them more [client/portfolio] responsibility."

The approach works, Kellogg declared, because "everybody has their own business and is visible to the board. I know each team's performance and contribution to the whole." The teams have been working together for about a year and are paid generous performance bonuses. "Each team is recognized for the growth of its portfolio," Kellogg continued. "You have to remind people that they have a vested interest in their team. Then you can just keep adding teams."

The divisions are also spread geographically, and even the head of the Boston-area division, Allyn Woodward, has been indoctrinated with the small-is-beautiful mentality. "Roger instills the 'close to the client concept,' " he told us. "Once you get big, you need to break up to keep close to the market."

Another advantage of the small unit is that it's "hard to create a clique," said Smith. It keeps everyone in earshot of each other. Smith puts his theory to effective practice consistently, even segregating the wire services department. "Now they're in a room where they can communicate," he reported. "I like openness, where people can spin around in their chairs and ask questions."

The effect on clients is palpable, Smith added. "The most frequent comment we get is, 'You don't seem like bankers, you seem like businesspeople." His retort: "We *are* businesspeople, we just happen to be in the banking business."

Smith explained that the latitude branch managers have isn't in what they offer, but in the way they offer it. "Our products are narrow in scope, but the trick is in how you tailor them to different clients'needs," he said. "In banking, everyone has unlimited 'no' power—people could say no to you all day long.

The first thing you do here as an account officer is ask, 'How can I say yes?' With us, account officers are the presidents of their own bank. If you have forty accounts, you're their president. I want the client to think you're 'It'— that's ownership.''

Three hundred years ago, the craftsman at his forge was a full-fledged businessperson. Thirty years ago, Ross Perot got fed up with IBM's stodginess (even then, as he saw it) and turned his aggressive EDSers into "can-do" entrepreneurs. Now Roger Smith has discovered (or rediscovered) the same formula at Silicon Valley Bank, as have Jack Stephens and Bain Farris at Lakeland and St. Vincent hospitals—and Jon Simpson at Titeflex. The "new" entrepreneur is the old entrepreneur—and more.

TOMORROW, THE WORLD

Can the businessperson idea be stretched even further? I think so. Michael Alexander explains in "Is There a Doctor in the Network" (*Computerworld*, December 9, 1991):

> The University of Pittsburgh Medical Center . . . will inaugurate this week a multimedia network that will permit neurophysiologists to assist in operations from a remote workstation. . . . Neuronet will link instrument racks in operating rooms to 100 HP Apollo . . . workstations at the seven hospitals that make up the medical center. . . . [It] will be used to transmit the brain-wave activity of patients undergoing neurosurgery in an operating room to a workstation. . . . The physiologist will [also] be able to see what the surgeon is seeing through his microscope during surgery as well as visually scan the operating room. Two-way voice communication will allow the physiologist to hear what is being said in the operating room as well as communicate with a neurotechnician. . . .
>
> "In complex brain operations, surgeons often encounter complications that require the assistance of a colleague," [Dr. Robert] Sclabassi said. "If the colleague was at another hospital, he or she would have to literally run to the operating room to scrub up and take a look. With this advanced network, a doctor will be able to walk to the closest computer terminal and attend the operation."

Or recall, in the Information Technology section, Chandler Stevens's discussion of "electronic organizations" and "expert networks." The Legitech Network he described connects state government science advisers. One queried the network with "What are alternatives to road salt for dealing with icy highways without polluting water supplies?" In short order, the questioner received a raft of helpful answers from around the nation. That is, we can readily imagine the truly informed-case-manager-cum-businessperson having a window on more or less the entire world. Tomorrow's one-person band can legitimately perform as a "global powerhouse."

In fact, there are precedents. Without the supporting technology (until recently), top university researchers have been at it for years: working with a small band of colleagues on the "home" payroll; performing research, then publishing it worldwide, in conjunction with other professors/miniteams/industrial and government labs from all over; consulting to corporations (and starting entrepreneurial companies—e.g., such researchers were/are the genesis and engine of the biotech industry); attending numerous conferences; accessing the world through leading-edge libraries (almost all in universities). These global pure-knowledge players were "informated" centuries ago. Now the railroad conductor, hospital care pair, insurance company case manager, and local banker are on the verge of joining their formerly exclusive club.

"BUSINESSING"

I'm loath to add more jargon. But damn the torpedoes. How about "businessing"? In the end, per Johnsonville's Stayer and Silicon Valley Bank's Smith, we are indeed trying "to business" everyone: to turn all employees into mom-and-pop enterprises, into real, whole businesspersons, responsible for customers from order to delivery of a service or product. "Businessing," as our cases suggest, includes at least these elements:

• Extensive cross-training, budget responsibility, "ownership of assets," substantial spending authority ("whatever you think you need"—almost), and quality assurance and management responsibility;

• the power (and requirement) to act on your own initiative and involve other functions without prior approval or second-guessing;

• responsibility for performing 80 or 90 percent of tasks that used to require numerous steps, numerous departments, and authority from several levels of management;

• having real customers, whose "cases" the "businessperson" grasps—and never lets go (i.e., being "businessed" means quarterbacking the services you can't personally perform, including calling in "more senior" superexperts if needed);

• informate I: Access to all financial information, real-time, from all functions, segregated by customer;

• informate II: Access to extensive nonfinancial info, such as scheduling data, including the ability to alter others' databases—e.g., schedule patient activity in other parts of the hospital;

• informate III: Access to expert systems (see Chapter 28), membership in a knowledge management structure (see Chapter 26);

- informate IV: "Global university" (e.g., ready access to electronic bulletin boards, external databases).

These elements, in turn, will only become real if the parent firm: (1) has significantly delayered; (2) is broken into mini-enterprises such as hospitals-within-hospitals (Lakeland, St. Vincent) or market-scale units (Chapter 18) with almost all functional staffs folded into such small units; and (3) permits easy conversation with "outsiders" of all stripes.

"The conversion of 'organization' into 'business' *always* strengthens corporate performance," Davis and Davidson conclude in *2020 Vision*. Always? And in italics? *Always!* And in italics (theirs)!

"Business"

At ABB, recall, CEO Percy Barnevik insisted that his newly formed 50-person profit centers are so effective because they have customers pestering them—that makes them a "real business." A sleepy Rochester, Minnesota, IBM development lab became the site for one of the company's (and the industry's) most successful products ever—the AS/400 midrange computer, which in 1991, along with related peripherals and services, generated over $14 billion in revenue! Many ingredients went into the transformation, but, according to project leaders Roy Bauer, Emilio Collar, and Victor Tang (in *The Silverlake Project*), none more important than learning to "act like a business." Things really started to pop when the group declared their virtual independence from corporate headquarters, and its culture-bound view, for example, of what customers the AS/400 should aim for.

"Business" is a magical word, it turns out. It implies autonomy, practicality, action-taking, self-sufficiency, and self-responsibility. In our biggest bureaucracies (private and public), these ideas have been absent for too long.

16

Basic Organizational Building Blocks II: Self-contained Work Teams

That 6- to 10-person Business Development Team which toils at Titeflex:

— includes almost all the company's old staff functions in its midst (e.g., most accounting and engineering, production scheduling, quality assessment);

— is self-managing and performs personnel evaluations;

— has customers;

— deals with vendors;

— invites in and goes out to visit customers and vendors on its own initiative;

— is involved in capital-spending proposals and decisions;

— seeks out new business on its own initiative;

— is a genuine profit-and-loss center.

Such a "work team" goes far beyond the early stabs at participative management. In fact, the evidence from Titeflex, ABB (its High-Performance Teams), and the likes of Johnsonville Foods suggests that these team-cum-small-businesses can enfold most of the world's work.

JOHNSONVILLE FOODS

> *Inc.* magazine: "How did you divide the company up into the appropriate teams?"

> Johnsonville Foods CEO Ralph Stayer: "I didn't. Why is that my problem? *They* divided it up."

Ralph Stayer joined the family-owned sausage-making company located in Sheboygan, Wisconsin, upon graduation from college in 1965 and took the reins from his father in 1978. "The business was growing very rapidly," he recalled when we spoke with him in 1988. "Yet my gut told me we weren't really special. When I looked around, people weren't having fun." He recalled an incident in 1980 that made a big impression. "I'd hired one employee early on, who was very competent," he told us. "Then one day it struck me that he was just a soldier, carrying out my orders. I tried to get him to take more responsibility, but he couldn't. I'd ruined him! A few years of my style had beaten the independence out of him." That's a harsh diagnosis, especially when self-administered—but Stayer was serious. "It wasn't because our employees were bad people," he added. "If anything needed fixing, it was me."

Experiences like this led to a wholesale transformation, best observed among the firm's *very* self-managing teams. Members in a typical dozen-person Johnsonville work group:

— recruit, hire, evaluate, *and* fire (if necessary) on their own;

— regularly acquire new skills as they see fit, then train one another as necessary;

— formulate, then track and amend, their own budget;

— make capital investment proposals as needed (after doing the supporting analyses, making appropriate visits to equipment vendors, etc.);

— handle quality control, inspection, subsequent troubleshooting, and problem solving;

— take on the task of constantly improving every process and product;

— develop quantitative standards for productivity and quality—then monitor them;

— suggest and then develop prototypes of possible new products, packaging, etc.;

— routinely work on teams fully integrated with counterparts from sales, marketing, and product development;

— participate in "corporate-level" strategic projects.

The secret to transforming sausage makers? "People want to be great," Stayer earnestly proclaimed. The boss himself? Highfalutin as it sounds, he said he wants everyone "to be the instrument of their own destiny. It is unconscionable for people not to have the chance to use their full talents."

It seems to be working. Johnsonville has grown from around $7 million (revenue) in 1981 to about $130 million in 1991. While the numbers are dandy, Stayer insisted that "watching people grow is my number one joy."

"Continuous learning" and "lifetime learning" are mere buzzwords in most places—but not at Johnsonville. Most workers, for example, take a full-blown course in economics, developed with the local community college. That's why they find it so "easy" to develop and track those budgets. At least as important, Johnsonville workers are among the 1 percent or less in the United States who are encouraged, with company financial support, to study *anything*—job-related or not. As one employee ("Member," per Johnsonville lingo) explained to me, "Look, anything you learn means you're using your head more. You're engaged. And if you're more engaged, then the chances are you'll make a better sausage."

Aspirations run high. While I was sitting in on the daily quality assessment meeting (consisting of a half-dozen workers with especially good palates), one woman sketched her scheme for becoming an expert trainer, who'd help out across the entire company. "I plan on retiring here," another worker told me. "I have a goal. I want to be a statistical-process-control coordinator, to go to all of our plants and work with people on projects, saving money, developing new programs, helping the company grow."

Johnsonville is a collection of projects. Each team is at work on projects. Each person is a project generator. Coping with the status quo is *not* the point. Moving forward is. Teammates deal harshly with any who choose to opt out of the "personal growth business."

To get a sense of how this exceptional story unfolded, ponder the words of a plant manager, two executive vice presidents, and CEO Stayer:

<u>Plant Manager</u>: "We're teachers. We help people grow. That's my main goal. Each person is his or her own manager. We're putting in a whole new bratroom [production area]. The people got a team together and sat down and decided how it should be laid out. I was involved as a coach. We don't have an engineering department that goes down there and says, 'All right, now we're going to modify this, we're going to modify that.' We have people in the plant who are looking at it and saying, 'You know, if we did it this way, if we put in this little piece, we could take this person out of there and we can run another forty pounds.' These people are industrial engineers. Farmers are engineers, they're businessmen, they're economists. They own and operate their own business. Each person at Johnsonville can do the same thing. . . .

"It was tough at first. We got Pride Teams* together, to sit down and

---

* The Johnsonville equivalent of quality circles, though not limited to people in the same function.

talk about situations in the plant, how we could make them better. People who didn't buy into it, given peer pressure, got out, were voted out of departments. . . .

"It's really exciting, to watch a person come out of high school, maybe not even out of high school. Pretty soon they're setting the schedules for the whole operation. They understand the inventories, the profit and loss, the budgets. . . .

You can do this anywhere. If people trust you, and they trust your motives and they trust that you're in it for them, not just for yourself."

EVP, sales and marketing: "I think the thing that's annoyed me for most of my career, particularly [during a decade-long stint at a big corporation], was spending more time trying to explain something I'd done than doing it. I'd spend four days out of the month preparing for an annual budget. Those were four days that could have been better spent working on the business. . . .

"We spend a lot of our time preventing the institutionalization of stuff that literally drove us out of those other places. We try to make sure that the systems do get put in place, but the systems are made to be broken. People come in with a mindset that they can tear this stuff apart, that they aren't stuck with it for the rest of their lives. They can change stuff. They're *expected* to change stuff. . . .

"The watershed for me was about two and a half years ago. I was still wearing some of my habits from my old career, and made the mistake of standing in front of this group of men and women and saying, 'Thou shalt not take vacations during this critical shipping period.' At which point my workers came back and said, 'Thou shalt not tell us when we can take vacations. We're adults, treat us as adults.' That was a critical moment for the organization. It was the day they stepped up to owning the business. And I backed off. Ever since then, they not only have been responsible for their own vacations, they've been responsible for structuring their own work, structuring their own budgets, for deciding, literally, every single significant aspect of their working life.

"For probably a year and a half before that, we were having monthly meetings, real informal, no rank stuff. I guess they had seen that I had a genuine desire to have a dialogue. There's a testing process. Finally, it comes through that it's okay to fistfight with me. They got to the point where they could say, 'Hey, he's got to put his money where his mouth is, and we might just as well get this over with now.' . . .

"We did something that had never been done [at an acquired plant in New Haven, Connecticut]. We introduced a customer to all the people who were going to make that customer's product. There weren't any sales guys in the room. It was the customer talking directly to the people who were going to build, audit, account for, order, spice for, package for, that customer. *No* sales and marketing types! They're out! The net effect was absolutely magic. There was awe on both sides. Line people [at the acquired plant] had heard about this magic 'customer,' but they don't sit across the table from him. But now they're being asked to innovate, give the customer new ideas, new products, that maybe they've never made before. We left that meeting with a plan for people from the plant to go out and build some new products to match the customer's desires and needs; [the plant workers] came back three weeks later and presented products that were unimaginable. One fellow even brought in some products he'd made in his basement!

"Employee involvement had really been botched up there [prior to the acquisition by Johnsonville]. People really didn't care. It wasn't from the heart. I don't really think [prior management] liked the people! They had consultants heaped on top of consultants. All the ideas were there. All the concepts were there. But it wasn't believable. You have to care. There has to be passion in it. There has to be emotion in it."

EVP, operations: "We don't need sixteen signatures to get something approved, to get it started. We don't have lines drawn on the floor. We roam, do whatever has to be done.

"You start out very slowly. Most of us are impatient. We might have a goal in mind. But we learned how to hold our tongues. As the trust begins to build, people begin to get on the bandwagon. There were a lot on the fence, there were a lot on the wrong side of the fence. There's a weeding process. Some drop by the wayside. They didn't want to be part of it. Some needed a little help to make the decision. . . .

"A big move was doing away with front-line supervisors. That doesn't mean that the functions of the supervisor went away, but the activities get dispersed among the people on the line. Many of our supervisors found other responsibilities, and they stuck around—but not as a supervisor. Our purchasing fellow used to be a supervisor. He found he wanted to go to something else, so he grabbed the purchasing responsibility. Another one is an assistant engineer. A couple of others went back into the crew. . . .

"Part of it is being yourself, twenty-four hours a day. Not having to put a mask on when you go to work, to be a different person than you want to be or can be. We ask ourselves frequently, 'What do you want to be when you grow up?' Some people laugh at that. They might—but I don't. I'm still growing up, and I want to continue to grow. I want to be productive forever. The Johnsonville way has so many parts to it, it's hard to pluck out one or two. People have asked me at times, 'Tell me about this or that part of your system.' I can't. I have to tell them about the *whole* system, because it is a picture. It's like a puzzle with missing pieces. If you don't see the whole picture, no one part of it's going to work."

Stayer: "First of all, you're going to get hired by your fellow workers. The whole interviewing process is set up to weed out people who need rank, need privileges, need structure. So you get that first feeling, 'Gee, this is a little different.' Second, you're going to get trained by your fellow workers, the people who do the work on the job. Third, they're going to tell you how your performance stacks up. They've developed graphs and data that help people chart their own performance. And you're going to get coached by them. They're going to take you under their wing and help you and make sure you understand what the program is. Your fellow workers are going to let you know what the performance standards are, and they're awfully high there.

"There's always this basic question when people hear about the Johnsonville way, hear about our dedication to people: They get it all mixed up. They think it's a real nice thing, that it's all fuzzy and warm. It's anything but that! It's far more difficult to work at Johnsonville than any other place. It takes a different class of person, a person who really wants to excel, because nothing else is accepted. We're here to give you an opportunity to achieve whatever it is you want to achieve in life. We'll also help you figure out what that is. We'll give you the resources to do it. We're also going to give you a little push in that direction. But if you don't have a goal, if you don't see yourself as improving, you're not going to make it here. It's that simple. Because you're going to be letting down not only yourself, but all of your fellow workers. . . .

"This is a way of life. You set the values that you cherish, that you will not deviate from. And then all of the other things flow from that. It's not that we put all these things in and 'fix' all these people with all these new programs. It's just the opposite. We fix *me* and our values first, then all the rest happens. If you're really going to change how you do things, you have to change everything."

Profit Sharing

Profit sharing is also part of the picture, as Stayer explained in a 1990 *Harvard Business Review* article:

> Every six months, we evaluate the performance of everyone at Johnsonville to help us compute shares in our profit-sharing program. Except "we" is the wrong word. In practice, performance evaluations are done by the employees themselves. For example, 300 wage earners—salaried employees have a separate profit-sharing pool and a different evaluation system—fill out forms in which they rate themselves on a scale of 1 to 9 in 17 specific areas grouped into three categories: performance, teamwork, and personal development. Scores of 3, 4, or 5—the average range—are simply entered on the proper line. Low scores of 1 or 2 and high scores of 6 to 9 require a sentence or two of explanation.

Each member's coach fills out an identical form, and later both people sit down together and discuss all 17 areas. In cases of disagreement, the rule is only that their overall point totals must agree within nine points, whereupon the two totals are averaged to reach a final score. If they cannot narrow the gap to nine points, an arbitration group is ready to step in and help, but so far mediation has never been needed.

All final scores, names deleted, are then passed to a profit-sharing team that carves out five categories of performance: a small group of superior performers (about 5 percent of the total), a larger group of better-than-average group of 20 percent, and a small group of poor performers who are often in some danger of losing their jobs.

The total pool of profits to be shared is then divided by the number of workers to find an average share—for the purpose of illustration, let's say $1,000. Members of the top group get a check for 125 percent of that amount, or $1,250. Members of the next group get 110 percent ($1,100); of the large middle group, 100 percent get $1,000, and so on down to $900 and $750.

Yes, people do complain from time to time, especially if they think they've missed a higher share by only a point or two. The usual way of dealing with such situations is to help the individual improve his or her performance in enough areas to ensure a higher score the next time. But overall satisfaction with the system is very high, partly because fellow workers invented it, administer it, and constantly revise it in an effort to make it more equitable. The person currently in charge of the Johnsonville profit-sharing team is an hourly worker from the shipping department.

WORK TEAM STATUS

Johnsonville is surely an exception, but there is, overall, significant progress to report in moving toward self-management. In "Workgroups in America Today" (*Journal for Quality and Participation*, June 1991), Peter Lazes and Marty Falkenberg presented a summary of their research, a useful examination of 22 randomly selected cases of new workgroup practices, all from manufacturing facilities in the U.S. and Canada. Nine were "greenfield" sites (new plants, start-ups) and 13 were "transformations" (redesigns of existing plants). The average new plant employed 260 people, the average transformed plant employed 1,140, and 10 of the 22 operations were unionized.

First, the authors looked at eight "technical support tasks" that are traditionally the responsibility of separate support departments: quality control, safety, equipment maintenance, engineering/equipment changes, choosing production methods, product design, customer/supplier relations, and problem solving. The average work group they studied was carrying out seven of the eight. Involvement in product design (teams at 12 of 22 locations) was least common.

Next came eight "coordinating and scheduling tasks," including setting production goals, materials management, preparation and/or monitoring of a team budget, task assignment, production scheduling, shift scheduling, break scheduling, and vacation scheduling. The average work group was at least partially responsible for five of those tasks. Task assignment was most common—groups at 19 sites were heavily involved in that. Preparation and/or monitoring of the group's budget was least common—but even here, work groups at 8 of 22 locations had some budgetary responsibilities.

Third, "group support tasks"—selection of work group members, selection of the group leader, training, performance evaluation (individually and/or as a group), discipline, design of the compensation system, and administration of the compensation system. Not surprisingly, work groups were less involved in these still sensitive areas. They participated in three on average, with groups at 18 of 22 locations involved in training (most common) and groups at 4 sites participating in external leader selection (least common).

Lazes and Falkenberg singled out the "integration of work groups with support departments" for special attention. Typically, the formal designation of liaison persons was the first step toward integrating work groups and support departments. In eight cases, support departments had formally designated coordinators to liaise with work groups; in most of these instances, the work groups also had designated a separate member to coordinate with each key support function (the liaison role typically rotated among all group members, shifting about once every six months). Three of 22 sites had gone all the way: Support departments had been disbanded, with staffers (maintenance experts, engineers, purchasers) merging into the work groups. "In essence, each team had its own mini-support department," the authors wrote. In 6 of 22 cases, Lazes and Falkenberg found that traditional support departments were maintained in more or less standard form, though even in these instances work group members carry out some of the departments' support tasks—e.g., statistical process control, quality inspection, basic safety tasks, preventive maintenance.

In 7 of 22 cases, the authors discovered that first-line supervisors had been eliminated. In another 6 cases, the number of supervisors had been reduced. Among the remainder, the supervisory role had been changed "from one of direction and control to one of facilitation, coaching, and communication."

Sweeping changes in compensation were also unearthed. Sixteen of 22 sites had moved away from pay based solely on job classification. "Three pay traditional job-based wages combined with some sort of gainsharing or group bonus plan, five use a skill-based system, seven use a skill-based system combined with gainsharing, and one uses an individual incentive plan," the authors observed. (Of the 6 that stood pat, 5 were unionized.)

Management had not branded as failures any of the work group development efforts. Twelve of the 22 plants reported significant productivity increases (up to 100 percent), while only 3 reported no productivity increase. (The remainder wouldn't disclose results.) Eleven reported improvement in quality, 2 no improvement, and 9 didn't respond. Six of 10 unionized plants reported a decrease in grievances (from 130 per year to 10 in one instance).

CLUSTERS: A COMPLETE ALTERNATIVE TO HIERARCHY?

Quinn Mills wants more! In *Rebirth of the Corporation,* he proposes a sweeping alternative to hierarchy and even to the latest experiments in self-management. His paradigm for zany tomorrow, like mine, is the professional service firm. He calls his model "the cluster organization" and argues for "dramatic change in the structure of the organization." Where hierarchy remains, he flatly asserts, "There cannot be any rethinking of the fundamentals of management."

Mills is careful to distinguish the cluster from most current experiments with self-managing teams (he calls such teams a "halfway house from hierarchy"). He defines a cluster as:

> a group of people drawn from different disciplines who work together on a semipermanent basis. The cluster . . . handles many administrative functions, thereby divorcing itself from an extensive managerial hierarchy. A cluster develops its own expertise, expresses a strong customer . . . orientation, pushes decision making toward the point of action, shares information broadly, and accepts accountability for . . . results.

Such largely self-sufficient clusters vary in size from 30 to 50 people, as Mills sees it, and are further subdivided into self-directed work teams of 5 to 7 people each (the scheme is close kin to ABB's profit centers and High-Performance Teams). In complex settings, you might find six flavors of cluster: a "core team," the new name for top management; "business units," which conduct business directly with external customers; "staff units," clusters with internal customers, but which operate in accordance with market dictates; "project teams," assembled for a specific improvement or strategic project; "alliance teams," generally "whole" ventures with outsiders; and "change teams," specifically created to modify broad aspects of the corporation's activities.

Four factors are essential if the cluster is to perform well, Mills asserts.

First, goals must be clear. "Each person must know and understand the mission of the team with which he or she works," he writes. Second, "to act on their own initiative, people must have the necessary competence. This requires not only technical specialization, but a grasp of the broader picture as well." Perpetual training, for instance, must be viewed as an investment rather than a cost. Third, Mills joins the rising chorus in insisting that information be freely shared: "To make the correct choices in local circumstances, people need local information [and] information about the overall setting in which they are acting." Finally, Mills declares, "people need to know they are trusted; that they will not be unfairly penalized for . . . failures."

The new information technologies enable the cluster form of organization to work. But networks of personal computers, Mills insists, "are not themselves new organizational structures as many have mistakenly concluded." They are, instead, "the infrastructure which underlies clusters." Most important, he claims, hierarchies cannot exploit these new technologies effectively, while clusters can.

Mills is at his best dealing with the common objections to clusters:

- "Clusters ignore the innate human need for hierarchies." To the contrary, Mills argues that "much of what we perceive as human nature in the workplace is nothing more than a thorough adaptation of individuals to a hierarchical context." Distinctions among individuals based on ability *do* exist in clusters. "Natural leaders emerge and play a disproportionate role in the activities of the group," he says, but a "formally designated hierarchy is not required for leadership to emerge." (This parallels our discussion about the difference between pecking orders and hierarchies.)

- "It is impossible to motivate people without the prospect of [traditional] promotion." Mills concedes the importance of promotion, but his research shows that recognition for job accomplishment and self-motivation are even more important. Tapping into these deep impulses will, he maintains, more than offset the absence of hierarchical rungs to climb. (I can see Johnsonville's Stayer nodding.)

- "Individual performance in a cluster will 'level down' to the lowest common denominator." Leveling down, Mills points out, is *more* likely to occur in a hierarchy than a cluster: "Why does any employee try to get away with as little work as possible? Because the game of trying to outsmart the supervisor is more interesting than the work itself." But there's no supervisor to outsmart in the cluster. Furthermore, Mills finds, "peers [in clusters], who depend on each other to carry part of the load, are very intolerant of shirkers." Our Johnsonville and Titeflex cases, among others, provide strong confirmation of this assertion (as do, of course, our analyses of professional service firms).

- "People will lose their individualism and privacy . . . in [clusters]." This is a possibility, Mills admits. On the other hand, there are counter-strategies—

such as continuing to ensure that individual performance appraisal is maintained and pronounced, providing individual work space as well as group areas, and working assiduously at "customized [personal] development plans for each individual" in the cluster.

- "If I do not have an important-sounding job title, I will not be able to get a good position in another company." Titles will virtually disappear in a cluster configuration, Mills agrees. On the other hand, he claims, so many companies are in a state of flux that job titles have already become virtually meaningless.

- "There will be no effective limit on mistakes made by employees in a cluster because there is no direct supervision." People on interdependent teams, Mills retorts, are especially "quick to note and object to errors" on the part of their teammates. Moreover, individual performance evaluation will continue to exist, weeding out those who "repeatedly make serious errors."

- "Clusters will take all the fun out of being a boss." Yes, Mills acknowledges, if fun was giving orders and acting in a high-handed fashion. But if fun is helping others grow (Stayer's kick), then clusters are made to order for the new-breed manager.

- "Managers will lose touch with their organizations." To the contrary, the few remaining chiefs will be mostly freed from rote work, Mills suggests. They will have more time, not less, to "spend on longer-term strategy and business-integration issues."

- "There won't be any middle managers left, and those of us who are middle managers will lose our jobs." Mills predicts there will be *more* middle managers in a cluster configuration! But there is a twist: The traditional "middle management tasks"—e.g., initiating projects that add value—will become part of everyone's job.

- "Companies that have experimented with organization structures like clusters have failed in business." Mills concedes the example of People Express, which more or less had a cluster format. He provides a cogent analysis of the company's problems, arguing that the novel structure wasn't People's killer. (I agree, though this is no place for a lengthy explanation. People's waterloo was founder Don Burr's out-of-hand dismissal of information technology's crucial role in the airline industry—e.g., American Airline's "dynamic pricing" strategy.) In any event, Mills says we should expect failures with a brand-new form of organization that flies in the face of hundreds of years of tradition. Most important, he insists that non-cluster forms of organization are simply not up to snuff in today's fast-moving business environment. When it comes to boasting of failures, traditional hierarchies are taking honors right and left!

- "The advantages claimed for clusters can also be obtained in a hierarchy." Sure they can, *in theory*, Mills admits. But only if "the managers and executives in it were to behave much differently from what is ordinary in a hierarchy." Remember our Union Pacific Railroad analysis: Elaborate decision-making processes could have been truncated *without* removing five layers of management in the operations structure; but the likelihood of much streamlining without the radical structural shift was nil.

Implementing clusters is no walk in the park. It calls for a strong emphasis on *cooperation*, and, paradoxically, an equally important focus on *individual* performance. "It's a real beehive," one manager who'd lived in a cluster told Mills. (Ah, the new-metaphor bug bites again!) "There is both competition among the members of a beehive organization, and mutual cooperation and support. It isn't just consensus and mutuality, as in Asia; or just individuals working under direct supervision, as in many American organizations. The beehives seem to be able to harness both the competitive and cooperative drives into a very powerful combination."

Mills supports his ideas with several solid, well-researched case studies of the transition to something like clusters in parts of the U.S. Army, General Electric, Square D, Volvo, Swissair, and British Petroleum. Add up the likes of Mills's research, Johnsonville's and Titeflex's experience, the work of Lazes and Falkenberg, and you've got an iron-clad case for optimism about the most extreme sort of self-management. Or do you?

BUT . . .

The fact is, I could have readily provided several well-documented counter-studies which suggest that the average work group implementation effort is leading to little or no improvement in competitiveness (productivity, quality, etc.).The problem stems from studying the work group idea in a vacuum. A progressive work team/cluster concept is not likely to yield much pay dirt unless, like Walsh (UPRR), Simpson (Titeflex), and Stayer (Johnsonville), you first delayer the organization and gut staff power (and numbers). And that's not all. Recall Walsh's adventure in Louisiana after the misbegotten drug raid. Recall Simpson's great crayon caper. And the Johnsonville workers' uprising over dictatorial vacation scheduling. These sorts of affairs add up to what I call the missing "x-factor." In a word, *trust*.

17

The Missing "X-Factor": Trust

When Warden Dennis Luther calls inmates "constituents," that's a maverick position.

CRAIG APKER
Associate Warden
Federal Correctional Institution
McKean

If you back a person into a corner and kick him and kick him and kick him, he will kick back. You've already backed the person into the corner by putting him in prison.

WAYNE SMITH
Associate Warden
Federal Correctional Institution
McKean

Trust? "Good stuff," you say. "Now let's get down to the basics: How many levels of management? Exactly what should work team responsibilities be?"

That's the way it usually goes. Trust? Of course it's important. But what else can you say? A lot, I suggest. I'll at least say a little. We've already seen trust on the railroad, trust at a sausage maker. Now we'll get serious—how about trust at a federal pen?

Warden Dennis Luther opened Federal Correctional Institution McKean, in Bradford, Pennsylvania, in February 1989. In mid-1992, a staff of 334 oversaw 1,261 inmates—the medium-security facility was already at well over 100 percent of capacity.

Luther is a career prisons man who told us, when we interviewed him in 1991, that he went into the profession "out of altruism" instead of joining the ministry, his second choice. In the mid-'80s, Luther turned around the Federal Bureau of Prisons' Danbury operation, probably the most troubled institution in the system before his advent. He has a track record as a maverick and risk-taker.

"I don't think prison has to be a constant negative experience for staff and inmates," Luther said. The prisoner's punishment is being *sent* to prison, he added. Punishing prisoners once they're inside is not the point. Luther insisted the prison can run smoothly if he can instill just that one notion.

AN UNORTHODOX CULTURE

"We could beat prisoners and build up hostility between the keeper and the kept," associate warden Wayne Smith told us, "but here we allow inmates to somewhat manage themselves." Establishing this new ethos hasn't been easy. Conservative staff members fought Luther under the generally unassailable banner of "compromising security." For example, when he decided to allow popcorn at special events like movies, some guards objected. Inmates would stuff the popcorn in the locks, they claimed. The popcorn was distributed. The locks stayed popcorn-free. (Not all staff can come to grips with the McKean approach. Luther eased out two associate wardens whose resistance persisted.)

Popcorn-free locks is the least of it, of course. Despite normal exterior security (electronically monitored chain-link fences, with coils of razor-sharp wire between them), you'll find no steel bars inside. Wooden doors to the prisoners' rooms are kept unlocked and, unlike most prisons, McKean houses inmates without regard to race.

Inmate Roger Fields, who was released in mid-1992, was my original contact (almost 10 years after *In Search of Excellence*, he became the first prison inmate to write to me). He reported with bemusement that "if the staff isn't responsive to Luther's ideas, he deals with them." Another inmate, Steve Monsanto, confirmed Fields's comment, relating a story that could only come from McKean: Shakedowns take place in every federal prison. In other facilities, the guards usually tear the con's cell apart. At McKean, though, after a shakedown guards must replace everything exactly as they found it. Monsanto remembered returning to his cell once, to find it torn apart by a new officer. He told a lieutenant, who told Monsanto to leave the cell alone. "The new officer will put it back," he said.

More tribute to what Luther calls "an unorthodox culture" came from Mike Eger, warehouse foreman and, when we talked to him, head of the American Federal Government Employees Local. Eger has been at McKean from the start, signing up a record number of charter members in the union local. Washington officials were concerned. No matter, it turned out. "I've never had a grievance or a ULP [unfair labor practice] since we opened in October 1989," Eger told us. "The warden here is different. He tries things, simple things that make our life better." Eger contrasted his McKean experience with a previous posting at Lewisburg, where inmates were constantly fighting and harassing the staff. "Inmates here have a choice," he said, "and that choice is a high degree of self-management." Yet, Eger quickly added, it's no picnic: "They're not getting any more than any other inmate in the system." As to Luther's magic elixir, Eger was clear: "The best thing about the warden is that he never lies."

Respect for the Front Line

The success in getting front-line staffers to treat inmates with respect is a direct reflection of the respect top prison management shows for those staffers. (Yes, the same old story: If you want the customer to be treated well, treat the person who deals with the customer well. Ho hum. Ever wonder why it's still such an exception? I do, every day.) Inmates are Luther's constituents. So are employees. Senior federal prison managers, Luther said, repeatedly overlook the role the front line can play. "Line-level people have good ideas, not only about how to do their job," he added, "but about how to do *your* job better."

Luther nurtures involvement by creating task groups for anything and everything. Task groups to explore using inmates in the nearby national forest. Task groups for expanding inmate programs, for teaching classes, for planning and putting on a community picnic. Such efforts are especially helpful in engaging those who normally aren't involved, he said.

"There's no correlation between creativity, intelligence, and [federal pay] grade level," Luther told us. "That's sweet music to most [McKean staff] people—but no one's ever told them that before." Luther expects staff contributions as a matter of course. At the biweekly meetings of department heads, for example, each attendee is expected to contribute at least one concrete suggestion for improvement.

The Line Staff Advisory Board, a rotating group of front-line workers, talks through suggestions, complaints, and rumors with Luther. Change comes all the time. Inmate food service workers, for example, used to be locked down (locked in their cells) when they weren't working. Now food service managers send them back to their dorm or to recreation when the job's done. Obvious? Not if you've spent a career being trained in *dis*trust.

FROM THE HORSE'S MOUTH

Maybe some of the ideas Luther espouses would be mouthed by other prison wardens. But one group is not likely to mince words—the prisoners themselves. My colleagues Deborah Hudson and Paul Cohen were allowed unfettered, no-administrators-present access to Luther's "constituents." Here's the sort of thing they heard: "I've been locked up fifteen years. I haven't seen people get along together regardless of race, creed, or color except here." "The warden channeled the staff so they treat the inmates like human beings." "I was awestruck. Two months after getting here I was still in a daze by the—I have to use the word—freedom." "There are very few incidents here. Why? Because inmates can use their skills and talents to benefit themselves and the institution. Where else could the inmates have a club with an office, their own phone, and the ability to talk to the administration whenever they want?" "This is as good as it gets inside. It's the best place in the system. You see an associate warden every day, and the warden every two or three days."

Abdul Adam was unofficial head of the prison's Sunni Muslims at the time of our visit: "I say to my people, if it gets any better, we're going to send for the wife and kids. Did I die and go to prison heaven?" Adam spent 10 years in Leavenworth, two in Terre Haute—where, reported one of McKean's associate wardens who "did time with him" (prison staff lingo), he was a first-class troublemaker. When new Muslim inmates got off the bus, they usually sought out Adam, and often asked him for a knife. "So we sit down and talk," he said, "and I tell them how it's run around here. They can't believe it."

Inmate Involvement

Regular "town hall" meetings with inmates are one part of a determined two-way communication process. Even more important, any proposed changes to regulations or procedures are brought to inmates first. The prisoners typically point out numerous subtleties which will help the program work better, or would torpedo it if not addressed, Luther said. In fact, inmate suggestions are now a routine part of McKean's day-to-day, culture: for example, recommendations about items to be offered in the commissary. (Sound small? Only if you're oblivious to prison psychology. Another "small" touch: The staff cafeteria serves exactly the same food as the inmate cafeteria.) The staff also conducts quarterly "customer"—that's right, inmate!—surveys.

The Inmate Benefit Fund

Attitude is all-important, but "structure" helps, too. Especially the McKean "clubs"—e.g., the Vegetarian Club, the Muslim Brotherhood, the Spanish Club. In addition to providing specific, useful outlets for inmates, the clubs also serve as "intake organizations" for arriving inmates—they're central, in fact, to transmitting McKean's unique culture.

The Inmate Benefit Fund, an umbrella organization representing all inmates, raises money, then spends it on charities, cultural affairs, leisure activities, and special programs. Inmates select representatives to the fund's board of directors, which also includes one senior prison staff member. The fund is audited annually by an outside CPA. "The strength of the Inmate Benefit Fund is that we can contribute to the running of the internal affairs of the prison," the prisoner who heads the Vegetarian Club told us.

The Inmate Benefit Fund is always moving, nudging. When Deborah Hudson visited, the fund was negotiating to become McKean's laundry vendor. Hudson also learned that the Music Appreciation Club was about to hold a fund-raiser—to expand its membership of 75 and to raise money to start a sheet-music library. (A club membership card permits you to check out musical equipment from the recreation center.) The Italian-American Club, 50 strong, had just held a fund-raiser, selling Italian meats and cheeses. Hudson was also invited to come back the evening of her visit to attend the West Indian Club's special ethnic dinner, followed by a video. (Subsequently, Hudson got a note from Luther, proudly reporting that the Inmate Benefit Fund's 1991 Christmas drive had netted $2,000 for needy local children. Overall, the IBF has raised more than $20,000 for local charities.)

"Thank You"

Father Henry Andrae, the Catholic prison chaplain, summed it up when he told us he'd gotten more thank-yous from McKean inmates in the last two years than during 12 years of teaching Catholic students. "The philosophy is 'whatever we can do to make this work better, let's give it a try,' " he added. "What's not accepted is, 'No, no, no, we can't have it, it doesn't work, go to your corner and shut up.' The philosophy is the same for staff and inmates."

Father Henry recalled a food strike right after the prison opened. It didn't turn into a major crisis, because the new leaders met, discussed the problem, and responded by communicating openly, honestly, and in a timely fashion with the inmates. Warden Luther said the strike "was a wonderful training experience. I'd open every prison with something like this! The issue is communication and responsiveness, and in a new facility, the staff was overwhelmed. The solution was walking and talking, getting out into the yard, comparing notes."

OK, OK, but does it work? In mid-1992, after more than three years of operation, the prison has had: no escapes, no murders, no serious assaults on inmates or staff, no sexual assaults, no suicides. McKean earned a 99.3 accreditation rating from the American Correctional Association, the highest in the Bureau of Prisons. "I've audited a hundred fifty prisons," the ACA's Richard Steinert told FCI McKean's staff, "and this is only the second one rated outstanding in quality of life for inmates and staff."

McKEAN'S CREDO: "BELIEFS ABOUT THE TREATMENT OF INMATES"*

1. Inmates are sent to prison *as* punishment and not *for* punishment.

2. Correctional workers have a *responsibility* to ensure that inmates are returned to the community no more angry or hostile than when they were committed.

3. Inmates are *entitled* to a safe and humane environment while in prison.

4. You must believe in man's *capacity* to change his behavior.

5. Normalize the environment to the extent possible by providing programs, amenities and services. The denial of such must be related to maintaining order and security rather than punishment.

6. Most inmates will respond favorably to a clean and aesthetically pleasing physical environment and will not vandalize or destroy it.

7. We do not treat all inmates alike any more than we treat all people in the "free world" alike. We must be sensitive to personality differences, cultural backgrounds, lifestyles and educational levels, and treat inmates as individuals.

8. Bringing racial bias into the institution that results in discriminatory actions can be every bit as dangerous to fellow staff members as the introduction of contraband.

9. Whenever possible, *provide explanations* for changes in policies and procedures that the inmate perceives as detracting from the quality of his life.

10. *Be responsive* to inmate requests for action or information. Respond in a timely manner and respond the first time an inmate makes a request.

11. *Be dependable* when dealing with inmates. If you say you are going to do something, do it.

12. It is important for staff to *model* the kind of behavior they expect to see duplicated by inmates.

13. The indiscriminate use of foul language by staff can only detract from the professional image staff must try to maintain.

14. There is *inherent value* in self-improvement programs such as education, whether or not these programs are related to recidivism.

15. Inmates need *legitimate opportunities* to enhance their self-esteem.

16. Inmates are to be treated *respectfully and with basic dignity.* Staff can treat inmates respectfully without compromising the essential element of professional distance.

*Written by Dennis Luther, and widely distributed at FCI McKean.

17. Be courteous, polite and professional in all dealings with inmates, *regardless* of their behavior.

18. Staff *cannot*, because of their own insecurities, lack of self-esteem or concerns about their masculinity, condescend or degrade inmates.

19. Some inmates are very intelligent or knowledgeable. Don't be threatened but, rather, capitalize on their skills.

20. Never, *never lie* to an inmate.

21. Inmates will cooperate with staff to a much greater degree if motivated by *respect rather than fear*.

22. Don't impose rules, regulations or regimentation that cannot be *reasonably tied* to the need to maintain order and security.

23. Stress the value of rewarding good adjustment with privileges and amenities.

24. Punish behavior that threatens order and security—swiftly and harshly.

25. Send clear messages regarding the kind of behavior that cannot be tolerated in an institution.

26. Inmate discipline must be consistent and fair.

27. Use *only* the amount of force, verbal or physical, needed to maintain order, security, and staff and inmate safety.

28. Do or say nothing to an inmate that you would not want to have videotaped for the warden's review!

Trucks and Trust

"Preston was just like all the other trucking companies," sales VP Paul Sims told us in 1989. "Management knew all the answers. If there was a question, management would make the judgment. No matter that the manager had seven years' experience, and the driver had twenty. The feeling was, 'I am the manager. I have the title.' When a guy didn't have the right attitude, I would give him workloads to straighten him out."

Then, in 1978, Will Potter arrived as CEO of the Preston, Maryland-based company. Potter announced to management—and the drivers—that *management* was the problem. Though Sims, then an assistant manager in the Canton, Ohio, terminal, admits he thought Potter "was nuts," he decided to hang around and give the new approach a try. (A lot of other managers bailed out.) After a seminar on "performance management," for example, he bought an easel and started "posting how productive we were, posting revenues and load averages." He was taken aback when drivers immediately started asking questions. "I'd show them their productivity for the day, and I'd draw a star or use a sticker when they did a good job," he recalls. "I saw these grown guys getting excited about this. If I got real busy in the morning and didn't put the figures up, the guys would come over to me and say, 'Sims! Put those figures up!' " All the involvement nearly wore Sims out. It got to the point where he was coming in at four-thirty in the morning and leaving at six at night, exhausted.

"So one day, I had three keys made to the terminal," he continued. "The morning shift came in and I put the keys down on the table. 'What's that for?' they said.

" 'So that you can unlock the door in the morning,' I said.

" 'What? You aren't going to be there?'

"I said, 'No, I can't keep coming in at four a.m. You guys work four-thirty a.m. to one p.m., but I have to stay until six and it's killing me.' And they said, 'What if we have a problem?'

" 'Solve it,' I said.

" 'What if we can't?'

"I said, 'Here's my number at home, call and wake me up.'

" 'You trust us?' they said.

" 'I wouldn't have made these keys if I didn't.' They couldn't believe it."

Now the workers do believe—and so does union leadership. "Preston is the most unique trucking company I've handled," we were told by Sonny Musso, then president of Merchandise Local Union #641 in New Jersey. "They don't just tell [drivers] 'You can do that.' They explain why, or why not. [The driver] can talk to the president or chairman of the board if he wants to." In fact, Musso became an unabashed salesman. "When I see a good account, I'll give them a call, suggest they should give the business to Preston," he said. "Preston pays attention to the people who do the work, which few companies do."

While hundreds of less-than-truckload haulers shut their doors following industry deregulation in 1980, Preston's fortunes have soared: Revenue has more than tripled, productivity improvement rivals that at the Union Pacific—and accident and grievance rates have tumbled. Tough customers like Charlie Corace, executive director for quality at McNeil Pharmaceutical, told us that the Johnson & Johnson subsidiary is looking at Preston "as a company to model ourselves after. I've become one of their biggest salespeople. I called the company I used to work for and told them about Preston, that it's the company they should be doing business with. . . .

"I now have a Preston truck on my credenza. People walk into my office and ask why. I tell them about what can be accomplished when you support your people. When I look at that Preston truck, I don't see the truck, I see five thousand people pulling together."

18

Basic Organizational Building Blocks III: Market-Scale Units (Buckyborgs)

The advantages of smaller size are becoming very great. Young graduates go to work for giant companies because they have a recruiter on campus and a training program. . . . They used to go from one big company to the next. Now they go from a big company to a medium-size company. When you look at who is exporting, it is not the big companies. . . . [Most U.S.] exporters of manufactured goods are medium-size companies, highly specialized.

I don't think big companies will disappear. I think that in the future it will be a strategic decision whether you want to be bigger or not, when in the past bigness itself was the goal. Some businesses will have to be very big, but I see more and more businesses where medium size is much better and where it simply diffuses results and destroys profitability to try to be big. It is becoming increasingly important to think through what is the right size.

PETER DRUCKER
Fortune, December 30, 1991

"Right size," as Drucker says, need not mean giant—as it almost automatically did for decades. In fact, the giants have led the way in either shedding assets (cutting fat, dumping misfit pieces of their portfolios) or reconfiguring assets into manageable hunks, or both (ABB bought stuff, trimmed fat, and reorganized into 5,000 autonomous bits).

Can we say anything useful in this madcap environment about "right size"? Yes! To begin with, it may be *much* smaller than you imagine—in any business you can name.

GOLDMANN PRODUKTION, THE 11-PERSON BOEING

There are two ways to color a candle. Most common, in the United States anyway, is "through coloring," which involves lots of inexpensive, fat-soluble coloring chemicals. The dipping and coating method uses expensive pigments that, unlike the fat-soluble variety, don't bleach out over time.

Goldmann GmbH, founded in 1919 by Sidney Goldmann to import boric acid from the U.S. into Germany, consists of three companies. One produces those expensive pigments—highly sophisticated compounds, not altered by sun or heat. They're also solvent-free and nonallergenic.

CEO Walter Goldmann's pigment production outfit, Walter Goldmann Produktion, with just 11 employees, has a whopping 50 percent share of the world market in this specialty niche! The growing, $5-million (revenue) firm envisions a possible breakthrough in the U.S. Several large American chemical companies plan to expand their production lines and use pigment dipping. If so, the likely source will be Goldmann or Bekro Chemie, another miniature German firm (which has the other half of the world market).

Whoever heard of an 11-person company with a heavy emphasis on R&D? Well, whoever heard of an 11-person company that has a 50 percent world market share? Two of Goldmann Produktion's 11 employees are full-time researchers, responsible, among other things, for an explosion in the number of proprietary mixtures the company offers—from 600 shades at the start in 1971 to about 10,000 today.

Goldmann Produktion's operation mirrors the best of German management practice. Worker "self-responsibility" is Walter Goldmann's constant cry. That, along with focus, listening to customers, an export orientation despite its pygmy size, and that continuing investment in R&D, has turned Goldmann's independent candle pigment chemical company into the Boeing of its field.

May the Best Garage Win!

You can do a lot with a very little money.

ROBERT KRIEBLE, Loctite
founder, lecturing Russian
officials on entrepreneurship in
early 1992

In late 1991, Wavetracer of Acton, Massachusetts, announced a "deskside massively parallel processing supercomputer" that caused a stir in the computer industry. The $85,000 to $150,000 machine, with 8,192 custom processors, measures just 8 by 23 by 29 inches, and runs on standard 110 volt current. In a Pentagon test, it demonstrated a 50:1 price performance advantage over the Cray XMP-48, a powerful supercomputer, though not Cray's most advanced machine anymore (the XMP-48 costs $15 million new). More important, Wavetracer's offering promises to bring supercomputer power to the desktop—opening the door to decentralized computational feats that were recently unthinkable.

If a big firm had tried developing such a machine, one industry leader told me, it would have taken three or more years and several hundred engineers, and R&D costs would probably have been $25 million to $150 million. Wavetracer, on the other hand, went from paper design to fabricated system in 18 months—a team of 10 engineers did the job with $2 million. In fact, the first pre-prototype was constructed from $14 worth of "stuff" from Radio Shack!

(And then there's the supercomputer that *New Yorker* author Richard Preston dubs "Gregory Chudnovsky's apartment." It's as fast as the $30-million Cray Y-MP-C90, one of the fastest supercomputers in the world. Built with $70,000 worth of parts, the m zero, as the immigrant brothers Gregory and David Chudnovsky call it, is performing unimaginable computational feats.)

BUCKYBORGS (AND MAGIC)

In its August 24, 1991 issue, *Science News* uncharacteristically gushed about, uh, "buckyballs":

The more they discover, the more researchers wonder whether there's anything [Buckminster] fullerenes cannot do. . . . The symmetric buckyball's 60 [carbon] atoms fit together so well that the molecule exhibits properties that make it seem like one giant "superatom." . . . It reacts with many substances and maintains its integrity under a variety of conditions. . . . [It] represents an intermediate scale between the atomic and macroscopic [levels]. . . . [Scientists] applied very large pressures to buckyballs . . . compressing the molecules to less than half their original diameter. And the buckyballs still bounced back. It's very resilient. . . . Fullerene fever has sparked a number of investigations into buckyballs' frenetic motion. There are 174 different ways that these things can vibrate. . . . Each buckyball could flatten a little and bulge at the side and then return to its round shape. Or the balls could expand and contract as if breathing. Or the pentagonal facets might push out as the hexagonal ones contract. . . . Then, too, the balls can spin freely and continuously, or sporadically in a ratchet-like fashion. Often, they move quite fast at high temperatures . . . tumbling around every which way. . . . Ordered or disordered, spinning or twisting, superconducting or lubricating, the superstar spheres display a lot of things that point to a lot of unusual properties.

Goldmann Produktion teaches us that "right-sized"—even in chemicals—can be 11 people! And maybe companies of more than a dozen or so are too big to invent nifty supercomputers. Maybe not, too. But it's not a silly suggestion.

I want to leave the dozen-person global world-beaters behind for now (we'll get back to them in our Markets and Innovation section with a vengeance), and turn to *magic*. These buckyballs may offer the clue. The wonder molecules have chemists on the edge of their chairs. By the standards of the molecular world, they're not tiny. They're not grand. They can have the bejesus beaten out of them and bounce back. Hey, they can vibrate 174 different ways—not bad.

Buckyballs—and Percy Barnevik—got me thinking. Barnevik has fallen head over heels in love with a *50-person molecule*, those ABB profit and loss centers. Some are bigger (up to 500 people—though they'll probably get busted up). Some are smaller (a dozen people, ABB's equivalents to Goldmann Produktion). But 50, give or take, is the very happy median.

With Messrs. Fuller and Barnevik in mind, I suddenly found myself tripping over the number 50/60 with great regularity. Britain's Richard Branson built a multibillion-dollar enterprise, mostly in the tough entertainment industry (records, an advertising company that uses dirigibles, etc.); before peddling his record companies in early 1992, he had a payroll of 10,000—grouped in 200 companies, average size 50 (and when the number got much beyond that, he'd swoop in unceremoniously and split the company up—to keep it agile and aggressive).

In the pages that follow, we'll examine several buckyball organizations, or "buckyborgs," as I call them. They encompass much of the commercial spectrum—media (Random House, International Data Group), financial services

(Acordia), heavy manufacturing (Chromalloy Compressor Technologies and, looking back, ABB). In each case, the "magic" number 50/60, more or less (35 to 200, actually) crops up as an effective—market-scale—unit size.

There's lots more to this story. For example, and again ABB is a case in point, there is power—and profit—to be reaped from cobbling together sizable collections of these units: e.g., being small and big at once. Neither Peter Drucker nor I have any problem with that. The point is not that "small is now always beautiful." It is that big is often ugly—in its current, still typically undifferentiated state (IBM's newly autonomous units, for example, are almost all still monsters).

What follows is hardly "proof" that the magic number 60, or 50, or 35 or 200, is right for every market. I will be pleased if you read through the cases and simply give me a "Hmmm. Interesting." (And I'll be thrilled if you start muttering things like "magic number fifty. How the hell can I get hold of Barnevik?")

Why 50?

18 October, 1991

Dear Tom:

You said you were fascinated by the number fifty, that corporations seemed most productive when they were composed of no more than fifty people. I worked in start-ups for years. You are right. After about 50 employees, companies are not the same. Certainly, between 80 and 100 employees, they lose their efficiency.

The answer might be simple, and it has to do with the ability to communicate effectively. After all, with 50 employees there are 1,255 mathematically possible *two*-person interrelationships. Today, when you can't partition tasks as was once the case, when groups form and reform, and people must work together as an efficient team, my mind is boggled that fifty is even an effective group size!

I also believe that at some point in an organization's growth, layers of management evolve—maybe it is at 50 employees. It is axiomatic that meetings attended by more than two layers of management are ineffective. This means that while it is difficult for people to work together in an unstructured environment, it is equally difficult to work in a structured environment.

Sincerely,
Dave Bonini

TP Note: Bonini works for the Silicon Valley arm of a major Japanese computer company. His unit (and *a fortiori* the parent firm) has far more than 50 people—and is doing well. Is Bonini writing his employer off? Hardly. It's just that there's something about this number worth our attention—particularly, as Bonini underscores, when accomplishing cohesive tasks is a must and yesterday's hyperspecialization is doomed.

IS THIS BOOK BROUGHT TO YOU BY: (A) FEISTY LITTLE KNOPF OR (B) GIANT RANDOM HOUSE, INC.? PICK (A), (B), OR (A) AND (B).

Liberation Management is published by Alfred A. Knopf. (Some call it the premier publisher in the American book industry—lucky me!) But the book is only "sort of" published by Knopf. It is also published by Random House, Inc., a $1-billion global enterprise (which in turn is part of the loosely linked, $10-billion Newhouse media combine, consisting of Random House and numerous newspapers, magazines, and cable television properties).

Random House, Inc. consists of a "daunting maze of divisions, imprints, and imprints within imprints," David Streitfeld wrote in *New York* magazine in late 1991. There's the Random House imprint within Random House, Inc. (Little Random, as it's commonly called), Knopf, Pantheon, Schocken, Villard, Crown (whose "family" also includes Clarkson Potter, Orion, Harmony, and Bell Tower), Times Books, Turtle Bay (new, with seven people), Vintage, Ballantine/Del Rey/Fawcett/Ivy, Fodor's Travel Publications, a juvenile division, the Outlet "promotional book" company, audio, video, and reference and electronics publishing divisions—and a score of international units from Toronto to London to Sydney to Auckland.

A market-facing/market-scale unit at Big Random, an "imprint" like Knopf, is a *very* small business—the size ranges from 2 people (Schocken) to 80 (Little Random), with 25 the average. Imprints "acquire" manuscripts or proposals (e.g., the right to Katharine Hepburn's autobiography) from an author or, more often these days, from the knowledge society's ubiquitous middleperson, an agent. Then the imprint oversees their editorial development, design, and production (the latter mostly done by outsiders), and marketing. Knopf, for example, employs 76 people: editorial, 30; publicity, promotion, advertising, and the sale of foreign and other rights, 21; design and production oversight, 23; finance, 2.

On the street-end of the business, Big Random has four distinct sales forces totaling nearly 180 salespersons; they peddle books and other products for Random's dozens of imprints, and also those of five otherwise unrelated

publishers, including Reader's Digest books; the sales operation is comple-
mented by a distribution scheme that includes three warehouses, in Westmin-
ster, Maryland, Avenel, New Jersey, and Jackson, Mississippi.

Collections of Compatible Intellects (Making Money!)

Big Random is in the business of developing intellectual property, chairman
Alberto Vitale told me in mid-1992, a process that he says can't be defined as
neatly as product development at a GE or GM. (True, but the point of this
discussion is that GE's and GM's worlds are becoming more and more like
Random's—much to the chagrin of many of those organizations' denizens.)
Vitale called an imprint "a company" and "a collection of compatible intel-
lects"—the sum of its editors' skills and zest. Radical decentralization is the
only possible structure, he claims, for maintaining "intellectual distinction"
among the jumble of imprints. To keep the creative juices bubbling, he almost
sighed, "You put up with a lot of nonsense, improvisation, a certain lack of
management professionalism [by Harvard B. School standards]." You tolerate
such confusion in pursuit of the "bottom line"—a bottom line, Vitale snapped,
that comes down to the answer to one question: "Do we have the books?"

"The price of freedom [for an imprint] is financial success," Vitale said.
He's not kidding. Random House, Inc. has a buttoned-down budgeting and
forecasting scheme, which even Vitale cheerfully admitted is "rigorous."
Moreover, peer pressure (among the heads of Random's imprints) keeps the
heat perpetually high. Though Vitale acknowledged that "intellectual talent
[i.e., an imprint] can go through periods of drought, maybe even several years
long," he quickly added, "If you're not upset when you perform poorly [fi-
nancially], you shouldn't be here."

Shortly after arriving at Big Random in 1990, Vitale proved that he meant
business by challenging longtime Pantheon publisher and book-world heavyweight André Schiffrin to put his house in good financial order after several
years of serious losses. Schiffrin refused—and was shown the door. (Some
claim that Vitale's predecessor, Bob Bernstein, was himself shown the door
because he wouldn't read Schiffrin the riot act.)

Squirrels' Nests . . .

My experience with Knopf, and Little Random before that, is small-company
to the core. You enter the unimposing lobby at 201 East 50th Street in New
York City, look for the name of your imprint on the elevator, and ride up to
the appropriate floor. There you're greeted by a receptionist in an unadorned
reception area. Well, maybe you are. Maybe you're not. The desk is often as
not unoccupied. Then, with or without guidance, it's into the: (a) labyrinth?
(b) squirrel's nest? (c) rat's nest? (d) beehive? Take your pick.

Each office is a crystal-clear declaration of individual independence. At
first (to this day, in fact, in my case), you are stunned to pass these little

dens—perhaps 10-by-10—knowing that the editors have, in many cases, dealt with the literary giants of our time, maybe for decades. When your manuscript gets to the copy-editing and design phases, you often go from 10-by-10 offices to 8-by-10 offices, virtual closets. In any case, your experience, from stem to stern, is one of intimacy—a far cry from most impersonal, big-corporate settings.

. . . and Corporate Muscle

Vitale insists that the squirrel's nests—and the energetic little imprints that encompass them—could not make it without Papa Random. Random House, Inc. has deeper pockets than any tiny stand-alone, can survive those occasional droughts at one or two imprints, provides useful specialized services (e.g., legal), and, courtesy its overall marketplace presence, can attract star talent. As to the latter, Vitale asserted that "being the company where every top editor wants to work" is his principal aim for the corporation.

Book publishing, as Vitale sees it, is about both sustainable quality (creating stable homes for superior editors) and raw opportunism. It is both a peaceable kingdom (editors working meticulously to shape a manuscript, a process that sometimes takes years) and, he said, "beyond madness" (the near-mindless scramble for the right to publish a Magic Johnson or a Norman Schwartzkopf, and, later on, the frenzy associated with hitting the street at the "right" moment and pushing the book into a *very* crowded marketplace in a *very* big way). Structurally, then, according to Vitale, Random House, Inc. is big *and* small—a blend of "reactive capability" (small) and "central services" (big).

The longtime publishing veteran contended that the Big Random difference is encouraging "freedom of individual expression" among editors and others ("without abdicating financial responsibility," he hastily added, for the umpteenth time). Such freedom to produce the best is a long-time Big Random tradition that Vitale clearly cherishes. It is certainly abetted by the overall Newhouse philosophy—*lots* of freedom, *lots* of responsibility to perform. (And don't forget to italicize "lots" both times.)

It's essential to understand how far the Big Random "model" goes beyond "decentralization" as it has been conventionally practiced by sizable outfits. The Random imprints are "small businesses" with exceptional autonomy, which must thrive or evaporate. But that's not the whole story: Random imprints have unmistakable "personalities" of their own that make each one more than a "unit" of Big Random. It is these remarkable differences of character among so-called "subordinate" units that allow the parent—as de facto portfolio manager—to thrive in its madcap marketplace. And it is just such distinctiveness of agile, modest-size units that I see as the premier requirement for tomorrow's corporate success in general. At Big Random, you'll find no better example of a tiny unit with its own signature than Knopf.

Sonny Mehta, Inc. (Mostly)

Knopf publisher Sonny Mehta jokingly told me he was attracted to books because he's lousy at math. Frankly, it's hard to imagine India-born Mehta being lousy at anything. His publishing career has consistently been marked by a strong independent streak, literary acclaim, controversy—and commercial success.

In 1987, S. I. Newhouse, Jr., talked longtime Knopf editor-in-chief Bob Gottlieb into running the increasingly frumpy *New Yorker* magazine (which apparently stayed too frumpy for Newhouse, leading to Gottlieb's dismissal in June 1992). As his successor at Knopf, Gottlieb hand-picked his old friend Mehta, then the publishing director of Pan Books in London. While some were irritated that Random House had reached across the Atlantic to fill what may be American book publishing's most prestigious slot, most gushed about Mehta's artistic and commercial instincts. In a major story in *Vanity Fair* at the time of the move, author Ian Jack summed up the "community's" feelings when he wrote that Mehta is "a man who in the judgment of his peers and rivals is an inspired finder and seller of books."

Mehta, who also heads the Vintage and Pantheon imprints for Big Random, has changed everything and nothing. Gottlieb, he said, was a one-man band. He allowed editors enormous latitude to develop books with their authors—but those books were always, in the end, those that Gottlieb wanted. Mehta has his passions for particular books, too (including Bret Easton Ellis's *American Psycho,* which he acquired for the Vintage imprint); yet he encourages editors to follow their own tastes in books to be acquired—and then permits them lots of space in the subsequent development process (albeit calling their attention, far more than was done in the past, to the financial aspects of publishing). In a sense, he's turning editors more or less into "publishers"—businesspersons per Chapter 15—in their own right.

Mehta, however, is his own chief marketing officer—and his business instincts are at the heart of an increasingly healthy Knopf. Moreover, he's sharpened the imprint's financial discipline. Before, he told me, all the numbers were kept in Gottlieb's head. Mehta has added a bit more formality to the budgeting process, without making it bureaucratic. He also makes it clear that he, not Papa Random, is master of Knopf's financial planning process.

I asked Mehta why such an independent force (himself) chose to take on the challenge of a little (in conventional terms) company as his next career step. He frankly admitted that he knew next to nothing about Random House, Inc. in 1987 when he signed on, but quickly agreed to come because of the unique standing of the Knopf imprint, which he declared to be one of a handful of the world's best. It also turns out that Mehta, literary to a fault though catholic in his tastes, is a compulsive marketer. He has a steely determination to connect with readers in large numbers, and have his books "make a difference in the world's conversation." Hardcovers don't sell well in Britain, Mehta explained, which is why he gravitated to paperbacks and Pan there. Hardcovers do sell well in the United States, where they play a central cultural role—none, perhaps, more than Knopf's.

Mehta is officially a corporate vice president of Big Random, though when we talked he seldom mentioned the parent firm, seemed to take its occasional political intrigues with a grain of salt, and admitted that being part of Random House *Inc.* per se hardly makes him tingle. It's books and new projects of all sorts, and linking up with readers, that get him animated.

Still, Big Random has its uses. Its pockets are deep, and, assuming that Mehta's own house is in order, he can get quick approval to proceed with almost any manuscript acquisition or other new project. Moreover, the big firm's powerful sales and distribution arm helps enormously in getting to those readers. Although Mehta is involved in the grubbiest details of marketing Knopf's 180 (more or less) new titles each year, he allowed as how he has little appetite for managing per se, and blanches at the thought of having to be involved in such things as sales force administration. "Even making decisions about replacing a receptionist who leaves is a nuisance," he said.

Will Mehta hang around at Knopf for almost two decades, as predecessor Gottlieb did? Will he finish his career there? Climb the Random House, Inc., ladder (such as it is)? Seek a bigger pond? One senses that he has little taste—or inclination—for climbing *any* corporate ladder. He is, however, perpetually on the lookout for opportunities to break new ground in publishing and leave his mark. (Mehta, make no mistake, is a hustler. But in the terms of this book—see especially Chapter 30—he is a "horizontal" hustler, oriented toward grand projects, not a "vertical" hustler, spending most of his time worrying about politics and perks.) As long as he can fit such opportunities into his Knopf, Vintage, and Pantheon portfolios, he'll probably hang on. Sonny Mehta is indeed a master in publishing's universe, but at this juncture he can probably do as much or more within the Big Random "family," albeit mostly unattached to that family, than anywhere else.

Does Mehta bring to mind a division general manager at a Fortune 500 company (I've met hundreds)? No! His views are clear, at times quirky, and always very independent. His potency in the industry is not matched by one in a thousand "division chiefs" in traditional firms. Knopf has become *his* imprint as it was Gottlieb's before him. Mehta is Mehta, and Knopf is Knopf-and-Mehta—and, marginally, part of a bigger entity. Mehta, who has a lawyer negotiate his financial arrangements with Big Random (he has no taste for it), reminds me more of someone like movie director Martin Scorsese: Mehta hooks up for a while with large outfits that provide the space for him to achieve sizable projects he thinks are important; he spends as little time as possible minding the corporate entity, performs in his own pond (and expands its diameter and depth accordingly), and mostly goes his own way. Attracting a handful of such fiercely independent people is a key—*the* key?—to the small-big success of Random Inc., the overall Newhouse organization, and perhaps 'most any firm these days.

INTERNATIONAL DATA GROUP

We think small is beautiful. If people have total control over their business, they will have the best possible emotional involvement.

> PAT McGOVERN
> IDG Founder
> *The Economist*, March 1991

Knows startups cold—grows by launching them constantly within his own company. Craves customer contact, responsiveness, speed; launched one IDG publication in just three days. More than any other CEO around, McGovern gets it: preach the mission, provide information, give folks plenty of rope—then get out of the way. . . . Another thing: has as much fun on the job as anybody we know. We like that.

> *Inc.*, upon naming PAT
> McGOVERN CEO of its "Start-up
> All-stars" in 1989

Each Wednesday, the mailman delivers *Computerworld* to my farm in West Tinmouth, Vermont. Running 125 or so dense pages, it declares itself "The Newsweekly of Information Systems Management." *Computerworld* (USA) is one of 180 titles, read by about 25 million readers in 59 countries, published by International Data Group.

In addition to its magazine operation (IDG Communications, which tallies over 80 percent of IDG's total revenues), IDG includes IDG World Expo Corporation (which produces conferences, seminars, and trade shows for the information technology industry) and the IDG Research Companies (which do market research and consulting for 3,700 corporate clients and oversee various industry databases). In 1991, IDG grew, as usual, by 25 percent or so, from a little over $500 million to about $650 million.

The company was founded in 1964 by MIT-graduate-turned-iconoclast-entrepreneur Pat McGovern, a frenetic world traveler who logs a quarter of a million miles a year tracking the ever-changing information industry—and easily keeps four full-time secretaries busy in the process. Industry luminaries such as Microsoft founder Bill Gates acknowledge the company, based in Boston, Massachusetts, as a major information-systems-industry player. (IDG's success also landed McGovern on the *Forbes 400* list of wealthiest Americans.)

Spinoff, Spinoff, Spinoff

> I'm convinced that our success is based on a decentralized approach to doing business, on our ability to stay "small." By doing so, we can evolve with the market and constantly identify new customer groups. . . . How can you create a small-company environment and still continue to grow and prosper? The answer is the networked corporation, and the facilitator is technology. Technology breaks down barriers that block the door to the next generation corporate environment. Networked computers, sophisticated but affordable communications capabilities, and strategic use of information systems suddenly create a myriad of possibilities.
>
> PAT McGOVERN
> *Chief Executive*, April 1990

IDG was only banking $1 million in annual revenues when McGovern decided to spin off his first independent business unit—and go international! "Pat had a vision many, many years ago that each market has to have its own set of publications, its own market research, all indigenous to that national market," IDG president Walter Boyd told us. Started in 1967 by the launch of *Computerworld*'s Japanese counterpart, *Shukan Computer* (now known as Computerworld Japan), the strategy has led to 80 globe-spanning business units today.

Speed. Responsiveness. Independence. Those are the watchwords. But McGovern and company give those oft-used words new oomph. One of its flagships, *MacWorld*, was announced the same day Steve Jobs announced the Macintosh itself. And in 18 months, starting in mid-1989, the company launched 16 publications in Eastern Europe.

Fritz Landmann, former president/publisher of *Computerworld*, came to IDG in late 1986 and started *Federal Computer Week*. "Pat literally handed me a check and said, 'Good luck. You have eight weeks to put out your first issue,'" Landmann told *Folio's Publishing News*. "Pat's great talent is in hiring talented people and then getting out of the way. He's very interested but not intrusive. I got action, action, action. At [a previous employer, such a] start-up would have taken six months."

The formula works. A remarkable three-quarters of IDG's publications turn profitable within the first three years—and fewer than 10 have failed. McGovern explained the genesis of his small-unit, spinoff philosophy in a 1990 article in *Chief Executive*:

> When I am driving along Route 128 in Massachusetts, or Route 101 in Silicon Valley, I use an eyeball measurement to evaluate the companies that line those highways. The number of cars in the parking lot after 6:00 p.m. is inversely proportional to the size of the company. . . . In the large companies, the parking lot is a desert. This phenomenon is one that reinforces a business lesson I learned right after graduating from MIT. I was associate editor of a computer magazine and my job was to travel around the U.S. and visit computer companies. I noticed immediately that the people I met at the smaller companies were more excited by their work, about product opportunities and contact with customers. The bigger the company, the less satisfied the people were. There was frustration with internal competition to get ahead, not to mention much less contact with the customer. The conclusion is obvious: small is better.

IDG's business units average 50 people each (yes, that number), and range in size from about 30 employees, in Argentina and New Zealand (overseeing three publications), to 200 employees at *Computerworld* in the U.S. The company has launched as many as 20 publications in a single year. McGovern explains how:

> IDG is able to respond quickly to opportunities because of its highly decentralized corporate organization. Our market research company, IDC, provides us with important guideposts. . . . As soon as IDC research, information sources and my own instincts developed during the years in the business suggest that a new market is ready for an IDG publication, I get involved personally. This means that I am on the spot in the country. If the situation seems favorable, we then survey prospective readers and talk with the principal potential advertisers. Once we are confident that a market is viable, my key task becomes finding the right local person to head the business. And finally, when the publication is launched, I put my trust in the managers I have hired.

IDG insists that its local chiefs start from scratch. "We have thirty-nine *Computerworlds* around the world," Boyd told us when we interviewed him in 1991, "and people think, 'Oh, you translate into that many languages,' but the fact is we don't translate at all. We start companies in each of the countries." Every *Computerworld*, for example, gathers stories of particular interest to its country, all written in the country's language. Feature advertising aims at that country's buyers, and the magazines are printed locally.

In 1990 *Boston Business Journal* profiled the entries of IDG and its competitors Faxon into the then-Soviet information technology publication market. Faxon simply printed more copies of its regular U.S. magazines. IDG's publication was written in Russian by Russian writers. "Surprisingly," McGovern said, "our market research shows that Soviets really don't want to read about U.S. success stories." The upshot: Faxon aimed to achieve profitability in Russia within three to five years, while IDG broke even on its very first issue of *PC World USSR*, based on circulation proceeds alone.

Local business units are further encouraged to expand and create additional publications. In fact, IDG headquarters will help out, paying up to $50,000 to research any interesting idea (such "R&D" was budgeted at $15 million for 1992). But one cardinal rule is observed: Every product must have a dedicated product champion. "You've got to have one person whose entire life depends on making that particular publication work," Boyd said. "Every time we've given in to not doing that for whatever reason, we've made a mistake." Business unit presidents are encouraged to start other publications, he added, "but then they must give up the publishership. We always try to be the market leader, and you need a focused champion for that." The genealogy of *Network World* is typical, *Folio's Publishing News* reported in 1990:

> The editors of *Computerworld* saw how important communications was becoming to companies. They also noticed a new group of managers emerging at those companies to oversee the networks of voice, data and video communications. They swiftly launched *On Communications*, a magazine with longer feature articles aimed at the managers of networks. It was put out twice as a supplement to *Computerworld*. The audience proved voracious, and *On Communications* became a monthly. . . . Finally, it turned into a weekly newspaper and was renamed *Network World*. . . . [It] turned profitable in 1989, just three years after the weekly's startup in March 1986. . . .
>
> Now *Network World* is about to sire its own spinoff: *Global Network*. . . . One of *Network World*'s senior editors pitched the idea to Gary Beach, the publication's president and publisher, last February. At a board meeting in April, he asked for test money. . . . The editor who conceived the launch idea, Steve Moore, is being made editor in chief of *Global Network*. . . . And so it goes at the IDG publishing think tank.

In addition to start-ups generated by existing business units, IDG also listens attentively to outsiders who submit business plans for new publications. "We look at a proposal and then might say, 'We love your idea. Come join us as a president and do your business plan,' " Boyd told us. "We do a fair amount of this, and we're like a magnet for people! They know our reputation, they know they can still function as an entrepreneur. They can get their seed money and their cash flow from us, but still have a very high level of independence." Over a dozen IDG operating companies have sprung from such over-the-transom inquiries. (The pervasive idea of "ownership" manifests itself in other ways as well. Thirty percent of IDG is currently owned by an ESOP, and McGovern is aiming for 50 percent employee ownership by about 1995.)

Global from the Start

"When we started, 78 percent of the world market for information technology was in the U.S.," McGovern told the *Boston Business Journal* in 1990. "Now it's 45 percent, and by the year 2000, it will be under 20 percent. So if you're not globally present, you're going to miss a vast majority of the opportunity." So far, IDG has mirrored the shift in the information-technology marketplace. In 1991, 53 percent of IDG's revenues came from outside the U.S., a figure expected to run up to 80 percent by the year 2000. Boyd claimed that the company is "probably fifteen to twenty years ahead of most [competitors] in the U.S., who are just now realizing that everybody has to be global."

But IDG seldom follows the easy path. Not only did it start overseas by taking on Japan, but it also has bragging rights as creator of the first joint venture—of any sort—in China. And the company launched Eastern European operations in Hungary in 1986; today IDG Hungary is profitable and employs 90 people who generate $5 million in revenue. Overall, *Computerworld* alone had editions in 22 languages and 50 countries by mid-1992.

A Lean but Persuasive Center

IDG's headquarters staff numbers just 20. Four are members of the executive committee (McGovern, Boyd, the executive vice president of finance, and the controller). They're assisted by a few financial analysts, administrative assistants, public relations staffers, and secretaries.

How do far-flung business heads communicate with headquarters? Directly! "There's *nothing* between the independent business unit managers and headquarters," Boyd insisted. "There's a direct link, and they get twenty-four-hour response from us. We don't have regional managers. We don't have product managers. Headquarters functions like a venture capital company. In terms of 'management layers,' we have none." (Note: *None.*)

Which is not to say anarchy reigns. One corporate ritual is the 11:11 executive committee meeting. "Every Monday of the year at eleven-eleven a.m., we either have to be in the conference room at headquarters or on the phone," Boyd declared. "We discuss any new business plans [IDG receives three or four each week], any new proposals, any variations from plan." The crucial Monday meeting underpins the group's ability to move fast. It's a rare issue that languishes for more than a week awaiting resolution.

And financial control *is* centralized. Each business unit, for example, electronically transmits a standard accounting report to headquarters every month, along with a page of commentary that, according to Boyd, "typically contains just major messages for us—changes in the competitive situation, the economic situation, social conditions." Unit managers must also submit 30-, 60-, and 90-day outlooks and a year-end forecast updated each month. An annual business plan must also be turned in—and once agreed to, it is to be met. *Or else.* "If an independent business unit manager misses three quarters in a row, then he gets the dreaded visit from me, at which time we suggest to him that it might be time to look for something else to do," Boyd said. "There are exceptions, like a major economic or social upheaval. But basically, if a situation is normal, we say, 'Lose three quarters in a row, and you're clearly not the right manager for us.' We feel that our presidents are very much in touch with their market. Once they make their commitment to us, we expect them to keep it." You can't defend yourself by ginning up timid projections, either. "Our stated corporate goal is to always grow revenues at twice the rate of market growth," Boyd explained. "If the market grows at fifteen percent, we want to grow at thirty percent."

For those who make it, the rewards are great—unexceptional salaries are accompanied by significant bonus potential. "The bonus is tied to the business plan and there's no top and no bottom on it," Boyd explained. "We agree once a year on a salary and bonus base. For example, we might say, 'Your salary is a hundred thousand dollars and you have a hundred-thousand-dollar bonus. The bonus will increase or decrease by the same percentage that your plan increases or decreases. If you do ninety percent of your plan, you get ninety percent of your bonus. If you do a hundred eighty percent of your plan, you get a hundred eighty percent of your bonus.' We like to keep base salary to no more than fifty to sixty percent of total compensation. We don't want people who want to work for a flat salary—those people don't interest us."

Train in Tough Times

McGovern is a nut about training. "We set aside for training an amount equal to three percent of our payroll," he told *Human Capital*. "Each business unit has those funds charged to its budget, so it's 'use it or lose it.' We build it in so a group that may have a difficult business year won't be tempted to improve its bottom line by cutting its training budget. . . . A unit having a difficult business year is often the one that needs to train the most, because they're clearly in a competitive situation where it's even more important to elevate the skills of their people. . . . We find the best return on any investment comes from training. That's better than putting in a new word processor or a color-separation system or labeling machine, because your rewards go for the lifetime of the employee rather than just for the lifetime of the equipment."

The center also requires each publication to do several customer surveys each year and insists that units do regular market research. Headquarters sends out an annual employee survey, too—workers rate their unit and immediate supervisors.

Support Operations Get the Market Test

Business units typically do their own editing, reporting, publishing, sales, circulation, marketing, and production. Accounting, market research, list rentals, and other support services are mostly contracted out. IDG has several "central service units" which perform these functions, but all are organized as separate companies—and business units are not required to use their services. "The service units have to sell themselves to the operating units on an annual basis to maintain their business," Boyd said. "That means that our central accounting group realizes that everybody who uses their services is a client, and thus treats them like clients. They have to give superlative customer service and their price has to be right. Headquarters will not underwrite *any* of their shortfalls. They go out of business if they lose their customers."

Keeping the center lean and publications entrepreneurial calls for eternal vigilance. "I constantly fight the spread of hierarchy and those who extol the top-heavy approach," McGovern wrote in *Chief Executive*. " 'Why don't you have central paper buying rather than each individual publication finding its own source?' the experts ask. 'Such economies of scale would certainly produce an immediate increase in margin,' they say. That may be true, but taking away operating freedom would cause key people to leave the company, and in a few years, stagnation would set in. If you allow a small group of people to take an idea, nurture it, build it and make it happen, the chances of success are enhanced beyond measure."

A "Networked Corporation"

"We *live* on electronic mail," Boyd said. "Everybody in the world is connected to our e-mail system." The company also set up IDG News Service, which gives all IDG publications access to the news stories of all other IDG publications.

Though following its own publications' advice and living the Electronic Age to the hilt, IDG is also master of high-touch—and spends lavishly on face-to-face get-togethers. Regular geographic meetings bring all units from a country together with Boyd, and product line meetings bring all *Computerworld, PC World, MacWorld,* or *Network World* staffers together. Function meetings gather salespeople, marketing people, or circulation people from hither, thither, and yon. An annual three-day worldwide fest is the icing on the cake. All these meetings transfer know-how, share information, and build up a sense of camaraderie between otherwise very separate operating units, Boyd claims. Concern with leveraging knowledge—and simultaneously maintaining entrepreneurial zest—never stops.

Cap Gemini Sogeti (and the Magic Number)

"Cap Gemini Sogeti, France's leading [information technology] services and software organization, has no centralized human resources department; instead the group's three divisions—France, Europe and the U.S.—are split up into some 250 autonomous branches, each comprising an average of 50 employees. The evolution of the group is like the growth of a cell; as soon as a branch reaches an unmanageable size, it is subdivided into two smaller branches.

"Each manager of a branch is in charge of a budget, and is paid by results. He also has sole responsibility for the organization of his human resources. This decentralized structure is well suited to the service company that provides custom-made services for its clients—and many companies in many sectors are becoming just that sort of service company.

"But accepting autonomy means accepting difference. A candidate is always recruited by his direct superior, even if the latter has only a few months seniority. 'This approach,' commented a manager, 'is simply a logical consequence of the philosophy behind decentralization—decisions should be made by those whom they concern.' This autonomy can lead to wide differences in practice between branches. Managers from neighboring groups are brought together for training. Cross fertilization of ideas is encouraged—but sameness is not enforced."

"Building Flexible Companies"
Business International Limited
1991

THE LITTLE ACORDIA GIANTS

Ben Lytle sits atop The Associated Group, a fast-growing, $2-billion (1991 revenue) corporation. The 7,000-person, Indianapolis-based outfit is divided into seven lines of business, such as health insurance and managed health care, including Blue Cross and Blue Shield of Indiana; life insurance; government program administration; and general financial services, including the investment-banking firm Raffensperger-Hughes & Co. (Insurance industry rating specialist A.M. Best gives The Associated Group one of the highest possible rankings, based on soundness of financial results.) Then there's the arm which packages, tailors, and delivers most of these services to carefully selected market niches—some 20 Acordia companies. CEO Lytle calls the Acordia idea, launched in 1989, "a totally new concept in the financial services industry."

SBUs a Disappointment

Appointed head of operations at The Associated Group in 1982, Lytle dealt quickly, and he thought decisively, with the big firm's obvious clumsiness. He created five Strategic Business Units (which expanded to become the seven lines of business described above). "But I found they weren't small enough or focused well enough," he told us in 1991. "In fact, the culture of the corporation didn't change that much. It changed for a handful of executives who now had strategic business unit accountability, but even they still thought like 'organization men.' They still thought about 'How many people do I have,' not 'How much money am I making?' They still thought about the internal measures of service, not external ones."

It would have been "extremely difficult to jump straight to the Acordia companies concept," Lytle asserted in retrospect, "so we spent almost five years in these SBUs, while we crafted the Acordia idea, which involved, first of all, a further breakup of the business units." (Today, those units mainly serve as "production" operations for the Acordia marketing and product development companies—see below.) The Acordia idea, Lytle added, also meant defining "narrower niches, creating separate legal corporations, and decentralizing several major functions that hadn't been decentralized when the SBUs were created.

"One of the biggest steps was to totally decentralize into physically separate facilities," he said. "I never will forget one exchange in the elevator. I was really excited about having gone from a functional organization into these major units. A claims processor was in the elevator, too, and I asked her, 'How do you like working in the new structure?' And she said, 'Oh, real well.' And I asked, 'Where do you work?' I was expecting her to say something like, 'I work in the Commercial Division, we support small businesses.' But she said, '14.' All that had changed for her was the floor of the building where she worked. Nothing else!"

The elevator episode "really made me take a look at how to change culture," Lytle reflected. "You have to change what people see, where they live, how they're paid, everything. So when we subsequently did the rollouts into the Acordia companies, we literally changed a lot of things about the way people lived. Our people even had to interview for jobs in an Acordia company. And we went to more at-risk pay, more incentive based on bottom-line results."

The Acordia Concept

At first blush, the formal definition of the Acordia concept—to "design, integrate, and administer insurance and financial-service products to specialized customer segments"—hardly sounds radical. Put another way: An institution (school, hospital, bank) currently purchases financial services from dozens of different agencies and administrators. An Acordia company's mission is to consolidate all that—"to bring these products together [for] our clients. . . . Acting as an integrator . . . we [will create and] assemble specialized product packages and service much of what we package, rather than leaving it to the insurance company, which may not be as responsive to our client's needs." The point, Lytle told us, is that "insurance and employee benefits purchasers are increasingly going to demand unique, customized, integrated solutions." That, he said, marks a sharp break with traditional, standardized, "take-it-or-leave-it" insurance products and services.

The Acordia solution is a passel of tiny companies, each aimed at a microslice of the marketplace. Or, in Lytle's words, a "network of small, independent specialty companies headed by entrepreneurial management." Lytle constantly underscored the word "independent." "These are *not* just operating divisions," he insisted again and again. (He's gone a long way to turn such rhetoric into hard reality. All Acordia companies, for instance, have their own chief executive officers and their own boards of directors, usually including outsiders.)

An Acordia company will serve—and attempt to meet all the financial service needs of—one industry (e.g., schools, colleges), one age group, or one geographic locale (e.g., 11 counties around Evansville, Indiana). So far, Acordia companies are serving city, county, and other local governments; colleges and universities; private and public secondary schools; banks and other financial service institutions; and providing products and services for senior citizens. The 1989 roll-out included 8 Acordia companies, and Lytle can imagine 100 within 10 years.

"An Acordia Company is much smaller than a large corporation," Lytle proclaimed in a recent speech, "but still a substantial business." The ideal size, he and his colleagues believe, is 65 to 100 people. In fact, whenever a company's population approaches 200, their plan is to break it up and refocus it on an even more precisely defined niche. The idea, Lytle said, "is to keep the CEO and the employees close to their customers." To further combat bigness within the small operations, workers have mostly been organized into self-managed teams with, Lytle adds, "direct accountability for a handful of customers."

Each Acordia company is designed to be *very* self-sufficient. Members include sales specialists, product designers, benefits analysts, claims specialists, and, especially important, experts on the customer segment the unit serves. For instance, former school administrators have been brought into the company that focuses on schools, financial consultants into the company aimed at the financial services industry, and so on.

One objective, have no doubt, is to hawk The Associated Group's broad range of products. The Associated Group's seven lines of business will probably remain major suppliers to the Acordia companies. On the other hand, if

Acordia CEOs can't find the financial products they need within The Associated Group's network, they're free to go outside. Toward this end, Acordia companies have already developed relationships with, for example, over 50 of the world's largest insurance providers.

It seems to be working. HayGroup's 1991 "management culture survey" for the Acordia companies found that about 98 percent of employee respondents agree that the "reporting structure facilitates decision making" (compared with about 45 percent for the industry as a whole). Seventy-nine percent saluted "freedom to take independent action," compared to an industry average of 40. And "innovativeness of decision making" was claimed by 92 percent, while the industry norm is 28. For a closer look, we examined four Acordia companies.

Acordia Collegiate Benefits

Acordia Collegiate Benefits inherited 23 college accounts from The Associated Group, and quickly determined that almost half were losing money. Among the parent's 2,000 accounts, the 11 losers were easily buried, but to the tiny Acordia company, chartered to turn a profit from the start, they stood out like sore thumbs. The intense scrutiny also gave Acordia Collegiate a chance to find out *why* the accounts weren't profitable, which in turn led to the development of new products.

CEO Sherry Nord illustrated her new company's approach. "Purdue University tries very hard to take care of its employees," she told us. "They had been operating a campus office where employees could come in and get their claims processed or their questions answered by other Purdue employees." The plan was self-insured and self-administrated, and costs were getting out of hand. "Purdue needed to increase the benefits," said Nord, "but at the same time keep costs down." Acordia Collegiate created a new, tailored scheme that would do just that. However, Purdue didn't want to shut down the campus office and lay off university employees.

"So they also asked us," Nord recalled, "if we would consider having their employees process claims on our system, with our people doing the audits on the claims, our people doing the training for their people, initial and ongoing. We said, 'Well, we've never heard of that being done before, but we'll be glad to try!' "

The request required the utmost flexibility. Acordia Collegiate would have to set up a remote site tied electronically to Acordia Collegiate, teach Purdue employees how to process claims and answer inquiries on claims, and all the while still handle claims submitted by health-care providers, auditing, back-end filming, and storage. It was, and is, a unique operation. Nord also pointed out that there could have been "a security issue, with other folks getting onto our system, but we were able to work that out. The result is that Purdue didn't have to lay off staff, Purdue employees still have a place to go and talk to real live human beings about their claims, but Purdue doesn't have to process anything itself."

Acordia Collegiate's narrow bead on colleges and universities has led to the development of new products with broad application. "After we became independent, we found out that the student market in the college and university arena was sorely in need of attention," Nord told us. "As a large corporation, [The Associated Group] was treating the student business just like any other group account. But we at Acordia Collegiate found that it's dramatically different from a normal group account, and that there were no products truly geared toward students." So a new product was developed, she said, which "we would never, as a big corporation, have done enough research to produce. That's too bad, because ten percent of the uninsured population in the U.S. are students in colleges!"

Nord also reported she can deadeye Acordia Collegiate's marketing. "When you only have thirty-five hundred prospects and you know who they are, you can put together some very clear, focused products. For instance, we only advertise in college and university newspapers or magazines. You don't put an ad in the *Underwriter* [a general-purpose insurance industry magazine] and hope that at least one college reads it! Our name recognition is growing more rapidly than if we were trying to peanut-butter the whole United States with Acordia." (Small equals *more* name recognition. Hmmm?!)

Nord is not surprised by Acordia Collegiate's success. "Decisions are made very quickly here," she said. "We're located within a hundred yards of each other and can walk across the hall and say, 'Hey, let's get together and talk about this,' and we can get the decision made literally within hours. Another advantage is that customers can get to me or a vice president or other officer of this company any day or any time by picking up the phone and calling us. Before, they very seldom if ever got to the head people. . . . We know exactly who the [customers'] people are, we talk to them, have interactive relationships with them. It didn't happen before. Now they tell us what's really on their minds."

Acordia Business Benefits

Acordia Business Benefits of Evansville, Indiana, has a potential market of just 11 counties. "We either make it or break it in eleven Indiana counties. If we don't do the job for these counties, we're out of business," CEO Russ Sherlock told us. "That means being uniquely responsive. For example, Indian Industries came in and said, 'We have this idea for a health-care program. We've developed it in concept, but we need someone to help us round off the edges. We've approached a number of other insurance companies, but they're just not interested in us, because we're only three hundred people, and we're the only people who have asked for this type of program.' We put our heads together and said, 'We can do that.' "

CEO Bob Griffin of Indian Industries likes what happened. "Acordia listened," he told us. "They thought our plan was good, and they worked with us on designing and implementing it. They designed special software for us and have been very supportive of our needs."

Sherlock understands why only his company leaped at such an opportunity. "I have to say that if I were a huge company in New York and some little firm in Evansville wanted to try something wild, I'm not sure I could dedicate the necessary resources," he said. "Look, if I had been with [The Associated Group's] Blue Cross or Blue Shield of Indiana in the old structure, there's absolutely no way I could have pulled this off in less than a year and a half. Instead, when Indian Industries came to us, we had the whole thing worked out in one and a half months."

Acordia Local Government Benefits

The first piece of business Acordia Local Government Benefits got was a direct result of its exclusive local government focus. The State of Mississippi put a retiree benefits program out for bid. About 10 companies responded. "Decision makers in Mississippi were impressed that we were totally dedicated to serving municipal employees," an Acordia Local Government official told us. "They felt that we understood their needs better than any of the other competitors. [Acordia Local Government] had no pricing advantage—the pricing was pretty much equal among the competitors, but Mississippi believed that we knew and understood them better." Mike Henning, CEO of Acordia Local Government, recalled that Mississippi also liked the fact that "we were small, yet backed by a very large financial organization, The Associated Group. Even though our parent is a two billion dollar company, we were an excited, entrepreneurial company that wanted to be sure we understood their needs."

Tom Archer, Acordia Local Government vice president of marketing, said that "the reception we get at the National League of Cities Convention is probably the clearest indicator that the customer likes our specialized services. Last year there were about eight hundred exhibitors, and we were the only health insurance carrier there. As the mayors came by, they'd ask, 'Oh, you do health insurance for cities?' And our response was, 'Yes, that's *all* we do!' They were consistently shocked."

Acordia Local Government offers a full menu of financial service products to local government employees: health, life, disability, dental, vision, financial benefits, and deferred-compensation programs. "But even more than that we offer a service," said Henning. "Our reps are really 'counselors' or 'consultants.' They help local officials through the budget process, planning, preparation, involvement with union negotiations. That's something people in this business were not used to seeing. They're used to an insurance peddler coming in and telling them, 'This is the price,' and that's that. Instead we work with them as a partner and help them control their overall costs."

Acordia Small Business Benefits

Keith Faller, CEO of Acordia Small Business Benefits, offered further evidence of the difference between the new "culture" and the old. Two months before his outfit officially opened, Faller acquired Plan Administrator's Inc., a small third-party administrator. "I knew the environment had really changed," he told us:

— "Only senior executive staff [at The Associated Group] ever made acquisitions in the past;

— "This time, no one other than my team ever visited the acquisition in person at their place of business;

— "I never provided more than ten pages of detail—acquisitions in the past took months and had reams of paper from accountants, consultants, and auditors;

— "The deal involved $550,000 up front and there was potentially $1.2 million dollars at risk—not huge money, but I didn't have a nickel at the time in our company's accounts;

— "I got closure on the deal from senior management after two short meetings and in less than thirty days—and most of that time was spent working the legal angle;

— "I was told, basically, 'It looks good, it fits your mission—you need to make sure you get the profits.'

"Nothing like it could have ever happened in the centralized organization," Faller concluded.

Struggling to Implement

Getting to success stories like these, especially in such short order, hasn't been all roses. "We put all the executives on electronic mail, car phones, home faxes, whatever they wanted," Lytle told us. "We wanted them wired up so they'd be able to talk to each other because they weren't going to have the staff support systems they'd had in the past. E-mail turned out to be a godsend. We also have an Executive Information System that captures information in each of the Acordia companies. Each of them can use it to look at the others, to see how they're doing.

"We had a few of our execs who had never used computers in their career, and they were looking at these things squinty-eyed, but they've gotten used to them and they use them as heavily as anybody else now. I literally threw the stuff at them. It was the reverse of our company history, where it was 'justify your car phone,' 'justify your home PC.' I said if they're an Acordia exec, they get everything.

"We also have a monthly meeting to present how we're doing, talk about different things people are trying. Each CEO presents what his or her company is doing. But the formal part of the meeting is really less important. I purposefully designed the meeting so that it has a long break at the beginning, a little bit of program, a long break in the middle, a little bit of program, and then a long cocktail hour with food afterwards, because that's where all the business gets done. On top of that, Acordia CEOs get together every couple of months or three months on their own—I don't have anything to do with it—and structure their own meeting around the things they're trying to get done."

(When Lytle talked about less staff support for the top dogs, he wasn't kidding! Since The Associated Group transformation began, five levels of management have been removed—two in the initial 1982 move to SBUs, one more in 1985, and another two when the Acordia concept was implemented in 1989.)

Along the road to change, Lytle has also been frustrated by difficulties at the front line. "We found that half, maybe less, of the people really thrived on learning new tasks and doing multiple jobs," he told us. "The other half really struggled with it, either intellectually or they were saying, 'How much more are you going to pay me if I learn this?' The mindset of some surprised us, since every employee survey we've done for the past ten years said they'd like more variety in their work." We're slowly winning it, and as new people are hired from the outside, they don't know that you're *not* supposed to be able to do all these tasks, so they just learn them right away."

In addition to new hires, Lytle depends on what he calls the "show-a-success" stratagem. "We let each company approach it in its own way," he reported. "Some retained a fair amount of specialization in the work, but put together multifunction teams—maybe three claims processors, two inquiry people, and an auditor make up a team. Others cross-trained each person within the team. People figure out what works best for them, then learn from each other. That's the beauty of Acordia. We have twenty experiments going rather than one centralized group trying to figure out how it should work."

New Big

In the end, the key to success at any Acordia company is perhaps very simple. It hustles any business it can in its niche—those hoops that Acordia Collegiate Benefits jumped through for Purdue—because it has no choice. As a small firm, it's cater to the customer's whims, or else!

Overall, as at ABB Asea Brown Boveri, Acordia has redefined the notion of scale. Scale today is mostly associated with knowledge, not lumpy objects. The point of the individual Acordia company is to be a giant, not a dwarf. That is, within the collective heads of its 65 or so employees, an Acordia company will know more about its customers (i.e., be bigger by the most important modern standard—targeted knowledge) than "bigger" (total bodies, total assets) competitors. Moreover, through wise use of its overall network of inside and outside companies, it should be able to bring a wider ("bigger") set of resources to bear, more quickly, more efficiently, and more imaginatively than "bigger" (again: bodies, assets) competitors.

More Getting Small to Get Big in Financial Services

"If Rolf Hueppi is right, the future of his Swiss insurance company is being shaped in Wisconsin's meat-packing plants. And on the shop floors of German retailers, in Swiss dentists' surgeries, and in the showrooms of auto dealers across the U.S. This eclectic batch of small businesses are some of the sectors Mr. Hueppi's company, Zurich Insurance Group [$14 billion in 1991 premiums], has already identified as its targets for growth.

"The aim is to transform Zurich from a sprawling multinational into a network of tightly focused operations structured around certain key markets. 'This is the evolution of the industry: The less specific you are, the more difficult it will be to survive,' Mr. Hueppi says. . . .

"Zurich's answer to the coming [European insurance industry] upheaval, from which Mr. Hueppi predicts a handful of European insurers will emerge as global players 10 years from now, is to cosy up to the customers it wants to keep. The underlying calculation is simple: A more concentrated marketing effort means lower overheads, and a closer customer relationship means more value added in the contract. Taken together, those two factors translate into higher profit margins.

"As an example, Mr. Hueppi points to one of Zurich's U.S. units, Universal Underwriters, which has a 26 percent share of the market for car dealers' insurance policies in the U.S. 'There isn't an auto dealers' convention that our guys aren't invited to. . . . You build an expertise around the customer, and that's an investment,' he says."

THE WALL STREET JOURNAL EUROPE
June 23, 1992

CHROMALLOY COMPRESSOR TECHNOLOGIES

Chromalloy Compressor Technologies is part of the Chromalloy Gas Turbine Corporation, one of five sectors of the $1.9-billion (1991 revenues) Sequa Corporation. Just another subunit? Wrong. Modest-sized CCT has broken itself into 16 independent companies. It's no stretch to say that each one is a legitimate, "huge" (new big) powerhouse in its chosen, tiny field.

"Focused management, focused product" is CCT's rallying cry. (Ditto Acordia!) Each specialty operation features state-of-the-art technology and makes all necessary investments to repair a handful of aircraft-engine components for major airlines. Such a strategy allows a CCT unit to be a clear-cut technology leader and to fully utilize its special equipment—because it can be a genuinely dominant *global* player in each v-e-r-y small arena.

Here are the specs on a couple of CCT's full-blown companies:

● <u>Panhandle Aeromotive</u> "provides specialized repairs to Pratt & Whitney JT9D, PW2000, and PW 4000 combustion chambers, plus other precision thin-walled, high-temperature turbine engine components. Extensive, innovative tooling and inspection facilities . . . and state-of-the-art robotic equipment identify this unit as an industry leader in its field."

● <u>Aero Services Technologies</u> is an "FAA certified repair station specializing in the modification and repair of turbine mid-frames for the General Electric CF6 family of engines. Among the state-of-the-art technologies employed is automatic TIG welding enabling the replacement of turbine mid-frame case and liner flanges. Aero Services Technologies a the leader with regard to incorporation of General Electric Service Bulletins 72–973 and 72–975."

Get it? Probably not. (I don't.) But one thing is clear: *Focus* is CCT's gig! On the other hand, CCT as a whole can bring to bear an extraordinary team of experts on a wide range of thorny problems.

CCT Companies: Independence *and* Shared Services (Small/Big)

A CCT company ranges from 18 to 70 employees and $5 million to $25 million in annual revenues. Each is very independent, with (1) complete, no-baloney profit-and-loss responsibility; (2) its own building, equipment, and management team; (3) the authority to seek out customers, hire personnel, purchase capital equipment; and (4) production, engineering, quality, sales, and technical customer support capability. (While each outfit has accounting staff and full-fledged financial responsibility, incoming receipts go to CCT, which also prepares reports demanded by corporate higher-ups.)

Make no mistake, CCT is as serious as Acordia about maximum company size. Chipola Aerotronics, in Marianna, Florida, started thinking spinoff when it hit 70 employees. Now it's reached 115 and has picked a site 26 miles away for a new company—which it plans to focus entirely on welding activities associated with Chipola's specialty.

The bitsy companies do benefit from shared support services provided by CCT, including building and grounds maintenance, government and public relations, new-site selection, and shipping and receiving. There's also a tiny group of highly talented engineers at the center, on call to deal with special problems. If there's a glitch in a part a CCT company ships, for instance, a specialist will rush to the customer site at CCT's expense, no matter who caused the problem. Furthermore, the center has invested aggressively in customer support technology; for example, QuickTrak is a state-of-the-art 24-hour telecommunications system that gives customers phone access to the status of any component being repaired—in English, Japanese, German, French, Spanish, or Korean.

Life at a Typical CCT Company: Aero Component Services

What's life like in one of the CCT companies? Consider 30-person Aero Component Services. Most line workers come aboard with little or no industry experience, which is the way CCT companies like it. Because of the intricacy of parts that cost $300,000 each, CCT companies find it easier—and more effective—to imprint their quality standards on "amateurs, rather than retrain employees from other outfits," we were told. The hyper-narrow focus of each company abets this thrust; workers needn't be trained on many components. Beyond their technical purview, though, all Aero Component Services workers are involved via self-managing teams in most aspects of the business—quality, reliability, and production techniques, for instance. (One success indicator: Revenue per employee runs a high $250,000 to $350,000.)

Look around Aero Component Services and you'll discover a treasure trove of state-of-the-art machinery. CCT outfits may be tiny, but they understand how their bread is buttered: Stay out front with technology—or else. Thus Aero Component Services, like every other CCT company, has the authority to purchase new capital equipment as required.

But how do potential customers discover such a small outfit? Aero Component Services has its own marketing rep, but also takes advantage of the group's pooled resources, such as "Technology Tours"—regular visits to the world's major airlines. For example, 1990's grand swing stopped at American, Delta, Northwest, and Continental in the U.S., and at SAS, Air France, Iberia, Swissair, British Air, and Aer Lingus in Europe. Technical specialists and other representatives from all the CCT companies were involved.

Advantage CCT

When the breakup of CCT into small companies was announced in 1990, customers thought management had lost its marbles. "Our concept suddenly meant that [an airline] customer, instead of dealing with one company, was dealing with ten," vice president Jerry Price told us. " 'We're trying to reduce the number of our suppliers and you're taking a quantum leap in the opposite direction,' they said. But I think experience with us has changed that. Customers are able to call one of our companies about a [very specialized] component and talk directly to someone empowered to make a decision, to expedite the part through the process if there's an unusual need. And the customer can say, 'We want to change and tighten the tolerance of a certain component'—and that'll happen overnight.''

Price enumerated several customer advantages flowing from the novel approach:

- Speed. Most CCT customers own expensive machinery to repair similar components, but one of their general-purpose machines will typically be used to process all manner of parts. That, said Price, "results in a severe queuing problem, which extends turnaround time." So CCT creates an individual company "with all the necessary machinery to repair one or a half-dozen parts, then does those parts for all airlines. By total focus and concentration on a product, we produce the part in twenty to thirty days that often takes an airline seventy to eighty days." If you fix parts fast enough, you can reduce engine overhaul time by as much as 50 percent. That in turn translates into a requirement for fewer spare engines, each of which may carry an $8.5-million price tag! At the very least, the CCT company's speed means that airlines can carry less parts inventory—no small thing when a part can run $300,000 a copy.

Speed is a cornerstone of CCT's operating policy, and CCT companies must be prepared to promise customers 30 days or less turnaround time, though they generally do much better than that. In fact, the little outfits are so fast they routinely serve European airlines—from Florida, remember. "If anyone had said we'd be sending parts to the U.S. for repair," a Lufthansa executive told Price, "I wouldn't have believed it could happen." But it is happening.

- Responsiveness to the customer. Small means less bureaucracy. Customers calling one of the small companies are immediately in touch with someone very knowledgeable *and* authorized to make decisions. Even the most expensive and complex special requests are ordinarily approved on the spot.

- Quality. Focus means that a CCT company has an opportunity to build towering expertise in its narrow product line.

- Lower costs. Labor costs are generally low, because CCT's tiny plants/companies are located in tiny communities with wage rates below those in metropolitan areas (where most airlines operate). In addition, CCT exec Jerry Melvin told us, "The work ethic in the smaller communities is much greater than in the larger ones. Most people want to stay in that small town, so they're much happier to work there." Greater efficiency thanks to less bureaucracy and sky-high machine utilization seals CCT's commanding cost advantage.

- Better management. Smallness, CCT managers say, means better understanding, better communication, a greater sense of community—and the ability to aim undivided attention at a single product and technology.

- <u>Constant upgrading</u>. Additional tooling, machinery, and expertise are constantly called for, given the rapidity of technological change in the industry. Once more, keen focus is a big plus—a CCT company is rarely late to the technology party. (It can't afford to be!)

- <u>The motivation of a stand-alone</u>. Each company strives to be the best in the world in its focused technology. It's always "on report," thanks to that no-bull P&L responsibility.

In sum, a combination of tiny CCT companies adds up to big. "Our competitors don't have the breadth of engines, engine models, or components that we repair as a collective group of companies," Price asserted. "One of our companies overhauls the JT8D intermediate case [a component of a Boeing 727 engine]. There are competitors doing the same component, but their organizations will be running multiple parts through their shop. We have a shop that only sees this one component. Our people know it intimately. Moreover, as worker experience with the component grows, and our experience at serving the unique expectations and requirements of each customer grows, we're able to provide Burger King 'have it your way' service."

CCT and its airline customers aren't the only ones sold on the concept. "We were very impressed with the facilities and the investment you made in the future of our industry," FAA Airworthiness Inspector Supervisor John Walker said in a 1990 letter to CCT. "I wish all repair stations felt the way you do, because it would make our job a lot easier." Praise like that from the nigglers (thank God!) at the FAA is uncommon, to say the least.

Brazil's Semco Goes Buckyborg

A little over a decade ago, Ricardo Semler inherited a company that was about to go broke. Today it's a vital 800-person enterprise. Among other things, productivity per employee grew sevenfold in the 1980s, despite the constant turmoil in Brazil's markets. (Semler's Semco makes a variety of products, including marine pumps, truck fittings, digital scanners, and dishwashers. It sells to blue-chip customers from around the world. Competitors, such as Westinghouse, are blue-chip as well.)

Semler began by splitting things up. "The first effect [of the creation of business units] was a rise in cost due to duplication of efforts and a loss of economies of scale," he wrote in the *Harvard Business Review* in 1989. "Unfortunately, balance sheets chalk up items like these as liabilities . . . and there's nothing at first to list on the asset side but airy stuff like 'heightened involvement' and 'a sense of belonging.'" Newly autonomous entities of 100 to 150 people each produced an immediate turnaround, however. Sales doubled within a year. Numerous new products, stalled for years in R&D, were unveiled. While Semler says he doesn't "claim that size reduction alone accomplished all this," he does suggest that it was the single most important element—for the simple reason that it put employees in close, human, nonhierarchical touch with one another. (Today, no more than one "layer" of management separates the front-line lathe operator from the division general manager; there were 11 layers when Semler arrived.)

Semler went on to explain, telling a tale reminiscent of Jon Simpson's at Titeflex:

> [We] immediately focused on one facility that had more than 300 people. . . . [It used] an MRP II system hooked up to an IBM mainframe with dozens of terminals all over the plant. Paperwork often took two days to make its way from one end of the factory to the other. Excess inventories, late delivery, and quality problems were common. We had tried various worker participation programs, quality circles, kanban [just-in-time] systems and motivation schemes, all of which got off to great starts but lost their momentum within months. The whole thing was just too damn big and complex; there were too many managers in too many layers holding too many meetings. So we decided to break up the facility into three separate plants. . . . [We] kept all three in the same building but separated everything we could—entrances, receiving docks, inventories, telephones, as well as certain ancillary functions like personnel management, information systems and internal controls. We also scrapped the mainframe in favor of three independent, PC-based systems.

Semler won't let grass grow between anyone's toes. As at Acordia and CCT, part of his creed is automatic division, like it or not. When a Semco unit hits the 100-person-to-200-person mark, it's split in two, "No matter what the economies of scale might be in theory," he said in a speech in 1990, "we find a way of segmenting it." Cribbing Mike Walsh's logic for sizing the UPRR's Top Gun units, Semler insists that such a procedure is required "so that people can know each other."

Semco's corporate staff numbers just 14. There's a single human resources officer, a legal officer, and a small treasury function that sticks around—but general managers are usually out and about, working on new business opportunities and visiting customers. It's a strong stimulant to local decision making. "There's no use consulting [the corporate center]," Semler asserts. "You won't find anybody. So you'd best make the decision where you are."

LIGHTLY LINKED MARKET-SCALE UNITS

What can we learn from these companies? Perhaps, in the past, a Chromalloy Compressor Technologies company would have been a "shop," a cost center. (At best: More likely, CCT assets, all half utilized, half out-of-date, would have been under one vast, undifferentiated roof.) But today, a new realization is emerging. Put an 18- to 70-person group together as a "company," with clamoring customers, full profit-and-loss responsibility, necessary equipment (and the authority to buy more if needed), and all appropriate functional skills—and you gain enormous power, without the extra costs that we've always assumed would flow from "duplication of services." At CCT, no such duplication occurred; yet the individual unit, in its small community, provides a full range of sophisticated services to a precisely targeted array of demanding global customers.

CCT is a brilliant case of "new small-big," of having one's cake and eating it too. It takes full advantage of the entrepreneurial drive of about 50 focused people. But make no mistake, CCT is also a potent network of companies. There is synergy: (1) a coherent philosophy; (2) some cross-selling; (3) group marketing affairs, such as the Technology Tours; (4) a handful of top-rank, on-call experts; (5) a few central support services; and (6) the comfort a big, bureaucratic customer gets from the fact that a CCT company is part of a stable corporation (Sequa)—comfort that would not likely be provided by a 50-person mom-and-pop, no matter how good, that just happened to open for business in Fort Walton Beach, Florida. The ABB, Random House, IDG, and Acordia stories are similar. Their ability to engender entrepreneurial commitment (that comes with "small") *and* harness the power of the network (big) is what buckyborgs are all about.

Are there precedents? When it was racking up one or two billion dollars in sales, Hewlett-Packard could still brag of something close to IDG's flavor of small-unit, entrepreneurial zest—i.e., the small-and-big structure. But it's lost a lot of luster and tended to centralize as it's become a true giant (though HP is working overtime today to regain some of its former entrepreneurial spark). 3M, my longtime favorite, has been able to retain surprising entrepreneurial, small-big zeal, while simultaneously taking advantage of its $13-billion (1991 revenue) network power.

Nonetheless, these new "market-scale" models are different from even the old HP or the current (and old) 3M. Though a reasonably consistent vision and set of values mark ABB, Random House, IDG, Acordia, and CCT, the architects of these schemes have created and/or allowed to flourish genuinely independent, entrepreneurial *companies* within a larger whole. Though there is systemic power, Acordia is a collection of *independent* companies (Acordia Business Benefits makes it in those 11 Indiana counties or shuts its doors). IDG is a collection of *independent* companies. Random House is a collection of *very* independent, *very* cantankerous imprints—remember our discussion of Knopf's Mehta.

The trick, in the end, is creating a new form of network and a new form of independent market-scale unit. "Network power" at ABB, Random House, or IDG is impressive and valuable, but not the product of big, central, overbearing staffs; and unit independence in these firms would turn most HP or 3M unit chiefs green with envy.

WHY A CENTER AT ALL? (THE SEARCH FOR SOUL I)

Goldmann Produktion, 11 strong, does business on its own—and the world is its oyster. Specialized publishers have grown exponentially in number, and in many cases distribution powerhouses like Random House are more than happy to peddle their wares. The next chapter is a special analysis of the ultimate market-scale unit, an independent 345-person global *monster*—Rational, a premier member of Germany's fabled Mittelstand (middle-sized company) sector. In Chapter 21, we'll discuss "supersubs" (super-subcontractors), Goldmann-size, independent specialists with enormous reach in their chosen tiny niches. That is, the new economic conditions, which blunt the old power of scale and call for astonishing adaptability, are spawning a deluge of completely independent, modest-size world-beaters.

Which raises an important issue: Is the network dimension so all-fired important? Why a collection of companies? Why a corporate center at all? Good questions! And there are no easy answers. (The rest of this book will mostly be devoted to wrestling with precisely these questions.) At this point, suffice it to say, based on the cases we've assessed, that there are some things a center can add:

- Point of view (vision? strategy?). I'd choose "point of view" in preference to either "vision" or "strategy." Ben Lytle has a clear idea of what an Acordia company is all about. That guiding idea brings some useful coherence to the enterprise. (CCT's uniform commitment to speed is another example.) On the other hand, Lytle's concept is anything but a detailed strategy that the independent units must follow. Some like the word "vision," and tag Pat McGovern and Ben Lytle as "visionaries." My problem, to be discussed later, is that some "visions" can become straitjackets, more constraining than even an elaborate strategy dictated from on high. And the point in the end, remember, is to engender flexibility, adaptability, and independence of *viewpoint*—so that the individual units can deal energetically and entrepreneurially with their fickle, fashionized micromarkets.

- Reputation for quality. ABB does lots of institutional advertising. Much of it is aimed at "branding" the widely dispersed firm's longtime commitment to and reputation for quality in *all* it does. Random House and IDG, though not institutional advertisers, also "stand for" quality within their big industries. CCT's overall commitment to quality keeps the FAA smiling.

- Methodology/disciplinary emphasis. IDG requires similar customer surveys for similar magazines (e.g., all *Computerworlds*), and there's an unmistakable "IDG way" of establishing, in short order, a new magazine. Beyond the general point of view, there's a reasonably well articulated "way we do certain things around here" that can add general value to networks of dispersed organizations aimed at roughly similar markets (e.g., information for the fast-moving information industry in IDG's case).

- Network to learn from. IDG created its own wire service. It also schedules numerous face-to-face get-togethers to enhance learning across the system. ABB will rise or fall on its ability to turn its little units in any "business area" into a learning network. So, too, the Acordia companies. (The development of formal knowledge management structures will occupy us in Chapters 26 through 29.)

- Big enough pond to attract stars and top talent in general. Though a would-be publisher's attraction to IDG is the opportunity to realize entrepreneurial dreams, there's also an attraction associated with a larger, established entity. Part of IDG's "network power" is its ability to attract energetic stars who are not quite up to going it on their own, but who are far too entrepreneurial for traditional corporations. IDG is also known, remember, as a good place to send business proposals—another "big pond" attribute not available to small, wholly independent entities. The Random House story is the same.

- Access to experts via rotation. One of the jobs of an ABB Business Area chief, recall, is rotating top talent through various small ABB companies in order to accelerate systemic learning, develop general managers (and globalists) quickly, and parachute needed expert skill into a local enterprise. It's one more advantage of the bigger overall pond.

- Selected central services. CCT reaps enormous benefits from the tiny pool of super-experts who can quickly resolve customers' thorniest problems. IDG and ABB have valuable central service units too, though the units are exposed to market pressures—local IDG and ABB companies can elect to purchase similar services from outsiders.

- Market power. If you're going to deal with American Airlines or Lufthansa, you'd better not come across as a pipsqueak. CCT doesn't—even though its *true* power is largely a product of purposeful pipsqueak-ism, those focused 18-person-or-so units. Likewise, ABB's power transmission arm can project a global market presence, even though many of its 25 independent businesses are smaller than a local competitor's.

- <u>Distribution muscle</u>. Random House, Inc. has the ability to push people around a little in the marketplace. In fact, I suspect that the only truly effective giants (in the "old big" sense) in tomorrow's world may well be distribution goliaths—Random House, UPS, Federal Express, Waldenbooks, Wal-Mart, Arrow Electronics. (In some industries, "product" companies are becoming distribution companies to some extent. In biotech, for example, Brobdingnagians like Merck and Eli Lilly are increasingly turning to outsider Lilliputians to do turnkey product development.)

- <u>Assurance of stability because of total size</u>. Recall that the State of Mississippi (customer) took a shine to Acordia Local Government Benefits because of its focus and responsiveness—but was comforted by The Associated Group umbrella. Similarly, the FAA (customer) likes CCT's focused, small units, but is reassured by the Sequa umbrella.

- <u>Deep pockets for speculative ventures</u>. IDG provides millions in seed money to individual magazines—president Walter Boyd called the corporate center a venture capital operation. "Big" Random House shells out millions for a book proposal—an out-of-reach number for a tiny independent publisher, the size of a typical Big Random imprint. There's value to such central kitties, though big-firm pockets can be too deep, stifling the would-be Wave-tracers—beware!

- <u>Enough "bigness" to attract investors</u>. Money flows more readily, like it or not, to an ABB than to a Wavetracer. Artfully concocted networks (see the Thermo Electron case, Chapter 34) can attract big investors for small, at times speculative ventures.

The trick is maintaining the fine line between "something" and "nothing," managing the big-and-small-at-once contradiction, as ABB's Barnevik puts it. At the "nothing" end of the scale, the larger entity becomes a financial holding company, and provides minimal leverage to its collection of enterprises. (It has no soul!) At the far end of the "something" scale, any one of these dozen raisons d'être for a center, let alone all 12 taken together, can add up to big-league intrusion—quashing the hard-earned, ever-fragile independence, spirit, entrepreneurial energy, and "must-serve-the-customer-or-die" zeal that the market-scale unit is designed to engender.

Barnevik was hardly the first to observe the importance of big-small tension. Seventy years ago, GM's legendary Alfred Sloan said that managing the ever-moving centralization-decentralization balance was the CEO's top task. (His current descendants at GM get damned low marks as jugglers.)

How easy it is for these eminently sensible central "contributions" to become overbearing! Hewlett-Packard divisions choked on central guidance in the 1980s. (IBM and GM have almost succumbed to it.) Though Barnevik speaks of balance (even though some have called his firm the world's most decentralized behemoth), it's Pat McGovern's passion for imbalance—"err-ing" unflinchingly on the side of independence—that we should attend to most assiduously in these off-center (bonkers) times.

Decentralization Redux?

This is not a chapter about "decentralization"! It speaks to something more profound—subsidiary-unit autonomy, independence, and personality achieved through a variety of devices (some reviewed here, many more to be discussed in the Markets and Innovation section), on an unprecedented scale.

The search for "balance" is not the main point. Don't forget, this book is subtitled "Necessary *Dis*organization. "Dis" is the main message in a fashion-ized world.

In this chapter, we've seen that the center can do some things to abet its collection of entrepreneurial companies. But the onus is always on the chief, as McGovern and Barnevik know so well, to keep his or her hand lightly on the tiller. It's ever so easy to destroy the sort of newfound zeal that grips Acordia Collegiate Benefits' CEO Sherry Nord today!

19

More Market Scale: Independent, Global, Mighty, and SMALL

Do your sums right, based upon gross domestic product or population, and you'll find that, relatively, Japan has four times more giant companies than Germany. Think about the German economy, if you do (very few do in the United States), and you'll likely think BMW, Daimler-Benz, chemical giant BASF, electronics giant Siemens. Those firms exist, to be sure, and have proud heritages (if not so much profit and growth these days). But they're not the heart of Germany's economic success—as measured in part by per capita exports that typically ran two and a half times higher than Japan's, four times higher than ours before the integration of East Germany (and since—so far).

Germany's secret is its *Mittelstand*. These middle-sized German companies—ranging from fewer than a dozen people (Walter Goldmann Produktion) to a couple of thousand (Trumpf, Chapter 35)—are focused, export-oriented, value-added obsessives. They amount to an old idea that has stood the test of time, and that is still ahead of its time. The best of the Mittelstand, in the fashionized, knowledge-based economy, define appropriate-scale/market-scale excellence. They include winners in low tech and in high tech. They "overcome" the world's highest wages by producing the world's highest-value products.

None does it better than Rational. With just 345 people on its payroll in 1992, the company is the "combi-cooking" IBM, DEC, and Fujitsu in one. It produces computer-controlled ovens that combine convection (forced air) and steam heat. Exports accounted for almost two-thirds of its $125 million sales in 1991 (up from $12 million in 1985), research is a priority, customization is routine, and the sticker price ($6,000 to $26,000) is stratospheric.

TOTAL CONCENTRATION

Why use a Rational combi-cooker? That's what we asked André Soltner, world-renowned owner-chef at Manhattan's Lutèce restaurant, in 1991. "We don't have much space here," he began. "An oven like this does a lot of work and doesn't take up much room. We can steam, we can bake, we can use the combi features such as steaming and then roasting—it's really three ovens in one. And it cooks very evenly: Chicken, for instance, roasts much better with the combi adding a little steam every half minute or so, which avoids our having to open the door to push a little water in somehow or other. Using the steam-only feature, we cook our asparagus, tomatoes, spinach, fish." Soltner, who had used the Rational product for about four years, added that it had "changed the way we do our cooking. I simply could not have the same level of service [for my guests] without this oven. It's one of the greatest inventions since I became a chef."

Things weren't always so rosy for Rational. In 1970, owner Siegfried Meister began resurrecting what he told us was "just another sheet-metal company." He moved into convection cooking and developed a fine oven, but others soon caught up. A battle royal ensued. Meister, who declares himself an archenemy of "destructive competition," had no intention, he told us, of "selling on price."

So he went out to the market and talked with professional chefs about new wrinkles. It's no secret that lots of cooking requires both steam and forced hot air. The chefs reminded Meister of that, and that no cooking tool could handle both chores. Meister, a technologist with any number of patents to his credit, went home and got down to work.

It took about eight years to develop the first effective "combi" and get it established. Despite the "obvious" need and numerous successful demonstrations, chefs were openly skeptical. They had a hard time believing that such dreams could come true. Meister and his colleagues picked up a customer here, a customer there—about 100 in all by 1984. No matter the difficulties, Meister decided to take the plunge. He shut down his successful convection oven line, which accounted for over half of revenue at the time (colleagues thought he was crazy, he admitted)—and poured all his and Rational's energy into the combi. "It was necessary to concentrate," he said. It turns out that Meister's on a mission: He believes he can drive convection ovens from the marketplace. But only if Rational keeps improving its pioneering product. "We're strong," he insisted, "because of our total concentration, our focus, our specialization." (Welcome to the Mittelstand!)

Rational has sold about 80,000 combi-cookers to date. You'll find them on a British submarine, the private yacht of a Saudi prince, a North Sea oil platform, and at Disney World (where they're used by the U.S. culinary team), Lutèce (as well as other chic restaurants around the globe), and numerous hospitals and universities. But the surface may only have been scratched. Commercial market potential, according to sales vice president Helmut Stempel, is 1.5 million units.

A DISTINCTIVE HARD/SOFT BLEND

While state-of-the-art software goes into the combi product, the trick at Rational (and the other German Mittelstand companies we examined) is equal respect for sophisticated software—and for handicraft. Most Rational employees, R&D engineer and shop-floor worker alike, are graduates of Germany's unique apprenticeship program. Meister claimed that the respect for material the program imbues is "just as important as when I went through it. The computer-driven brain in the combi-cooker is important. But the oven has a lot of mechanical parts, too. They have to work with the utmost precision."

A German line worker echoed his boss. "We try to make the product better every day," he said. "Take the welding. If we find a little bit of metal inside the machine which might disturb the customer, that they might rip their clothes on, or whatever, we try to fix it. The main thing is the quality of the product." But suppose it's a little weld on the back of some panel that no one will see, I asked. "It's not a matter of the customer seeing it or not seeing it," he snapped. "The idea is to present the ultimate in quality. And if he sees it or not, well, that's not our problem."

(Meister is critical of some of his American colleagues. "They consider the electronic parts, the software, all-important," he said. "They say it's eighty percent of the product. But I don't think so." He contrasted the Japanese—and Germans—with Americans. "The Japanese also look at the entire product," he told me. "They don't separate things like you do, saying that the 'software is most important, the mechanical unimportant.' ")

SYMBIOSIS WITH THE "TARGET"

I've written extensively about customer focus. But I learned a lot, was humbled in fact, by my visit to Rational. For one thing, there are signs all over the plant, "Gut genug? Der Kunde entscheidet." ("Good enough? The customer will decide.") Then there's Meister's insistence—and I heard this not just from him but all over Germany, from the front line to the front office—that profit is not his primary concern. Solving the customer's problem is his consuming passion. "All decisions are held up to the standard: Do they benefit the customer?" was the way sales chief Stempel put it. And this from a line worker: "Make life simpler, easier for the customer, that's what it's all about." Another: "Everything for the customer." And another: "We have a new generation of oven, in production just six weeks. It opens on the right-hand side. One of our clients asked if we could also have it open on the left-hand side. We went off to research, and they said, 'Well, yes, but it will take time. He wants it in a week, and we can't do that.' So we got together [in the factory] the next day and decided to proceed anyway. The client got the oven on time, with the feature he wanted." When I suggested that such customization would surely break the bank, I was quickly rebuked. "We do anything the client wants us to do," the worker replied. "One wants the handle up, another wants the handle down. I honestly don't think there's anything we wouldn't do."

There were times when I thought I'd run and hide if I heard "target group" one more time. That target group is professional chefs. Rational lives for them. "This is very, very important," Stempel reminded me again and again. "The basic philosophy is the most important thing," Meister said. "We repeatedly talk about our reason for existence, to give the best to the target group." Stempel explained Rational's success by referring to the "vision," the "colorful pictures that Herr Meister paints for everyone." Meister used the same language. "I paint pictures, try to bring the idea to life, over and over again." The picture Meister paints? "Simplifying daily cooking jobs for chefs all around the world," Stempel almost shouted at me.

"We have three hundred forty-five people here thinking combi-cooking every day," the sales chief continued. "No competitor can boast of fifteen years of total concentration on combi-cooking." The future? Meister insisted he won't carry more than 400 employees on his payroll. But after expected growth and more subcontracting, the 400 will be all the more focused on a few skills unique to combi-cooking. The last 15 years was all about concentration. Tomorrow: *more* concentration.

Research absorbs 10 percent of all employees. Simply put, no other competitor, including any number that are dozens of times bigger than Rational, can boast a 30-person research activity aimed exclusively at combi-cooking. A customer visiting Rational's research area will see 30 machines, Stempel told me. "Every one of them will be a combi. When he visits a competitor he may also see thirty machines in R&D, *if* they let him in. But maybe one out of the thirty will be a combi." In fact, Peter Huber, head of R&D, insisted that letting customers into R&D is part of Rational's strategy. "We want them to see our R&D, to know how hard and exclusively we're at work improving the combi technology," he said, "pouring resources on in a way that no one else can match."

The Customers' "Lawyers"

Rational can boast of 12 full-time chefs, who in turn claim experience in some of the world's leading kitchens. "They're lawyers for our customers," Meister told me. Other competitors, Stempel said, might have "one or two chefs, but usually none." Those chefs are responsible for many of the features, technical and nontechnical, which set the Rational product apart.

It seems so obvious. But apparently it's not. No one else has them. Rational does. The chefs are constantly out and about, cooking at food fairs around the world, training chefs who've just bought the Rational product, giving demonstrations in one of any number of training centers owned by Rational or one of its distributors. And listening, listening, listening.

Staff chef René Markus described a typical visit to a recent purchaser of a Rational cooker. "We go out," he said, "look at the menus that they offer, provide advice on how to best use the combi to exploit those menus." And if one of those customers calls, from anywhere, and wants a staff chef from Rational, quick, the chef hits the road—at Rational's expense.

The easy, open relationship the chefs maintain with R&D and the shop floor is almost as important as their dialogue with customers. Head chef Josef Meringer described "cooking with our engineers," leading them to better understand the world of the kitchen. In addition to such live demos, any number of practical tools keep the staff chefs in touch with R&D and product planning. According to sales chief Stempel, the firm doesn't rely on market research surveys of its clients. Instead, he told me, "It's a matter of constant feedback, sitting down and discussing things." For instance, there's a monthly *jour fixe*, an established day when chefs, product managers, and R&D people meet. The chefs are "not like salespeople," Stempel pointed out. "They speak the language of our customers."

Stempel went on to list a number of other activities that buttress the vital keeping-in-touch process. For instance, all field-service techs spend at least four to six weeks working on the line in the factory, he said, "feeling the material, getting an understanding of how it all fits together." And all sales and marketing people serve a stint in the kitchen—a week in a hospital kitchen, another week in a hotel kitchen, another in a restaurant. The objective, Stempel said, is "feeling life in the kitchen, the daily problems of the customer."

No Barriers to Communication

Open communication is a key to success. R&D chief Peter Huber made it clear, for example, that all Rational's staff chefs feel perfectly comfortable "calling me directly, or the software engineer who's working in the area, when they have a problem. And the service trainer—when he comes back from a trip around the world, he always stops by, gives R&D feedback."

The combi's astonishingly user-friendly operating panel is typical of the by-products from the close—and mutually respectful—relationship between the chefs and the engineers. Stempel is amused at the complexity of some competitors' operating panels. "I saw one once at an exhibition in Vienna," he recalled. "There was a little piece of paper attached to the operating panel explaining the symbols—to the company's *own salesmen*. It's unbelievable—but true." He shook his head and added, "If those symbols, made by engineers, couldn't be understood by their salespeople, think about how the [potential customer] feels."

Or take the case of the skinny thermometer. The combi-cooker, like some others, comes equipped with a meat thermometer. But how should it be designed? "The engineer says it would be better if the stick is thick," head chef Meringer told me. "That means greater safety, a longer lifetime. But for us chefs, it's important that the stick be very thin. With a thick stick, we put a big hole in the roast beef, and you can tell when you slice it. We don't accept that. You as a restaurant guest shouldn't accept it either."

The chefs were clear: "We need a thin stick for the meat thermometer. It could be broken, but that's the engineer's problem. Our problem is the roast beef." Animated discussions took place among the engineers, the chefs, the salespeople. The chefs were insistent. So were the engineers. Meringer chuckled as he recalled the exchange. " 'You're stupid chefs,' they said. 'What do you know about metal?' So we kept discussing it, and, in the end, we found the right solution [a pretty thin stick, with lots of strength] for chefs all over the world. This is so important to us."

SELF-IMPOSED SIZE LIMITS

Will Meister stop at the 400-person limit he's set? Stempel is openly skeptical. But if not 400, then something pretty close to it. "We don't want a thousand or two thousand people," Stempel told me. "That's not our objective. We want to be innovative, we want to focus on know-how, not putting up more bricks, more buildings, big factories, and things like that. We really want to emphasize the innovative power of the company."

That translates, as Meister sees it, into "doing in-house what we can do better than others, and giving to outsiders anything else." He calls it the "strategy of the prolonged workbench." To oversee his unusual approach, Meister has "created two different 'heads of production'—one for production done in the company and one for work done by subcontractors. They're in a kind of competition. Each wants to prove that his workers can do the best components, provide the best quality. [In the case of the outside production head, "his workers" don't work directly for him.] Then afterwards, we'll decide when each component will made."

The production boss in charge of subcontracted work would normally be in "purchasing"—in Germany or America. "But we don't want things to be 'purchased,'" Meister said. "We want to enlarge our production, not just in-house and not just by investing capital in [our] plant. We want to do it outside. Maintaining our standards, our insistence on just-in-time production, is only possible if you treat outside work like production of your own."

But no matter how much work is subcontracted, Meister is bound and determined to "maintain the feeling for the [whole] product." Toward that end, he insists he'll always hold on to at least one machine associated with each major production activity, so that Rational can co-lead technology advances with its subcontractor partners.

Meister's approach to production is mirrored in relationships with the other important category of outsider—distributors. Rational typically seeks out relatively small distributors that can become true partners, share its philosophy, grow with the firm—and, most important, concentrate on the combi product.

THE FLEXIBLE RATIONAL WORKER

Think about Germany, and you probably think discipline, rigidity. Discipline, yes. But rigidity is a different story. In fact, discipline, especially self-discipline, allows for the underlying conditions which engender maximum flexibility. Production head Bernhard Hintersberger recalled his experience at giant Siemens. "In such a place," he told me, "it always takes step after step after step to communicate with another department." But at Rational, by contrast, "You can go to the telephone, you can reach any employee, you can reach [R&D chief] Huber. You can tell him something, work out a problem on the spot."

Good enough, I conceded, but does it work the other way? What about the factory workers? Hintersberger was clear. It's commonplace, not unusual, for them to go directly to him or even Meister. In a subsequent conversation with four plant workers, I asked whether Hintersberger had been telling the truth. "It's absolutely true," one shot back, and then went on. "Anybody here on the production floor, anybody wherever in this company, can call anybody else. We can call Herr Meister, Herr Stempel. You can page him, call him on the phone. And we do it." The worker was eloquent in describing why such communication is vital: "It's essential, because you need to make decisions very quickly. It's important for us not only to be able to talk to the next level, but two levels up." (Could I have been conned? Yes, but I don't think so. The worker's body language said, "How could you ask such a silly question?" As I heard the same tale elsewhere, and at a tavern or two, my skepticism receded.)

Workers also contrasted Rational with bigger companies. "Companies like Siemens are just not very flexible anymore," one worker said. "They can't modify their products as quickly as we can." Stempel pointed out that there's "feedback every day at Rational [from the marketplace]. In bigger companies, it's often ignored." He reflected on 20 years spent working in Germany for Hobart, the big American kitchenware maker. Engineers and marketing people rarely talked, he said. Marketing people were generally unwilling to consider ideas that might be appropriate to the German market, but not necessarily to the American market. (Stempel tried to get Hobart interested in the combi idea, but it was dismissed as "of no interest to the American market." Take that, Chef Soltner!)

Discipline, Self-discipline, "Self-realization"

The no-walls, easy-communication story was at times hard to fathom. In my tour through German firms, for instance, I invariably bumped into large quality-control departments. The new American theory (that is, the Japanese theory, which we've imported) is that quality control should be turned over to the worker; there's no need for a quality-control department. Yet the German approach seems to work, and apparently isn't as dispiriting to workers as it is in the United States—where quality control is the cops policing idiots (those workers). I asked a Rational quality-control officer, Roland Klages, whether he wasn't, in the end, a cop. I got an earful: "We might look like policemen [quality people wear different-colored jackets], but that's not our job. We're a bridge between production and the customer." Klages insisted that his job was supporting those in the plant. "Everybody makes mistakes, and if you make a mistake, that's fine," he said. "The issue is how people treat each other. And here it's a matter of respect for the worker."

That might sound like motherhood and apple pie, but I think, instead, it's one of the special attributes of the German working environment. Almost everyone in the plant has been tempered by that apprenticeship program. Workers *are* competent, and are *perceived* as competent. The point, production chief Hintersberger said, is not discipline, but "self-discipline." There's mutual appreciation for skill and craftsmanship—among, say, the production worker, the engineer, and the quality-control person. The time spent learning respect for material and precision during the lengthy apprenticeship program provides a strong basis for subsequent respect on the shop floor. Such grounds for mutual respect are absent in most U.S. operations, where the "worker" hasn't been indoctrinated in such basic skills, and the hands-clean "boss" wouldn't know the results of their application even if he were staring at them.

The idea of self-discipline has a concomitant—"self-realization," as Hintersberger labels it. A failure to achieve "self-realization" is the reason he left Siemens. And, for that matter, the reason Siegfried Meister never went to work there in the first place. "My family was civil service, teachers," Meister said. "They told me, in effect [as a young engineer], 'Go to Siemens, get a secure job.' But I didn't want to do that. I wanted to have more possibilities, to move something." And "to move something" is a phrase you often hear from Meister. Young engineers at Rational, he insists, "feel that their efforts can make a difference, right away. And incidentally, their job is as secure here as at a giant company. If you really want to move something, you're far better off here."

20

Networks I: Farewell Vertical Integration, Welcome Networks

The supreme challenge of the 21st century will be the ability to manage projects that transcend all the conventional boundaries, whether to produce global products or prevent global warming. The bureaucracies of the Industrial Age, with their rigid focus on in-house protocols, will appear to the new intercorporate transcontinental networks like old Royal typewriters do to PC users.

JESSICA LIPNACK AND JEFFREY STAMPS, on challenges facing McDonnell Douglas
St. Louis Post-Dispatch,
December 22, 1991

Our economic future hinges on information technology and biotechnology. In these two industries, new-form "organizations"—find them if you can!?—are emerging to deal with rapid scientific progress and an explosion of entrepreneurs. Almost every new product in biotechnology, says Dartmouth's Brian Quinn, comes from a one-of-a-kind "company" that's really a complex network. The industry is marked by extreme specialization: Some companies are stars at certain aspects of basic science, others are masters of pilot-plant development, others' meal ticket is commercial-scale production, others handle clinical trials, and others still, including some of the biggest pharmaceutical houses, dominate the complex marketing, selling, and distribution activities. Ditto Silicon Valley. Products there are usually birthed by unique networks. The idea of vertical integration is anathema to an increasing number of companies. Most of yesterday's highly integrated giants are working overtime at splitting into more manageable, more energetic units—i.e., de-integrating. Then they are turning around and re-integrating—not by new acquisitions, but via alliances with all sorts of partners of all shapes and sizes.

STRAWS IN THE WIND

Financial services are de-integrating fast. Recall the analysis of the industry by Steiner and Teixeira in the Information Technology section: Enterprises are focusing on the few things they can do with distinction, then shipping out the rest of the work to a growing number of entrepreneurial firms, often outside the "industry." (Industry in quotes, because financial service firms are really packages of service activities, most of which are unrelated to finance—e.g., data processing, legal affairs, etc.) And sluggish automobile companies have gone off on a farming-out binge. Once they only "outsourced" secondary components; now they're even starting to ship out R&D. (And if they don't de-integrate, they're at least pushing internal components units, for example, to sell their products on the open market—like "real businesses.") And more:

• Robert Reich, *New Perspectives Quarterly,* Fall 1991: "When an American buys a Pontiac Le Mans from General Motors, he or she engages in an international transaction. Of the $20,000 paid to GM for the car, about $6,000 goes to South Korea for labor and assembly; $3,500 to Japan for advanced components such as engines and electronics; $1,500 to West Germany for styling and design engineering; $800 to Taiwan and Singapore for small components; $500 to Britain for marketing; and $100 to Barbados or Ireland for data processing. The rest—less than $8,000—goes to strategists in Detroit, lawyers and bankers in New York, lobbyists in Washington, insurance and health-care workers all over the country, and GM shareholders—most of whom live in the U.S., but an increasing number of whom are foreign nationals." (So much for "Buy American" campaigns.)

• *The Economist,* September 29, 1990, reports on $77-million (1989 revenues) International Automotive Design. Founded in 1976 by John Shute, IAD now has 1,300 employees in America, Europe, and Japan. The firm is sought out by carmakers for several reasons: Some have scaled back in-house design facilities. Some are deliberately placing projects with companies like IAD to foster a fresh perspective. But above all, IAD is quick. Its main business, *The Economist* says, "is turning ideas on a computer-aided design screen into a prototype which senior executives can drive. . . . This is how the [Mazda] MX-5 was born. The original concept and styling came from Mazda's R&D center in Irvine, California. An IAD prototype was shipped to California so that Mazda officials could drive it in the 'target' market. The company knew it had a hit when motorists in Santa Barbara chased after the car to ask where they could buy one." (Fifteen years ago it would have been unthinkable for automakers to subcontract the tasks IAD now routinely performs for them.)

• Kevin Done, *Financial Times*, March 6, 1991: "Ford has signed a contract with Yamaha of Japan for the design and development of a small engine to be used in its European car range from the mid-1990s. . . . It is the first time Ford has contracted out such an important element of its mainstream engineering development program, and the first time it has turned to Japan."

• "Giant Firms Join Outsourcing Parade," *Computerworld*, page 1, September 30, 1991: "Dramatically staking out new territory in the outsourcing user and vendor landscapes, General Dynamics Corp. and Computer Sciences Corp. teamed up last week on a ten-year computer services contract worth an estimated $3 billion."

• In late 1991, McDonnell Douglas sought an encompassing partnership with Taiwan Aerospace (implementation, as of this writing, is problematic). To become competitive with Boeing and Airbus in commercial aircraft development, the firm sought to de-integrate. In fact, *The Wall Street Journal* (November 15, 1991) reported that McDonnell Douglas only planned to hold on to "the three most important jobs": design, final assembly, and flight testing.

"NEW SIZE" = NETWORK SIZE

In the 1990s, corporate ethnocentrism will . . . give way to corporate collaboration. . . . The concept of the corporation as one entity, fortress-like and independent, will decline and the concept of corporate partnering will rise. . . . [C]ompanies will concentrate on what they do best and align with other companies having something valuable to offer that is integral to their service [offerings].

LEONARD BERRY AND A. PARASURAMAN
Marketing Services

What *is* size? For a couple of hundred years, it's characteristically meant *owning* as much as you can of the action. In *The Visible Hand*, which traced the emergence of modern Industrial Age enterprise, Pulitzer Prize–winning business historian Alfred Chandler called the wholesale shift toward vertical integration in the late 19th century the ultimate step in "perfecting" modern enterprises. And indeed, given the importance of reliable supplies of raw material such as iron and oil in yesterday's economy, and general uncertainty due to limited communications capabilities (no electronic data interchange!) and transportation, having everything under your direct control—under your roof, if possible—made some sense.* No more.

For one thing, lumpy raw material is yielding to ephemeral brainpower as the source of most value-added. And brainpower, unlike an oil field or coal deposit, is fickle—dispersed, ever changing. Also, thanks to the new technologies that provide the ability to communicate and coordinate in a virtually error-free, paperless way (courtesy EDI, the favorite of outfits as different as GM and Wal-Mart), companies can have their cake (reliability) and eat it too (take advantage of others who are more effective at a special task). In the end, though, there's one paramount force: Innovation and flexibility, today's imperatives, are ipso facto at odds with owning all the resources.

Amidst all this, old ideas about size must be scuttled. "New big," which can be very big indeed, is "network big." That is, size measured by market power, say, is a function of the firm's extended family of fleeting and semi-permanent cohorts, not so much a matter of what it owns and directly controls.

The newly de-integrated company/network form of "not-a-company company" ("not-an-organization organization"—whatever) is troublesome to conceive—and a downright pain to manage. When we talk about subcontracting nowadays, for example, we're not talking about the old form of the thing, where a company's engineers develop product specs in a vacuum, its purchasers mindlessly select the low bidder from among any vendors they can find in the yellow pages—and the manufacturing gang gets stuck with the often as not poor result. The "new subcontracting" (I'll disavow the prefix "sub" momentarily) is about networks and relationships among *equals* (and, you should pray, "betters"). Learning how to manage networks of relationships among equals/betters becomes a primary managerial chore for the "organization." Very few have a clue as to what's up. (Among big firms, the likes of Apple and MCI have come further than most. Control-bent oldsters like GM and IBM have the longest road to travel.) How many training courses does your organization have on "managing relationships with outsiders"? How many that *all* managers must attend? That non-managers (i.e., everyone) must attend? These are the kinds of questions we must be asking.

---

*Recall the panic after the OPEC oil shock of 1973. It led Du Pont, for example, to acquire huge Conoco, a move which has distracted the chemical giant from core chemical-business issues, at a time when its product lines are facing numerous challenges from specialist competitors in a fragmenting marketplace.

THE FLEXIBLE, NETWORKED WORLD
OF MCI

If you recognize that there's a constant pressure to institutionalize rigidity, that there's a normal tendency to try and institutionalize the status quo, then what you have to do is institutionalize change, the exact opposite.

BILL McGOWAN
Interview with the author, 1989

The late Bill McGowan's MCI, the David that beat up Goliath AT&T, has become a behemoth in its own right. Yet wander around MCI today and, despite its size, you're most immediately struck by the vigor, energy, barely controlled chaos—even though MCI's business is running a telecommunications network, where major operating errors simply aren't OK at all.

Part of the explanation is a lean organization structure. When we interviewed him in early 1989, McGowan bragged of having "far fewer middle managers" than other firms the same size. Middle rungs on hierarchy's ladder, he said, slow things down, filter useful information, stop decisions from being made. "Most middle managers are really 'human message switchers,'" he went on. "They gather information, they collate it, collect it, distort it a little bit, hold on to it a lot—because information is power; and then they distribute it. All that takes a long time and is very expensive. It stops the decision-making process cold." And that won't do, for MCI or anybody else.

MCI's philosophy is clear: "freedom *and* responsibility." Ops chief Dick Liebhaber insisted that MCI is "no nursemaid." People get "responsibility they never dreamed of, an opportunity to grow, to shape your own job, to do business with less hierarchy," he told us. But if you're "not suited for this environment, you leave. It's not a paternal company." Overall, Liebhaber claimed, MCI is nothing less than a brave "social experiment." And that experiment in wide-open internal management is mirrored in the firm's unique approach to "outsiders."

Subcontracting a Way of Life

MCI reaps the benefits of over 9,000 research and development engineers *not* on its payroll, a senior vice president of advanced technology who *doesn't* develop technology, and a research and development complex in Richardson, Texas, where *no* R&D takes place. The R&D facility is known as an "engineering developmental lab," because that's where technologies developed by dozens of independent contractors from all over the world are tested, perfected, and then integrated into the MCI network.

MCI took to subcontracting because it had no choice! Back in 1968, when the company was founded, no one in the United States would sell it operating equipment. So MCI sought out international suppliers and created telecommunications services using hardware and software developed in whole or in part by others. Now, in an industry where new products routinely become obsolete in a year, MCI claims that it's more efficient to spend time looking for innovative subcontractors than developing its own technology. "I have access to the intellectual assets of nine thousand [other firms'] engineers," Liebhaber said. "If I did my own development, what would I have, five hundred engineers?"

MCI's advanced-technology staff of 12 or so constantly searches the world for leading-edge technologies, Liebhaber told us. (As one result, the company started using fiber optics, designed by Corning Glass, before its competitors.) Furthermore, to induce subcontractors to push their technologies to the limit, the company uses two suppliers for every network function—fiber optics, switching, etc. It then uses automated measurement systems embedded in the network to track the reliability of the vendors' equipment. Contracts are renewed from year to year. "Our suppliers know very quickly that if they provide equipment that doesn't work [or isn't] advanced technology, they aren't going to be a supplier very long," Liebhaber declared.

For example, two large companies, one U.S. and the other Japanese, supplied MCI with laser technology that powered fiber-optic cable at a capacity of 405 megabytes per second (which translates to simultaneous transmission of 6,000 phone calls per second). When the second vendor jumped to 565 megabytes, it won the contract to provide laser technology for all of MCI's new routes. When the first vendor later jumped to 810 megabytes, it won the next contract. "If we had been buying from just one vendor, we'd probably still be at 405," Liebhaber said. "If I'd developed my own equipment, I'd probably still be at 405!"

Vendors who lose out on new contracts aren't discarded. For instance, the "losing" laser-technology supplier still has equipment on MCI's network and is eligible for new contracts if it improves its technology. "MCI sticks with every potential supplier," Liebhaber told us. "Suppliers basically want to be the best and we help them reach their objectives by providing high standards. Sticking with creative vendors also means that MCI will help out if and when the vendor's quality falls short—working together with them on quality control projects aimed at bringing performance up to snuff.

In an apparently odd twist to this "partnering" saga, Liebhaber claims he will not permit a vendor to custom-tailor its product to MCI's needs. Having equipment tailored to your own needs is the same as developing technology on your own," he flatly asserted. "You get to depend on it and get stuck in the technology rut." But MCI does keep in close touch with its vendors' product development efforts. That way, the firm has a head start in figuring out how to use new product as soon as they're available.

MCI also routinely seeks out partners to do tasks outside the company's purview. For instance, when MCI needed part-time telemarketing reps a few years back, it decided to subcontract. "Our business isn't dealing with the complexities of work schedules for part-timers," Liebhaber said. "I'm trying to learn how to provide quality service. I think the most successful businesses today are businesses that have these partnership-like arrangements, where there is something to be gained by each participant."

Using networks of subcontractors can lead to some interesting relationships. There are times when MCI is simultaneously providing a service to a customer, subcontracting a service from that customer—and competing with the same firm. "We have to remember which relationship we're working on when we're talking," Liebhaber told us. "When competing, I deal with a firm just the way I deal with any other competitor." He added: "If you can manage those three relationships in a very rational way, you're a winner. You're each taking strengths from the other."

Though MCI has quickly become the second-largest telecommunications network in the U.S., it still has no plans to produce its own technology. Nor does Liebhaber spend sleepless nights worrying about MCI's ability to come up with new products and services on its own: "It's how you put it all together that makes the difference. That's where we add the value. You see, we understand our business. Our business is not engineering or manufacturing. Our business is service. So it's how you put the pieces of technology together— that's MCI's creativity. We know those are our strengths."

DIFFERENT WAYS TO SLICE THE CAKE

I have to keep networking everywhere, looking for good partners.

> Stephen Wayne, CEO
> Sasson (1991 sales, $256 million;
> employees, *nine*)

Mostly owing to the accident of its birthdate, AT&T does lots more itself than MCI. But these two are not the only sharply contrasting set of direct, powerful competitors. The diagram opposite, adapted from Brian Quinn's *Intelligent Enterprise*, displays 1989 sales per employee and the value of plant and equipment as a percentage of sales for three companies—Apple Computer, IBM, and Digital Equipment. To be sure, the trio doesn't make exactly the same set of products, but they're roughly comparable. Differences in product line in no way explain the fourfold variation in output per employee, or the threefold difference in plant and equipment as a percentage of sales, between Apple on the one hand and IBM and Digital on the other.

Different Strokes for Different (but Apparently the Same) Folks

	Sales per employee	Net assets as a percent of sales
APPLE	$369,593	18.4
IBM	$139,250	63.0
DIGITAL	$ 84,972	44.6

I'm not contending that IBM and Digital are doing it "wrong," that Apple does it "right." My bias lies in that direction, but I needn't go so far to make my point—which is simply that three organizations we think of as "computer companies" have chosen entirely different ways to do business. Moreover, the numbers are consistent with experts' views of the three. Digital, though changing somewhat of late (in response to a string of tardy new products), has long been known for doing it all: If they didn't invent it themselves, then it wasn't worth talking about! IBM was cast from the same mold. Apple, though not the most extreme case in the industry, can fairly be called a "network company." Managing relationships is as big a deal at Apple as at MCI. (Not coincidentally, MCI holds about the same edge over AT&T in sales per employee as Apple holds over IBM.) While Apple attends to some crucial tasks itself—mostly design, engineering, assembly, and marketing—it also, again like MCI, happily farms a lot out.

(It's interesting to see that firms are starting to focus on these formerly unsung statistics. For example, Sun Microsystems, which already contracts out an enormous amount of its tasks, aims to surpass standard-setter Apple by raising revenue per employee from about $200,000, in late 1991, to $500,000. How? Contracting *more* out!)

When we picture Japanese companies, we often imagine monoliths—huge, orderly firms churning out standard goods. Well, as is so often the case, we've got it wrong. Fact is, the average giant Japanese company—Nissan, Fujitsu, Canon—is a network, with exceptional reliance on small (even tiny) subcontractors. The "parent" retains some critical functions, and that's about it. Consider, for example, the $4-billion (1991 revenue) Kao Corporation, Japan's premier packaged-goods firm. The 6,700 employees on its payroll translate into about $600,000 in revenue per employee—50 percent above Apple's number.) Sara Lee, typical of big U.S. and European packaged-goods firms, has a cast of 100,000 supporting $12 billion in sales—five times more people per revenue dollar than Kao. Furthermore, some 2,800 of Kao's 6,700 employees—a stunning 42 percent—were in research and development.

Now think about Apple, Kao, and MCI, so different in level of vertical integration from their principal competitors. Kao has a powerful consumer franchise in the huge Japanese market (and is expanding rapidly overseas). Apple has a powerful consumer franchise throughout the U.S. and much of the world. MCI has a well-anchored franchise in the U.S. and, increasingly, abroad. That is, Kao and Apple and MCI have global market clout and presence. Yet they don't "do" as much as their principal competitors. They farm out many chores (and parts of all chores) and focus their work forces on ideas—engineering, new-product development, advertising, and so on. World-wide Apple-power, Kao-power, MCI-power, then, is mostly network/partner power, not do-it-yourself power.

POWER, VERTICAL INTEGRATION, AND "NEW SCALE"

Market power is no longer proportional to size as measured by vertical integration, or number of employees on the payroll. In fact, power today is, arguably, inversely proportional to "vertical integration size." The vertically integrated firm grows too sluggish, cuts itself off from too many rich sources of innovation, and cannot shift gears easily.

Instead, success in the marketplace today is directly proportional to the knowledge that an organization can bring to bear, how fast it can bring that knowledge to bear, and the rate at which it accumulates knowledge. Market power mostly derives from one's skill at bringing together the best network of insiders and "outsiders"—to take advantage of a fleeting (a few years at most) opportunity. The ability to bring knowledge to bear fast is, in turn, largely a function of:

— the reach of the firm's "network," including insiders and outsiders of any size, from anywhere;

— the density of the network, meaning (1) the variety of network partners brought to bear on the particular project and (2) the intensity of the relationships one has that can be called upon at a moment's notice;

— the network's flexibility and skill at quickly reconfiguring.

By definition, such networks include but are not limited to: (1) suppliers, (2) suppliers' suppliers, (3) distributors, (4) franchisees, (5) other middlemen, (6) customers, (7) customers' customers, and (8) other specialized resources such as university professors and consultants.

Thus, modern market power stems mainly from resources you don't own or "control" in the old, hierarchical sense. In fact, in a "knowledge-based society," where ideas-added to any task are the chief source of value, one does not, by definition, "own" *any* resources. Voluntary contribution of the imagination (there's no other kind, which is the point!) by every on- or off-the-payroll person is the new name of the new game.

"New" Core Competence (Soul II)

None of the above implies that a critical mass of key skills is not important. Remember, McDonnell Douglas intends to keep its design, final assembly, and flight-testing skills/activities intact if it completes its deal with Taiwan Aerospace. MCI is clear that its special competence is putting together new telecommunications packages that can, at the drop of a hat, serve a customer better; rapidly and effectively integrating the work of outsiders is also a special strategic competence MCI seeks to maintain. Or recall Rational: Despite a whopping market opportunity, CEO Siegfried Meister won't let the company top 400 people. As business increases, he will subcontract more and more. But he's out to build an ever-stronger set of core competencies—e.g., via the cadre of staff chefs and the massive R&D operation (relative to his competitors and the size of his niche). Rational is also honing its skill at managing interdependence, via the co-head of outside production idea.

So critical mass and core competence are very much alive and well in this age of "network-power." However, that's not to say it's easy to define critical mass or core competence! Moreover, when an area is designated as a core competence, subcontracting *part* of it probably makes sense. Then the trick becomes figuring out how much to subcontract without losing distinctiveness. BMW, for example, may soon decide to allow outsiders to produce engine blocks, a core competence area that it's zealously kept to itself in the past. Yet BMW has no intention of letting its skills in this all-important area atrophy. To the contrary: Given the importance of engine blocks, it is imperative that BMW maintain the skill necessary to manage the technology and work as an equal with any number of clever outsiders. (Also see page 334.)

Oddly, the more important a "core competence" area is, the more important it is to inject that area with powerful subcontractors, to whom the in-firm experts must listen. We'll delve into this more in the forthcoming Markets and Innovation section; for now, it's enough to note that sadly, but predictably, the more significant the core competence, the smaller the odds that resident experts will listen to *anyone*. Extreme organizational measures that amount to inoculating yourself against yourself are required to keep new blood and new ideas flowing in critical competencies.

It's essential to understand that maintaining a critical mass in a core competence area needn't mean assembling a cast of thousands. That is, critical mass in even the biggest firm could well translate into a group of 10 to 30 stellar players, supported by a perpetually revolving set of outsider (university, small firm, etc.) experts—e.g., MCI's itinerant band of a dozen staff technologists in quest of the best technology/partners. Remember, "new scale" overall is a "network" idea, not an "ownership" idea. Likewise, new critical mass/new core competence can be achieved by an "affinity group." A critical mass for knowledge development (of the sort found at universities, an increasingly good model for a knowledge-based company) is characteristically achieved by "teams" of no more than a dozen experts—from a half-dozen locations in a half-dozen countries on three continents. Terms like "affinity group," "extended community," and "university" are essential to the evolving notion of an effective force that can cope with volatile times.

SUBCONTRACTING PROS AND CONS

Organizations have to build structures that explicitly encourage assimilating external technologies. . . . [They] should do more than hire a few "technology talent scouts"; they need to create organizational parity between internal and external development. . . . Companies should also consider a "tax" on internal research and development projects: Set aside 10 percent to 15 percent of the funding to acquire external technologies, such as licenses, university relationships and outsider expertise. Management should insist that all innovation-development reviews include a discussion of how a new product or service might be assembled from external sources.

MICHAEL SCHRAGE
The Wall Street Journal,
January 14, 1991

Assume for a heartbeat that it makes sense to consider subcontracting *everything*. Over the last couple of years, we've challenged participants at our executive seminars to consider doing just that. Some important ideas have emerged from their deliberations.

- The shift to subcontracting applies to everyone. Of course, subcontracting is a growing issue for AT&T, IBM, BMW. But it's as much an issue for my $10-million (revenue) company. Where is *our* value-added? What are *we*? What shouldn't *we* be doing? Our communications arm has revenues of about $4 million, and five employees—that is, sales per employee run more than twice as high as Apple's. The minuscule "division" (actually, remember, a company in its own right, one of five that make up The Tom Peters Group) works "with" others in accomplishing television, audio, and book publishing activities. To use Brian Quinn's term, it's an "intellectual holding company"— its only assets are ideas, some brand equity/identity (a modicum of market power), *and* an ability to work effectively with a variety of network partners.

- The chief objective of extensive subcontracting is innovation. MCI and Apple live in frantic marketplaces, and they mostly use outsiders to help them keep pace with change. Subcontracting is hardly a new idea—we've typically gone outside to pursue efficiency. But in our brave new world—where every good is a fashion good—breaking out of habit patterns is an institution's premier challenge. Only constant, intimate commerce with outsiders will begin to do the trick. Of course, lots of subcontracting per se doesn't guarantee innovation. There are clever subs and dull subs. At this point, I'm simply trying to make the case for the vigorous consideration of subs in the first place.

- Efficiency is a side benefit of subcontracting—but not through a "hire"/"fire" approach. Huge firms are finding that effective subcontracting with moderate-size, highly focused partners almost automatically abets efficiency (e.g., CCT). Perversely, smaller firms, with little overhead and the ability to act with blinding speed, tend to be much more efficient than large outfits which choose to do "it" inside. The efficiency comes from the nature of the sub, not because, as has been standard practice, subs can be brought on board when demand is high, dismissed when demand is low. Such an idea is anathema in the new subcontracting context; if we're talking about developing "network partners," then treating "subs" as expendable resources is a grave mistake.

- Subcontractors should work on everything—including research and development. Networker Apple has retained the lion's share of the "thinking function" within its walls. Nonetheless, Apple is the master at using subcontractors in the brain sphere—from software writers by the thousands to independent contractors who add pizzazz to anything Apple does. (It sometimes seems hard to find a clever person in the San Francisco Bay Area who *hasn't* done a special project for Apple!) And remember MCI's 9,000-person engineering "staff"—which really boils down to a dozen people working to find and effectively use 9,000 engineers in *other* firms.

- Train, share values, share information, and invite "outsiders" to participate in everything. An effective collection of "outsiders" must work as a coordinated whole. That means focusing on network management per se. In particular, "outsiders" must be treated as insiders. For example, "outsiders" must have instant access to virtually all information, including the most proprietary, of its network partner. There is a catch, however. If "insiderization" of outsiders becomes extreme, you lose the very freshness you were attempting to gain from the subcontractor in the first place. Some would argue that you can avoid debilitating dependence on subs by setting high annual improvement targets. That's a useful step, but not adequate. One reason: "Improvement targets" involve today's goods. The innovation imperative should keep us scouring the world for subs who unexpectedly leap-frog current partners' offerings.

- The cry from the executive suite should become "Prove it *CAN'T* be subcontracted!" The burden of proof should be on internal units to show why they should continue to exist. Most important, the "make"/"buy" decision must be made in a "fair fight"—for example, the internal unit should be fully and fairly costed.

- If you decide not to subcontract a task, require the group performing it to sell a substantial share of its output on the "outside," at market prices. If you're not willing to go whole hog with the sub idea, at least *simulate* the marketplace. (This includes all staff functions, too—à la ABB.)

- "Don't sub your soul." This was the advice of a senior Federal Express officer attending a seminar where our "subcontract everything" challenge was laid down. In the end, there must be an "it" that makes an Apple Apple, an MCI MCI, a Kao Kao. But determining the "it" that amounts to *soul*, or what's special or integral about the organization, is getting ever harder and changing dramatically.

Pitfalls of Excessive Subcontracting . . . Maybe

Participants in our seminars by and large buy the idea of paying much greater attention to de-integrating and to shipping out lots more than they do today. Nonetheless, serious concerns surface.

- The sub that knows your secrets has you by the throat. If multiple subcontractors aren't available, dependence is an automatic problem.

Rejoinder. MCI shows the way in fighting dependence. It insists that subs provide a standard rather than gold-plated, customized product and sets tough standards (i.e., be best in class, worldwide). MCI also never ceases to search the world—literally—for ever more and better subcontractors. Upon finding a candidate special, MCI tests a newcomer's mettle with a tiny piece of business.

Sure, if there is truly one and only one vendor available, you've got a dependence problem. (Although that doesn't necessarily mean you should do the job inside: Who's to say that you can do it better, dependence or not, than that sole source supplier?) In part, though, increased dependence throughout the network is precisely the point; in return for accepting mutual dependence, the yield is presumably more innovativeness, more flexibility, more efficiency. The "cost" to the subcontracting firm is a necessarily heavy investment, which most don't make, in learning how to manage dependent relationships effectively.

• Subs who learn your secrets are likely to expand into your business.

Rejoinder. *C'est la vie!* That won't silence you, but *c'est la vie* has its place. To deal in a fast-paced, ever-changing world, you must create networks quickly to exploit *fleeting* market opportunities. Put together the best network possible to deal with today's opportunity, then hope for the best.

Mostly, though, remember that we're talking about a brand-new ball game in "supplier relations." When a sub encroaches, it's usually because (1) you were casual about initial selection; (2) you subjected the sub to constant niggling of a sort which would erode any relationship; and/or (3) you didn't make a real investment in partnership—and the development of mutual trust—from the start. Lesson: If you don't want subs to screw you, quit screwing them. Another part of the answer is to work only with "the best." The best are invariably preoccupied with doing their own thing ever better— and getting into your business would usually be a distraction. Moreover, "the best" at anything usually have great integrity.

• There are major economies of scale associated with components production (and the production of services, for that matter). If different outside vendors are supplying various parts of my firm, I'll end up denying our internal component maker access to the whole firm—and thence the possibility of achieving maximum scale economies.

Rejoinder. Let's forget the fact that the scale economies are invariably wildly overrated. If the topic is security (Guardsmark, see page 320), parking (Professional Parking Services, see page 318), training on special equipment (Skonie, page 325), it's the sub who usually brings the scale economies! Remember CCT: Its 50-person units are *bigger* than $12-billion American Airlines—when it comes to a particular engine rotor. As for the in-house producer being allowed to serve a big company (yours) on a silver—i.e., monopolistic— platter: It's the single best way I know to insure that inefficiency will reign. That internal producer needs to *earn* its way to any scale economies by winning fairly fought marketplace battles (see page 342).

• If the subs are far away, then the "soft"—but essential—intimacy and learning that come from day-to-day contact will be absent.

Rejoinder. First, familiarity often breeds contempt. The accounting department on your payroll typically has the accountant's contempt for non-accountants. If accounting is subcontracted, on the other hand, the outside provider will at least hide the contempt beneath a serious effort to satisfy the customer in order to retain the business. More important, interesting stuff is going on all over the planet—in any discipline you can name. While there may be some loss from the absence of geographic proximity, you must presume that it will be repaid by the cleverness of the very special sub you worked so hard (shades of MCI) to ferret out. Once again: You'll just have to invest in learning how to work with distant partners—e.g., don't chintz on travel authorizations, even in tough times (especially not in tough times).

- Isn't a subcontractor's loyalty suspect by definition?

Rejoinder. Subs are loyal as all get-out, if chosen carefully. If you're worth a hoot, good subs would like to grow their business with you over the long haul. Moreover, subs—more than your own people—typically have a pressing profit-and-loss orientation that gives them a compelling reason to deliver the highest level of satisfaction possible, and not let you down on the "soft" factors such as loyalty. Furthermore, in a world more sensitive to networks and relationships, subs with reps for disloyalty will find their gooses cooked, fast. Would you hire a sub who'd cheated on your archrival? Not if your head's bolted on right.

Each objection is fair and reasonable. And it turns out that there is really only one antidote—working like hell at network and relationship management, at finding and nurturing superior subcontractors. Alas, these tasks/skills are usually honored in the breach.

NETWORKS, SUBS (AND SOUL III)

Consider this assessment of the publishing industry that appeared in *The New York Times* ("Book Notes") on July 31, 1991:

Move over, publishing houses, and make way for the industry's latest creation: the editorial boutique. Two trends are giving the boutiques a boost. Editors at big publishing houses are overburdened and do not have time to edit all manuscripts. Moreover, several hundred people have lost their jobs in publishing over the past year, and some of them have decided to establish their own free-lance editorial operations.

"Publishers are throwing off more and more functions because it saves them time and money," said Jim Frost, who left Warner Books last year after being asked to give up his post of editor-in-chief. He has now set up his own company, the Philip Lief Group, Inc., which does free-lance editing.

Recently, for example, Delacorte, a unit of Bantam Doubleday Dell, asked Mr. Frost to edit "The Small Book," by Jack Trimpey, which describes a recovery system for alcoholics. Mr. Frost was given the job shortly after Delacorte acquired the work in a $250,000 two-book deal.

Asked why Delacorte had done this, the book's official editor, Emily Reichert, said, "We wanted it out as soon as we possibly could, and we realized that we needed someone to come in and do substantial and very time-consuming work." She said that it was the first case she knew of in which Delacorte had used an outside editor.

Laurence J. Kirschbaum, the chief executive of Warner Books, said that his house now gives about 10 percent of its list to outside editors, adding, "I think that you are going to see more and more of this." . . ."The way it is going," [said publishing consultant Lorraine Shanley], "publishers are going to become more like distribution systems with editorial functions farmed out elsewhere."

Many publishers are resistant to that notion. But the economics of modern publishing in media conglomerates seems to have opened the way for the boutique doing everything from line editing to the "packaging" of books: That is, the complete preparation of a work to the point where the publisher merely has to manufacture and distribute it.

Perhaps tomorrow's only "big" (more or less "old big") firms will be distribution outfits. That's the gist of the story here. But where's soul in all this? "R&D" and "product design" in publishing are mostly performed by authors and editors. Authors have always been "subs." (And other tasks, from indexing to dust-jacket design to printing, are also usually subbed.) But now editing is being subbed, too. If you sub "R&D" and "product design," what are you left with? Surely a big dent in soul.

On the other hand, big publishers (so far) all maintain at least an elite cadre of "acquisitions" editors, who bring authors to the house and manage long-term relationships with authors important to the house. (This cadre is perhaps analogous to MCI's itinerant band of a dozen super-engineers pursuing new technologies from around the world.)

The big publishers, then, are expert at "network management" (authors, agents, subbed non-acquisition editors, designers, etc.) and marketing/distribution. Yet there is a danger here. There is an elusive "something" that makes, say, a Knopf a Knopf. It has to do with the cadre of super-editors (who, at Knopf, not only acquire manuscripts but also painstakingly reshape them)— and with the cadre of copy editors (master craftspersons who mostly oversee the work of outside subs), designers, and others who carry the Knopf lore and contribute to the "Knopf feel" of a/this book.

Messy, eh?

21

Networks II: The World of the SuperSubs

In 1990, I gave a speech at a Marriott hotel in Orange County, California. It was at noon. Traffic was badly congested. Yet the Marriott clan did a remarkable job of valet parking, unloading over a thousand people in an amazingly short period of time. It was better than that. They did it with panache—a look of hustle, crisp uniforms, a smile for every patron, and nary a dented door.

Various companies, including Walt Disney Productions, had bought tables for this public television fund-raiser. In the midst of my remarks, I turned to the Disney gang and said, "Even *you* could learn from the way our friends at Marriott handled the parking!" Applause followed. Many others evidently had noticed the extraordinary parking act. After the talk, a young man introduced himself as the cofounder of Professional Parking Services, Inc. It turned out that his outfit had done the "event parking" for Marriott.

Welcome to the world of super-subcontractors, or "supersubs." They're the ones who make it possible for an MCI or an Apple—or a Marriott—to de-integrate and win by doing so.

PROFESSIONAL PARKING SERVICES, INC.

Ron Cribbet, general manager of the San Ramon, California, Marriott when we spoke to him in 1990, chose not to have his own parking department. "I try to stick to the knitting," he told us, then added, "Besides, we just aren't valet parkers."

Enter Paul Paliska. He once worked as a bellman for Cribbet, observed parking problems firsthand, and decided he could do it better. With his brother Stephen, he formed Professional Parking Services, Inc., in 1984. When the Irvine, California, Marriott (where I gave that speech) developed parking problems, the Paliska brothers were ready to go. By 1992, they were employing 600 valets at 80 hotels and restaurants. They also do the parking at numerous "special events" in Hollywood and elsewhere.

But PPS claims it can do more than just park cars—it wants "the front." That is, the hotel doorman's work, too. At some sites, such as the San Ramon Marriott and the Westin South Coast Plaza in Orange County, PPS has won the whole works.

Like almost any discipline when you look beneath the surface, valet parking is more complicated than it appears. The Paliska brothers are masters at putting the "guest" (their term, swiped from Marriott) first. They also are masters of quality control, worker scheduling—and risk management. (PPS insures clients like Marriott against damage to parked cars. Thanks to its track record, PPS can get better rates than its "bigger" employers—because PPS is in fact "bigger" at the narrow task it performs.)

Effective recruiting is essential. (Of course, you say. On the other hand, what's your impression of the average valet-parking attendant?) Prospective PPS employees, Stephen Paliska says, must be clean-cut, courteous, and able to communicate well. PPS also departs from the norm by taking training seriously. "Our training philosophy is to steal the best training ideas from the hotels we work with," Stephen told us. New employees study and are tested on a 10-page booklet, and attend an orientation course at a Southern California Red Lion hotel on how to open car doors for women, park cars, write up tickets, and so on. Next, they're assigned to a location, each with a designated trainer to work on local details—the locations of ballrooms and bathrooms, and whom to get in touch with at the hotel for this guest request or that.

Marriott's Cribbet waxes poetic about PPS. "They give great service, pay attention to things like uniforms, and train their people the Marriott way," he said. In fact, PPS sends employees to Marriott training programs. "That's fabulous," Cribbet added, "because it helps them understand our philosophy, how we treat the guest. The customer sees the valets as being associates of Marriott." (I did!)

Cribbet was more than willing to have PPS take over the doorman function at San Ramon. Before doing so officially, PPS valets had routinely handled the front when the doorman wasn't around (on break, for instance). "They did such a great job with it," Cribbet told us, "that it seemed right to turn the responsibility over to them." The service is especially helpful at a nonurban hotel like the one in San Ramon. In such locations, Cribbet pointed out, doormen "don't make a lot of money. They don't get the tips that the doormen do who work downtown in a large city. Getting a doorman out here is like finding a needle in the haystack." PPS does it for him—hey, doing so is a PPS core competence (a large part of its soul).

It hasn't always been smooth sailing. There have been conflicts between Marriott bellhops and PPS valets, Cribbet admitted. If the PPS valet comes into the hotel and can't find a bellhop, he'll go ahead and deliver the customer's luggage to his or her room. But when bellhops complained, Cribbet would tell them, "You'd better not abandon your post!" He added, "We deal with such conflicts by looking at who was best taking care of the customer." The local PPS supervisor also attended Cribbet's weekly senior staff meetings, something he said he had to force other valet companies to do.

If a customer says a valet nicked his car, PPS will have it fixed, no questions asked, Cribbet told us admiringly. If a customer says money was stolen from his or her car, PPS will refund the money. Cribbet could remember only one instance when PPS didn't automatically fix or refund. A car mysteriously disappeared from the parking lot, and the customer claimed he was a stereo sales rep who'd had a ton of equipment in the vehicle. Cribbet laughed, recalling that the automobile was "worth about thirty-nine dollars, with a stereo system worth about sixteen thousand." PPS agreed to replace the car and the stereo system—if the sales rep could either produce a sales receipt for the car stereo, or get a note from the company that had loaned him the system. PPS also notified the police. It turned out that the "rep" had stolen the car.

GUARDSMARK

Based on the company's brochure, you'd think you were about to do business with Tiffany's. The cover, printed on the highest-quality paper, is conservative gray, slashed by a small silver stripe; "Guardsmark," in raised letters, appears on the right side of the stripe; below that, in elegant, larger embossed letters: "Edge." That is, "Guardsmark Edge."

But it's not Tiffany's. Or perhaps it is: Guardsmark is the Tiffany's of the security business. Founded in Memphis in 1963 by dapper Ira Lipman, it's become the 6th largest security firm in the U.S. (out of 13,000), with annual revenues of roughly $150 million. Eight thousand Guardsmark employees work in 400 cities.

Overall, security services (including guards on a Marriott or Apple payroll) are growing at 15 percent a year. Industry revenue is ticketed to top $50 billion by 1995, and specialist security firms like Guardsmark are capturing more and more of the total each year—e.g., 65 percent in 1988, up from 55 percent a decade earlier. But the industry is rife with problems.

Questionable front-line employees top the list. "Unfortunately, too many of the security guards working in the United States today are unqualified, dishonest, unreliable, and violent," Ira Lipman said in a speech to the University of Maryland Institute of Criminal Justice and Criminology. "Many of them use drugs and have criminal records. . . . This lack of quality—caused in good part by the lack of a responsible attitude among owners—is the major challenge facing the private security industry today." Lipman offered appalling statistics: "In the early seventies, the owner of a security-services firm in Pennsylvania discovered that 10 percent of his security force had criminal records. . . . [O]f all the security guards in New York state in 1980, 66 percent had arrest records. In California, 20 percent of all applicants for security licenses have conviction records."

The 40-year industry veteran admits to losing business when the client's only consideration is price. But Lipman made his priorities clear in his University of Maryland speech:

> I've spent my entire career in private security and devoted all my energy to creating a company that is unique in the industry. . . . If there is any secret to our growth over the years, it is that quality should not be considered a relative concept by business owners but as an absolute. . . . Putting principle above profit has cost us over the years, at least in the short run. Disarming our security officers [Guardsmark was a pioneer in doing so] lost us many customers who thought their security required a Wyatt Earp or Doc Holliday to keep the peace. Our selection, training, and supervision programs created overhead costs that kept us out of the running for very competitive contracts that centered on price as the determining factor. Fortunately, there's always a market for the quality leader in any industry. Proving that to skeptics in the private security industry was a great challenge.

The Hiring and Development Edge

Lipman's company brochure gives away all his secrets. Recruiting tops the list—the brochure's first section is "The Edge in Selection":

> Every person who becomes a Guardsmark security officer has been thoroughly interviewed and investigated before receiving final approval from Corporate Headquarters. . . . The 24-page Guardsmark employment application covers the past ten years in the applicant's employment and residence histories, as well as complete life medical history. A notarized explanation is required for any gap of 30 days or more in employment history. . . . All previous employers over the past ten years are contacted and questioned concerning the applicant's employment record and eligibility for rehire. We also contact current and former neighbors and interview character references submitted with the application. . . . For every applicant, police records are checked and fingerprints are taken, unless prohibited by law. . . . No veteran with a discharge under less than honorable conditions is ever considered for employment, and this infor-

mation is verified. . . . Polygraph testing is requested of all employees, unless prohibited by law.

Only 2 percent of applicants survive such screens. Lipman claims that it's "tougher to become a Guardsmark security officer than a police officer in most communities." (*Time* reported in early 1992 that Guardsmark's "record in 1991 was more than twice as clean as that of the New York City Police Department.") While the company espouses decentralization in general, it keeps a strong hand on the recruiting tiller (its soul!). A headquarters Selection Controller rides herd on every hiring decision.

Guardsmark also emphasizes "The Edge in Training." In the first phase, the brochure informs us, the new hire must master a 113-page training manual. Then there are video training tapes produced by the in-house training department. On top of that, "all Guardsmark security officers receive no fewer than four regular training sessions per month. . . . [And] with every paycheck, security officers receive a detailed security training bulletin which is included in a continuing security notebook." Such training, one of many signs of the firm's commitment to its employees, helps keep turnover at less than a fourth of the industry average. (Above-average pay doesn't hurt either.)

Total Dedication

The final section in the brochure, titled "The Full Service Edge," describes numerous services available to clients and nonclients. The firm's Technical Services Division, an independent consulting and research arm, conducts security surveys and undertakes special projects, such as antiterrorism assistance. For a fee, Guardsmark will conduct site security surveys for nonclients, write a 40-to-60-page report with summary recommendations, and create a "customized, detailed manual [that] provides a basis for the organization's subsequent security methods, standards, and procedures."

Even the largest corporations would be hard-pressed to make this kind of commitment to their own security operations. Guardsmark, as a meeting with Lipman or a glance at his promotional material demonstrates, is very serious, very professional, very committed. Like the Paliska brothers in parking, Lipman has turned a mundane activity, low on many corporate managers' lists, into solid gold—and a first-class service.

WORDS AT WORK

News of WordRight Express Editing—the name WordRight has since been changed to Words at Work—arrived at my office in a faxed press release, dated April 10, 1991. It read in part:

Executives, managers, entrepreneurs and staff of any profession who are facing the crunch of deadlines without a professional wordsmith on hand can fax letters, reports, proposals or articles to (617) 338–8954 and receive an edited version by fax within 24 hours. WordRight's editors/wordsmiths fix punctuation and grammar faults, remedy awkward word use, rectify lapses in clarity and append suggestions for how the writer can better meet his or her communicative purpose.

It was sweet music to the ears of the top salesperson at a giant company. Booking $2 million in sales each year, she's on the road most of the time—and regularly corresponds with her boss by faxed memos. But, like many, she is petrified of writing. Enter Words at Work. The sales superstar quickly became one of the top clients of Words at Work president and founder Susan Benjamin. Before long she was routinely running draft memos past Benjamin (via an exchange of faxes) before faxing them back to home-office brass.

Words at Work, the subcontractor, is itself a network of subcontractors. ("Independent contractors" in IRS-ese.) It helps with those memos for the boss, but more often Words at Work's clients are young businesses. Words at Work treats them as partners, creating press releases, newsletters, sales brochures, and the like. By mid-1992, the two-year-old firm was serving over 150 clients, from Alaska to Maine. About half use the firm's services regularly.

Words at Work works out of a small office in Boston (*and*, de facto, the homes of its subcontractors), thanks to the great fax miracle. In that sense, it's a technology-based, fully networked, thoroughly modern corporation. On the other hand, the service it delivers is as much hands-on consulting as efficient "wordsmithing."

"Writing is something everyone has a lot of anxiety about," Benjamin told us. "We try to build relationships with people so they feel more comfortable. We try to help them, give them the information they need. We believe that editing is a type of teaching." So when Words at Work processes a document, the customer gets more than line edits. For one thing, there's always a detailed critique. Moreover, whenever Benjamin assesses potential subcontractors, she includes an interview over coffee. "I want to make sure they have an encouraging personality to help them work better with our clients," Benjamin declared.

In fact, Words at Work insists it wants to work itself out of business with some clients. On the one hand, Benjamin reported, clients "get a document from us just like they would from an ad agency." On the other hand, "They develop skill in creating it—something they'll have forever, that will help their business. We're not finished with a client after one job, but we do want to show them they can save money by doing a lot of the work themselves. We don't want our clients to be dependent on us forever." But, she quickly added, "Most stay with us even as, along the way, they become better writers."

A Full-Service Operation

Like Guardsmark, Words at Work is a "full service" enterprise. Products include:

Editing, including express editing. Words at Work offers three editing services—"regular" (three-day turnaround), "rush" (24-hour turnaround), and "super-rush" ("within hours—call first"). Prices, in mid-1992, ran from $20 for the first page and $10 for each additional page for the regular services to $30 for the first page and $25 for each additional page for the super-rush service. The insistence of clients pushed Words at Work to offer the super-rush alternative, but it cuts into Benjamin's sleep. "It's like being a doctor. I feel I'm always on call," she told us in 1991. "Clients have the home phone number of the person they're working with. The other night I was giving a dinner party and got an emergency client call at ten-thirty p.m. People call me at home on Sunday night, because they're working on something that's due Monday morning."

On the morning we interviewed Benjamin, she'd gotten a call from one of her regular clients, an insurance company employee seeking emergency advice: The client was preparing a letter in response to a customer complaint, and couldn't come up with a positive opening. Benjamin provided an on-the-spot fix. More typically, a call about a 10-page proposal will come in to Words at Work at, say, 2:00 p.m. The client immediately faxes the document and will likely get it back via fax, edited, by 7:00 p.m. Words at Work only asks the client for billing information and the editing format—for example, does the client want the editor to write directly on the manuscript, or on a separate sheet of paper? Most of the company's work is not emergency editing, although most of the emergency work turns into repeat business. "Someone might have used us once with a fax service, then they want a fifty-page proposal edited and dropped in the mail," Benjamin told us.

Personal consulting. A few clients work with Words at Work continually. One is a senior scientist "who's a lousy writer," according to Benjamin. The long-term list also includes a bank president—and several professors. As per Benjamin, the latter "must write and publish, but many of them don't have an interest in writing. Their writing is very general, there's no strong tone—and we try to help them with such problems."

In-house seminars. Words at Work also acts as a communications consultant to companies. Its subcontractors might spend up to five days at a client firm, teaching a customized seminar on letter and memo writing. Instructors are usually experts in the client's field.

No Staff and a Talented Network

Benjamin is Words at Work's only full-time employee. She subcontracts administrative tasks, as well as editorial chores. Minimum specs for her editorial contractors are impressive: at least 10 years' experience as a writer/teacher; graduate-level degree in English, writing, or a related subject or a degree in a specialized field, such as law or finance; some corporate experience, either on the payroll or training and teaching corporate employees. "We really want our subcontractors to be vital in what they do, whether it's financial writing, real estate, or legal," Benjamin stressed. "They need to be in touch with the industry. For example, if they're going to work with a real estate client, then they should currently be writing for real estate publications."

Benjamin also insists that her subcontractors work for other firms. "Being out there makes them more in touch, helps them have a better understanding of the needs of specialized clients," she claimed. (There's a switch: Words at Work says you're valuable only if you're *not* committed full-time!)

A glance at the curriculum vitae of a typical Words at Work contractor confirms Benjamin's recruiting skill and penchant for quality: ". . . 25 years as an award-winning editor, journalist and columnist for newspapers and magazines in New York, Chicago and Boston. . . . Has published more than 300 articles in trade magazines and contributes regularly to *The Office, U.S. Banker, Financial Services Week* and *Insurance and Technology*. . . . Corporate clients have included the public relations departments of IBM, Wang, Alloy Computer, Stratus Computer and the Saddlebrook Corporation."

To sum up, Words at Work can bring to bear, for clients of any size, the power of its rich network. Few medium-sized companies, or big ones for that matter, can boast of its skill bank or responsiveness.

THE SKONIE CORPORATION: THIS SUPERSUB DOES "SOUL" (SOUL IV)

A hospital that spends $200,000 on a blood chemistry analyzer, say, will probably send a lab staff member to the instrument manufacturer's for a week to learn to use the equipment. Upon her or his return, the device is shipped and set up in the hospital lab.

End of story? Hardly. At this point, it's quite possible that a contractor working as part of the network of the $4-million (1991 revenue) Skonie Corporation sets out for the hospital to conduct several weeks of "on-site hand-holding," as Skonie founder Valerie Skonie calls it—e.g., training all shifts on the new instrument, assessing its performance, and determining how many supporting "consumables" (filters, pipettes, etc.) the hospital will need.

Why don't equipment manufacturers do that follow-up training? It's a long story, but the nub of it is that equipment producers have traditionally shortchanged training in favor of selling. Then came Skonie, the company based in Sausalito, California, that mastered this arcane, vital art.

Skonie as Network and Recruiter Extraordinaire

Skonie Corp. has a full-time staff of seven. It is a subcontractor to medical equipment makers—and it provides its own carefully selected subcontractors to work with the equipment makers' customers. Skonie is a key but unsung player in the equipment producer-trainer-customer network. "Clients"? Skonie has all sorts: The equipment producer. The end user in the hospital. Subcontractors* to Skonie who do the "real" work of training the end user on the producer's equipment. Valerie Skonie's "aha" was seeing a business in this jumble.

The Process

Skonie prefers to hook up with an equipment manufacturer several months before release of a new product. That way, its trainers are ready to go from the start. But the firm is also frequently called in when a manufacturer has unexpectedly strong sales of a new product: The manufacturer's salespersons (or in-house trainers) get swamped by end-user training needs and neglect their selling chores.

In fact, the heart of Skonie's business proposition is acting as the manufacturer's "customer training department," as Skonie put it in a 1990 interview, and freeing up its salespersons to sell. "The salesperson is probably one of the most expensive people on their payroll," a Skonie manager told us. "He should be out selling, not installing. We tell the client, 'Let us get someone who's more cost-effective to do that work for you.'"

Skonie works with about 80 subcontractors. A lot of the firm's value-added is its skill at recruiting, selecting, and coaching those contractors. "We don't look for the best person in a city [where Skonie needs trainers]," Valerie Skonie told us. "We look for an *absolute* level of quality. We can go to a city and unearth fifteen candidates, but come back with nobody. There's a tendency to want to come back and say, 'This is the best person.' And I always have to say, 'The best person in the group may not be good enough for us.' My role is to constantly remind people of that."

Among other things, the screening process includes a training demonstration—candidates bring in a complicated piece of equipment they're familiar with and train *Skonie* on it. Valerie S. looks for very specific traits: How do

---

*The language can get messy. Skonie officially calls itself a "broker," its trainers "independent contractors." Such distinctions are of vital importance, it seems, to the IRS. To us, to aid our examination of the network idea, Skonie is a supersub which uses subs—period.

candidates set expectations (do they spell out how long the training program will take?); when do they get the "client" involved (how early?); how frequently do they check on the "client's" feelings; etc.

Once appropriate trainers are lined up for a job, Skonie Corp. presents them to the manufacturer for approval—which almost always ensues. "We've turned finding the right contractors into a science, and our clients know it," Valerie S. claimed. "We can spend up to four months looking for someone. We've developed a really good reputation for our ability to find people who are often, clients say, better than their employees." She insisted that it makes perfect sense that her independent trainers outshine payroll employees: "They're willing to take risks, to take responsibility for their work. There's a whole different set of motivators going on with people like that."

No Easy Sell

Despite a proven track record, Skonie still has a tough time worming its way into a manufacturer's heart. "Potential clients generally see merit in the idea, but a sale often takes several years of 'staying in touch,' " Valerie S. told us. "Then, all of a sudden, the client has a need, a new product or product promotion, a hiring freeze, or something that creates the perfect climate." When that happens, she's typically in clover. "Once a client has a chance to try it, they can see for themselves that the benefits far outweigh the risks," she said. "Our clients become our best salespeople."

Skonie's work with what is now one of the firm's biggest clients began with a small trial. The manufacturer was conducting seminars for end users at its headquarters and needed an extra trainer on occasion to handle especially large groups. The contractor Skonie provided established the firm's reputation. Two and a half years later, when the manufacturer released three new products, Skonie was hired to do training on the premises of end users. Another success followed, and now Skonie provides most of the manufacturer's field training support. "We went from one person for two and a half years," said Skonie, "to a peak of sixty-two people with that contract."

Finding a Hole

Valerie Skonie worked for years in a hospital lab, then became a product trainer for a Silicon Valley company that was setting up a medical division. Then the firm fired its regional sales manager—and suddenly she was Western regional sales manager, with responsibility for 14 states. She quickly noticed she no longer wanted to "waste time" training. "A lot of companies used their salespeople to train customers," she recalled, "but I realized that, much as I was more of a trainer than a salesperson, my new priority was to sell."

Skonie subsequently became a product manager for the company, which was manufacturing equipment for several bigger firms to sell under its own label. One of her jobs was teaching the big firm how to teach its salespeople to train end users. "The salespeople didn't care," she said. "It was a joke. I watched and said, 'This is a disaster. Nobody cares about training.' "

She decided there was a better way, and persuaded her customer to let each of its 10 salespeople find contractors to do end-user training. Sounds good. But it didn't work. The salespeople didn't know how to pick trainers. "What if I take on all this stuff," she mused, "the hiring, recruiting, bookkeeping—and grooming trainers for the job?" In February 1980, she did just that—and after five months of wearing out shoe leather made her first sale.

Valerie Skonie has translated her experience on the road as a salesperson into business advantage. "When you have a fourth of the country [as your sales territory], it really plays havoc with your quality of life," she said with passion. "I sensed that there were a lot of people who would love to do these jobs, but couldn't do them full-time, and wouldn't put up with all the traveling. Ultimately, such people would do a better job if they had the freedom to create their own work schedule." And that, she added emphatically, "is what we're proving."

Skonie tests her theories in her own business. When we visited her, a temporary office worker was handling administrative chores. Skonie Corp.'s chief financial officer is also an independent contractor. Valerie S. was uneasy about farming out such a crucial task, but recalled thinking, "If I don't take that risk, how can I ask my clients to?" She summed it up this way: "I try to run my business the same way that I suggest to clients. I'm sensitive to clients' issues. I like having [independent contractors] around me. I think they enjoy their work more, and are willing to work harder when they work. They can give me a hundred and fifty percent when they're here. I think you get a quality of output that you can't always get with a full-time person. Not only that, but you also provide these people with the opportunity to write the script for their life, for their careers."

In an in-house organ, Valerie Skonie wrote that "Our skill is finding superb people and orchestrating the relationship between the client and the contractors so that everyone gets what is ultimately needed for everyone to win." If I'd led off with that quote, you would have snickered. But a decade of success suggests that Skonie Corp. and its network colleagues are doing just that—and inventing a new form of organization along the way.

Soul (Again)

The Skonie story amounts to "subcontracting soul"—or something close to it. If the essence of business success is repeat business, then Skonie Corp. "does soul" for medical equipment manufacturers: The service Skonie performs amounts to the most tangible evidence of the producer's level of concern for its end-user customers. If an end user's lab staff is poorly trained, the instrument will never realize its potential, and the odds of a repeat sale will drop precipitously.

THE SUPERSUBS IN REVIEW

• Recruiting muscle. Each of the companies we examined knows much more than its often more muscular clients do about recruiting the region's/nation's best in its given field. In retrospect, it's "obvious" that a supersub's most important skill—its soul!—is recruiting. (If that's so clear for supersubs, why not for everyone else? I'm continually astonished by how little *strategic* attention many—most?—pay to recruiting.)

• R&D prowess. Thanks to narrow focus and total concentration, the supersubs pay enormous "research attention" to their task—security, training hospitals in the use of complex equipment, parking cars.

• Scope. Though Skonie has only seven full-time employees on its payroll, it's *huge*—it has access to (and detailed knowledge of) a much bigger network of superb practitioners (contract equipment trainers) than clients 1,000 times its nominal size. So, too, Words at Work, Guardsmark, and Professional Parking Services: In their hyper-narrow specialties, their reach/breadth of knowledge is awe-inspiring!

• Mastery of relationship management. Tomorrow could bring contract termination. Their positions always precarious, these firms are fanatics about the management of multiple relationships—with purchasers of their service (corporate purchasing departments, equipment manufacturers), contractors (in several cases), and end users (hotel guests, hospital lab techs). Unlike an in-house staff department, the supersub that fails to serve the end user well is headed for deep trouble, quick.

A THEORY OF "SUB"-CONTRACTING

Remember that old Groucho Marx line, "I wouldn't join any club that would have me as a member"? How about this variation: "I wouldn't want to work with a subcontractor who'd have me as a partner." In tomorrow's increasingly competitive world, I suggest, my variation is the appropriate beacon. The supersubs are the reason why. But to deal with—and take full advantage of—these stellar performers of often unsung, but often vital, tasks, we need some (more) new imperatives:

• Only work with subcontractors so good they wouldn't want to work with you. It's a strong way of saying work *only* with the best. It's not a matter of "us" doing "them" a favor, but of "them" doing "us" a favor—or, one hopes, each of us doing the other a *big* favor by joining a special network for some period of time. It's the way I look at it in my own business: I am stunned by the energy and talent of the people who work with me in "sub"-contracting roles. I'm honored by their presence. Somehow, I don't think that's the attitude Ford has toward, say, its mirror-making vendors.

- Given the volatile world marketplace, your demands as "prime" contractor on "sub"-contractors must be outrageous. One of the principal reasons for wanting to work with the best is to be able to demand the impossible in good conscience. In order to react opportunistically to the latest marketplace wiggle, you must be able to ask "subs" to adapt to ever-shorter response cycles necessary to fit your ever-shorter response-cycle needs. (We're all hopelessly entangled in each other's spiderwebs these days.)

- You must command an "unfair share" of attention from your "subs." Forget altruism! Since your "subs" are the best, customers are beating down their doors. Since they are the best, they will doubtless give virtually all those customers "very good" service. But you want more than very good service: You want outrageously good service. And that's only going to happen if *you* work constantly to make your "subs" heroes.

- Your "sub"contractors must be very healthy financially. Nickel-and-diming "subs" was always stupid. Now it's insane. I want the impossible from my "subs"—which means I want them to be financially healthy enough to aggressively push the state of the art in technology, training, etc.

- Forget the prefix "sub." One simple alternative is "contractor." Another is "external associate," as distinguished from the "internal associates" on your payroll. Nitpicking the language is not small-mindedness. Words are important—and "sub" carries lots of baggage, all bad in a world where speedy response to fast-shifting times means trust and mutual dependence, with the lawyers left at home.

(More) SuperSubs, Big and Small

- On March 11, 1991, *Financial Times* of London ran a special supplement on "contracted business services." It reported "the rapid, worldwide growth of the business support service sector [which] reflects a revolution in boardroom thinking over the most cost-effective and efficient way to run a company in today's harsh, highly competitive corporate environment." Among other things, *Financial Times* examined more than 50 European support-service companies totaling over £1 billion in annual revenue—e.g., Sunlight, in textile rentals (launderable workwear, linens, surgical gowns), and BET, in building maintenance.

- A September 11, 1991, *Wall Street Journal* headline read, "Small Companies Thrive by Taking Over Some Specialized Tasks for Big Concerns."

The article began: "Last October, National Steel Corp. streamlined operations in a peculiar way: It spun off its mailroom. Executives at the steelmaker's Pittsburgh headquarters still get letters. But another firm, Ameriscribe Corp., sorts and distributes them. The New York company also handles all of National's major copying work."

The *Journal* went on to report that Mobil had subcontracted refinery maintenance to Serv-Tech, AT&T had subbed credit card processing to Total Systems Services, and Whirlpool had hired Kenco Group to manage its distribution centers. A researcher at the U.S. Bureau of Labor Statistics called such supersubs "a major growth industry on the American scene."

● "Need a CFO, call Arthur." No, the ads don't say that, not yet anyway. But if you're tired of keeping your books, you can give Arthur Andersen a try. "Freeing today's leaders to shape tomorrow" is the registered service mark of the $5-billion accounting firm's new Contract Financial Management (CFM) service—which will take over all your accounting activity (putting some or all of your accountants on Andersen's payroll) and provide you with a chief financial officer to boot.

CFM was launched in 1989 in response to stymied growth opportunities (the Big Six accounting firms have already divvied up most potential audit clients)—and an increasing willingness of companies, bent on getting lean and concentrating on core skills, to contract *anything* out. (Continental Bank, on a crash diet, stunned the business community in 1991 when it farmed out *all* its legal affairs.) Early clients of Andersen's CFM range from midsize manufacturers to a division of British Petroleum (Andersen took on 250 BP employees); the firm is betting on CFM to produce hundreds of millions in revenues by the mid-'90s. "The corporation is becoming unbundled," Gary Peterson, who heads Andersen's CFM operations, told us. "One day you're going to meet ten different people working for a company—and they'll be from ten different companies' payrolls."

OTHERS WITH SOUL ALLOW YOU TO DUMP NONESSENTIALS: THE (MOSTLY) GOOD NEW-NETWORK NEWS, OR SOUL V

What's the relationship of parking to soul? Running a hotel is as tough a job as I can imagine. Providing matchless yet economical guest service is a pain. It's helpful for the hotel keeper to be able to focus on the basics and dismiss other important but secondary chores—parking for special events among them.

But "dismiss" is a dangerous—and unnecessary—word to use. The great news: For every service, no matter how *apparently* mundane (and what, *appar-*

ently, could be more mundane than parking?), there is, out there *somewhere*, an energetic entrepreneur who's as passionate about his task as Seymour Cray is about the next generation of supercomputer.

Okay, I'm a snob. I find it tough to imagine being "passionate about parking." One wonderful thing about the structure of the increasingly entrepreneurial economy, however, is that it provides us with parking fanatics! The Marriott hotel manager sweats the tiniest detail of the way his guests are being treated within his four walls. But he can take some comfort in knowing that PPS execs are sweating, too—and maybe even more than he, because as entrepreneurs their reputation and economic viability depend upon making him *very* happy.

Catch-21.9: So What Is Essential?

Of course, there's a monumental catch. How do you tell the difference between soul and *not*-soul? Can McDonnell Douglas be dead certain (page 304) that the three tasks it plans to retain after de-integration—design, final assembly, flight testing—are enough to allow it to (1) remain distinctive and (2) control the overall process of aircraft development, sales, and support so as to command a global market presence? (A lot of the answer for such a "prime" contractor which subs a lot depends on its skills at network/project/interdependence management—see Chapter 24.) Or how about that Marriott property manager? I dismissed parking a "non-soul" for Marriott. Hold on! Parking is arguably a prime—*the* prime—contributor to the event attendee's important first *and* last impressions of Marriott. It's no stretch to say that PPS is doing "soul work" for Marriott.

It all adds up to Catch-21.9—at least. On the one hand, you can relieve yourself of "unnecessary" burdens (like parking), and turn them over to a stellar supersub. On the other hand, the "unnecessary" skills may turn out to be "soul" (i.e., critical).

But who cares as long as they're done well (à la Professional Parking Services, Skonie)? You'd better care! The tricky question is how much is too much. So you "give up" parking. Then "the front." Then audiovisual services for conventions. Why not housekeeping? (Hospitals have thrived subbing housekeeping to ServiceMaster.) Et cetera.

As the et ceteras add up, there's less and less left of you. After decades of excessive vertical integration, and given the newfound requirements for innovation/adaptability, that's mostly good. But at some point, "there's no there there" any longer.

When do you slip over the line from "wise de-integration" (necessary disorganization, eh?) to "no there there"? No easy answers await. In fact, the whole business only gets more confusing.

Soul's Tricky New Look: "Horizontal Soul"

Consider the very profitable and strategically advantageous information systems arm of AMR (American Airlines' parent). AMR's dynamic pricing process (which exploits its information systems to the hilt) has been, some say, American's most important strategic lever. Moreover, sales of AMR's information systems capacity to third parties have at times generated more profit than flying people around. So: What if AMR had subcontracted all its information systems work to EDS 20 years ago? The odds are EDS would have done a competent, efficient job. But would EDS have provided the same flair that AMR information systems whiz Max Hopper and chairman Bob Crandall did? Don't bet on it!

In fact, the AMR example opens a fresh can of worms. "Soul" is increasingly found in "horizontal" rather than traditional, "vertical" processes. Go back to ABB. It has important, traditional "vertical" skills—e.g., engineering excellence in certain fields. Yet its most precious—and unduplicatable—competence may well become its T50 process for cycle-time compression. Or reconsider International Data Group: It's a powerful niche player in the computer industry ("vertical soul"). Yet its distinction lies at least as much in its "horizontal soul"—e.g., its well-honed process for creating quick start-ups. EDS, too, makes no bones about the future. "Vertical" Strategic Business Units bring home most of today's bacon, but the new "horizontal SBUs" (which leverage knowledge across the corporation) are its chosen path to a healthy tomorrow.

Boeing makes about 35 percent of the value that goes into one of its planes. Engines, electronics/avionics, seats, and even large portions of the fuselage are made wholly by outsiders. Some say that Boeing's true soul is its mastery of "systems integration." Likewise, MCI's true soul is systems/network integration. Retaining/building excellence at that *alone* does not seem to handicap MCI in its battle against AT&T (which boasts awesome engineering talent, including a peck of Nobel laureates at Bell Labs). Arguably, MCI's lack of in-house talent is an advantage—the company thrives on its quick-change artistry, while AT&T is captive to massive in-house engineering (no matter how talented) and production (sluggish operations, by definition, in *any* $63-billion outfit).

Elusive "horizontal soul," then, includes the likes of (1) EDS's "horizontal SBUs"; (2) Union Pacific's 106 newly identified horizontal processes; (3) ABB's T50 program; (4) Titeflex's "culture of velocity"; (5) IDG's business creation skills; (6) MCI's systems integration/network management talent; (7) the supersubs' recruitment skills; and (8) the project management capabilities of Boeing, Fluor, Bechtel, et al.

Soul can come from the strangest places! It's dangerous to do too much yourself today. And just as dangerous to guess wrong about the odd crannies from which full-blown, marketable soul can emerge.

A corporation's top team must work overtime at de-integrating to stay innovative and flexible (without de-integrating to the point of meaningless-ness). But the gang at the top must also work overtime determining what and where soul is, can be, might be, ought to be, for now, for the future. The choices are tough. The consequences are enormous. Inflexibility kills fast today. On the other hand, "horizontal" soul worth billions (those systems integration skills at Boeing) takes decades to develop and imprint on the market. Go figure!

Slippery "New Soul" in the Auto Industry

In a 1989 MIT working paper titled "Collaborative Manufacturing," MIT's Charles Sabel, with Horst Kern and Gary Herrigal, examined subcontracting and soul—old, new, and changing—in the world auto industry:

Firms are drifting . . . willy-nilly and for reasons they seldom articulate . . . away from [their limited] interpretations of new supplier relations [aimed at] cost cutting [and] towards a disconcerting view in which the design and production of an automobile requires collaboration of many specialized firms, none of which could complete or even organize the task alone. At the limit—and that limit is already being approached by at least one major producer—the car company would become a kind of higher order design house and marketing agency. Its chief function would be to coordinate the work of other design houses [the system suppliers], assemble the subassemblies, and distribute the final product. . . . [T]he traditional [auto] manufacturer would become at best a primus inter pares, at worst a "value-added remarketer" or "systems house": the computer industry's unlovely names for firms which buy components from sophisticated specialists and combine them in the ways that respond to the needs of particular markets. . . .

[Automakers must distinguish between] systems . . . which the company *must* make if it is to retain its competitive identity and advantage, and those it *can* make, but might well subcontract to suppliers with independent design capacities. . . . [Most conclude that] *anything* could be designed and produced outside; and what appeared at any moment as an immutable list of "must" and "can" components was really nothing more than the current, revisable, collective judgment regarding which components it was *opportune* to make. . . .

BMW has moved most decisively towards collaborative manufacturing. Fifty-five [to] 75 percent of the total production costs come from out-sourced parts. Eighty percent of the parts purchased

involved important collaborative work with a specialist subcontractor.
. . . Growing emphasis on collaboration has turned in-house
manufacturing at BMW increasingly into a strategic learning process.
[The ultimate in "horizontal" soul!—T.P.] The idea is to establish a
system in which the firm continuously learns from its suppliers without
becoming intolerably vulnerable to them. . . . Recently there was a long
dispute between purchasing and engineering about whether to stop
producing cylinder heads in-house. The decision was to keep production
inside because BMW did not want to transfer a crucial proprietary
casting technology to a supplier. But all parties agreed that it was
unlikely that such production would remain in-house for long.

22

Networks and Markets I: A First Look at "Marketizing" the Firm

Hard as it is for bosses to accept it, head office delivers many services in the same way as would an outside subcontractor. So make [all services] compete with outsiders. Only keep the function in-house if headquarters wins a contract.

"Farewell HQ"
The Economist, March 24, 1990

The division managers pay for the headquarters services from their own budgets. If they think they're paying too much for support staff, we simply eliminate the [headquarters] job.

Robert Potter, President
Monsanto Chemical Company
Fortune, April 6, 1992

Recall ABB's big, bloated central staff units of yesteryear: CEO Percy Barnevik let almost a third of the staffers go. About a third went to the firm's line businesses. Most of the remaining third stayed with the staff units, which were transformed into freestanding service centers. The latter now must compete for line units' business, at market prices. Take, for example, the ABB World Treasury Center based in Zurich. It employs 200 people, who are in 10 treasury "companies." Simon Holberton of the *Financial Times* reported in early 1991 that the 10 "serve the financial requirements of ABB's industrial business units. However, they also operate as independent profit centers. In their dealings with the business units, they operate at market prices—they compete head-on with banks for [the business of ABB's 1,300 companies]—and it is in the trading and management of the funds they receive that they make profits attributable to the [central] treasury."

Staff units at a few other companies have found novel ways to make big bucks. *CIO* magazine (April 1991) reported that, as part of an aggressive effort to market the services of what had been a "staff" function, Pittsburgh's Mellon Bank brought in $350 million from data processing performed for 700 "outside" customers in the financial industry. *CIO* continued:

> Competitors include not just other banks (such as Citicorp) but also EDS, IBM and Systematics. . . . [In late 1990], for example, Mellon beat out seven competitors to win a multi-million dollar . . . contract from the $4.5 billion Dollar Dry Dock Bank of White Plains, New York. Dollar Dry Dock wanted more than just leased [computer power], however. The two banks entered into what Dollar Dry Dock Executive Vice President and CFO Charles Richardson calls a "hybrid relationship." Some of Dollar Dry Dock's software will run on Mellon's iron, but over the six-year duration of the contract, the New York bank will also [begin to use Mellon's applications software]. . . . Mellon also intends to hunt for customers outside the banking industry and has considered forming alliances . . . in order to expand its . . . services.

The GM Automotive Components Group includes seven parts divisions. Each division now competes with outsiders for GM business. And each one is peddling its wares outside GM—to the likes of Chrysler, Ford, and any number of Japanese domestic plants are customers.

In sum, one of the last of the centrally controlled economies is coming under the market's sway—not Cuba, but the centrally controlled, nonmarket arenas (e.g., components, services) that dominate the *inside* of the traditional, vertically integrated corporation. Corporate executives wax eloquent about the market, but part the curtains at most of the enterprises they run and you'll find the most outrageous inefficiencies in the provision of services and components—abetted by the absence of market forces.

THOMPSON PUBLISHING GROUP MARKETIZES "STAFF" SERVICES (AND EVERYTHING ELSE)

In 1991, $17-million (revenue) Thompson Publishing Group decided to get *more* vertically integrated—but with a twist. It created a telemarketing "department" to serve the company's 40 newsletters and manuals.

Make that potentially serve—because president Richard Thompson was clear that the new in-house staff would have to compete with outsiders for the publications' business. The telemarketers would also be expected to win outside contracts. "Why pay for outside services if you can do better inside?" Thompson told us in 1991. "And if you *can* do it better, why not sell outside yourself?"

Today, 80-person Thompson Fulfillment Services—located in Salisbury, Maryland, 100 miles from Thompson Publishing's Washington, D.C., headquarters—handles telemarketing as well as circulation, mail list management, customer service, accounting, and warehousing services for Thompson Publishing and others.

In fact, all Thompson employees feel the pressures and incentives of the marketplace. The publications themselves—covering regulatory compliance issues for various industries—are organized into four autonomous business units. Each is managed by "associate publishers who are responsible for their own bottom lines," Thompson said. "They can use Thompson Fulfillment Services or not." Associate publisher Stephen Munro uses Thompson Fulfillment, but keeps in touch with outside service providers: "We're always solicited by fulfillment organizations, so we know the costs of services outside." He pointed out that Thompson Fulfillment does have the advantage of familiarity with the complicated specifications of Thompson publications—most of which are individually collated, loose-leaf references running hundreds of pages. Nevertheless, shopping around lets Munro know that "we get the best service at the best price. And if that changes, we'll go elsewhere."

For her part, Thompson Fulfillment's general manager, Karen Lankford, takes nothing for granted with her in-house accounts. "I see them as my best clients and harshest critics," she told us. "They expect more from us than from an outside vendor, and we try to give them more." The associate publishers, who are encouraged to test her against outside telemarketing services on every campaign, sometimes do opt to give telemarketing work to outside firms, citing their closer location or satisfactory relationships that predate the creation of Thompson Fulfillment. For its part, Thompson Fulfillment now does 15 percent of its total business outside of Thompson Publishing, and expects that to grow to 25 percent within the next two years and to 50 percent within the next five. Thompson Fulfillment is, of course, responsible for its own P&L, and virtually all of its component activities—systems, fulfillment, customer service, and telemarketing—also operate as individual profit centers.

Thompson Fulfillment chief Lankford has taken to the new mode of operating with a vengeance. She recently leased warehouse space at a separate location in Salisbury, even though additional space was available in her main building. Lankford told us with some satisfaction that building management "thought we'd lease more space from them just because we're here, but I found cheaper space somewhere else, and we can pass that savings on to our customers." In a similar vein, Richard Thompson also recalled asking Lankford to develop a program for assessing the characteristics of an effective telemarketer. "She told me, 'It's a good idea, but where's the profit for us?' " Thompson said with a laugh. "So I created a budget on the corporate side to pay for her time to do the study."

Lankford and finance VP Joe Ozalas have developed a detailed reporting system that breaks out the cost of every task, from accounting to warehousing. Publications are billed accordingly. "Money comes out of their budgets and into ours," said Lankford. "In the corporate budget, it 'zeroes out' in the end, but for the divisions, it's real cost and for us it's real income."

Thompson Publishing Group's free-market experiment began in 1987, when the company reorganized its editorial staff into autonomous units, each responsible for the writing, marketing, and production of its own publications. "I tried to create for the [associate publishers] a job I'd love to have," Richard Thompson said. "It's a chance to run their own business and make their own decisions." Moreover, the change liberated Thompson himself from the "day-to-day headaches" of managing, and allowed him to focus on "coaching and creating new businesses."

Associate publishers cooperate by comparing notes on similar problems, but the groups also compete. For example, Richard Thompson periodically circulates a list of new publication ideas to each associate publisher. "I put everything up for grabs," he told us. "Any associate publishers with time or interest can bid on developing a new [publication]. If no one picks up on it, I figure it was a dumb idea." Associate publishers are also free to acquire outside publications—with all costs showing on their own P&Ls. And Richard Thompson offers incentives for starting new publications. Bonuses are based on each group's growth and profitability (which means, of course, that associate publishers investing in new business—like "real" businesspeople—must sacrifice short-term bonuses for bigger potential long-term payouts). Spurred by the new scheme, Thompson Publishing Group has grown at a 20 percent annual clip since its inception in 1987, and introduced 35 new publications along the way.

Emancipated Reporters

They call themselves "clusters"—groups of six to nine reporters, editors, photographers, and graphic designers. The clusters are part of a new approach to the newspaper business that has been adopted by the *London Free Press* (London, Ontario). The independent units, which have absorbed about one-third of the newsroom's editorial complement, "generate, research, write, and illustrate their own ideas," according to *The Globe and Mail* (Toronto). But they are not guaranteed space in the paper! They must "sell their ideas to whichever section of the [paper] they can. . . .

"Reporter Peter Geiger-Miller, 51, a veteran of 27 years in newspapering, was a member of the prototype 'environment' cluster," *The Globe and Mail* goes on. "He says the experiment was a great success. . . . 'It was thoroughly enjoyable. We wrote for every section of the paper—homes, sports, business—so, from my standpoint, it was very emancipating, a chance to take a different approach to stories.' "

Not everyone takes such a positive view. Nonetheless, the experiment continues—newspapers in Canada as well as the U.S., confronted with sluggish or falling revenues, are clearly in need of a shot in the arm. This may be it.

HEWLETT-PACKARD INTEGRATED CIRCUITS UNIT TESTS ITSELF IN THE WORLD MARKET

According to sales manager Richard Duncombe, on November 1, 1987, Hewlett-Packard's integrated circuits unit transformed itself "from a cost center into an independent financial entity." It began to bid globally for external sales. Competing against other leading vendors, such as Toshiba and AT&T, the IC division ($200 million in 1991 revenue) has been successful in winning contracts for specialized applications.

Since HP insiders don't have to buy from the IC unit, Duncombe told us in 1991, it has long competed with outsiders "on an equal basis" and gets "fair market value" for its expertise. "It's not a cost-plus or anything like that," he said. "Within HP, we sell to the computer systems organization, the computer products organizations, the measurement systems organization, and many other operating divisions." In fact, the IC unit serves 45 of 52 product divisions and supplies parts for a majority of HP's 12,000 products.

Having captured most of the internal market, the unit has taken dead aim at the outside world. "We look for relationships more strategic than buy-sell," Duncombe reported. "We work with [outside customers] to develop new products that will also be attractive to our internal customers." He added that, in selling to outsiders, the unit gets "a real-world measure" of its strengths and weaknesses. "We learned that we're strong where we didn't think we were, and *how* weak we were where we thought we were weak. It's a calibration. When you do a silicon IC process it's expensive. You can't afford to miss the mark. And selling outside keeps you straight."

MIDLAND CABINET LETS THE MARKET TURN WORKERS INTO "BUSINESSMEN"

Robert Boynton, Jr., owner of Midland Cabinet Company of San Carlos, California, promotes entrepreneurship among his 20 employees—and improves customer service along the way. Employees can use Midland's new multimillion-dollar facility after hours to work on outside jobs. Boynton charges them 10 percent over materials costs. Workers have to be on board for three months before getting a key, which allows them to come in on their days off.

Boynton refers customers directly to his employees if a prospective job is too small for Midland to do profitably, or if the shop is too busy to take it on. Some Midland employees do a dozen or more outside jobs a year. The privilege broadens employee skills and improves their business acumen, workers claim. They learn how to set prices, negotiate their own deadlines, and cut down on waste time, which makes them faster and more effective during the regular workweek as well. Boynton doesn't manage the relationship between employees and their customers once a job is referred. The worker is fully accountable—to himself *and* his peers. "One guy wasn't delivering well at all, and that hurt everybody's credibility, but the boss wants to keep this privilege going because it broadens us," one cabinetmaker told us. "The guy did finish the job, but not without a lot of nagging. He wasn't reprimanded but he eventually left [Midland]. The company stays out of it, but if you mess up, they definitely won't recommend you for other jobs." Employees are also responsible for judging whether or not their extra jobs will eat into their energy during the regular workweek.

Workers end up learning so much about running a business that a half-dozen cabinet shops have started as spinoffs from Midland. Boynton is a proud papa. He adds that having his cabinetmakers build their business skills and learn to deal effectively with customers shows clients that Midland workers can handle any job—large or small.

MARKETS, MARKETS, MARKETS

These three cases cover a surprising amount of ground, and give an inkling of the scope of the marketizing idea.

— Small line units have their own P&Ls and can even acquire businesses on their own (Thompson).

— Line units can reject the offerings of the service-staff units for whatever reason they choose (Thompson, Hewlett-Packard).

— Staff units are expected not only to compete for line unit business, but to garner a substantial share of their revenue from outside sources (Thompson, HP).

— Workers are made more business/market-conscious by being encouraged to take on outside, for-profit tasks (Midland).

— It makes sense for tiny companies (Midland with 20 employees) as well as monsters (HP with a payroll of 90,000).

Stir in the likes of ABB and Mellon Bank—and you begin, I hope, to see the potential. But the issue is not beyond debate.

AN EXCHANGE: "MARKETIZING"

I received this letter shortly after we devoted a 1991 issue of our newsletter to "marketizing":

Dear Tom:

The concept of turning cost centers into profit centers can certainly increase attention to quality and service, since the operating unit must now try to improve the bottom line. While I am generally in favor of this concept, I would like to point out one caveat. Forcing a unit to become a profit center may actually cost the entire company money.

For example, suppose the Gadget Division of Gizmo Inc., a profit center, needs to purchase widgets. They can do so internally (from the Widget Division, also a profit center) or purchase them from another company. Gizmo's Widget Division can produce the widget for $1.00. The other company can produce that same widget for $.75. The industry standard markup is 100 percent, so that Gizmo's Widget Division would want to charge $2.00 while the other company will charge $1.50.

If the Gadget Division buys internally, they are out $.50 per widget, so they will wish to purchase externally (according to your advice). However, the *entire company* is still better off if the widget is purchased internally. Each widget purchased externally means that Gizmo Inc. is out $1.50 (the price Gadget pays). If purchased internally, Gizmo Inc. is out only $1.00 (Widget Division's actual cost). Additionally, no jobs or resources are wasted in the short run.

There may be a need for Gizmo's management to set better transfer prices and shore up the performance of the Widget Division, but these are side issues. In the interim, Gizmo's bottom line is benefitted by *not* turning all divisions into competitive profit centers.

I wrote this note because I have seen this profit center idea work against the best interests of a previous employer. On the other hand, I am now working for a very lethargic cost center which could stand to implement many of your ideas in this and other matters.

Regards,

Seth Steingraph
Marketing Engineer
Hewlett-Packard

I replied as follows:

Dear Seth:

Gadgets needs widgets. It goes to the *internal widget supplier* (INT) and an *external widget supplier* (EXT) for bids. INT quotes $2.00, EXT quotes $1.50—all as you said. Now what?

In the real world, Gadgets most likely goes back to INT and says, "You'll have to give me a better deal." What's INT's response: First, INT will probably argue a value-added case: "Our mean time between failures is lower than EXT's." "We have extra functions/features." "It will be easier for you to keep an eye on us because we're nearby." Etc.

Gadgets responds by questioning INT's mean time between failure data. And adds: "You guys [INT] always show preference for our Big Sister Division. So in a pinch, you'll screw us—with corporate's blessing." (Gadgets knows Gizmo corporate is counting on Big Sister Division for an earnings boost this year—hence Gadgets may well be right about INT's prospective behavior.)

So INT goes back to the drawing boards, as would a "real company" with non-competitive costs. INT decides to come down in price to $1.60 *and* simultaneously launch a long overdue initiative aimed at, among other things, paring costs from $1.00 to $.80.

The $1.60 is in the ballpark, and Gadgets is willing to make a deal with INT, given written reliability-of-supply assurance. Selling at $1.60, of course, violates Gizmo's 100 percent markup rule, so INT now has a problem with carping corporate (as a "real business" with pinched margins would) that can be answered only with a credible plan to get those costs down to $.80 fast.

Suppose INT *does* trim costs to $.80 and also offers some special features. Not only does INT keep Gadgets' business (legitimately!), but it now finds itself in a position to win substantial business beyond parent Gizmo's doors. (My general bias is for Gizmo corporate to have set a hard and fast target for outside sales by INT—10 percent, say, within two years; a minimum of 25 percent in five years.)

Consider another scenario. After some wrangling, suppose INT has come in at $1.60, as I said. Naturally enough, Gadgets now goes back to EXT, a hungry, market-share-driven Japanese supplier, which says margins-be-damned, we'll come down from our original $1.50 offer to $1.30.

Now INT *is* in a pickle. Its managers don't see how they can get costs down to $.70, in order to bring their price including appropriate margins down to an in-the-ballpark $1.40. Odds are they're wrong, and maybe this shock will finally force them into a *radical* restructuring. But suppose they're right. What then? The best bet for INT may be to stoke innovation's fire and try to leapfrog EXT, by producing a next-generation widget that Gadgets will drool over—along with enough outsiders to make INT/Gizmo's R&D expenditure worthwhile. (This is essentially what Intel did years ago. It bitched and moaned about the Japanese "dumping" DRAMs in pursuit of market share. But faced with the facts, it got out of the DRAM business, bet the farm on innovation—and produced a string of pathbreaking microprocessors that led to fast growth and almost obscene profits. Meanwhile, the relentless Japanese pursuit of volume to achieve efficiency led to staggering industry overcapacity—and, eventually, a financial bloodbath.)

In any event, I see this "marketized" give-and-take as clearly in Gizmo's best *long-term* interests. Without the market pressure, INT continues to limp along, probably getting a little less competitive each year. With market pressure, there's a good chance that INT can shape up, keep Gadgets' business fair and square, *and* become competitive on the open market.

Equally important, by keeping the deal straight (i.e., not forcing Gadgets to pay the in-house supplier that extra $.50), the heat of accountability on Gadgets is searing. If Gadgets misses margin targets, its managers can't complain to Gizmo corporate chiefs at year end that "dealing with INT at $2.00 instead of EXT at $1.50 did us in." And if Gadgets' managers do make a legitimate deal at $1.60 with INT, and INT *does* stiff them on schedule in favor of Big Sister Division—even then they can't complain. Their supplier welshed on its commitment. Gadgets still takes the heat from corporate for missing its goals, but vows to do no more business with INT at *any* price. Just like the real world!

And more: Now and again, Gizmo may find that an innovative, market-pressured unit like INT hits one out of the park, leading all of Gizmo off in a valuable new direction. In the wildest case, a market-pressured components unit like INT may become Gizmo's main growth/profit engine. Gadgets may become the also-ran. The odds of this are low, but they're virtually zero if INT is *not* subject to the market's discipline.

In sum, Gizmo is better served in the long haul by *dis*investing in units like INT if such units cannot achieve world-class levels of price/performance—assuming there are multiple, alternative, reliable outside suppliers (which, these days, is usually a safe assumption). To be sure, if Gizmo does disinvest in components-making arms like INT, it *must* retain crucial engineering/design capability that allows it to creatively work with/manage relationships with top outsiders.*

If Gizmo can't build a sustainable competitive advantage in components arenas such as INT's, then Gizmo probably ought to be investing its discretionary dollars in Gadget or other/new Gadgets-like divisions where, presumably, Gizmo has a greater proprietary skill set/edge (more "soul"). Given today's market volatility (in your [electronics] industry, a product "generation" for INT is probably a year, tops), Gizmo simply can't afford to have *any* long-term, non-competitive hangers-on muddying its portfolio.

Thanks for your letter.

Sincerely,

Tom Peters

P.S. This response only covers the sterile "logic of the case." Creating a trustworthy accounting scheme and a corporate culture that supports market-based behavior and thrives on creative relations with outside network partners is the essential art upon which this concept ultimately rises or falls.—T.P.

The Case for Ownership

Money is made by setting de facto standards.

Bill Gates, Microsoft
quoted in Robert X.
Cringely's *Accidental
Empires*

Bigness rarely leads to promised efficiencies (scale economies). And bigness invariably crunches innovativeness ("big, flexible" is a joke). Besides, "new big" allows you to be powerful, while shipping out lots of work to supersubs that are your betters.

So why even consider being "old big"? Because it's easier to push people

---

*This, recall, is the trick at MCI and BMW, and the essence of Rational's "extended workbench"/"co-head of production" model.

around, that's why. (Ask any neighborhood bully.) When GM talks, thousands of suppliers are all ears—even today. When IBM gets the sniffles, thousands of vendors get colds—even today.

Economic research provides a raft of consistent evidence that cartels (de facto standard-setters—e.g., price "standards") seldom last. Railroad cartels in the U.S., near the end of the last century, quickly dissolved into bickering. Nothing much has changed: In April 1991, 21 computer industry firms, including heavies such as Digital Equipment, created the Advanced Computing Environment. ACE was a coalition dedicated to establishing industry standards for lots of things—and aimed at denting IBM's still enormous clout. A year later, for a variety of reasons, ACE was in disarray. IBM, though bloodied, was unbowed.

No one could have predicted the reasons for ACE's failure. But wise heads should have been able to predict the end result. Which brings us to yet another slippery network/soul issue.

Networks, I'm more or less claiming, are the best/only way to be responsive today. I've also claimed that midgets—e.g., stovemaker Rational—can be global giants. I don't mean to waffle on either claim. I do mean, however, to acknowledge the wisdom of the Bill Gates epigraph ("Money is made . . .").

Sun Microsystems licenses advanced technology to all comers—in undisguised hopes of creating one of Gates's "de facto" standards (see Chapter 34). Boeing farms lots out, but (like BMW) retains "systems integration" all to itself—which helps it call many a shot with many a big vendor (e.g., GE's multibillion-dollar aircraft-engine operation).

Trying to establish standards, for Sun, Microsoft, or Boeing, is risky. But the payoff can be enormous. And don't hold your breath waiting for "networks" to defy gravity and establish the sort of bully-power that can stand the test of time.

23

Networks and Markets II: The Pursuit of Power

Several years ago, senior executives from Procter & Gamble and Wal-Mart met for two days to explore how they could jointly apply quality management principles to the disposable diaper business. As a result of this meeting, a team of Procter & Gamble employees moved to Bentonville, Arkansas, Wal-Mart's headquarters, to work with Wal-Mart executives on productivity and quality issues. Wal-Mart has increased its Procter & Gamble diaper business by 50 percent and cut inventory . . . by 70 percent because of this collaboration.

LEONARD BERRY AND A. PARASURAMAN
Marketing Services

In a strategic alliance, one or both of the partners want to assure that the other cannot have an affair with a stranger. But we cartel officials are more for free love.

WOLFGANG KARTTE
President, German Cartel Office,
on the proposed linkage of
Allianz (Europe's largest
insurer) and Dresdner Bank
Financial Times, April 22, 1992

Compete by collaborating in order to avoid competing? Excuse me?

You learn it on the first day of your first economics class: Smart businesspersons seek monopolies. Because as Willie Sutton said about banks, that's where the money is. (Which is why smart governments try to keep smart businesspersons from achieving monopolies.)

Rational's Siegfried Meister is a smart businessman. He designed a good convection oven. Others caught up. He said he disliked "destructive competition" (competing on price, which decimates margins), so he boldly shut his successful convection oven line down—to pursue monopolistic profits through an unassailable advantage in combination-cooking technology.

Now Meister is collaborating more—i.e., subcontracting out more of this and that. But he's collaborating to concentrate. He wants to keep his firm energetic (400 people tops), but he wants the 400 to devote themselves to a handful of areas where he can leverage his almost monopolistic skills in combi-cooking (e.g., *more* R&D).

On March 29, 1990, Sara Lee executive Keith Alm gave an impassioned speech about strategic alliances:

> Competition by collaboration. . . . P&G has practically *defined* packaged goods marketing and now they are *redefining* it in terms of exciting and innovative new partnerships—strategic supplier and customer alliances that will see them into the next century. . . . We are creating *shared destinies*. And increasingly, the basis for these shared destinies is *shared information*. . . . *The new currency is knowledge*. . . . Visionary suppliers—like P&G and Sara Lee—are beginning to create *knowledge-based* partnerships to share business and *information* with their largest customers. . . . The idea is to . . . create clearly superior customer value that *shuts your competitor out*—preempts him, while creating a *sustainable balance of power* between partners. . . . There has to be a marriage—right through the distribution chain to your customer . . . through strategic alliances with *first mover* retailers . . . The major retailers around the world are moving toward cooperative alliances with a select few suppliers.

Keith Alm is clear. (As was P&G when it lovingly approached Wal-Mart—see the epigraph.) Collaboration? Networks? Alliances? He's for 'em all. Why? Day one of economics class—the pursuit of monopolistic power ("*shuts your competitor out*"). I'd bet that the biggest cloud on Alm's horizon is anxiety about maintaining enough clout, vis-à-vis a monster like Wal-Mart, to hold onto a "sustainable balance of power between partners." Metternich and John D. Rockefeller would clap their hands with delight!

Yes, Alm makes the requisite bow to "clearly superior customer value." It reminds me of the thoroughly democratic words in the old Soviet constitution. But the primary intent is unmistakable.

"Strategic alliances" are the rage. And when MCI joins up with a clever, moderate-size technology partner to inject innovation into its network, fast, I applaud. Just as I applaud when a big, smart medical equipment producer seeks out Skonie Corp. to train its customers. (Make no mistake, though. Valerie Skonie seeks monopoly no less than Keith Alm: She wants to have *all* the best medical equipment trainers in her matchless, she hopes, network.)

Does the consumer gain value from the marriage of P&G and Wal-Mart? Should we applaud? The consumer probably does gain value. But we should *not* applaud. Why? Because the consumer probably gets value only *at first*. Most monopolies add value *at first*. (After all, they *become* monopolies because they've been doing something very well.) But then sluggishness sets in: i.e., fear of trying the new, because, hey, why screw up your current monopolistic advantage?

Back to MCI. Ops boss Liebhaber, though an urgent seeker of competitive advantage, is a self-interested *anti*-monopolist. (Hmm?) Liebhaber doesn't want to *make* anything. Why? Because bureaucracy is bureaucracy, and he would soon become victim of an in-house monopolistic engineering department (to justify the investment in the in-house department, he'd have to feed it *some* business—even if a little Taiwanese supplier could do part of the job faster, more cheaply, and more innovatively). So Liebhaber seeks to maintain his advantage by *not* tying himself to in-house sluggishness—and by always keeping at least a pair of contending vendors on the hook.

The good news (mostly): Monopolists almost always choke on their greed. They fight innovation. And fight. And then, and it can take a long time, they invariably get toppled by an upstart.

German Cartel Office chief Wolfgang Kartte is right to call strategic alliances among ponderous giants "voluntary renunciation of competition"—and to vow to quash them. But what about business chiefs? Well, they should listen to Kartte. The *pursuit* of monopoly power—of a crushing strategic advantage through a de facto research monopoly in combi-cooking, for instance—leads to innovation. But, eventually, it results in resistance to change. For the corporate boss, the trick, examined in detail in the Markets and Innovation section and hinted at in the analyses of IDG, Acordia, and CCT, is to engineer competition against yourself: At once to try and attain a "crushing" advantage (as a 35-person CCT company does in repairing one kind of aircraft-engine turbine blade), and to keep fresh by creating more and more largely independent 35-person powerhouses.

Collaboration and networking, government approval or disapproval aside, is great stuff—and deadly—in equal measure. "Compete" by collaborating in order to avoid competing. And then go stale. Catch-22, anyone?

24

Networks III: Life in Networked Organizations

People who write history as a succession of great men underestimate the importance of the network.

JONATHAN MILLER
quoted in Michael Schrage's
Shared Minds

We've examined the bits of networks, such as the supersubs, and
discussed some firms, such as MCI, which have purposefully chosen to "do"
relatively less than their peers and farm out more. We've looked at the pros
(many) and cons (which the pros outweigh—but see Chapter 23 and Markets
and Innovation) of alliances of all sorts. But what is it like to *live* a networked
life? How, for example, do you "manage" one of the world's largest conventions with a full-time staff that you could almost fit in a phone booth?

THE NATIONAL RESTAURANT ASSOCIATION ANNUAL CONVENTION

It's always held in Chicago during the third week in May. It
boasted the U.S.'s largest annual trade show registration in 1990—108,731
people. It's the National Restaurant Association (NRA) convention, 1,800
exhibitors strong, featuring marathons, distinguished speakers, and a whiz-
bang culinary team competition.

The American Culinary Classic

The NRA convention has to compete vigorously to attract customers. For one thing, other national trade shows that restaurateurs might attend move from one attractive location to another, year after year. But only McCormick Place in Chicago can handle the NRA's numbers, so it's Chicago or else. Competition from spiffed-up regional restaurant shows is intense as well.

Enter Michel Bouit. NRA convention chief Dick Gaven got him to head the 1991 convention's American Culinary Classic. Competing were fifteen teams from around the world, including the U.S. Culinary Team.

A typical national culinary team consists of three hot-food cooks, a pastry cook, and a team captain. At Frankfurt's renowned international restaurant trade show, cookoffs work like this: Teams submit a favorite recipe, then prepare it on the spot for judging. The NRA in 1991 took a different tack: The evening before the cookoff, each team got a "mystery box" containing various ingredients (selected in accordance with international food competition requirements—teams draw numbers to determine who gets which box), then had a half hour to turn it into creative recipes. They practiced that night, then arrived at McCormick Place at 6:00 a.m. on the big day. At noon, each team served 80 portions to judges, then another 280 to ticket-holding members of the general public.

Quarterbacking the big NRA cookoff gave Bouit visibility—not immaterial, since he'd like to head the American Culinary Federation some day. The NRA's Gaven enticed him with the promise of publicity, then gave him a couple of thousand bucks to cover incidental expenses. For two years, Bouit visited competitions, called on chefs and culinary teams, drummed up interest in the NRA event. He also pulled together an extensive network. For example, various chefs from around the country were talked into acting as "hospitality ambassadors" for the teams (translation: finding drivers to ferry around the visiting chefs). ARA, the giant food service company, agreed to sponsor a party for the teams. Syracuse China sprang for special commemorative plates. Another convention exhibitor provided chairs for the big day. Another coughed up silverware. And so on.

A Fragile Yet Robust Network Churns Out Precision *and* Novelty

The NRA's American Culinary Classic provides a glimpse of network manager/NRA exec Gaven's life. You could say Bouit was a subcontractor to Gaven. (Gaven doesn't look at it that way. Bouit was a comrade-in-arms, as he sees it.) Bouit, in turn, worked intensively and personally with a separate, extensive network of "subcontractors" to cobble his event together. In fact, just about everything associated with the NRA convention is subcontracted. (The full-time NRA staff, which runs the convention, more or less numbers seven—see below.)

Scrounging, nudging, and cajoling were the names of Michel Bouit's game—the commemorative plates, the chairs, the silverware. All in all, hundreds of "staff" were eventually involved in just the one event, from paid ushers (one of several hundred "official" subcontractors) to those volunteers who chauffeured the culinary teams around.

It is a complex mess. Yet given the increasingly competitive context and the high expectations of NRA members (the trip-of-the-year for most), Gaven's extensive, half-cocked "organization" has to work perfectly the first time! In Gaven's world, it is *always* the first time. There are significant differences in each convention and its players—no one show is like any other. In sum, what Gaven oversees must be very reliable, very dependable, very predictable—and very new, very exciting, very different. And all this courtesy of a full-time design/oversight staff that amounts to about one-tenth of one percent of those who are involved in putting on the show itself.

Gaven spends the year hyping the next show, sorting through the results of the latest show, working on relationships—with VIP attendees, exhibitors, culinary teams, scores of Michel Bouits. Exhibitors whose performance is humdrum, for example, have to be weeded out from time to time. Then there's the growing market-driven need to put on a raft of very special events to give the show a perpetually fresh flavor. The Culinary Classic was one. So's a highly publicized 10-K race, in its 11th running in 1991. "Some guy suggested it," Gaven said matter-of-factly, "so we gave it a try." Now "The Main Course: The World's Most Hospitable Race" alone has a $50,000 budget and draws over 3,000 contestants. United and Delta airlines provided prizes in 1991. Others got into the act too, giving out T-shirts to tout the race and so on. Each such event becomes the big show's signature for some sizable number of attendees. For example, Gaven claimed that numerous convention attendees bubble about the race, yet have little else to say about the rest of the NRA show. Others will form their impression of the show based on something they may not have even seen! "Three thousand people will see some big-name speaker, like Norman Schwartzkopf," Gaven told us. "Then ten thousand will *say* they saw him. After all, they meant to go!" That is, lots of those who don't go to such events still feel they were part of something exciting just because Stormin' Norman was there. ("Oh, I saw Norman Schwartzkopf at the '92 NRA".) And that, after all, is the point if Gaven is to entice them back to Chicago next year—and the next, and the next. . . .

Special events come and go. Gaven has taken a chapter from 3M's book—"make a little, sell a little, make a little more." And if it doesn't sell, don't make any more. The NRA Wine Classic had been around for a while, but Gaven could never push attendance at the wine tasting competition much above 1,000. That wasn't enough for a "big" event, within the context of the larger objectives of the show. After four years of adjusting and trying, he killed it. Such creation and destruction are the essence of his ever-gyrating game (carnival!).

The Little Band of Jugglers

But how do you "run" such an affair? Gaven handles promotion and NRA board politics. Andy Wroblewski is the full-time director of exhibits, sales and operations. He and Mary Pat Hoffman work at keeping current exhibitors happy and manage a network of part-time telemarketers who seek out new exhibitors. Lennie Torres rounds up about 14,000 hotel rooms and manages relations with the city's hoteliers. Her system is primitive, which doesn't bother Gaven in the least. Torres, he says, is a master. Gaven has to decide what to subcontract, what to keep to himself. He could, like many other local trade show honchos, subcontract the arrangement for hotel rooms to Chicago's Convention Bureau. But having those rooms ready, Gaven insisted, is too important to farm out. (Booking rooms is *soul*.)

Then there's Theresa Struppa. Gaven's worked with her for 14 years, but can't seem to remember her title—or if she has one. She handles registrations. Making badges is soul, too, and kept in house—a little machine cranks out 300 per hour. One man, Ainsley Wareham, "does all eighty-thousand-plus of them," Gaven told me. When I talked with Gaven in 1991, Wareham was full-time at Burger King, and working part-time for the NRA at $6.00 per hour. To hear Gaven, he may be the most important person in the organization. He also runs the mailroom and does pretty much anything and everything that anyone asks. Wareham loves Gaven, and Gaven and the NRA team love Wareham. There are two other more or less full-time members of the convention management team—a data processor, Carmen Laureano, who also handles the administrative details of hundreds upon hundreds of contracts, and Judith Fay, a secretary.

That's it!

Network Meister Gaven

As I see it, Dick Gaven is the classic "new look" network manager. (It's old look, old hat to him—but decidedly new look to denizens of vertically integrated firms.) He's very personable, wanders incessantly, plays the phones like a master—and works ceaselessly on relationships. Gaven has a well-developed knack for ferreting out the likes of Michel Bouit. And no one I've met more instinctively gives others full credit for numerous things he's had a hidden hand in. Ideas surface all the time—Gaven lets them bubble up, gain support, then gives them a try, nudges them forward. If they work, with the right players in place, fine. Push harder. If they don't, that's OK too. Don't lose sleep—just move on.

Hang out, talk up, nudge, cajole, praise—these are the apparently pedestrian skills that Gaven has mastered. But they add up to very nonpedestrian results: the premier status the NRA event maintains in the multibillion-dollar world of conventions.

TPG COMMUNICATIONS: WHERE'S THE BEEF? (SOUL VI)

The essence of *any* "firm" is ever more elusive. Hotel companies rarely own hotels these days. An insurance company or some other big financial institution usually does. Almost every "thing" the hotel firm "owns"—brand loyalty, service management skills, information systems and databases, financial deal-making skills—is intangible. But in cases like Marriott's, the value of those intangibles adds up to billions of bucks.

To maintain such value is increasingly a matter of building and nurturing dense networks. Even my own tiny company is enmeshed in (and busy creating) a "spiderweb" of shifting, complex relationships with a host of tiny and huge outsiders. In particular, the five full-time employees of Tom Peters Group Communications (TPGC) spend most of their time scouring the globe for the best partners to parlay "soft" notions into "hard" products—and, ultimately, into cash (about $4 million in revenues in 1991).

For video "products," for instance, we work primarily with Video Publishing House (star of the Dallas Organization, remember). The $14-million industry leader in training videos gathers top directors (subcontractors), arranges funding, and finds the right airspace (such as PBS) for our shows. The "only" things Video Publishing House "does" are overall program conception, marketing, distribution—*and network management.* (Plus about a thousand other "little" things that make its soul different from the souls of others—i.e., elusive *Video Publishing House-ism!*) The story is repeated with virtually all of TPGC's other "products": Licensed workshops are produced around the world by CareerTrack of Boulder, Colorado. Audio products are mostly joint-ventured with Nightingale-Conant of Chicago. (Both market-leading firms are themselves networked to the hilt.) We conceive, research, and write a monthly newsletter, but Berkeley-based InfoCom Group markets and administers it (supported by numerous subs of its own). And the weekly TV spots I used to do were produced and directed by dozens of independent "firms" from around the world, depending on my location at the time. (Sometimes the producer would be a one-woman band with an audio subcontractor. Sometimes it would be a special-services arm of a huge corporation.)

What a tangle! I'd hate to have to draw an organization chart of the relatively simple activities (by Marriott's standards) I've just described.

How is it tied together? First, through a clear concept—i.e., *soul.* We think we know what we're about. By subcontracting most everything, we focus on those few items where we have a strategic edge. But no one is "in charge" in the classic sense. We view Video Publishing House as *our* subcontractor. They view us as *their* subcontractor. Who's right? Both of us. Neither of us. Each will do well to the extent that the other does well: It is a relationship based upon unequivocal mutual dependence. (In mid-1992, another video company suggested a project to us that was irresistible. We decided to bring VPH in on the act, even though there was no technical reason to do so. The nontechnical reason was to demonstrate that we were "in it together" with our important partners.)

Why don't we pursue some of the forgone revenue (the $20 million or so difference between our communication arm's booked revenue and its products' retail value) by producing, marketing, and distributing our own TV shows, audios, and newsletters? (Or even books: Several entrepreneurial sorts, including a couple of engaging Dartmouth MBA students, have proposed self-publishing schemes.) Simple: Each "sub"-task is highly sophisticated and specialized in its own right. Fat chance that we'd match the patiently honed skills of our partners at any one of these activities. Each, after all, is as obsessed with constantly improving its narrow-gauge strengths as we are about improving ours. And that's the larger message: We're not "obsessed" with the ins and outs of newsletter marketing, for example—but the world increasingly offers the likes of us a choice of entrepreneurs and specialists, big and small, who are.

This isn't a "great company" story. I think we're good, but this recitation isn't an advertisement. The point: Our now-you-see-it, now-you-don't, find-it-if-you-can, it's-changed-since-yesterday structure—a *non*structure by the last several hundred years' standards—is quickly becoming the norm, from bitsy us to humongous MCI.

July 1991: A Day in the Life of Alison Peterson, Networker

Alison Peterson, who heads Tom Peters Group Communications, is our Dick Gaven. For a week, Peterson recorded what she was up to. A typical day, chopped into 15-minute chunks, went like this:

8:00	Cleaned company kitchen (rotating duty): "What a pit!"
8:15	Call to video partner. Fax to Korean partners [who are starting to distribute our products].
8:30	Evaluate subcontractor working for CareerTrack.*
8:45	Ditto.
9:00	Call VPH, call one of VPH's subcontractors.
9:15	Faxes to various customers.
9:30	Evaluate CareerTrack subs.
9:45	Call to VPH subcontractor.

*We and CareerTrack co-create seminars, then they stage and market them via a global network of trainer-subcontractors. Though CareerTrack has a tough quality-control regimen, we review seminar transcripts and have the right to reject trainers (see below).

10:00	Call to customer.
10:15	Evaluate CareerTrack subs.
10:30	Call to VPH subcontractor, write memo on that call to Tom [yours truly].
10:45	Ditto.
11:00	Evaluate CareerTrack subs.
11:15	Ditto.
11:30	Ditto.
11:45	Fax to German subcontractor doing research for book [this one!].
12:00	Lunch with marketing VP of another TPG company.
12:15	Ditto.
12:30	Ditto.
12:45	Ditto.
1:00	Ditto. [More than an hour for lunch, Alison?—Tom.]
1:15	Review current version of new video, prior to conversation with VPH.
1:30	Ditto.
1:45	Ditto.
2:00	Ditto.
2:15	Phone call to VPH.
2:30	Ditto.
2:45	Phone call to another of VPH's subcontractors.
3:00	Ditto.
3:15	Phone call to CareerTrack re subcontractor evaluations.
3:30	Phone call to potential seminar partners.
3:45	Prepare for meeting tomorrow with [our CFO].
4:00	Miscellaneous administrative tasks, most dealing with "outsiders."
4:15	Ditto.
4:30	Ditto.
4:45	Phone call to Tom re video project.

5:00   Review manuscripts associated with another video project.

5:15   Ditto.

5:30   See you tomorrow!

SUMMARY

	Hours	Percent
Own Company Administration	0.75	8
Other Tom Peters Group	1.25 (lunch)	13
Venture Partners/Subcontractors	7.00	74
Customers	0.50	5

Peterson is probably a typical new-look network manager—about three-quarters of her time is spent dealing with partners! Those hours devoted to evaluating CareerTrack's subcontractors reveal one of the crucial subcontracting/networking issues. Our reputation rises or falls, as we see it, on our partners' performance. Peterson spends a couple of days each month evaluating their trainers by listening to audiotapes of their performances. (Various members of our staff, often not from TPGC, and friends all over the world also drop in on seminars.) From all that, she/we:

—learn new twists, customer interests;

—maintain active involvement in assuring product quality (and make it clear, just by time spent, that we are insistent about maintaining that quality);

—give voluminous, detailed feedback to our partners (including kudos and occasional recommendations to drop a speaker).

The effort constitutes maintenance and protection of our "soul," relative to this important relationship.

There turns out, then, to be a lot of "beef" in this story. It's just not the sort we've been used to. We "control" key relationships mostly by investing time in them. We retain (often via contract) substantial formal authority, but work like hell *not* to exercise it. Our effectiveness is wrapped up in Peterson's skill (like Gaven's) at developing and nurturing numerous levels of relationships of significant economic value—and in not using formal sanctions except as a last resort.

MANAGEMENT MAXIMIZERS

When Management Maximizers (M^2) founder Marion McGovern took maternity leave in 1990, she did just what her firm recommends to its clients and queried the M^2 network for a replacement CEO (!). Enter Nancy

Macchia, a former vice president in sales and operations at the Bank of America, who did so well that she became one of the firm's shareholding partners.

Of course it wasn't quite that easy. First McGovern had to figure out what Macchia was to do. Which meant figuring out what McGovern herself did. McGovern considered herself the small firm's chief PR and marketing person. But after reflecting and counseling with her colleague, co-founder Paula Reynolds, she concluded that her special skill was client service—which therefore became Macchia's chief task as substitute boss.

Started in 1988, M^2 tallied $1.2 million in 1991 revenues, and expects billings of $5–$10 million by 1994. On a day in mid-1991, 25 members of M^2's "network" were ensconced in executive or senior project management jobs.

One of M^2's very first senior executive placements was at Lucasfilm. Personnel director Lori McAdams was about to take maternity leave, and McGovern's fledgling firm dug up a half-dozen replacement candidates—including Patsy Murphy, a former personnel officer at NBC who'd been working independently for about three years. Murphy filled in more than adequately for McAdams, and ended up staying at Lucasfilm to do special tasks after McAdams returned to work.

Since then, M^2 has provided about 125 "substitutes," including replacement CEOs and CFOs. In addition to Lucasfilm, clients include Union Bank, Clorox, Pacific Gas & Electric, Visa, First Nationwide Bank, Hewlett-Packard, Safeway, Windham Hill, Oakland East Bay Symphony, and FMC.* Jobs filled include: controller/CFO for a biotech startup, permanent part-timer, three days a week, based on $75,000 per year in compensation; interim CFO for a consumer goods company, $140 an hour; contract recruiter for a huge telecommunications company, $65 an hour; product manager for information services product repricing, $100 an hour; business strategist for an environmental services company, $100 per hour.

M^2 is a product of the times and a harbinger of times to come. Surveys show that 2 million Americans work as part-time, independent professionals. In the San Francisco Bay Area, where M^2 is headquartered, roughly 60 percent of companies of at least middling size use contract middle managers. More narrowly, there is, as of this writing, a growing, $75-million-a-year market for replacement *executives*, M^2's bailiwick.

The Art of the (M^2) Deal

M^2's meat and potatoes is an extraordinarily accomplished network of 2,000 professionals, averaging 15 years of experience (the average member has held

*Despite the heft of this list, most M^2 clients are midsize firms. Such outfits tend to run lean and have a tough time covering for an absent senior manager. Most big firms, the M^2 founders report, are still fat enough to absorb the temporary loss of a "key" exec without feeling any compelling need to replace the absent person.

several middle management positions). Over half have advanced degrees, and almost half run their own independent consulting businesses. About 60 percent are women.

At the start, M^2 got lots of publicity in conjunction with the "mommy track" issue. Indeed, any number of M^2's initial placements, and a few of its current placements, are execs replacing execs on maternity leave. Replacements for people taking leave of one sort or another constitute one of four varieties of slots M^2 typically fills. The others are interim managers—jobs filled on a full- or part-time basis because of management vacancies caused by an unexpected departure or corporate decision to downsize; permanent part-time people—to fill slots (including very senior slots) that will no longer be occupied by full-time people; and project professionals—who can step in and handle specific projects in, say, marketing, finance, human resources, or manufacturing. In this last role, M^2 positions itself as an alternative to pricey consulting firms such as Booz, Allen (where McGovern once worked) and McKinsey.

If you want to infuriate the founders, call them an "executive temp service" or, worse still, a "body shop." While they'll admit to the technical validity of both monikers, their marketing objective is to move beyond the typical temp "feel." The special M^2 difference (soul), the founders suggest, is a unique, artful ability to create a match between highly talented network members and clients in pursuit of senior specialists—and to fully specify the nature of the job to be performed (the sort of thing McGovern did for herself when she took leave from her own firm).

Not surprisingly, M^2 sports a computerized database and has figured out, over time, how to fill it with useful, accessible information. Nonetheless, the art that goes beyond the cold qualifications in the database is what adds distinct value. The company charges a lot for its services and seeks to earn its keep by purposefully seeking out assignments where it can play an expansive role in filling a critical slot. Perversely, in the case of the most senior placements, M^2's customers have seldom thought through the departing exec's chores. Yet effectively specifying principal tasks is a must—since an M^2 network replacement exec is expected to hit the ground sprinting.

When it comes to technical skills, M^2 execs acknowledge that most of their network members are "overqualified." That's as it should be. A job's technical requirements are unlikely to throw the replacement for a loop. The M^2 network member's true key to success is "political skills"—which depend in turn upon the M^2 replacement manager getting a "full cultural core dump," as co-founder Paula Reynolds put it, "whose calls to return, whose not to return, and so on."

Bringing In Business

In mid-1992, M^2 was getting a half dozen or so customer inquiries per week. A couple were still of the "do you do this?" variety, according to Reynolds, though she happily reported that callers "at least know we don't do the replacement secretary stuff." To spur growth, M^2 hired its first full-time, outside sales person, Claire McAuliffe, in October 1990. She adds four to six prospect calls per week to across-the-transom inquiries. Hooking a client usually takes several months. Consider a placement agreement to provide a project manager for about six weeks to a small financial services firm, Working Assets: The CEO wanted to bring in-house the customer service function now being performed by her long-distance telecommunications vendor. M^2 found two superior candidates who would figure out (in those six weeks), how to get the job done. One's a technologist who could potentially create a proprietary service system for the client. The other is a customer service specialist, whose shtick would be the human resource aspect of bringing the function in-house. M^2 execs hoped eventually to place both candidates with the client—but had just gotten their toes in the door with a brief "see how it works out" assignment for the technical person, Shari Guilfoyle. (Guilfoyle is a typical M^2 network member. A 1979 San Jose State University grad, she was manager, then vice president of shareholder relations, at Benham Capital Management Group from 1984 to 1990. As VP, she supervised a staff of 85 and a $3-million budget—and managed an ops center responsible for handling over 100,000 calls per month. A telemarketing program she created produced $100 million in new accounts in its first year of operation. In April 1990, Guilfoyle founded her own management consulting firm.)

McGovern insists that the sales function is crucial. The biggest competition in M^2's loosely defined "industry" is New York-based Interim Management Corporation, and McGovern attributes a lot of its success to a full-time, seven-person sales force. "The service needs to be explained, then explained again," she said. Because of its New York location, Interim is rarely a direct competitor. At this point, most exec replacement business is local, and M^2 does have narrow-focus, local competitors such as Palo Alto's Adams & Allgood, which specializes in providing temporary marketing and sales people to high-tech firms. But formal competition isn't M^2's worry. As Reynolds put it, "Our biggest competitor, bar none, is 'I know someone who. . . .' " That is, the haphazard "networks" of pals that individuals in potential client companies call upon when the need for a replacement manager or project honcho arises. M^2's chief selling task, then, is demonstrating that the breadth and depth of its network, and its ability to achieve unique fit and task specification, are of greater value than that random assortment of available friends that come to the minds of prospective-client execs. Since most prospective clients, at this juncture, have so little experience with part-time execs and interim project managers, they have a tough time conjuring up the difference between "good fit" and "bad fit," or between a "network" of 10 pals and M^2's well-vetted 2,000.

"Getting It"

Despite consistently positive customer feedback, repeat business has not met the M^2 founders' expectations. As of this writing, about 25 percent of placements come from past customers. Even the happiest customers "don't quite get it," McGovern laments, when it comes to understanding how best to exploit M^2's unique network resources.

Part of the problem is a failure to comprehend how the world is spinning these days. One constant client objection, Reynolds and McGovern report, is, "If these people [network members] are so good, how come they aren't working full-time?" McGovern and Reynolds rebut with, "They're so good, they don't have to work full-time!"—that is, M^2's network by and large consists of confident professionals who have chosen to turn their backs on the traditional rat race.

The M^2 founders argue, and I agree, that the purposefulness and commitment of their average network member are frequently higher than those of the average payroll employee, including senior managers. "These are people who put their reputation on the line every day," McGovern almost shouted at me during our interview. There's no tomorrow for a contractor who messes up! Reynolds added that an M^2 network member "tends to be much more self-motivated, more of a self-starter than the average, even good payroll employee in a good company. M^2 network members are secure people, comfortable with themselves, comfortable that they can get up to speed quickly in 'most any setting." (Skonie Corp.'s Valerie Skonie would smile, I'm sure.)

Managing M^2

M^2 shares a tiny office in San Francisco's financial-district. Employees include the principals (only McGovern is full-time), sales manager McAuliffe, salesman Dick Knock, and office manager, coordinator, and overall administrator Yolanda Pacho. Part-time support staff, mostly college students, provide further administrative assistance. M^2's controller is part-time, from the firm's network. When special tasks surface, the company again looks to its network.

"Look at our corporate identity project," McGovern said. "A little firm like ours is using the resources of some of the most talented people in the nation on a very part-time, very affordable basis. That's what it's all about." M^2 can also brag of a highly involved advisory board, consisting of a senior vice president at Charles Schwab, Clorox's director of marketing, Pacific Gas & Electric's treasurer, and an EVP at Wells Fargo. Among other things, this august band adds credibility to the still oddball M^2 concept.

Cofounder Reynolds likened M^2's internal management process to an earlier stint in a congressional office. "You're expected to get a lot done, cover a broad range of issues, and get it done fast," she said. "Yet no one who can help you works directly for you."

Networking: A Day at M^2, July 12, 1991

Let's take one last, close-up look at "network management." Marion McGovern and her colleagues let my colleague, Kathy Dalle-Molle, follow them around for a day.

July 12, 1991: 8:00 to 10:00 a.m. Marion McGovern writing follow-up letters to potential clients. Nancy Macchia trying to find subcontractors for a new job that came in yesterday afternoon. Client (new) is Rucker Fuller, an office furniture retailer opening a showroom this fall; needs someone ASAP to coordinate the opening. Position is part-time through October. McGovern and Macchia decide to search the database for subcontractors with experience in event planning, sales and marketing, and maybe real estate. "This is an interesting position to fill," Macchia says, "because there are a lot of different skills at work. It's not like filling a financial analyst slot."

They search the database by industry, in this case public relations as the primary category and real estate as secondary. (They can search up to five industries at a time.) Database search is performed by one of two part-time college students, and Macchia reviews the resultant list of more than 100 possible candidates. She remembers a few. For most, she'll pull files—a subcontractor's file contains a résumé, work samples, the M^2 application, interview notes (if there was an interview), notes about positions the subcontractor has been contacted for and/or filled, etc. Macchia selects three candidates, calls them. Two aren't around (typical), one is a no-go.

(Rucker Fuller has also asked M^2 to fill a part-time strategic marketing/ sales position; Macchia hasn't begun that search, since the position doesn't open for 30 days. M^2's salesperson, Claire McAuliffe, got both orders from Rucker Fuller, then turned them over to Macchia. Macchia says it's usually not necessary for her to visit the client if McAuliffe has already been there. M^2 execs get back within 24 hours to clients who place orders to let them know if they've surfaced potential candidates. In another 24 hours, they deliver résumés and a cover letter, or report that they haven't been able to find anyone who's available. By that point, McGovern or Macchia has usually interviewed candidates. If a client is in a desperate rush, the M^2 team saves time by limiting their scan to previously interviewed network members.)

On July 12, M^2 has one other new-client job in process. Five other jobs are also active—clients are meeting candidates, reviewing résumés. And another five client inquiries are pending: One firm wanted M^2 to fill four positions, but suddenly reorganized and the positions are now on hold; another was redefining the project, another needed higher-level management approval. (In situations like this, Macchia follows up with the client once a week.)

Macchia now decides she's uncertain about the hourly rate Rucker Fuller has in mind for the event planner. She calls her contact in Rucker Fuller's organization; he's in a meeting, and she leaves a message. (Macchia later says Rucker Fuller didn't balk at a suggested $100-per-hour fee.)

Macchia calls a subcontractor who'd interviewed a few months ago for a job at Wells Fargo Bank (to oversee development of a new product). The bank has been sitting on the job order for six months. Though impressed by M^2 and by the subcontractors they'd interviewed, Wells Fargo hasn't filled the position. Macchia sent a letter to her client at Wells yesterday, saying, "I assume the project has gone away. I hope you'll call us in the future, etc." Now she's letting the subcontractors who had interviewed know the state of play. (Macchia spends most of her time on the phone—calling subcontractors to let them know the status of a position they've interviewed for, finding subcontractors for a position, talking with new and existing clients. That is, keeping everyone plugged in.)

10:00 a.m. to 12:30 p.m. Meeting with Linda Rosso, a subcontractor (part of the network) who's been working for the last six weeks on M^2's new marketing communication plan. Rosso conducted interviews with all of M^2's principals and numerous subcontractors and clients. She found that it takes clients a long time to figure out what M^2 does. She also says that M^2's early "mommy network" publicity could be a liability. (For the next several months, Rosso will act as M^2's de facto marketing director. "Obviously, we couldn't afford to hire her as an employee," McGovern says, "but five thousand dollars here, ten thousand dollars there, that we can handle.")

12:30 p.m. to 2:00 p.m. Paula Reynolds and Rosso go to lunch together. Macchia leaves. McGovern asks Macchia to bring back a big container of coffee yogurt, which she eats while continuing to work.

The VP of human resources at Smith & Hawken frantically called McGovern yesterday afternoon. Needs to hire another HR manager, but can't until November. The company's CFO, who met Reynolds at a social gathering a few months ago, gave Reynolds' card to the HR VP and suggested that she see if M^2 could help. Hours are flexible. M^2's subcontractor would primarily be responsible for developing a new performance appraisal system and for counseling managers about the company's termination policy. HR VP tells McGovern there might be other work, too.

McGovern has had the database searched for personnel management and codes A, C, and E—e.g., A is "strong generalist." Now she goes through the printout, circling the names of people she knows would be good for the job—one, for instance, is a former HR manager at the retailer Cost Plus. She also highlights "maybes." Naomi Hayashi, an M^2 part-timer and student at San Francisco State, pulls the files on top choices and those McGovern doesn't know. McGovern will call five prospective candidates.

McGovern's also trying to find a candidate for Fair Isaac, a local credit-ratings firm. The company needs help setting up a system to provide credit ratings to insurance companies. McGovern thinks she's found the perfect candidate: "When I called one of his references, the guy told me, 'There's no person better in the world for this job.'" He's very senior, however, so she wants to develop other options—"They might want a worker bee," she says.

(Throughout the day, McGovern calls clients and subcontractors, determining interest in the various positions. She also keeps in touch with McAuliffe, who calls several times. McGovern also reviews the approximately five résumés/network applications that come in each day. First she checks for accuracy. For example, one applicant has marked law as a functional skill, but his résumé shows that while he has previously worked in a law firm, he's not a lawyer—he prepared budgets for lawyers. Another applicant used to be director of events for Caesars Palace. He's exceptionally well qualified, but McGovern decides he doesn't merit an interview because M^2 doesn't get many calls for such a unique set of specs.)

2:00 p.m. to 2:45 p.m. Macchia interviews a potential network member, referred by another network member who also happens to be a former client. Macchia finds the applicant is unemployed, looking for permanent, full-time work. (Macchia had called the candidate with a client need in mind that matched the applicant's skills. Job involves creating a direct-mail program for a new product.) Macchia pointedly reminds the applicant that, as a condition for getting the interview, she must make a commitment to the full term of the job—no backing out if a full-time job offer comes along halfway through the assignment.

2:45 p.m. to 3:30 p.m. Macchia returns a couple of subcontractors' calls concerning the Rucker Fuller job. Discusses the position, their interest, how they'd sell themselves for the job, asks them how *she* should highlight their experience when she talks to the client.

McGovern making calls to subcontractors for the Smith & Hawken job. She's faced with a potential problem, because all her candidates are senior people—she must find someone she likes with less experience, in case that's what Smith & Hawken wants.

3:30 p.m. to 4:30 p.m. McGovern, Reynolds, and Macchia meet at this time every Wednesday. McGovern leads the meeting. Macchia talks about Rucker Fuller. McGovern reviews Smith & Hawken. Broderbund Software has canceled a work order—Macchia to find out why. A technical writing position at Syntex has been on hold for two weeks. U.S. Instrument Rentals is interviewing candidates sent by M^2. Reynolds suggests that Macchia follow up with a potential investment-banking client who's looking for a controller. McGovern reports that McAuliffe has met with the CEO at Working Assets— M^2's newly placed subcontractor "is a great fit," the CEO says. McAuliffe is trying to get Working Assets to commit to Phase II of the project. Reynolds asks her partners if they're getting testimonials from these clients.

The group decides they need a better voice mail system. McGovern suggests that Reynolds call one of their network members who's a specialist in that area. (The network member has spent the last five months on a client project that was supposed to last a week.)

Reynolds starts a discussion about the Linda Rosso meeting. They decide how much to spend on the marketing program, where they can cut corners. Discuss draft of a new sales letter that McGovern wrote but Rosso hated. Rosso's revising it, will fax it first thing tomorrow. All agree that Rosso will "report to" McGovern. Reynolds makes sure everyone knows who they're supposed to follow up with, who has lead on each project.

Discuss new tag-line on their logo: "Expertise in interim management services" or "Excellence in. . . ." Reynolds wonders about sending the new marketing plan to the board of advisors. They decide to send it to the three marketing people on the board. Reynolds will call them, tell them it's coming, set up a lunch meeting to discuss.

McAuliffe isn't at the meeting—Reynolds wants to make sure she'll be informed about what has transpired.

4:30 p.m. to 5:30 p.m. McAuliffe returns from sales calls. She usually spends two days on the road (one in Silicon Valley, one in Marin County and the East Bay), another day making sales visits in downtown San Francisco, two days on follow-up with existing clients and miscellany. McAuliffe averages 8 to 10 client meetings a week. Today, she was in Silicon Valley, meeting with the CFO of a medical instruments firm and the finance vice president at Franklin Fund. Also supposed to meet with someone at Sun Microsystems— when she arrived, she was informed that the person couldn't make the meeting, so she stopped in to see another client at Sun.

"Days in the life of" managers are usually revealing. On the one hand, whether the subject is Joe Doaks, Marion McGovern, or Senator Self-important, much of the content is the same—wheedling, cajoling, nudging, chatting, pursuing "fit." On the other hand, this report *is* different. M²'s principals are constantly mindful of their network. Most traditional managers downgrade the importance of networks, adopting at best a "let the network manage itself" attitude (and at worst a "what a silly pastime" attitude). Not M². Their network is their lifeblood.

As a networker, M² also has to take the long view, tiny firm or not. We saw lots of effort devoted to today's jobs. But a lot of attention was also paid to jobs on hold, and to network members who might not be utilized for months, if ever.

ROIR/RELATIONSHIP POWER

ROI. Return on investment. Important. ROIR. Return on investment in relationships. More important!

We all invest in relationships. It's only human, off the job or on. But today's wisest firms, it seems, are those that are tops at consciously investing in relationships—steadily, over time, with a purpose and a passion. But even the stellar, pioneering outfits (Apple, MCI, Skonie, M²) don't try to *measure* it. And that's a mistake. More important still: measuring *cumulative* investment in relationships, *rate* of investment in relationships, rate of *increase* in investment in relationships, and so on. (E.g., I didn't know, until we did this research, that our Alison Peterson spends 74 percent of her time on "network partner relationships." If I'm wise, I'll resample in a year, and worry if that number has dipped—especially if it has dipped in favor or more inward-focused activities.)

Recall that new hires at EDS are immediately plunked down at a customer operation. From day one, they are steeped not in technology qua technology, but in putting the customer first. Most EDS "war stories" are about going the extra mile for the customer. The physical proximity of EDSers to customers is still a notable difference from many of the company's competitors. It all adds up to a phenomenal investment in close customer relationships. Think back to those staff chefs at Germany's Rational: What else are they doing, day in and day out, except cumulatively out-investing competitors (in a measurable way) in developing close relationships with professional-chef customers?

Or view Silicon Valley Bank through another lens. It's a pipsqueak compared to many of its neighborhood competitors. Yet it wins big in its chosen market, serving emerging-technology businesses. Why? A senior officer at the bank put it simply: "We've invested more in relationships with [local] venture capitalists, we know them better than our competitors." Those venture capitalists, in turn, steer startups toward the feisty bank. Look again at Management Maximizers, Skonie Corporation. These are small firms with big aims. Leaders are betting their companies, pure and simple, on investing more, more quickly, than others in network- and relationship-building.

Americans talk about relationships in nefarious terms when the topic is the Japanese. Theirs is a more relationship-based society than ours. Getting near the inner circle is often next to impossible for outsiders. Oddly enough, there's a rather close parallel between American frustration with Japanese clubbiness and the frustration CDC, Honeywell, Burroughs, and others used to express about IBM. In the typical Western tradition, IBM's competitors believed they should win, no ifs, ands or buts—because they had "better equipment." I can't judge whether or not it was better. I do expect it was often at least the equivalent of IBM's. On the other hand, IBMers were masters at "controlling the account." That's another way of saying they had patiently, and expensively, invested more than any of their competitors in relationship-building at the highest levels in customer firms. This was not a function of IBM's giant size. The relationship investment strategy can be traced back to the second decade of this century: When IBM was smaller than Silicon Valley Bank, Thomas J. Watson, Sr., was investing in relationships to a degree that others weren't.

Want to make a change in your overall business strategy? Try changing the "relationship investment pattern." Success today mostly comes from the integrated efforts of networks of peers. A sneaky opportunity lies in relationship investment. Most give it lip service. For a few, like Marion McGovern and Valerie Skonie, it's a passion. Make no mistake, it's a matchless opportunity.

And Women Shall Lead the Way!

> All the early franchisees were women, and that pleased me—I was comfortable with that. I could see that men were good at the science and vocabulary business, at talking about economic theory and profit and loss figures (some women are, too, of course). But I could also see that women were better at dealing with people, caring and being passionate about what they were doing. In my experience, women were less likely than men to believe that the joy of business was contained in the bottom line.
>
> ANITA RODDICK
> Founder, The Body Shop
> *Body and Soul*

In *The Female Advantage,* journalist Sally Helgesen examines the management styles of four exceptionally successful female executives. Above all, the quartet emphasize relationships. They picture themselves, they tell Helgesen, at the center of a "spiderweb" (there we go again!), not at the top of a pyramid. "Network," "relationship," "spiderweb," and like terminology—seldom heard in the Green Bay Packers' locker room—are the staples of Helgesen's pioneering work. Case in point: Helgesen's exemplars see interruptions as natural—and fruitful. While typical males see interruptions as irritants (according to research), women are more likely to see them as opportunities to work on cementing a relationship with an insider or outsider, to say thanks or otherwise show respect to a valued subordinate.

Women tend to put relatively more emphasis on the long term, Helgesen finds. It's not that her female chiefs have better long-range plans than men. Rather, they tend to see everything in a larger, longer-term context. Former Girl Scouts boss Frances Hesselbein, for instance, considered herself part of a "continuum that links the past, present and future." Helgesen also points to extensive research by Dartmouth business school professor Leonard Greenhalgh, who finds that women are better negotiators than men: Men focus on wins, losses, and competition. Women "treat negotiation within the context of a continuing relationship," Helgesen says; they bend over backwards to make the other party a winner in his/her own and the world's eyes.

The successful women chiefs also emphasize "closeness to," rather than "distance from," other members of their team. They practice "inclusion" rather than "exclusion," she adds. They are far more willing than men to distribute and share information. Less surprising, but no less potent because of that, women tend not to make the distinctions men make between their jobs and their lives. Values of nurturing and caring lived in one context (life) are naturally carried to the other (business).

Helgesen argues persuasively that this different style of management is peculiarly appropriate to today's commercial venue. In the age of the brain worker, self-motivation, counseling rather than order-giving, listening rather than shouting, and developing a rich and dense set of relationships/network partners rather than seeking to control all contingencies are made to order.*

My colleagues and I questioned Helgesen about her work:

<u>What surprised you about your findings?</u> "For one thing, men have responded positively. A lot of men have had very bad experiences in hierarchical corporations. They look at the book and say, 'That was the problem! The guy was hoarding all the information. He was more concerned about his position than the company as a whole, and the way it was structured reinforced that.' "

<u>How can women managers best deal with resistance to change in the organization?</u> "Listen to the people who are resisting, take that into consideration, and use it in a positive sense. It's a disarming technique. People who resist something expect *not* to be listened to, so they start backbiting or turn around and try to spread negative propaganda within a company. Remain aware of that and draw people who are resisting into the process by making them feel involved."

<u>What can men learn from women managers?</u> "The primary thing they can learn is that gathering information—and disseminating information—are *both* signs of strength. Holding it is not! One thing the women in the book said is that if you think of yourself as being in the 'center' instead of at the 'top,' it allows you to be much more flexible. Men are also going to have to learn to become more multifaceted in their identity, less identified solely with their position on the job, but taking their identity also from their family life and their life in the community.

"Hierarchical structures are male. They were devised in the public

---

*Helgesen used Henry Mintzberg's research methodology as her jumping-off point. Her diary analyses of how women execs actually spend their time were modeled after his pioneering effort. The contrasts she observed, then, were not relative to an abstract, prototypical male, but to Mintzberg's meticulous diary analyses of men. True, Mintzberg's work is 20 years old: But does anyone think men have fundamentally changed their behavior patterns since 1970?

sphere when it was dominated by men. That's what we all need to learn to get away from, because it's no longer practical, it's no longer efficient, it's no longer the best way of doing things. How much stronger to pull the best out of people, offering guidance and direction, but giving them room to grow! You take greater advantage of their skills and you also take a certain level of anxiety off yourself—you enjoy it more."

25

The Quest for Metaphors IV: The Imagery of Dynamics and Connectedness

> After, when they disentwine
> You from me and yours from mine,
> Neither can be certain who
> Was that I whose mine was you.
> To the act again they go
> More completely not to know.
>
> ROBERT GRAVES
> "The Thieves"

> Most managers get into trouble because they forget to think in circles. [They] continue to believe that there are such things as unilateral causation, independent and dependent variables, origins and terminations.
>
> KARL WEICK
> *The Social Psychology of Organizing*

The network model is hard to grasp, trapped as we are by traditional, linear, Cartesian modes of thought. For some, though, non-linearity is like breathing. And it's to them we turn, in our continuing quest (Quest for Metaphors IV) for new models, new metaphors, new mind maps.

We are so set in our ways that we fail to realize that there are robust mental frameworks that have stood the test of time, and that offer genuine, full-fledged alternatives to our normal modes of thought and conventional imagery. Frankly, it's hard to overestimate the degree to which we are subconsciously governed by old maps. When we Americans think strategy, often as not we think football. What a disaster! Football fields are circumscribed. Opponents show up at a set time to play. When a whistle blows, both sides stop. And so on. That's a long way from the dizzy doings of M^2's world.

QUANTUM MECHANICS' ANTIREALISM

Anyone who is not shocked by quantum theory has not understood it.

NIELS BOHR, physicist,
father of quantum mechanics

Einstein said that if quantum mechanics is right, then the world is crazy. Well, Einstein was right. The world is crazy.

DANIEL GREENBERGER
theoretical physicist
quoted in *Scientific American*
July 1992

Quantum mechanics is weird. I've read perhaps a dozen popular books on the topic—e.g., Nick Herbert's *Quantum Reality*, Fritjof Capra's *The Turning Point*, Michael Talbot's *Beyond the Quantum*, John Gribbin's *In Search of Schrodinger's Cat*, Danah Zohar's *The Quantum Self*, Gary Zukav's *The Dancing Wu Li Masters*. Though originally trained as a scientist, I understand little more about quantum mechanics than when I opened the cover of the first one. But I have been devastated and emotionally affected. It doesn't add up. And that, more or less, is the point.

"I remember discussions with Bohr [in 1927] which went through many hours until very late at night and ended almost in despair," quantum pioneer Werner Heisenberg wrote in *Physics and Philosophy* in 1958. "And when at the end of the discussion I went alone for a walk in the neighboring park, I repeated to myself again and again the question: 'Can nature possibly be as absurd as it seemed to us in these atomic experiments?'" At the heart of the despair was the disappearance of the "old" reality, of Newton's lumps—discrete protons and electrons that could readily be pictured in a clearly comprehensible, sun-and-planet atomic structure.

"So far, 60 years into their young history, quantum physicists still find themselves wholly unable to explain how there *can* be an everyday world—the world of tables and chairs, rocks and trees, etc.," Danah Zohar writes. "This 'anti-realist' view . . . is influenced by the bizarre and shadowy nature of quantum-level events, where nothing in particular can be said to exist in any fixed place and everything is awash in a sea of possibilities. . . . Quantum-level material, we must remember, is not very 'material.' . . . In place of [atoms depicted as] tiny billiard balls moved around by contact or forces, there are what amount to so many patterns of active relationship, electrons and photons, mesons and nucleons that tease us with their elusive double lives as they are now position, now momentum, now particles, now waves, now mass, now energy—and all in response to each other and to the environment."

It is the World of the Odd Names. Gluons and gravitons. Muons and leptons. Tauons. Quarks. Charms. And it's not even clear that these subatomic "particles" exist! Relationship becomes *everything*. Physicist Fritjof Capra explains in *The Turning Point*:

> Discovery of the dual aspect of matter [its behavior as both particle and wave] and of the fundamental role of probability has demolished the classical notion of solid objects. . . . The solid material objects of classical physics dissolve into wave-like patterns of probabilities. These patterns, ultimately, do not represent probabilities of things, but rather probabilities of interconnections. Careful analysis . . . in atomic physics has shown that the subatomic particles can have no meaning as isolated entities, but can be understood only as interconnections. . . .
>
> Subatomic particles, then, are not "things" but are interconnections between "things" and these "things," in turn, are interconnections between other "things" and so on . . . As we penetrate into matter, nature does not show us any isolated building blocks, but rather appears to be a complicated web of relations. . . .
>
> The conception of the universe as an interconnected web of relations is one of the two major themes that recur throughout modern physics. The other theme is the realization that the cosmic web is intrinsically dynamic.

The quantum world, Capra insists, turns conventional thinking upside down, in a way that perhaps only poets have understood in the past (see the Robert Graves epigraph). "Whereas in classic mechanics the property and behavior of the parts determine those of the whole," Capra writes, "the situation is reversed in quantum mechanics: It is the whole that determines the behavior of the parts."

I don't intend to "explain" more (truth is, I can't), but simply to point out that quantum mechanics, which has trumped Newtonian physics the way the car trumped the horse (horses were fine at the time and still have their place), is the best explanation we now have of the "physical" world. It's an explanation wholly at odds with the deterministic, Newtonian past.

Since we have typically turned to the physical sciences for our social "science" models, the time has surely come to look hard at the implications of quantum mechanics for organizations. At least we should worry about our lingering devotion to Newtonian models of organization structure. In fact, organizational arrangements emerging in our highly interconnected, fast-paced, intangibles/knowledge-intense, relationship-driven global village seem far more consistent with "quantum reality" than "Newtonian reality." Relationships. Networks. The intangibilizing ("informating") of everything. "Spiderweb" organizations. All these ideas are of a piece with the elusive (key word!) principles of quantum physics. At the very least, admitting the possibility of a quantum analog in new organizational models may make the big band of "tough-minded-and-proud-of-it" among us feel better—it amounts to an impeccable anchor in the physical sciences for these odd new ways of getting things done.

AUSTRALIA AS A MUSICAL SCORE

And now for something *completely* different! Forward into the past. Progress from the world of muons, tauons, and quarks to Australia's aboriginal world, as described by Bruce Chatwin in *The Songlines*. Forget, once more, Newtonian metes and bounds. Property, property rights, and "organization" among the aboriginals were conceived as a maze of one-dimensional "lines" that were "sung." We should, Chatwin writes, "visualize the Songlines as a spaghetti of Iliads and Odysseys, writhing this way and that."

Songline mythology dates from the Dreamtime, the aboriginal word for the creation. "On the morning of the first day," Chatwin tells us, "each of the Ancients . . . put his left forward and called out a . . . name. He put his right forward and called out [another] name. He named the water-hole, the reedbeds, the gum-trees—calling to right and left, calling all things into being and weaving their names into verses."

Descendants of the Ancients took up the songs and passed them along as they traveled over the countryside. "The whole of Australia could be read as a musical score," Chatwin observes. "There was hardly a rock or a creek in the country that could not or had not been sung. . . . Providing you knew the song, you could always find your way across country." The first time a pregnant aboriginal woman felt her baby kick, she gathered the elders, who "interpret the lie of the land and decide which Ancestor walked that way, and which stanzas will be the child's private property. They reserve him a 'conception site'—coinciding with the nearest landmark on the Songline."

To keep the songlines alive, aboriginal "song owners" periodically met at the Big Place: "One after the other, each 'owner' would . . . sing his stretch of the Ancestor's footprints. Always in the correct sequence! To sing a verse out of order was a crime [which usually] meant the death penalty. . . . [To forget one's song] would be to un-create the Creation."

Aborigines used songlines in commerce, too. "The trade route *is* the songline," Chatwin writes. "Songs, not things, are the principal medium of exchange. . . . A man's verses were his title deeds to territory. He could lend them to others, he could borrow other verses in return. But one thing he couldn't do was sell or get rid of them." In a description that could easily have come from a textbook on quantum physics, Chatwin talks about trading relationships among widely separated tribes: "To move in such [a parched] landscape was survival: to stay in the same place suicide. [Everything] depended on being able to leave [a given locale]. Every [aboriginal] hoped to have at least four 'ways out,' along which he could travel in a crisis. Every tribe— like it or not—had to cultivate relations with its neighbors. What the whites used to call the 'Walkabout' was, in practice, a kind of bush-telegraph-cum-stock-exchange, spreading messages between peoples who never saw each other, who might be unaware of each other's existence."

Confusing? Of course! But the bedrock (is *that* the right image?), again, is a metaphor that is "relationship-driven," not "thing-driven"—and a far cry from traditional hierarchies. Moreover, isn't this spaghetti of one-dimensional songlines as valid a model for organizing space as the 246, two-dimensional, trapezoidal "towns" (and 8 "gores") that "cover" all of Vermont? The point is that songlines: (1) existed and worked for thousands of years; (2) are as plausible a way of organizing as any alternative model; and (3) may, surprisingly, *better* describe today's corporate environment than traditional hierarchies, organizational maps, and voluminous strategic plans. (Oticon's Lars Kolind, recall, gave us "spaghetti organizations"—Chapter 13.)

HARLOT'S GHOST

It was once again pure coincidence that decided the future. It was pure chance that we had not yet left the apartment when the Compagnie Générale Transatlantique phoned, the same call, probably, that I had heard about an hour ago, but hadn't been able to answer, a crucial call it was. My passage to Europe could only be booked if I called at once, by 10 p.m. at the latest, with my passport. All I mean is that if I hadn't taken the little appliance apart the call wouldn't have reached me and this would have meant that my voyage would never have taken place, at least not on the ship on which Sabeth was traveling, and we should never have met, my daughter and I.

MAX FRISCH
Homo Faber

To read Max Frisch, Paul Bowles, Gabriel García Márquez, Anton Chekhov, Jane Smiley, Malcolm Lowry, or Norman Mailer is to consume a rich diet of relationships, chance, interconnectedness, muons, songlines, things large within small, small within large, things within things that nonetheless encompass things that are beyond them. Perhaps there are Cartesian novels, hierarchical novels, Newtonian novels. If so, one presumes that they have been quickly—and mercifully—consigned to literature's dustbin. The richness of life, which we accept as private selves and when we turn to novels or poetry, seems abandoned at the front door of the business or public agency establishment.

I have long written about the perceptual attributes of products, the overwhelming importance of a caring response following a snafu (how you handle a mistake is as important as having the product work in the first place!), as well as the organizational conundrums discussed above. These "odd" ideas are more consistent with the convolutions within convolutions in Norman Mailer's *Harlot's Ghost* than in Peter Drucker's latest pronouncements (or mine).

Can novels and poetry be considered a "metaphor"? Perhaps, perhaps not. The point here is the dogged pursuit of un-ordinary analogs. If fiction and poetry (drama, opera, etc.) capture life better than other cultural media, and who would disagree with that, then why not think of fiction as a model for organization? After all, isn't that what the quotation marks around "organization" are all about? Organizations are fiction—especially the knowledge-based, professional service firms that are tomorrow's best models.

A TRIP TO KUNMING

And now, from the guidebook *Southwest China Off the Beaten Track,* a "Daoist tale":

There were two travelers, one eager to be in Kunming the next day, the other, a Daoist, was also heading to Kunming. Together they went to the train station and were confronted by a long, disorderly queue at the ticket window. Once in line, the first traveler yelled at people cutting in, and, when possible, physically ousted them. After an hour's wait, he reached the ticket window and demanded a hard sleeper on that afternoon's train. *Meiyou* [there are no] hard sleeper places, [he was told].

Swearing and complaining, he was able to purchase a standup ticket. The traveler triumphantly fought his way out of the crowded train station only to find that his friend had disappeared.

The traveler, much agitated, waited angrily in the smoky waiting room before struggling onto the train. All the seats were already filled, causing him to vent his frustration in a loud voice, thus alienating the Chinese passengers. Feeling ill-used by people who only wanted his FEC [Foreign Exchange Currency], he refused to eat or upgrade to the soft sleeper offered by the conductor. He demonstrated his contempt for everyone by standing for 18 straight hours to Kunming. When he arrived, the city did not live up to his extravagant expectations, built up during his hellish train ride. The traveler hated Kunming in particular and China in general.

Three weeks later, he ran into his old companion at the Emei train station. After telling his own tales of woe, he asked the Daoist about his experience in Kunming. His friend replied, "I don't know. I'm still on the way. When I saw there were no hard sleeper tickets on the train, I made for the bus station. Before I got there I met a truck driver over a bowl of noodles, and went to his home village for a festival. There I met some fellows going north by bus. We made some great side trips together, then I joined a family returning home by boat. When train tickets south proved hard to get, I went hiking in the countryside instead. As you can see, I've enjoyed the way to Kunming and may actually reach the city before I leave this country."

And what, you might reasonably ask (now thoroughly frustrated), is the relationship of a Daoist tale to modern market economies? Everything, I suspect. In turbulent times, taking pleasure in the incomprehensible process of discovery—and not assuming that things can be planned—is paramount. It's one more story about relationships and waves, not charts and particles.

ORGANIZATIONS DON'T EXIST, DO THEY?

The real problem is that we are used to looking at the world simply. We are accustomed to believing that something is there or it is not there. . . . Our experience tells us that the physical world is solid, real and independent of us. Quantum mechanics says, simply, that this is not so. . . . [According to theoretical physicist Henry Pierce Stapp], "If the attitude of quantum mechanics is correct . . . then there is no substantive physical world, in the usual sense of this term. The conclusion here is not the weak conclusion that there *may* not be a substantive physical world, but rather that there is definitely *not* a substantive physical world." . . . This is not only different from the way we have looked at the world for 300 years, it is *opposite*. . . . What we experience is not external reality, but our *interaction* with it. . . . The world consists not of things, but interactions.

GARY ZUKAV
The Dancing Wu Li Masters

When I was at McKinsey, it occurred to me that consultants could be divided into two sorts. One took great static pictures of a market, a competitive situation, a corporation. The other saw people, relationships, processes. It's barely an exaggeration to say that the twain never met. It takes total concentration to take a picture of a market. It also takes total concentration to sniff, sense, feel the ebb and flow of power and relationships.

Particles and Waves

Pondering such differences is abetted by returning to the strange world of quantum mechanics. Consider Werner Heisenberg's "uncertainty principle." We can know where a subatomic particle is. Or where it's going. But we can't know both. Period. Moreover, the better the bead we get on where it's going (its momentum, for example), the more we lose sight of where it is. In other terms, subatomic "stuff" can be described as particles or as waves. The solid, particle view used to dominate. Now the wave idea has gained prominence. So, too, goes the new world of "organization." Yes, I *should* always use that word *organization* in quotation marks. To use the word without the quotes is to suggest the thing is real and has a discrete location. (Frankly, even quotes don't do the job. The word itself carries too much solid, pyramidal, particulate baggage—no matter how hard you try to "fuzz" it up.)

Maybe organizations were close to real at one point: In a world dominated by the predictable rhythms of agriculture, where nothing much changed from one year to the next—or in a later world dominated by changes that took years, which gave most of us time to adapt to new inventions. In a world where markets were reasonably stable, with 2-, 5-, or even 15-year product development cycles acceptable (15? that's how long it's typically taken Mercedes to fully redo a model), the Newtonian view was just dandy. Headquarters were tall buildings. They "looked like" the organization—the hierarchy—they enfolded. Factories were big, lumpy. And General Electric was General Electric, not GE. International Business Machines was not IBM. Kentucky Fried Chicken was not KFC. It was Newton's world, all right.

Then that world went gooey on us. All goods—"hard" (materials) and "soft" (movies, records)—became fashion goods. Volatility became the norm.

Ambiguity dominated. Just as the rise of quantum mechanics has vaulted the ephemeral wave from a distant secondary spot in the physicist's explanatory arsenal to a pinnacle high above Newton's clockworks and billiard balls, the volatile competitive environment is vaulting the "squishy side" of "organization" to the top. Organization charts (which bear an eerie resemblance to Newtonian models of atoms), corporate towers, and procedure books (which purport to be inclusive wiring diagrams) are being supplanted by spiderwebs, improvisational theater, carnivals—and electronic bulletin boards. (Consider Sears and Wal-Mart. Sears conducts business—slowly—from a 110-story, Newtonian tower. Wal-Mart has a three-story headquarters imbedded in one of the world's most advanced information technology spiderwebs.)

Hard and Soft Imagery

What is an "organization"? (Of the in-quotes sort.) Take one more look at the Dallas Organization, EDS, M^2, Imagination. Groups, including "outsiders" (that one should always be in quotes, too, since outsiders are now insiders and borders have become transparent . . . and . . . and . . .), coalesce somehow, for a while, get a "job" done—*job* also deserves quotes, since the ability of any job to dominate a market for a long period of time has disappeared in every business. (And the "job" is creating a "product"—increasingly soft. And the core "skills"/soul are increasingly "horizontal"/integrative/soft . . . and. . . .)

The new ideas/images *are* important (you have to have some definition, don't you?), and they are misleading. They are helpful: They give us alternative *hard* images; rather than call it all "fluff," call it a "spiderweb." They are unhelpful: They still, at their core, leave us with a sense of the concrete.

Can You Find Your Organization?

Quantum physicists refuse to acknowledge that the chairs they sit on are really there, that they even exist. The odds are high that the chair exists right now ("It's a good working hypothesis," a physicist friend mused). But they can't prove it. Everything is in flux. Everything *is* flux. Particles are only more or less likely to be at this more or less place than that, depending more or less upon what's happening with other particles.

So, too, organizations. You're sitting in the Ingersoll-Rand Industrial Power Tool Division headquarters, a *building* in New Jersey: *Where* is that Project Lightning Team, anyway? More fundamentally, *what* is that Project Lightning Team? At that instant, a group of people—engineers, manufacturers, purchasers, accountants, marketers, salespersons, industrial designers, and maybe even a supplier or two—are off talking with a real end user in a Caterpillar factory.

Project leader Jim Stryker lived in a Newtonian world—the New Jersey headquarters. So he put together a three-and-a-half-foot Newtonian chart, which made the big boys in New Jersey feel on top of things. But the "magic"—recall the barbecues, the team-building activities, the serendipity of the motel parking lot "drag test"—was the waves, the very fluidity of it. The *energy* of first out-of-town trips for old Ingersoll-Rand hands, *the new relationship with* the industrial designer, *the new relationship with* distributors, *the new relationship with* material-supplier Philips and grinding-pad producer 3M— that's what allowed Ingersoll-Rand to compress time dramatically, to create a genuinely novel product.

If you're lucky, your organization—that is, "organization"—*doesn't exist.* You can't find it. People aren't in their offices. They're not doing what they're "supposed" to be doing—not passing papers to and fro, not watching the very Newtonian clock crawl toward 5:00 p.m. They're violating Newtonian precept after Newtonian precept. They're talking with this person and that, building this relationship and that, attempting to intercept wacky information streams via some elusive electronic network. Somebody's just headed off to Japan on a lark—that is, the unlikely pursuit of a connection, a partner, a *feeling* for the phenomenally volatile and mysterious Japanese market.

Where *are* they, damn it? If you can answer that question, you're Newtonian—and in trouble. In the old days, we wanted an answer to that question. "They're in the factory." "He's in his office." "I can get him when I need to." (A lot of people are still playing this game, and have used the fax, e-mail, etc., as the new Simon Legree: This time ole Simon is a wireless pager rather than a policy manual. But it's still a *cord*—and that, make no mistake, is a problem in a volatile world.)

Ambiguity defines the market. So doesn't it follow, as day follows night, that ambiguity must *be*—or "be"—the organization? Um, how do you do a "charts-and-boxes" depiction of ambiguity?

3M's No-Building Building

Consider 3M's giant Austin, Texas, electronics operation. In deference to the market's new pace, 3M has slashed product development cycles in the last few years from a couple of years to a couple of months. 3M sells a product all right—a cable, connector, whatever. But top 3M marketers told me in 1990 that they really "sell a process"—a process that allows 3M to create a customized solution to a customer's needs more effectively (faster, more cleverly) than a competitor can. It's "my flow chart versus my competitors' flow chart," they said. Instead of lump, think flow chart, which of course is about relationships. Bye, Isaac Newton. Hello, Niels Bohr.

Another part of the new "3M" in Austin is its new building—a physical configuration designed to negate normal physical configurations. It is an anti-configuration configuration. It's a design to foster waves—to increase the probability that a useful particle (person) will come into contact with another useful particle. People are "designed in" closer together. Functions are jumbled to cause chance connections. Blackboards and couches and coffee machines are placed next to bathrooms (creating so-called "interactive nodes") to up the odds of productive interchange. If that's not wave thinking, I don't know what it is.

Somebody did build the building, I'll grant you. Somebody made the blueprints. Somebody laid the pipe. Somebody wired it all up. Nonetheless, it's an anti-building building, aimed at facilitating 3M's new anti-product product environment.

Frolicking Rolodexes

Recall our discussion of master networkers. They're tops at "playing the phones," "managing the Rolodex," dealing with the relationship (ROIR—return on investment in relationships). It's a very non-organization organization way of thinking about things. Try imagining an organization as a collection of frolicking Rolodexes. It's a long way from traditional org charts.

Capitalism without Untidy Capitalists

It's discouraging! *Dynamics* is not taught in most economics courses. There's a lot to say for simple, Newtonian supply-and-demand charts. If you don't know them cold, you're not going to understand much about economics. (If you don't know Newton, you'll be hard-pressed to embrace Heisenberg.) But supply and demand as a *snapshot* doesn't mean a darn thing. Supply and demand *over time* is the whole story. It's hard to think about, hard to conceive: Most dynamic supply-and-demand representations, such as "spiderweb" supply-and-demand charts (yes, spiderweb is the word economists use) are clumsy efforts to illustrate the dynamic in a two-dimensional way.

But some people, some marketers—Les Wexner at The Limited, for example—are dynamicists. They "feel" the flow of the market. Economics commentator George Gilder chides most economists. They've made the science live up to its dismal moniker, he says. They love capitalism, but don't like capitalists. Capitalists/entrepreneurs—like Wexner—disturb, disrupt, make waves.

NECESSARY DISORGANIZATION

"If you really believe in quantum mechanics, then you can't take it seriously," Univeristy of Chicago physicist Robert Wald said in the *The New York Review of Books*. Alternatively, if you really believe in "organizations," then you can't take them seriously. To take organizations seriously is to go Newtonian—to focus on the charts, the boxes, the job descriptions, the specifiable. Not taking organizations seriously is to relish a wave-like environment, where relationships are paramount; where launching scattershot attacks on markets (via a motley collection of buckyborgs) is essential; where projects are king; where volatile networks filled with subcontractors conquer markets; where renegades and disrupters are cherished for the mess they make; where breaking yourself up before a raider does is the ultimate wisdom; where *necessary disorganization* reigns.

Organizations don't exist, do they?

26

Knowledge Management
Structures I: Taking Knowledge
Management Seriously

Learning is the new form of labor. [It's] no longer a separate
activity that occurs either before one enters the workplace or
in remote classroom settings. . . . Learning is the heart of
productive activity.

SHOSHANA ZUBOFF
In the Age of the Smart
Machine

"Soft" now dominates. "Hard" has been eclipsed. Knowledge is
all-important. Bringing knowledge to bear, quickly, is critical. We've discussed
new structures which have dramatically enhanced the flow of information. But
we have largely ignored, until now, the following question: If knowledge is the
source of most value-added (from minor improvement projects to rapid development of new families of products), how do organizations accumulate it, how
do members of dispersed organizations learn from one another?

Recall ABB: Its power transmission group, though by far the world's
largest player in its industry segment, consists of 25 units in 17 countries. Many
of those units are smaller than their largest local competitor. Why not sell the
little units off to their managers? ABB's answer, in a nutshell, is the promise
of learning. "We want to create a process of continuous expertise transfer
[among the twenty-five units]," ABB's Sune Karlsson said. "If we do, that is
a source of advantage none of our rivals can match." The smallness of the
individual power transmission unit begets appropriate responsiveness; but the

expectation is that incessant collaboration with fellow units will allow any one unit to bring to bear all of ABB's formidable power transmission knowledge, gleaned from thousands of projects executed throughout the world.

Ah, you say, got it. Off we go to talk to the information technology wizards. Let's construct a state-of-the-art e-mail network, and get on with communicating in this "dispersed network" of modest-size ABB units. Not a bad idea. But, it turns out, it's only a small part of the answer. Wise application of information technology is a necessary, but far from sufficient, condition for knowledge management success. What else is required? Lots! Moreover, very few people—even ABB, in my judgment—have thought very intensively about the process of capturing and then applying knowledge within a newfangled crazy-quilt "network" ("spiderweb," etc.) and applying it systematically.

KNOWLEDGE MANAGEMENT STRUCTURES AND THE NEW ORGANIZING LOGIC

"Learning organizations" have become a hot topic. I like the moniker. But I prefer an alternative: *knowledge management structure,* or KMS. (Don't let the word "structure" mislead you. As you'll see, there's an important structural element to the idea. Yet there is much more—and most of it is *soft.*)

Before defining the beast, though, let's review the bare-bones case that has brought us to this point.

1. The "fashionized" marketplace demands *de-coupling/agility* as never before. The logic behind the ABB, IDG, and Acordia structures is market-driven. Only modest-size units, more or less, are adaptable enough and responsive enough to stand a chance in today's zany public utility, materials, electronics, or financial services marketplaces. The answer: Old corporate edifices must be de-integrated/de-coupled.

2. To achieve appropriate de-coupling/agility, we must *destroy* headquarters and functional staffs. It's not enough to decentralize and create business units on paper. We've been doing that to little avail for decades. As we saw in the Union Pacific, ABB, and Acordia cases, the middle management layers and functional staffs must be virtually destroyed if autonomy is to get much beyond lip service. (Or the staffs/HQs should be tiny in the first place, as at IDG and CNN.)

3. The "fashionized"/"knowledge-added" marketplace demands *expertise* as never before. There is a wretched paradox on the loose. Survival calls for de-coupling and dismantling staffs. Survival also comes from smarts— which require us to tap into deep, broadly based corporate/extra-corporate knowledge structures (like that of ABB's power transmission group). But how

do we act small (agile/market-scale/de-coupled) and big (system smart) at once?

4. To develop necessary expertise, we must simulate functional staffs *without* bureaucracy and *with* global reach. There's nothing wrong with the staff *idea*. Old-fashioned staffs, after all, were intended to be mechanisms for knowledge accumulation and dispersal. The problem was: (a) they learned that power stemmed from hoarding knowledge; (b) top management leaders began using staffs as cops; and (c) the ponderous staffs slowed decision-making intolerably. So we still need—need more than ever—to bring extended knowledge to bear, but without the old, slow, political, I'm-the-expert-and-you're-not structures.

5. To simulate functional staffs without bureaucracy, we must build spartan, global knowledge management structures (KMSs). The knowledge/expertise idea must be kept alive, expanded in fact—but recast in modern terms. An answer is the "learning organization"/knowledge management structure concept. It amounts to a revolutionary new, nonbureaucratic approach to doing the work of developing experts/building expertise in ways that enhance the power of market-scale units, but don't encumber them with imposed bureaucracy.

6. The essence of an effective KMS is *advertising, marketing, packaging, incentives, big travel budgets, and the psychodynamics of knowledge management*. The crux of the issue is not information, information technology, or knowledge per se. It's how, for example, you get busy people in those miniature ABB units to want to contribute to the KMS. The answer turns out to lie more with psychology and marketing (of knowledge within the "family") than with bits and bytes.

THE PSYCHODYNAMICS OF KNOWLEDGE MANAGEMENT

When I was at McKinsey, the surefire success formula was to throw very bright, aggressive people at a client problem. It was assumed that we would automatically get smarter over time. We'd learn from our clients, learn from our colleagues, work on two or three projects a year, frequently shift industries; we were continuously exposed to different peers and leaders, often from different countries.

Things have changed. Knowledge management and knowledge integration—and the learning process per se—is markedly different at McKinsey in 1992 than in 1980. For one thing, the firm has a secret weapon—Brook Manville, who, when I talked with him in mid-1991, sported the formidable title of Director of Knowledge Management. It's exaggerating to declare that Manville sits at the apex of some "alternative pyramid" (opposed to the company's normal office/project structure), like ABB's Business Area dimension to its matrix. But his charter does suggest a new set of important concerns at McKinsey. In fact, the company's managing director, Fred Gluck, now talks about maintaining the "balance" between "serving clients" and "creating knowledge."

Most talk about "learning organizations" is maddeningly abstract or vague—and perpetually falls short on the specifics. McKinsey, on the other hand, has taken the idea further than any other big company I've come across. Its leaders don't feel that they have the luxury of living with abstractions. The analysis that follows, like the saga of developing the Cyclone Grinder at Ingersoll-Rand, is long on detail, for it is in the detail, and in the flavor, that most of the clues to constructing an effective KMS lie.

Structure

Brook Manville works most closely with one of McKinsey's few senior administrative officers, Bill Matassoni, director of communications. Manville is more or less the knowledge business's "Mr. Inside," overseeing the firm's effort to develop and disseminate learning internally. There's also a more or less "Mr. Outside"—Alan Kantrow looks out for the "external" publications that spring forth from McKinsey. On the one hand, Kantrow aims to establish a public image of McKinsey at the cutting edge of business thinking—hence an attempt to get consultants quoted in *Fortune, Business Week, The Economist* and other prestigious magazines. But Kantrow's effort is also essential to the overall knowledge development process. Getting busy consultants to spend lots of time preparing articles for external publication is vital to inducing forward thinking that rubs off inside the firm.

Manville, however, is our focus. The "structure" that's "beneath" him consists of 31 "Practice Centers." (Let's be clear: In no sense do these centers "report to" Manville. Each one is *very* independent, as we shall see in the detailed assessment of one of them, the Organization Performance Practice.) Thirteen, called "clientele centers," are oriented toward *industries*—banking, insurance, energy, electronics; the other 18, called "centers of competence," focus on *functional specialties*—organization performance, marketing, operations. Every Practice Center has a wholly voluntary leadership cadre of consultants. All Practice Center "members" are volunteer consultants, too. Practice Center membership ranges from a handful to a hundred; the numbers fluctuate wildly, depending on whether or not the center's topic is "hot." "Center" is a state of mind, not a physical location—though most Centers do have a full-time administrative staff assistant, who usually (but not always) hangs her or his hat in some corner of the leader's home office.

Philosophy

About five years ago, director of communications Matassoni was tapped to think about "it"—something to do with "learning." But development of a more effective "learning system" didn't tickle his fancy—"a bunch of library shit" is what he called it. Given the low status of such activities at McKinsey in those days, he was certain he'd "get no credit" for time spent on such a pursuit. The head of the library in the New York office was supposed to help Matassoni, but got promoted and disappeared. Matassoni turned to Manville for help. The classics scholar, who'd also developed computerized databases, was an inspired choice.

Manville described his approach as "moving beyond 'we're-smarter-than-anybody-else-and-that's-enough-to-maintain-our-advantage' to 'every-engagement-as-a-learning-opportunity.' " (Remember: "Engagement" equals "client project" in company jargon.) Matassoni emphasized to us that necessity was, as usual, the mother of invention. "McKinsey [and a handful of others like it] used to have an armlock on top business school grads," he said. "But no longer. Our clients have hired people like us [for their own payrolls] and have them all over their organizations. Very smart analysts are no longer a scarce resource—and just throwing very smart people at a problem, as we did, is not enough anymore." In fact, McKinsey has taken the threat seriously enough to alter its "fundamental value proposition" to something like this: "Professionalism [McKinsey's long-term competitive advantage] plus consultant skills plus institutional knowledge equals client impact." Emphasizing systematic development of consultant skills, beyond catch-as-catch-can, is new. And putting institutional knowledge development and application on a par with the other two amounts to a dramatic shift of emphasis.

Manville, sounding like CNN's Ted Turner, went on at length about "internal knowledge *on demand.*" That is, creating the ready ability to tap into what people have learned—*and* creating the motivation to put such learning into various databases and Practice Centers to begin with. In simpler terms, the centerpiece of the effort, Manville said, is to "put people in touch with other people" and information. Putting people in touch with others, which used to be a casual, personal process, is now becoming more systematized (a necessity in a $1-billion outfit); the overall knowledge-building process will, according to Manville, allow people "to extend their personal networks, fast and efficiently." Quids and quos—getting *and* giving—are important. "Every engagement gives you a chance to contribute something back," Manville entreats junior consultants. "Knowledge development is a professional responsibility." Though helping others out even when you're busy as hell has long been a part of the McKinsey culture, the idea of formally contributing to institutional learning was alien a decade ago.

Marketing

Hooking busy consultants, obsessed with today's client, on the new priority is not easy. The Practices must simply resort to hardball salesmanship. "They should think about growing their 'mind share' with consultants throughout the firm," Matassoni said. "The post-merger management specialist [who deals with special human and strategic concerns that crop up after big mergers] should have the attitude that 'I want to get my Practice's ideas looked at by an increasingly large number of people around the firm.' " In fact, the knowledge management gurus are pushing Practices to survey consultants to find out what they need to know and want to know; based on survey findings, "formal Practice agendas" are formulated.

Does It Pay Off?

Putting recognition for knowledge development into the personnel evaluation process is vitally important, and there has been some progress. For example, Manville and Matassoni claim that "it's almost imperative to have publications in your portfolio" when you come up for promotion. If you haven't contributed to the knowledge base, you're looked at somewhat askance. Manville glowed as he described a call from a member of the Directors Committee (the group responsible for promoting people to the top rank at McKinsey). A candidate was hovering on the cusp of selection/rejection. He'd contributed rather significantly to a Practice area. "How often has [his] intellectual 'framework' been used?" Manville was asked. Given the increasing sophistication of the knowledge-management effort, Manville reported that he was able to offer more than anecdotal evidence. For example, he could cite 131 successful project proposals that had mentioned so-and-so's approach explicitly; he could also refer the caller to several seasoned project leaders who'd used the "framework" in their client work.

More broadly, the "indirect payoff" of engaging in knowledge development, Manville emphasized, is "getting your name around, which makes you more valuable in the McKinsey network world. You get called more often, you're positioned to be recruited for better assignments, you get much broader exposure."

Databases and Publications

McKinsey's dusty archives have begun to come alive. The top-of-the-line database/archive, called Firm Practice Information System, "went electronic" in 1987. It was primarily used for accounting in the past. Now Manville wants to turn it into a "marketplace of readily accessible ideas." Getting good, timely information into the FPIS has become one of his obsessions. Manville uses carrots *and* sticks: For example, you get no "charge code" (the basis for billing clients) until you provide the FPIS with a two-page summary of how you're going to approach a project. Moreover, every three months each project leader gets a printout of what he or she has put into FPIS. It comes with an insistent plea for updating: For example, the project leader is asked whether she or he has learned *anything* that could be helpful to others. (A typical reply—"The XYZ team has developed a PC-based demand model for North American farm machinery, etc., etc.") The best of these "learnings" are subsequently published in a widely distributed monthly print document. Ever the pragmatist, Manville insisted that one of his principal chores is "mercilessly dunning" project leaders to supply updates to FPIS. Taking such apparently mundane tasks seriously is near the top of the list which discriminates between knowledge management on paper and knowledge management that is effective in practice. (Manville eventually wheedles a response to about 80 percent of his requests for updates. About 30 to 50 percent report something new, specific, and applicable to a wide audience. Manville estimated that about 20 percent are "really new"—with potential lasting value to McKinsey.)

The other principal, centralized, on-line information system at McKinsey is the more yeasty Practice Development Network, or PDNet. Its contents are organized around the 31 Practice Centers. By early 1991 the Organization Performance Practice, for example, had inserted 531 documents into PDNet and was adding about 7 a month. Overall, the network, updated weekly in New York, held 6,000 documents in mid-1991.

PDNet captures what Manville called "core documents from the Practices." What's the definition of "core"? A key to the success of McKinsey's knowledge management process is allowing users and decentralized experts to define what's important! "The Practice leaders tell us what's 'core,' what's not," said Manville. The process of adding to PDNet, he noted, is very "democratic at the input stage." Anything that anyone from the Practice wants to include is OK. But Manville also oversees a vigorous "gatekeeper function at the user interface." That is, PDNet is weeded annually. Practice leaders are asked to jettison material that is outdated or is not in demand by consultants.

Manville acknowledges a significant strategic dilemma, generic to knowledge managers. On the one hand, he wants the network to be friendly—not overmanaged, not bureaucratic. He wants to develop enduring, endearing relationships with his knowledge "suppliers," the Practice people, all volunteers, who see their every new thought as Einsteinian. On the other hand, he understands his role as a "wholesale broker" of knowledge: The harried user-consultant in the field doesn't want a bulky PDNet loaded with garbage—thence the need to weed.

All this leads to numerous minute operational considerations. For example, Manville said he "doesn't want librarians to do the abstracts" of PDNet documents, as has often been the case in the past. Why? He wants the project creators to do it, because their language is closer to the end user's—it is precisely upon such subtleties that the overall system rises or falls, that system use increases or decreases.

Documentation also includes the Knowledge Resource Directory—"McKinsey's Yellow Pages," one consultant called it. Updated annually, it provides a guide to who knows this about that. For a given Practice, you'll find a listing of members, other experts, and core documents that can be retrieved from FPIS and PDNet.

There are also Center Bulletins from each of the 31 Practice areas, featuring new concepts the Practice wants to parade before all the firm's consultants. And Applications Bulletins—practical, one-page papers written by consultants that are widely distributed, and appear at the rate of two or three per week. While one observer noted that Applications Bulletins are of "uneven quality," many do matter and are used, according to Manville's meticulous surveys. (Some acknowledge a bit of a "churning effect"—a consultant creates Applications Bulletins to "check a box" while wending his or her way toward partnership.)

The average Applications Bulletin offers sanitized, nonconfidential information about a recent study. It also includes an explicit effort to enhance networking. Each Bulletin lists everyone who's been involved with the idea that's described, and provides names to contact and/or references to pursue for further information. And in yet another effort to create metrics and provide feedback, Manville now tracks requests for Applications Bulletins. Practice leaders get regular reports on how frequently their Bulletins are asked for, which turns out to be a helpful measure of usefulness as perceived by the internal client.

(More) Internal Marketing

Matassoni talks about PDNet document preparation in unabashed marketing terms. The objective, he tells would-be consultant writers, is "propose, position, proposition." Matassoni hounds people to get their input right, to make it as attractive as possible to potential users. Matassoni and Manville also want the PDNet "supply/demand process" to become strategic. As they see it, PDNet document usage figures should shape the agendas of the 31 Practices. Document usage numbers provided to Practice leaders, Matassoni added, should be seen as "sales leads." To tout their Practice, leaders should provide information consistent with the demands of consultants in the field. Moreover, if the Practice leader thinks a document is terrific (hardly unusual), but it's not being used, then Matassoni proposes a practical strategy—recast the document into terms that "make it attractive." If customer service concerns "are hot [they are], then, Mr. Practice Leader, reposition your obscure financial analysis scheme in terms that link it to customer service needs!"

In a lengthy conversation, Manville, a database professional, rarely resorted to database terminology. "Knowledge" is not the technical accumulation of information, as he sees it. The crucial factors are the format of the information, the credibility of the information, the zippiness of the information, the degree to which it's attached to credible people, and instant availability. All this constitutes "the last ninety-nine percent"—beyond mere construction of effective, efficient, on-line databases. Though databases are imperative, databases alone do nothing for you—often *less* than nothing. (Less than nothing: "Good" databases can provide a false sense of security. To be good—e.g., massive—is not necessarily to be useful or used, let alone the basis for corporate strategic advantage.)

THE ORGANIZATION PERFORMANCE PRACTICE

The Organization Performance Practice, or OPP, leads the pack at McKinsey in organizing for knowledge development. It's also one of the biggest Practices: About 50 percent of McKinsey's studies have a "significant organizational component," OPPers say, up from about 25 percent just a few years ago.

OPP Structure

Two senior partners—Jon Katzenbach from New York and Ed Michaels from Atlanta—are de facto "Practice leaders." They're part of an eight-partner "leadership group." (Six of the eight are Americans, one is French, one is Canadian.) "Below" the leadership circle you'll find some 60 "members of the Practice." Membership criteria: These generally senior consultants "like to do" organization work—and contribute documents to the Practice.

There are some other loose categories of OPP consultant-experts. First, project managers on cases with a "significant organization component," but who have not previously shown a distinctive interest in the organization area; this group is singled out because it holds special knowledge that can be used by others. "Repeat callers" to the Rapid Response Network (see below) also make the "friends of the Practice" list—the three staffers who administer the network are out-of-the-closet marketers, who make a major effort to lasso more consultants into organization work (they assume a repeat caller to the RRN is ripe for proselytizing). There are also several organization "specialists," including two former Harvard professors. They're part of McKinsey's relatively new specialist career track. (Those hyper-experts, however, even in the "new" McKinsey, are expected to bill half their time to clients.)

In an unprecedented initiative aimed at bringing "new blood" into the Practice, the OPP invented the Client Service Center in 1991. About 15 project managers have committed to a 12-to-18-month stint working full-time on OPP-related projects. Teams headed by these specially designated project managers will always involve expert partners from the Organization Performance Practice as advisers. The group also convenes monthly to swap experiences.

It adds up to an imposing array of semispecialist talent—all volunteers except for the pair of former professors. But the loose confederation is not enough. The budding OPP experts need support—and, more important, their burgeoning collective competence must somehow be made readily available in a friendly fashion to the other 2,900 widely dispersed consultants (half of whom, remember, are engaged in work with at least OPP overtones). Enter the OPP administrative scheme in general, and the maestros of the Rapid Response Network in particular.

Breathing Life into the OPP: The Rapid Response Network (RRN) Is Created

Organizational librarian Jennifer Futernick joined McKinsey in 1981, just before I left. She and a New York counterpart now in the strategy Practice were the only full-time administrators/expediters in the quarter-baked "Practice business" at that time. When I was involved in "organization stuff," from 1976 to 1981, most of our attention went into figuring out what was happening in the outside world, then trying to transmit that knowledge to consultants—through clumsy paper documents and a handful of five-day training sessions, mostly for very senior consultants. Such activities, with many twists, turns, and enhancements, sputtered along over the next eight years. But in early 1989, the OPP took a big—and organized—step forward. The eight-person leadership circle spent two days in Rockport, Massachusetts, noodling about a new vision for the Practice. They decided to shift emphasis from figuring out what was going on in their discipline beyond McKinsey's borders to "capability-building"—working to dramatically enhance the organizational consulting skills throughout McKinsey.

Doug Smith, a partner from New York, and Lynn Heilig, a former consultant and now an OPP specialist in Atlanta, took on the task of inventing some sort of "network" that would provide quick, useful information (documents, access to experts) to any consultant, anywhere, confronted with an "organizational problem." At the time, requests to the OPP for information were mostly funneled to Futernick in San Francisco. She was (and is) a walking encyclopedia—and her office was a jumble of paper files. (Had she been struck by a bus in 1989, most of the "competence" of the OPP would have vanished.) In a way, Smith and Heilig were seeking to formalize, systematize, and extend Futernick's catch-as-catch-can activities.

But how? A hotline? E-mail? Formal? Informal? Should they piggyback off of the FPIS and PDNet, which were just getting off the ground? Or did they need their own computerized database? Eventually, and in spite of some concern about duplication and complication within and beyond the Practice,

Heilig, Smith, and the OPP leadership group concluded that they needed a new, unique dedicated system. Heilig found an acceptable software package, DataEase, and the OPP spent $180,000 modifying it, upgrading it, and getting it running. The nub of the scheme was computers, printers, and a new database to be managed by Heilig, Futernick, and Nancy Taubenslag, the third member of what I call the OPP Three.

At a meeting in Nice, France, in April 1990, the new service, dubbed the Rapid Response Network, was announced with fanfare to the OPP's 60 members, even though the software wasn't fully operational. Uncharacteristically for "buttoned-down" McKinsey, the network "launch" even included T-shirts and mugs emblazoned with the RRN's logo. In the fall of 1990, the RRN went on-line—accompanied by lots of skepticism. First, the fear of confusing overlap with other McKinsey databases. Then a vague but even more important concern that the RRN would distance consultants in pursuit of information from the members of the Practice. The old "scheme" (i.e., scrounge around in your personal network in pursuit of help) was messy, and hit or miss. But at least there weren't any formal filters. The new worry was that the RRN would become a "layer"—and besides, the gatekeepers, Heilig, Futernick, and Taubenslag, were not "normal" consultants. "We'll have to talk with lower-level people," went the lament. "We'll lose access to partners." "We'll become isolated." (Recall our earlier discussion of "class" at McKinsey: Non-consultants have been dismissed—by consultants—as "not real people," often in just such language.)

All the forebodings could easily have been justified, which is why this knowledge management "stuff" is so tricky. Had the OPP Three been power-mad bureaucrats, the RRN would have been stillborn. They were anything but. (Which is almost a problem for this analysis: They are so damned selfless that you wonder, as in the Ingersoll-Rand case, about the odds of replicating the process.)

The RRN at a Glance

Think of the Rapid Response Network as a phone, not a computer database. It rings in Atlanta (where Heilig hangs her hat), but via voice mail Futernick and Taubenslag regularly take requests and go to work on them. (Taubenslag, a former McKinsey consultant, is now a part-time subcontractor who works from her home near Manhattan.) About 120 queries come in each month, roughly 25 percent from outside the U.S. (about 60 percent of McKinsey's consultants are outside the U.S.). It takes two or three hours to respond to a "normal" request, and the requesting consultant typically ends up getting a half-dozen appropriate documents—from the RRN database, FPIS, or PDNet—and a few experts to call (more on that later).

The RRN database held 700 documents in mid-1991, and was growing by 70 entries a month; it can be accessed by 60 subject heads and 150 key words.

RRN documents include internal Practice presentations (general and detailed), relevant letters of proposal, sanitized documents from client work, OPP-related book reviews, and journal articles. There's also information on experts—mostly from McKinsey, though leads on a handful of expert McKinsey alumni (*not* including me) are available as well.

The On-Call Consultant

The On-Call Consultant, or OCC, is an essential—and unique—part of the RRN. At Nice in April 1990, all 60 "members of the Practice" agreed to be OCCs. That is, they promised to make themselves available, several weeks each year, to chat with consultants throughout the firm grappling with organization problems. Furthermore, they agreed to guarantee they'd get back to any caller within 24 hours—they knew from the start that dependability had to be the signature of the process (an eye toward "marketing" again.).

During a "duty week," an OCC typically spends a half hour or more a day on a couple of calls. Julien Phillips, a key member of the Practice for the last 15 years, is the patron saint of OCCs. He is renowned for spending hour after hour on the simplest request from the most junior consultant. (Think of Phillips as the OPP's human equivalent to the serendipitous Ingersoll-Rand "drag test." Without such a saintly, selfless senior figure, it's possible that the RRN idea would have lacked the special tone that clearly sets it apart. More generally, it is precisely such subtleties—or strokes of luck, depending on your view—which make or break knowledge management schemes in general.)

The Artistry of the OPP Three

It's impossible to overemphasize the importance of the way the OPP Three approach their jobs. For example, they are the ones who decide when to refer, or not to refer, a query to a given OCC. Though customer-oriented to a fault, the trio also are *very* conscious of "managing" the OCCs individually and as a group, so as not to overburden them. (And "overburden" has a different meaning for each of the 60 perpetually harried OCCs.) Managing these "psychodynamics of the network" as the OPP Three's Taubenslag tagged it, is arguably their most important contribution.

The marketing-minded OPP Three look at their job as reaching out, not just reacting. They talk easily about "catching young consultants early," providing extraordinary service so that "repeat business" is high. They shamelessly hawk their wares. Stickers with the RRN phone number are slapped on all Practice documents shipped to consultants. A Practice brochure for the RRN automatically goes out with each OPP document PDNet spews forth from New York or London. A snazzy annual report, the first of its kind at McKinsey, provides details of accomplishments, "customer" feedback, and a catalog of available services. (A section of the report is reproduced on the next page.)

OPP 1991 Annual Report, p.11.

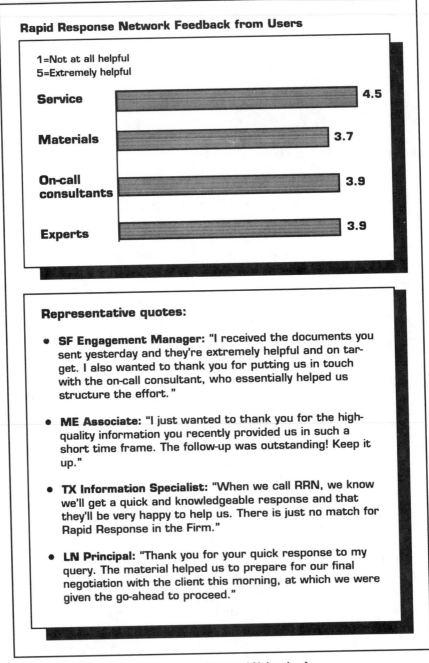

Rapid Response Network Feedback from Users

1=Not at all helpful
5=Extremely helpful

Service — 4.5

Materials — 3.7

On-call consultants — 3.9

Experts — 3.9

Representative quotes:

- **SF Engagement Manager:** "I received the documents you sent yesterday and they're extremely helpful and on target. I also wanted to thank you for putting us in touch with the on-call consultant, who essentially helped us structure the effort."

- **ME Associate:** "I just wanted to thank you for the high-quality information you recently provided us in such a short time frame. The follow-up was outstanding! Keep it up."

- **TX Information Specialist:** "When we call RRN, we know we'll get a quick and knowledgeable response and that they'll be very happy to help us. There is just no match for Rapid Response in the Firm."

- **LN Principal:** "Thank you for your quick response to my query. The material helped us to prepare for our final negotiation with the client this morning, at which we were given the go-ahead to proceed."

(SF=San Francisco; ME=Melbourne; TX=Texas; LN=London.)

A Day in the Life of the OPP Three

Lynn Heilig recalled a typical day in May 1991. Six calls came in. First, a request for information about the organization of finance departments in global firms, to support a new McKinsey project; pressing issues included centralization and decentralization, the importance and application of information technology. In response, Heilig conducted an FPIS database search, among other things. She ended up shipping out a batch of documents and recommending several experts to be contacted. The second call came from a Los Angeles consultant, concerning an energy-industry client who was reorganizing. Heilig sent out material responsive to a broad question about appropriate line and staff roles and corporate reorganizations in general. The third query came from a consultant working on a letter of proposal for a possible new project. He wanted the scoop on McKinsey's experience in a special area. After another FPIS search, the consultant was given a list of several people to contact. (The office librarian should have handled this one, though Heilig did so, since she was contacted—and, as usual, went overboard with an eye on marketing and future business.)

The fourth request came from a senior Los Angeles partner who wanted some "client-ready material"—off-the-shelf diagnostic tools that could be applied *immediately* to his project. Heilig queried the RRN and PDNet databases. Sixty documents and 83 experts spewed forth. Six documents seemed especially useful. The problem: They were all over the place (including Australia), and a couple were confidential, requiring a release by the senior consultant involved. Nonetheless, she tracked down whom and what she needed, with a lot of help from her extended "network," and the material went out on time. (Again: Such tenacity adds enormously to the perception of RRN's responsiveness, and gives the Practice enhanced credibility.) Heilig also recommended two experts. The fifth request involved a new project in the life insurance industry—not surprisingly, "delayering" was the issue. Once more, appropriate documents were dispatched and three experts were recommended. (Not incidentally, the three were past "users" who'd been actively engaged with the RRN within the previous four months—thus the network builds!)

The final query came from a consultant working with another energy-industry client. He wanted to know how line business units should measure and evaluate corporate staff services. The consultant thought he ought to create a survey, but wasn't sure it was the right thing to do. If it was, he wanted a set of survey forms—*now!* Heilig provided some documents and also referred him to the on-call consultant and two other experts.

Jennifer Futernick, like Heilig, handles three to six calls a day. Futernick also calls herself a "scout" for external material (a nice complement to her colleagues' internal orientation): She's an assiduous book review reader, for example, and when she's pulled together a critical mass of relevant reviews, she sends them out to members of the Practice.

Follow-up is as important to the OPP Three in building clientele as handling incoming requests with dispatch. Nancy Taubenslag is the designated follow-up specialist. On a typical day in early 1991, she placed follow-up calls to 15 RRN "customers." (Her computer is programmed to "tickle" her seven days after *every* RRN request.) She got through to five. One bitched—he had called the RRN, searching for information unrelated to the OPP, and was unhappy. Irrational as his reaction was, Taubenslag treated him as a potential "convert," and provided some advice. Two others gave the RRN an unequivocal thumbs-up on the material they'd received. The final pair needed more information—and additional experts to contact. Why hadn't they called the RRN again on their own? "Who cares?" Taubenslag said. The point was that the seven-day tickler provided an opportunity to offer more service to these customers—and sink the Practice's hook in a little deeper.

Taubenslag also performed one long-term follow-up, resulting in a half-hour discussion about lessons learned from a study. She transcribed the conversation within the hour, then sent it out to the reporting consultant for review, asking him to send back an approved version to be put into the FPIS, within three weeks. (When she does her seven-day follow-up, Taubenslag asks if she can call the "customer" when his project is complete. If the answer is yes, she activates another tickler to remind her to do so.)

There are a host of other "minor" aspects to the follow-up process. When a consultant gushes about the work of an on-call consultant, for example, Taubenslag will likely send that OCC a thank-you note. If the OCC is junior, she makes sure to send carbon copies to others in her or his "network."

The OPP Three Loves You!

The OPP Three is a caring group. It shows and it makes all the difference. They don't view their primary objective in narrow terms (codifying learning, managing a database), but as "helping consultants ask better questions," "making organizational consulting a key McKinsey skill."

Heilig, Futernick, and Taubenslag also chatter a lot about "mutuality of support" and "collegiality." Such talk is essential to the overall knowledge-management idea. The OPP center is unique within McKinsey—a principal reason is that the OPP Three amount to a "critical mass" which is missing in many other McKinsey Practice areas. Such ideas as "critical mass" (soul!) and "mutuality of support" (soul!) within the group that "administers" such a program are of the utmost significance (along with a hundred other "details"). Boil it down, and the OPP Three are in the business of generating interest in and enthusiasm for their Practice. Their cheerleading skills are at least as important as their encyclopedic technical knowledge.

In the end, I can only urge you to reread this case *slowly* in a week or two. In these few pages, literally hundreds of subtleties have surfaced—insisting that consultants rather than librarians write the FPIS summaries, allowing the new RRN database to be incompatible with the others in order to spur the OPP champions on, 24-hour service guarantees by the OPP on-call consultants, the emphasis on "marketing" by everyone involved, etc. Yet if we truly see the "learning organization"/"knowledge management" idea as essential to competitiveness, then we *must* learn from examples like this, and learn, above all, from those gory details. McKinsey has been at formal knowledge management for a half-dozen years and, despite a thousand lessons learned (most the hard way—how else?), Manville would be the first to acknowledge that he and his colleagues are barely out of the starting blocks. The outline on the next page summarizes a few elements of the McKinsey KMS.

But Is It Relevant to Me?

But are this case and set of specs relevant to, say, ABB? Yes, unequivocally. ABB has demolished most of its expert-staff structures—but it's determined (1) to build knowledge and transfer learning effectively among 1,300 companies/5,000 profit-and-loss centers, and (2) to do so without re-creating, even indirectly, a new, ponderous expert-staff apparatus. ABB, then, like McKinsey, will be dependent on volunteerism and "soft" incentives (power transformer boss Sune Karlsson said as much—see p. 51). It's my bet that ABB and, say, Union Pacific will end up with learning structures that look a lot like McKinsey's. Hey, Brook Manville is that rare McKinseyite who really is a staffer (with no expectations of billability to clients). But guess what? McKinsey's clients have been battering down *his* door to get a glimpse of the firm's pioneering approach to knowledge management.

FI GROUP'S "FLYING SQUADS"

In 1962, Steve—that is, Stephanie—Shirley decided to have a baby, but her employer (Britain's big computer company ICL, now owned by Fujitsu) wouldn't accommodate her need for odd hours. So Shirley took care of herself, founded FI Group—and invented a way of working that's as advanced as any in the world. (Stephanie switched to "Steve" to get a foot in the door—in the early 1960s, "Stephanie to see the chief" usually got the door slammed in her face.)

With approximately £25 million in revenue, fast-growing FI Group is one of the United Kingdom's largest information systems houses. It "employs" 1,000 or so people at any time; about two-thirds are women. Yet the firm's full-time "core" is only 250—150 responsible for managing projects and "core competences," 100 doing administrative chores. The rest are "freelance associates," called upon as needed from a database/network of 5,000 qualified, independent professionals to execute FI's sophisticated client projects. They're required to work at least 20 hours a week, and they do about one-third of their

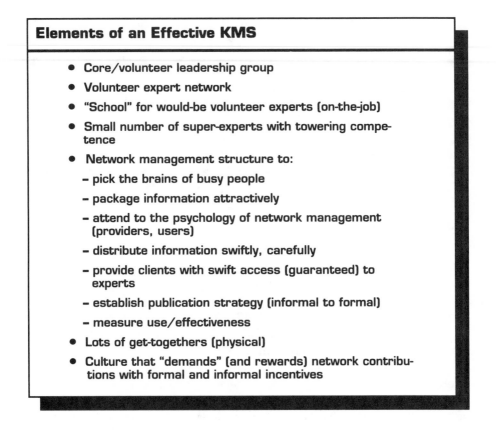

Elements of an Effective KMS

- Core/volunteer leadership group
- Volunteer expert network
- "School" for would-be volunteer experts (on-the-job)
- Small number of super-experts with towering competence
- Network management structure to:
  - pick the brains of busy people
  - package information attractively
  - attend to the psychology of network management (providers, users)
  - distribute information swiftly, carefully
  - provide clients with swift access (guaranteed) to experts
  - establish publication strategy (informal to formal)
  - measure use/effectiveness
- Lots of get-togethers (physical)
- Culture that "demands" (and rewards) network contributions with formal and informal incentives

work at home; the rest takes place on customer premises or in one of FI's new Work Centers. Looked at from a different angle, over 500 "FI people" are at work in hundreds of different "sites" (including homes) on any given day (FI inspired Charles Handy's "scattered organization" imagery—p. 150). Complex, long-duration software support and maintenance projects account for most of FI's bookings. Clients include Britain's blue-chips, such as Sainsbury's, Unilever, Shell, and British Telecom. A typical project: FI Group created a sophisticated purchase order scheme for Tesco, the huge British bakery firm.

Fleshing out the dispersed working scheme and establishing the matchless standards of quality necessary to build credibility for such an odd institution (especially given FI's *very* conservative client base) kept Shirley's platter full in the early years. But now Chief Executive Hilary Cropper, who came aboard in 1985, is at work on "phase two"—turning FI "from 'production'-led to 'marketing'-led." Creating market-focused divisions was step one. (That shift also involved "pushing middle management out into the divisions" to head off incipient bureaucracy.) Developing proprietary information systems products that can be "branded" and sold, with minimal tailoring, to numerous clients is next up. The mainspring for accelerating product development is "capturing know-how," Cropper told me in 1991. She insisted that it will be "FI's crucial, long-term competitive advantage."

But how do you rapidly capture knowledge in a uniquely dispersed organization mostly made up of part-timers? Cropper's answer is "flying squads," which absorb about 12 of the core cadre. Squad members move from project to project in an ongoing quest for useful knowledge that can be turned into products with widespread utility. A flying squad member may hang around for three months on a three-year project. She or he wins acceptance on the always harried teams by helping out with day-to-day chores, Cropper claimed, and then can go about the main task of codifying ideas that can be used by others. Cropper went on and on about "writing it down"—the whole idea of systematic learning, she said, is completely counter to FI's normal, on-the-fly culture. (Ditto at McKinsey.)

The product development process spurred by the flying squads is picking up steam. "We're slowly learning how to do it," Cropper said. Project teams, she added, "always are creating new competences. The flying squads are people in the middle who seek to extract those competences from individual team members, then codify them. Such codification was ignored before, because of the dispersed nature of the organization."

(Beneath such a bare-bones description are a thousand subtleties. For example, FI Group has long put out a strong emphasis on collegiality and self-discipline. Then, in 1991, founder Shirley decided to reduce her shareholdings dramatically and sell a majority interest in the company to its employees, including the freelancers. Abetted by interest-free loans, 72 percent of the employees bought shares in the initial offering.)

CRSS, THE SCIENCE OF LISTENING AND LEARNING TOGETHER

CRSS, a $472-million (1991 revenue) Houston firm, performs construction management and civil and mechanical engineering, and develops and manages power cogeneration plants—and it is one of the world's premier architectural firms. Architecture is its roots, and CRSS's remarkable record includes designing some of the world's most complex projects. Its approach to working with its clients is what sets the company apart. Amazingly, CRSS architects established, and then maintained for over four decades, preeminence and competitive advantage via one "simple" tactic—*taking listening seriously*. CRSS builds on *listening*, worries about *listening*, works ceaselessly at improving its *listening* skills. CRSS's technology of listening turns out to be a benchmark knowledge-management saga.

In 1948, CRSS founder Bill Caudill won a contract to design a schoolhouse in Blackwell, Oklahoma, 525 miles from his College Station, Texas, "headquarters" (a cramped office over a grocery store). He and partner Wallie Scott determined the requirements, concocted the design, then toted their plans to Blackwell. The school board rejected their work out of hand. Caudill and Scott listened respectfully to their client's concerns, went home with tails between their legs, made all the changes requested, toted the new plans back to Blackwell for a second try. The school board tossed them out again. And again. Then a fourth time.

"Patience, enthusiasm, and money were running short," Caudill later wrote in *Architecture by Team*. "Finally I said, . . . 'Wallie, we are going to lose our shirts if we don't do something quick. How about you and me loading the drafting boards in your car (my car was so old it wouldn't stand the trip), driving into Blackwell and squatting, like Steinbeck's Okies, in the boardroom until we get the damn plans approved?' So we did. We drove in on a Sunday night and early Monday morning we had our 'office' open for business—in that boardroom. We never dreamed that fourteen years later we would be doing the same thing in the Harvard Faculty Club with a team of nine architects/engineers working with twelve distinguished professors. Frankly, all we were interested in was to 'get the damn plans approved.' And come Friday night in a meeting with the board and the administration in the same room, the plans were 'approved with unanimous enthusiasm.' But a lot happened between Monday morning and Friday night."

Willie Peña, a founder of the firm, recalled in a 1989 interview the amusing scene, as recounted by Caudill and Scott. The folks of Blackwell, he told me, stayed far away from the youthful duo ("college boys") at first. But after a day or two, a member of the board wandered by, asked a question, made a little comment about, say, the location of a cupboard, a lavatory, whatever. Gradually those visits became regular. Thus, Caudill wrote, "in trying to find a way to lick the distance problem, we happened upon a truth that should have been obvious to us all the time—the clients/users want to get into the act of planning, and when they do, there is no reason not to get approval, because then it is automatic. . . . Throughout the years of our practice we have [also] learned that clients/users' involvement generally ensures better facilities."

And that's that—more or less. But, as is often the case, the apparently simple ain't when you look up close. The intensive, interactive design and joint learning process—today meaning "squatters' teams" (still called that) that often number 20 or 30 on big projects—was ridiculed by the haughty architectural establishment for years. Architecture's Leonardo da Vincis said that art and creativity would invariably be sacrificed if client involvement became the norm, especially in such a pronounced fashion. The dregs of that ridicule linger to this day. That's one reason this still odd way of doing business—hanging out, squatting, call it what you will—remains as strong a competitive advantage as it was following the Blackwell incident almost half a century ago.

CRSS staffers give the approach high marks. "The client's part of it," one young architect told me. "They stay up all night, just like you do. You bring your drawing tables, you paper the wall with 'snowcards' [which depict ideas and concepts—more later]. You eat and often even sleep in that place. You want a little catnap, you go out in the hall and lie down for a few hours, then work a little longer. They get a kick out of it, the interaction, the feeling. From their point of view, you're really committed to *their* project and *their* problem. You get a lot further down the road than you would using any other process."

Teams include many disciplines from the client organization and from within CRSS. Take the design of the headquarters for 3M's electronics sector in Austin, Texas. 3Mers involved in facilities planning, finance, and the like, from corporate headquarters in St. Paul, Minnesota, participated. So did 3M marketers, salespeople, and engineers from Austin. On the CRSS side, there were architects of various stripes ("programmers," "designers"—see below), construction managers, engineers, and so on.

3M electronics execs bubble about the building *they* invented (together with CRSS), and contend it's been a prime mover in dramatically paring product development cycle times (see also p. 379). After working with CRSS, a Toyota product development executive went home and effectively applied the process he'd learned in Houston—to the creation of three new car models.

Teamwork and Programming

There are two key ideas here—teamwork and programming. "Team action is difficult to understand," Caudill wrote in *Architecture by Team*. "Architectural training was anti-team. The truth is that we were trained to bully, to tell our clients what they should have. And I thought what they should have was 'me.' My own design. My current taste. My convictions, if not prejudices. I greatly admired the famous architectural hero who had the courage to tell the client to go to hell if that client had the audacity to interfere . . . or complain that his roof was leaking."

Buttressing and complementing the team idea is the rigorous CRSS discipline of "programming." "CRSS' main contribution to the [architecture] profession has been in the programming aspect of our architectural practice and in our acceptance of the premise that better buildings result when the client/users are on the planning team," Caudill wrote. "This has led us to the development of new methods of serving our clients, in creating new ways for team communication such as analysis cards, the squatters, the user/architect clinics . . . . In particular, the firm has developed two sorts of specialists—one called 'programmers,' the other 'designers.' "

CRSS management is adamant that the programming mindset is different from the designing mindset. The reason: Programming must be kept separate if listening and learning from the client are to get their proper, all-too-rare share of patient attention. The main idea behind programming: "If programming is problem seeking, then design is problem solving," Peña, Steve Parshall, and Kevin Kelley say in another CRSS book, *Problem Seeking: An Architectural Programming Primer.* Do designers program? They can, but [programming] takes highly trained architects who are specialized in asking the right questions at the right time, who can separate wants from needs, and who have the skills to sort things out. . . . Most designers love to draw, to make 'thumbnail sketches' as they used to call them. . . . They can be serious deterrents in the planning of a successful building if done at the wrong time. . . . Before the whole problem is defined, solutions can only be partial and premature. . . . The experienced, creative designer withholds judgment, resists pre-conceived solutions and the pressure to synthesize. . . . He refuses to make sketches until he knows the client's problem."

Peña, one of the last of the original Caudill team, is the high priest of programming. Though a jolly soul at 72, with a mischievous gleam in his eye and a hearty laugh, he is stern and forbidding when it comes to protecting these principles. The rigidity of his views comes in for a fair amount of carping in the halls of CRSS, despite the firm's (and Peña's) distinguished record. Yet Peña, like Caudill before him, is used to that. Patient listening, and segregation of programming and design, remain unusual.

Brown Sheets, Snow Cards, Etc.

Supporting the concept of programming/listening/learning team architecture are dozens of detailed devices, discovered and honed over the years. For example there are "brown sheets" and "analysis cards," each aimed at promoting more thorough understanding of the client's problem, which leads in turn to involvement and more effective design. Consider, from *Problem Seeking,* "Guidelines for the Preparation of 'Brown Sheets' ":

> Brown sheets graphically indicate [facility] space needs which have been derived from project goals, facts, and concepts. They are intended to project the magnitude of numbers and sizes. A client and a designer can visualize the number and sizes of spaces more easily if they are indicated graphically and to scale. . . . One glance [at the brown sheets] can tell where the major allocations of area have been made, the predominance of small spaces requiring a higher percentage of circulation spaces, or the unjustified equal size of different functional areas.
>
> The first purpose of brown sheets is to present the area requirements as determined during the interviews. . . . The second purpose of brown sheets is to serve as work sheets during work sessions. For that purpose they are made of informal materials that not only lend themselves to revision, but even invite revision. (Computer-made brown sheets lack this quality.) . . . Brown sheets are sized to a format suitable for viewing by groups of 10 to 20 people. Therefore, facility titles, area figures and the white area squares must be clearly visible.

We observed a session with a dozen or so CRSS and 3M team members. Walls were peppered with strange configurations of what I learned were "snow cards" (more formally, "analysis cards"). Development, use, and manipulation of an average display of 150 5-by-8-inch snow cards turns out to be the essence of programming. The details from *Problem Seeking*:

The face of [an analysis] card has an almost imperceptible, non-photo-blue grid based on 0.5 centimeters. The grid is helpful in sketching diagrams, charts and even in lettering. . . . The card is made of 100 pound pasted Bristol stock. . . . The cards are relatively small and easy to handle. They are deliberately kept small to accommodate only one thought, one idea, simply and economically stated. They should encourage a sharp focus on each card. . . . The cards are small enough to force the avoidance of unnecessary detail. . . .

Deal with [an analysis card] as if it were a telegram. Think what must be said. Reduce it to one thought. Put it down graphically with very few elements. Write it out with very few words. Add color only for emphasis or for coding. . . .There is a certain look about good analysis cards. The bad ones are generally too bold and heavy or too delicate and light. . . . Label the drawings properly. Reinforce the drawing with a short sentence. . . . Use letters one-eighth inch high or larger. Use a number-two pen or wider. . . . "Think" cards are done quickly by anyone who has a bit of information for consideration. . . . "Working" cards are sketched carefully enough to clarify the thinking. . . . "Presentation" cards are meticulously drawn for greater precision. . . . All cards are process documents and as such should have an informal, loose look as opposed to final documents. . . . Encourage everyone on the team to produce the initial analysis cards. Remove those inhibitions caused by the high standard of "presentation" cards. Promote the production of "think" cards.

[Analysis] cards may be used freely, sorted and grouped in sequence. They're best used as a wall display—tacked and grouped under the process sequence of Goals, Facts, Concepts, Needs and Problems. . . . Typically, interview notes and pre-programming information lead to the making of analysis cards. These are displayed and tested during the work sessions. It is a process of *feedback* and *feedforward*. . . . A wall display of analysis cards makes it easy to test the interrelationships among Goals, Facts and Concepts which leads to Needs and eventually to the Statement of the Problem.

100-Pound Pasted Bristol Stock

Why, in this book on general management, cite in detail the specifications of CRSS's analysis cards? For the same reason I dragged you through a morning in the life of McKinsey's Nancy Taubenslag. Moving "learning organization" and "knowledge management" from flavor-of-the-month to half-century strategic advantage is as much about 100-pound pasted Bristol stock as it is about the high-sounding distinction between programmers and designers.

(MORE) LEARNING TOGETHER: WHOLESALE MINGLING

The Buick Reatta Craft Centre (BRCC) in Lansing, Michigan, was a failure that's been a raging success. Buick Reattas were discontinued when sales fell below expectations; nonetheless, the transformation of the former Oldsmobile forging plant to a new-look factory and avowed "idea incubation center" paid off. The plant is now ticketed to build GM's first electric car.

Nothing at BRCC was more intriguing than the wacky arrangement, literally "designed" on a napkin (and never written down in much detail), between Buick and giant paint supplier PPG. The BRCC Paint Shop was managed by a PPG employee, Steve Nowak, who reported to the BRCC operations manager. Nowak's paycheck said PPG, and he managed budgets for his PPG technical service and sales division—and for the BRCC Paint Shop. Nowak commanded PPG supervisors, who in turn managed hourly GM (BRCC) workers, all UAW members. (PPG also placed other sales and technical support reps in satellite offices—on the BRCC plant floor.)

Painting cars is a complex process, GM plant manager Jim Rucker told us in 1991. "On the fly, it's extremely hard to know exactly what the cause-and-effect relationships are when a problem arises." Did it come from workers applying the paint? Or was the paint itself flawed? With the new arrangement, Rucker said, "There's no need to waste time arguing or trying to find that out for the purpose of pointing fingers and laying blame. You're really just trying to solve the problem." Before, he added, PPG would imagine that GM wasn't doing all it could to solve the problem. GM in turn felt PPG wasn't looking hard enough.

But the joint learning process went beyond solving today's problems. PPG employees, for example, worked with GM counterparts to modify the painting robots to improve efficiency. A PPG executive was quick to tell *Ward's Auto World* that by doing so, "[We] were working on a way to cut down the amount of paint we sell. But we aren't in favor of waste of any kind, that's the point."

Plant manager Rucker bubbled about the possibility of continuous improvement processes that marry the two organizations. "Think about the learning curve," he said. "What organization makes paint and applies it? None! This new hybrid sees all sides, all the variables of the process at once, and it's easier to improve the product and the application process when you've got all that knowledge in one place." In the end, he added, "when something goes wrong, yeah, the organization is leaner and meaner and you can solve problems quicker. But you mainly ought to be thinking about when things are going *right*. How do you *learn*, how do you get *better*?"

The BRCC/PPG program also incorporated futuristic twists. For instance, GM's advanced engineering department, PPG's paint labs, and EDS's computer mavens worked on special robotics for paint delivery, monitoring, and self-correction. (The idea originally came from GM hourly workers aiming to eliminate the need to constantly adjust their robots.) GM and PPG officials told us that all aspects of the BRCC "experiment" were successful. The scheme will live on, somehow or other.

QUAD/GRAPHICS: EDUCATION "Я" US

We're a know-how company, a knowledge company, an R&D company. And that means we're also a people company—because where else are the ideas going to come from? And that's why we have to spend so much time on . . . education. Because unlike some high-tech company out in Silicon Valley . . . we don't hire a lot of engineers. The average employee that joins my company looks like a loser. They are the kids in the class that didn't go on to college, who didn't make it in school for some reason, and in many ways have nowhere to go. And what we do is get them to elevate their sights, to become something more than they had ever hoped to be. Instead of thinking of themselves as printers, we get them to think of themselves as trained technicians who run computers that run the press. . . . You can't have a technology company without also being a training company. And this is something we understood from the beginning. . . . And so on Monday, Tuesday, Wednesday and Thursday, employees will run the presses, and then on Friday, they go to school. It's a tremendous development system—the kids really take off.

HARRY QUADRACCI
Chief Executive Officer
Quad/Graphics, *Inc.*, 1986

Harry Quadracci, like Ralph Stayer at Johnsonville Foods, is an articulate proponent of what I call "organization-as-university." Both Johnsonville and Quad/Graphics are explicitly set up as learning institutions.

Quad/Graphics is a half-billion-dollar growth company (also see p. 146). Its reputation is outstanding: state-of-the-art presses, superlative responsiveness, top-drawer quality. But its true distinction is a matchless commitment to learning. Quad's "trick" is simple: All employees are "students" from the moment they sign on. Mostly on autonomous 6-person press teams, they're hired by "sponsors" (peers) and directed by "mentors" (not bosses). To become a mentor yourself, you must survive Quad's one-year training "boot camp." Furthermore, you don't get promoted, from a typically grueling entry-level job, until *you* have trained your successor!

Quad employees get paid for a four-day, 40-hour, flex-time week. Then there's that voluntary fifth day—without pay—in the classroom. About half show up. In 1991, employees who chose to attend training courses averaged 200 hours in the classroom. (Employees *are* paid for a two-week introductory course.)

Learning and teaching, as Quadracci tells it, are the only routes to job security. So everyone teaches her or his would-be successor, and everyone also has the opportunity to become a classroom teacher. Quad/Ed, the firm's training arm, has five staff trainers—who mostly help line workers with teaching techniques. Any worker who wants to teach a course, on anything, is welcome to do so. "Grab three people, get them into a classroom, and you're on your way," a Quad/Ed staffer told me. In fact, there are close to 200 volunteer worker-trainers, each of whom donates an average of 10 hours a week to teaching.

Quadracci himself plays teacher to his workers, conducting numerous sessions in the firm's Little Red School House. He also teaches classes for customers. (Quad customers are welcomed with open arms into all the firm's plants. Quadracci insists that line workers are his sales force. "Selling," he said, "is done in the plant." And, indeed, on any given day you'll find customers and Quad workers, age 18 and up, working on printing-improvement projects.)

The company also organizes R&D as a training and joint learning activity. Quad/Tech (the R&D arm), with ceaseless worker input, constantly experiments with the firm's $6-million presses, getting them to perform tricks that their manufacturers never imagined. (Quad/Tech, for better or worse, perfected the device that blows subscription cards into magazines.) Such perpetual improvement has propelled Quad ahead of its competitors.

So whether it's the basics for teenage pressmen, customer projects, or R&D, Quad/Graphics' approach has one theme: education. It is, pure and simple, an unabashed learning machine.

A LEARNING/KMS TYPOLOGY

From these cases, and a few that came before, we can concoct a typology of sorts:

- Formal KMS. The "McKinsey model," or systemic knowledge capture and management as a strategic aim. McKinsey, FI Group (flying squads), EDS (centers of service, horizontal SBUs), and ABB (the Business Area mechanism, centers of excellence) are barking up this tree.

- The Technique of Joint Learning. CRSS has thought through the process of joint learning more thoroughly than any firm I've come across. David Kelley Design and Chiat/Day/Mojo seek advantage in much the same fashion.

- Schoolhouse. Quad/Graphics epitomizes the schoolhouse model/corporation-as-university. Johnsonville Foods is on the same wavelength.

- Total Integration/Symbiosis. PPG's relationship with BRCC is the benchmark when it comes to integration/symbiosis with outsiders. EDS is close.

- Learning Network. MCI is as good as its energetic, entrepreneurial network partners. And no better. The shifting MCI network *is* the "corporation"—and its learning device. Apple is also master of this process.

Learning Devices Galore

The cases in this chapter emphasize learning and knowledge management. But it turns out that we encountered a rich array of learning devices in earlier examples, too. The chart on pages 408 to 412 summarizes—and evaluates—21 cases. Learning processes are divided into four critical areas:

— Learning with clients. Beyond routine market research, focus groups, etc., how does the organization achieve symbiosis and constant learning exchange with clients?

— Learning from outsiders. How does the organization tap the knowledge of consultants, academics, universities, subcontractors, community leaders, and various others not on its payroll?

— Learning from each other. How is knowledge passed on within a group, from group to group, from division to division, or even from sector to sector within the organization?

— Systemic knowledge capture and dissemination. Per McKinsey, is there a systemic scheme *at a strategic level* for capturing and disseminating knowledge? Is a full-blown learning mechanism in place?

Learning Processes at *Liberation Management* Companies

COMPANY	LEARN FROM CLIENTS	LEARN FROM OUTSIDERS	LEARN FROM EACH OTHER	SYSTEMIC KNOWLEDGE CAPTURE DEVICE	COMMENTS
David Kelley Design	S	S	S	S	Projects are everything; multidisciplinary training; brainstorming; early/continuing client involvement in a structured way; only accepts assignments "we can learn from"; physical layout abets interaction; all kibitz; shift from industry to industry; value-added comes from process of inducing creativity; institutionalized playfulness; Stanford University (outsider) connection; curious chief (David Kelley).
McKinsey	S	A	S	S	Projects are everything; heavy client involvement from the outset; formal knowledge management structure; project rotation gives multi-industry exposure; hires academics in small numbers to emphasize functional excellence; outside publication strategy; superb word-of-mouth network; norm of reciprocity (you're expected to help others no matter how busy you are).

S = State-of-the-art.   G = Good.   A = Average or weak.

FI Group	S	A	G	S	Projects are everything; "flying squads" created to capture learning; emphasis on creating products based on such learning; easy electronic communication; new Work Centers abet team interaction.
EDS	S	A	G	G/S	Projects are everything; on-site with the client from day one; emphasis on horizontal SBUs to disseminate "products" across industries; Centers of Service supplement horizontal SBUs; acquisitions to fill knowledge holes; superb word-of-mouth network; ethos that gives "points" for giving up "your" people to work on others' projects.
Chiat/Day/Mojo	S	G	S	S	Projects are everything; unique client involvement in creative affairs from the start; account managers' support of creatives; physical layout induces interaction; creatives kibitzing; strong, independent advocate for the consumer.
CRSS	S	G	S	S	Projects are everything; value-added strategy based on (1) technology of client involvement; (2) team-based architecture; (3) separation of "programming" from "design."
ABB	G	A	S	S	Structure (P&L centers) that forces high customer contact; Business Area structure (spartan, roving teachers) that is de facto KMS; learning/knowledge transfer is ABB's strategy.

S = State-of-the-art.   G = Good.   A = Average or weak.

COMPANY	LEARN FROM CLIENTS	LEARN FROM OUTSIDERS	LEARN FROM EACH OTHER	SYSTEMIC KNOWLEDGE CAPTURE DEVICE	COMMENTS
Dallas Organization	S	S	S	A	Every event means working together with new people, picking up new tricks necessary for survival in a tough environment, where word-of-mouth reputation is everything.
MCI	G	S	S	G	Learning from subcontractors, then applying knowledge to customer-partners is MCI's value-added strategy; easy interchange, create-a-project; chatty e-mail system; high tolerance for failure; low tolerance of bureaucracy.
CCT	S	G	G	S	Structure makes it incumbent upon each tiny unit to be more expert than any competitor (or customer) in the micromarket area in which it competes; sees more customers/problems relative to one aircraft engine part than anyone else; tiny central staff of super-experts.
Quad/Graphics	S	G	S	S	"Start teaching you on day one"; "you are teaching others in a couple of months"; "Little Red School House"; "anyone can start a new class"; teaching/learning is normal and the basis for value-added; quickly sells new process improvements to competitors, so heat always on to improve; customers always in the plant; line worker as expert/salesperson.

S = State-of-the-art.   G = Good.   A = Average or weak.

Imagination	S	S	S	G	Projects are everything; everybody helps out everybody else; lots of kibitzing; anybody does anything; constant push to be more creative, better than yesterday; physical space fosters easy interchange; only accepts challenging assignments; makes space on payroll for stars, even if no assignment available; actively curious chief (Withers).
Johnsonville Foods	G	G	S	A	Acquiring new skills and learning/growing individually is the corporate ethos and value-added advantage; teams work on new products and capital-goods proposals with vendors, customers.
Ingersoll-Rand's product development approach	S	S	S	S	Multi-function learning; constant customer/vendor/outsider contact; scheme for replicating process; attention to "soft" aspects of learning (e.g., barbecues).
Titeflex	S	S	G	A	Business Development Teams are in direct contact with customers and vendors; ethos of easy exchange; driven to constantly improve.
Rational	S	S	G	A	Staff chefs are in direct contact with customer; "live for the customer" is the corporate culture; customize everything; easy contact among functions.

S = State-of-the-art.   G = Good.   A = Average or weak.

COMPANY	LEARN FROM CLIENTS	LEARN FROM OUTSIDERS	LEARN FROM EACH OTHER	SYSTEMIC KNOWLEDGE CAPTURE DEVICE	COMMENTS
IDG	S	G	G	S	Entrepreneurial unit structure forces customer contact; minimal bureaucracy ("no layers"); frenetic, peripatetic chief; well-oiled mechanisms to induce cross-unit learning (formal and informal); aims to attract independence minded stars.
UPRR	A/G	A	G	S	Cross-functional contact and customer contact now easy/routine; 106 "horizontal" processes identified for improvement amount to a systemic knowledge management scheme; all personnel "informated."
Oticon	A	G	S	S	Projects are everything; no limits to job; "culture" of fluidity ("do whatever makes sense"); almost no bureaucracy.
Buick/PPG	S	G	G	S	Wholesale intermingling adds up to unique day-to-day contact/learning strategy; intermingling expanded to special, long-term projects.
Véronique Vienne	S	S	Not Applicable	G/S	Career is viewed as string of learning and improvement opportunities; only works with people she can learn from; insatiable quest for more useful experiences; minimal fear of failure (in the traditional sense).

S = State-of-the-art.   G = Good.   A = Average or weak.

27

Knowledge Management
Structures II: Getting Physical

By 1993, IBM's British division will have all 1,000 of its headquarters employees working in "non-territorial" offices—
places where they have no desk to call their own. . . . Digital
Equipment Corp.'s subsidiary in Finland has equipped offices
with reclining chairs and stuffed sofas to make them more
comfortable and conducive to informal conversations and the
swapping of ideas. Companies such as Apple and General
Electric are experimenting along similar lines.

The Economist
March 7, 1992

My big dictionary sat on the bookshelf beside the fireplace in the
living room. I'd use it every week or so. A while back, I put it on a table in the
hall, open to the last word I'd looked up. Now I use it once or twice a day,
sometimes more.

It may almost be the age of those teraflop computers (which will process
one trillion instructions per second), but plain-vanilla physical location—
whom and what you hang out with—is decisive to learning. I use that dictionary much, much more for one damn reason: It's there.

It turns out that physical location issues are neither plain nor vanilla. In
fact, space management may well be the most ignored—and most powerful—
tool for inducing culture change, speeding up innovation projects, and enhancing the learning process in far-flung organizations. While we fret ceaselessly
about facilities issues such as office square footage allotted to various ranks,
we all but ignore the key strategic issue—the parameters of intermingling.

NEW "NEIGHBORHOODS" SPEED UP PRODUCT DEVELOPMENT

> Clusters need an environment in which people can see one another easily, and therefore are encouraged to communicate. In the past companies wanted to avoid this situation believing that when people were talking, they were taking time away from work. But as work comes to involve . . . more judgment about specific situations, efficiency can be increased when people consult quickly about how best to handle a circumstance.
>
> D. Quinn Mills
> *Rebirth of the Corporation*

The seven-story glass and granite pyramid rising above the cornfields near Grand Rapids, Michigan, is visible for miles. But it is not a monument to corporate ego. Rather, the structure is designed expressly to reshape the product development process at Steelcase, the $2-billion (1991 revenue) manufacturer of office furniture.

Steelcase aims to cut product development time in half by grouping together, in multidisciplinary teams, 575 designers, engineers, and marketing and purchasing people. (They were previously scattered through three buildings.) Michael Nowik, chairman of the 13-person materials management group, told us that within two weeks of moving into the $111-million Corporate Development Center in May 1989, he noticed a "reduced number of [formal] meetings and a less formal, more effective flow of information and dialogue. Now, questions and decisions are resolved much more quickly and easily."

Steelcase employees were involved in planning the building, which incorporates, among other principles:

- Functional diversity. "The only way to break down barriers is to bring people into closer contact. The goal is not 'homogenizing' the organization, but helping different groups accept and respect different ways of thinking and working," we were told by Franklin Becker, Cornell University professor of facility planning and management, who consulted on the project. The Corporate Development Center does this through "neighborhoods" of diverse disciplines grouped together for the duration of a project.

- Spatial mobility. "No single office, no matter how well designed, is likely to support all the tasks and activities and forms of interaction in which workers are involved," Becker said. Thus, the Corporate Development Center uses multiple work areas: individual workstations, common work areas, dedicated project rooms (where designers can spread out materials and experiment with products), break areas, and enclosed offices at the top of the pyramid (available temporarily to anyone needing a quiet place to work).

Becker argues that the building is not necessarily "efficient" (people may have to walk farther than before to get a cup of coffee or use the rest room), but it is "effective," promoting greater interaction and innovation. Managers from all functional departments work in an accessible "directors' cluster" in the center of the building. And, according to Becker, the building's atrium lobby, cafeteria, break areas, and escalators also "support face-to-face contact and spontaneous communication."

Michael Nowik said that working in the middle of his group encourages "a more effective, relaxed style of management. People don't come to their boss's office on bended knee. The building promotes a style of management where I can be an integral part of the team, and become a facilitator more than the 'boss.' "

Bring 'Em Home

"Over time as the company had grown, [its] functions had become geographically spread out. . . . Styling was done in the East and human factors analysis was done on the West Coast. Prototypes were constructed in Asia, tested in the U.S. and then handed off to manufacturing facilities both in the United States and in Asian countries. This lack of co-location was an important difference between this company and its fast-innovating competitors. . . .

"Because of the separation of functions, [people assigned to] the program . . . worked on several projects at once. Progress of these projects was coordinated by computer-based scheduling routines that moved them from formal review to review. Because of the physical separation of activities, program participants had to travel a great deal, even within a building. Program managers themselves, who were highly paid, walked between two and nine miles a day performing their tasks. On average, more than 25 percent of their time was lost walking from one task to another, and another 25 percent was spent in coordinating meetings, leaving less than 50 percent of their time available to add value.

"In contrast, fast-innovating competitors concentrate their program resources not only in one city but in one building and on one floor. The manufacturing facility is also in the same building or in one nearby. Communication is almost instantaneous. Problems can be quickly resolved not only because they are more visible to all but because the feedback loops for information are short."

GEORGE STALK, JR., AND
THOMAS M. HOUT
Competing Against Time

HANG OUT WHEREVER IT MAKES SENSE

Martin Beck is president and CEO of Fitch RS, a $35-million (1991 revenue) design consultancy based in Worthington, Ohio, that uses multidisciplinary teams to design consumer products and store interiors, and to execute corporate/brand identity programs. The firm's 500 employees occupy five farmhouses (called "pods") on 15 acres of rolling meadows. To serve clients effectively, Beck urges his employees to tinker with their work space. As a result, walls, windows, doors, and halls change frequently. Beck says he doesn't buy the argument that limiting such construction/destruction would save money. (Fitch RS invests about 1.5 percent of annual revenue in remodeling.) "Everything costs," he told us in 1990. "People have things in their businesses they don't think of as costs. They have guards at the door to keep employees from walking out with things. We don't have guards at the door. We have carpenters. The worst cost is being in a building that doesn't let you work."

Pencil lines on the ceiling show the previous locations of office walls that employees have moved. Some workers have opted for cubicle partitions with arty cutouts, others for antique desks instead of the company-issued white slabs. Yet few employees abuse their freedom to tailor their space. Instead, the nature of the project dictates whether they will have cubicles or bookshelves or walls.

Even though employees work on multidisciplinary teams, those with similar job duties are divided into departments housed in separate rooms. But staffers go where the project dictates. If they need to work in large groups, they congregate in specially furnished conference areas they've nicknamed "war rooms." If work can be accomplished by two people, they meet in a department office. If the work can be completed solo, the staffer stays at his or her desk—or works at one of the picnic tables outside when the weather permits. If teams need to focus on long-term projects or whole departments need to be near each other, they move.

For example, the firm's retail designers, who plan store interiors, were spending more and more time with the communication department's designers (who specialize in product packaging) in one of the firm's war rooms. "We thought it might be easier if we just moved the two groups closer together," we were told by Dan Dorsey, associate vice president for retail. The subsequent move has caused staffers in both departments to view their tasks differently: Since they work side by side on a project, staffers view their clients' needs more holistically. According to Dorsey, this shift has occurred at the same time that clients' design needs are changing. For instance, manufacturers are beginning to open stores to sell their own products. Since the combined departments at Fitch RS are familiar with both product design and retail space design, they can create more integrated designs for such clients.

Not everyone was happy about the move. The market strategies group, which used to be located next to communications, was afraid their relationship with that group would weaken if the departments were separated. (Market strategies works closely with communications by conducting surveys and developing strategies to present a product to the marketplace.) But Fitch RS promotes a philosophy of letting coworkers do whatever it takes to get the job done—and the retail designers wanted to hang out with the communication designers, and vice versa. So that was that, and though Bill Burke, VP market strategies, admitted he "kicked and hollered a bit," he soon realized "retail was very cramped and couldn't exhibit their wares very well. It seemed to be logical for us to move." Now that his department is in its new space, his staffers have tightened bonds with other departments, like product design and corporate marketing. "Actually this space has worked very well for us," Burke confessed.

Even the accounting department gets caught up in the act, shifting among the five pods. "I think that's the way it should be because our main purpose is to help the designers do what they do," said Paul Casper, VP finance and administration. But that doesn't mean his department automatically accepts all the firm's quirks. Casper told us he dislikes the formless, "design-as-you-work" environment that designers seem to thrive on (although he does use some designer tools, like fiberboard walls to hang important papers on). Nonetheless, the designers' theory that the worker should shape the work space instead of the work space shaping the worker is alive and well in Fitch RS's accounting department. Casper pointed out that his staff decided who should sit next to whom based on work flow.

Fitch RS has another way to spur thinking about the relationship between the workplace and people. It has developed an Exploratory Design Laboratory that not only helps solve clients' problems, but in the process experiments with new ways of working and using the workplace. It feeds those ideas back to the company. For instance, to make the company's centralized library more accessible to employees, Fitch RS is planning to divide it into small libraries placed throughout the complex.

Clients also are asked to shape Fitch RS work space to suit their projects' needs. (Clients frequently visit the facility and can either stay in a nearby hotel or room with Fitch employees.) They help build structures needed for presentations and they move walls when the work area needs to be enlarged. Thus clients take greater ownership in the process and can better implement the project back in their own organization, observed senior VP John Rheinfrank. (It's an interesting variation on the CRSS theme—see Chapter 26.)

"Clients say, 'I wish we could have a facility like this.' Not because it's pretty, but because it actually works and is conducive to the ways of thinking that we're trying to engender," Duncan Sutherland, VP, Exploratory Design Laboratory, told us. "What most businesses are still trying to do is shoehorn people into a facility concept that's based on an industrial metaphor. That's what we've changed and why clients like this so much. Our goal is to have the idea of 'facility' disappear and the work itself come to the surface, so we really need to rethink the relationship between the people and the workplace." The facility is "not just a shoebox," Sutherland added. "It's an integral part of the organizational strategy. It will become a powerful tool to accomplish a company's mission and not simply be a way to keep rain off and make sure people happen to be there."

WELCOME TO THE PLANT, BEAN COUNTERS

The high-tech Coca-Cola and Schweppes Beverages plant in Wakefield, England, is the biggest of its kind in the world, shipping 11,000 cans and bottles every hour. To facilitate teamwork, speed, and efficiency, Coke designed the new plant to house almost all 100 employees—including engineers and office workers—within sight of the shop floor.

The plant is organized around cross-functional teams of five or six people. Workstations are designed to accommodate the needs of each. For instance, teams of production workers and maintenance engineers work side by side on the line; space for their tools and parts is within reach. Besides that, each team has its own "line cabin" where it can meet, sip tea, and discuss problems away from the noise of the production line.

In fact, only the plant's computer operation is separated from the production floor (because of the technical need for climate control); all other offices—accounting, purchasing, personnel—overlook the production or warehouse facilities. Everybody is close to the action, and as a result problems on the line can be quickly corrected.

"We've taken people from diverse backgrounds and they've helped each other," operations manager Nick Bolton told us in 1990. "Some people can now have detailed technical discussions, though a few months ago they had never been in a canning plant."

Lounging with Your New Teammates

Suppose you have a critical 90-day (or nine-month) project, and you're insistent that the accountants, MIS gang, operations bunch, distribution team, and sales folks ought to join the designers and R&D people from the outset. But you're reluctant to put them together for reasons of cost, disruption, and the like. So the team's accountant, say, works with the group six hours a day, four days a week. She invariably darts back to her accounting department office each afternoon to "tidy up loose ends." She riffles through her in-box, chats with one or two colleagues, pokes her head into the boss's office. Who cares?

You'd better! After all, she's comfortable (15 years) with her band of fellow number manipulators. She rolls her eyes as she tells an old accounting pal about the financial naïveté of "those primitives in sales [on the project team]." She and a departmental colleague plan a Saturday-night outing or at least a 30-minute stop at the local lounge Friday evening— where more "smart us, dumb them" war stories will doubtless accompany a glass or two of Chardonnay.

Kiss goodbye project-team camaraderie, mutual appreciation, and zeal for completing the task. I'm all for the Saturday-night soiree or the lounge stop with a workmate, but I just wish it were the team's number cruncher getting together with the team's salesperson. And so it would have been, more likely than not, if the planners had had the sense, clout, or resources to put that project team in one place, preferably in a rented building two miles from headquarters—and next to that lounge, which would in and of itself have dramatically enhanced the odds of after-hours team member chats.

THE "TRANSNATIONAL" PHENOMENON

Chris Bartlett and Sumantra Ghoshal coined the phrase "transnational corporation." They claim, in their book *Managing Across Borders: The Transnational Solution,* that the fluid nature of markets has made old organizational models obsolete for multinational corporations. In the past, most companies opted either (1) to keep most power concentrated at headquarters (with co-located "central global product managers" setting worldwide business strategies), or (2) to devolve almost all power to "country bosses." Instead, Bartlett and Ghoshal counsel doing whatever makes sense for a particular line of business.

CSC Europe

CSC Europe is a $200-million, 2,000-person part of $1.7-billion Computer Sciences Corporation. In 1991, to prepare for a more integrated Europe, CSC changed shape. Chairman John Thompson explained in the 1991 CSC Europe annual report:

We find little added value in a headquarters staff "coordinating" transnational activities, so we have closed our former headquarters office in Brussels; those functions which provide specialized services are now located in whichever line organization suits them. . . . Of course, we still need central competence in, say, banking, but we maintain that competence wherever our banking specialists live, and they in turn network with others in each of our country organizations. Rather than gather all that competence together in some central headquarters, we disperse it across Europe.

Note the close parallels with ABB's 65 Business Area teams and McKinsey's 31 Practice Centers. CSC's Thompson still uses the word "central" ("central competence in, say, banking . . ."), but by that he *now* means a collection of experts hanging out wherever they wish or wherever it makes sense, and gaining strength through networking. Thus CSC Europe reaps the harvest of concentrated expertise without the bureaucratic shenanigans that invariably accompany powerful players gathered in a single central location—especially one within ear's range of the big cheese. I call his approach "new central" (concentration/centralization via network, with a potential critical mass physically located wherever it can be most effective); it's close kin to the "new big" idea introduced in Chapter 20. It's also another splendid illustration of the matchless (yes, matchless) importance of physical variables.

GM Europe

In recent years, General Motors has had a string of successes in Europe. There are many reasons, but shifting the continental headquarters is one that several experts point to.

GM's European operations were run by its German subsidiary, Opel, headquartered in Rüsselsheim, Germany. As a result, *The Economist* reported in 1991, "GM's top European managers used to be swamped by German issues and the day-to-day problems of running Rüsselsheim, [GM Europe's] biggest manufacturing complex. A further difficulty was that Rüsselsheim employs generations of workers from the same family. That meant there was stiff resistance to change—and to investment in manufacturing facilities outside Germany."

Frustrated GM execs decided to move to a neutral site. In 1986, the European headquarters was shifted to Zurich—and a more pan-European mood is reported to have emerged almost overnight. (Moreover, the then European boss, Jack Smith, deliberately chose a building that could only hold 200 people—to dramatically underscore his essential "lean and mean" philosophy.)

IBM

IBM is a master of international business (Royal Dutch Shell may be its only peer). It has long understood the importance of being an "insider" away from home. But when it comes to "the real thing," product strategy, Armonk (headquarters) has held almost all its cards close. That may be changing. Consider this *New York Times* report, filed from Tokyo in April 1991:

> When IBM introduced an array of small portable computers in the United States recently, something was missing. The company said it would be months, maybe a year, before it brought out its first super-lightweight notebook-sized computer, which can fit in a briefcase. But if you live here in Japan . . . you can buy one made by the International Business Machines Corporation this week. That is because IBM is under mounting competitive pressure from Japanese makers, led by Toshiba and NEC, who have created a billion-dollar market in the most portable of portable computers. So the American company is rushing a new notebook machine into Tokyo's neon-lit electronics stores this week. . . .
>
> "It's a new approach," Nobuo Mii, who heads the manufacturing and technology side of IBM Japan, said recently. "There are a lot of technologies in Japan that we have to exploit more fully. And the best place to test the technology is right here, against the best Japanese manufacturers. So we now have the mission to develop some of these technologies for IBM around the world." In fact, IBM says that the eight-pound laptops introduced in the United States two weeks ago will be the last models developed in America. From now on, they will all come from IBM Japan.

"Learning organization"? What's *that*? If you want to "learn" about notebook computers, go to where the leaders in notebook computers are—and send your Mr./Ms. Notebook there, and let him or her set your strategy from there. Is that so tough? (Yes, many would answer, in practice.)

PROXIMITY ON A GRAND SCALE: VALLEY POWER

In "The Origins and Dynamics of Production Networks in Silicon Valley," a 1990 conference working paper, University of California professor AnnaLee Saxenian describes brand-new forms of broad-ranging supplier-buyer relationships, which she claims are fundamentally changing American business in high-tech industries, and beyond. As usual, necessity has been the mother of invention. "The rising costs of product development, shortening product (life) cycles and rapid technological change," Saxenian says, have led Silicon Valley firms, among others, to adopt these pathbreaking ways of doing business.

Of course the Silicon Valley companies could simply have gobbled one another up, doubtless forming sluggish mega-firms. (To its detriment, the pathetic European electronics industry has mostly followed such a combinatorial path.) Instead, the Valley's outfits have usually chosen to take advantage of their rich setting and create extensive, collaborative partnerships. Benefits from the resultant "network firms," as Saxenian labels them, are considerable. Companies, she says, can stay focused on what they know best (and advance in carefully selected areas), spread risks (cost and technology), move fast (by involving all parties from the start), and push multiple sources of innovation onto the market at one time.

Sun Microsystems, founded in 1982 and a $5-billion (revenue) company by mid-1992, is a classic example of the new breed. Sun's founders, Saxenian writes, "chose to focus on designing hardware and software for workstations." Though it "stuffs" (assembles) some of the printed-circuit boards that are at the heart of the machine, basically Sun manufactures almost nothing—even final assembly of the workstation is done by an outsider. The company purchases application-specific integrated circuits (ASICs), disk drives and power supplies as well as standard memory chips, boxes, keyboards, mice, cables, printers and monitors from suppliers. Jim Bean, Sun's VP of manufacturing, insisted to Saxenian that the firm never considered vertical integration—given the presence of hundreds of sophisticated operations in Silicon Valley, each investing heavily in staying at the leading edge in the design and manufacture of their specialty. "If we were making a stable set of products," he added, "I could make a solid case for vertical integration." But product life cycles are far too short for such a strategy, and technology is changing too fast. "The guiding principle for Sun," Saxenian concludes, "is to concentrate its expertise and resources on coordinating the design . . . of a final system, to advance a few critical technologies, and to spread the costs and risk of new-product development through partnerships with suppliers."

Saxenian provides the helpful example of Sun working with Cypress Semiconductor to develop a sophisticated microprocessor, the brains of a workstation. A team of 30 engineers from both companies worked at a common site for a year, "combining Sun's Sparc architecture and knowledge of systems design and software with Cypress' integrated circuit design expertise. . . . This core team was supported through constant feedback from the product development, marketing and testing specialists in each firm." Developing and managing such mutual learning experiences, per se, is at the heart of Sun's overall corporate strategy. (On the next product round, after Saxenian's research, Texas Instruments did a more thoroughgoing job of collaborating with Sun—and took a lot of business from Cypress, leading to the latter's first-ever layoffs.)

Sun is a high-level "systems integrator." But how do such convoluted relationships look and feel from the other end of the food chain? Saxenian examines a group of firms called "contract manufacturers," particularly those involved in the assembly of printed circuit boards. They were historically labor-intensive and not very technologically sophisticated—that is, at the low end of the technology scale. But even that's changing, she found. Consider Flextronics: "During the 1970s, it was a small, low-value-added, 'rent-a-body' operation"; as of 1990 it had become "the largest contract manufacturer in the region, [offering] state-of-the-art engineering services and automated manufacturing," Saxenian writes. The company has developed long-term relationships with large neighbors such as IBM, Hewlett-Packard, Sun, and Apple Computer. No mere servant, Flextronics provides important innovations which are reflected in each big customer's products.

Out of these intensely intertwined destinies comes something even more elusive, yet arguably more important. Saxenian labels it "joint learning." As suppliers are "increasingly treated as equals in a joint process of designing, developing, and manufacturing innovative systems," she says, "the suppliers themselves become innovative and capital intensive producers of differentiated products." In the end, Saxenian claims, Silicon Valley is "far more than an agglomeration of individual technology firms. Its networks of interdependent yet autonomous producers grow and innovate reciprocally."

PEOPLE WHO GROW UP IN ANNAPOLIS LIKE OYSTERS

Could it be that simple? Move functions closer together at Steelcase—and major shifts in crucial interaction patterns occur in *two weeks*? (And don't forget our imagery there: Steelcase calls the new interdisciplinary team spaces "neighborhoods"—nice!) Giant GM Europe moves away from its parochial German moorings and turns "pan-European"—almost overnight? CSC Europe deals with the new Europe by scrapping its headquarters in toto and letting folks go wherever it makes sense for them to be; and IBM, in a big break with tradition, does the same thing—at least in the "notebook" computer market. And could it even be that Silicon Valley's enormous power is mostly proximity power?

My conclusions: It may be almost "that simple." I'm supported by a ton of research. At the macroeconomic level, Michael Porter, in *The Competitive Advantage of Nations*, demonstrates the remarkable power of dense, local learning networks to establish global industrial supremacy. (For more on Porter's thesis, see Chapter 34.) At the microeconomic level, MIT's Tom Allen has been studying physical layout for decades. He observes order-of-magnitude differences in frequency of contact—when people move together or apart by just 10 or 20 yards or so. Studies in social psychology demonstrate that people who are thrown together invariably come to appreciate—and more, *like*—one another. Get the bean counters and the manufacturing blokes together, as Coca-Cola/Schweppes did, and you'll soon find accountants with grease under their fingernails and manufacturers gabbing about cost variances. (And they'll also, the research shows, probably begin bowling together—with their families—in a few months.)

There are people who grew up, as I did, in Annapolis who don't give a hoot about oysters, boats, or the Navy. And there are people in Billings, Montana, who love boats, the Navy, and oysters. But it's obvious, isn't it, that regardless of the reason you live in Annapolis (e.g., accident of birth, like me), the odds are dramatically higher that you'll like "sea stuff" more than if you first saw the light of day in Billings? Of course, it's obvious. Of course, "odds are dramatically higher." Of course—except we seldom think of such things when we're designing corporations.

28

Knowledge Management Structures III: Knowledge Bases, Expert Systems, Computer-Augmented Collaboration, and the Potential of Information Technology

IBM is taking physical factors seriously to abet rapid learning—creating those "nonterritorial offices" in its U.K. operation to foster interchange among staffers from different functions, moving full responsibility for its notebook computers from "headquarters" to Japan—to be at the industry's epicenter. But it's also using its own technology to great effect: In the late afternoon, an engineer at the Thomas J. Watson Research Center in Yorktown Heights, New York, uses the internal e-mail system to query thousands of IBM engineers around the globe, and in the morning he finds a dozen answers from "colleagues" in a half-dozen countries awaiting him.

But, as we saw at Titeflex, there's nothing automatic about the effective application of advanced computing devices. If used unwisely, the computer can hinder more than help. (The Titeflex Genesis Team, assembled to hasten order entry, was a *physical* response to overcomputerization of the wrong sort. Putting five folks who were formerly parts of multiple functions in a circle turned out to be just what the doctor ordered.) Despite more lousy experiences than good ones to date, the power of the electron is gradually being harnessed to augment human interaction and long-distance learning. That was precisely the story of McKinsey's Rapid Response Network. The "psychodynamics of network management" *are* critical—but make no mistake, the RRN is a child of the Information Age.

BUCKMAN BETS ON KNOWLEDGE TRANSFER

As we move toward the chaos of the future, the progress of Buckman Labs relative to other companies will be determined by the growth in the value of knowledge that exists within the company. . . . The acceleration of knowledge transfer is how we will grow this collection of individuals that we call Buckman Labs into what it can be. . . . [Our] strategic advantage lies in the leverage of knowledge.

BOB BUCKMAN
Chairman, Buckman Labs
Speech to company marketers
May 1992

In 1991, Bob Buckman, chairman of $200-million (revenues) Buckman Labs, hurt his back. While at home playing with his computer, he got to thinking. And from those thoughts, mediated by pain, came his obsession with "knowledge bases." A couple of months later, he wrote me: "I have concluded that the system we need should have the following characteristics: (1) it should reduce the number of transmissions of knowledge between individuals to one, to achieve the least distortion of that knowledge; (2) everyone should have access to the knowledge base of the company; (3) each individual should be able to enter knowledge into the system; (4) the system should function across time and space with the knowledge base available 24 hours a day, seven days a week, since the company never closes; (5) it should be easy to use for those who aren't computer experts—be searchable on every word in the knowledge base; (6) it should communicate in whatever language is best for the understanding of the user [Buckman competes in over 60 countries]; and (7) as questions are asked of the knowledge base by the users, and answers given, it should be updated automatically—the accumulation of technical questions and answers would generate our knowledge bases for the future."

A lot has happened since then at the Memphis-based specialty chemical company, culminating in the reorganization of all information systems activities into a new entity called, simply, the Knowledge Transfer Department. Its goals are to:

1. Accelerate the accumulation and dissemination of knowledge by all Buckman Laboratories associates worldwide.

2. Provide easy and rapid access to Buckman Laboratories' global knowledge bases.

3. Eliminate time and space constraints in communications.

4. Stimulate associates to experience the value of enterprise knowledge sharing in servicing customers.

5. Respect the dignity of each individual by cultivating an environment which enhances his or her professional development, and recognizes each as a valued member of a service-oriented team.

Buckman, who spends heavily on research and development, says that knowledge transfer expenditures are running as high as R&D expenditures—which is fine by him. Yet he acknowledges that he has a long way to go, and in fact guesses that full-scale implementation won't come until 1994. But he knows what the stakes are if he gets it right. The privately held firm was evaluated by Goldman, Sachs in 1990. Its market value was $175 million higher than its asset value. That difference, Buckman bluntly asserts, is the knowledge employees hold in their collective heads. And it's that difference that he plans to build upon.

"Knowledge is acquired on the front line, moves up the organization, is sifted, digested, rearranged and then disseminated back to the front line," Buckman said in a late-1990 speech to his planners. "The knowledge that each of us acquires will have a different meaning to each of us and will have a different meaning to those to whom we transmit it. The more steps in the process, the more the knowledge changes and the more stale it becomes." If the firm could effectively accumulate and disseminate knowledge, he concluded, "we would have over 520 brains connected in real time across time and space available for any problem. We all need to realize that the best brains in the company on a particular subject frequently are not in the U.S. company, or in marketing services in Memphis, or in research and development, but are spread out around the world. Our computer system for technical questions and answers will give you access to everyone. When you pose a question of the system, you may be surprised at where the answer will come from."

Since that 1990 talk, Bob Buckman has become even more strident. Buckman Labs' new approaches to "knowledge processing," he said in a 1992 speech to his marketers, "are profoundly antibureaucratic. . . . [T]he most powerful individuals in the antibureaucratic future of Buckman Labs will be those who do the best job of transferring knowledge to others."

Amen!

DIGITAL EXPLOITS ITS NETWORK
PRODUCTS FOR INTERNAL LEARNING

Bob Buckman understands the ultimate potential of electronic knowledge transfer better than anyone I know. But some firms are further along than he is with the nitty-gritty of implementation. *Sales & Marketing Management* reported in 1990 on Easynet, Digital Equipment's "flexible information network," which aims

> to make the salesperson a more productive member of a cross-functional team whose expertise may include sales, marketing, finance, engineering, support services, software and training. . . . Easynet . . . links all sales, marketing, and service personnel in 500 offices in 33 countries [and makes it] easier for customers to place orders electronically, . . . facilitates communication between sales reps and corporate support resources, . . . [and] provides sales people with some 50 major sales and marketing [software applications packages] from qualifying leads to post-sale servicing. . . . Every DEC sales rep has an Easynet account and can access it from the office, customer site or at home via a PC or terminal.

Robert Hughes, then DEC's VP of U.S. sales and marketing, described the bold Easynet vision: "Satisfy any customer's need for any of DEC's 100,000 products or services electronically in zero seconds at zero cost." Yeow! Then Hughes offered *Sales & Marketing Management* dramatic early evidence that this audacious goal is not science fiction: "We recently executed a large sale to Pacific Telesis. The sales manager for the product was located in San Francisco, the industry marketing group in Massachusetts, the project manager in Washington, the software manager in Los Angeles, the vice president who made the pricing decisions in Santa Clara, and the support people in Maryland. The project was carried out almost entirely by electronic conferencing. Because the customer was tied to the network, he received status reports electronically." *Sales & Marketing Management* reported that "sales reps have been quicker to take to the new modus operandi than their managers." Hughes wasn't surprised: "It was an obvious thing from their point of view, because the customers were crying for it. It's tougher for managers, because they've been geographic kingpins."

EXPORTING KNOWLEDGE MANAGEMENT
CAPABILITY (FOR PROFIT)

Federal Express is a leader of the pack in developing information systems aimed at keeping its customers informed and serving them better (the firm has a staff of 950 programmers in Memphis and Colorado Springs). But it's figured out that it can turn its *internal* knowledge management skills into new business. FedEx's Business Logistics Service Area, *Business Week* reported in May 1992, bags $400 million in revenue from "managing inventory and shipping for such companies as Laura Ashley."

FedEx is hardly alone. Motorola applies its communications networking skills to managing entire communications operations for customers. And Baxter I.V. Systems, part of Baxter International, has developed a new service business that will take over the mixing of all drugs into I.V. solutions for a hospital ("patient-specific intravenous-solution compounding," in Baxter's words); hospital staff pharmacists currently do most such mixing..

Kennametal, a producer of metalworking and mining tools for more than half a century, is a most unlikely player in this game. It developed a state-of-the-art inventory management system for itself. Then it figured out that it had a salable service. "Kennametal," *The New York Times* reported in May 1992, "now stocks and manages the tool storage areas for some customers."

Expert Systems Tap Deep Knowledge

"Artificial intelligence" gurus promised the moon. And scared a lot of us to death. They sang of a revolution that would replace skilled professionals. Yet the first "AI" applications seemed trivial. So what's the deal?

In *The Rise of the Expert Company* (1988), pioneer and renowned AI scholar Ed Feigenbaum and his colleagues, Pamela McCorduck and Penny Nii, provided practical examples—21 cases of expert-system development from the manufacturing sector (e.g., Northrop, Navistar, FMC, IBM, Du Pont, Westinghouse), the service sector (e.g., American Express, Arthur Andersen), and the public sector (The British National Health Service, The British Pension Advisor). Japan's pathbreaking firms were also examined—Kajima in construction, Canon, Fujitsu, steelmaker Nippon-Kokan, Toyota, and Nippon Life.

Perhaps the most exciting story comes from Du Pont. The chemical giant certainly wins the numbers game hands down: By mid-1988, Du Pont had 200 expert systems up and running—a staggering number, considering the authors' estimate that only 1,500 expert systems were operational (in the world) at the time. A whopping 600 more were in the works!

"Mike-in-the-Box" is the name of one of Du Pont's expert systems. The real Mike is the company's best at purging a distillation column of impurities, one of the most demanding tasks in the world of commercial chemical engineering. A lot of the real Mike's expertise has been boiled down to hundreds of "rules" and captured in an expert system run on a PC. (Almost all of Du Pont's applications are PC-based.)

The overall Du Pont AI champion, Ed Mahler, oversees a "pirate-ship operation" with a tiny full-time staff. He largely eschews giant investments and instead urges engineers to spend just one month and about $5,000 to $10,000 developing each new system. The pleasantly nonthreatening term for a Du Pont AI system is Partners for Experts.

(Mike-in-the-Box has company around the globe. To wit: "God in the works," the captured expertise of an aging, irreplaceable blast-furnace expert at Nippon-Kokan; "Geoff's Book," thousands of rules from the head of the top estimator at building contractor Lend Lease of Australia; and J. A. Gilreath, Schlumberger's ace oil field data interpreter, whose expertise is now enshrined in that company's Dipmeter Advisor system.)

The bottom line that Feigenbaum et al. report is impressive. At IBM Burlington (a massive semiconductor operation), an expert system has bestowed a 10 to 20 percent increase in throughput—it adds up to tens of millions of dollars in annual savings from just the one system. At The British National Health Service, a demanding and critical evaluation task that took six experts two hours is now done (better) in nine minutes. At American Express, the "decline rate" (decisions not to grant credit) has been reduced by fully one-third; the value of the single new AI system that makes it possible was estimated at $27 million a year. A Westinghouse system (a new service the firm sells to utilities), aimed at enhancing the utilization of giant electric-power generation turbines, contributes a whopping $3 million per year per customer machine. And an AI system that aids product design at Canon has made scarce, highly skilled designers of TV-camera lenses fully 12 *times* more productive.

The cognoscenti argue about the importance of various forms of more linear (traditional AI) and less linear (neural networks, abetted by superfast parallel processing machines) computing schemes. I have neither the inclination nor the talent to enter the debate. I do conclude, however, that any senior manager who isn't at least learning about expert systems, and sticking a tentative toe or two into AI's waters, is missing a significant opportunity.

COMPUTER-NERD CEOS

Bob Buckman wants to start a "real-time," multicontinent, 520-person "conversation." DEC wants to do the same thing with even more people in more places. McKinsey's Rapid Response Network, with a passel of incentives and a heavy dose of psychology, is an effort to start a conversation among busy, far-flung consultants who presumably have a lot to teach one another.

Still, most CEOs have shied away from the computer, according to industry consultant Mary Boone in *Leadership and the Computer* (1991). A few, however, are like Bob Buckman and have used it effectively to spruce up communication in their companies—and to accelerate the pace of systemic learning:

- Richard Pogue is managing partner of the global law firm Jones Day Reavis & Pogue (1,200 attorneys). The outfit is "technologized" from stem to stern, via electronic document exchange (even with clients), computer-based research, and computerized dockets. Pogue himself is an e-mail addict, Boone reports. He insists the medium is a major spur to keeping communication "personal," collegiality high, and far-flung offices part of the team. E-mail, he adds, lets people "converse" with him who otherwise might be too intimidated to drop by his office. And while a memo may sit in his briefcase for weeks, the psychology of wanting to wipe that screen clean impels Pogue to respond almost instantly to his 35 to 40 daily electronic messages.

- Chairman Burnell Roberts of huge Mead Corp. is hooked on e-mail, too, calling it "a marvelous facilitator" and noting its surprising "intimacy." Boone adds that Roberts and his colleagues also built a unique global database of people they've gotten to know here and there. When Roberts goes overseas, for instance, he'll tap into the database to survey possible contacts; the constantly expanding network is essential to Roberts's global team-building and knowledge-capitalization efforts. Roberts is also a regular user of Mead's on-line human resource system. He told Boone that he likes the unfiltered information it provides on up-and-comers. Top management, he surmises, is more likely than conservative personnel staffers to consider job candidates with unconventional profiles.

- William Esrey heads United Telecom (and, thus, US Sprint). He also touts e-mail for opening "a dialogue" with employees at all levels, from all over the firm. "[They] feel that they are dealing directly with me," he says, and speak differently than if the communications were being screened by staffers. (Esrey promulgated a few e-mail "rules." One urges users not to take even a second to go back and fix misspellings or other glitches. "The idea is that you communicate [with no fuss]," he emphasized.)

But e-mail is only the start for Esrey. At US Sprint, for instance, he played a hands-on role in developing an on-line program that provides cash flow/cash position figures, updated daily. That system, he told Boone, went a long way toward getting everyone focused on cash management. Esrey regularly taps into *external* databases as well. For example, his desktop system is keyed to perform an hourly search for news on principal competitors. He also merged extensive external data into internal financial databases, to help promote what he calls a culture change from internal to external awareness.

- CEO Richard Crandall's Comshare, Inc., pioneered executive information systems. Crandall sets the tone by using his company's products to the hilt. (A surprising number of computer/software chiefs don't.) Like United Telecom's Esrey, Crandall relies on external databases to keep direct tabs on competitors and the industry. He also waxed eloquent to Boone about getting data before it's edited by well-meaning staffers: Crandall pictures himself as an "interactive navigator" amid a swirl of raw information available at his fingertips. Crandall also likes to build on-line measures and quick feedback loops for everything. Customer satisfaction is his hobby and obsession—and he aims to make it everyone else's as well. On a daily basis, Crandall's system tracks the rate of customer problems solved, and even charts the number of visits by important customers (or potential customers) to Comshare; the latter turns out to be an ingenious leading business indicator.

NOT SO FAST?

Issues raised by Boone's 16 CEO interviews are, of course, complex. When, for instance, does incisive probing go beyond directing attention toward key initiatives and become power-sapping micromanagement? And how about the case of Aetna Life & Casualty president Ron Compton: He confessed to Boone that he has an active e-mail hookup on his sailboat. Ye gods!

Recall our hymn of praise in the last chapter to learning through physical proximity. The electron can be a major hindrance. For instance, a friend at Hewlett-Packard told me that the firm's fabled MBWA (managing by wandering around), which has been so important to maintaining entrepreneurial informality in the face of staggering growth, has been blunted by what the natives call MBSA—managing by *screening* around. While some who wouldn't have communicated with others now do so thanks to e-mail, wandering "is becoming a lost art," he said. "People are glued to their screens. Some don't look up from one day to the next."

Thomas Winship, retired editor of the *Boston Globe*, takes a similar valid lick, in an August 1991 article in *Editor & Publisher:*

There is no turning back to the typewriter-hot type days. The electronic newsroom has wrought too many miracles in production, cost savings, speed and efficiency. However, a psychological downside does exist. . . . More and more "bigfoot" reporters and columnists now work at home or go directly to their assignments from home. They seldom are seen at the water cooler. Example: Peter Gammons, the dazzling baseball writer, agreed to go to work for *Sports Illustrated* only if he could continue to work out of his home in Brookline, Massachusetts, on a home computer supplied by S.I. He files from home or the ballpark, does not even have a desk at *Sports Illustrated* in New York. Gammons represents a growing work pattern. [But] when the stars don't come to the office, it greatly diminishes the spirit, atmosphere and inspiration of the newsroom, especially for the young journalists who learn so much by schmoozing with those who have made it. . . .

"The newsroom sure isn't what it used to be," says Arthur Gelb, who recently retired as *New York Times* managing editor. "In times past, reporters and editors used to retire to the local saloon to collaborate, talk to others, and chew over how they should have handled stories." Now, Gelb has observed, "reporters talk to computers rather than to each other." . . .

Too often editors and reporters give, take and discuss story assignments via electronic message. It is just too easy for an editor to message instructions to a reporter or photographer rather than to get up off his backside and walk across the room to discuss a story in a give-and-take discussion. Or when in angry disagreement, what an easy way out it is for reporters or editors to vent their feelings via message rather than have a face-to-face confrontation. . . . Creating more togetherness is a tough one. One answer is holding more staff meetings and group discussions. Another is to subsidize a local pub.

The "clear" answer to the dilemma Boone and Winship describe is *do both*. On the one hand, mash people together to enhance project-team effectiveness (Oticon's mobile carts, 3M's "interactive nodes," Steelcase's "neighborhoods," IBM's "nonterritorial offices"). On the other hand, give them ready electronic access to insiders (as IBM and DEC do especially well) and outsiders, by the thousands, of all stripes, from all over. Or follow the IDG model: Create a "networked organization," with the electron as networker-in-chief; then spend money like crazy to bring people from all over the globe together on a regular basis.

But such a "clear" answer is, of course, glib—as the Hewlett-Packard vignette points out. Has HP "learned" more from linking up electronically than it has lost from the dent put in managing by wandering around? Solomon couldn't answer that. E-mail can be quite chatty. But even at its best, it's no local pub. Look back at Saxenian's description of Silicon Valley's strength: Some say conversations in the weight room at Santa Clara's yuppie Decathlon Club have given birth to more fruitful new products than many large nations have produced.

COMPUTER-AUGMENTED COLLABORATION, TRANSFORMING HUMAN INTERACTION FOR LEARNING'S SAKE

On the one hand, expert systems, electronic bulletin boards. On the other, former *Boston Globe* editor Thomas Winship's concern for the passing of heated debates at the saloon after work. Iconoclastic columnist Michael Schrage deals with both phenomena: His vision is electronic and utopian—and he understands that fully exploiting the new technology means much more than raw information-processing speed and capacity. "What's necessary isn't more communication," Schrage writes in *Shared Minds: The New Technologies of Collaboration*, "but rather a different quality of interaction." That new quality, he asserts, is collaboration:

> Real value in the sciences, the arts, commerce . . . comes largely from the process of collaboration. What's more, the quality and quantity of meaningful collaboration often depends upon the tools used to create it. . . . Collaboration is like romance . . . It can't be routine and predictable. People collaborate precisely because they don't know how to—or can't—deal effectively with the challenges that face them as individuals. . . . The issue isn't communication or teamwork—it's the creation of value. Collaboration describes a process of value creation that our traditional structures of communication and team work can't achieve.

Devising collaborative environments is the most significant organizational task confronting today's companies, Schrage claims. "Creative people must use their skills to devise environments that foster their work," psychologist Howard Gruber told Schrage; to do so, "they [must] invent new peer groups appropriate to their projects." The mecca of collaborative systems is Xerox's Palo Alto Research Center. Xerox's Terry Winograd and Fernando Flores, Schrage says, dismissed "the conventional perception of an organization as a bureaucracy or as clusters of teams and individuals: They see the organization as a 'network of conversations' where the design of communication doesn't just link people and places but also coordinates conversations for action."

Schrage contrasts a "communication-oriented environment," where "people discuss what they want to do and then go off and do what they think they've agreed upon," with a "collaborative environment," where "people spend as much time understanding what they are doing as actually doing it. . . . The thing that distinguishes collaborative communities from most other communities," he observes, "is this desire to construct new meanings about the world through interactions with others."

Schrage's research mostly deals with the new tools of collaboration. "No matter how novel, organizational structures aren't enough," he insists. "You need rooms to meet in, lights to see by, computers to link to, telephones to talk through. . . . Tools are, literally and figuratively, the way people come to grips with their work." Can there be, he wonders, such a thing as "convivial tools"? Conviviality, Schrage writes, "offers a different context in which to view the design and use of the organization's tools. . . . The desk is designed for individual use. So is the phone. The personal computer is just that: personal.

. . . The photocopier supports high-speed duplication of . . . individually generated memos and reports. On the surface, there's nothing wrong with that: Individuals need tools to support their work. There is nothing in the office, however, explicitly designed to support collaboration. . . . Tools designed to support collaboration will be qualitatively different from tools designed to support individuals."

The box is not entirely empty. "The felt tip pen and the paper napkins are collaborative tools," Schrage writes. "The blackboard [is] an astonishingly reliable and resilient collaborative tool. [It] may have served us well for hundreds of years, but maybe it's time for a change." Enter computer-augmented collaboration:

[Xerox's] Bernard DeKoven discovered that computer-generated shared space was the best way to get people to participate playfully in meetings. . . . [Xerox's Colab includes a] large screen [which] becomes a community computer screen where everyone can write, draw, scribble, sketch, type or otherwise toss up symbols for community viewing. It's shared space. People can produce on it or pollute it. . . . [The] traditional notions of conversational etiquette go out the window. . . . One person [may write] a controversial message on the community screen while another talks about something else. . . . Ostensibly, there may seem to be nothing revolutionary here, but exploring ideas and arguments in the context of shared space can completely transform conversation. The software injects a discipline and encourages people to create, visually and orally, a shared understanding with their colleagues. The technology motivates people to collaborate. . . .

When ideas become objects that can be [physically] manipulated, meetings become more concrete. . . . In this environment, oral contributions aren't the only way to participate. People can silently enter ideas for community consumption. Instead of having to wait your turn and risk having the glimmer of an idea evaporate into the ether, you can enter it into a special window on-screen without orally interrupting what's going on. . . . There is a complete record of what data, icons, and processes float across the shared space of the community screen. . . .

"Scroll wars" . . . "window wars" . . . The medium . . . engenders its own idiom and humor. When people dwell for too long on a point, some prankster might thrust the clock icon right into the middle of the screen, enlarging it to humongous size, and letting it tick away. People get the message. . . . Being in [an EDS] Capture Lab meeting is not unlike being in a production room editing a movie or being in the control room in the van directing the coverage of a football game. . . . There's a kinetic quality to the discussion and people feel that their words are tangible things—that they can reach out to the screen and move them around, edit them, blow them up or file them away. . . .

These rooms evoke different behaviors because they are designed to evoke different behaviors. Conversations have a different quality and urgency in these collaborative environments because the technology makes it easy to share information in profoundly different ways.

Not that it all happens automatically. "Fuzzy thinkers and people who have difficulty articulating their thoughts are penalized," Schrage, who is neither, acknowledges. "Participants who shotgun comments and digress look like muddled thinkers. Perhaps people defer too willingly to the glib participant who's always ready with a facile phrase." Despite such concerns, Schrage is an enthusiast. "The implication is clear," he writes. "Both executives and middle managers will spend a greater portion of their time collaborating on documents deemed important to their organizations. Budgets, training procedures, strategic plans, quarterly reports, and other documents will increasingly be produced collaboratively in real time, not processed in long cycles of draft and revision."

Schrage's enthusiasm is merited. And it should be taken with a grain of salt. Merited, in that almost everything we've said in these pages is in accord with his call for new forms of collaboration to aid knowledge workers, from the Union Pacific Railroad to McKinsey. On the other hand, extensive research on cognitive styles, for example, suggests that people vary greatly in their thinking habits. Some do well in open exchange. Others listen quietly to a three-hour debate, without making a single contribution—then take a walk in the foothills and produce a synthesis that moves several steps beyond the group's product. (And a few sit and listen for months, even years, then produce a genuine breakthrough—if their firms, with or without computers, are smart enough to tolerate the silence.) Schrage's love affair with the new tools doesn't scuttle the long-standing, well-placed fears that committees—no matter how terrific their tools—far more often rein in than spur creativity. In the vibrant software industry, for example, a surprising share of pacesetting products has come from bearded computer geeks living alone, deep in the hills of Northern California or Oregon. The relative absence of such geeks—and foothills—is among Japan's biggest disadvantages, vis-à-vis the U.S., in the software "race."

Electronic Communities

In the Summer 1991 issue of *Whole Earth Review*, Howard Rheingold takes a page out of Michael Schrage's book and writes of the enormous potential of creating electronic communities:

In the age of mass media, citizens and grass roots groups need an equalizer. The combination of personal computers and the telephone network might prove as important to citizens in the information age as the printing press has been for several centuries. The use of electronic mail services, computer bulletin-board systems, and computer conferencing systems as channels to make decisions and disseminate information can help grass roots political organizations, nonprofit groups, and other public interest groups to gather critical information, organize political action, sway public opinion and guide policy making. . . .

Tens of thousands of [computerized bulletin-board systems] are in operation in North America alone, most of them in people's homes, most of them single-line operations (which means that only one person can access the BBS at a time), many of them devoted to a specific area of interest (. . . politics at the left or right, skateboards or science fiction, computer games or ecology). BBSing has created a full-fledged subculture, with national conventions, paper publications, and local social events, all organized on-line. . . . There are even global networks of BBSs.

But the technology is far from the whole story. There must be motivation to make the connections. Rheingold continues:

Dave Hughes figured out how to use a BBS to exert political leverage on local government. Ask anybody in Colorado Springs, where Hughes made his first foray into electronic democracy because he wanted to find a way of letting local vendors, who had been shut out of bidding on the county computer contract, air their complaints. The press logged on, asked questions on-line, and confronted the county commissioners with the complaints and the facts they had compiled. "It got so hot that county staff members were observed reading from BBS printouts at the podium during formal readings," Hughes recalls. "In the end . . . the commissioners knuckled under, went to bid, the whole inefficient and incestuous system was exposed, and today there is a whole new approach to information management in the county. The key was that members of the press, who knew that something was wrong but lacked the technical expertise to ask the right questions, were able to use my BBS to meet, efficiently, with a wide range of experts, and thus tackle a difficult form of investigative journalism." For his next foray into BBS politics, Hughes invited a candidate for city council to post his views on Hughes's BBS, and to respond to questions from voters. The candidate was elected, and the councilman continues to use the BBS to communicate with his constituents.

AND DON'T IGNORE "CYBERSPACE"

In late 1991, The MIT Press delivered up *Cyberspace*. One chapter, by Steve Pruitt of Texas Instruments and Tom Barrett of EDS, is titled "Corporate Virtual Workspace":

The traditional equation of "labor + raw materials = economic success" is rapidly changing as American businesses approach the global, highly competitive markets of the twenty-first century. Strategic advantage now lies in the acquisition and control of information. . . . Corporations . . . are becoming bewilderingly diverse and geographically far-flung. The ability to bring dispersed assets effectively to bear on a single project or opportunity is becoming increasingly difficult. . . . The lumbering bureaucracies of this century will be replaced by fluid, interdependent groups of problem solvers. . . .

We believe that cyberspace technology will be a primary drive toward new corporate architectures. The technology will enable multidimensional, professional interaction and natural, intuitive work group formation. The technology will evolve to provide enterprises with what we call Corporate Virtual Workspaces (CVWs) as highly productive replacements for current work environments. . . . Having no need for physical facilities other than the system hosting the CVW, the cyberspace corporation will exist entirely in cyberspace.

With little need for startup capital, cyberspace corporations will form quickly around an individual or group of individuals who have identified an opportunity and formulated a market plan. Additional cyberspace workers will quickly be gathered from previous endeavors or new talent will be recruited. Profit shares will be apportioned across participating members.

The cyberspace corporation may provide a single product or service and then disband, or it may be formed with a longer-term vision and remain to serve the product's market. Other cyberspace firms may specialize in assuming ongoing maintenance of products if the developer decides to pursue other market opportunities.

Cyberspace corporations will be very fast-acting and transient. They will be composed of bright, creative, high-tech nomads who will coalesce into work units for dynamic market opportunities. Personnel turnover will be high as tasks are completed and cyberspace workers decide to migrate to other opportunities. As new corporations form, cyberspace workers may find themselves working periodically with the same people. A very productive informal network will form as cyberspace workers leverage their rich set of experiences and contacts.

Right On! (Sorry)

Do we really need such terms as "cyberspace" and "corporate virtual work-space"? On the one hand, such flighty terminology evades the practical concerns that former Union Pacific boss Mike Walsh and McKinsey's Brook Manville must deal with. (After all, aren't computer-augmented UPRR conductors and McKinsey's Rapid Response Network operating in a corporate virtual workspace?)

On the other hand, we do need to be stretched. The UPRR story really does amount to a lot more than "getting folks from multiple functions together with the aid of modern electronics and telecommunications." I side with Schrage (et al.). There's an opportunity—and a necessity—to reinvent the way humans converse ("convivial tools"?) to get things done. I hope these pages are loaded with helpful details. I also hope that the new language, even if irritating, is a constant reminder of just how fundamental this shift to a "knowledge-based society" really is.

29

Knowledge Management Structures IV: Developing and Tapping Expert Power in the Hierarchy-less Organization

Social workers are like all professional groups. The whole basis of their professionalism is that they know better. . . . Professionals naturally resist any suggestion that other people could do their jobs just as well with less training or no training at all, and what they fear most is that people could manage without them. . . . Every profession, as George Bernard Shaw observed, is a conspiracy against the lay person. Keeping professionals under control will always be a struggle. The aim must be to reduce their power, to increase the citizen's redress against them, to make them more accountable. Above all, we should question the extent to which we need them at all.

PETER WILBY, reporting in
The Independent (London)
April 14, 1991

We are shifting beyond traditional hierarchy. Splitting firms into bits is part of it. Breaking down functional barriers is another. Both ideas suggest dramatic improvements in communication among formerly isolated functional baronies, and the demise of most middle ranks in those baronies, so that the front-line players in one function can readily deal with front-line players in another (to get today's task done, to improve a process, to fix a problem, or to take advantage of a fleeting market opportunity with little or no muss and fuss). But one can go much further—toward the wholesale destruction of the functions themselves and, then, to "projectizing" the entire firm.

A "NEW LOGIC OF EXPERTISE"

Functions, functional stovepipes, whatever, "are history," as the kids say. But before initialing the epitaph, let's remember why those stovepipes grew so tall in the first place. As organizations became complex (e.g., nation-spanning), the demand for "white-collar" talent grew exponentially—enter, for example, the railroads' big, expert mechanical, engineering, finance, purchasing, and personnel departments. Now we are "destroying" those "functions." Implied, if we're not very careful, is the denigration of expertise per se. That's hardly the point. To the contrary, in our knowledge-based society, expertise (and thence knowledge management) has never been so important. It's just that we can't abide the conventional form in which it has been offered, which slows things down and, à la the old Union Pacific, disempowers those closest to the action.

These chapters on knowledge management structures amount to a search for a "new logic of expertise," fit for the fashionized marketplace. Let's now sketch the evolution of expertise in the corporation, from its useful beginnings 125 years ago to the heights of wretched excess it reached in the 1980s, to a revised look for tomorrow. The from-yesterday's-to-tomorrow's-expertise argument is summarized below:

1. <u>Our experts were not as expert as we thought</u>. The *idea* animating the functional organization made lots of sense: It takes a lifetime to learn, and then keep up with, your discipline. But as functional bureaucracies grew, that wasn't always how things turned out. A not especially cynical executive described the loss of a veteran functional specialist/"expert" this way: "It's not as if we lost twenty-three years of experience. We lost one year of experience, repeated twenty-two times." Tragically, the average central staff expert isn't so expert after all. Unfortunately, "learning" has not been very near the top of the priority list in the typical purchasing, accounting, training, or personnel department—and that's saying it kindly.

"Experts" were transmogrified mostly into "policemen," overseeing the manual that defined their function's responsibility to the corporation. Yes, the manual changed every year. But the changes usually amounted to additional "not-to-do's" rather than "how-to-help's." So the typical expert became a drag on action, Mr. (or, of late, Ms.) "Why-it-can't-be-done-that-way." While systematic evidence is scant, my observations over the last quarter century suggest that the average "expert"—on a big corporate staff, at least—probably doesn't devote more than 5 percent of his time to learning new techniques. (Sure, he might go to the annual meeting of the Electronics Industry Purchasing Officer Trade Association, but it's mainly to see old buddies from last year and have a company-paid week on the town.)

Such a state of affairs would be unusual for effective, independent "professionals"/"experts" who perform in the marketplace. To stay in business, whether surgeons or independent CPAs, they must devote lots of "homework time" to learning the newest twists and wrinkles. By contrast, how many corporate purchasing department staffers do you know who religiously—once or twice a week, say—do real "homework," such as reading journal articles, as the *average* surgeon or independent CPA does? Not many, I fear.

2. <u>Furthermore, the functional disciplines are not so arcane/complex as the experts made them out to be</u>. As the Peter Wilby epigraph suggests, it's fair to say that one of the roles of experts is to surround their disciplines with witches' brew, hubba-hubba, and other trappings that make them *appear* to be very difficult, and inaccessible to anyone other than a master. Yet as companies have turned over accounting chores to the front line (save the most complex SEC reporting), they've invariably found, if their commitment has been genuine, that the *average* front-line person can quickly take on lots of the routine, and even not-so-routine, work. So, too, with purchasing, engineering, selling, even (per the strange ways of Johnsonville's Ralph Stayer) strategic planning.

One of the holy writs of the quality movement has been "get rid of the quality department." Prior to the surge of quality concern in the '80s, Americans had been accumulating "expertise" in quality for 50 or more years. However, it turned out that people at the front line were fully capable of doing fishbone cause-and-effect diagramming, Pareto analysis (counting errors by a more complicated name), and any number of basic (and advanced) statistical manipulations—and they had a lot better idea about what ought to be measured/counted than distant staffers. (The "expert" staffers didn't even do Pareto analyses until they were pressured from the outside—at which point they began claiming that only they were fit to do them.)

3. <u>Which is not to say there is no need for expertise</u>. When I cry "destroy the functions," I'm not suggesting that accounting and purchasing and MIS and quality and production scheduling aren't important. They *are* important. Expertise in these areas is imperative! Firms need more of it, not less of it. The expert work must be done. The issue is how—and where—to do it. And the answer, increasingly, is that it need not be done in isolated, "on-high" (corporate, sector, group, division) functional departments given to overseeing thousands of pages of stagnant, ever more elaborate (not to be mistaken for clever) manuals.

4. Most experts/expertise should be—and can be—shifted to work teams/
manufacturing cells/clusters/project groups. At Titeflex, recall, the production control operation disappeared, instantly "excessing" some 30 "experts."
Most ended up within new manufacturing cells. They took the legitimate part
of their expertise closer to the action, as part of a coherent, self-contained
"business"/team. As a rule of thumb (per the likes of ABB), at least 80 percent,
and perhaps 95 percent, of "experts" at the division, group, sector, or corporate level can be folded into self-contained operating units, project groups,
clusters, manufacturing cells.

There are a host of ways to approach the issue. At General Electric's
lighting panel boards operation in Salisbury, North Carolina, for example,
self-managing teams semiannually elect persons to fulfill expert roles—e.g.,
quality, safety and housekeeping, training, production scheduling. (I'll talk
about how such persons can become/stay skilled later.) At Johnsonville
Foods, the would-be quality guru of a team more or less elects herself—i.e.,
expresses an interest and starts taking courses. If she demonstrates competence
to her teammates, they'll likely appoint her lead person for, in this case, team
quality. (And she can even aspire to be a roving super-expert, helping other
teams—if those teams want help and deem her work to be of value.)

5. There is/can be/ought to be a vestigial structure to oversee this new
scheme. Consider GE's lighting panel boards operation again: Elected team
leaders in a given discipline meet with each other and an "adviser" on a weekly
basis to discuss activities/problems/opportunities. The adviser can be a genuine expert in a given discipline (finance, human resources) or simply a senior
manager, from any function, who volunteers to act as overseer (coach, cheerleader) for a discipline. The OPP Three at McKinsey plays a similar role in a
very different setting—administering an area of expertise for thousands. At the
highest level, each of the 65 bare-bones Business Area staffs at ABB performs
a like mission for its numerous companies and profit centers.

6. There _are_ clear responsibilities that a "coordination group" or individual team member responsible for expertise takes on. Coordinators/designated
experts/emergent experts take on responsibility for education: their own and
that of others. "Others" might mean (a) the rest of the team in the case of a
team-appointed quality coordinator; (b) a group of team quality coordinators;
or (c) the entire plant or division in the case of an "emergent" quality expert
who takes it upon himself or herself to teach an important skill (as at Quad/
Graphics, Johnsonville).

The new-look coordinator/expert's activities might include: (a) perpetually surveying the field, reading the literature, attending appropriate seminars
and courses; (b) calling in a consultant, for a lengthy analytic engagement or
to give a short course, say, to quality coordinators, selected work teams, or the
unit/plant/division as a whole; (c) taking "sabbaticals" to update or expand
skills (a work team's quality coordinator, for example, might go off to a

customer operation or a university to pick up a particular technique that can subsequently be transplanted back into his or her unit); (d) becoming a "rover" for three to nine months, teaching others within work groups/cells/ clusters/project organizations some particular, or generic, skills which he or she has mastered; and/or (e) forming special project teams to accomplish a one-off "expert" project (for example, revising project accounting practices).

7. <u>The bottom line is volunteer-driven, speedy learning.</u> All of the above is marked by *volunteerism* (people stepping forward and deciding they want to be experts, as at Johnsonville, Oticon, Quad/Graphics, or McKinsey) and *perpetual learning* (finding out what's going on, passing it on to others, and having the "space," including time and financial support, to do just that). Ideally, there will be no "average" team members! Each member should choose a special skill area in which she or he then behaves in a decidedly *un*average fashion—i.e., assumes fairly broad responsibilities. The new requirement for the typical worker, then, is three major steps beyond yesterday's "pair of hands": She or he should (a) be multiskilled; (b) choose and master an area of special competence; and (c) transmit that special knowledge to others, within and beyond the work team's borders.

8. <u>And there may still be a role for a "central staff."</u> A bare-bones "central" activity, in any given skill area, could consist (or not) of the following:

— No one. Let the coordinators at the team/unit level be wholly responsible. Or use self-managed coordinator groups (quality, etc.) for maintaining/enhancing special knowledge.

— An executive who takes on, as an ancillary task, oversight of a skill area—acting as facilitator to the various groups/teams/projects/local experts/coordinators.

— A tiny, *non*-expert staff. At the Union Pacific Railroad, for example, strategic planners are not "professionals," but line operatives who move into the function for a couple of years. (It amounts to a win/win situation. Such strategic planners have no stake in building up a bureaucracy—it will only come back to haunt them when they return to the line. Moreover, they will return carting an invaluable experience.)

— A tiny staff of more-or-less permanent experts, who spend 75 to 90 percent of their time "on the road" (in the factory, at other operations), acting as "consultant to" basic business units, showing up only when called.

— A tiny group of "consultants," as above, plus one or two of the "world's greatest" in a given area. Value-added in the corporation increasingly comes from nontraditional sources—information systems, accounting, purchasing, quality, distribution. (Rather than the old favorites—marketing, sales, engineering.) Companies ought to do "traditional" R&D in such areas, and should therefore try to engage a handful of wild, woolly, dedicated wizards who can conjure new ways of using these disciplines to reinvent the enterprise. For example, in companies with over $250 million in sales, consider creating corporate vice-presidential positions for the following: (a) knowledge management, (b) perceived quality and brand equity management, (c) innovation processes, (d) time-based management, (e) industrial design, and (f) horizontal-systems integration. But note: Incumbents—"horizontal vice presidents"?—should each be supported by no more than two full-time professional staffers.

Review this discussion. The role of special, professional knowledge is exalted, not dismissed. However, very nontraditional approaches are suggested for tapping into and applying knowledge—approaches that keep "experts" from becoming internally focused, creating grand baronies, or oriented toward police work (maintaining their function's "integrity" and hoarding information/knowledge at the expense of the wider organization's total learning).

As usual, there is a caveat. Tomorrow's "suits" must truly believe that the average person is able to learn the rudiments of computers, accounting, purchasing, quality, statistical methods, engineering, and so on. Otherwise, the front line will smell the mistrust from the top, and none of this will come to pass.

Going Home

For the last 100 years or so ("specialization" has been on the rise for 175 years, "professionalism" for 125, "M.B.A.-ism" for 50), we've assumed that there is one place where expertise should reside: with "expert" staffs at division, group, sector, or corporate. And another, very different, place where "the (*mere*) work gets done." The new organizing regimen puts expertise back, close to the action—as it was in craft-oriented, pre-industrial revolution days. (And it utilizes the new technologies to allow widely dispersed front-line experts unfettered access to one another.) We are not, then, ignoring "expertise" at all. We are simply shifting its locus, expanding its reach, giving it new respect—and acknowledging that *everyone* must be an expert in a fast-paced, fashionized world.

The New-Look Professional Takes Stock

David Maister, a Harvard Business School professor turned consultant, is the premier student of professional service firms. He has examined how such firms maintain—or lose—their knowledge-based edge. Then he took a long look at himself. Here's an excerpt from Maister's "How's Your Asset?":

At the end of my first full year as [an independent] management consultant . . . I decided to take stock. How healthy was my career? I quickly discovered a disturbing paradox. My income statement was fantastic, but my balance sheet was deteriorating so badly I was in danger of ruining my career, i.e., going out of business.

Just before starting my consulting career I had published a few articles which had caught the attention of my target clientele. . . . The consequence was that I was incredibly busy. . . . But was my business (and/or my career) truly healthy? . . . The first group of assets on which my career was based was my inventory of knowledge and skills. Professionals get paid for their time, but that's not what we sell. We sell knowledge and skill. The second (potential) asset was my client relationships. Much to my surprise, I discovered that both had deteriorated badly.

The problem with my knowledge and skills was that I hadn't learned anything new. By definition, the unsolicited phone calls requesting my services had been for things that I was already known for. Even though each client project was customized (to a degree), I found myself doing basically very similar work for a variety of clients. I had not added to my abilities. What was even more shocking (and depressing) was the realization that not only had I not grown my asset, but its value on the market was going down—rapidly. Left untended, knowledge and skill, like all assets, depreciate in value—surprisingly quickly. . . .

It . . . became clear that my client relations would have a high value if and only if the next time the client had a problem in my field of interest, I had a high probability of getting the job. . . . But the truth was, that wasn't the case. I realized that having done "one thing" (or a limited set of things) for a wide variety of clients meant that I really hadn't developed relationships that promoted the chances of me getting their next (interesting) assignment. . . .

In sum, I learned that unless I actively worked at it, my career prospects would inevitably decline, even when (or perhaps especially when) I was making lots of money. Having a good current year financially was clearly a necessary condition for my success, but it was far from being a sufficient condition. Keeping my career moving forward, even staying level, was going to take conscious effort. . . . .

That's what I learned in my first year. Since then, I have learned that these experiences were not just the problems of the early stages of a career. In fact, the more "successful" I got in later years, the greater was the temptation to exploit existing skills and relationships and the harder I had to work to make sure that I didn't just cruise, letting my balance sheet slip away unexamined.

After having observed thousands of partner-level professionals in a wide variety of professions in numerous countries, I conclude that [these lessons apply] not only to me, but to every professional, at any stage in his or her career. . . . Whether you are 25 or 55, you will always need to worry about where your career is going from today. As you think about your career, here are some questions to ponder: In what way are you personally more valuable on the marketplace than last year? What are your plans to make yourself more valuable in the marketplace than in the past? What specific new skills do you plan to acquire or enhance in the next year? What's your personal strategic plan for your career over, say, the next three years? What, precisely, is it that you want to be famous for?

30

The Trauma of Buying into "Horizontal," "Whole," and "Learning to Learn"

The project at the end of the millennium is to go against fragmentation. . . . I sense that this is true in all fields.

ILYA PRIGOGINE, 1977
Nobel prize–winner in chemistry
New Perspectives Quarterly
Spring 1992

Learning to learn as a matter of (corporate) course, taking the broader view (the essence of learning for the work team or buckyborg) is an enormous issue. It requires a new "sociology."

GOING "HORIZONTAL"

"The traditional job descriptions were barriers," a Motorola exec was quoted as saying in *Target*, the journal of the Association for Manufacturing Excellence. "We needed an organization soft enough between the organizational disciplines so that the hand-off process was fuzzy, so that people could run freely across functional barriers or organizational barriers with the common goal of getting the job done rather than just making certain that their specific part of the job was completed."

I get a real buzz when I hear Motorolans using words like "soft" and "fuzzy." Motorola is a hard-nosed, engineering-driven firm. But it was among the first of the elderly giants to recognize that such functional barriers must be destroyed. And getting comfortable with words like "soft" and "fuzzy" is imperative to that process. (More imagery.) That's one good reason why organization charts are so damned misleading today. Just try and capture the essence of M^2 on an $8\frac{1}{2}$-by-11-inch piece of paper!

But if you could, your diagram would be oriented at a 90° angle to normal organization pictures. Roald Nomme, a former Scandinavian Air System executive, comments that a customer experiences the airline "horizontally"—a baggage handler at the front entrance to the airport, then a check-in desk person, then a gate person, then a flight attendant, and so on. The customer has an overall "SAS experience." That customer's "slice" is antithetical to the conventional way firms have been "organized." While the customer's view is completely horizontal, the functionally conceived organization goes about most of its work via vertical, often noncommunicative "departments" (baronies, fiefdoms, imperial states).

And one more. Consider a hotel: Each worker you connect with—at the bellstand or front desk, from room service or housekeeping—is normally part of a different, "vertical" (functional) department. Yet your experience of the hotel is completely "horizontal." You experience "Hyatt." You don't think of "an experience with Hyatt's housekeeping *department*," "an experience with Hyatt's room service *department*," etc. So it is, too, in your dealings with IBM, Buckman Labs, or MCI.

All the Way Over, Damn It!

It's difficult to exaggerate the importance of this idea. Or its special relevance to a fashionized, high-speed world. Customer perceptions are "horizontal." Fast product development is "horizontal." Partnering and networking are "horizontal" (the spiderweb versus pyramid imagery). Learning is "horizontal." Not "substantially" horizontal. Not "significantly" horizontal. All-the-way horizontal!

"Horizontal" versus "vertical" is a highly abstract formulation, I admit. But no idea—not one—in this book is more important. Flip that axis. ABB is starting to, via its T50 process. The Union Pacific is on its way. David Kelley Design and Imagination and McKinsey and M^2 and EDS and CNN were born that way.

One, Two, Three, all together, *flip that axis.*

THE "SOCIOLOGY" OF GOING HORIZONTAL

In 1991 Gary Kasparov successfully defended his world chess title. Do you suppose, with that bridge crossed a second time, he's now looking for a "promotion"? A chance to move "up the ladder"? Could Kasparov be lobbying to become head of the International Chess Federation? How silly, eh?

If you laughed at this example, why do you also laugh at the idea of "horizontal promotion"? Because the fact is, it must become part and parcel—a social mainstay—of the new, hierarchy-less, horizontal, project-driven organization. There's not going to be much of a pyramid left to climb.

So how will people get their kicks—their bucks, their psychic compensation? For hundreds of years we've enjoyed the perks as much as the pay increases: the car, then the bigger car; the secretary, then a pair of secretaries; various stages of progressively greater isolation in our offices.

Honestly, now, that's the *real* "career progression," isn't it? Office in a bullpen. Then four-foot partition. Ceiling-to-floor partition. Secretary's desk outside. Secretary gets an attached office, too. Now add an anteroom. Then on to the executive corridor, with a "general pre-anteroom," followed by your own anteroom. Now add security guards. Joy of joys, the real world never intrudes anymore!

Ho, ho, ho! But many at my seminars don't laugh. "They," I am repeatedly told, want those trappings. Not "*we*," mind you. "*They*." "They" have great difficulties with the idea of shifting to a horizontally driven organization. I am sympathetic. We in the U.S. have a more substantial entrepreneurial bent than almost any other nation. It's OK for a young American to aspire to entrepreneurship, to go to work in a smallish company. But it's not *that* OK. Down deep, most parents hope that their Janie or Johnny will go into engineering at 3M, marketing at PepsiCo, financial services at Morgan Guaranty, and so on. We may be a lot "better" than the average German on this—but the more apt phrase is probably "somewhat less worse." We still admire those huge firms, and want, for our son and daughter (and ourselves), progression "up the ladder," with all the attendant trappings.

(The issue is especially nettlesome—even poignant—for women and minorities. In the last 20 years, they have finally begun to "make it," in fairly sizable numbers, into the middle and upper-middle reaches of the hierarchy. And now that hierarchy is fast disappearing before their eyes—along with the toehold so painstakingly gained. There are no easy answers. For me to try and sell the joys of "horizontal promotion" to a woman or African-American held back for years by the old-boy network is the worst sort of hypocrisy. I do offer a ray of hope: Because women and minorities have only recently joined the middle management ranks, they are less likely to be caught up in its bureaucratic ways; and many, frustrated by the glass ceiling, have already struck out on their own. Perhaps members of an M^2-like network, they are in the vanguard. It's the old-boy club that will, I suspect, eventually be at a disadvantage, because of the inflexibility of mind that club "membership" carries with it. The problem is that in the short run, the "outsiders" newly arrived to middle management may bear the brunt of the cuts, while the senior old boys will mostly remain in place.)

For large firms trying to "go horizontal," shifting the locus of prestige from "going up" to something much more fundamental—"Doing something more interesting than you've done before"—is a monstrous hurdle. It's one *more* reason, I can't help adding, that the professional service firm, with its wholesale project orientation, is such an apt model for the future—especially an apt "social" model. The average denizen of a professional service firm who does well on project X (helping a modest-sized company with this or that) aspires to a bigger team, a bigger and more complex and challenging problem. Such an aspiration may indeed have several dimensions of "more." But "more" (more complex, etc.) is *not* the same as more "up." To the contrary, the aspiration is unmistakably "horizontal"—to stay with the project team, the real work of the organization, but to do it in a context that provides increasing complexity and excitement (and, over time, remuneration). At McKinsey, the majority would rather be known as "the guy/gal who's got Hewlett-Packard [as *my* client]" than "the XYZ office manager."

Sure, at McKinsey or EDS, or even Imagination, there are some who take a shine to "firm politics." And God bless them, said most of us at McKinsey in my day. There is a need to "manage," even in the very horizontal and project-oriented firm. Those willing to do so were heaven-sent. (Especially since they weren't more highly compensated than the top project consultants.)

The world's best poker players don't hanker for jobs in casino management any more than Kasparov wants to be a chess bureaucrat. The average world-class pianist doesn't aspire to be musical director of a symphony company. And the average writer doesn't aspire to be a publisher, either. In fact, in most walks of life—outside big, industrial-revolution organizations—it is "normal" to want to "do something better/more interesting," not to "move up."

There's not a shred of self-sacrifice involved in all this. There's no pining for sackcloth. Indeed, at McKinsey as in major league baseball, the stars—the very best project-team consultants—make a ton of money. As they do more and better, they make more money—and few are known to turn down raises. In fact, like ballplayers, they want to make more, and want everyone to know it. The bucks are mainly a way of "keeping score," for senior McKinsey directors every bit as much as for José Canseco.

Fine, you say. But how do I bring about a corporate social revolution in which horizontal movement is revered? A few gutsy champions in the organization who are willing to take on an exciting "horizontal" task, rather than make the next, "normal" move up the hierarchy, can send an important signal. A participant at one of our executive seminars did just that. He'd recently been promoted "up" into top management. Finding that committee meetings were filling his days and keeping him from implementing changes he deemed imperative, this fellow stunned colleagues by initiating a demotion for himself and taking charge of a moderate-sized operating unit "down" the organization. While it's too early to tell, his outrageous act may serve as a beacon to others in the firm, encouraging others to risk the unconventional. (At the very least, he reports, he's having a lot of fun.)

At the Union Pacific Railroad, former chief Mike Walsh perpetually talked up "going horizontal"—leading important projects not associated with steps up the ladder—as the essence of career progression. Pay schemes, of course, must reinforce such budding resolve. There must be hard, visible evidence, for example, that stellar researchers who continue to produce, but don't wish to manage research activities, can earn as much (or more) as those who opt for high-sounding administrative posts. Semco's Ricardo Semler did this with a maverick band of innovators who didn't take a shine to management; their charge was, instead, to create new product lines—and they shared significantly in the profits when they did so.

The path to the more distant future is less murky. You begin at the beginning—with "straight talk" at the outset of the recruiting process, making it clear that "getting ahead" means moving laterally, perhaps even "downward" upon occasion, to build skills and tackle more challenging assignments not necessarily associated with "ladder climbing." To abet this, in modest or immodest fashion (it's very immodest in consulting firms—where project work starts on day one), new hires should quickly (within weeks?) become part of a project team. If steps "through" ("up?") more challenging projects are demonstrably the norm from the start, then the attraction to the trappings of hierarchy never gets established in the first place.

"Horizontal promotion" is a necessity, not a nicety, in a world of fast-changing, fragmented markets. Companies by and large will grow in a "flat" rather than pyramidal direction—à la IDG, CCT, and Acordia. When a monolithic, functionally organized chemical company wakes up and finds 80 percent of revenue coming from specialty—fashion/boutique—chemicals, then its organization had best become all-the-way "horizontal," fast.

ACQUIRING PERIPHERAL VISION

Wal-Mart's matchless information systems allow it to make decisions with blinding speed. Despite the power of the high-tech scheme, though, top Wal-Mart execs still spend at least two days a week in the marketplace. Ask why and you get an unenlightening "Because it's the right thing to do." Say what? In *Future Perfect*, consultant Stan Davis helps explain when he describes top foreign exchange traders as "intuitive, [having] an inner sense of oneness with currency flows. . . . They see things as a totality." An inner sense of oneness with the market—that's precisely why those top execs at Wal-Mart religiously schmooze in the stores each week!

In any event, the need to speed up all processes, work with more partners in more complex networks, and bridge any remaining functional barriers within the firm means that all employees, top boss to temporary broom-wielder, must learn to think in "wholes." (We need "metaphors of wholeness," Shoshana Zuboff writes in *In the Age of the Smart Machine*.) But such an innocent-sounding requirement runs counter to our long-standing penchant for increasing specialization. By the end of World War II, we had disaggregated whole jobs to the point where some plants had 500 hourly job classifications. (Recall that St. Vincent Hospital in Indianapolis had almost 600 specialties—see page 229.) Sadly, this glorious history has turned on us with a vengeance, now that new foundations for competitive advantage are emerging.

False Start

> The myth is that learning can be guaranteed if instruction is delivered systematically, one small piece at a time, with frequent tests to ensure that students and teachers stay on the track. . . . Nobody learns anything, or teaches anything, by being submitted to such a regimen of disjointed, purposeless, confusing, tedious activities. Teachers burn out, pupils fall by the wayside, and parents and administrators worry about the lack of . . . progress . . . or interest.
>
> Frank Smith
> *Insult to Intelligence: The*
> *Bureaucratic Invasion of*
> *Our Classrooms*

The place where an emphasis on "wholes" and "horizontal" might begin, our schools, is one of the worst examples of verticality and fragmentation. "The large high school," said Ted Sizer, head of the Coalition of Essential Schools, in an exchange reported in *Harper's*, "is a product of the so-called efficiency movement, the pre–World War I fantasy that, following [time and motion expert] Frederick Taylor's industrial principles, saw the school as a place where certain rivets were hammered into the heads of indistinguishable units, each of which was called a child."

Alas, in the K-12 system today we find:

• Steep administrative hierarchies. New York City's public school bureaucracy, for example, has an administrator-to-student ratio that's 60 *times* higher than that of the more "wholistic," classroom-focused New York City parochial school system.

• "Vertical" aspirations. "Principal" is actually short for principal teacher. Sadly, most principals today avoid the classroom like the plague, and aim only to get out of the school and get on with climbing the administrative ladder.

- Micromanagement. "Downtown" (the administrators) often requires teachers to prepare detailed lesson plans—and then turns around and prescribes exactly what should go in them. Under the benign heading of "coverage," for example, you might well find a mandate to handle the Civil War in 2.3 class hours, with 9 minutes allotted to the Battle of Gettysburg. Honest! To engage students, Sizer contends in his masterful *Horace's Compromise: The Dilemma of the American High School*, they must understand why they are asked to do something, must comprehend that the material they're confronted with "leads somewhere," must somehow be allowed to take "ownership of exercises." Teachers, says Sizer, should be providing "fewer answers and insisting [that students] find the . . . answers themselves." Learning, he adds, "is messy [and] explaining must be incessant." The problem: The system doesn't trust teachers or students, doesn't tolerate messiness, doesn't allow time to explain. Ironically, Sizer continues, "It is the athletic coach, often arrogantly dismissed by some academic instructors as a kind of dumb ox, unworthy of being called a real teacher, who may be the school's most effective teacher of skills." The athletic coach *does* coach, *does* demonstrate, *does* take time to explain—and "downtown" offers no objections whatsoever.

- Fragmented days. A typical school day is chopped into 50-minute bits called "classes." Ridiculous, yes. But that's only the start: Mix in public address system interruptions, constant assemblies, and other disruptions—and forget getting involved in learning. What *should* happen, according to Sizer, adds up to "less is more," one of his most oft-repeated rallying cries. Translation: "Fewer areas taught in longer blocks of time," with plenty of space for coaching, explaining, and personalization. "As the major goal of education is developing the intellect, the very exercise of explaining ends and means and gaining agreement is itself educational," Sizer notes. "The essential word throughout is *why*, which is the central interrogative of all learning." The props under the learning, examining, questioning classroom are philosophic. "Respect more and patronize [students] less," Sizer demands. "[Teachers] can help by trusting, asking much and holding [students] accountable." The classroom, he adds, should become a place of high expectations.

- Monster schools that destroy a sense of community (wholeness). Pioneering New York City principal Deborah Meier argues that only smaller schools will permit effective teacher empowerment, engender trust that comes from knowing one another, head off bad behavior, and support the teaching of civic values (through communal involvement in the successes and failures of daily life). "Unless schools think small," Meier wrote in *The New York Times* in September 1989, "no reform is possible." The answer: Think buckyborg and replace industrially inspired memorization factories with units of 250 or fewer students. That doesn't mean we need to torch the big schools. "Large school buildings can house many schools," according to Meier. In East Harlem, for example, 51 autonomous, independent schools are nested in 19 former big-school facilities.

- Fill-in-the-blanks tests and workbooks that turn teachers and students into automatons. Life is not about filling in the blanks. Neither is learning! Sizer encourages "final exhibitions" of learning—high school equivalents to college theses.

- Students as "rivet heads." Students aren't treated as active learners, according to Sizer. Instead, they are assaulted with irrelevant bits of knowledge in narrow subject areas, taught in tiny doses. Students are not passive receptacles, Sizer points out, although we often treat them that way. "The contrast between energy on the [after-school] jobs and lassitude in the classroom is striking," he adds. Kids understand the game and become "good at dumbness. The most important strategy for [classroom] survival is docility." Sizer provides a striking example from his research:

> Brody [a teacher] finally turned to history and announced that the purpose of this class was "to cover Chapter 6." . . . [He] moved through the text, slowly asking a question of no one in particular and then slowly answering it himself. The students quietly watched this performance. The door to the classroom was open, and three times student messengers from the office came in and consulted with Brody. . . . After each interruption, Brody continued. Several students had their notebooks open, but neither they nor anyone else took notes. . . . [T]he class eventually petered out to a quiet, genial chatter between Brody and the students. Brody ended the session with the announcement that a test would be given later in the week and that "you should know what will be on it." That much was clear: The questions that Brody had been himself asking were copies (it soon became clear to me) of those at the chapter's end in the text. These were what was expected. Memorize those, and you're home. . . . It would be nice to report that Brody's class is an exception. It is not. The agreement between teacher and students to exhibit a facade of orderly purposefulness is a Conspiracy for the Least, the least hassle for anyone. . . . This was a happy school. Attendance was up. Fights were down. Scores were up (from abysmal to merely embarrassing). In all, that school was a place of friendly, orderly, uncontentious, wasteful triviality.

"Doc" Littky's Gospel of Projects, Wholes, and Horizontal

There's Sizer's "Brody." And then there's Winchester, New Hampshire, high school principal Dennis Littky, whom I interviewed in 1988 in connection with a television show. Projects? Wholes? Horizontal? Learning to learn? "Doc," as he's called, could have written the book on it.

Julia B. Thayer High School's principal, teachers, parents, other community members, and students spent over a year hammering out their one-page "Philosophy and Goals" statement. Consider the third and fourth sentences: "We want to develop the desire for the skills necessary for continuous learning. We must educate our children in the most appropriate way so that they can become the best they can be." It wasn't easy to write, but it was easier to put on paper than to execute. Especially when the 300 Thayer High students, in a community fast losing its industrial base, had the nickname "the animals," a fair indication of their low discipline level and the very low level of self-esteem that went along with it. Teachers' esteem was at rock-bottom, too.

But today, under Littky's watchful eye, Thayer classrooms buzz, a direct outcropping of his philosophy of engagement. "The classes where the kids enjoy, there is no behavior problem," Littky said, "and the kids enjoy when they're involved. If they're doing a science experiment, and they're doing it because they care about it, then they don't sit back and draw pictures and yell at the teacher."

Consider:

The "Thayer 500 (cm)" group lab problem 2: The concepts of potential and kinetic energy can be demonstrated with the help of an automobile. Problem: For this lab, your group is challenged to create a racing vehicle which shows how potential energy can change into kinetic energy. Your group will have five days to construct an entry into the official "Thayer 500 (cm)" race. The racecourse will be on the floor of Room 5 and will consist of a tape trace 500 centimeters in length.

Rules: (1) Your group must work alone. (2) You may only enter one vehicle. . . . (3) There is no limit to the position or amount of dead weight placed in, on or around your machine as long as it is attached to your machine and finishes with your machine. No pulley systems may be attached to your vehicle. (4) You may not use any electrical devices. . . . (9) All materials used must be found or inexpensive. (10) You may not start your vehicle using any outside force other than gravity.

Evaluation: Evaluations will be based on: completion of daily records sheets, group effort and finished product. . . . Good luck!

Though I'm a credentialed engineer, I don't remember much about potential and kinetic energy. I bet that's because my tenth-grade physics teacher, a fine enough fellow, didn't have the imagination or energy to create the "Severn [my high school] 500 (cm)." But Mrs. Toner, who taught eighth grade at Thayer High, did. And engaged her kids. It almost seems superfluous to add that they learned more than if their "goal" had been to ace a multiple-choice or fill-in-the-blanks test.

There's nothing "soft" about all this. It's not a reversion to the well-intentioned but often misguided "do-whatever-you-want" philosophy of open classrooms in the 1960s. Littky and his teachers are rigorous and emphasize the basics in a set of precise "exit skills" to be achieved in every course. But rote memorization is out (yet another form of specialization—heaven forbid that we should design tests that can't be electronically marked), and essays are in. "You still need your timelines," said one history teacher, "but they're not an end in themselves." Instead, the facts are almost always embedded in something vital—applying the study of American history to the 1992 presidential elections; employing the axioms of both a science course and a politics course to analyze the acid rain issue, so important to rural New Hampshire.

Littky spoke about the four "Rs" rather than the characteristic three. He added *responsibility* (for self and others) to reading, 'riting, and 'rithmetic. Ever so gentle, yet commanding more respect from students and teachers than any leader I've observed anywhere, he is masterful at engendering self-responsibility. "I'm in the bathroom with five kids who are hanging out," he recalled, "and I said, 'Look at this joint.' And they said, 'Yeah, it's sick, isn't it?' Even though they, probably, were the ones who put their cigarettes on the floor and knocked down the tiles. And I said, 'What can we do? Would you guys be willing to paint?' 'Yeah.' 'Would you be willing to come in on the weekends?' 'Great.' 'What color?' 'Er, ah, blue, I think, would be good.' I went out, got the paint. They came in, boys who barely could come to school during the week came in on a Saturday, and we painted all day. They were proud of that place. So that's the kind of thing that gets kids committed to something." Now the bathroom is the kids' responsibility—not Doc's, the teachers', or the custodial staff's.

But it's not that Littky thinks rules are useless. To the contrary. He's a demon about them. Yet his philosophy about regulations is unconventional in school circles, to say the least:

"There were a lot of rules here. Lots of negative notes going home, so everyone was afraid of school. You open up a letter from school, and it had five things saying your kid's horrible in this, horrible in this, horrible in this. . . .

"We sat down in advisory committee and asked kids what the rules should be. Kids did surveys. We finally put down the ten things that kids thought needed rules. Then the faculty and I came up with the rules, then sent them back to the kids, back to the staff, then passed it back and forth until we finally came up with some very clear stuff.

"It was all built around respect. We don't have a lot of rules. We have a few rules, and we're very clear that we don't tolerate breaking them at this school. Everybody knows them, and that's it. Even though they might have been the same rules that they'd had before, the kids had been involved. We weren't tricking anybody: They went through the process, and we went through the process."

Nonetheless, in a refrain that FCI McKean's warden Dennis Luther would understand, Littky is under perpetual pressure to add more regulations:

"I've learned that one of the problems with public schools is they build their rules and actions because of what one kid does or two kids do. One kid writes on the wall, or does something during class, and so they punish everybody by putting hall guards in, because of that one kid.

"The hardest thing is when somebody messes up, and my custodian comes in and says, 'They broke this! There should be a teacher guarding it at all times.' I've got to step back and say, 'That's one kid who did it, and I'm not going to ruin it for everybody else, and I'm not going to set rules for everybody else.' And I also have to say to myself, 'Well, it didn't work, I'm going to get burned sometimes.' "

When he arrived at Thayer, Littky said, his biggest problem "was that no one, teacher or student, felt good about themselves or what they were doing." So he built esteem by giving trust—and expecting it in return. "He has a relationship with every child in that school," one local school board member told us. "He always treats everyone with respect. He loves those kids and they know it." She also claimed that he changed the tone of the school from defeatist to positive in a host of little ways. "First thing you saw before were notices on the board that someone had detention," she recalled. "Now there are always bright and happy things [such as announcements of individual achievement] on the bulletin board. That, itself, makes students take pride." A teacher added, "If you expect that kids are going to write on the wall, they will, OK? And if you expect the teachers can't do something, or won't do something, they won't. He always expects the best of you."

In fact, the process Littky undertook with teachers is a carbon copy of the one he used with students. Many teachers in America today, and at Thayer before Littky, are as demoralized as their students. "The school was falling apart," said one teacher, who went on to describe the absence of goals and the lack of self-respect on the part of students and teachers alike. So Littky urged autonomy. " 'Try it' are his favorite two words," another teacher told me. Yet another bubbled about "the freedom to teach. . . . There is no set curriculum. You're not required to cover material at a certain rate." But, once again, that's not a sign of laxity. Littky constantly nudges, pushes, and cajoles everyone to do more, to reexamine *everything*. "It's exhausting, confusing, frustrating," one teacher declared, "but without it I'm not sure what I'd do. I can't imagine doing anything else, except constantly evaluating and re-looking at what's done, to try to make it better." One of her colleagues exclaimed, "I enjoy teaching again. I *love* teaching again. There is a sense of . . . joy about it, and there is hope."

You don't suppose we could talk Littky into running GM, do you?

31

Trust, Respect, and the Mindful Organization

The only way to make a man trustworthy is to trust him.

HENRY STIMSON
U.S. Secretary of War in
World War II

One day, at a nursing home in Connecticut, elderly residents were each given a choice of houseplants to care for and were asked to make a number of small decisions about their daily routines. A year and a half later, not only were these people more cheerful, active and alert than a similar group in the same institution who were not given these choices and responsibilities, but many more of them were still alive. In fact, less than half as many of the decision-making, plant-minding residents had died as had those in the other group. This experiment, with its startling results, began over ten years of research into the powerful effects of what my colleagues and I came to call *mindfulness*, and of its counterpart, the equally powerful but destructive state of *mindlessness*.

ELLEN LANGER
Social psychologist, Harvard University
Mindfulness

Look back and ponder:

- Dennis Luther instills a culture of respect and trust at the Federal Correctional Institution at McKean, Pennsylvania—with staff and inmates alike (both firsts). McKean gets the highest rating given by the American Correctional Association and, after three years of operation, reports no murders, no escapes, no serious assaults on inmates or staff, no sexual assaults, no suicides.

- Mike Walsh comes from a modest job at Cummins Engine to the chairmanship of the Union Pacific Railroad. He lays off 10,000 people, yet the unions admire him, old-line managers change their ways, 100 years' worth of bureaucratic excess is erased in 5 years. The "trick": trust and respect. After a misbegotten drug raid in Louisiana, Walsh hops in the company plane, dragging his top officers with him, hightails it to the scene—and publicly apologizes to the assembled railroaders for management's despicable act of mistrust. Claiming that most fellow CEOs "badly underestimate" the amount of change the work force can handle, Walsh turns over responsibility to the front line almost overnight—and opens the books to everyone. One long-time railroader, now a UPRR exec, says: "We're letting people do what they wanted to do, and were capable of doing, all along."

- Will Potter, a banker, comes to Preston Trucking in 1978. In front of a group of truck drivers, he says that management is to blame for shabby past performance. He offers up the miracle cure to management and workers: trust and respect. Paul Sims, a low-level department manager at the time, is appalled. But wanting to stay employed, he tries. Worker response to a tad of respect, trust, and open books overwhelms him—in a matter of *days*. A little over a decade later, Preston is productive, profitable—and judged by outsiders to be "one of the 100 best companies in America to work for." Teamsters Union officers direct customers to Preston. Blue-chip customers like Johnson & Johnson and 3M say that *they* can learn a lot about employee relations from these maverick truckers.

- In another Teamster stronghold, at the birthplace of the industrial revolution in America, another miracle of trust and respect occurs. Jon Simpson arrives at the limping hose maker Titeflex. Customers are screaming. He unplugs the fancy computer system, drags the furious customers down to the front line, and instructs his front-line workers to "do it"—fix the problem for the customer as they see fit. He opens the books, confers with the unions, dumps first-line supervisors, installs self-managing teams in short order—and achieves a spectacular turnaround in 90 days.

- In 1974, within hours of joining up at McKinsey, I'm sent out on my own to a client operation. For reasons I can't fathom for another decade, McKinsey trusts me to do the right thing. I do. ("Men who experience a great deal of accountability make accurate decisions"—industrial psychologist Karlene Roberts. See below.) McKinsey, despite numerous competitive challenges, remains one of the premier professional service firms in the world, and doubled its revenues between 1986 and 1991.

But we still don't get "it":

• A 1990 survey by the Gallup Organization for the American Society for Quality Control finds a great divide between rhetoric and reality: "The picture emerging from this study of the work force is that of a group of people whose talents, abilities, and energies are not being fully utilized for quality improvement—arguably the most important objective facing American business today. . . . This survey reveals a lack of participation. . . . Some may be turned off by what they perceive as a gap between the company's talk and action on quality."

• A 1991 *Harvard Business Review* survey of business leaders worldwide reveals that less than 20 percent of respondents share significant strategic information with their employees. (They don't share with anyone: About one-quarter say they "never" share strategic information with customers, and a quarter also report "never" involving customers or suppliers in new-product planning.)

• In a 1991 ISL International survey of Canadian executives' opinions, only 7 percent of participating presidents and vice presidents rank themselves at 9 or 10 (1 = "strongly disagree"; 10 = "strongly agree") in response to the statement "Most of the employees in our organization feel that they, as individuals, can make a difference in terms of helping the organization to compete more effectively." (Half the chiefs gave their firms—i.e., themselves— grades of 6 or less.)

• Britain's Joshua Tetley pub chain considers establishing a "100 club." Members of its 20,000-person work force can qualify (for "club" membership, and a few prizes) if they can recite the names and drinking habits of 100 customers. A top manager scoffs that Tetley will be "lucky to get one" employee who can or will pass the test. The program is approved anyway, and within a few months, over 500 employees know more than 600 names (and drinking habits) each, and one bionic chap can recall over 2,000. Thanks for the faith, boss!

This book lays down a daunting challenge to bosses and workers. (Or, rather, this book assesses the challenge that the *marketplace* is laying on companies.) The average worker—hose maker, trucker, railroad conductor, or management consultant—"will be expected" to:

—work mostly in self-managed project teams;
—shift team membership periodically;

—learn several, formerly "professionals only" skills, and achieve towering competence in one or two;

—work constantly with customers and vendors;

—take the initiative consistently and invent improvement projects as a matter of course.

That is, the employee "will be expected" to do these things *if* the company plans to survive, and *if* top management trusts workers (and supervisors and customers and vendors) to get on with it. The last "if" is the $64,000 question upon which the effectiveness of the newfangled organizations hinges: No trust equals no project organization equals no removal of layers of middle management equals no willingness to share strategic information equals no multi-skilled training equals no self-management (team or individual) equals no intimate "outsider" (customer, vendor, partner) involvement—equals no dice. That's the equation which cannot be avoided or evaded.

The Boss Will Not Approve Travel

"Don't show any purchase orders to Ralph S. Heath III. He just might set them on fire. The president of Ovation Marketing, Inc. in La Crosse [Wisconsin] already has done that once, and the message apparently has been burned into the minds of his employees.

"Purchases and travel budgets had to be approved by middle management and Heath until the end of last year. Then Heath issued an order. Employees were told to approve their own expenses. Heath found out it was easier to issue the order than make it work. A couple of weeks later, he was still being swamped with purchase orders. 'They weren't quite comfortable with the new responsibility,' he recalled. 'So I decided it was time for a meeting.'

"He explained again that requisitions were now an individual responsibility. Then he set fire to his stack of purchase orders. The demonstration was effective. He hasn't received a purchase order since. The change has been effective in more important areas, too. Six months after the beginning of the experiment, Heath has found:

—"Ovation's travel expenses are down 70 percent.

—"Entertainment expenses have dropped 39 percent.

—"Car mileage costs have declined 46 percent.

—"Office supply expenses were reduced by 18 percent.

"Better yet, Ovation's business is up 16 percent in this same period, compared with the first half of 1990.

" 'It's an interesting phenomenon,' Heath said. 'We clearly demonstrated that by giving control to the associates, they are actually more careful with spending than I was because now it's their responsibility.' Heath added that Ovation Marketing, which was founded in 1978, uses the same concept in generating its advertising programs. Individuals charged with designing a creative marketing program are responsible for the final product, not middle management or Heath."

KEN BREKKE
La Crosse Tribune
September 2, 1991

CATCH-22 (NO HALF-TRUST)

Create an institution where people aren't *allowed* to be curious, and people *won't* be curious. Pretty soon bosses, with a ton of corroborating evidence, will solemnly intone that "most people aren't curious." From there we begin to wonder whether they can "handle all that change." So we take half-steps toward structural reform. And we lose the ball game.

The nub of the problem: There's no such thing as half-trust. "Push the needle all the way over," said the UPRR's Walsh (and he did). "Men who experience a great deal of accountability make accurate decisions"—that was the No. 1 conclusion University of California Professor Karlene Roberts reached after a multiyear study of decision making under pressure at nuclear power plants, on aircraft carriers, and among air traffic controllers. (In Roberts's study, summarized in the July 1989 issue of *Smithsonian*, the most effective leaders gave underlings lots of responsibility, eliminated hovering supervision despite the fact that lives were on the line—and then demanded results.) And remember Secretary of War Stimson: "The only way to make a man trustworthy is to trust him." In short, you'll never know until you try. You *must* let go if you expect people to respond. The offering of trust must at first be *unilateral* on the part of management. Trustworthiness, tomorrow, comes only after granting trust in the first place—today. Obvious? Of course. Honored in the breach? Usually.

As one executive (and private pilot) put it, "The instructor pilot can't 'half' sit next to you doing your first solo." To be sure, the would-be soloist must first pass "ground school." Nonetheless, the initial by-yourself flight can occur (in the U.S.) after only 10 hours in the air! Obviously, not many first-time soloists are lost, or the FAA would change the rules. That is, people routinely live up to "impossible" challenges—if managers have the nerve to set out those challenges in the first place and then get out of the pilot's seat.

And "nerve" is the right word. Make no mistake, what Mike Walsh, Jon Simpson, Will Potter, and Dennis Luther did was nervy. It took guts. Or, rather, it took enormous belief in people.

Why? Why? Why? Why does trusting people take such a leap of faith? Why do we insist upon calling leaders who trust people "gutsy" (as I just did)? Go back to the Ellen Langer epigraph: Engage patients at a nursing home— *just let them mind their own plants*—and twice as many stay alive, compared to the "mindless" contingent. What the market demands, I conclude, is mindful organizations. (Which will be the product of trust granted with gusto—QED.)

Room to Learn: Louis Agassiz

Louis Agassiz as a Teacher (by Lane Cooper, 1917) includes recollections from distinguished scientists who studied under the renowned Harvard zoologist—and exceptional teacher. One recounted his introduction to Agassiz: "I had assigned to me a small pine table with a rusty tin pan upon it. . . . When I sat down before my tin pan, Agassiz brought me a small fish, placing it before me with the rather stern requirement that I should study it, but should on no account talk to anyone concerning it, nor read anything relating to fishes until I had his permission to do so. To my inquiry, 'What shall I do?' he said in effect: 'Find out what you can without damaging the specimen; when I think that you have done the work I will question you.' In the course of an hour I thought I had compassed that fish. . . . I was anxious to make [a summary report] and get on to the next state of the business."

But Agassiz paid no attention to his student that day, the next, or during the following week. So the novice, after suppressing his impatience, took another look, and then another. To his surprise, he learned more: "I set my wits to work upon the thing, and in the course of 100 hours or so thought I had done much—a hundred times as much as seemed possible at the start."

Agassiz eventually responded: "On the seventh day came the question, 'Well,' and my disgorge of learning to him as he sat on the edge of my table, puffing his cigar. At the end of the hour's telling, he swung off and away, saying, 'That is not right.' " Reluctantly, the student went back to his rusty tin pan. After another week of hard, silent labor, he had results that astonished him and passed muster with his taciturn teacher. Agassiz acknowledged the student's success by bringing him a big pile of bones, with the order to sort them out.

Much more agonized examination was in store, with stupendous results: "Two months or more went into this [second] task with no other help than an occasional looking over my grouping with the stereotyped remark: 'That is not right.' Finally the task was done, and I was again set upon a remarkable lot of specimens representing 20 species of the side swimmers. . . . I shall never forget the sense of power . . . which I felt in beginning the more extended work on a group of animals. I had learned the art of comparing objects, which is the basis of the naturalist's work."

The manager's job is like that of the teacher. She or he has but one objective: pursuing improved performance by fostering long-term personal (and team) engagement, learning, and continuous development. It takes deep immersion and a lot of frustration to comprehend any topic, from the nature of a specimen in a glass jar to the workings of a small corner of a distribution center. Moreover, it's clear as day that the average worker, like the good student, is an avid would-be learner—if only we had the moxie to create workplaces that resemble Agassiz's lab a bit more.

" 'THEY' WANT . . .": BULL!

There is no end to the " 'they' want" objections managers raise. For example: " 'They' *want* structure." Bull! No, that's not fair. If "they" *do* want structure, in 9 cases out of 10 it's because "they" don't trust "you." People who want detailed policy manuals (and any number do), as well as those who wish to have the security of a union contract, usually do so because they don't trust management to hold up its half of any bargain.

The Control Paradox

Accountability. . . . Delegation . . . Teamster hose makers on self-managing teams out visiting customers and vendors. Are mistakes made? Of course! And the likes of Titeflex's Simpson would be the first to say so—with delight. No mistakes, no learning. Any idiot knows that. Sadly, a lot of industrial managers have behaved like idiots for the last 150 years.

It does get a bit noisy. "Timid men prefer the calm of despotism to the boisterous sea of liberty." The author: Thomas Jefferson. His words, I suggest, speak exactly to today's corporate environment. All too many of our chiefs, at the work group or division level, seem to prefer calm despotism of their own making to the boisterous liberty of a genuinely empowered work force.

Calm despotism may have had its place when the market was calm. But markets have clearly turned boisterous. Boisterous competitive circumstances call for boisterous individuals, boisterous teams, boisterous buckyborgs, and boisterous corporations. It's about that simple.

Which leads to an extraordinary paradox: You are out of control when you are "in control." You are in control when you are "out of control." The executive who "knows everything," who is surrounded by layers of staffers and inundated with thousands of pages of analyses from below, is "in control"— just like those central planners in the engine rooms of the former Soviet economy. In reality, he has the *illusion* of control. Tons of paper. Reports on *everything*. A staff of hundreds of gofers and yes-men at his beck and call.

In fact, you really *are* in control when thousands upon thousands of people, unbeknownst to you, are taking initiatives, going beyond job descriptions and the constraints of their box on the organization chart, to serve the customer better, improve the process, work quickly with a supplier to nullify a defect. If the system did allow you to "know" all this, the following would occur: (1) staffers would interject, impose their expertise, and at the very least slow things down; (2) the all-important "they" wouldn't take the initiative in the first place, because "they" would know what was coming—delay, reworking of the idea—from those hordes of staffers in various layers throughout the organization.

Another, rather perverse, way of looking at the control issue: If you can answer the questions that make it to your desk, something's wrong with your system. The chief—supervisor (if any are left) of the 15-person team, division general manager with 4,000 people reporting to her—gets paid, 100 percent as I see it, for dealing only with dilemmas that *cannot* be dealt with by those closer to the action. If you can readily answer the questions that come to you—what weight machine to get for the new health club, which office supply company to use for pencils and paper clips, what car types to buy for the sales force— then "they" aren't stepping up to the plate. (Doubtless because you haven't allowed them to!) Look at the queries that come your way in the course of the next week. If they aren't imponderables, if you can answer most of them, then take a serious look at your system—and wonder why such stuff makes it to your in-box and distracts you from the issues that you *should* be dealing with.

AUTOCRATIC DELEGATORS (MORE PARADOX)

Mike Walsh is not easy to love. Among other things, he's an autocrat. I would hate to be on his wrong side. (Ditto McKinsey's de facto founder, Marvin Bower: And I *have* been on his wrong side.) Yet Walsh understands "letting go" almost as well as Professor Agassiz did. He turned enormous authority over to the field, with virtually no accompanying training at first. (It came years later.) On the other hand, consider the Louisiana incident again: Walsh made it clear that he would not tolerate drug use—and he would not tolerate deception of employees. It was an autocratic, unilateral, uncompromising declaration. Walsh set a clear moral tone: trust given (unilaterally); responsibility, reliability, and accountability expected in return. Asked what he liked best about Warden Dennis Luther, McKean's former union chief Mike Eger replied, "He never lies." Luther's formula: trust given, responsible behavior expected in return.

MCI delegates, delegates, delegates. Managers say they "can't find anyone who will make a decision for them"—which is another way of saying it's up to them, which they quickly figure out. Delegation? Yup! But, MCI exec Dick Liebhaber snaps, "We don't coddle." His is a severe institution. The freedom is heady. The performance expectations are Olympian.

The freedom I experienced at the McKinsey Marvin Bower created was exhilarating. But for seven years I also suffered from almost constant headaches because of the expectations. In McKinsey's "ambiguous," project-centered, never-work-with-the-same-people-twice world, the standards of integrity and attentiveness to clients and peers were skyscraping. I paid through the nose for my freedom, in other words. (And, mostly, it was a good bargain—though it took me years to see it that way.)

Lots of companies decentralize. It happened in the 1950s, and it's been happening in the last few years, with a vengeance (à la ABB). But most chiefs, sad to say, blow it on "both" scores: (1) They only half let go (which may be worse than not letting go at all), and (2) they fail to establish heartfelt (and Maalox-slurping) accountability. They "half-trust." They half-delegate. They half-coddle. And then they wonder why not much happens.

My list of "top three" delegators consists of Mike Walsh, Pat McGovern (IDG), and Percy Barnevik (ABB). My top three autocrats are Mike Walsh, Pat McGovern, and Percy Barnevik.

Go figure! (I devoutly hope you do.)

32

Beyond Hierarchy

Modernism, which dates from the late 19th century, is . . . associated with mass production, uniformity, and predictability; post-modernism with flexibility, choice, and personal responsibility.

> MICHAEL PROWSE, "Post-
> modern Test for Government"
> *Financial Times*, April 21, 1992

As a scientist, I would say that one cannot speak at all about linear progress. . . . And we certainly cannot speak about destiny. What one can speak about, however, is novelty and "rules within randomness."

> ILYA PRIGOGINE, 1977
> Nobel prize–winner in chemistry
> in *New Perspectives Quarterly*
> Spring 1992

While we teach many of the right things in our MBA programs, we don't teach some critical things we ought to teach . . . like leadership, vision, imagination and values. . . . The major reason we don't is because if we teach those untaught things it will become more difficult to teach and to justify what we already teach. So we have built a weird, almost unimaginable design for MBA-level education. We then lay it upon well-proportioned young men and women, distorting them (when we are unlucky enough to succeed) into critters with lopsided brains, icy hearts, and shrunken souls.

HAROLD LEAVITT, professor
emeritus, Stanford University,
in "Educating Our MBAs . . ."
*California Management
Review*
Spring 1989

Beyond hierarchy! Oh, really? Percy Barnevik and Mike Walsh have devolved enormous amounts of responsibility. But both still have a very firm hand on the tiller. And the operations, sales and marketing, and finance departments at the Union Pacific Railroad have hardly disappeared—though they are much slimmer than before and are working together with unprecedented ease. What about the Acordia companies and IDG? Unit chiefs have lots of clout, but there is also pronounced system-wide discipline, even if it is exerted by a minuscule center.

Okay, vestiges of hierarchy do remain, even in the "exemplar" firms I've identified. But let's take a different tack. Not so very long ago, in 1967, John Kenneth Galbraith declared in *The New Industrial State* that all our material wants would be fulfilled—thanks to the automaticity of profits thrown off by near-perfect, giant American corporations, run by an elite of managerial technocrats.

Now, just a quarter-century later, outside members of the board almost throw out the chairman of General Motors. IBM management, with much applause from the sidelines, considers dismemberment ("Breaking Up IBM"— *Fortune* cover, July 1992). And in May 1992, *Business Week*'s cover blares, "Johnson & Johnson, A Big Company That Works!" (Yes, even an exclamation point.)

That's right, we are now stunned when a big outfit *does* perform well—and note that *Business Week* feels pressed to add, also on the cover, that "J&J's secret is keeping its business divided into small pieces. Managers are given a free rein to take big risks. . . . But they better produce." So much for managerial technocrats in tall towers atop steep functional bureaucracies.

THE BERLIN WALL AND THE AGE OF REASON CRUMBLE

Abolishing its planning department might be the best thing a company could do for its shareholders—or so says a report from management consultants at . . . Deloitte Haskins and Sells. Looking at total returns paid to shareholders . . . by 75 British companies over the past three years, the report shows that firms without central planners tend to produce higher returns. . . . The main problem seems to be that firms with a planning department are more likely to build empires. . . . Too bad the 29 companies with planning apparatchiks are so wedded to them: Firms that thought their planners had contributed "a great deal" to results had few of the high performers among their number.

"The Planned and the Damned," *The Economist* February 18, 1989

It seems no accident that the earth-rending reassessment of paths to satisfactory corporate performance is occurring at the same time that totalitarian states are collapsing and nondeterministic models are coming to dominate science. Vàclav Havel, addressing world business leaders in Davos, Switzerland, in March 1992, called the collapse of communism "an end not just to the nineteenth and twentieth centuries, but to the modern age as a whole . . . the proud belief that man, as the pinnacle of everything that exists, was capable of objectively describing, explaining and controlling everything that exists."

Wasn't the old Union Pacific's structure, cobbled together in a different environment and with access to technologies different from today's, a hubristic exercise in "controlling everything that exists"? Wasn't it the dispassionate algorithms underpinning the old Union Pacific, and Sears and GM and IBM, that fired Galbraith's imagination? ("The size of General Motors is in the service not of monopoly or the economies of scale but of planning," Galbraith wrote in *The New Industrial State*. "And [thanks to] this planning—control of supply, control of demand, provision of capital, minimization of risk—there is no clear upper limit to the desirable size.") Even Peter Drucker's magisterial *The Practice of Management* (1954) was one long diatribe against intuition— and one long paean to hyperrational approaches to harnessing large numbers of people in large organizations.

Only 15 years ago, choruses of tribute to the power of centralized strategic planning were sung in business school classrooms across the land—and around the globe. By 1989, however, sounding rather more like Vàclav Havel than like the business school professors they are, Gary Hamel and C. K. Prahalad were writing, in a landmark *Harvard Business Review* article:

As "strategy" has blossomed, the competitiveness of Western companies has withered. This may be coincidence, but we think not. . . . Typically, competitor analysis focuses on the existing resources . . . of present competitors. . . . The lesson is clear: assessing the current tactical advantages of known competitors will not help you understand the resolution, stamina, and inventiveness of potential competitors.

The authors went on to suggest that firms should worry more about creating competence to respond to the unknown—something akin to Prigogine's "rules within randomness" or Johnson & Johnson's flexible collection of smallish, risk-taking, accountable enterprises.

The Carpet Is Thick, the View Magnificent, the Profits Stink

"Ed Brennan, a third-generation employee at Sears Roebuck who rose from the shop floor to become its chairman, sits in Chicago's 110-story Sears Tower and ponders a question about capital expenditure. The carpet is thick, the view magnificent, and Mr. Brennan does not appear to know the answer.

"An adviser interjects. The required figure will be disclosed in the retail and financial services group's annual report. Perhaps he could search it out and communicate later? Mr. Brennan, mollified, delivers a homily on the dangers of statistics.

"By chance, an identical conversation had arisen weeks earlier. The setting had been the spartan headquarters of Wal-Mart, an aggressive discount chain which recently ousted Sears as America's top-selling retailer. Don Soderquist, Wal-Mart's [vice chairman], had nipped into a neighboring office, cornered the finance director, and extracted the answer. It took two minutes and there was no minder in sight."

Financial Times
May 12, 1992

TOOLS OF CONVIVIALITY, WORK AS DIALOGUE

What happens when we flatten the hierarchy? We get a little less of the same thing. Even though there are fewer levels of management, people still suppose that their box is sacred territory which [must] be defended at all costs. Organizational flattening . . . does not fundamentally redefine relationships between people and functions in the organization. Functions still work sequentially, making decisions from fragmented perspectives.

> Suppose, instead, we were to think of ourselves and our positions within the organization not as fixed little empires, but as resources available to others. If we were to see ourselves not as boxes but as nodes in a network, not as cogs in a gear but as knowledge contributors . . . . In the network enterprise, each position . . . represents a person with capabilities, skills and experience. Instead of mutually exclusive tasks (jobs) and departmental assignments (charters), enterprises blend the talents of different people around focused tasks.
>
> CHARLES SAVAGE
> *Fifth Generation Management*

Mere "flattening" is not enough, says Savage. (Recall that Quinn Mills argued that where hierarchy lingers, "there cannot be any rethinking of the fundamentals of management.") Savage goes on to discuss "work as dialogue," an idea which gets at organizations (including "outsiders") as collections of ever-forming, ever-dissolving, ever-changing, multi-functionally skilled project teams—involving, per the Oticon model (Chapter 13), everyone. Work as dialogue is reminiscent, in turn, of Michael Schrage's new forms of collaboration and electronic "tools of conviviality"—Schrage's book, remember, was titled *Shared Minds*.

Neither Savage nor Schrage—nor Oticon's Lars Kolind nor CNN's Ted Turner—is an anarchist. There are some rules (called values) at Oticon, and a clear philosophy guides Turner Broadcasting/CNN. After all, we've devoted many a page in this section to "soul," my preferred term for rules, values, vision, philosophy, whatever. Oticon has soul. So, too, Rational and Random House. (Even the ephemeral "Dallas Organization" had soul.) Yet none of these "organizations" bears much resemblance to the GM Galbraith spoke of so adoringly in 1967 or, sadly, to today's GM, following lots of well-intentioned but ultimately nonrevolutionary change.

Work as dialogue, shared minds, and the floating crap games of project teams (of insiders and outsiders) "tied" together by soul of some sort—that's the mostly elusive "stuff" that adds up to "beyond hierarchy." But "mostly" is a key word. For we have also found companies that are already far "beyond" traditional hierarchy—the professional service firms, CNN, Oticon, and even a monster heavy-industrial outfit, ABB.

No, none of these firms is "without" hierarchy, let alone pecking orders. But "beyond"?—indeed they are, by the standards of the last couple of hundred years.

ORGANIZING'S NEW PARADOXES

On the one hand, we're going beyond hierarchy, and trying to liberate almost everyone in the organization. Yet that liberation leads to many a sleepless night—the result of membership in project teams with sky-high standards, imposed mostly by oneself, but by demanding peers as well. This paradox, one of several, is the heart and soul of the bold new journey on which we've embarked.

- Organizing/focusing and dis-organizing/de-integrating. Our model firms are getting "more organized" and more focused—putting together tightly tied networks and largely self-contained units, from care pairs to multifunction teams to independent business units that take responsibility (*with accountability*) for a whole task. At the same time, the same firms are *dis*-organizing (creating passels of very independent subunits, selling off misfitting pieces of business portfolios) and *de*-integrating (subcontracting this, that, the other, and at least part of *everything*).

- "Smaller" and "bigger." The "company," as we have known it, tends to be getting smaller, as it subcontracts more and more tasks, breaks itself up voluntarily, and focuses more on the few tasks at which it can add special value. On the other hand, to execute a particular strategy or develop a particular product/product family, the company is often as not, even if it's a genuinely tiny firm, embedded in an extensive ("big") network. The network, for a while, *is* the company (no quotes!). That is, firms are getting smaller and bigger at once. Or try it this way. "New big" means a small to modest-size unit that's a de facto *giant*—i.e., best-in-class at a key task, such as an Acordia, CCT, or IDG company. "New *big*" also means network big—i.e., a powerful, temporary collection of potent *midgets* and potent, autonomous, and accountable *bits* of larger firms.

- Accountability and teamwork. With the failure of grotesque overspecialization and the overdetermined, nonaccountable matrix structure mostly behind us, and the need to develop products and bring them to market more quickly before us, all signs are pointing toward more accountability—for the work team, the market-scale business unit. Yet that accountability is embedded within a necessity to support other network partners. Professional service firms such as EDS and McKinsey, and new network firms such as MCI, demonstrate the plausibility and effectiveness of the "do both" approach.

- Autonomy and partnership. Individuals are becoming more autonomous, with responsibility for creating projects and managing their careers, on or off corporate payrolls. And they are engaged in more partnering activities—

depending more on each other as teammates, and on other members of an expansive network that invariably includes numerous "outsiders."

- More specialty/expertise development and less specialist/expert staffs. Developing value-added skills becomes more important than ever, and each team member and each team/business unit becomes more responsible than ever for developing special knowledge. On the other hand, old-fashioned centers of expertise (which often weren't very expert)—those vast, functional staffs—are going,going,gone.

Add it up, and you get something rather surprising. There's no rejection of the past in all this! Expertise is more important than ever, not less. And bigness has its place. However, expertise is being changed, altered almost beyond recognition (closer to the line, everyone's responsibility). So is big (mainly emanating from temporary collections—networks—of very small, focused, and autonomous bits).

Amen, Maybe!?

In September 1991, for the first time, I exposed a group of executives to the full thrust of this book. The 80 people present came from as far away as Malaysia, Brazil, and New Zealand. The firms and agencies represented covered the full spectrum of the private and public economy. Among them: 3M, National Semiconductor, James River (forest products), Sara Lee, World Bank, Dayton Power and Light—and the AARP and the County Council of South Glamorgan, Wales. Near the end of a grueling five-day seminar, my colleagues and I asked everyone to indicate his or her comfort level with the central notions by assessing four statements cast in purposefully extreme language.

First, "You understand and accept 'fashion' as the 'right' metaphor." Some 57 percent called it "safe" (the most "comfortable" ranking); 30 percent said "risky" (the middle category); and the remaining 13 percent opted for "dangerous." (Breakdowns by industry reveal little; the attitudes of those in the public sector were only a bit more cautious than those of their private-sector counterparts.)

Next, "Create mini-strategic business units everywhere": 55 percent safe; 35 percent risky; 10 percent dangerous.

Then we tested the project idea—"Everyone and everything organized around projects." This got the most support, with 61 percent judging it safe, 33 percent risky, and only 6 percent dangerous. Ah, home free? Hello, projects. Bye-bye functions.

But wait. The last statement was "Destroy functional departments." And the rats turned on us! Twenty-one percent said safe, 23 percent risky—and 56 percent went for "dangerous."

It's a bloody mess, is what it is, mate. Fashion, yup. Tiny units, okay. Projects, amen. But rip the heart out of the functional departments—not so fast, lads. Percy Barnevik, Jon Simpson, and Lars Kolind aren't alone, but they don't have much company yet either.

LOTS TO DO

The best—and most important—news is that "they" (you, me, your local Teamsters worker) can cope. Véronique Vienne, jobhopper extraordinaire, gets it. Marion McGovern of M^2 gets it. And so does Inge Christophersen at Oticon—a "secretary" (in days gone by) turned multiskilled member of a shifting portfolio of project teams.

But hold on. Though Inge Christophersen may well get it, that doesn't mean that this "stuff" is a walk in the park. Christophersen's colleague, economist Soren Holst, lamented that lots of "old look" Oticon managers (and nonmanagers) were not measuring up as new look project-team leaders. Warden Dennis Luther had to bounce a pair of associate wardens who couldn't "get" the idea of "respect for inmates" through their noggins. And "even" David Maister, lifelong student of professional service firms, has had to learn new tricks to build his "assets" (e.g., learn how to keep learning).

McKinsey, that group of consummate knowledge workers, is desperately trying to figure out just what the hell knowledge is—it's farther along with "knowledge management" than most, but at the same time barely out of the starting gate.

"Starting gate"? That's a pretty lumpy object—and hence a lousy image. For the problem is that the starting gate in our fashionized marketplace is constantly shifting position. Only opening yourself up wide to perpetual destruction (beyond Beyond Hierarchy?!) offers hope for renewal. How do you do that? Willing exposure to the market's fickle gales is the only answer that seems to make sense.

V

Markets and Innovation: The Case for Disorganization

PROLOGUE: DECONSTRUCTING THE CORPORATION

Lenin once said that the capitalists would supply the rope for their own hanging, and in a way he was right. As market forces and the rise of the information age ultimately forced the unbundling of the Soviet Union, so they are forcing America's largest economic organizations to break up into more efficient pieces. If you've grown accustomed to a sheltered life inside a really large corporation, take pity on the unemployed apparatchiks at the Kremlin. The next Kremlin to fall may be your own.

PETER HUBER
"The Unbundling of America"
Forbes, April 13, 1992

Imperial Chemical Industries P.L.C., Britain's largest industrial company, reported gloomy results today, but its shares soared as it announced plans to split itself in two.

The New York Times
July 31, 1992

On December 25, 1991, the Soviet flag flying over the Kremlin came down. Thus ended a misguided 74-year experiment in central planning. One month earlier, IBM announced it was in effect breaking itself up into 13 pieces, thereby doing voluntarily what it had fought for a decade to keep the U.S. Department of Justice from doing in the 1970s. (In January 1982, IBM's stock market value was $34 billion; by June 1992, according to *Fortune*, it had increased 65 percent to $56 billion. In 1982, AT&T agreed to bust itself into eight pieces—AT&T and seven "Baby Bells." Over the next 10 years the value of all combined Bell entities shot from $48 billion to $180 billion, a 275 percent jump. Is there more to the two companies' stories than not splitting up versus splitting up? Maybe. *Maybe not.*)

Crackup, the word of the '80s, now, even more so, of the '90s. Big firms routinely find that the value of their constituent parts—if severed from the head—is several times greater than the current whole. ABB buys up everything in sight, then smashes it into tiny bits in the boldest organizational experiment in decades. Japanese firms go on a mad spree of spinning off entrepreneurial units, reversing decades of concentration. The average size of firms in developed countries plummets. Germany's matchless, and virtually unstudied, post-World War II economic record turns out to have been borne mostly on the backs of dynamic, fiercely independent, middle-sized firms, called the Mittelstand.

The preceding section spoke of organization. This one speaks of *dis*organization. And no "device" disorganizes more effectively than the market. Thence the title of this section, Markets and Innovation. The need for innovation on an unprecedented scale is a given. The question is how. It seems that giving the market free rein, inside and outside the firm, is the best—perhaps the only—satisfactory answer.

33

The Exaltation of Mess, or Learning to Love Chance

> The 2 prime movers in the Universe are Time and Luck.
>
> KURT VONNEGUT
> *Hocus Pocus*

Do everything right, all the time, and the child will prosper. It's as simple as that, except for fate, luck, heredity, chance, the astrological sign under which the child was born, his order of birth, his first encounter with evil, the girl who jilts him in spite of his excellent qualities, the war that is being fought when he is a young man, the drugs he may try once or too many times, the friends he makes, how he scores on tests, how well he endures kidding about his shortcomings, how ambitious he becomes, how far he falls behind, circumstantial evidence, ironic perspective, danger when it is least expected, difficulty in triumphing over circumstance, people with hidden agendas, and animals with rabies.

> from Mel's journal in
> *Picturing Will*,
> a novel by Ann Beattie

Elephants have a hard time adapting. Cockroaches outlive everything.

PETER DRUCKER

interview in *Forbes*

August 19, 1991

The message from the Beyond Hierarchy section was paradoxical. We loudly sang the praises of independent units—Lakeland Regional Medical Center's "care pairs"; the thousands of 50-person profit-and-loss centers at ABB; the 50-or-so-person independent companies at Chromalloy Compressor Technologies, IDG, Random House, and Acordia. But we endorsed networks and connections with at least equal enthusiasm. Overall, in fact, the *organizing* message carried the day. Now the time has come to emphasize *dis*organizing's vitally important role in an economic world gone bonkers.

IBM decentralizes. Then decentralizes again. Then decentralizes one more time. And joins in alliances with this company, then that company. But it's still too sluggish by a mile. (And can't gather the nerve to deconstruct its monster sales organization). The long 80-year-old shadow cast by even a diminished corporate headquarters thwarts initiative after initiative. "Like nearly every other clever product from IBM," Robert X. Cringely wrote in *Accidental Empires*, the innovative database language SQL "had been developed in secret. [The development group] lied about it, then finally showed it to the big shots who were too impressed to turn the product down." *The Wall Street Journal* filed an eerily similar report on IBM's 1990 Nobel prize–winners for superconductivity, J. Georg Bednorz and K. Alex Mueller: "The two scientists hunted quietly, telling a supervisor a half-truth, and steering a curious visitor off track. . . . The issue is a sore point now for IBM brass."

But at least SQL survived and the furtive scientists got their Nobels. An even more damning report appeared in *Upside*, in a May 1992 analysis of why IBM backed out of an agreement to use NeXT Computer's pathbreaking "object-oriented" operating system:

> What finally did in Nextstep was the internal politics in the highly political world of IBM. . . . When the Nextstep deal had been cut, the IBM workstation systems division [was] run by Andrew Heller . . . a particular partisan of Nextstep. . . . At the time . . . Heller had good access to chairman John Akers. But Heller [saw Nextstep as an alternative to technologies that] were favorites of long-time IBMers. The old guard was wary of challenging existing, and highly profitable, software systems. . . . According to an IBM insider, "IBM simply couldn't afford to put that good a solution on [its existing operating system]."

What's the answer? Markets! "The only true decentralization is a spin-off," University of Maryland professor Julian Simon wrote to me, commenting on an article of mine that he felt let IBM off too lightly. "IBM breaks up operations into several 'independent' parts, and at the same time appoints a czar to oversee them."

IDG and Acordia spin out units at a tidy clip. But even they wouldn't pass Simon's demanding test: You've got to *sell* it to its managers or the public, then let the market have its way. In the next chapter (Violent Market-Injection Strategies), we'll see some who come close to attaining Simon's ideal—for example, Thermo Electron and Teknekron.

Keep it hooked together lightly, but pursue some synergy (ABB)? Sell parts of parts to the public (Thermo Electron)? Sell everything off eventually (Teknekron)? Play the automatic division game when units hit a certain size (CCT, Acordia, IDG)? Or don't allow yourself to grow too big in the first place (Rational)? Frankly, I'm not sure what the answer is.

But I *am* damned sure that the fashion message is right! Every market is exploding, microtizing. There isn't time enough to think. Besides, tangles of causes and effects are far too complex to sort out, whether your business is haute couture, software, materials, chemicals, travel services, or movies. Everyone, from everywhere, is leapfrogging everyone else. Product development cycles, regardless of industry, have shrunk to a year or so at most. And "cycles" that last mere weeks aren't uncommon. (Look, it's taken me five years to complete this book. These days, the likes of Waldenbooks have enormous impact on market acceptance and sales. Suppose Walden takes a shine to the book, puts it on the cherished front shelf. Great! That gives it *two weeks* to prove itself. If not, it's off to the back shelves, then out the back door. That's life. For you. For me. Bye-bye five years.)

If you're IBM CEO John Akers, it's no longer sufficient to pray that a couple of guys in Rüschlikon, Switzerland, will cheat, not tell their supervisor what they're up to, and bag a couple of Nobels for you. Survival? I'm with Peter Drucker. This is the era of the cockroaches.

What follows will be bitter medicine for most:

—Things are moving too fast for us to sort out logically what's going on. Our understanding of cause and effect is hopelessly incomplete, frightfully misleading, and getting worse by the day, increased computer power notwithstanding. (Know any good programs that would have guessed how much we'd love visible bubbles and pumps in our athletic shoes?)

—So disorganize!

—And keep disorganizing!

—Try anything! The more screwups the merrier—don't get caught up in endless rehashing. You must recover quickly, then try something else.

—And, oh yes: Maybe break the joint up. Sell off the most effective commercial units. (I'm not kidding.)

—Hurry!

MESSY MARKETS

I love markets. I admit it. I love radical decentralization. I am an enemy of elaborate plans. An ally of hasty action. An enemy of excessive order. A friend of disorderly trial and error—especially error.

I am an ardent admirer of F. A. Hayek. It is wretchedly unfair to summarize his 22 volumes of collected works in a paragraph. But here goes. "The market economy is not [the] product of deliberate design," he wrote in his slim 1988 book *The Fatal Conceit*. "It far surpasses the reach of our understanding." But, he adds, it's not just that markets are messy and complex; they're also not fair. Success does not necessarily—or even all that often—go to those who have worked the hardest (i.e., "deserved it"). In short, the success or failure of a product in the market is due to a lengthy, complex, loosely linked chain of circumstances, wholly unpredictable at the time a decision to launch a product or new business is made.

I Kin Read Writin

"More than fifteen years elapsed between the invention of the typewriter and its first real marketplace success," Cynthia Monaco reported in *American Heritage of Invention and Technology*. It was patented by Christopher Latham Sholes in July 1868. James Densmore subsequently paid $600 for 25 percent of the rights to that patent. He figured on sales to "literary and professional men who would value the opportunity to see their work in print," Monaco says.

Sholes and Densmore didn't sell a single typewriter at the 1876 Centennial Exposition in Philadelphia, although, according to Monaco, "people stood in long lines to purchase slips of paper with personalized, typewritten messages." By 1880, 12 years after the invention, just 5,000 machines were in existence.

The problem: Eloquent script was a significant part of an executive's presentation of himself. Thus the chiefs of the day (and their well-trained clerks, who actually pushed the pens) saw no reason to resort to some newfangled, mass-produced, mechanical device. One of the earliest companies to perceive the value of these odd-looking machines, and to make regular use of them, was Sears Roebuck. But even Sears found that it had to continue to send handwritten letters to its farm customers—who were likely to take offense at communications produced by typewriter. Monaco relates that one Kentucky mountaineer, after receiving his first such communication, wrote back, "You don't need to print no letters fer me. I kin read writin."

Embrace Failure to Discover Success

So hail the wacky power of the market—the bubbling brew, the constant hubbub of trial and error, of works and products and projects in progress, the sorting out of winners and losers for hopelessly complex (and invariably "unfair") reasons.

The market is frightening, even terrifying. It's not pretty. It's surely irrational. Yet over the long haul, the unfettered market *works* for the most rational of reasons: It produces *more* experiments, *more* tries, *more* wins, *more* losses, *more* information processed (market signals)—faster than any alternative.

Ah, yes, those losses. That's another little irritation: The essence and engine of the market economy is failure. Not success. Success, statistically speaking—inside the firm, in an industry, in a region, in a nation—is merely the occasional (and usually accidental) by-product of the far more numerous failures. It's difficult to swallow. It always has been. But the concept must be swallowed—today more than ever. In marketplaces gone nuts, from the competition among symphonies to the competition among running-shoe producers, not understanding the zaniness, not developing strategies that acknowledge the zaniness, is the kiss of rapid death.

The market: Yes, I love it! Outside the firm. *And inside the firm.* My belief in the ability of market forces alone to provide "guidance" and sort things out is the reason I've taken to titling speeches "How to Destroy Your Company Before a Competitor Does." That's right: *destroy!* Products, product lines, companies, and industries are overturning one another with shocking rapidity. Only those who have the guts to embrace failure eagerly and to disorganize purposefully and perpetually even have a chance. Incidentally, I'm not sure that they have that much of a chance, either. (More on that in Chapter 40.)

THE VIGOROUS PURSUIT OF SERENDIPITY

Chuckle if you will at the ancient hunting "strategy" of Labrador's Naskapi Indians. I take it seriously. So does organization researcher Karl Weick, reporting in *The Social Psychology of Organizing*:

Every day the Naskapi face the question of which direction the hunters should take to locate game. They answer the question by holding dried caribou shoulder bones over a fire. As the bones become heated they develop cracks and smudges that are then "read" by an expert. These cracks indicate the direction in which the hunters should look for game. The Naskapi believe that this practice allows the gods to intervene in their hunting decisions. The interesting feature of these practices is that they work.

To see how . . . think about some of the characteristics of this decision procedure. First, the final decision about where to hunt is not a purely personal or group choice. If no game is found, the gods—not the group—are to blame. Second, the final decision is not affected by the outcomes of past hunts. If the Indians were influenced by the outcomes of past hunts, they would run the definite risk of depleting the stock of animals. Their prior success would induce subsequent failure. Third, the final decision is not influenced by the typical human patterning of choice and preferences, which can enable the hunted animal to take evasive action and become sensitized to the presence of human beings.

Well said! Yet maybe Dr. Claire Lewicki, a fictional character in the 1990 movie *Days of Thunder*, says it better than Weick, or even Hayek. Her comment to race driver Cole Trickle (played by Tom Cruise): "Control is an illusion, you infantile egomaniac. Nobody knows and nobody controls anything." When a product becomes a roaring success—*In Search of Excellence*, the Apple II computer—it's for a thousand, or more likely a thousand thousand, unchartable reasons. Such is life.

Don't get me wrong. I'm not against hard work. It's imperative. The problem is, lots of people work hard. Lots of people are smart. Lots of people work hard *and* are smart. Take, once more, the revealing case of IBM, home to a lot of very smart, very hardworking people. Yet its matchless success from 1960 to 1985, I contend, was largely a matter of luck.

Tom Watson Sr. went to work around the turn of the century for National Cash Register. NCR boss William Patterson was a pioneer who emphasized service and paid attention to people—not exactly typical in those days. Watson Sr. learned at Patterson's feet.

In 1913, Watson bought the Computing-Tabulating-Recording company, forerunner to modern IBM. He emphasized people and service—obsessively. The small company prospered. When electronic computers reared their head in the post–World War II environment, Watson Sr. was not very keen on them. His hard-won customer base was happy with their mechanical punch-card machines. Why rock the boat? It was his renegade son, returning to the fold after some rather frisky years, who forced Pop into the computer business.

Watson Sr.'s abiding emphasis on service and people stayed firmly in place, however. And it turned out to be the right idea for the time. Thirty years

(Drawing by Cheney; © 1990 The New Yorker Magazine, Inc.)

ago, recall, computers were used for trivial functions, such as payroll process-ing. Moreover, they weren't all that reliable. The people in charge of comput-ers at corporations were rarely experts at first; they were more likely senior accountants, pressed into heading nascent computer operations because rou-tine accounting activities were the first to be automated.

Most of Watson's competitors, such as William Norris at Control Data Corporation, were first and foremost technologists. Unlike Watson Sr., they loved their clever machines and the whole idea of the computer revolution. Like the Barney Oldses of a half century before, they emphasized gee-whiz technical features, hired technical salespersons to sell those features, and could never get over the fact that Watson Sr., selling to conservative accountants-turned-computer-barons, was winning big with what they considered un-imaginative products. In short, IBM was a service star in an era of malperforming machines. And it worked in spades.

Then the worm began to turn, probably starting with the onslaught of Digital Equipment's minicomputers. The worm writhed its damnedest in the mid-'80s. Computing became reliable. The payroll checks went out on Friday afternoon without a hitch. Computing also became decentralized, and ma-chines and systems were sold beyond the boundaries of the "glass house" and the purview of the corporate vice president for information systems. More-over, that corporate VP was now usually an expert, not a transformed accoun-tant interested in protecting himself at all costs against failure; and the new chief-cum-expert wanted to experiment, to do it his way, to mix and match IBM equipment and the products of others. Suddenly companies run by experts who could help you solve your specific problems (the longtime Digital strength) started to look very good. Result: IBM suffered setback after setback at the hands of everyone from the Apples at the "bottom" of the market, to the Digitals and HPs in the middle, and the Crays and Thinking Machines at the top. Once best known for "awesome service," IBM suddenly became more known for awesome arrogance, bureaucracy, overconfidence, and attention to the *wrong* customers.

So the era of IBM's preeminence *was* largely serendipitous. Sweat, toil, and tears? Sure. But all those exertions just happened to be in an arena—service—that paid off big *in the specific context*. (Maybe I'm not alone in this analysis. Tom Watson Jr., quoted in *Computerworld* in June 1992, said he had considered titling his autobiography *The Right Place at the Right Time*, or *Blind Luck*—he chose *Father, Son & Co.* instead. Too bad.)

The nature of IBM's winning hand itself sowed the seeds of maladaptability. The firm is now working overtime to try and look more like companies it dismissed in the past—HP, Apple, Sun, Dell, et al. It doesn't take a genius to predict that it will never again be the dominant player it was in the '70s: Each bit of IBM now marches to the tune of someone else's drummer.

(On these matters I speak from experience. *In Search of Excellence* is a garden-variety "excellent" product—a pretty good product blessed with impeccable timing. "Timing" is a word that businesspersons by and large prefer to "luck," because it makes it sound as if you might have played at least a little role in the outcome. What was the magic of *In Search of Excellence*? It was launched during the month in 1982 when U.S. unemployment hit 10 percent for the first time since the Great Depression. People were in the midst of a big "downer." And the book purported to be about "great American companies." Moreover, the best-selling management books of all time up to that point—*Theory Z, The Art of Japanese Management*—had said, in effect: "Everything that's good and new in management is going on in Japan." The authors of those books, all close colleagues, had gotten to the market a year before Bob Waterman and I did. Our delay, which irritated us at the time, was a godsend—yet another synonym for luck. People were fed up with "their" message, and welcomed ours. *In Search of Excellence* was about wacky ideas—"the rational model has led us astray." If they'd been presented by a professor, well, forget it. But our book came out in a conservative black-and-gold cover and was supported by a conservative consultancy, McKinsey & Company. I say all this, I reiterate, with the benefit of hindsight. We had not a clue about the importance of these or a thousand other things at the time.)

In 1989, Continental Bank chairman Tom Theobald was quoted in *Fortune* as counting himself lucky in implementing a major change program. The bank had been at death's door, he said, so people had listened when he'd called for transformation. They had no choice. I thought it was a remarkably candid comment by CEO standards—and sent Theobald a note saying as much. He wrote back:

> Thanks for your note. With the exposure to corporate America that comes from our business relationships, I am pretty much convinced that the willingness to change co-relates mathematically with the proximity to financial disaster. And even then, it doesn't always materialize!

We are, in short, caught on the horns of a dilemma. To thrive as a corporation, you must passionately pursue the perfection of the products or services that have vaulted you to success (e.g., old IBM). However, to survive for the long haul, you must passionately pursue the destruction of what you have created. The question: Can you passionately pursue perfection and destruction simultaneously? It's not clear.

"The only way to gain a modicum of control," one exec attending a seminar said, "is to acknowledge that you are out of control." If you admit to the vagaries of the marketplace (luck, timing), to quote Mao Zedong, you must "let a hundred flowers bloom, a thousand schools contend." (Mao himself hardly did that, of course, but it's still a great idea—and to the point.) The grandees at Johnson & Johnson, PepsiCo, 3M, IDG, and ABB mostly get it. Damn few other grandees (of large companies, large museums, or large public agencies) do.

To summarize, consider the following logical propositions, about an illogical world, purposefully parsed to annoy and irritate:

—Success is due to luck.

—Success carries within it the seeds of failure.

—Long runs on Broadway are rare.

—Serious renewal and genuine transformation are virtually impossible.

—You may *survive* success, but it is most unlikely that you will be *interesting* again.

—Planning only hinders, and the ever-popular "culture transformation programs" are a snare and a delusion.

The "answer"? Destruction, mostly. How? The following, discussed in more detail in several chapters to come, may be helpful: (1) violent market-injection strategies (subjecting business units to unfettered market discipline); (2) voluntary dismemberment ("raiding yourself"—before the raider comes calling); (3) perestroika inside the firm (how to be procapitalist *inside* the corporate moat, especially among staff service functions); (4) inundation by outsiders; (5) headquarters (literal)/staff destruction; (6) *"de-verticalization"* (subcontracting damn near *everything*)—oh, and (7) *don't* listen to customers (or rather, listen and don't listen with equal vigor—I'll come back to this one).

The odds of redefining an industry are low, looked at from the perspective of any single giant, stable firm—or from the perspective of any one entrepreneur a venture capitalist bets on. On the other hand, given the power of the law of large numbers over time (and not so long a period, these days), the odds of having an industry redefined out from under your feet are amazingly high. Retailing in the U.S.: It's been upended by Wal-Mart, The Limited, Toys "Я" Us, The Gap, Home Depot, and a dozen others—in just the last 10 years. The newspaper industry has been wrenched off its foundations by efficient direct-mail advertising and *USA Today*—and phone companies and cable companies are about to do even more damage to the papers. Turner Broadcasting and CNN—and cable television in general—have ripped gaping holes in the Big Three TV networks. Apple, Dell, Everex, Sun Microsystems, EDS et al. (et al., et al.) have redefined computing. AMR, with its extraordinarily efficient use of information technology, has reinvented the airline industry. MCI and McCaw Cellular have set the telecommunications industry on its ear. (And the split-up of ICI—see the second epigraph on page 479—may, according to some, foreshadow wholesale restructuring and unbundling in the world chemicals industry.) Could you or I have predicted any of this? And who the players would be who'd lead the charge? Fat chance! But the fact that we're such crummy prognosticators doesn't mean that the odds of any industry's redefinition aren't high. And that is precisely my point.

Internal to the corporation (should you keep it intact), the only possible winning idea is to allow the redefiners—damnable rogues, that is (see Chapter 38)—to have their way, even though they may crush today's top-performing products. (And laugh while they're at it.) Sadly, most companies aren't ready for such quirky doctors and bitter medicine. And, indeed, if you take the medicine too early (ah, the vagaries of "timing"!), you may end up doing yourself in before you ever become an "in" to undo. That is, too early to change is just as bad as too late. Tough!

Even a touch of cynicism may help. The Allied air forces effectively raided the German war ministry headquarters on November 22, 1943. "Although we have been fortunate in that large parts of the current files of the ministry have been burned and so relieved us for a time of useless ballast," wrote Nazi armaments minister Albert Speer, "we cannot really expect that [the Allies] will continually introduce the necessary fresh air into our work." Sarcastic or not, Speer had a point. Look at Wal-Mart's spartan "headquarters" ("Greyhound Bus chic," one wag called it; "Formica couture," said another). Then look at the lingering opulence at hapless Sears Roebuck. Is it treasonable to suggest that Speer was on to something, no matter who his boss was?

BEWARE THE FALSE PROPHETS OF COMPREHENSION

I devoured James Gleick's book, *Chaos*. It certifies a notion dear to my heart—that the messy aspects of phenomena are the most important. Before chaos theory, for instance, scientists taught us that big effects were generally the result of big causes. Now chaoticians are suggesting that "small changes in initial conditions" have enormous consequences. Suppose, for instance, that on the way to work you're bonked on the noggin by a flowerpot that falls from a third-floor window ledge. What complex chain of events in your life, the life of the third-floor tenant, the building's architect, etc., led you and that flowerpot to meet up? And if, say, your grandfather had altered his pattern infinitesimally 73 years ago today, aren't the odds high that this morning's accident would never have happened?

Burgeoning computer power helps us create models that track Gramps and take into account long, convoluted chain reactions. As a result, chaos theory will doubtless make major contributions to the likes of weather forecasting (showing how a tiny disturbance hither generates a monster storm yon) and medical science (explaining the mysterious turbulence that marks the heart's functioning).

But beware the inflated promise of chaos theory! Be warier still of adherents who propound its immediate application to business strategy. As I was talking with one colleague about some zany market phenomenon, he chimed in with, "Chaos theory will demonstrate that this isn't chaotic at all." He could be right in a narrow, technical sense. But I wouldn't bet your company on it.

Consider this excerpt from *A Random Walk Down Wall Street*, in which economist Burton Malkiel pokes fun at star stock pickers:

The contest begins and 1,000 contestants flip coins. Just as would be expected by chance, 500 of them flip heads and these winners are allowed to advance to the second stage of the contest and flip again. As might be expected, 250 flip heads. Operating under the laws of chance, there will be 125 winners in the third round, 63 in the fourth, 31 in the fifth, 16 in the sixth, and eight in the seventh. By this time crowds start to gather to witness the surprising ability of these expert coin-tossers. The winners are . . . celebrated as geniuses in the art of coin tossing—their biographies are written and people urgently seek their advice. After all, there were 1,000 contestants, and only eight could consistently flip heads.

I've got to admit that I've penned similar tributes. Celebrating such "heroes" is part of our everlasting, compulsive need to explain. It's given us cave drawings, Greek mythology, Newtonian physics, quantum mechanics, and now chaos theory. Our drive to know has been the engine of modernity.

Or has it? The fact is that the astonishing power of all capitalist economies, and especially the American economy, stems from having arranged things so that we don't have a clue as to what's up! Our numerous winning entrepreneurs, despite what passes for analysis in their after-the-fact autobiographies, are more or less lucky finalists in the business start-up version of Malkiel's Wall Street coin-toss. We have an "unfair share" of Bob Swansons (Genentech), Michael Dells (Dell Computer), and Craig McCaws (McCaw Cellular) because, generation after generation, we induce an inordinate number of our prodigies to "flip coins."

So let's hold the applause for chaos theory. Instead of the frantic pursuit of total comprehension (via central-control schemes), let's revel in our very *lack* of comprehension! While less successful businesspeople retain consulting chaoticians to construct ponderous models aimed at explaining what went wrong yesterday, the champion entrepreneur gets in another 10 tries, one of which just might click. At this point, anyway, it's criminal to waste precious days trying to figure out what Granddad might have done differently 73 years ago to keep that flowerpot from beaning you this morning.

The Anatomy of a (Planless) Summer Vacation

If I hadn't had to go to the bathroom at *precisely* that moment, things would most likely have worked out differently. We're used to eye-catching stories like that after an airplane crash: The person, delayed in snarled traffic, missed the fatal flight by 90 seconds. Dramatic? Absolutely. But it turns out that all of life is like that. And if we've got the guts to acknowledge it, then we'll pursue very different business strategies than if we think we can control fate through clever plans.

My wife and I landed at the Grenoble airport. Our bags were slow to come off the aircraft, so I went to the toilette. Returning to the baggage claim area, I passed a kiosk selling some very helpful guides for 69 francs (about $13). They detailed hundreds of nifty-looking hikes—right in the area where we were staying. I thumbed through a couple, then bought the lot (six).

The next morning, ensconced in a rented cabin nestled in the French Alps, we picked one of those hikes. It was fantastic, and a pattern of daily hiking, which we hadn't planned, was established.

What if the bags hadn't been delayed five minutes? What if I hadn't made that pit stop? Would it all have worked out the same way? The answer, if you're at all honest with yourself, is "of course not."

That's not all that happened on the trip. For about 18 months, I'd been practicing "aerobic walking" (or "walking"—some call it "dork walking"; it's not very pretty). When I started I could barely manage 1.25 miles at 14.5 minutes per mile, three or four times a week. Today I average 5 miles, up and down Vermont's mountains, at 11.25 minutes per mile, six or seven times a week. The latter numbers reflect a breakthrough that occurred during that vacation in the Alps.

I arrived in France determined not to let my walking habit slip, but I was panicky because our cabin was situated at about 5,500 feet. I imagined nothing but agony from walking at that altitude. I started tentatively and managed about 1.5 relatively slow miles and a 750-foot ascent the first day. (A victim of my preconception of agony, I was in agony.)

On our second Alpen day, my wife and I happened to take a brief after-dinner drive and discovered a lovely village at the end of our road (where I walked). It was about 4.5 miles away and up 2,500 feet (at 8,000 feet). Getting to that village and back became my vague "walking fantasy." Over the next few days, as I adjusted to the altitude, my walks got a little longer, a little higher, a little faster. But the village at the end of the road was as elusive as ever.

The "breakthrough" came 10 days into our stay. My wife and her daughter wanted to explore a wild trail beyond the end of our road. "I'll walk up," I nonchalantly proclaimed, "and meet you on the far side of the village." I took off, walked my usual distance uphill (about 2.5 miles by then), and ran low on oxygen. But I was damned if I was going to be discovered in a panting heap by the roadside! I knew I could walk fast, though not speed-walk, almost *any* distance; and that's what I determined to do—and did. I made it to the village before Kate and Sarah arrived by car, and greeted them by holding out an insouciant hitchhiker's thumb.

The next day I easily speed-walked to within a half mile of the village. The day after, I made it to the village going full bore. Two more days and I'd passed the village and gone another half mile up a steep trail. I ended the trip routinely walking 7 to 9 miles, ascending over 2,500 feet, at a fast clip. When I got home to Vermont, where my walk had plateaued for months at 3.5 miles and 12 minutes, I began to walk 4.5 to 6 miles at that 11.25 minutes-per-mile average.

This little vignette, I contend, reveals the typical tangle associated with the accomplishment of *anything*. And I grossly oversimplified even this trivial case. (Suppose, for example, Kate and Sarah had gotten the urge to ramble past the village 5 rather than 10 days into our trip. At that early juncture, I'd have had plenty of reason not to "take on the big goal." Et cetera.) In any event, here are some "lessons" from the mountain:

—*Memorable goals do help, but most emerge by chance.* I accidentally discovered my village in the mist and attributed all sorts of heroic properties to it. Before that, my abbreviated walk was just a miserable, painful trek leading nowhere except up, up, up an endless, dusty road.

—*Emotion is essential.* There was no way that I was *not* going to meet Sarah and Kate at the end of that road.

—*How you do it is irrelevant, but once you've done it, it's done.* I "decided" that it didn't matter how slowly I walked to the village. So I made it—slowly. The point is, I made it. The following day I did it fast, simply because I knew I could do it at all.

—*None of it was planned.* Beyond a vague desire to "keep up the walking habit on vacation," I could not have imagined such perfect and complex circumstances for spurring me to bust loose far beyond my prior persistent "limits."

Are these "lessons" from a trivial walk in the hills applicable to the complex world of business? You bet:

— *Treat accidents as allies.* Effective leadership consists of opportunistically responding to accidents, not wasting precious time lamenting the unfairness of untoward circumstances (weak knees, steep hills, new competitors).

— *Make room for people to become self-motivated (e.g., promote accidents and cheerlead for those who respond to them).* Only goals that we discover ourselves and which give us an ego stake ("meet Sarah and Kate at the distant village or bust") will animate us to struggle onward.

— *Don't overplan.* The typical plan is meaningless, the goals lifeless—and everything changes in the process anyway.

"Society has become unmanageable as a result of management," writes researcher Henry Mintzberg in *Mintzberg on Management.* " 'Professional management' is . . . an invention that produced gains in organizational efficiency so great that it eventually destroyed organizational effectiveness." That loss of effectiveness, Mintzberg argues, comes from ignoring the "commitment of individual flesh-and-blood human beings." Managing by accident, making friends with happenstance and enemies of dreary plans, is a useful antidote to "professional" management run amok.

Ah, if only the stuffy bastards in the boardroom wouldn't think so much! If only they'd get out and actually meet a customer. If only they'd let the crazies loose. If only they had the will to destroy their forbears' creaky creations. If only . . . If only . . .)

34

Violent Market-Injection Strategies

The thematic terms are . . . *autonomy, experiment,* and *diversity.* . . . The underlying source of the West's ability to attract the lightning of economic revolutions was a unique use of experiment in technology and organization. . . . The key elements of the system were the wide diffusion of the authority and resources necessary to experiment; an absence of more than rudimentary political and religious restrictions on experiment; and incentives which combined ample rewards for success . . . with the risk of severe penalties for failing to experiment.

NATHAN ROSENBERG AND
L. E. BIRDZELL, JR.
How the West Grew Rich

In the title of this section, you'll find markets *first,* innovation *second.* It's increasingly clear to me that in a topsy-turvy world, where all goods are more or less fashion goods, only egging on the market to fully buffet each and every part of the firm will increase (to a satisfactory level—maybe!) the possibility of corporate survival, and, occasionally, excellence.

EXALTER OF UNTIDINESS

F. A. Hayek was that rare economist who was also a first-rate historian. And to the faithful economic historian, like the meritorious novelist, the mess is the story. Hayek describes fitful economic (and human) progress as a direct function of rich, volatile, unpredictable experimentation in the marketplace. (He calls the global economy "the most complex structure in the universe"—inherently incomprehensible.) It's not pretty, but it's increasingly clear that it works far better than any alternative.

Tumbling into Hayek—yes, I started reading him by accident, appropriately enough—was a profoundly exhilarating experience. He mustered hard empirical evidence to buttress his case (in those 22 volumes of collected works—I'm not through all of them yet). My introduction to Hayek made me vow that I'd never again accede to the forces of order—the dogmatic strategic planners, the hierarchists, the central controllers who try to convince us that order and success are handmaidens (oh, what a comforting illusion, as Hayek points out so eloquently); that if we can just get the plan right, goodness will surely follow. To revel in disorder and the joys of accidental discovery. That's the magic of Madison Avenue and of Hollywood. Of Silicon Valley and once, long ago, of Detroit.

Where's the Mess?

After two years I have not been able to get rid of the smell of central planning.

> VLADIMIR DLOUGHY
> Minister of the Economy,
> Czechoslovakia, on the offices
> he inherited from the
> Communist regime in 1988

There is no hope for the state enterprises.

> Anonymous Chinese
> economist, quoted in *The New
> York Times*, December 18, 1991

In 1991, I glanced at *Marketing Strategy: A Customer-driven Approach*, by Professor Steven P. Schnaars. Then I dug in. It's a useful book, neatly summarizing the important positions taken by today's marketing and business strategy gurus: the successes and stumbles of the Boston Consulting Group's market share/"experience curve" approach in the 1970s; the pros and cons of

Harvard professor Michael Porter's three "generic strategies"; the strengths and weaknesses of the PIMS (profit impact of market strategies) database. And so on.

I took notes. Then, as I prepared to write this section, I reviewed my scribblings on Hayek one last time—and ripped up my notes on *Marketing Strategy* with anguish, anger, even disgust. Why? Nowhere in those tidy pages (presented as a primer for business students) was there even a hint of the richness, messiness, and uncertainty of markets. Of the disorder, fun, and enthusiasm—and agony and despair—of markets. (No, not untidiness "of" markets. Untidiness *is* markets.) To the contrary, the possibility of conquering markets with a sound plan and a little more market research could be found on any page. Not in *these* pages. You'll quickly find that messiness is the message here.

F. A. HAYEK: THE MESS IS THE MESSAGE

To understand innovation in a frantic world, like it or not, we need to go back to the economic basics. Not the dull basics of supply and demand curves that you and I first learned, but the real basics—the hurly-burly of economic life. Friedrich August von Hayek long ago dismissed traditional macroeconomic thinking, for he was the exceptional observer who examines the raw essence of markets. Consider the circumstances that led to the emergence of markets, upon which Hayek speculates in *The Fatal Conceit*:

> Only a few, relatively small localities would have provided small bands of hunters and gatherers all that even the most primitive tool-using groups need for a settled existence. . . . Without support from fellows elsewhere, most humans would find the places they wished to occupy either uninhabitable or able to be settled only very thinly. Those few relatively self-sustaining niches that did exist would likely be the first in any particular area to be permanently occupied and defended against intruders. Yet people living there would come to know of neighboring places that provided most but not all of their needs, and which would lack some substances that they would require only occasionally: flint, strings for their bows. . . .
>
> Confident that such needs could be met by infrequent return visits to their present homes, they would stride out from their groups, and occupy some of these neighboring places, or other new territory even further away in other parts of the thinly populated continents on which they lived. The importance of these early movements of persons and of necessary goods cannot be gauged by volume alone. Without the availability of imports, even if they formed only an insignificant fraction of what was currently being consumed in any particular place, it would have been impossible for

early settlers to maintain themselves, let alone to multiply. Return visits to replenish supplies would raise no difficulty so long as the migrants were still known to those who had remained at home.

Within a few generations, however, descendants of these original groups would begin to seem strangers to one another; and those inhabiting the original more self-sustaining localities would often begin to defend themselves and their supplies in various ways. To gain permission to enter the original territory for the purpose of obtaining whatever special substances could be obtained only there, visitors would, to herald their peaceful intentions and to tempt desires of its occupants, have had to bring presents. To be more effective, these gifts had best not satisfy everyday needs readily met locally, but would need to be enticingly new and unusual ornaments or delicacies. This is one reason why objects offered on one side of such transactions were, in fact, so often "luxuries"—which hardly means that the objects exchanged were not necessities to the other side. Initially, regular connections involving exchange of presents would probably have developed between families with mutual obligations of hospitality. . . .

The transition from the practice of giving presents to such family members and relations to the appearance of more impersonal institutions of hosts or "brokers" who routinely sponsored such visitors and gained for them permission to stay long enough to obtain what they needed, and on to the practice of exchanging particular things at rates determined by their relative scarcity, was no doubt slow. But from the recognition of a minimum still regarded as appropriate, and of a maximum at which the transaction seemed no longer worthwhile, specific prices for particular objects will gradually have emerged.

In this description, the complexity of what Hayek calls the "extended [economic] order" appears. And along with it, and quickly at that, the "unknowability," in any exhaustive sense, of even the simplest extended order. The connections have already become far too rich and too dense to map.

Extended trade, Hayek observes, emerged before agriculture—in the Paleolithic Age, some 30,000 years ago. To move trade beyond the narrow immediate locale, some small number of guiding traditions and rules proved essential. (It is important to note at the outset that those "rules" were not, as the term might imply, the product of planning. Some societies accidentally fell into such practices, Hayek asserts. They prospered. The practices—"rules"— they had stumbled upon were copied and spread.) Above all, he avers, private property was the cornerstone for all that followed, the very basis for organized trade and thence the painful movement from small, isolated savage bands or tribes to widespread, interdependent modern civilization.

The "extended order" began around the Mediterranean. Societies there were the first, according to Hayek, to accept "a person's rights to dispose [of property], thus allowing individuals to develop a dense network of commercial relations." Private property, Hayek insists, also enshrines, by definition, the primacy of decentralization. The right to dispose of one's assets provides the basis for dealing with—or not dealing with—others of one's choosing (the most fundamental definition of decentralization).

The intellectual problem that was Hayek's preoccupation (and amply illustrated by the long extract) is this: The dense, decentralized network that emerges quickly becomes unknowable. Moreover, the chief vehicle which moves economies and civilization forward is unplanned experimentation by and among millions of individuals (billions today) who do not know one another. Along the way, successful experiments are emulated. (Some very few experiments are immediately successful, for the "right" reasons—i.e., according to "plan." The rest that are successful emerge, over time, for the "wrong" —i.e., unplanned, unimagined, mostly unimaginable—reasons.) Unsuccessful experiments, the vast majority, simply drop by the wayside. Thus the process of economic expansion is humbling, irrational, and—in principle—not amenable to centralized planning and control. "Order generated without design," Hayek wrote, "can far outstrip plans men consciously contrive." He adds that the "extended [economic] order resulted not from human design or intention but spontaneously. . . . Evolution leads us ahead precisely in bringing about much that we could not intend or foresee."

(Hayek's use of "evolution" and terms derived from evolutionary theory such as "blind variation," "adaptation" and "selection" is no accident. Indeed, he takes pains to point out that Darwin was singularly influenced, 20 years prior to publication of *Origin of the Species*, by reading Adam Smith's *The Wealth of Nations*. The proper credit for evolutionary theory may lie almost as much with Smith's brilliant notion of the "invisible hand" as with Darwin's rich observations during the voyage of the *Beagle*.)

But those, yesterday or today, who are under the spell of the invisible hand are faced with a dilemma: First, they/we cannot fully "understand" how the market works, given its extensive nature. Second, the market serves no purpose "that one can specify fully in advance." And third, it produces results that are "not immediately observable" (i.e., results clouded by those tangles of causes and effects). But these three properties, Hayek points out, are *the* defining bases of testable, modern scientific hypotheses. That is, this extended, unknowable, unplannable, unspecifiable market order flies squarely in the face of the Enlightenment, of Cartesian logic and of scientific reasoning—all that has defined intellectual "progress" for the last several hundred years.

Part of the problem is egocentrism. "Intelligent people," Hayek wrote, ". . . tend to over-value intelligence and to suppose that we must owe all advantages and opportunities that civilization offers to deliberate design." To the contrary, Hayek insists, for instance, that Europe's "extraordinary expansion in the Middle Ages" was a product of "political anarchy." The anarchy per se produced the diversity which led directly to modern economic "order."

The rowdy capitalist towns of the Renaissance in northern Italy, southern Germany, the Low Countries, and England were an inexplicable new species—which launched modern market economics.

Joyous Anarchy

So much of economic success—Silicon Valley, Taipei, Hong Kong, Guangdong, Hollywood—has to do with anarchy. The "magic" of Silicon Valley lies as much in the bars and the squash courts as in Stanford University's fertile labs. It is the anarchy itself that "produces" the high volume of chance connections, the oft-told motivational fables. It is the energy from the critical mass—a statistical artifact, product of the law of large numbers—that makes Silicon Valley what it is, and makes it almost uncopyable. You could physically construct a Silicon Brasília, but you'd be hard-pressed to initiate the wild, untrammeled growth that created California's matchless economic hot spot.

On the one hand, Hayek argues persuasively that rules are imperative to progress (in very small number: private property, enforceability of contracts). On the other hand, freedom is maximized—as is wealth and the fruits of civilization in general—precisely because these rules are *impersonal.* They guide vast numbers of relationships among large numbers of people unknown to one another; their content and minimalist nature spawn decentralization rather than centralization. And maximizing decentralization, Hayek claims, by definition maximizes experiments—thereby maximizing the number of "blind variations" (the evolutionary model) from which unpredictable but useful outcomes (called "selective retention") can occasionally occur.

Hayek further claims that "all evolution rest[s] on competition. . . . [Useful knowledge] arises in a process of experimental interaction of widely dispersed, different and even conflicting beliefs of millions of individuals. . . . [Rules aimed at] repressing differentiation due to luck . . . would have scotched most discoveries." Hayek cites the preeminent philosopher of science, Karl Popper, who wrote in *Conjectures and Refutations* that there can be no final knowledge, only "suggestions" (hypotheses or conjectures) which are supported for a time, then subsequently overturned (refuted) by better but still necessarily inconclusive "suggestions"/conjectures. "Our aim," Popper added in a passage admiringly quoted by Hayek, "must be to make our successive mistakes as quickly as possible."

Which leads us back to Hayek's disdain for modern macroeconomic reasoning. He contends that it "conceals the character of competition as a discovery process." (Some maintain that the connection of markets and spontaneous discovery is Hayek's most profound contribution.) Hayek hammers away at the importance of disorderly decentralization as "the only way to make use of [widely] dispersed information in its great variety. . . . Decentralized control of resources, . . . through [privately owned] property, leads to the generation and use of more information than is possible under central direction. [As Popper said,] 'To the naive mind, that conceives of order only as the product of deliberate arrangement, it may seem absurd that in complex conditions order and adaptation to the unknown can be achieved more effectively by decentralizing decisions.' "

Yet another problem for rationalists, Hayek says, is that diversity of wants/tastes/values—which directly creates relative scarcity, and indirectly creates the price mechanism—is "not an attribute or physical property possessed by things." It is completely subjective. (Fashion!) The creation of products, markets, and trade itself is "simply" a by-product of playing up to different tastes among different individuals. "To serve a constantly changing scale of values," Hayek acknowledges, "may indeed seem repulsive." Economists, he asserts, have wrongheadedly regarded the daily elbowing among merchants in the marketplace as "superfluous . . . a methodological mistake. . . . Activities that appear to add to available wealth 'out of nothing,' without physical creation and by merely rearranging what already exists, stink of sorcery."

Why spend so much time on Hayek? Simple. To fail to appreciate—in the fullest sense of that term—the richness, passion, and raggedness of the market mechanism is to be unprepared to lead a firm (or a regional or national economy)—especially in today's unhinged global marketplace. There is no doubt that economists and planners don't much like bawdy capitalists. There's no place in the Chase Econometrics Model (or the General Motors strategic plan) for destabilizers like today's Steve Jobs, Ted Turner, Al Neuharth, or yesterday's Thomas Edison, J. P. Morgan, Andrew Carnegie.

Propositions from Hayek

• Liberty/wealth ("civilization") is due to "extended order"—i.e., trade over distance where producers and distributors and buyers are *not known to one another.*

• The extended order is based on a few overarching "rules"—e.g., private property, enforceable contracts. (The rules did not emerge as the product of planning!)

• Following a few uniform, impersonal rules maximizes variety. Variety (the product of competition/decentralization) in turn is the key to discovery and hence the creation of wealth.

- *Intangibles*—money and banking, differing tastes—are *the* basis for the extended order. *All* value (trade) is a function of intangibles/human relationships, *not* physical properties (e.g., intrinsic "quality" of the objects per se).

- Value stems from rearrangement/rearrang*ers*. Brokers, etc., are *more* important than "producers."

- Growth stems from trial and error, competition, the survival of (and imitation of) the successful. (The successful seldom know they will be successful. Success invariably stems from unintended consequences, from endless strings of unpredictable causes and effects.)

- Decentralization/decentralized processing of information (and the trial-and-error, often "lucky" discovery of preferences/tastes) is the key to the extended order. More information, *by far*, can be processed more quickly in a "disorganized" (decentralized) system—i.e., more chance, unpredictable-in-advance connections occur, which lead to more "blind variations," thence, eventually, more "selective retention." (Not for sure, of course. "Selective retention" is a probabilities game.)

- Success doesn't necessarily come to those who "deserve it" and is not a matter of "fairness"—because of the complexity of the system, which leads to long chains of unintended consequences, with *long-term* effects which can rarely if ever be anticipated at the moment by even the most brilliant prognosticator.

MICHAEL PORTER: AN UNLIKELY PRINCE OF DISORDER

The most competitive industries in all the European nations were those where capable national rivals were pressuring each other to advance: German cars and chemicals; Swiss pharmaceuticals, heating controls and flavorings; Swedish heavy trucks, paper products and machinery; Italian clothing and factory-automation equipment. In contrast, widespread collaboration was a sign of decline, or of government inter-vention preserving uncompetitive rivals.

Some people think Japan's success is due to cartels and collaboration. It is not. In the industries in which Japan is internationally successful, it has many committed, fiercely competing local rivals. Its nine car makers, 15 television-set manufacturers, and 10 fax producers show how local rivals, each with only a modest share of the home market, can prosper abroad through rapid upgrading and the impetus to compete globally. The same is true in Korea. MITI, Japan's industry ministry, has failed repeatedly when it has tried to consolidate industries (e.g., in cars, steel or machine tools).

MICHAEL PORTER
The Economist
June 9, 1990

Say "Michael Porter" and buttoned-down techniques for corporate strategy analysis come to mind. Harvard's Porter earned his renown at the pinnacle of business-strategy thinking by teaching people how to get organized, how to analyze their "business systems," how to out-plan competitors. But that was before *The Competitive Advantage of Nations*. It took four years of painstaking research in 10 countries. And fills 855 pages. But you can boil Porter's magisterial work down to just three words: "vigorous domestic rivalry." That is: Firms that engage in the most intensive competition in their home market tend to improve fastest. Nations that encourage such unvarnished local rivalry tend to perform best. Correspondingly, those firms and nations that limit vigorous competition and the number of competitors perform most poorly.

Porter exhaustively examines industrial competition in Denmark, Italy, Korea, Singapore, Sweden, Switzerland, the United Kingdom—and of course Japan, Germany, and the United States. He was motivated by what he felt was the failure of accepted economic wisdom to explain what's happening in today's global economy. Surprisingly, he and Hayek end up in the same place—as avowed allies of virtually unrestricted market forces, as princes of disorder.

Porter's approach is fresh. (Indeed, some have compared it in scope and originality to David Ricardo's theory of "comparative advantage.") He is unique in concluding that the right analytic focus for explaining modern economic performance is neither the individual firm nor aggregate macroeconomic forces; instead, it is the industry or industry segment. "This book," Porter writes, "is about why nations succeed in particular industries." The centerpiece is a mother lode of case studies—e.g., the German printing press industry, the American patient-monitoring device industry, the Italian ceramic tile industry, the Japanese robotics industry.

Porter finds that a handful of nations dominate any one industry or major industry segment. Moreover, vital competitors tend to be tightly bunched in a narrow geographic area *within* a nation. An unabashed globalist in perspective, Porter nonetheless ends up insisting that the nation and region have never been more important. "Competitive advantage," he concludes, "is created and sustained through a highly localized process."

To examine that localized process, Porter concocted the national "diamond"—four forces, acting in concert, that determine national competitiveness in any industry. First, "factor conditions." A large labor pool and extensive natural resources are no longer decisive for the achievement of economic advantage, he argues, but "advanced factors" are—data communications, the pool of engineers and scientists, university research in sophisticated areas.

"Demand conditions" come next. Consider Japan's success in TVs. The U.S. got a clear jump in television production. But Japanese demand took off for a host of reasons, and its market became saturated before ours. Japanese firms, therefore, were forced to make massive efforts to reduce costs, and to add numerous new features in order to survive in their crowded home market. In the process, they almost inadvertently ended up capturing global leadership with their superior products. (Such demand characteristics mark almost every one of Porter's industry studies. The seemingly insatiable U.S. demand for health services, for example, has helped make us a world-beating supplier of medical equipment.)

The third element is "related and supporting industries." Take Italy's dominance in footwear. Strength in the final product (shoes) is supported by, and dependent upon, parallel strengths in processed leather, leather-working machinery, and specialized footwear design services. Likewise, Italy's leadership in the lighting industry is abetted by its leadership in the related furniture industry; and vice versa. (AnnaLee Saxenian's analysis of Silicon Valley provides strong corroboration: Localized, mutually dependent innovation throughout the "food chain," from circuit-board assemblers to systems integrators, is the region's hallmark. See p. 421.)

"Firm strategy, structure, and rivalry" is the final factor. Porter insists that few industries will emerge from a nation as global powerhouses unless all four forces are pulling together. But he quickly adds that vigorous domestic rivalry is first among equals, with "especially great power to transform the diamond." Domestic rivalry feeds on itself. New competitors emerge within the country. The roiling local cluster of competitors spawns spinoffs and start-ups. Intense, close-at-hand rivalry also tends to enhance the other three facets of the diamond: "Advanced factors," such as university research, are driven by a rich nearby mix of companies concentrating on a small number of fields. Rivalry fosters domestic demand, by creating unexpected consumer desire for the most sophisticated products from these energetic industries. (It's the age-old chicken-and-egg conundrum. The Japanese are relatively wealthy and live in small homes. In part, their addiction to consumer electronics is a by-product of lots of dough and not much space. That, in turn, fuels a vigorously competitive consumer electronics producer sector. Which leads to an outpouring of exotic and unexpected new products, some of which are scarfed up by those voracious consumers with wads of discretionary cash.) Finally, hot domestic rivalry encourages and puts severe pressure on "related and supporting industries" to upgrade.

The most useful measure of national economic strength, Porter argues, is productivity. He contends that national productivity is less a function of traditional macroeconomic policy levers (e.g., managing money supply) than of government programs to induce "relentless improvement" and "stimulate dynamism and upgrading." Spurring such dynamism, he adds, "leads to competitive advantages, not short-term cost advantages" that could theoretically come from combining big industrial firms by relaxing antitrust enforcement.

No nation can dominate industries across the board. Therefore, Porter concludes, "Efforts to preserve all industries will lower the national standard of living." Furthermore, nations that support collusion and try to put all of an industry's eggs in one basket (attempting to create a dominant "national champion" company, a favorite French strategy) are doomed to fail. They end up suppressing rather than inducing the necessary energetic *domestic* rivalry.

Porter on Policy: Hail Trust Busters and Free Traders

Some of Porter's resultant policy advice is music to liberal ears. "Education and training are decisive," he writes, and the "single greatest long-term leverage point available to all levels of government." Porter stresses the crucial role of K-12 schooling, research universities, and vocational education. He also favors stringent product safety standards, chiding the U.S. for having lost its leadership in this area; nations with the toughest standards force their home companies to upgrade products in a fashion which abets long-term global industry advantage. And Porter insists that strong antitrust enforcement is "essential"—there is, he says, no more important lever for stimulating domestic competition.

Others of Porter's suggestions will thrill conservatives. The provision of "breathing spells" for beleaguered industries is ludicrous, he claims, and rarely if ever leads to improvement. He also blasts import restrictions of all stripes.

Then there are a few proposals that will infuriate almost everyone. Porter favors a strictly limited role for increasingly popular cooperative research efforts. They usually stifle domestic competition, as he sees it. Porter also questions inter-firm cooperation and strategic alliances. His research suggests that such corporate hugfests "usually undermine competitive advantage" and "sap rivalry." It's also easy to go too far in protecting intellectual property, Porter claims. Speeding up the rate of diffusion of innovation, not slowing it down, is the desired end which excessive copyright protection hobbles.

Add up Porter's suggestions, and you get a formula for maximizing the force of the market's winds—and a set of prescriptions that Hayek would surely have applauded.

HI HO DESTRUCTIVE COMPETITION!

Most business people view universities as quiet, calm, out of touch—that is, "ivory towers." Rubbish. In fact, worldwide (few cultural differences on this score), they are home to energetic competition. Losers often weep. Occasionally they commit suicide. These days, Big Science at universities may call for more teamwork to conduct ever grander experiments. But have no doubt about what the Fermi lab high-energy physics "team" is up to: destruction of the ideas of others, supplanting them in a decisive, ego-crushing fashion.

Scientific and economic progress are products of destructive competition. Period. Copernicus *overthrew* the myth of an earth-centered universe. And the transistor dethroned the vacuum tube. Speaking of vacuums, the electric home vacuum mercilessly crunched those wonderful old carpet sweepers. (Remember them?) As the word "destructive" suggests, such competition is seldom pretty to behold, in big-university settings, in the semiconductor and soft drinks marketplaces—or *within* the corporation. But the absence of tidiness, and grudges held for decades (the spice of research-university faculty life), are no cause to reject the process, or the result.

Private railroaders greedily butted and shoved one another around in the two decades after the Civil War. Bloodthirsty, destructive competition led to massive overbuilding—fully 20 percent of all previously laid track had to be abandoned in the last 15 years of the 19th century. What a waste, eh? Hogwash. First, that vicious competition led to remarkably rapid track-laying and associated technological and administrative breakthroughs. Arguably, the railing of America was shortened by a quarter century thanks to vigorous local Porterian rivalry. Testimony to the value of that energetic competition is what transpired when collusion usurped it: Railroads cozied up to each other, then the government stepped in with regulations to curb the most wretched excesses of collusion (uh, "strategic alliances")—and America's premier business pioneers (those self-same railroads) quickly turned into bloated, noncompetitive national jokes.

The absence of vigorous competition has a ripple effect. Former Union Pacific Railroad chief Mike Walsh points out one side effect of the fact that deregulation came to trucking before railroads: Diesel engines in locomotives are relatively underpowered and inefficient compared to those in trucks. Why? Different technologies? Forget it. Bare-knuckle competition among newly deregulated truckers quickly induced bare-knuckle competition among related suppliers—e.g., trucking's diesel engine providers (Porter's model again). That process was absent in the still regulated railroad industry. The diesel producers were mostly the same for trucks and railroads. No matter. There was no automatic spillover to railroads—until deregulation and competitive pressure began to ride the rails, too.

Chairman John Akers is blasting away at IBM's innards. Why? He's not reacting to newfound strength at Germany's Siemens or even Japan's Fujitsu. Instead he's cowering before a frustrating, diffuse attack on IBM by Hewlett-Packard, Cray Research, Convex, Sequent, NCube, 3-Com, Intel, Cypress Semiconductor, Sun Microsystems, ASK, AST, Microsoft, Dell, Acer, Apple, Compaq—and several *tens of thousands* of other outfits you've never heard of. Akers claims 50,000 competitors.

Yet some policy gurus say Silicon Valley (and the American electronics industry in general) is home to excessive, destructive competition—i.e., destructive in that it wastes scarce national resources such as engineering talent. Lots of firms do go out of business. And many others scratch out a living, but produce no memorable products. Is engineers' time spent at such firms "wasted?" To the contrary. Engineers at failed firms arguably have the highest, not the lowest, rates of learning—which is subsequently applied in zillions of other settings. I'll admit that the Valley's doings ain't pretty to watch at times. Especially since so little of the churning occurs for "logical" or "fair" reasons—if you believe that the best plan and the cleverest idea should always win. But it's the most *constructive* destructive competition this country has seen since the days of those miserable SOBs who built the railroads and steel mills, dug the coal mines, and drilled the oil wells. (Want to get a bead on heavyweight, bloody—literally—competition? Read about the old coal-mine bosses in Pennsylvania. And remember the results: the coaling of America in record time—which, in turn, directly powered our dramatic, rapid drive to economic superpower status.)

Now shift your sights to the innards of the firm. A decade or two after some new technological discovery is made and initially commercialized (e.g., autos in the first decade or so of this century), brutish technological competition gives way to vigorous polishing of the apple—a search for efficiency, leading to the likes of Ford's mass production techniques. After most significant gains from the efficiency wars have been realized, surviving giants usually settle down and become sluggish and complacent: Witness the decidedly gloves-*on* tiff over tail-fin supremacy that marked the U.S. auto industry in the unglobal 1950s. In the case of U.S. autos, destructive competition, which waked up the whole industry after four slumbering decades, came from outsiders.

First VW tried to teach us that all cars need not resemble tanks. Cute, we said as one, but irrelevant. Then the hungry Japanese auto bosses (ruthless, not just vigorous, rivals) reinvented the entire industry.* Pity that the Big Three,

---

*To go back to Hayek's theme, unintended consequences reigned. Matching their infrastructure (narrow roads, no oil), the Japanese produced relatively light, fuel-efficient autos—which just happened to coincide with the OPEC oil shock. But not even the oil shock could keep Detroit from responding to change by doing more of what it had always done—building big cars. Consumers "conspired": After Oil Shock I had played out, we resumed our love affair with big cars, taking the pressure off our automakers. Only Oil Shock II brought us to our senses, by which time the Japanese beachhead was well established. *C'est la vie.*

like the railroads before them, failed to engage more quickly in serious competition *inside* the individual firms. Suppose General Motors, for example, had in 1973 dismantled its several-thousand-person headquarters in Detroit and moved, with an ABB-like staff of 150, to the epicenter of the emerging American economy, to Los Angeles, Dallas, or Atlanta—that is, had tried to destroy itself before Nissan (et al.) did it the favor? The problem: It's the rare established corporation that's capable of self-destruction unless it has been bred into the firm from very early on (see the cases below for a few who are productively suicidal).

Modernity has its downsides. Some are so serious—destruction of the environment—that they make the whole idea of "progress" seem dubious. But if you buy the idea of progress, on net, then you must, as I see it, buy the idea of competition. And, like it or not, competition that breeds efficient (rapid) overall progress is destructive. Yes, some temporary "network of loving partners in strategic alliance" may produce today's scintillating product. But if there is a somewhat more scintillating product before dawn tomorrow, which is increasingly likely, don't count on it coming from yesterday's perhaps useful strategic alliance. And if tomorrow's exciting product is a real leap forward—which destroys your product, your morale, and your bank balance—I'll almost guarantee it won't have come from yesterday's winner or alliance partners.

If you want good advice on destructive competition, forget the blather you read about Japan's keiretsu combinations. Behind a lineup of serene faces lie effective street fighters. A glance at an unemployment map of the state of Michigan will show you exactly what happens when complacent firms (ours) fail to engage in destructive (i.e., serious, swift, fundamental) competition.

Smart Chips from Vigorous Rivals = U.S. Success

The U.S., it's said, is "coming back" in semiconductors. Actually, we were never "away," save in the laments of nouveau establishmentarian semiconductor bosses and Harvard economics profs bent on making Industrial Policy. As "smart" (so-called "design-rich") chips have become the cornerstone of the huge market and commodity chips have lost their luster, Americans are recapturing overall market share—and building a bulging, vital smart-chip lead. Make no mistake, the success is mostly a tribute to many half-sung, vigorous, take-no-prisoners, small- to moderate-size companies—and a few viciously competitive, ungentlemanly giants like Intel, which has been spurred on by its upstart rivals and an ungentlemanly CEO (Andy Grove) who wouldn't last a day in the GM boardroom.

ECON 101—YOU NEED IT

The first chapter of this section examined the role of chance in economic life. The first dozen or so pages of this chapter examined the messy fundamentals of the market mechanism. Is all this a diversion? "Why Econ 101?" you might ask.

Nothing is more important to the basic argument of this book than acknowledging the role of virtually untrammeled market forces—in these volatile times. Most businesspersons cheer markets in general, and probably secretly admit that 99 percent of the reason they're where they are is "lucky genes." But these "facts" are ignored when it comes time to design the organization—especially an organization fit to ride out tomorrow's, and the day after's, competitive gales.

Some, however, large ego or not, get it. They watch bureaucracy and sluggishness creep into their recently feisty firms. And they do something about it.

THERMO ELECTRON'S PUBLIC SPINOFFS

In 1956, George Hatsopoulos got his Ph.D. in mechanical engineering from MIT. With $50,000 from his friend Peter Nomikos in hand, he promptly founded Thermo Electron Corporation. The company went public in 1967. (Nomikos is still a major shareholder.) With sales of $805 million (1991), Thermo employs slightly over 6,000 people and spends a heady 8 percent of gross revenues on research and development: It was tagged a "perpetual idea machine" by a Wall Street analyst quoted in *Research and Development* (Thermo won the magazine's "Corporation of the Year" award in 1989).

"My idea was a broad-based technology company that would work simultaneously on lots of ideas that were risky," George Hatsopoulos told us in 1991. "But if any one of them worked out, we would be profitable." Thermo currently participates in six major businesses, all in some way related to the application of thermodynamics: instruments (Thermo's largest and most profitable business); biomedical equipment; cogeneration (i.e., design and construction of cogeneration, alternative-energy, and biomass-fueled power plants); manufacturing process equipment (e.g., paper-recycling equipment and electroplating systems); advanced technologies (including electro-optical systems and signal-processing lasers); and services. Sales have nearly doubled since 1987, and non-U.S. business accounts for about a third of Thermo's revenues.

The most potent embodiment of the "perpetual idea machine" notion is Hatsopoulos's unique organization structure. To keep the entrepreneurial juices flowing in an increasingly large firm, he constantly spins off substantial minority interests in what others would call "divisions" to the public.

Thermo currently has seven publicly traded subsidiaries. Thermo Process Systems, Inc., for example, develops metallurgical heat-treating systems, thermo waste treatment equipment and services, and aerospace heat-treating services; it's 74 percent owned by Thermo Electron, with the public owning the rest. Thermedics, Inc., 60 percent owned by the parent, develops instruments for detecting explosives, drugs, and carcinogens, and also develops biocompatible polymers. Thermedics is also unique to the Thermo Electron family in having subsequently spun off subsidiaries of its own to the public—for example, Thermo Cardiosystems, Inc., which creates pneumatic and electric cardio-assist devices (Thermo Electron and Thermedics combined own 55 percent of this spinoff's spinoff). In addition to the publicly traded subsidiaries (including subsidiaries of subsidiaries), there are also three subsidiaries in which private investors have minority interests of about 5 percent.

Thermo also has several divisions—such as Thermo Fibertek, Tecomet, and the Peter Brotherhood—which are still wholly owned by the parent. And several of the spinoffs have wholly owned, highly autonomous subsidiaries. At some point, any of these units could go partially public.

Motivations for Spinning Off

Spawning nonstop entrepreneurial behavior has been George Hatsopoulos's obsession from the start. He's long rewarded employees with stock options, for instance. His motto is "let the market decide." That's essential, he claims, in an R&D-driven company. (And what company, from the new restaurant across town to the software start-up down the block, doesn't need to be "R&D-driven" in a knowledge-based, fashionized market?)

Compensation based solely on current financial results doesn't cut the mustard, Hatsopoulos says. A division might spend like crazy on research, but come up with a portfolio of high-potential innovations. In the process, though, short-term earnings might decline. Value has been created, but how do you measure it? And how does top management reward it? Hatsopoulos put the question this way: "Can you imagine me arbitrarily doubling the bonus of the division whose earnings went down fifty percent [because of hefty R&D spending] and only giving half a bonus to a division whose earnings increased fifty percent? No matter how much I explained, I'd be spending all year trying to keep people from getting demoralized." Stock options turn such judgments over to the marketplace, and Hatsopoulos claims the public mart does a good job of taking research investment into account—so long as analysts can understand the company's strategy (see below).

The stock-option strategy worked well, execs say, during the firm's roaring '70s, which were marked by 20 percent a year growth. By the beginning of the '80s, however, Thermo had grown and diversified to the point where even rewards based on stock price had become only loosely related to individual performance. "The stock price might go down because one division did lousy, while another did very well," Hatsopoulos told us. "Everybody was getting rewarded the same way, regardless of whether they were contributing or not." Hence the decision "to separate the company into several public companies. It would be a new kind of management structure. Each part of the company would have its own stockholder constituency that would vote with their pocketbooks on how the individual division is doing."

Hatsopoulos admitted that spinning bits of a corporation off to the public is not an original idea. On the other hand, Thermo's approach mocks conventional wisdom. "Spin-offs in the past were done with peripheral businesses," he said. "Our strategy was to take our *core* businesses public. That had never been tried, and to my knowledge others haven't done it to this day." John Wood, CEO of Thermedics, the first spinoff, added, "Before we arrived on the scene, 'spinoff' might have implied 'How do you get rid of a dog?' We've used it in quite the opposite way: 'How do you take a *jewel* and raise money to finance its growth more rapidly than you could afford to if it remained part of a larger corporation—and at the same time offer strong incentives to the management team to make it successful?' "

Thermo execs acknowledged that, at first blush, the new structure makes the parent look like a holding company. "We are *not* a holding company," John Hatsopoulos, Thermo CFO and George's brother, snorted. "We are a totally unified company with common goals and interests, giving an opportunity to investors and employees to benefit from the success of a spinoff." It's all about having the best of all possible worlds—"a small company incentive-wise and a big company service-wise," as John Hatsopoulos sees it.

John H. pointed out another difference between Thermo's spinoff strategy and that of others: The parent doesn't sell shares of the spinoffs; the spinoffs do it themselves! "If the parent company sold the shares," he told us, "it would suggest we're looking for money for ourselves. If the spinoff sells its own shares, they're doing so because they need to fund their own growth." Furthermore, John H. claimed that Thermo "has never sold a single share of any of our subsidiaries and taken the money for ourselves. We allow spinoffs to sell shares to raise money. If they need a lot of money, and that would endanger our controlling interest, then we [parent Thermo] participate in *buying* shares."

Structure and Incentives

Spinoff management teams are ordinarily granted stock options that add up to 8 to 12 percent of ownership in their company. Total compensation for spinoff CEOs, however, encourages a broader look. An average package includes 40 percent options in their own spinoff, but also 40 percent options in the parent—and 20 percent options in sister spinoffs.

Despite such efforts to foster a corporate perspective, spinoffs are designed to be independent. For one thing, each one has its own board of directors, typically consisting of members of Thermo Electron's top management, the spinoff CEO, and two outside directors. For another, "We try to avoid transactions between units," George H. said. "We do that by having each unit in a significantly different business." On the other hand, he added, "there's a constant sharing of experiences and learning; one division will often volunteer to support another that may, for example, need certain key individuals." Thermo encourages transfers from company to company to broaden executive experience, cross-pollinate ideas—and keep that fragile but vital "sense of the whole" intact.

The corporate center offers a variety of services to spun-off units, which typically sign an initial three-year service agreement—which is invariably renewed. "For one percent of its gross revenues," John H. told us, "we will provide the spinoff the services it needs to face the world." (He implied that it is a very good deal—i.e., somewhat subsidized.)

These services include cash management, pension fund management, leasing, customer financing, investment banking services including investor relations, administration of employee benefits, executive recruiting, SEC filings, and patent and trademark protection. The center also offers more general services including technological assistance (access to specialized expertise in various technical disciplines), corporate development (assistance with business planning and analyses of acquisitions—several of the subsidiaries have made their own small acquisitions), and market planning and development (including assistance with economic forecasting and, if useful, high-level corporate contact with select key customers).

"I really believe in small companies," George H. said emphatically. "But small companies have big disadvantages. They don't have the support, the financial and management resources that big companies have. So you have to find a new structure for U.S. industry that combines the advantages of small companies and the support of large companies. My own answer is to have a bunch of small companies in a family, which gives them financial and management support and strategic direction. But at the same time they are acting as though they are independent companies with their own constituency of stockholders."

(Consider Random House and IBM, IDG and Thermo, for a moment. Random has very independent "imprints" and IBM is *trying* to turn its 13 Baby Blues into very independent units. Nonetheless, both firms have purposefully retained brawny, mostly centralized distribution schemes—i.e., potent sales forces. IDG and Thermo also provide their very independent subsidiary units with useful central services—but don't encumber them with a central sales force. "Encumber," of course, is in the eye of the beholder. Random CEO Vitale and IBM CEO Akers would call their potent distribution arms "soul," though critics of IBM, at least, point to the anticompetitive effect of the firm's big distribution arms. IDG and Thermo don't find soul in central distribution—and different industry structures alone don't explain their radically different strategy. Nobody said this was easy.)

Run-up to Spinoff

"Throughout the company we probably have a hundred things in very, very early stages of development," Thermo executive vice president Robert Howard told us. "People always find a way to do the initial work—doing it at night, attempting to take it far enough to demonstrate some credibility. Then, maybe the discoverer wants to run an experiment which will cost, say, thirty thousand dollars . That can be authorized within the division. If the expense is a hundred thousand or more, however, that affects the division's or spinoff's bottom line, and at that point the idea would be reviewed on a wider basis." The corporate center on occasion provides patient money to fund a project as it moves through various stages of development. Or government grants or industry support might be sought. (Such grants, from the likes of the Gas Research Institute, the National Institutes of Health, and the Jet Propulsion Lab, account for nearly half of Thermo's total R&D budget.)

As it gathers steam, a project might be converted into a wholly owned subsidiary, which, among other things, prepares its management for subsequent spinoff status and public ownership. Two or three more years (Tecogen) to a decade (Thermo Instrument Systems) may pass before public spinoff.

"When the possibility of success is on a reasonable footing and you can see the shape of the business that will develop around the new opportunity," Thermedics CEO John Wood told us, "it's time to go public." If capital requirements are modest—$3 million to $10 million—Thermo might decide on a private placement, selling about 5 percent of the stock to select investors. The chief motivation for such a modest placement is the chance to give significant stock options to the spinoff management team. As for jumping all the way to public ownership, "the project has to require substantial capital, have the potential of growing thirty percent a year or more, and exhibit the depth of management necessary to handle the pressures of work in a public company," CFO John Hatsopolous explained. "The public is a much tougher boss than we can ever be. They can fire you on an instant's notice by selling your stock. We can't hire and fire managers like that!" Once Thermo makes such a decision, then it must satisfy the investment bankers. "That's equally hard," John H. reported, "because we have to convey a *concept*. When [prospective spinoffs] are first offered [to the public], they are selling at a [price-to-earnings ratio] that reflects future earnings, not current earnings." It helps a lot to have an investment banker who buys the overall Thermo scheme. Lehman Brothers became an ally and partner, after lots of hard selling on the part of Thermo's senior officers.

Thermedics, the First Spinoff

Thermedics, which recorded profits of $4 million on $32 million in revenue in 1991, was spun off in 1983 to develop heart-assist devices. Related research began at Thermo Electron in 1965, funded by grants from the National Institutes of Health. "The work continued until the early eighties," Thermedics CEO Wood explained. "At that point, top management realized that the effort going into developing a mechanical heart was a relatively small activity submerged within a much larger Thermo Electron. If we spun off Thermedics, we'd give investors a chance to invest directly in that particular research. We also recognized that somebody in a small group working for a large company probably wouldn't see his or her successful efforts directly rewarded by a change in the [parent's] stock price. By creating a spinoff, we could offer stock options to the management team—they could see their successes or failures much more directly."

Thermo had "a tremendous amount of technology in a small group" working on the heart-assist device, John H. recalled. "But the group was getting lost. Its management came to us and said, 'How can we make a contribution here? We are a one-to-two-million-dollar subsidiary, and it looks like it'll be five more years before we grow to substantial size. Other groups at Thermo can get a single order that's ten times our total size! We just can't make an impact this way.' So we had to find a way to remedy that."

Right after spinoff, "we were very small," Wood said, "with only about thirty people. We depended on Thermo Electron for virtually all of our services. We'd use their purchasing agent to buy things for us, their human resources, finance, accounting." Things have changed, but Wood nonetheless appreciates the continuing link with the parent. "Thermo Electron, for instance, has a full-time patent counsel," he explained. "When we have a question, I can pick up a phone and get an answer, in effect, from a high-quality law firm that I couldn't afford if we were a small company on our own. The same is true with finance. We pool our cash with Thermo Electron, which has a full-time treasurer investing several hundred million dollars; he's able to get more attractive rates than we could. Investment banking is another advantage—our offerings have been underwritten by quality firms. Our bond offerings were guaranteed by Thermo Electron, which allowed us to raise money that would otherwise have been unavailable. We also have an awful lot of talent we can lay our hands on, and yet maintain the spirit and flexibility of a much smaller company."

But when Thermo subsidiaries go public, they must start behaving like a public firm. "Since we were an R&D company at the time of our spinoff in 1983," Wood reported, "we didn't have strong sales and marketing expertise. We wanted to beef that up and to acquire a volume manufacturing capability as well." So what did Thermo Electron's brand-new spinoff do? It made an acquisition! "We acquired a company called Corpak, which is a major supplier of enteral feeding systems," Wood told us. "They're in Chicago, and we've moved some of our products there. Although Boston is a great place for doing R&D, it's not so good for high-volume manufacturing because of [high] labor rates."

Since its initial public offering in 1983, Thermedics has initiated several more rounds of equity and bond financing. And it's made several acquisitions besides Corpak, including Universal Voltronics—which Thermedics purchased from parent Thermo Electron. Universal, a $1.5-million (revenue) business, makes trace-detection instruments, which, for instance, measure nitroglycerin in the blood of heart patients. (On it goes: Nitroglycerin is also used in explosives. When the FBI learned of Thermedics' research, a whole new business family was born—bomb detection. Thermedics' product, EGIS, is used by airports to detect bombs in luggage. That business is growing so fast that—natch!—Thermedics recently created a wholly owned subsidiary, Thermedics Detection, to accelerate commercialization.)

In 1988, Thermedics broke new ground within the Thermo Electron family by deciding to spin off its own public subsidiary, Thermo Cardiosystems. The reasons mirrored those which had led the parent to spin off Thermedics in the first place: a potentially important product in development and a pressing need for capital. "We sensed that government funding [to support product research] was falling off," Wood said, "yet our clinical success with patients using our devices was very impressive. So we needed more cash to continue development and replenish the loss of a couple of million dollars a year we'd been getting from the federal government." In January of 1989, Thermo Cardiosystems' initial public offering (IPO) raised $17.5 million. Wood underscored the tie between the ability to raise money and what he calls a "pure play." Thermedics, he said, "was originally formed as a 'pure play' in the biomedical area. But with the addition of these detection instruments and our new business of polymer products, we had developed diverse business lines. The creation of Thermo Cardiosystems allowed the investor to refocus on the heart-assist pump itself."

"Pure Plays" Yield Market Value

The "pure play" concept is important. CEOs of "conglomerate organizations," such as GE's Jack Welch, constantly snarl about the low prices of their shares. But the handful of critical security analysts who track a company simply can't get a clear line on such diverse enterprises, which feeds their inherent conservatism. What applies to a GE—which is in such diverse businesses as financial services, entertainment, aircraft engines, and locomotives—also applies to the difference between *moderately* focused

Thermo Electron, *substantially* focused Thermedics, and *precisely* focused Thermo Cardiosystems. In short, the more exact the focus, the greater the ability of analysts to get a confident bead—for better or for worse—on the unit's future.

Thermo Technologies Corporation: Letting Go of Central R&D!

The July 1991 spinoff of Thermo Technologies Corporation (subsequently renamed ThermoTrex) represented a next step in the evolution of the Thermo Electron model. The $17-million operation was Thermo Electron's central R&D arm—in a company known for the effectiveness of its centralized R&D. Now even that unit was to be fully marketized.

The R&D Center had been the birthplace of all the divisions which became Thermo subsidiaries. As divisions peeled off, the center would replenish itself, mostly by seeking more outside development contracts. But by 1987, it was spinning things off so quickly that it was down to just $4 million in sales. Then Thermo Electron acquired Western Research Corporation (WRC) in San Diego, an R&D company with about $15 million in sales—and a brand-new group of technologies. Thermo's R&D Center and WRC merged to form Thermo Technologies Corporation. And promptly went public.

Thermo's top team was clear about the need to make the bold move. "Thermo Technologies Corp. had three very promising technologies that could lead to products addressing very large markets, but their commercial development was going to consume a [big] R&D expense," Executive Vice President Robert Howard explained to us. "A public company [Thermo Electron] can generally afford only so much for R&D—given investor expectations about quarterly and annual earnings. And we had so many other promising projects on the boards that we couldn't support them all. We'd already made commitments to several projects, and these new opportunities [from the combined R&D Center-WRC organization] came on top of that. So we decided to sell an interest in the public [via TTC] to get the twenty million dollars they needed."

Typical of new Thermo public spinoffs, TTC consists mostly of R&D staffers. As time goes on, said Howard, "they'll add sales and marketing people, and develop manufacturing capability, as we've done with all our internally grown businesses." And, of course, the odds are high that TTC itself will spin out new subsidiaries, given the troika of exciting technologies it's pursuing. "Within three years or so," Howard told us, "we see TTC's wind-shear detector really blossoming as a commercial product. We might very well spin it off then."

In the End Small (and Big)

Spinning off has so far allowed Thermo Electron to retain its entrepreneurial spark. When Thermo Process Systems CEO Walter Bornhorst explained going public, it wasn't hard to understand why. "You feel a lot more pressure from the stockholders than you do from management," he told us. "It's also nice to believe in the company and invest your money in what you're doing. I took all the cash I had and bought the stock, because I had a lot of confidence in the team of people we had." People who are owners, he added, "are less concerned about their job titles and exactly where they stand in the company, and much more concerned about making the company successful. They tend to do whatever it takes, because they all have a stake in it."

The spinoff strategy has also allowed Thermo Electron to accelerate the growth of new businesses. CFO John Hatsopoulos said he's been pleasantly surprised by the market's reaction: "We got an added bonus—the price of the parent stock started *rising,* because analysts can now judge the value of the parent by seeing the value of the spinoffs, multiplied by the percentage of parent ownership. They add it up and what they thought was value X is really two X." But the new little public companies also benefit enormously from Thermo's overall financial strength. When Thermo Cardiosystems was about to be spun off, the market for IPOs was very weak. So Thermo Electron, EVP Howard told us, "guaranteed people who invested in Thermo Cardiosystems that at the end of a certain period of time, if they chose, they could have their money back. They would lose the interest, but the initial investment would be returned." Needless to say, since the value of the Thermo Cardiosystems investment has tripled since 1988, no investors have asked for refunds.

Thermo Electron's leaders are convinced they can reap the benefits of bigness and smallness simultaneously—a virtual must, as they see it, in today's volatile environment, which requires both constant renewal and the simultaneous ability to project significant market power. Yet in the end, the continuing entrepreneurial zest is what counts most. "We have a variety of new ventures and many entrepreneurs," CFO John H. concluded. "If you don't have this kind of a culture, what are you going to spin out? Most companies don't have many new ventures. Sure they have wonderful established businesses, but they lack the venture spirit."

Cray Cracks

Supercomputer standout Cray Research came to a fork in the road in 1989. It was essential to place a big bet on the nature of the next-generation product. Two very different approaches were under consideration. Cray execs felt—with rare and admirable honesty—that their strong "culture" would prevent them from giving both novel approaches a fair try. So founder Seymour Cray split himself off and created Cray Computer, only 10 percent owned by Cray Research. The decision, says computer-industry guru Esther Dyson, "was a clear-eyed recognition of the advantages of concentrating corporate energies, emotional and managerial, on a single project. . . . Cray will become two smaller, focused companies—one seasoned and one upstart—fighting fair and square in the marketplace." (As of this writing, the upstart is taking its lumps, which may be the strategy's best advertisement. If Cray Research founder Seymour Cray had stuck with the bigger firm, he'd doubtless have played havoc with its activities by pigheadedly defending his own approach, thereby consigning both efforts to purgatory.)

CYPRESS'S FRISKY SATELLITES

There is new strategic logic in our business: Think small, think flexible, think efficient. Corporate size is no longer an intrinsic asset in competing with Japanese conglomerates. The availability of cheap, high-performance desktop computers (essential to designing new chips) means that ever-smaller companies can play and win. With 22 employees and an investment of only $7 million, Ross Technology, a subsidiary of Cypress, brought to market a chip set more powerful than the leading Intel 80486 microprocessor.

T. J. RODGERS, founder
and CEO, Cypress
Semiconductor
Financial Times
August 13, 1991

Good luck on finding a business as tough as semiconductors. Big, market-share-gobbling Japanese companies. Big, ferocious American companies. Droves of entrepreneurial start-ups pursuing domination of a niche. Product "life" cycles of six months not uncommon. In the midst of such madness, few have performed better, and shoved the giants aside from time to time more ferociously, than Cypress Semiconductor. T. J. Rodgers's firm boasted $287 million in revenue in 1991, but there's no room for gloating (as a mid-1992 downtick in performance demonstrated). *The* issue, as Rodgers sees it, is maintaining the entrepreneurial vitality that marked the firm as a start-up.

"When we hit about fifty million dollars," Rogers told us in 1991, "I felt that the company was getting too big for me to run on a daily basis. So in 1986 four profit-and-loss centers (divisions) were created. More success. A hundred million dollars in revenue. But each stride only made Rodgers's nerves jangle more. He began to observe lethargy—"a sort of entropy effect, a wind-down effect"—creeping into the feisty company.

"If start-ups are so good, if they work so well, if those were the good old days," Rodgers figured, "then let's have some more of the good old days!" At that juncture, he "began to fund 'start-ups,' remote from Cypress—different building, different president, different board of directors." Each subsidiary company was created to attack a carefully defined market—and each aimed to combat the dreaded "plant manager disease," as Rodgers calls it.

Consider Cypress's first subsidiary, Fab II, founded in 1986. "Ordinarily," Rodgers said, "you think of a wafer fab [semiconductor fabricating operation] as a place where you hire a new vice president and give him a charter to go build the plant, then turn it on." But Rodgers vividly recalled his previous experience, at Advanced Micro Devices, with new remote plants. "If you put yourself into the plant manager's shoes, you observe a very different set of motivators from those that spurred the entrepreneurs who started the company," he said. "The founders were concerned about cash flow and diluting their equity in order to raise necessary cash. But when you start a new plant, although nominally it has an entrepreneurial aspect associated with creating a new entity, the fact is that none of those old motivations are there.

"A plant manager knows he'll get fired for the number-one sin—not bringing new capacity on line, on time. If he slips one or two quarters, it'll put a big dent in the parent company's P&L and threaten his job. As a result, the primal motivation of plant managers is *not* to minimize cash flow, *not* to balance the risk of buying insurance in the form of extra equipment and people against getting [his equity] diluted. That's because he has no stock to be diluted."

As a result, Rodgers claimed, the plant manager "always wants *more* equipment and *more* people, to guarantee that, in the worst case, when half his equipment is broken, he still has the resources to get the job done." The chief executive, on the other hand, worries about return on investment—and tries to *minimize* capital purchases. The result is an endless debate, which, according to Rodgers, the president usually loses. "I'm a good debater, I'm technical, I'm very difficult to bullshit," he said. "But the fact remains that the company will get big enough and complicated enough that I will continually lose the arguments, even when I'm right. If the motivations are wrong, the plant manager will eventually amass sufficient data, using his army of people to make presentations and demonstrations to prove his point—which he had arrived at prior to collecting any of the data—that he needs *more*, because *more* guarantees his job." Rodgers called it "a sick way to run a company."

Back to 1986: In the midst of protracted warfare with that Fab II chief,

Rodgers remembered "looking at him and saying, 'What if I give you a two-million-dollar bonus to start up Fab II and do it right?' That got his attention! But 'the bonus' wasn't really a bonus—it was an *anticipated* capital gain *if* he met his business plan."

The new model was launched. As per Rodgers, "Instead of having a 'plant,' we'd have 'a company.' The 'plant manager' would be president. The company would have a separate board of directors and would be incorporated in Texas, not California like Cypress. It would have a business plan. Today it makes wafers and sells them. It has two or three customers, not just Cypress— although we are the predominant customer. And we funded the business plan and the plant exactly the way a venture capital firm would: The 'start-up' had to produce a classic pro forma profit-and-loss statement, a cash flow statement, a balance sheet."

The pro forma cash flow statement predicts the start-up's maximum, cumulative negative cash flow—which is the amount of capital a firm typically needs to "raise." Based on that, a traditional start-up can figure what percentage of its ownership it will have to sell to fund operations. If the new start-up's managers miss that target and require more funds (and can find a funder), more of their precious stock must be issued. That, of course, reduces the prospective value of their personal shareholdings at the time of an anticipated initial public offering.

Rodgers plays it straight. When considering a new operation, he goes to investment bankers and shows them the business plan. He asks what the "start-up" should be worth, on the market, in three years—if its objectives are realized. In this case, though, Cypress will be the market, and the subsidiary's employee-owners will subsequently "sell" their shares back to the parent. Rodgers also decides what the start-up team's rewards should be, assuming expectations are met—for example, he told us, "something like a five-million to eight-million-dollar reward for creating a twenty-million-dollar (revenue) wafer fab or microprocessor company, with twenty percent operating profit." (Rodgers would like the *average* employee to own about $100,000 worth of stock if things pan out.)

If the investment banker says that such a new "company" should have a market worth of $75 million, and Rodgers wants to offer a $7.5-million potential incentive to the start-up team, then that team will get 10 percent of the total stock issued. Rodgers pointed out that it's up to the new company's president to divide up the stock. For example, people brought in at a higher salary get more stock than those starting at a lower salary; those who come aboard very early, when the risk is highest, get more than those who come later.

Rodgers offers the new company's employees two kinds of stock options. First, options in their start-up, set up so that they become fully vested on the date Cypress plans to "buy back" the start-up's stock. The second set of options is in Cypress stock. Though issued when the start-up is formed, the Cypress stock doesn't begin to vest until the date Cypress plans to buy back the start-up (then vesting ensues over the next four years). Suppose the buy-back of the start-up occurs after three years of operations. According to Rogers, employees have a three-year-old, "very attractively priced set of Cypress options. Maybe they got their Cypress stock [options] at five dollars a share when they joined the start-up. Three years later Cypress is selling at twelve-fifty a share. They're just beginning to vest, so if they leave the company, they are walking out on a big sum of money."

Rodgers insisted that the approach has dramatically changed the tenor of relations between Cypress and its subsidiaries. The dialogue between Rodgers and the new subsidiary chief (and his management team, all of whom own lots of stock) is no longer "between me, the conservator of dollars, and the president [of the subsidiary], the wheedler of funds." Now when Rodgers argues, he often takes the *opposite* tack with that new company's president: "Why don't you buy twenty steppers [the principal machines used in semiconductor production]? I'd love to write you a check for twenty-million dollars—and take up *all* the stock in your company. Then I won't have to pay you *anything* later on! How many steppers would you like? My checkbook is open."

This time the subsidiary chief sings a different tune. " 'We need only two steppers,' he tells me. All of a sudden the entire motivation becomes that of a start-up owner as opposed to that of a plant manager," Rodgers said. "Before that, he was just spending, trying to perform against plan. It wasn't until the [new] corporation was created that the sensitivity of 'it's *my* money' as opposed to '*their* money' started to set in. Instead of [the start-up team's] creative genius being aligned *against* me, arguing about why they needed *more*, their creative genius is allied *with* me. Instead of their treating my every suggestion ('Can't we save money by doing X?') as a threat, the way most large units in large companies treat the CEO's ideas, they begin to treat them as opportunities to conserve their equity position."

The new approach also allows Rodgers to attract a different caliber of leader than he could before. He pointed to Roger Ross, a key technologist from Motorola who came to Cypress to start up Ross Technology (mentioned in the epigraph). "I could never have gotten Roger Ross to be a division head in my company," Rodgers told us. "On the other hand, Ross was attracted to the middle situation, halfway between employee and entrepreneur. He runs his own company as president, has his own board of directors—but he has the advantages of Cypress's worldwide sales force, and some other things that Roger Ross, who is a computer architect, might not want to spend time trying to develop. It's not clear that Roger Ross knows how to sell silicon in Germany, but he is a superb architect. So he opts for the path where he has the independence he wanted, but some support from a corporation, in this case Cypress."

(The parallel between Ross and Knopf publisher Sonny Mehta is almost exact. Mehta is a successful "architect" with an openly expressed lack of interest in the ins and outs of sales force management—but he's a valuable arrow in the quiver of Random House CEO Alberto Vitale. See Chapter 18.)

The nub of it, Rodgers concluded, is that "the start-up mentality has caused performance in our new fabs to be, literally, two or three *times* more efficient than in the money-wasting giant companies that spend two or three hundred million for a single wafer fab."

Owners' Incentives

Body Shop founder Anita Roddick understands the perils of ownership dilution. After an initial success, she decided to expand. Banks wouldn't touch her young and quirky operation with a 10-foot pole. But a friend, Ian McGlinn, offered to provide Roddick $7,000—in return for 50 percent ownership.

Roddick quickly struck a deal. (There was little alternative other than knocking over a few 7-Elevens.) In 1992, McGlinn's stake was worth $250 million! Roddick claims she'd gladly do it all over again. Nonetheless, it's a vivid illustration of dilution—and a Technicolor reminder to business owners to do their best to conserve cash.

TEKNEKRON'S "OPEN CORPORATION" MODEL

Chances are you've never heard of Teknekron Corp. Formed in Berkeley, California, in 1968 by disgruntled big-company refugees and a few Berkeley professors, the information technology pioneer has been growing 40 percent a year, and boasted revenues of $225 million in 1991. Founder and CEO Harvey Wagner claims his "open corporation" model provides a unique approach to moving innovation swiftly from lab to marketplace.

T. J. Rodgers, Thermo's Hatsopoulos brothers, and Wagner all argue that the U.S. doesn't want for ideas waiting to be commercialized. "The main problem has been in moving innovation to the market," Wagner wrote in the Summer 1991 *California Management Review*. He blasts our biggest companies for failing to commercialize "the transistor, the UNIX operating system, reduced instruction set computing (RISC), relational databases . . . and user-friendly personal computers." In each case, a giant's research lab hatched the idea. But, Wagner asserts, "the development of large markets was left for others, usually American entrepreneurial startups." What's missing? According to Wagner, "an 'innovations transfer' force—some sort of catalytic agent—between the company's research laboratory and its product divisions."

Enter Teknekron! Wagner's formula is patiently to transform talented, energetic youngsters into high-tech entrepreneurs by connecting them to both sources and users of innovation. Typically, two budding entrepreneurs, painstakingly recruited to Teknekron a couple of years after attaining an advanced technical degree, become the basis for a start-up. When their venture has grown, several years later, to about 25 employees, it becomes one of Teknekron's "affiliated companies." If the affiliate succeeds, *total* spinoff from Teknekron is the final step.

Teknekron currently averages three or four startups per year. Since 1968, 11 units have graduated to full-fledged "affiliated company" status. Four have gone public (100 percent) or been bought by large corporations (e.g., Litton, TRW). Six are still growing as affiliates. One was disbanded. (About a dozen other start-ups never made it to affiliated-company status.) Overall, Teknekron is guided by a lean central staff of 15, not including the entrepreneurs.

Why not make the new operations independent from the outset, as Cypress does? "[It] misleads everyone . . . into believing that the venture has attained the maturity . . . that one associates with a going concern," Wagner says. "I am convinced that new entrepreneurs should be led through a series of achievements that successively give them more autonomy and control." (The Cypress story, of course, features seasoned Roger Rosses, not wet-behind-the-ears youngsters.) Wagner also has unshakable beliefs about incentives: "All rewards should follow performance, not precede it." Teknekron entrepreneurs don't get equity until their unit is successful enough to merit affiliated-company status—though the parent does pledge that "a prescribed fraction of the affiliate's stock will be reserved for staff members," Wagner writes. "Who gets how much is a judgment . . . made by the affiliate's president in consultation with its Board."

In Wagner's self-proclaimed "school for entrepreneurs," the green start-up team is immediately thrust into the marketplace. "The initial focus on marketing," Wagner says, "immediately connects the entrepreneur to a user of innovation." In fact, Teknekron's permanent staff members often accompany the entrepreneurs on early sales calls. (Almost all Teknekron start-ups aim to develop sophisticated, customized equipment, working as partners with sophisticated end users.) Teknekron also maintains special links with suppliers of new ideas. For example, Wagner and his colleagues try to " 'marry' the entrepreneurs in each start-up with compatible academics, who become 'academic principals' of the new venture."

Though Wagner sees the "open corporation" approach as a generic answer to technology transfer problems at big firms, he acknowledges the difficulties. For one thing, a Teknekron start-up's characteristic 8-to-15-year gestation period is hard for an earnings-obsessed giant to abide. Nonetheless, the company's sterling track record warrants serious consideration by midsize and large firms alike.

HAVING YOUR CAKE AND EATING IT, TOO

These three models are among the best of the "have your cake and eat it, too" bunch. There are distinct skills that parents Thermo Electron, Cypress, and Teknekron bring to the party (as do IDG, The Associated Group, and Chromalloy Compressor Technologies). The three parents understand the center's value (per Rodgers's comments about what Roger Ross could do for him, and what Cypress could do for Roger Ross). Yet in all three cases, the abiding thrust is "let the market motivate—*and decide*."

Is there any inherent reason why the Thermo model, say, could not be applied to General Motors? No! In fact, EDS is close to the Thermo model— i.e., some of its stock is publicly traded, and CEO Les Alberthal must worry about public shareholders. There's also no inherent reason why the EDS/ Thermo model could not be applied to GM's auto operations. The Saturn "division," in fact, was the first independently incorporated subsidiary established by GM since 1921 (though it's still 100 percent owned by the parent). I suspect that selling part of Saturn to the public would spawn useful independence among Saturn's leaders and the rank-and-file alike. I'd certainly consider buying Saturn stock, while I wouldn't be caught dead with GM shares. (Hear that, GM chairman Bob Stempel?—assuming you're still chairman when this book comes out.)

VIOLENT MARKET-INJECTION STRATEGIES

Let the market decide. That's the message from Hayek and Porter to Hatsopoulos and Wagner. Here, in summary, is a sampling of no-nonsense (violent) market-injection strategies:

- <u>Sell off all or part of new units</u>. This is the route taken by Cypress, Thermo Electron, Teknekron, Cray Research—and very few others. It's my belief that something like these models should become the norm in any industry you can name.

- <u>License your most advanced technology to all comers</u>. Quad/Graphics boss Harry Quadracci is a contrarian when it comes to most aspects of management, but nowhere more than in product development. He underwrites a sizable R&D unit, Quad/Tech (see also p. 406). But as soon as Quad/Tech develops something interesting, buttons it down, and gets it ready for routine application within the firm, Quadracci licenses/sells the new technology to anyone who's interested—including his chief rivals! His reasoning is straight-forward: There's no such thing as "proprietary" today. Somebody, he argues, whether a rival or an outsider to the industry, will quickly copy anything Quad does. The company's "defense": Via jury-rigged devices hung on every machine in its plants, Quad has long been at work on the next generation of innovation (and the next)—while Quad/Tech polishes current innovations for widespread sale. By selling off (for a tidy profit) his newest technology as soon as it is refined, Quadracci keeps the heat perpetually turned up under himself.

Sun Microsystems practices the same religion, and reaps many benefits from quickly peddling its newest technologies. Innovative licensees—IBM, Digital Equipment, and Toshiba, among others—end up enhancing the technology to Sun's subsequent benefit. Licensing also spearheads Sun's efforts to establish industry standards, by getting its technologies, directly or indirectly, into lots of hands, fast. But once more, keeping the heat turned up under itself may be the most important objective. "Proprietary technologies, Sun's managers reckon, tempt companies to relax," *The Economist* reported in 1989. "Knowing that competitors will share basic technologies makes employees concentrate on staying ahead . . . by innovating faster."

- Destroy your most profitable products. An old-line materials manufacturer is developing a half-dozen new technologies, some with exceptional potential. Several are ready for the marketplace, and have been tested successfully with leading-edge customers. Now is the hour to launch an outright market onslaught. But the tradition-clad company's heartland operations, which boast many profitable, market-leading products, have balked. Managers in the old divisions see the new technologies (unproven in their minds) as direct threats to their "cash cows." To say there's a battle royal going on is gross understatement. "The thing about it," one new-product chief told me, "is that they say our 'unproven' technology is attacking some of their 'new' technologies. True, [the company] hasn't been *selling* some of their products all that long, but their core technology is over forty years old! Who do they think they're kidding?"

A few *do* get the message, like Sun Microsystems (again). "We wouldn't hesitate to bring out a new product at a price performance level that absolutely destroyed an existing line," then Sun vice president Carol Bartz told George Stalk and Tom Hout (*Competing Against Time*). "Why should we wait for the competition to do it?" But even in the wacky world of computers, Bartz acknowledged, such purposeful cannibalization is "a brand-new concept . . . we've proved you can make money doing it."

Don't forget Rational, either: Chief Siegfried Meister shut down his successful convection oven line when it accounted for over half of his sales—and was turning a profit. There was no other way, he felt, to force his team to concentrate on the risky, high-potential combi-cooker business. Talk about nerve! (Sure, Meister could have failed, and then I wouldn't have written about him. Right? Right. But that's no call to dismiss such wild strategies—after all, these are wild times. Moreover, history is on my side. It turns out that the risks associated with management teams holding on to "cash cows," and choosing not to cannibalize a successful product family until it's too late, are far higher than the risks involved in selling the cow too soon. Besides, Meister's spot on: Without total attention, no combi success. It was tough enough to sell the newfangled machines *with* total attention.)

The late Emil Martini, longtime chief of Bergen Brunswig (the second-largest pharmaceuticals distributor in the U.S.), told me in 1989 that there's a single question he pestered his colleagues with: "How do we obsolete ourselves?" Bergen Brunswig has been a distribution systems technology leader for decades. But the company lives in fear. "Obsoleting" itself—working to cannibalize leading-edge services—is seen as the only practical defense against sprightly competitors. Procter & Gamble and 3M have practiced this discipline to great effect for decades. It's not pretty—none of the strategies in this section are—but it works. (Of course, there are no sure things. The P&G "model," for example, has blemishes. Chief among them: Even the "cannibals" at P&G—brands attacking other brands in the same family—have frequently become big, bureaucratic, and dull.)

- Insist that every element of the firm—even staff—demonstrate "fitness to compete" by selling a substantial share of their products or services to the outside world. "A key factor for success in components," McKinsey's Kenichi Ohmae wrote in the November/December 1988 *Harvard Business Review*, "is to sell about one-third to internal users, one-third to domestic competitors, and one-third to global competitors, so that the component division is fully exposed to the external wind." This "strategy" was discussed in the Beyond Hierarchy section—it's being followed by the likes of General Motors, Hewlett-Packard, and little Thompson Publishing Group. But Ohmae's strictures add an important twist—setting rather precise targets for outside sales by internal units. Remember my "exchange" with the Hewlett-Packard engineer (page 342): If such targets cannot be achieved, I'd propose dumping the internal unit—sell it or shut it down.

- Force "fitness to compete" among support functions (components producers, staff service units) by allowing—and even encouraging—close-to-the-market units to purchase any and all goods and services from outside vendors. This is the mirror image of the previous point. Bell Atlantic and AT&T are among the growing number following such a strategy. Both have created numerous, largely autonomous close-to-the-market units. Such units are permitted—even encouraged—to buy products and services from the "best" source, even when they could readily purchase such products and services from an internal operation.

- Subcontract extensively. As we saw in the Beyond Hierarchy section, MCI makes nothing—by choice. Its small but potent "R&D" activity is principally designed to attract vendors—of any size, from anywhere—who can provide something clever to hang on the MCI network, to better and more rapidly serve its customers. MCI figures the marketplace does a better job of providing it regular, up-to-date infusions of innovation than any internal research or computer units ever could. That, of course, is the message of this chapter.

35

The Market's Will Be Done: The Mighty German Mittelstand

The shift from the big to the midsized enterprise as the economy's center of gravity is a radical reversal of the trend that dominated all developed economies for more than a century.

PETER DRUCKER
*For the Future: The
1990s and Beyond*

Buried deep below the headlines of sensational business successes and innovative breakthroughs lies a quiet inconspicuous source of wisdom on global competitiveness. Germany's small and midsize companies.

HERMANN SIMON
"Lessons from Germany's
Midsize Giants"
Harvard Business Review
March–April 1992

When business policy debates arise in America these days, we instinctively ask, "How does Japan do it?" Shelves in the business sections of bookstores creak from the weight of texts, from learned to stupid, on Japanese management. Japan does lots that we can learn from (and vice versa). But what about Germany? That's the question I began asking almost four years ago.

For one (big) thing, Germany's export record is miles better than Japan's (and more miles still better than ours, on a per capita basis)—despite stratospheric wages and minuscule workweeks. Yet you'll find no books, or even chapters of books, on German management. That's not all you won't find. You won't find many German companies you've heard of, either. The 1989 *Business Week* recitation of the globe's 1,000 biggest businesses really got me thinking: There were 353 entrants from the U.S., 345 from Japan, and 30 from Germany. Huh?

The answer to "huh?" is Mittelstand—you've already met two of its stellar members in these pages (Goldmann Produktion, Chapter 18; Rational, Chapter 19). Max Worcester, an Englishman who sits on the board of the *Frankfurter Allgemeine Zeitung*, hosted a "get to know the Mittelstand" meeting that I attended in December 1990, in Munich. My subsequent research led to a PBS television show on the Mittelstand ("Germany's Quality Obsession") in May 1992. Along the way, I learned a lot about this semisecret German economic phenomenon.

Thousands upon thousands of Mittelstanders (about 300,000 in all) dominate global micro-niches. Combi-cookers and other high-value kitchen equipment? Yes (Rational et al.). Niche chemicals? Yes (Goldmann Produktion et al.). And textiles, too!

I say textiles, "Hong Kong" pops into your mind. Try again. The world's No. 1 textile exporter, by far, is Germany. Its $11-billion textile export tally was a third above No. 2 Hong Kong in 1990. Who puts such numbers on the board? Mostly the likes of 85-person, $18-million (1990 revenue) Wilhelm Zuleeg. How? "We have the most modern factory and no machine older than five years," company president Stefan Zuleeg told *Business Week* in late 1991. The product of the computer-controlled looms provides, the magazine reported, "high-fashion fabrics for some of the world's swankiest designers, including Cerutti, Anne Klein and Georges Resch."

Business Week also discovered other dominant midgets:

—G. W. Barth makes machines for roasting cacao beans. Like Zuleeg, Barth CEO Karl Mayer-Potschak has invested like crazy in new technology. The small firm (just 65 employees) boasts 70 percent of the global market!

—Panther follows a typical Mittelstand strategy of being "the big fish in small but rich ponds," *Business Week* says. The "Munich-based [company] . . . and its high-tech equipment unit make state-of-the-art cameraman's chairs, used for filming movies. They were the first to install a computer in the chairs, giving photographers the ability to program the chairs' movement." The five-year-old outfit has grabbed a 50 percent share of the European market, and is hard at work boosting its 10 percent share in the U.S.

The Germans are careful to point out that theirs is a "social market economy," not a market economy. That's meant a healthy welfare state—and more stability at huge firms than one finds in the U.S. But as full-scale European integration looms, Germany has had to rethink its economic policy. It turns out that giant German firms are in anything but great shape—witness a 1990 *Forbes* report claiming that 200 of the 300 business units at mighty Siemens were losing money or barely breaking even. The saving grace, whether market economy or social market economy, is the decidedly nonbureaucratic, pro-competition Mittelstand. Rarely the recipient of direct government or financial-market support, Mittelstanders have gone their own way—and are now role models for us all. A visit to a toymaker and a machine-tool producer provides some more clues about how it happens.

GEOBRA/PLAYMOBIL: PRODUCT, PRODUCT, PRODUCT

The one clear message is that "simplicity" in a company's product range, customer base, organization structure, and business system is key to corporate success.

GÜNTER ROMMEL,
McKinsey & Co., on that firm's
1991 study of excellent German
midsize companies

On pages 12 and 13 of the 1990/91 Playmobil catalog, you'll find a colorful family of construction toys. One "unit" is a bulldozer, with detachable driver. There's also a road-repair crew; workers all have safety hats, and international-standard signs and other safety gear are included. You'll even find the construction boss's shack, complete with, among other things, a transit-toting surveyor. The next two pages of the catalog feature rescue-operation sets: an ambulance with crew (and wheelchair and stretcher); a firetruck with appropriate personnel; a police helicopter; a coast guard rescue boat; a hospital (consisting of an operating room with a surgery team of three and a patient; a hospital bed, including colorful yellow bedside flowers—and a visitor). Other settings: a complex farm scene, a full-blown circus, various water activities (windsurfers, fishermen, divers, diving-control raft), a polar set (snowmobiles, explorer's tent—complete with a bearded explorer), a space-exploration scene, a pirate ship, and, yes, cowboys and Indians.

It wasn't like this in 1876, when Geobra, Playmobil's parent company, was founded in Zirndorf, Germany, a small town outside of Nuremberg. The firm made various stamped-metal consumer and industrial products, then switched to metal toys (e.g., telephones and cash registers) after World War II. The remarkably successful Playmobil product line was launched in 1973, under the tutelage of fourth-generation family leader Horst Brandstätter (the Geobra name comes from his predecessor, <u>Geo</u>rg <u>Bra</u>ndstätter). In 1991 the firm tallied sales of more than $250 million. It employs 2,000 people, about 1,200 in Germany. (The main factory is a 500-person unit in Deitenhofen, near Zirndorf; there's another 500-person operation on Malta.)

The mighty-midget-as-global-star shines here as at Rational. Exports account for a little more than 50 percent of Playmobil's revenue. Via subsidiaries or distributors, Geobra maintains a presence in over 40 countries, and has won acclaim far from home—Playmobil's new circus set, for example, captured Holland's toy-of-the-year award in 1990. Exporting has been no walk in the park, however. Brandstätter admitted to some frustration in the U.S.: Our emphasis on TV advertising and toys with gizmos is inconsistent with the Playmobil ideal. And Asia? "It's so far away, so difficult to understand," Brandstätter sighed. (German success in Asia in general has been underwhelming.)

Don't bother looking for Playmobil on the mass marketers' shelves in Germany, the United States, or anywhere else. Instead try high-end specialty retailers: F. A. O. Schwarz in the U.S. (and Vermont Toy Chest in tiny Manchester Center, Vermont, near my part-time home), Harrods in London, Mitsukoshi on the Ginza in Tokyo, and Printemps in Paris.

In May 1991, Horst Brandstätter, in a most un-Germanic open-necked shirt, and I sit in his stylish new office. We're about to begin taping an interview for television. But he is uncowed by the mass of high-tech equipment that surrounds us. Brandstätter is perpetually animated; he draws pictures with his hands in the air, grabs a piece of paper and sketches an idea. There's an irrepressible twinkle in his eye, as you might expect of a toymaker. But make no mistake, he's chosen to compete in one tough business! Brandstätter attacks it in a typical German Mittelstand way, with a crystal-clear sense of what he's about, and an abiding focus on product excellence—or "product, product, product," as he put it on several occasions.

"In the U.S.," Brandstätter says, "an executive exclaims, 'What a wonderful year, what great profits.' But we have a different philosophy, one that focuses on the product in the long haul." Brandstätter admits that "I sound like a preacher, but if you want to make a good product [in our industry], you have to think exclusively about the toy and the child. You can't think about sales volume." Mittelstand to the core!

Design of the toys is obviously important. But it's not the whole story. Brandstätter, like his Mittelstand kin, spares no expense in manufacturing—first and foremost the art and science of precision mold making. Some 4,500 Playmobil molds are valued at $100 million. (Multi-metal molds for big toys, such as pirate ships, can weigh two tons.) Factory equipment, including high-tech injection-molding machines, adds another $100 million to the investment scorecard. Ten thousand different parts in 350 colors that go into about 60 million toys per year are the result.

Stirring the Child's Imagination

Hans Beck, one of the people to whom this book is dedicated, took his apprenticeship as a carpenter, then spent years restoring old furniture. In 1948, he emigrated from East Germany, and in 1958 he got word that Geobra was hunting for a toymaker. That wasn't his specialty, but he talked Horst Brandstätter into taking him aboard anyway.

Over the next 10 years, Brandstätter and Beck engaged in an extraordinary dialogue. Hard as it may be for American managers (even business owners) to fathom, Brandstätter gave Beck a decade to play, to observe, to learn. Beck would carry an idea to Brandstätter. Brandstätter would go home, think about it, and come back the next day with a rebuttal. Along the way, mutual respect grew. Finally, in the early 1970s, the Playmobil toy line was born.

Simplicity, fantasy, system—those three words capture the magic. "This is a toy the child can apply his fantasy to, can change at every moment," Hans Beck told me. "He can create new ideas, new stories, new interactions." The idea, per Brandstätter, is "not that the toy has to *do* something, but that the children do something *with* the toy."

Hans Beck is a taciturn man (Horst Brandstätter assured me that this is as true in his native German as in English). I sat in his office for an hour, enchanted, watching him carve soft plastic. He was whittling a coat for a dachshund which would make its way into a new Playmobil winter scene. Beck was surrounded by sketches and models in various stages of progress. His concentration was singular—even with me, five other people, and a pair of TV cameras and associated equipment in the room. His identification with the toys and the children he serves is obvious to the most unschooled observer.

The heart of the Playmobil scheme is an innocuous yet compelling four-inch-high figure which displays no particular mood. "It's neutral," Beck said, "not a great man or a little man. I wanted to make a toy that could force the children to use their fantasy." Despite the yelps from typical buyers at huge retail chains, and, occasionally, from parents (at least at first, before they observe their children becoming mesmerized by the toys), you'll find no bells, no whistles, no electronics. "Kids get bored with toys that 'do something,' " Brandstätter insisted. "They use them three times, then run out of stories, and put them aside." Not so that Playmobil figure, to which the child can assign almost any personality. (Since undertaking this examination of Geobra, I've stumbled across a dozen "Playmobil parents" in the U.S. Without exception, they marvel at the ceaseless fascination the toys provide. Hey, *I* love them!)

There are numerous twists. Simplicity on another dimension: You can bend a Playmobil figure into a sitting position, but you can't adjust its legs separately. "[The complexity is] what buyers want, but not what the child wants," Brandstätter explained. "The child couldn't keep the toy steady [with legs that moved independently]." At this point in my interview, Brandstätter stopped, picked up several toys from his desktop, and started to play as if I weren't there. "The children like simple things," he began again, a moment later. "They have ideas you and I cannot see."

But there's also an intriguing dimension of complexity, which nonetheless remains true to the larger Playmobil theme. Toys are never conceived of one at a time. Each one fits into—and is sold as part of—a mini-setting, with at least a couple of characters, a piece or two of equipment. Those mini-settings, in turn, are always part of larger settings like the ones I described at the outset—a construction site, a circus, etc. It aids the fantasy, yes. It's also not a bad sales idea! A typical box shows several other small settings which fit into the big scene; customers regularly return to buy additional bits.

A Tough Sell

"What makes this business difficult," Brandstätter declared, "is that grown-ups have to solve children's problems. How do they do it? In most cases, they go into stores all around the world, look at what's selling, buy samples, take them back home. Then key people sit around and say, 'This item is selling well now. How can we make something like it which will sell even better?' " For example, buyers for mass merchants practically begged Brandstätter and Beck to develop Olympic Games theme sets in 1988. But, Brandstätter told me, "Mr. Beck says this doesn't fit our system. The Olympics is about individuals. Where's the team? [Almost all Playmobil settings feature people working in groups.] The children will be frustrated, Mr. Beck says. They'll buy it, use it a few times, then leave it alone." Schemes like instant plastic Olympians, said Brandstätter, moving closer to me and boring in, "are oriented to grown-ups, to corporate buyers. We hear so many funny things. 'This needs an extra feature.' 'Why don't you add electronics?' But that's not the way to make a toy. It doesn't, in most cases, have anything to do with the child's needs."

Brandstätter illustrated by explaining why he and Toys "Я" Us buyers never hit it off. They examined a line (about 200 items) that Playmobil offers as a complete set. "The Toys "Я" Us people said, 'We'll take this, this, this, this,' " Brandstätter recalled, "just ten or fifteen pieces. But think of it like an alphabet. Suppose the buyer said, 'Nobody wants a Y. I only want an A, E, R—and very cheap!' We told them it wasn't possible. The children have part of the system, then they want to add to it. The mother goes to the store, but the store doesn't have the missing bits." (In fact, Playmobil requires even the smallest specialty retailer, like my friends in Vermont, to purchase at least 54 items.)

Big retailers in general are the scourge of Brandstätter's existence. "I had some Canadians in my showroom a couple of years ago, a small retailer and a group from a large retailer," he remembered. "We were talking about the sets. I asked the big retailer's buyer, 'Do customers come in with a piece of paper and a number on it, to ask for specific items?' 'Never,' he said. 'Do you ever visit the stores, see the people?' I said. 'Yes, yes, yes,' he said. 'But allow me to say that maybe you *saw* the people,' I said, 'but you didn't *look* at them.' Then I asked the small retailer the same question about people coming in with numbers on bits of paper. He said, 'Oh yes, about seventy percent come in with the number on the paper. And if they don't get what they want, they don't buy anything at all.' Now I ask, what do you think about offering only the As, the Es, the Rs? And when the people come in and want a Y, and don't get it? They're finished with us."

Polishing the Idea: R&D and Mold Making

Beck and Brandstätter are in their 50s. The Playmobil scheme is in their bones. But how do they keep it alive and moving? Part of the answer is an 80-person research and development/design activity, a separate legal entity headed by Beck. The aim: "to carefully build a development company, to come to understand, as well as Mr. Beck does, what the requirements of the [end] users are," said Brandstätter. "It will take ten or twenty years."

The "end users" help. Children deluge Playmobil with about 100 letters a week. I reviewed a few with Mr. Beck, who showed no signs of being jaded after reading thousands over the years. He'd hand me an elaborate sketch submitted by a child, wonder at the beauty of it as though he'd never seen such a thing before. "Elaborate" is often the right word. Letters sometimes go on for pages, amplified by drawings that clearly took days to produce—sometimes encompassing whole new scenes for Playmobil to consider. The best of the lot are circulated through the R&D operation. There's also Playmobil Park, part of Geobra's sparkling new headquarters. As the name suggests, it's a place for children to come and play—with Playmobil toys, of course. Each month, 5,000 to 10,000 children and parents go there to frolic. Specially trained observers, designers, and sometimes even Hans Beck sit down with the children and watch them play. The day I visited, almost 50 children (and 20 or so parents) were busily engaged. It was evident in a flash that Beck has found the formula—the children, without exception, were clearly engrossed by their fantasies, creating dozens of rich dramas before my eyes.

Remember the concern with getting everyone turned on to "wholes" that marked the Beyond Hierarchy section (see especially Chapter 30)? A few years back, the U.S. toymaker Mattel invited Beck and Brandstätter to visit its Los Angeles R&D operation. About 500 designers were hard at work creating toys for the giant firm, Brandstätter told me. Mr. Beck was dismayed, he added, because "they were so specialized, so separate from one another." That's completely contrary to Playmobil's design philosophy. "We want one person to do *more* of the work, create the *whole* line," Brandstätter explained. "How else do you get the overall feel?" At Playmobil, three-to-four-person teams develop a complete setting from start to finish.

Playmobil's R&D group is held in high esteem, but not much higher than the mold makers. Constructing a mold can take 8 to 10 weeks. The hard work and skilled craftsmanship are essential. "A bad-quality product cannot be a good product, no matter how well it's designed," Brandstätter snapped at one point. "We have a fine *idea* behind Playmobil, but the users' expectations get higher and higher."

In fact, concerns about mold making's central role in an ever more competitive marketplace led to an extraordinary investment of $30 million in the new headquarters building. Putting mold making and R&D/design under one roof was the chief aim. (Shades of Steelcase—Chapter 27.) Since 1989, when the building was first occupied, the interchange between the two all-important groups has improved dramatically, Brandstätter declared. Workers and managers concurred. One senior mold maker told me he pops into Hans Beck's office, or that of another designer, once or twice a day. When the mold makers were miles away, grouped with the factory team, almost all contact with designers was by phone.

The Factory

You'll find three classes of worker in two distinct parts of the Deitenhofen factory.* The injection-molding operation features 200 expensive, computer-controlled (as of late) "machines." Running them is not much of a chore, and machine operators are not highly skilled. It's the technicians who *maintain* the injection-molding machines who are the factory's stars, and most have gone through the rigorous German apprenticeship program. There's also a low-skill assembly area, mostly populated by women with minimum training, including a number of foreign ("guest") workers.

(Despite what smacks of dramatic status differences, wages are closely bunched. Technicians' base pay was about $24,000 in 1991, compared with $22,000 for mold-machine operators and $20,000 for assemblers. An R&D staffer in Zirndorf made about $32,000.)

Kurt Gertler, who's been managing the factory for a decade, talked on and on about his wondrous machines. He became glum, however, when he turned to his "people problem." Born in 1944, Gertler lamented the lack of worker motivation today. It's not just at Geobra, he quickly added, but throughout German industry. "People don't want to take responsibility," he told me. Quality circles have been tried, he insisted without much passion, but to no avail. He didn't point fingers at the foreign workers. New German apprentices "are no better," he avowed.

---

* Deitenhofen produces Playmobil's most complex parts. Malta produces simple, light, easy-to-ship parts. About 200 German "home workers" use equipment provided by Playmobil to make odds and ends in their own shops.

What's the story? To me, the factory was a gem. It was spotless. Everything about the work environment was professional. Product quality is sky-high—the statistics say so, and so did my careful inspection of the toys. "I like to work hard," Gertler told me. It felt like a major understatement, and maybe it explains a lot. Germans Gertler's age grew up with post–World War II scarcity and had to hustle to survive. Now the hunger, literal and figurative, of 1946 is long gone. My eyes told me that, though they're no longer hungry, the Germans at Deitenhofen—and elsewhere—are hardly lethargic; but then, I'm not Kurt Gertler.

Advantage, Mittelstand

Though Brandstätter has never worked for a big company, he's clear about the Mittelstand's advantage. Topping his list is a "better understanding among all the people who work here." Big means fragmented, as he sees it, a loss of feel for the whole, too many delays, and an intolerable distortion and dilution of the original vision. Next, a commitment to the long haul—it's only possible, according to Brandstätter, in owner-controlled companies. A big-company president, even in Germany, will be interested in performance over the next three or four years, Brandstätter claimed, "but my concern is performance in ten years, twenty years." Finally, there's the singular focus on the end user. Brandstätter gets at it in a peculiar way. "Some say I should have a board of directors," he told me, boring in once more. "They don't understand. That board wouldn't understand our company, wouldn't understand the children." Always, in the end—the product, the children, the vision.

Unlike factory boss Gertler, Brandstätter is not given to decrying the lack of worker motivation. He sees the changing times as an opportunity. And, not certain that I'd understood, he took pains to write me a few weeks after I visited him:

> In the days of slavery, people were motivated with the help of a whip. In the machine age, earlier this century, workers were motivated by piece wages. Working conditions were often inhuman, and only gradually started to improve thanks to trade unions that represented workers' interests. From 1945 onwards, people in Germany were motivated by the spirit of reconstruction. Until we became well fed!
>
> In our affluent society, even a lot of money isn't a sufficient motivation. After all, everybody has almost everything [they need]. What is needed [in the future] is the entire community's will . . . a commitment to the company and themselves.
>
> Our Playmobil House [the new headquarters complex] is generally described as especially progressive. It's often said that the working conditions are especially good, the surroundings very pleasant. The design of our home was proof of the high esteem in which I hold our employees. It

was meant to—and indeed has already begun to—give them a basis for being especially proud of the company, which is a prerequisite to their doing the utmost for our company.

TRUMPF, THE MARRIAGE OF HARD AND SOFT

Every five years the world has totally changed.

> BERTHOLD LEIBINGER
> CEO, Trumpf
> Interview with the author

Berthold Leibinger was ready to begin his apprenticeship in 1950. His only means of personal conveyance was a bike. So, he told me in a 1991 interview, he sought an employer-sponsor within biking distance of home. The employer turned out to be Trumpf. Today Leibinger heads the German Machine Tool Association, is a confidant of the prime minister and a spokesman for the Mittelstand, and owns 73 percent of $475-million (annual revenue) machine-tool producer Trumpf. The stellar firm's brochure begins: "The quest to create the perfect machine. It's a goal we all share at Trumpf." If that sounds pretentious, then you've got a lot to learn about Leibinger, Trumpf, and Germany. The funny thing is, you see, Trumpf means it.

"The Quest to Create the Perfect Machine"

The machines Trumpf makes nibble, punch, cut, and bend metal; prices range from $200 thousand to $1.3 million, Cadillac country in the machine-tool business. They cut with super-alloy metals and, more recently, lasers. The firm was one of the first to introduce computer-numerical controls (so-called CNC) into the German machine-tool market, the first to introduce laser cutting. A big Trumpf machine can hold up to 400 different punching tools at one time, and apply them in complex computer-controlled sequences needed for intricate jobs. The company's principal market is big machining shops, where the transport of materials is crucial—it also sells automated handling systems that can manage over 40,000 parts.

Trumpf is global through and through, with exports amounting to almost 60 percent of total revenues. The firm boasts two U.S. factories, in Farmington, Connecticut, and Wilmington, Massachusetts. Some Trumpf machines have been designed largely in the U.S. In fact, Trumpf machines engineered and made in the U.S. account for half of Trumpf's Asian sales.

Almost 12 percent of Trumpf's 3,000 employees are in research and development. Ten years ago, of 105 R&D engineers, about 15 percent were software specialists. Today there are over 100 software engineers on Trumpf's payroll (80 or so working at the basic machine-language level, 15 on applied software programs, and 7 on customizing software to meet specific customer needs), amounting to almost a third of the R&D payroll. The metal benders at Trumpf, then, are keeping up with the times. If further proof is needed, you'll find it in this excerpt from an article in the March 1991 *Trumpf News*, bulletin of the firm's U.S. operations arm:

> Trumpf Industrial Lasers [TIL] has added telediagnostics to its full range of service department capabilities, allowing users of Trumpf laser equipment to correspond via telephone and modem with TIL service engineers for quick and accurate diagnostics of operational problems without incurring unnecessary down times. The telediagnostic service contract enables laser operators to link their laser control unit to one of the computer terminals at TIL's Wilmington, Mass., headquarters. There, laser service engineers can monitor all laser operational parameters down to printed circuitboard level and communicate with the laser operator through on-screen computer sentence cues requiring keyed responses. Once the problem is found, TIL engineers will walk users through the steps to correct the situation and if a part is proven to be faulty, a replacement can be overnighted for installation and, if necessary, a service engineer will hand-carry the part for an on-site call.

Mittelstand Is "Personal"

Some call Berthold Leibinger the Mittelstand's high priest. When he answered my question, What *is* a Mittelstand company?, he began hesitantly—"If only we knew." Then, quickly and typically, he went on to elaborate with Trumpf-like precision. A Mittelstand company is (1) "a company of medium size, which is owned by one family or a few owners" who are (2) "dedicated to a core business and stick with that core." Furthermore, (3) "the will of the owner should be visible," and (4) "the owner should provide continuity; the family sticks with the business through ups and downs." Leibinger believes that this last point is "essential to the stability of [the German] economy."

Some of Leibinger's colleagues added to the definition of Mittelstand. Ludwig Litzenberger, head of sales and a member of Trumpf's board, emphasized "personalization." "Everyone's contribution is clear," he said. Rosmarie Klamt, head of international sales, insisted that even major decisions at Trumpf can be "made in a day"—her definition of Mittelstand. She began work as an apprentice at a giant company, where she stayed 10 years. There, she said, "You just have your little part. Here, everyone can see the whole business."

Frank Schädler, who runs Trumpf's customer support activities, launched his career at a giant German auto company. (With a smile, he refused to tell me which one.) "At Trumpf," he said, "I don't feel like I'm a little cog in a big wheel. I can see my ideas applied to a new machine, often in a matter of a few months. There are only a few bosses here and there's very easy communication."

Trumpf's Customers: Mittelstand Serves Mittelstand

During my visit to Trumpf's demonstration center, I ran into one of Trumpf's classic German Mittelstand customers, Huber GmbH, a metal-fabricating firm that opened for business in 1923 and now has 25 employees. It mostly serves the electronics industry, making such things as stamped metal plates for computer carriages. (Firms such as IBM Deutschland and Hewlett-Packard GmbH are nearby.) Given the rapidly shifting nature of its customers' requirements, Huber needs flexible machines that can efficiently handle very short production runs.

Consider: A business chief, in his mid-50s I'd guess, running an ancient, 25-person shop making mundane metal parts. In the U.S., at least, such specs would hardly lead you to expect progressive behavior. Germany is different. I found the boss man hovering over a computer terminal with one of Trumpf's software engineers. The young woman was demonstrating an $80,000 software upgrade, which had been on the market for just three weeks; Huber's chief planned to put it on one of his Trumpf machines, and was anxious to get it adapted to the requirements of his product line.

This surprisingly typical German small businessman turned out to be an investment fanatic, who had four big Trumpf machines when I met him in 1991; though he hadn't yet bought a laser cutter, he was on the lookout for one as his No. 5 from Trumpf. Providing this sort of customer with the flexible tools he wants, then customizing the product to meet his specific needs, has been Trumpf's signature.

A Commitment to Innovation for the Customer

"If I had to single out one factor that's led to our success, I would say it's our constant dedication to innovation, in our products, our attitude toward new markets, and in our internal organization," Leibinger said. "We say, it's a rule really, that if we haven't reexamined every factor associated with doing business at least once every four years, then we haven't looked often enough." To support his claim, Leibinger pointed to the 60 percent of current sales that come from products introduced in the last three years. But isn't that much change inconsistent with the stratospheric quality of Trumpf's machines? I asked. Doesn't it amount to chaos? "That's the whole art, the whole art,"

Leibinger shot back. "It's like walking a tightrope. If you stand still you will fall down. If you run too fast you will also fall." (Despite the impressive new-product figures, Leibinger later admitted that the darkest cloud on his horizon was a shortage of the creative, entrepreneurial sorts needed to build a "healthy future" for Trumpf.)

Leibinger dwelt at length on managing the contradiction between focus and flexibility, which he translates as staying glued to the industry and customers you know, then changing everything to meet those customers' changing needs. "We're in the machine tool business, and that's that," he said . "But you keep looking at the process, always from the customer's view. What benefits can the tool bring? What's the best method for solving the customer's [metal-fabricating] problem, whether it's mechanical, electronic, steel, diamond tool, or laser?"

Germany doesn't have American-style MBA factories (aka business schools). And German execs don't subscribe to the American overemphasis, as they see it, on marketing concepts. But look again at America's core marketing ideas: Harvard guru Ted Levitt, for example, has long pushed the idea of a "market-driven company." Germans would sneer at the phrase. But, in fact, they "live for" their market without using the language. (We use the language, but seldom live the message.)

Playmobil's Horst Brandstätter talks product, product, product—and says he won't have an outside board because they won't understand "the children," who are his "target." Rational's managers talk ceaselessly about "the target," the 1.5 million professional chefs around the world they are determined to serve. Leibinger talks about the "best method to solve the customer's problem." Sales chief Litzenberger rambles on—and on—about "after-sales service, user training," and a host of other "user benefits." In fact these firms don't live "for" the customer, or even "with" the customer. The customer—Zen-like—is *one* with them. And that customer, at Trumpf as at Playmobil and Rational, is the *end user*—not the distributor, purchasing agent, or user's foreman. Rational makes ovens for chefs. Playmobil makes toys for children. Trumpf makes machine tools to serve machinists. Period.

Keeping Up

But how do top Trumpf managers fend off entropy and keep the now-sizable institution focused on change? In part, Leibinger says, it's a matter of perpetual retraining in new technologies. And that brings him to the unions, his partners, as he sees it, in pursuit of change. Leibinger cherishes the close union-company relationship in Germany, and compares it favorably to the situation in the U.S., where he had many years of hands-on experience. Sharing all information in a timely fashion is a critical part of that relationship. In fact, there's a legal requirement in Germany that all employees receive a quarterly "state of the company" situation report, including the nitty-gritty of the balance sheet and profit-and-loss statement.

(Actually, the picture is not quite so rosy as Leibinger painted it for us in mid-1991. With wage rates compared to those of principal competitors soaring, giant German companies have begun something approaching a mass exodus from the Fatherland—e.g., BMW's mid-1992 decision to build a huge plant, its first outside Germany, in Spartanburg, South Carolina.)

Staying flexible also comes from a "constant dialogue with our customers," Leibinger said. And make no mistake, the boss is part of that dialogue: Each year, Leibinger attends and makes detailed sales presentations at machine-tool trade fairs in Germany, Japan, the United States, France, the United Kingdom, and Switzerland. But, Leibinger also stressed, almost everyone at Trumpf, including R&D staffers, is regularly pushed out into the field, to attend fairs, analyze competitors' equipment, and spend hour upon hour with customers.

Leibinger also pointed to the composition of Trumpf's main board as a source of renewal. Five of the seven members are engineers, one's a physicist, and number seven is the finance man. Leibinger made it clear that finances are important, but he was equally clear that his company survives because of product and innovation—"finance should be kept in its place." That place, I sensed, is a distant third after science and engineering: Once more, product, product, product, the Mittelstander's lifeblood—it runs unmistakably even in the veins of the board.

"User Benefit"

Trumpf builds machines that offer the customer extraordinary flexibility. On top of that, Trumpf, like Rational, will customize to meet special needs. Increasingly, customization is translated into software terms—"adjusting the intelligence of the machine to meet specific customers' demands, to deal with the unique flow of data in the customer's computer system," was the way sales chief Litzenberger put it.

Litzenberger invariably returned to "user benefit": It's not a matter "of a few more holes per minute [punched by the Trumpf machine]. It's flexibility, making parts that normally could not be made on such machines." Litzenberger, like most of his Mittelstand counterparts, never strays far from the idea of direct value-added for users. He can't. The Japanese, for example, have a major price edge over Trumpf—an advantage that was markedly enhanced by the 25 percent decline of the yen relative to the Deutschmark a couple of years ago. "But we can't waste time complaining about currency fluctuations," Litzenberger insisted. Instead, the charge is clear: Get on with adding *more* value, *more* flexibility. Trumpf and Germany will thrive by charging a lot more for their products—then earning every D-mark of the premium.

"Stunning" is the only way to describe Trumpf's training and product demonstration center at its Ditzingen headquarters, 15 miles outside of Stuttgart. The design is crisp. The cleanliness stuns you. Modernity shines from every corner. The day I visited, a French customer team and a Chinese delegation were on hand. About 100 prospective customers per month pass through the center. The "hook" is simple: Customers are encouraged to bring plans with them for the most difficult part they need to produce. Typically it's something that they can't make on machines they own. Trumpf programs a demonstration machine to do the job, and almost invariably delivers the "impossible" finished product—by the end of the day.

Frank Shädler, who runs the center, explained its mystique to me by claiming that Trumpf "sells ideas." The "idea" is for customers to understand that Trumpf machines can do things they hadn't even imagined. Shadler wants visitors "to go away having *learned* something, not just having seen a machine."

A visit to the demonstration center is invariably accompanied by a visit to the factory next door. Again, visitors see Trumpf's excellence in the glistening floor on which they walk as well as in the glistening Trumpf machines making Trumpf machines. Is "glisten" an overblown word? Trust me, it isn't. (I called on a rare, relatively successful American machine-tool maker a few weeks after visiting Trumpf. I'd like to report that its demo center sparkled. It didn't. Clean, yes. But sparkle? Glisten? No. No. This place was OK, and then some. Trumpf shouts "excellence" at you.)

Typical customers end up sending several employees to the training center next door to the demonstration center. The 19-teacher operation, which claimed 3,000 "students" in 1991, spends 80 percent of its time teaching customers 50 different courses in CAD/CAM programming, operations, maintenance, machine-control systems, laser systems, and laser cutting technology. Trumpf's 250 service engineers are the targets of most of the rest of the center's educational effort, which includes extensive language training.

"Soft" or "Hard"?

The training center reflects today's increasing emphasis on machine-tool brains. Within its 11 classrooms, I found 3 machine tools, 22 workstations for programming, and 15 computer-numerical control (CNC) simulators. Is Trumpf, then, becoming a computer company? "No, we are *not!* We are *not!* We are really not!" Leibinger exclaimed. (Yes, three times.) "In the international market, German industry has a strong position in tangible things. The Japanese dominate the world market in electronic components. And the Americans are still the best software architects. Our special talent is combining technology—mechanical, electronic, software—into sophisticated systems of high-quality, *tangible* systems."

Leibinger recalled a visit from some MIT and Harvard professors not too long ago. They stopped at nearby Mercedes, Bosch, and IBM Deutschland, then as an afterthought added "two smaller companies" to their list, including Trumpf. Later, one wrote Leibinger: "He told me that twenty years ago he'd advised New England industries to get out of the textile-machine business, the machinery businesses in general, because 'These are industries of the nineteenth century, connected with steel and oil and so on. And the future is computers, software.' Now, he said, 'We come back and visit Germany, find a booming economy—and you're still producing those machines of the nineteenth century.' "

Leibinger admitted the machines "are totally different, a mixture of electronics, software and the mechanical." Still, he insisted again, "The center of our business is the *machine*. The tangible world remains, but it's changed, that's all. It's being penetrated by new technology, which is the fascination of our industry." Thirty percent of an automobile's value will come from electronics in the year 2000, Leibinger explained, "but it will still be an auto. It will still need reliable suspension, a quiet motor, and, and, and. The tangible side of the product is still very, very important to maintaining a competitive edge."

Dan DeChamps, who runs Trumpf's U.S. operations, says that about a fifth of the total value of a Trumpf machine now comes from the software brains. When I asked him whether Trumpf is not a thinly disguised computer company that also has some metal boxes to sell, he echoed his boss. " 'Thinly disguised' is simply not a correct statement," he retorted. "The share of electronics in a modern machine tool is certainly getting larger and larger. It supplements, and sometimes substitutes for, very expensive mechanical components which are not as efficient or as reliable. Nevertheless, the mechanics, the motion system of a machine, still contributes in a major way to the durability, the quality, the precision of the machine. If you don't produce rails and guides and racks and pinions that are very, very accurate, you will never have an accurate machine tool, no matter what your software and electronic controller do."

Germany's Matchless "Dual System"

Leibinger claimed that the distinctive hand-head mix characteristic of Trumpf's machines is partially a result of the fabled German "dual system," the apprenticeship scheme that emphasizes—for three-quarters of Trumpf workers and two-thirds of all German workers—a balance between theoretical classroom work and practical handwork. (The U.S. business lexicon these days is replete with references to "multiskilled workers"—as if it were a recent invention. The hand-head blend for workers dates back centuries in Germany.) Leibinger admitted that when he was an apprentice he thought he was spending "far too much time learning to do [metal] filing. We'd file six or seven hours a day—looking at the clock." He chuckled and said he can "still remember exactly where that clock was." But such discipline is important, he added, as important in 1992 as it was in 1950—the "sense for the material" is as much a part of a machine tool as those software brains, he said again. Then he went even further, and called the dual system "the backbone of Germany's ability to build quality products."

There are 120 or so apprenticeship trades in Germany, including flower-arranging. "In every case, you learn to do something very professional with your hands," Leibinger said. Then it was back to his favorite theme: "We don't live in a software world. Many people thought that software would be the future of mankind. But we need an automobile to drive around in, an elevator to take us up and down, a pencil to write with, a tablet to write on. We live in a tangible world. We have to be able to work with our hands." Then he told me a "little story" that circulates at Trumpf:

> Some young apprentices were complaining that they spent too much time on manual work. One of my colleagues took a group of them into our packing department, where we had one man who builds the crates for one of our machines. He was chopping wood to form the joints. He used his hatchet, very, very quickly, very, very precisely. My colleague said to the boys, "Look at that. He's achieved that level of precision and speed only because he's done such things thousands of times." That has a little bit to do with why we still believe that manual work is important.

The U.S. overemphasizes head skills, as Leibinger sees it. The German mechanic who was an American immigrant, he said, "feels that 'My son has to go to college.' So everybody goes to college. The social status of manual work in the United States is too low. Few Americans can do manual work exceedingly well. And that brings quality down."

A continent away, Dan DeChamps once again echoed his boss. "Filing is a hand skill that's necessary to finding out what metal is all about, how it behaves, what it does and what it does not do," he said emphatically. "And the machine tool is, after all, still designed to change the form, the shape of metal. Metal will always behave the same way, whether we have software or not. The evolution of the machine tool is so fast that the details of what I learned in school have become totally outdated. On the other hand, the feeling for what it means to bend something, to punch a hole, will never change."

Sales chief Litzenberger disagreed with his colleagues; he said that Trumpf *is* mostly in the software business these days. Nonetheless, he, too, under-scored the need for mechanical excellence. "We take our apprentices to the electronic shop, show them how to write software, how to make printed circuit boards," he said. "But we still feel it's very important for young people to work with material, to get the feel of the material in their hands, to know what metal working—which is our field, after all—is all about, what you can do with metal. Our apprentices take to both traditions: the electronic, and the filing. Sure, the accent has changed toward electronics and software. But you can't do without touch!"

Young Trumpf workers added their two bits. "It's still important to get a feel for the material you're working with, so you learn something about sheet metal—from filing sheet metal," one told me. But shouldn't the apprenticeship more accurately reflect the importance of the new technologies? No, said a first-line supervisor: "You have to spend time learning how the material feels. The computer is not going to give you a smooth surface. The mechanics, in the end, do that."

There are clouds on the horizon. Though Leibinger criticized the knee-jerk tendency of American youngsters to aim for university, Trumpf apprentices claimed the same thing is happening in Germany. "Metal working, the machinery business, is just not attractive for many people who finish their basic schooling," one said. "It's not that my generation is lazy, at least as I see it, but this business has a reputation of being 'dirty work.' Most young people today want a clean job, a quiet job, a desk job."

Public Support for Worker Education

When I visited Trumpf in mid-1991, the payroll included 82 "industrial" apprentices and 25 "commercial" apprentices (the latter heading toward administrative jobs). Trumpf shells out about DM 100,000 ($65,000) per apprentice during the three and a half years each spends in the program. The first year of the apprenticeship is by and large devoted to manual work—that is, filing. During the second year, apprentices rotate through various departments in the factory, starting to develop that special "feel for the whole" (the company, the product, the end user, how it all fits together) that's almost unique to Germany. The remainder of the program emphasizes computers, programming, and machine-control systems.

On-the-job training at the company, in company classrooms and on the factory floor, absorbs four days of an apprentice's week. (The company has three full-time instructors overseeing its apprenticeship program.) The fifth day is spent at a state-run school. Peter Feigel, who teaches Trumpf apprentices at the local state school, pointed to another crucial aspect of the dual system which is almost entirely absent in the United States—the smooth, seamless relationship between local industry, the voc-tech schools, as we would call them,* and state-level government. Feigel, a state employee, regularly visits the companies his apprentices work for; he's in constant contact with those firms' foremen and engineers, discussing individual apprentices and future training requirements.

Given the shortage of skilled workers in Germany, all Trumpf apprentices are guaranteed a job with the company if they complete their program. Most take Trumpf up on its offer, then stick around. For example, all 12 apprentices from the 1976 program are still at Trumpf. Many Trumpf workers go on to

---

* Sadly, though in part deservedly, "voc-tech" has a mostly negative connotation in the U.S.—the reject "track." The baggage Germany's apprentice program carries is positive.

additional schooling. Sometimes it's at night, financed by the company. But government support is available for those who choose to move ahead on their own—for example, 30-year, interest-free loans for training aimed at upgrading skills. (In the U.S., only training clearly associated with your *current* job earns even a tax break—and good luck getting an education loan as an "adult." Talk about shortsighted.)

Trumpf U.S.A.

Leibinger lit off his U.S. operations in 1967, to service machines exported from Germany. Today, Dan DeChamps' Trumpf U.S.A. employs 220. It sells, services, manufactures, and is increasingly involved in product development. To meet American customers' needs, for example, the company modified the Trumpf 260 metal-punching machine, and wrung $100,000 from its $400,000 price tag. DeChamps insisted during our interview that the resultant 260A is the equivalent of its predecessor in precision and punching speed; the only difference is that some features have been removed and its range slightly reduced. "Downsized, eh?" I said. "*Right*-sized," DeChamps shot back. Either way, the new 260A is not only selling like hotcakes in the U.S., but is doing very well in France and the United Kingdom. Not in Germany, however. The typical small businessperson in France, England, or the U.S. buys machines that are "the right size for today's work," DeChamps said. The German "overkills," loves his machine, scarfs up those new features, and wants to be "ahead of his needs"—remember Huber, the 25-person shop that boasts of four Trumpf machines.

Products made by Trumpf U.S.A. and sold in America usually displace Japanese machines. Thanks to the simplification of the 260A, for example, Trumpf is now more or less competitive with the Japanese on price—i.e., the Trumpf machine is "only" $30,000 to $45,000 more than the similar Japanese product. DeChamps was clear that Trumpf's U.S. strategy is the same as Trumpf's German strategy. "Sell the value-added, but keep the price within reach," he said, adding, "We will not sacrifice our product philosophy for market share." Do the Japanese do that? I asked ever so innocently. De-Champs smiled.

The sales chore in the U.S. is not easy, DeChamps acknowledged. Germans buy Trumpfs, he said, "because they always have." In the U.S., if price is the whole game, they mostly buy from Japan's Amada. If he gets a chance to sell "features and customization," then Trumpf has a solid shot. In fact, Trumpf U.S.A. has had remarkable success at customer sites where engineers are heavily involved in, or dominate, the purchasing process. But when big-company purchasing departments call the shots, it's a different story—TQM rhetoric notwithstanding. One American giant, held up as an example of enlightenment by many, only requires machines to be working 80 percent of the time. "Any old, cheap junk" will meet that standard, DeChamps sneered.

But the customer refuses to pay a penny more for Trumpf's greater reliability, so DeChamps is out of luck.

Living for Quality at Trumpf U.S.A.

Over time, Trumpf's U.S. manufacturing operations have imported fewer and fewer components from Germany. Take one of the laser machines: At the start, 80 percent of its parts came from Germany, DeChamps figured; today that's down to less than 10 percent. The U.S. share could be even bigger, he claimed, admitting with some irritation that specifications written in Germany frequently lead to a de facto requirement for German components. (The Trumpf approach to supplier relationships in the U.S. mirrors its approach in Germany. "We simply don't try to squeeze the last penny out of a vendor," DeChamps declared. "We firmly believe that the vendor has to have healthy margins, if we want the level of quality, innovation, and on-time support that Trumpf demands.")

Peter Demjanovic, a German line worker who transferred from Ditzingen to the U.S., insisted that Trumpf U.S.A. quality is clearly better than that of Trumpf Germany. "It's like the little brother syndrome," he said. "The U.S. has to do it better to keep the Germans out of our hair." Joe Christian, an American who works for Trumpf U.S.A., is a refugee from now-defunct Bridgeport Machine Tool Company—where his father had worked before him. "Quality is the name of the game here," said Christian. "My dad was taught to make as much money as he could, as fast as he could, for himself. He believed and saw the company as one vast source of money. Neither he nor I ever thought, 'This is a customer's machine. The customer is waiting for it. It has to work for the customer.'"

The secret? "Quality can only be produced, not controlled," DeChamps said. "Create appealing conditions, give people a sense of organization, and allow them lots of room to display individual initiative." He added that American workers have been "at least as successful" as their German counterparts. He attributed much of that to the hiring process. Joe Christian recalled "a very intense interviewing process. I came in for three separate interviews, all of them at least an hour or an hour and a half long. They'd quickly get the mechanics out of the way, then move to the personal: 'Where do you want to be?' 'Where do you want to go?' 'What do you want?' They were looking for a personality that would fit in, an outlook that would support the company philosophy." They got it with Joe Christian, and almost all of his 2,999 counterparts around the world of Trumpf, who continue, in dead earnest, their "quest to create the perfect machine."

CHARACTERISTICS OF GERMANY'S
MIGHTY MINNOWS

There are superb "Mittelstand" companies in America, Japan, and Sweden. And not so great Mittelstand firms in Germany. Nonetheless, a consistent (and coherent) set of characteristics seems to mark Germany's unusually high share of middle-size "giants":

- Focus. The Mittelstander, with 11 or 3,000 employees, sticks to his knitting. Recall that at Trumpf new products introduced in the last three years account for 60 percent of all sales—and software engineers are now about a third of a huge R&D operation, double the share of a few years past. Nonetheless, such big, new twists are in service to one invariant idea: bending, stamping, and crunching metal for demanding customers. Rational's commitment to combi-cookers alone, despite a wide range of impressive technical and marketing skills that might be applied to other fields, is equally pointed—and limited.

- Small means strong. Rational is a giant through and through—not a pigmy. It's the IBM of combi-cooker producers. In its little, global market slice, it's dominant, in control. Rational's Meister says he won't let the firm grow to more than 400 people: He's subcontracting lots more these days and further sharpening his focus on the handful of critical skills which can add to his competitive advantage/niche dominance.

- _Symbiosis_ with the end user. Geobra finds a host of clever ways to stay close to its toy-using kids. Rational is in sync with its customer-chefs. Trumpf is married to its customers' machinists. None relies on "market research"—but all three do spend lavishly for hands-on customer contact, customer training, and shockingly rapid and extensive customer service. Though the trio assiduously attend to their distributors and customers' purchasing people, the unmistakable bias is toward the _ultimate_ user—the kid, the chef, the machinist.
(My German Mittelstand friends don't know it, and didn't say it, but they taught me to use the word "symbiosis." These outfits—Playmobil, Trumpf, Rational—are in synch with their end users in a way I frankly find impossible to spell out, or reduce to any checklist. My translator gave me the first clue. She kept saying "identification with the user." At first, I assumed she meant "close to the customer." Now I know I was wrong. "Identification with"/end user is much, much more than "close to"/customer. See also Chapters 45 and 47.)

- Big spenders where it counts—i.e., for the customer. The top Mittelstanders charge a healthy premium for their goods and abhor discounting—it cuts into the margins they need to invest in state-of-the-art everything. Unlike most modest-size American companies, they spend like drunken sailors on customer contact, service, R&D, and plant machinery. Remember that Geobra has over $100 million invested in the precision molds from which its toys are made (and spent another $30 million "just" to get designers and mold makers within hailing distance of each other).

• <u>Soft and hard</u>. Germans in general, and the precocious Mittelstanders in particular, are masters of *blending*—feel *and* precision, metal *and* electronics. The lengthy apprenticeship program that seasons two-thirds of Germany's workers teaches a "sense" for material (wood, plastic, metal) and precision. Then this craft sense is skillfully combined with state-of-the-art electronics, software, lasers, etc.

• <u>On the leading edge, where it matters</u>. Germany gets a rap for being behind in the Electronic Age. That's true if the measure is computer, semiconductor, and software production per se. (SiemensNixdorf, Germany's leading computer company, is almost an embarrassment.) But the criticism is off target when it comes to applications: Witness all those software engineers in Trumpf R&D; CAD terminals that may outnumber lathes (computer-controlled lathes, of course) at Geobra; Rational's combi-cooker, which is an electronics marvel with user-friendly controls that could be the firm's least copyable advantage. (The oven controls are another intriguing combination of soft and hard—blending the sensitivities of the chefs, the software engineers, and the experts at metal bending on the factory floor.)

• <u>Pipsqueak or not, the world is their oyster</u>. Say "global," and "big" automatically comes to mind—on our side of the Atlantic. (Though we're getting better—see p. 563.) Not so for Rational's Meister, Trumpf's Leibinger, or Geobra's Brandstätter. Each of their firms sells from half to two-thirds of its goods *outside* Germany. It's not so much that the companies had global strategies from the start. They didn't. Instead, customer word-of-mouth pulled them, over time, into foreign markets. Then they went about the task of patiently building a reputation in country after country—always taking care to insure that the infrastructure (i.e., the ability to provide timely, attentive service) needed to support future sales thousands of miles from home was put in place ahead of demand.

• <u>The long view</u>. The micro-marvels are in for the duration. Working at product acceptance, creating an unassailable research advantage, and building global markets takes years—and years. Our Mittelstand chiefs talk in terms of decades, not quarters. (That's a misstatement: They rarely *talk* about the long haul—instead, every action underscores their lasting commitment to product, end users, industry, employees, vendors, and company.)

• <u>Obsessed with improvement (small and big), not competitors</u>. Trumpf's Leibinger says that every element of the firm must be reexamined from the ground up at least once every four years. Rational works obsessively at staying ahead of the competition—it means a thousand tiny touches that customers feed into the company *and* basic (by industry standards) R&D. Yet these Mittelstand chiefs seldom discuss the competition, mainly because they are the market pacesetters. They do run perpetually scared, talking on and on about marginal and basic improvement. (The abiding passion for improvement and abhorrence for the status quo reminded me so much of the late Sam Walton—an American Mittelstander in spirit who happened to build a $50-billion company.)

• <u>A disciplined but flexible work force</u>. You won't find songbooks or morning calisthenics at Germany's Mittelstand companies! You won't even come across quality-circle meetings or statistical process control charts. (I found nary a one of either.) You will find discipline and an obsession with craft. But such discipline is not synonymous with rigidity or group-think. To the contrary, Germans I talked with (boss and young worker alike) are proud of their ability to make a continuing contribution as individuals, and to move ahead as individuals. (For example, a couple of years after gaining an apprentice certificate, you can begin a program to become a "master"—another lengthy process which ends up with creation of a "masterpiece," the craftsman's equivalent of a Ph.D. thesis.)

• <u>No walls</u>. The firms I observed were marked by open, easy, free-flowing (albeit professional) communication. Mold makers at Playmobil routinely cross organization-chart boundaries to talk with toy designers—without suffering any bureaucratic delays. Customer-applications software programmers at Trumpf chat daily with software programmers in research and development. Rational's chefs have a constant dialogue with R&D people and factory people, too, without having to "go through channels." In fact, "channels" are rarely—never?—discussed. People get on with their "it" with haste and order, but org charts, manuals, and the like are conspicuously absent.

• <u>Quality shoppers, quality producers</u>. The Japanese taught us that quality is about quality circles, statistical process control charts—and getting rid of quality inspectors (turning the inspection task over to the workers). Yet the Mittelstanders we met all had sizable quality-assurance departments (which seem to act as cheerleaders for quality, not cops). But the tip-off about German quality comes from several 19-year-old apprentices, who lectured me about their willingness as consumers, despite low salaries, to pay an extra Deutschmark or two for the best.

The pervasive attentiveness to quality is abetted by an overall corporate passion for product (see below), characteristic Mittelstand focus, the apprenticeship program, peerless manufacturing equipment, glistening working environments, and marked respect for individual craftmanship. It adds up to a centuries-old "quality mind-set," never more valuable than in today's demanding marketplaces. And forget the loose talk about Germany becoming "a nation of rich, fat shopkeepers"—the drive of 1946 may have dissipated some, but slovenliness has hardly become a German characteristic.

• <u>Product! Product!</u> The product is the raison d'être, the breath of life, for the stellar Mittelstanders we visited. Rational's Meister goes on and on about painting mind-pictures to keep employees focused on his precious combis. At Geobra/Playmobil, we found the legendary Hans Beck—taciturn master carver of plastic and genius creator of toys; he is one with his small customers and exemplifies the product focus around which the entire firm revolves. Trumpf's Leibinger holds numerous patents—he's obsessed with product, and isn't a bit shy about it.

But product, like Mittelstand (so much more than "middle-sized"), has a different meaning than in America—an encompassing meaning. It's more than the object (the oven, the toy, the machine tool) or the service provided. Product is at once the thing you can touch—and the overall corporate "signature" (headquarters, furnishings, booths at trade shows), the overwhelming commitment to R&D, to the end user, the flexible organization structure. The product, that is, is everything. All are in service to this rich vision/definition.

- Personality. Is personality encompassed in product? Yes. Is product encompassed in personality? Yes. Either way you parse it, these firms, for better or (in other cases) worse, are a blinding reflection of a strong, focused personality who puts his stamp on everything from product design to headquarters carpet. And the chiefs are clear about it. Discussing his larger purposes, Leibinger closed by saying, "I hope that my personal life, my presence, my energy, can be seen as an example to everyone." To separate product, personality, and corporate character is an impossible task.

Germany's behemoths are arguably as sickly as America's. Germany's Mittelstand sparkles. Moreover, in marked contrast to the U.S., even big-company German execs readily acknowledge the preeminent role the mid-sized mega-sector plays in their country's success, at home and as the planet's premier exporters.

The German Mittelstanders are independent in spirit and practice—almost to a fault. They understand the good thing they've got going, and are openly contemptuous of their nation's Goliaths. They don't want to grow up to be like Siemens!

One at a time, the Mittelstanders have lots to teach us about the enormous potential of focused (fixated), global, modest-size firms. Their passion for product, end-user symbiosis, and bold investment sets them apart. Their ability, though sometimes only a few dozen strong, to invent and then overwhelm a global micro-niche is singular.

Looked at as a group, the Mittelstand is a matchless advertisement for the limitless power of armies of modest-size, niche-market-obsessed attack units—which is, of course, what Percy Barnevik aims for *within* ABB. To learn of the German Mittelstand is to shake conventional, "globalist" business wisdom (only the huge will survive) to the core, and to open our eyes to a genuinely original model of effective, large-scale economic organization.

Is the picture I paint too rosy? Yes, in the sense that there are lots of lousy

Mittelstanders that hardly resemble Rational, Playmobil, or Trumpf. No, in that German economic statistics—and the Mittelstand's unmistakable role in their achievement—speak for themselves.

More "Mittelstand": The Third Italy

"The Third Italy [contrasts with] the underdeveloped South and the old 'Industrial Triangle' of Turin-Genoa-Milan. [Stretching] from the Venetian provinces and parts of Lombardy in the North, through Bologna, Florence, and Ancona to Bari in the South, [its products include] knitwear, woolen and silk textiles, shoes, furniture, ceramics, tiles, musical instruments, special machines, hydraulic devices, agricultural implements, motorcycles, steel. . . .

"[The Third Italy] played a crucial role in Italy's emergence during the 1980s as [a leading] exporter of clothing and textiles . . . footwear and . . . machine tools. . . .

"[The key is] small firms producing specialized goods in short runs . . . using advanced technologies which are at once highly flexible and no less efficient than those employed by larger companies. [You find widespread use of] computer-controlled machine tools in metalworking shops, electric-arc smelting and continuous casting in steel mini-mills, microprocessor-controlled sensors in ceramic kilns, computer-aided design and cutting in knitwear and garments, high-performance water/air-jet and projectile looms in textiles."

> "Lessons for Enterprise Culture from the Third Italy,"
> *Quarterly Enterprise Digest,*
> October 1989 (*QED* is a publication of
> Britain's 3i, the world's largest
> venture capital firm)

36

"Marketizing's" Imperatives I: Rethinking Scale

The most suspect of [scale] advantages is the only one asserted by traditional economists: namely, economies of scale
in manufacturing. In the last decade, it has been discovered
that such economies can be achieved at extremely low levels
of production, and that these economies are often outweighed by the *dis*economies that occur when one tips over
into large-scale manufacturing, *dis*benefits that come from
the loss of human scale and the increase in bureaucracy.

> JAMES O'TOOLE
> University of Southern California
> "Big or Small?"
> unpublished paper, 1991

There are two ways to compete. In stable conditions, you plan
and you compete on scale. In unstable times—and by the way,
entrepreneurs create these instabilities—you live by your
wits. Living by your wits, by acts of intellect, means being
flexible, innovative, being willing to try and put yourself out of
business before someone else does.

> DICK CAVANAGH, coauthor,
> *The Winning Performance:*
> *How America's High Growth*
> *Mid-Size Companies Succeed,*
> interview with the author

Hey, size works against excellence.

BILL GATES, chairman and
founder, Microsoft
Upside, April 1992

"Although Japan has announced its intention to become a world leader in biotechnology," Gene Bylinsky wrote in the August 12, 1991, issue of *Fortune*, "it is hopelessly behind." Merck and Johnson & Johnson saved the day for the U.S., eh? Not exactly. Our winners, Bylinsky reported, are a pack of relative unknowns—Amgen, Genzyme, Immunex, Xoma, and Centocor, among others. The U.S. aces, which "the Japanese lack," according to Bylinsky, include "top scientists willing to help start pioneering new companies and venture capitalists ready to back them." One of those aces, ImmuLogic Pharmaceutical CEO Richard Bagley, a veteran of SmithKline and Squibb, said of our pharmaceutical giants, "It isn't clear that just because they're big they're going to survive."

Revolutionary technologies grow like dandelions in my lawn in Vermont. Entrepreneurs come out of the woodwork around the world. Centrally planned economies stagger, then collapse. ABB's Percy Barnevik predicts that two-thirds of Europe's big businesses will go bust after full-scale economic integration. The Fortune 500 loses its grip—see the figures in the chart* on the next page. What gives?

Instability, mostly. Call it fashionized markets, those technology revolutions (very plural), the rise of new market economies. For whatever set of reasons, the evidence is unmistakable: Big ain't what it used to be. (In fact, it never was what it was promised to be. But that's another story; and, besides, why beat dead horses?)

Still, Professor James O'Toole is led to ask, "Is it better to be big or small?" And then to answer: "Obviously, it is best to be both at the same time." That, in fact, is precisely the message of the Beyond Hierarchy section. (O'Toole, like me, slams manufacturing scale economies, but acknowledges the "big power" of an imposing market presence.) I attempted to redefine scale. On the one hand, I exhorted and exhorted again about focused and flexible, self-contained units—two-person "care pairs" at Lakeland Regional Medical Center, dozen-person teams at EDS, and mini-business units and buckyborgs, ranging from 10-person Business Development Teams at Titeflex to gangs of 100 or so at ABB, IDG, and Acordia. These midget "enterprises" are almost independent businesses, empowered to do whatever it takes to serve

* Adapted from *From the Ground Up: The Resurgence of American Entrepreneurship*, by John Case.

The Flow and Ebb of the Fortune 500

YEAR	EMPLOYMENT (millions)	PERCENT OF GNP
1954*	8	37
1959	9	40
1969	15	46
1979	16	58
1989	12.5	42
1991**	11.9	40

* First year of published rankings.
** Most recent rankings.

the customer. So small *is* beautiful! But wait, I said. There's also that "new big," the muscle of energetic networks—the way ABB tries to take advantage of a collection of smallish units which add up to the biggest power transmission business in the world, the way MCI revels in making nothing and working through a collection of network partners to innovate faster than more vertically integrated competitors like AT&T.

So "do both," eh? O'Toole is right. Case closed. Hold on again. The jury's still out on ABB. "Network big" could easily become sluggish and even anticompetitive (Sara Lee's Keith Alm, remember, wants to use "alliances" to foreclose competition). Thermo Electron took us past the "Beyond Hierarchy" section, illustrating company-held networks where the public owns pieces of most divisions (an enormous psychological and real step toward ultimate independence, albeit with a little network power in place). And don't overlook Germany's potent micro-monsters, from 11-person Goldmann Produktion to 3,000-person Trumpf: They are small to smallish, yet global in reach and totally independent (unlike smaller companies in Japan, they rarely are wedded to one or two or a handful of big-company customers), with no desire to grow up to be like Papa Siemens.

WILL WE EVER LEARN?

The average bank merger in the 1980s didn't cut costs, didn't raise productivity, and actually made the combined bank slightly less profitable.

Business Week
August 17, 1992

Forget the nuances—"new big," "network big," etc. In the U.S., at least, there's a lingering love affair with big—*old* big. Consider *Business Week*'s editorial of July 29, 1991: "Two-bit labs can't make megabuck materials." There's a materials science revolution going on, we're told. And *Business Week* characteristically insists that we should copy the Japanese model (*Business Week*'s version of it)—get organized and subsidize almost any American firm or laboratory that's interested, as long as it's a big one. The same issue of the magazine, incidentally (incidentally?), features the Chemical Bank–Manufacturers Hanover merger. Put the two slugabeds together, we learn, and, by golly, you'll have "No. 2 in the U.S." (behind sickly Citicorp)—"but just a distant also-ran globally." An "also-ran"? By what measure? Since when is $135 billion in assets too small to be effective? And by the way, who says big is better in banking anyway? *Business Week*, that's who. (So don't be put off by the detailed performance figures the same magazine publishes each year that demonstrate the opposite—nor by the epigraph above, from an article that appeared just a year after the Chemical–Manny Hanny get-together.)

Such headlines are the least of it. Despite the disarray in the Fortune 500 (and the fact, if you look up close, that they're madly de-integrating, selling off bits, subbing anything and everything, marketizing subsidiary units), very few weeks pass without calls for copying Japan's keiretsu-style links among big manufacturers, big suppliers, big bankers, big customers. Let's call it "super-mega-network-redoubled-Fortune-500-big." A lot of academic economists still love it (Harvard's and MIT's industrial policy gang and many, many others—exceptions like Mike Porter are rare). Members of the business press love it (a lot of them). Congressmen love it. Love—yes, love. Down deep, we're all Texans at heart: We love big and bigger, and positively adore biggest. How else, other than perpetually unrequited love, can you explain our intransigence in the face of overwhelming evidence? As we dismantle our biggest companies, we try just as hard to link what's left in a passel of those airtight strategic alliances. And then, if you're IBM's Akers, you continue to wonder why 50,000 competitors, most of them microscopic, are eating your lunch.

EUROPE AND JAPAN RETHINK
(SOMEWHAT)

So 1960s-style conglomerates bombed in the U.S. (*Nobody* disagrees about that.) So our big companies are splitting up. So what? In preparation for the open market of 1993 and beyond, Europe has gone on a merger binge. Natch. It's an unmistakable plunge toward bigness for bigness's sake—old bigness for old bigness's sake. ("Hey, Europe's gonna be big. So we better be big." That seems to capture the depth of most companies' thinking.) On the other hand, some *have* gotten the word. ABB, of course. Siemens, in response to the shabby performance of two-thirds of its business units (p. 000), "packed off 40,000 of its head office staff to front-line jobs in marketing and finance," *Forbes* reported in May 1990. And Holland's once-mighty Philips has shed 100,000 jobs in the last five years, largely by selling off misfitting bits of its portfolio.

"Overall size is largely irrelevant for competitive advantage," Michael Porter wrote in *The Economist* in 1990. "Diversification to build size for the sake of size is exactly the wrong strategy for most European companies . . . today—the American example [of the 1960s] is a poor one to follow. Instead, [European companies] should be narrowing their range of businesses and investing to build focused international market position in core businesses, readiness for the competitive challenges ahead." Commenting in the Fall 1989 issue of *Sloan Management Review*, London Business School professor Paul Geroski makes a similar point about European firms: "On the whole, the evidence suggests that the benefits of scale are modest. . . . [I]n the vast majority of [European] markets, the probable consequence of 1992 will be an increase in product variety." Geroski provides, as partial support for his hypothesis, a comparison between Britain (with a disproportionate share of huge companies) and Germany (with its exceptional dependence on the Mittelstand). "The [British] tend to manufacture relatively standard products in long runs, . . ." he writes. "German . . . manufacturers, by contrast, produce a great variety of high-quality goods in small batches. . . . Surprisingly enough, this strategy has involved no apparent sacrifice in productive efficiency—German output per employee is roughly twice that in the U.K."

America used to be the model for "big-is-great." Now Japan is giantism's supposed paragon (big-is-great, round No. 2). Well, we had some of the story wrong all along—e.g., big Japanese firms were always much less vertically integrated, and made much greater use of very small subcontractor "shops," than big American or European firms. But that's the least of it. As Americans look East (to Japan), the Japanese, ironically, are looking West (to America and, to some extent, to Europe) for more decentralized business models. Furthermore, lifetime employment, never what it was cracked up to be, is shriveling. Promotion in big Japanese companies is increasingly on merit, rather than on seniority as in the past. And big Japanese firms are creating droves of independent subsidiaries to inject entrepreneurialism into their sleepy (as they, if not we, see it) midsts.

With the sharp rise of the yen (and wages) and extraordinary competitive threats from close at hand (for example, Korea's Samsung is now world leader in four-megabit DRAMs, the hottest of the commodity semiconductors), Japanese companies are shipping more and more routine production offshore—while turning their own focus to brainwork and value-added tasks in general, just as the Americans and Germans did before (and are increasingly doing). Also, faced with a labor shortage, giant Japanese firms are belatedly paying more attention to the role of their subcontractors. To date, most subs have been treated shabbily, jerked back and forth at will to deal with the vagaries of the big firms' product demand. That's pushed the subs, in turn, toward labor-intensive rather than capital-intensive organization (labor is the only valve you can turn on and off in a hurry—forget lifetime employment among subs). Now, greater concern with subcontractors' technological grounding is becoming the norm—Japan wants, and needs, its own high-tech Mittelstand.

Big Japanese companies, with Sony in the lead, are madly shuffling their decks, shifting their emphasis from exports to multinationalism—moving production, and clout, out of Japan. Big firms' offshore units are being given much longer leashes by Tokyo. And offshore execs are attempting for the first time to become insiders—outside of Japan. (As well they might! Part of the almost thoughtless rush to "multinationalize" on the part of Japanese firms is in response to restrictionist-minded European Community bureaucrats—who seem even more tetchy about controlled-by-Tokyo behavior than their American counterparts.)

Add these factors up, and you have the makings for a banzai attack on old big. "The era of mass production is over and that will transform the whole nature of our industrial system," economist Tadao Kiyonari of Hosei University told *Inc.*'s Joel Kotkin in 1990. "The key company of the future will have fewer than 150 employees." That may be a way off, but unprecedented change is clearly afoot, whether Americans and Europeans are "happy" about the pace of change in Japan or not.

WHAT "SMALL" MEANS (AND DOESN'T)

Question: We keep reading about the improving Colorado economic climate; yet, conversely, we receive reports of mounting layoffs. How can the situation be improving in the midst of layoffs?

Response: The answer is simple: small business.

PATRICIA SILVERSTEIN
Board of Economists of the
Rocky Mountain News
February 1992

As Big Banks Fire Staff, Small Ones Are Hiring

Headline
San Francisco Chronicle,
July 16, 1992 (based on an
analysis from *American
Banker*)

So what is "small"? What is "big"? There are few slipperier questions.

- <u>Small does not necessarily mean tiny</u>. There is a certain minimum size, perhaps, which must be obtained to be effective, particularly as a global marketer. (Fifty people? 100? 250?) Mittelstand companies routinely violate such "rules"—it's not uncommon to find firms with only a couple of dozen people dominating a global micro-niche. But by and large, this section is not meant to be an advertisement for changing the world with three people in a garage in Milan, Osaka, Palo Alto, or Nuremberg. (Though it's happened before, is happening now, and will happen again—remember supercomputer maker Wavetracer of Acton, Massachusetts, Chapter 18.)

- <u>"Networks" are changing the definition of big</u>. As information technology and new management techniques assist people in learning how to work together, the ability to achieve "scale-power" in the absence of vertical integration is growing by the day. Maybe ACE didn't succeed in establishing uniform standards in the computer industry (p. 000), but "network big" is far from impotent.

- <u>Big is not big is not big</u>. ABB oversees a $28.9-billion firm with a corporate staff of 150: Its flavor of "big" is obviously unlike big at the centralized, staff-laden enterprises that are still so common to Europe and North America. "Thermo Electron big," with different publics owning pieces of divisions, is not like "3M big" (much more decentralized than most its size, but far from Thermo's level of subordinate-unit independence). And big in Japan, changing or not, is different from big in the U.S. or Europe; among other things, as noted, Japan depends on subcontractors much more than Americans or Europeans do (the picture is murky, since lots of Japanese subcontractors are very dependent upon and perhaps only somewhat de-integrated from the giants).

- Almost all big firms are working overtime to try and act like small firms. Competitive pressure, out-of-whack costs, enlightened application of information technology, the still volatile "market for corporate control" (i.e., the threat of raiders), and newfound obstreperousness of outsider board members (demanding executive accountability) have all conspired to induce big firms to try and get into fighting trim: shed misfitting bits of portfolios, create more autonomous subsidiary units, hack away at central staffs and group staffs and division staffs. In many respects, this is the "best" anti-old-giantism argument: If big is so damn good, why is almost everybody big (even if they've just become huge on purpose via mergers—e.g., ABB) working overtime to emulate small?

- The somewhat small are kicking the stodgy big around. When you look at where big firms, from IBM to Du Pont, are taking their lumps, it's more often than not at the hands of focused pipsqueaks. Furthermore, and this is "crazy" by old (1982) standards, it's now commonplace to find big firms by the trainload making pilgrimages to interesting smaller firms to try and figure out what's going on.

- "Different strokes for different folks." I'm prepared to argue that one strategy (more de-integration) is better than another (less de-integration), for a company or an economy. But if you demur, at least grant me the plausibility of an alternative strategy. To wit: If Japan is "winning in modern markets with big" (which is not how I see it), and if Korea is "winning in modern markets with big" (courtesy its handful of Chaebol-monsters, like Hyundai and Lucky Goldstar), then let me point out the following: Germany's Mittelstand (the basis for Germany's out-exporting the Japanese); America's vital, entrepreneurial South, Southwest, and West, compared to its sluggish, less entrepreneurial Northeast and Midwest; China's entrepreneurial Guangdong province vs. the state-enterprise-controlled interior provinces; the entrepreneurial "Third Italy" vs. the torpid, big-firm-dominated "Iron Triangle" (see p. 552); and Taiwan, as rich and entrepreneurial as Korea is rich and Chaebol-dominated.

Part of the issue is perceptual. We "see" lots of Japanese and Korean products, because both nations specialize in mass-consumption goods—Sony Walkmans, Toyota Camrys, and Lucky Goldstar VCRs. We don't "see" so much from Germany—W. G. Barth's cacao-bean roasters, Panther's high-tech cameraman's chairs, and Rational's ovens are backstage stars. This is true even of the U.S.: We run a trade deficit in many visible consumer goods (cars, consumer electronics), and a whopping surplus in less visible "capital" goods—many produced by unsung small or midsized companies—and intangible, less visible services.)

- Big is not necessarily rich. We know not all big firms do well (record numbers have been losing money). And neither do all big countries (witness

Russia, China, India). A study by economist Robert Summers, cited by *Business Week* in 1990, concludes that per capita incomes, overall, are slightly lower in countries with larger populations and land area. Smaller countries, like smaller firms, he observes, tend to focus.

- <u>Technology and brainware's dominance are taking the scale out of everything</u>. "Taking the scale out of everything"—that's the way steel mini-mill potentate Ken Iverson of Nucor Corp. put it. He and fellow mini-mill operators have taken most of the scale out of steel—and most of the wind out of big steel's sails (see *American Steel*, by Richard Preston). "The newest technologies (flexible manufacturing, faster computers, and better telecommunications) have reduced the optimum size of many businesses," *The Economist* reported in early 1990. "The odds are that they will reduce it even further." Quite simply, there's no longer any justification for 7,000 people under one roof to produce an automobile or "least cost" steel ingots. Though economies of scope—e.g., market power, which can often be realized via networking—remain important, and in some cases are of growing importance, economies of manufacturing scale can hardly be said to exist anymore. From Germany's textiles to Cypress's semiconductors and Titeflex's hoses, "maximum" manufacturing effectiveness can be achieved in small/smallish settings. Must, in fact, be so achieved: Old giantism and knowledge-based value-added "production" (which is the mainstay of all developed economies) are simply incompatible. You do brainwork in groups of tens, not thousands. (Revisit our discussion of all-firms-as-de-facto-professional-service-firms.)

- <u>America's biggest troubles have by and large come in "concentrated" industries</u>. In virtually every industry—consumer electronics, robotics, commodity semiconductors, automobiles—where the U.S. has been pounded by the Japanese, for example, we have had fewer competitors and a higher "concentration ratio" (a higher percentage of industry sales from fewer companies) than they did. Also, recall Michael Porter's evidence in support of "vigorous domestic rivalry" as the wellspring of success in a given global industry.

- <u>Don't forget "breakup value."</u> Many are taking a revisionist hacksaw to the '80s. I would argue that the "break-up-the-giant-corporation" '80s were mostly a success, albeit a painful one. (The fact that voluntary breakups are the '90s rage offers support for my view.) There was wretched excess, to be sure (working off the U.S. corporate debt bulge, for instance, cooled off the world economy in the early '90s). Yet more got done, faster, to start the wholesale repositioning of the American economy for the Post-industrial/Information Age than I, for one, would have imagined. "Start," of course, is the key word. Cutting and slashing and demolishing do not a sound strategy make. On the other hand, it's impossible to create a forward-looking, flexible strategy until the cutting and slashing and breaking up are largely done—e.g., ABB, the Union Pacific Railroad.

- <u>Most of the recent manufacturing surge in the U.S. is thanks to smaller companies</u>. Though big manufacturing outfits have made considerable productivity strides (which have regularly been in the news) in the last ten years or so, it's their smaller, unsung brethren (rarely in the news) that deserve the real kudos for jolting U.S. manufacturing productivity back on track, from the beleaguered Midwest to the Pacific shoreline. (The Los Angeles Basin, on the back of tiny firms rather than defense contractors, has become America's manufacturing leader—low-tech and high-tech, including textiles.)

• It's getting smaller out—period. New research reveals a dramatic drop in the average size of firms in Britain, Germany, and the United States. "Between 1975 and 1985 average numbers of employees per firm declined by 20 percent," *The Economist* reported in 1990, in an article titled "The Incredible Shrinking Company." (The figure opposite depicts the shift.) The decline, first thought to be a result of computerizing rote functions, is explained "by firms narrowing the focus of their activities [and becoming] less vertically integrated." The computer does play a role, but *not* as a labor-saving device. Instead, *The Economist* continues, it "encourages the substitution of markets for hierarchies"—i.e., facilitates more subcontracting and networking.

• All the major "forces at work"—technology, the burst of new competitors, uncertainty and upheaval in financial markets, the emergence of the "global village"—are dissipating old big's former (and, again, historically overstated) advantages. It really is almost that simple.

• Rising tides lead to diversity and variety, not uniformity. With rising incomes, the integrated European scene will be marked by increasing *variety* of tastes, not greater uniformity. Serving disparate tastes calls for more agile firms. What holds in Europe is increasingly true in Japan, Korea, and Taiwan—and will perhaps be the case in much of Latin America, Eastern Europe, and parts of the former Soviet Union by the end of this decade. (Even in the United States, regionalism in marketing is on the rise—giving another edge to more specialized firms.)

• Almost every product is being reinvented. Cars and materials are being transformed. Houses are getting smart. Et cetera. As a result, almost *every* industry is experiencing entrepreneurial rebirth—which, in turn, is one more nail in the coffin of clumsy, traditionally configured giants with an entrenched point of view.

• Competitive battles are Niche, Inc. vs. Niche, Inc.—not Monster, Inc. vs. Monster, Inc. The banking industry, for one, is no longer marked by the old, across-the-board sort of rivalry—Chase vs. Citicorp. Instead, the industry's signature is discrete battles for supremacy in hundreds of niches—e.g., student-loan processing. With that shift of emphasis, the power of old-fashioned enormity has largely been erased: Most banks are rapidly specializing and shedding hunks of their portfolios where they have no special advantage; and they're shipping out more and more work to subcontractors. Banking's story is software's story is materials' story is biotech's story. It does mean the

Average size of industrial firms

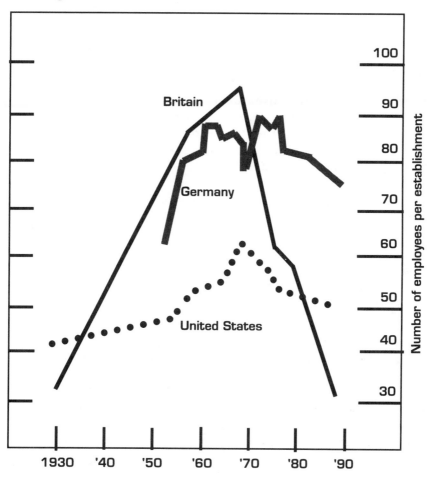

Britain

Germany

United States

Number of employees per establishment

100 90 80 70 60 50 40 30

1930 '40 '50 '60 '70 '80 '90

emergence of another flavor of "new big" (besides network big); that is, "giant" in a razor-thin "arena"—e.g., the Acordia company that wants to be the most potent financial service firm in 11 southwestern Indiana counties, or the 35-person CCT unit that wants to own the world in the maintenance of a single type of Pratt & Whitney aircraft-engine turbine blades.

 • Embracing moderate size does not mean eschewing global aspirations. The German Mittelstanders are a leading case in point, as are the miniature denizens of "The Third Italy." If "global" is the watchword, and it is, that hardly translates into an endorsement of old-style giantism. (U.S. exports are booming. And U.S. small firms are getting in on the act in a big way. Though overall figures are hard to come by, *Business Week*, for example, felt confident in declaring in mid-1992 that the new small-firm export surge is "vital to sustain[ing] growth in exports." Read *World Trade* these days, and you'll be regaled by saga after saga of tiny American firms with enormous reach.)

Add up these 17 points. Stir in Hayek, Porter, and the analyses from our Beyond Hierarchy section. Is B-I-G dead? Old big, yes, as I see it. The massive, vertically integrated enterprise, the giant factory fit for the ages—is *dead*. Moderate-size and focused (New Big I) is alive, very well, and getting better every day. New Big II, the fluid, flexible "learning networks" that may exist within a firm (ABB, IDG, Thermo Electron) or among sets of related firms (MCI and friends, Sun Microsystems and friends) is looking pretty good—and offers at least a slim chance of having the best of big and small at once. But my "conclusion" needs to be tougher: Beware of big, even network big, in a world come unhinged. (At the very least, promise me you'll consider posting over your desk the Peter Drucker epigraph that launched this book: "The Fortune 500 is over.")

Perky Baltimore!

"American orchestras have traditionally been divided into the Big Five and all the rest. Chicago, Cleveland, Philadelphia, New York, and Boston are America's world-class orchestras: they are supposed to attract the most distinguished music directors and guest conductors and to play the best; they record and broadcast their concerts on radio, and sometimes on television; they tour the planet. They make music for posterity. The rest, in this scheme of things, are compensation for less fortunate local communities.

"Things are not quite so clear-cut anymore. The Big Five have become sleeping giants, lulled into mediocrity by stuffy programming and uninspiring leadership; and at a time when the major orchestras are falling consistently short of expectations, more attention is being paid to the ensembles of Baltimore, Los Angeles, St. Louis, and, lately, San Francisco. Record companies are flocking to their orchestras, and so are audiences when they tour. . . .

"What most distinguishes the would-be second-tier symphonies these days is a certain freshness to music making. What attracted so much attention to the Baltimore Symphony's Beethoven in Carnegie Hall last summer, for instance, was not [director David] Zinman's interpretations but his experimenting with historical performance practices, such as his adopting Beethoven's rarely followed metronome markings. His was a new and different Beethoven—light, refreshing, and fast as the wind, if perhaps too featherweight for some tastes. And adding to the musical excitement in

Baltimore is the orchestra's composer-in-residence, the irreverent and riotous Christopher Rouse."

From "Sleeping Giants
and Nimble Dwarfs"
Connoisseur, November 1988

MAKING "IT" WORK I: CELEBRATING THE INVISIBLE HANDS

The vertical and totalitarian structure of the Tawantinsuyu was without doubt more harmful to its survival than all the conquistadores' firearms and iron weapons. As soon as the Inca—that figure who was the vortex toward which all the wills converged searching for inspiration and vitality . . . was captured, no one knew how to act. And so they did the only thing they could do, with heroism, we must admit, but without breaking the 1,001 taboos and precepts that regulated their existence. They let themselves be killed. . . .

Those Indians who let themselves be knifed or blown into pieces that somber afternoon in Cajamarca Square lacked the ability to make their own decisions either with the sanction of authority or indeed against it and were incapable of taking individual initiative, of acting with a certain degree of independence according to the changing circumstances.

Those 180 Spaniards who had placed the Indians in ambush and were now slaughtering them did possess this ability. It was this difference, more than the numerical one or the weapons, that created an immense inequality between those civilizations.

Mario Vargas Llosa
Harper's Magazine
December 1990

The power of Adam Smith's "invisible hand" is precisely its invisibility. No controller is needed to cause maximum economic well-being. Masses of individuals, almost all unknown to one another, make self-interested, independent choices—which turn out to coincide with the greatest good.

In fact, the presence and intrusion of controllers bent upon comprehension destroy the invisibility, and quickly sap the vitality of Smith's market Eden. (Of course, "maximum economic well-being" and "greatest good" should not be confused with engineering "optimum." Markets are very sub-optimal, in the normal sense of that term—i.e., compared to a frictionless world. It's just that there are no frictionless worlds, and markets are far less sub-optimal than planned systems—in the real, friction-filled world.)

Take a close-up look at "decentralization." Most business observers vigorously applaud the idea of chopping up big concerns, and even not-so-big ones, into moderate-sized, focused hunks. Yet decentralization, when it really works as at IDG or Thermo Electron, reduces hierarchical impedance in a way seldom realized in traditionally "decentralized" (on paper) organizations. The market's winds howl through the insides of IDG and Thermo, allowing numerous, independent, invisible hands (and heads) to propel the firm forward vigorously, if on a largely unforeseen and unforeseeable zigzag path.

To sign up for true decentralization, then, is to celebrate invisibility. It's well worth celebrating. The seldom-sung characteristics of the truly decentralized, largely invisible-from-the-top "unit" summarized here add up to an impressive endorsement for letting go (and another endorsement for smaller-than-traditional scale).

- <u>More information processed</u>. Market economies, in their maddeningly imprecise fashion, end up processing much more information than "command" economies. Instead of central plans and numerous controllers, there's the hurly-burly of middlemen, opportunists, and entrepreneurs—all jostling to take advantage of scarcities, short-term price distortions, emergent technologies, and subtle consumer preferences. (What "controller" would have foreseen the "need" for 41 varieties of Tylenol?) So, too, in the truly decentralized firm: People at the front line at Titeflex, with little or no fuss, readily seek out others (insiders or outsiders) to obtain a variety of useful, timely information to solve problems or take advantage of fleeting opportunities. In the centralized firm, by contrast, rigid and segregated information-processing rituals based upon rules from on high restrict the volume, timeliness, breadth, and usefulness of information flowing to those who need it most. (Of course, the additional volume of useful information within the truly decentralized firm is invisible to the "top," as in Smith's model of whole economies—it is thence unseen by senior controllers, which gives most such dispositionally mistrustful controllers the heebie-jeebies!)

- <u>Increased oddball connections</u>. The essence of creation—in all endeavors—is chance connections between ideas and facts that were previously segregated. Entrepreneurship à la Silicon Valley or the Third Italy, the engine of any market economy over time, is the direct by-product of chance, of convoluted connections among ideas, needs, and people from hither, thither, and yon.

Market economies provide incentives for more entrepreneurs to emerge and randomly connect with heretofore inchoate needs. When true decentralization holds sway inside the firm, large numbers of people seek out—or come randomly in contact with—others "beyond their job descriptions," thus surfacing opportunities and getting problems solved with cleverness and dispatch. (Consider that word "cleverness": It has little to do with IQ. Cleverness is mostly the post hoc assignment of "intelligence," which in fact is mostly a function of bumping into neat ideas—and that happens a lot more under conditions of true, messy decentralization.)

- Less distorted information. Hierarchies distort, abstract, and delay information processing—by their very nature. The accelerator in an effective market economy is the increasing volume of unfiltered, "real-time" information about prices and perceived values the world over, processed by those who can do something with the information in a hurry. Decentralized operations of the sort found at Thermo Electron or IDG allow everyone concerned to gather and use undistorted information directly from the source—the customer, the distributor, the vendor, a fellow front-line employee on another team.

- More "parallel processing." Computer mavens are buzzing over the potential of parallel, as opposed to sequential, processing of information. In unfettered markets, parallel processing is the norm: Suppliers, producers, middlemen, and consumers are dealing regularly with one another—and the same information—all at the same time. In truly decentralized corporate operations, engineers, accountants, marketers, salespeople, and manufacturers from various entities (supplier, corporation, distributor, customer) work "all at once" to try things, fix things, and exploit opportunities. On the other hand, centralized and functionalized operations by and large process information "sequentially": One fiefdom deals with an issue, then it's passed on to the next and the next in due—and delayed—course.

- More "front-line-to-front-line" contact. In decentralized organizations such as McKinsey, workers nearest the action make up their own minds about whom they need to deal with in order to behave most effectively and efficiently. The result, more unfettered front-to-front communication than in centralized operations, is more than additive: Such rich contacts over time lead to cumulative individual, group, multigroup, and network learning, and to increased readiness to respond to unforeseen difficulties or opportunities without the intervention of intermediate-level "processors"—i.e., staff "experts" and "middle" managers.

- Shorter feedback loops. When you're close to the scene, unimpeded by a cumbersome superstructure, and getting in your licks, you "hear" more quickly about whether an idea—new product, new technique—works. You can adjust faster, toss out useless schemes faster, improve faster. Market economies perform well because feedback loops are relatively short, and undistorted signals (more timely, closer to the action) rapidly inform large numbers of people that they are on the money, off the money, or halfway in between—in any event, giving impetus for an immediate next adjustment/try. The "magic" in the genuinely decentralized unit is the same.

• Increased "at bats." Given reasonably smart, energetic folk (invariably a fair assumption), success at anything is mostly a function of the number of times we try something. Market economies succeed by maximizing the number of tries by individuals, entrepreneurs, firms. The same holds within a firm such as CNN or Imagination. Assuming equally energetic and talented people in a centralized and decentralized corporation, the decentralizer wins hands down. Less time and effort are expended processing information through the hierarchy, and more time and effort are directly aimed at marketplace "at bats" and real-time problem solving to respond to customers or other close-to-the-action business needs. (Though systemic learning in such dispersed institutions is not necessarily efficient—hence the likes of the knowledge-management effort at McKinsey.)

• More "luck." Hayek is clear that marketplace victory does not always, or perhaps even often, go to those who "deserve it." Instead, victory goes to those who happen to be in the right place at the right time. Controlled economies (and controlled corporations) tend to work on the "deserve it" principle. Their orderly, hyperrational approaches (e.g., to resource allocation) shut off the possibility of the largely lucky accidents we call progress—the Apple II, Post-it Notes, FedEx, CNN. True decentralization simply maximizes the odds of a firm's getting lucky, by putting lots of energetic, empowered people "in the market's way."

• Higher accountability. Since information is less distorted, feedback loops (positive or negative) are shorter, and there are more tries in a market economy, accountability is *automatically* maximized. So, too, in the corporation: In the old days at motorcycle producer Harley-Davidson, for instance, six months of parts inventory dangled from the plant's ceiling, borne by an advanced, centralized materials handling system. The handlebar maker, for instance, was automatically *un*accountable—precisely because the handlebars she made today wouldn't be used by a final assembler for another 180 days. Now, with only a few minutes' worth of parts inventory in-plant (Harley has gone to a "just-in-time" scheme), the assembler screams bloody murder if there's a handlebar defect—and knows whom to scream at. Moreover, the person screamed at can respond, because her out-of-adjustment machine tool only drifted out of adjustment an hour ago, rather than six months ago. (And since she gets regular feedback, her tool rarely gets far out of line—which means she seldom gets screamed at.)

• Less "control" (in the traditional sense) in a truly decentralized system, which equals more control in the more important sense of responsiveness to real (volatile) conditions. The former Soviet economy was "under control."

Yet it regularly reported shortages among almost all basic consumer goods. No one "understands" the U.S. economy—and virtually nothing is out of stock. One economy, ours, is "out of control" in commonsense terms—it's thoroughly incomprehensible (complex macroeconomic "models" notwithstanding). And that's precisely why it's "in control" in fact. The old Soviet variety was "in control" in a commonsense fashion (you could point to a detailed plan for everything) and out of control in fact—precisely because it was comprehensible. Ditto corporations: 3M is out of control by most standards—thousands of unseen, internal entrepreneurs are beavering away on odds and ends of projects, following the company's "make a little, sell a little, make a little more" beacon. But 3M is in control compared to big corporations in general, precisely because all those eager beavers are working mostly independently to cope with ever-changing market conditions. Most other companies, like the old Soviet economy, are still guided by comprehensible master plans that shrivel the human spirit, delay useful signals—and thence reduce at-bats.

(Is there ever a case for tight control? You bet! The controls over our nuclear arsenal are tight. Thank God. But think about why: Because we don't want to use the system! The last thing we want is rogue missile-launching cowboys. In a volatile market, though, there is a premium on rogue missile-launching cowboys. In fact, progress is mostly the product of rogues—see Chapter 38.)

We're faced with a major emotional paradox. Most readers of this book are in favor of markets and dismiss centrally planned economies. Yet most readers of this book, being human, are antsy when they feel "out of control"— and thence routinely resort to rules and master plans to get "back in control." The problem: Those master plans help us achieve a sense of control at the expense of real "control" (i.e., the ability of the organism to respond automatically to altered and unpredictable circumstances) that can only come when we let go of the master plans. Addressing this problem may be the chief task of tomorrow's managers. In the past, when market feedback loops were much longer, we could at once maintain the illusion of control—plan! plan! plan!— and survive. But with feedback loops shriveling to nothing, it's no longer possible for us to maintain the illusion—and survive.

Beware Auto-Correlation! (When "Decentralization" Isn't)

IBM scored a major success with its AS/400 minicomputer. The key: The gang at Rochester, Minnesota, who made the thing more or less quit listening to IBM headquarters. They effectively declared their independence.

In the past, IBM's minicomputer ventures, influenced by the firm's leaders, who had cut their teeth on mainframe computers, had largely been aimed at meeting the needs of IBM's dominant mainframe customers. But a renegade

Rochester chief decided to go back to the drawing boards. He found that most minicomputer market growth was not coming from IBM's old-line mainframe customers. So he oversaw development of a machine that was targeted at new customers—in the process, he often operated at cross purposes with the powers that be at headquarters.

The moral of this story: To use statisticians' terms, IBM's AS/400 operation amounted to a "statistically independent" roll of the dice. Apparently robust statistical findings are frequently clouded by "auto-correlation." That is, seemingly independent events are anything but. Instead, they are mostly by-products of what's gone before. For example, an "independent" minicomputer division turns out to be indirectly handcuffed to the giant's longtime mainframe "culture"—what it does today, no matter how freestanding it may look on the organization chart, is mostly a product of what happened yesterday, and, for that matter, 75 years ago when the firm was founded.

Most corporations are frustrated by auto-correlation. They may think their divisionalized structure means that unit bosses will be making statistically independent tries. But they are usually wrong. Dead wrong. The central corporate culture casts a long, and long-lasting, shadow at IBM, GM, Du Pont—and even at ABB, EDS, and McKinsey. There is a value to uniformity (doing it "right" the first time), and a price (doing it the same way every time in a variable environment).

In today's madcap world, bits of firms must produce something approaching statistically independent tries—if the outfit as a whole is to up the odds of success in markets where attacks are coming fast and furious from unknown, unexpected quarters and competitors. The likes of Random House (remember Knopf's Sonny Mehta—p. 265) and IDG mostly get the point. Few others do.

Oddly enough, statistically independent tries also end up producing more home runs. The problem with corporate auto-correlation is that everyone pretty much thinks alike and takes the same level of risk. All tries are tightly bunched: In statisticians' terms again, the standard deviation of the population of market tries is low. With statistically independent tries, you dramatically up the odds of strikeouts—and of the occasional double, triple, or home run. Partial "proof": The top-performing, most innovative units of big firms are often those farthest from home. It can be the best of all possible worlds; the far-flung unit benefits from the parent's aura (e.g., global presence), without being hogtied by its "do it my way" corporate culture.

To Fight Auto-Correlation: Open Your Wallet

In 1989, A. T. Kearney, the consultants, released a study of long-term performance among our really giant firms—the Fortune 200. Using financial data from 1971 through 1987, they turned up 13 companies (e.g., Emerson Electric, H. J. Heinz, 3M, PepsiCo, American Home Products) that markedly outperformed the other 187. Closeness to the market (abetted by a ratio of corporate staff to total employees half that of the also-rans) was one factor that distinguished the 13. Another was sky-high spending authority: Division general managers among the winners could spend $20 million on their own signature—10 times more than their counterparts among the also-rans.

Twenty million is big bucks. But then we get to thinking, "Yeah, but those companies are *so* big." Okay, I've "downsized" Kearney's findings: $20 million in spending authority at a $5-billion company (the median size of a Fortune 200 firm in 1989, when the study was done), for instance, corresponds to $400,000 of spending authority for division general managers at $100-million (revenue) companies—and $40,000 in spending authority for unit chiefs (who'd probably be running $1-to-$2-million "outfits") at a $10-million firm!

Look at the Kearney finding through another lens. I contend that big chiefs who allow their division bosses high monetary discretion have done *something* at least to fight off auto-correlation and create the impetus for a sizable portfolio of experiments ($20-million "bets," unscrutinized by beady-eyed big-firm staffers). It's not that the chiefs need particularly brilliant division managers (I'm only half being facetious); garden-variety, aggressive division managers—who are allowed to do something substantial—will do.

It should come as no surprise that PepsiCo is among A. T. Kearney's 13. Former Pepsi-Cola boss Roger Enrico told *Fortune* in 1989 that he'd signed Michael Jackson to the first multimillion-dollar contract for a commercial without telling then-chairman Don Kendall. Kendall is a tough cookie. But that's precisely the sort of independent, imaginative behavior Kendall expected—nay, demanded—from his unit bosses.

Better Engineering? Fewer Engineers!

"To help U.S. industrial competitiveness, large engineering organizations need to be restructured, downsized, and redeployed. . . . Engineering organizations are perhaps the most fertile breeding grounds for rampant managerial incompetence. As engineers, we excel at designing and building oversized organizations, endless processes, and an almost unbounded succession of rules—the foundations of bureaucracy and the bane of productivity and creativity. We have evolved to the point of being totally rewarded on the basis of input (budget and organizational size) and not of output. Increasing the budget to raise output is the most timid bureaucrat's logic.

"But only rarely are budget and output correlated. Anthony Wang, head of Computer Associates International, Inc., reduces project staff to speed up a late product. . . . Large staffs are required because the heads don't understand the technology. Just after Seymour Cray produced the CDC

6600 in 1965, Thomas J. Watson, Jr., president of IBM Corp., wrote a memorandum to his staff in which he said: 'Contrasting [Cray's] modest effort [by] 34 people including the janitor with our vast development activities I fail to understand why we have lost our industry leadership position by letting someone else offer the world's most powerful computer.'

"Cray's comment was simply: 'It seems Mr. Watson has answered his own question.' . . .

"I have found that in order to get the number of staff on a project down below 50 (six teams, say, of six or seven), we must have exceptional, and very broad engineers—something most large engineering organizations discourage. The product quality and performance that results is usually outstanding. Furthermore, productivity is more than an order of magnitude greater than that found in the typical large organization. The vast array of new computer-aided design tools provides exceptional productivity gains and allows a small, bright staff to design very complex products in a very short time. . . .

"To cut the size of [central] engineering organizations by a factor of four or five, one [redundant] part should move into manufacturing, another into marketing and sales to learn and solve real user problems, and another should go back into the educational stream as either producers or consumers. [Others] should be encouraged to leave the company and start up new ventures based on the company's technology—but for various reasons, this is usually irrelevant to, incompatible with, or too creative for, the company's business objectives.

"Removing the nonproductive cancer that has spread through engineering and manufacturing will hurt, but it is the only way to survive competitively."

> C. GORDON BELL, computer pioneer
> "The Fewer Engineers
> Per Project, the Better"
> *IEEE Spectrum*, February 1989

Note: Gordon Bell once told me, "I've never seen a job being done by a five-hundred-person engineering team that couldn't be done better by fifty people."

MAKING "IT" WORK II: LEARNING TO RESPECT SMALL MARKETS

The Economist reported in 1991 on Japan's penchant for "product churning": "When developing a new product, Western firms use a 'rifle' approach, testing the market constantly and revising the product each time until it exactly meets the customer's need before launching it." Japanese manufacturers, by contrast, "tend to use a 'shotgun' approach. For instance, around 1,000 new soft drinks appear annually in Japan, though 99 percent of them vanish within a year. New product ideas are not tested through market research, but by selling the first production batch." *The Economist* provided the further example of a Sharp hi-fi with two compact disk players instead of one. Sharp's "experts" were openly skeptical about the need for such an oddball configuration, but they forged ahead anyway. Kids lapped it up, unexpectedly using the machine "to mix tracks from separate CDs onto tapes." The obvious lesson: You won't know whether you've created a niche/filled a customer's latent needs until you try.

"Most large markets evolve from niche markets," Silicon Valley marketing legend Regis McKenna claimed in a 1988 *Harvard Business Review* article. Sounding like Acordia's Ben Lytle and former Titeflex president Jon Simpson, he added that the niche market "teaches many important lessons about customers—in particular, to think of them as individuals and respond to their special needs." Effective electronics firms such as Convex Computer and Tandem, McKenna said, have learned to develop products for small markets by teaming software and hardware development engineers, quality experts, manufacturers—and customers. "Apple's experience with desktop publishing shows how companies and customers work together to create new applications—and new markets," McKenna declared. "Apple entered the field with the Macintosh personal computer, which offered good graphics and easy-to-use features. But desktop publishing didn't even exist then; it wasn't on anyone's pie chart as a defined market niche, and no one had predicted its emergence. Apple's customers made it happen."

In contrast, McKenna said in a *San Jose Mercury News* interview in 1989, IBM has lost out by dismissing small opportunities: "IBM was founded by a salesman, and every [chairman] has been a salesman. They created a very sales-oriented culture, very protective of market share. [IBM is] reluctant to introduce new products that might advance the state of the art at the expense of its existing products. The mentality is to maintain the status quo and move very, very carefully. . . . A lot of the technical people I interviewed at IBM were frustrated. They were unable to see their innovations and their new technologies brought to market. IBM would not enter a market until it was at least $100 million in size. A lot of companies have established very strong positions by the time they lead a market to $100 million. IBM missed the real revolution in [numerous] other areas. . . . The guerrillas are winning."

The idea, then, for chemical makers, financial service providers, software creators, or computer firms is to forget trying to control the pace of product evolution and instead use your talent to jump smack-dab into the tumult of the market. In "Corporate Imagination and Expeditionary Marketing" (*Harvard Business Review,* July–August 1991), Gary Hamel and C. K. Prahalad dismiss those companies "that simply ask customers what they want and end up as perpetual followers" and companies that try to push "customers in directions they do not want to go." Conversely, they praise firms such as Motorola for attempting to stay one step ahead, trying to "lead customers where they want to go before customers know it themselves." They add: "Market research and segmentation analyses are unlikely to reveal such opportunities. Deep insight into the needs, lifestyles, and aspirations of today's and tomorrow's customers will."

"Deep insights"? Doesn't that lead us right back to the Acordia units and the Ingersoll-Rand Cyclone Grinder team? Recall that the Ingersoll-Rand team "found" big lumps of tape on the ends of grinders—operators had put them there to keep their hands from slipping down onto an abrasive tip spinning at 35,000 revolutions per minute. How did Ingersoll-Rand "find" the tape? For the first time in the Power Tool Division's history (maybe the industry's history), manufacturing sorts and engineers and purchasers and accountants were working together, with marketing and sales people—on the scene. They went out and schmoozed with users—end users, the real people who use the tool eight hours a day. There was something special about that joint experience, all eyes watching a user.

The Cyclone Grinder's success is teaching Ingersoll-Rand about "deep insights" and "expeditionary marketing." It's teaching the company that with deep insights, "commodities" can become non-discounted, value-added solutions to customer needs. But, again, value-added only flows from listening "with" and respecting the *end user*—i.e., moving far beyond the high-sounding but often barren "ask customers what they want" that Hamel and Prahalad dismiss. It's a "small market" approach which can explode into a huge array of valuable products/micro-niches: Just ask Trumpf or Rational!

I recall discussions with managers at Procter & Gamble a half-dozen years ago. To be worthy of consideration for funding at P&G, a product family "line extension" had to aim for hundreds of millions of dollars' minimum annual revenue. The problem: The world doesn't work that way. (Not any more, at least.) In package goods, where P&G mostly competes, genuinely novel product entries—e.g., the burgeoning value-added market in prepackaged meals—have initially occupied little niches. Ignoring these pipsqueak products/niches is ignoring the direction in which the overall market is most likely to move, until, as perhaps at IBM, it may be too late to make a serious comeback.

Michael Porter has often chided CEO Jack Welch for insisting that all GE units rank No. 1, No. 2 or No. 3 in their industries. I think Porter's exactly right, if you use (as Welch apparently does) an overall measure of market share—e.g., "share of the global appliance market," "share of the global computer market." Focusing on overall share pushes you automatically toward schemes that will kill you in the long run. You will emphasize commodity (high sales) approaches and browbeat customers into hanging in with your aging technologies. You will dismiss small tries as inconsequential, be too focused on today's revenue to attend to Rational-size opportunities (or to defend yourself against a horde of Rationals until it's too late). Even Thermo Electron, tiny beside GE, decided that it couldn't adequately attend to niche opportunities unless it set its little (compared to the parent's overall size) spinoffs almost free.

Farmers and Hunters

Ponder medieval warrior Genghis Khan and the "Mongol horde." What comes to mind? Probably something like Webster's definition of horde, "a teeming crowd"—that is, the image of mass, bigness.

But that's wrong. Writing in the June 1988 issue of *Success*, business analyst David Rogers points out that the Mongols, on their way to conquering the greatest contiguous land mass ever controlled by one government, consisted of "a group of freelance bandits," whose basic building block "was a man on a small horse." The horsemen, almost always badly outnumbered in any local conflict, "could sprint to a point of attack, change direction at a second's notice or disperse to muster up later. The key principle was the autonomy of the small unit; it was big enough to mount an offensive, but small enough to retreat quickly."

Maneuverability, then, was the hallmark of the Mongols' strategy in war. As a basis for business strategy, the idea is brilliantly extended in an unpublished paper by Swedish business professor Gunnar Hedlund. In "Milking Cows versus Going Hunting: Conceptions of Corporate Strategies," he contrasts an "A-mode" of strategy, based on the agricultural model of civilization, with an "H-mode," which takes us back to earlier times when hunter-gatherers dominated the land. Hedlund argues that the H-mode of competing is more appropriate to the frenzied marketplace than the A-mode. He examines the two models along four dimensions.

First, the *environment*. Is it stable or chaotic? "The whole thrust of the agricultural revolution," Hedlund claims, "was to make the environment *predictable*. The fight was against the hazards of relying on the fluctuating supply . . . of wild animals. . . . True, there would be good and bad crops, but with foresight, technology and storage of food, difficulties would be overcome." By contrast, "the situation of the hunter-gatherer . . . is unpredictable. Last year, caribou was plentiful in the West; this year the herd may have migrated to the East and be greatly diminished." Hunters don't waste time making predictions; they know they have minimal control over their environment.

What has this to do with corporate strategy? "Everything!," according to Hedlund. "The idea that you can know what is around the corner of time is the foundation of most planning systems," he writes. "Even though the track record of forecasts is dismal, firms continue to work as if prediction were possible."

Hedlund moves from environment to *strategy*, counterposing "harvesting a location" (the A-mode strategy) with "search by locomotion" (the H-mode). When the agricultural mentality held sway, people sought large plots to take advantage of scale economies. Farmers would stake out a good position and remain there, "defending themselves against the attacks of the barbarians from the mountains, and making peace or cartels with [their neighbors]." By contrast, the H-mode strategy "builds on locomotion. It is crucial to be able to move, to search for new opportunities, to use the good years, not to hoard, but to go over to new mountains, to try another type of [fishing] net." Hedlund draws an analogy to today's mercurial business environment, claiming that rapid product development and niche-creation are the most likely paths to survival.

Next, Hedlund considers *structure*, comparing the "hierarchies" of the A-mode with the "flexible bands" that marked the H-mode. Traditional bureaucratic structures, which presuppose knowledge of what the organization will have to do in the future, won't work in today's uncertain environment. Silicon Valley, Hedlund reminds us, bears little relation to the Nile Valley.

The final distinction is *leadership practice*. H-mode leaders, Hedlund reports, were heroic, yet egalitarian—and true strategists. In hunting tribes, leaders had to be expert hunters who had performed proven feats, in order to know what to do as well as to be able to inspire fellow hunters. Hedlund characterizes the relationship between leader and follower in the H-mode as one of "joint pursuit." But in the agricultural mode, he writes, there is more "distance between the serf and the feudal lord than between the most inferior and the leader of a hunting band. Slavery thrives best in large-scale agricultural settings. Humans are 'resources' as much as anything else."

Summing up, Hedlund speculates that this "analogy is much more than an amusing but idle exercise. All firms in the industrialized world are coping with the drastic changes in their environment. . . . The message is the same: You cannot predict or control the environment. No established position is secure, and nurturing the capacity for change, on the basis of distinct and unsurpassed skills, is the only guarantee for a chance of a decent continued life."

37

Marketizing's Imperatives II:
Try It! Break It! Touch It!

If you can make it crudely, you can make it fast and it doesn't
cost much. [Then] you can test it easily . . . fix it crudely.

> PAUL MACCREADY, on
> developing the featherweight
> Gossamer Condor aircraft
> *Insight*, June 25, 1990

The logic behind establishing market-scale units, dismantling
hierarchies, simplifying systems, and allowing market winds to blow a gale
inside the firm boils down to two words: *Do it!* Fragmented, knowledge-based
markets *demand* that all firms behave as the Ingersoll-Rand Project Lightning
team did. Look at it (end users). Get out there (everyone). Try it (the prototypes quickly produced by Group Four, the industrial designers). ABB's 50-
person profit-and-loss centers come to life because they're out there, in the
market, unimpeded from trying things with real customers. Ricardo Semler
said he dismantled Semco's bureaucracy and formed small, autonomous, intimate business units to "free the Thoreaus and Tom Paines," to set rebels loose
to work directly with customers. So, too the Acordia, CCT, and IDG units. So,
too, the tiny teams at EDS, McKinsey, and David Kelley Design.

TRY IT. BREAK IT.

The only way, in the end, to cope in a fashionized market is to
try it. Forget plans. Forget market research. Just do it. In *The Cuckoo's Egg*,

astronomer/computer buff Cliff Stoll describes how he pursued a lawbreaking computer hacker; to collar resources for the project, he adopted the philosophy of fellow Berkeley physicist and Nobel laureate in physics, the late Luis Alvarez. Stoll recalls an exchange between the two:

> "Dead ends are illusory," [Alvarez told me]. "When did you ever let a 'Do Not Enter' sign keep you away from anything? Go around the brick walls. When you can't go around, climb over or dig under. Just don't give up."
>
> But who's going to pay my salary?
>
> "Permission, bah. Funding, forget it. Nobody will pay for research; they're only interested in results. . . . Sure, you could write a detailed proposal to chase this hacker. In 50 pages, you'll describe what you knew, what you expected, how much money it would take. Include the names of three qualified referees, cost-benefit ratios, and what papers you've written before. Oh, and don't forget the theoretical justification.
>
> "Or you could just chase the bastard. Run faster than him. Faster than the lab's management. Don't wait for someone else, do it yourself. Keep your boss happy, but don't let him tie you down. Don't give them a standing target."
>
> That's why Luie won a Nobel Prize. It wasn't what he did, so much as how he went about it.

Physicist Richard Muller, writing in *Nemesis*—an examination of the theory that a giant meteor hitting the earth caused the extinction of many species, including dinosaurs—tells another Alvarez story:

> I was helping another graduate student, Dennis Smith, mount a large photomultiplier tube in the Cerenkov detector, and I dropped it. It imploded just like a TV picture tube, with a loud and sickening crash. I had just destroyed $15,000 worth of hardware. Dennis consoled me. It could happen to anybody, he said. I thought it might be the end of my career. Fifteen thousand dollars was twice what I earned in a year as a research assistant. Some of the money would be recovered by firing me.
>
> A short time later I saw . . . Alvarez, and confessed what had happened. "Grrrrrrreat. . .!" he roared, and put out his hand as if to congratulate me. He shook my hand vigorously, but I protested. "Welcome to the club," he continued. "Now I know you're becoming an experimental physicist." To become a real member of the Mafia, you have to murder someone. To become an experimental physicist, Alvarez seemed to feel, you had to destroy some expensive equipment. It was a rite of passage. "Don't do anything differently," he advised. "Keep it up."

Chase the bastard. Don't wait for some one else. Grrrrrrreat, you busted it. Our job today is to create organizations not where people "do it right the first time" (what an absurd idea), but where people get on with it—"crudely," per Paul MacCready's advice from the opening epigraph. Doing it right is fine. After all, and "after all" included thousands of missteps, Luis Alvarez eventually did win a Nobel prize. But doing "it" at all, getting started, is even more important. Michael Dixon, longtime observer of successful entrepreneurs, engineers, and scientists, writes in the September 7, 1990 issue of the *Financial Times* that "every one" of his subjects in a recent study "denied planning out the work intellectually before tackling the practical tasks." Instead, the "decisive thinking was somehow embedded in the doing." They thrived by "relying fundamentally on intuition." ("I do it by *feel*" was the response of one subject, who captured the spirit of many others.) All of this, Dixon adds, flies in the face of the "plan-then-do approach," which dates back at least 2,450 years to Plato."

Ah, yes, the rub: two and a half millennia of conventional wisdom down the drain. But leave it to Jesuit-trained Harry Quadracci, Quad/Graphics' boss, to say it best: "Using plans . . . is like firing a cannonball. It's fine if you're shooting at a castle. But markets today are moving targets. The only way to hit them is to launch your business like a cruise missile: You fire it in the general direction of your objective. Then its own . . . systems adjust its course as it draws near [the target]."

Getting It Right the Second Time

In *Getting It Right the Second Time*, Michael Gershman jams 47 fact-packed cases into 256 pages. All teach one lesson: Keep trying, try anything, and maybe, if you're lucky, you'll get it right someday. Gershman acknowledges that "some products become immediate successes." But these exceptions are so rare as to be uninteresting. (A University of Southern California study he reviews evaluated 6,695 new food products introduced in the U.S. between 1970 and 1979. Only 93, or about 1.5 percent, ever achieved sales of $15 million or more in a year.)

Did you realize that modern PepsiCo went bankrupt *three* times before it got on track? Or how about the ultimate macho consumer franchise—Marlboro? It started out in 1924 as a premium-priced, nonfiltered blend of Turkish tobaccos aimed at women! Thirty years later, after dozens of variations on different themes, it took off. Others who got it wrong time and again (before eventually lucking out—uh, getting it right) include 7-Up, Quaker State, Quaker Oats, Life Savers, Yoplait, Tupperware, L'eggs, Wrigley's gum, Kraft cheese spreads, Cracker Jack, Hoover vacuums.

You learn, between the lines, that if you become successful it will usually be at the wrong time, for the wrong reason, after any number of false starts. Moreover, simply throwing more money at failing products is almost always a deadly mistake, Gershman tells us—though such products can subsequently become successful under wildly altered conditions (different timing, different product attributes, different marketing, different distribution). This doesn't help you figure out when to pull the plug the first time, always a critical and seldom-studied point; but it does suggest unmistakably that many new ideas had best be floating in many sinks if you intend to succeed in the end.

"THE MOST GODAWFUL MESS YOU EVER SAW"

Back to the Project Lightning team. Back to 10 eyes (finance-trained, marketing-trained, production-trained, engineering-trained) watching the Medieval Warrior (end user) at work. You can't "see" or "feel" unless you're out there. (Obvious? Not if you've hung around most American corporations, even circa 1992.) You can't "leapfrog" competitors or turn commodities into value-added brainware without "touch."

Touch, feel, see: They are miracle drugs. I fear that respect for touch, feel, and see has been lost within most of our big, traditional organizations. (Or maybe we never had it in the first place—recall Trumpf's Leibinger on Americans' unwillingness to file, file, file.) What a tragedy—and no one is more eloquent about the reasons why than the late Richard Feynman,* in *Surely You're Joking, Mr. Feynman:*

> When I got to Princeton, I went to [a] tea on Sunday afternoon and had dinner that evening in an academic gown at the "College." But on Monday, the first thing I wanted to do was to see the cyclotron.
>
> MIT had built a new cyclotron while I was a student there, and it was just *beautiful*! The cyclotron itself was in one room, with the controls in another room. It was beautifully engineered. The wires ran from the control room to the cyclotron underneath it in conduits, and there was a whole console of buttons and meters. It was what I would call a gold-plated cyclotron.
>
> Now I had read a lot of papers on cyclotron experiments, and there weren't many from MIT. Maybe they were just starting. But there were lots of results from places like Cornell, and Berkeley, and above all, Princeton. Therefore what I really wanted to see, what I was looking forward to, was the PRINCETON CYCLOTRON. That must be *something*!

---

* Interesting, isn't it, that we keep turning to the very top scientists, especially physicists, when we need to find "extreme" examples of hands-on experimentation?

So first thing on Monday, I go into the physics building and ask, "Where is the cyclotron—which building?"

"It's downstairs, in the basement—at the end of the hall."

"In the *basement?*" It was an old building. There was no room in the basement for a cyclotron. I walked down to the end of the hall, went through the door, and in 10 seconds I learned why Princeton was right for me. . . . In this room there were wires strung *all over the place!* Switches were hanging from the wires, cooling water was dripping from the valves, the room was *full* of stuff, all out in the open. Tables piled with tools were everywhere; it was the most godawful mess you ever saw. The whole cyclotron was there in one room, and it was complete, absolute chaos!

It reminded me of my lab at home. Nothing at MIT had ever reminded me of my lab at home. I suddenly realized why Princeton was getting better results. They were working with the instrument. They *built* the instrument; they knew where everything was, they knew how everything worked, there was no engineer involved, except maybe he was working there too. It was much smaller than the cyclotron at MIT, and "gold-plated"?—it was the exact opposite. . . . It was wonderful! Because they *worked* with it. They didn't have to sit in another room and push buttons!

A Matter of Learning to "See"

Kimon Nicolaïdes's *The Natural Way to Draw* has been called the best how-to book on any subject. Understand what Nicolaïdes is saying, and you'll have taken a big step toward understanding even better why the Princeton cyclotron was so successful—and why Ben Lytle's Acordia companies model is working so well.

There is only one right way to learn to draw and that is a perfectly natural way. It has nothing to do with artifice or technique. It has nothing to do with aesthetics or conception. It has only to do with the act of correct observation, and by that I mean a physical contact with all sorts of objects through all the senses. . . . Don't worry if for the first three months your studies do not look like anything called a drawing that you have ever seen. You should not care what your work looks like as long as you spend your time trying. . . .

I believe that entirely too much emphasis is placed upon the paintings and drawings that are made in art schools. . . . Unfortunately, most students, whether through their own fault or the fault of their instructors, seem to be dreadfully afraid of making technical mistakes. You should understand that these mistakes are unavoidable. THE SOONER YOU MAKE YOUR FIRST FIVE THOUSAND MISTAKES, THE SOONER YOU WILL BE ABLE TO CORRECT THEM. . . .

Look at the edge of your chair. Then rub your finger against it many times, sometimes slowly and sometimes quickly. Compare the idea of the edge which the touch of your finger gives with the idea you had from merely looking at it. In this exercise you will try to combine both those experiences—that of touching with that of simply looking. . . . Move your eye *slowly* along the contour of the model and move the pencil *slowly* along the paper. As you do this, keep the conviction that the pencil point is actually touching the contour. Be guided more by the sense of touch than by sight. THIS MEANS THAT YOU MUST DRAW WITHOUT LOOKING AT THE PAPER, continuously looking at the model. Exactly coordinate the pencil with the eye. Your eye may be tempted at first to move faster than your pencil, but do not let it get ahead. . . . DEVELOP THE ABSOLUTE CONVICTION THAT YOU ARE TOUCHING THE MODEL. . . .

[On drawing models taking active poses]: As the model takes [this or that] pose, you are to draw, letting your pencil swing around . . . being impelled by the sense of action you feel. Draw rapidly and continuously in a ceaseless line, from top to bottom, around and around, *without taking your pencil off the paper*. Let the pencil roam, reporting the gesture. YOU SHOULD DRAW, NOT WHAT THE THING LOOKS LIKE, NOT EVEN WHAT IT IS, BUT WHAT IT IS *DOING*. Feel how the figure lifts or droops, pushes forward here—pulls back there—pulls out here—drops down easily there. . . . If the model leans over to pick up an object, you will draw the actual bend and twist of the torso, the reaching downward of the arm, the grasping of the hand. . . .

I must admit that I'm close to dumbstruck by the regularity with which I come across stories like this—Feynman, Nicolaïdes, whomever. *M inc.* published an excerpt from Michael Bamberger's *To the Linksland* in May 1992. The author, a longtime golfer stuck in a performance rut, talks about the breakthrough that occurred after he worked with the legendary Scottish instructor John Stark. Bamberger had tried every technique in the book, he thought. But Stark sent him back to basics: *"Hear* the sound that the shaft makes as it comes through the air; *listen* to how rhythmic and sweet that sound is. . . . Those are the lonely sounds of good golf. Bamberger goes on to report that "I found it immediately effective. . . . By concentrating only on the sound I seemed to lose the irresistible urge to hit the ball hard, and my downswing was smooth, less rushed. . . . I remember the pleasure I felt then, the intellectual and sensory pleasure of being totally consumed in my effort to hit good golf shots and my increasing success." Ah, the miracles that occur, with easel or 4-iron, when one puts down the manual—and touches, listens. . . . How did we get it so wrong?

ALWAYS A NUMBERS GAME IN THE END

Consider new-product development. It's a low-probability game, no matter how much you plan or how often you survey current customers. There are so many variables—*literally millions of variables*—that go into any new-product success. There are variables that deal with the *technology* (design, engineering, manufacturability, quality, serviceability, etc., etc.). Variables that deal with *distribution* (who, in what channels, takes how much interest in the product, for what reason, when). And variables that deal with *customer use* (the lag time between the development of a new product and its routine adoption, even when dramatic and unmistakable benefits are evident from the outset, often runs to decades—and almost always occurs via a convoluted, totally unpredictable path). Not to mention variables that involve *competitors* (big competitors, small competitors, domestic competitors, foreign competitors, competitors from previously noncompetitive industries—e.g., toolmakers like Kennametal getting into tool-room management). And *generic uncertainties* (coups, countercoups, energy cartels, inflation). Multiply, as you must, these and other clusters of variables, and the odds of succeeding on any one "at bat" are all too close to zero.

Which leads to the obvious conclusion: Innovation, in the end and no matter how well thought out, in business as in science or art, is almost always a numbers game. Lots of tries, lots of time spent with progressive end users, lots of tiny markets attacked—and maybe a hit or two will ensue now and again. Sadly, though my point seems so obvious (for the ages, and especially today), it is seldom reflected in corporate innovation strategies, which all too typically depend upon a small number of ponderous projects. Such an overanalyzed, under-touched approach is implicitly based on the notion that "if we throw enough money at it, do enough market research, surely something good will happen." Wanna bet?

Coping with the "Risk-Free Society"

The late Henry Fairlie wrote a chilling 1989 cover story for *The New Republic*, "Fear of Living." In January 1967, he noted, "The first Apollo space craft caught fire during a test on the launch pad. Three astronauts were killed, the nation was shocked and horrified, all the more so because the screams and scrambles of the astronauts could be clearly heard." After a brief delay in manned flights, the Apollo program resumed with strong public support; within 18 months, Apollo 11 landed on the moon.

Fairlie contrasts the Apollo tragedy to the 1986 Challenger disaster. "The prevailing mood in America so panicked NASA that it took almost three years to send up another shuttle," he observes. "In the 19 years between these tragedies, the idea that our individual lives and the nation's life can and should be risk-free has grown to be an obsession . . . threatening to create an unbuoyant and uninventive society."

With madness afoot in every marketplace, glory, I predict, will go to leaders in firms who attack the future with the most zest, the most tries, the most failures. This is the worst of all times to engage in perpetual analysis, and to run from risk, from action-taking—and mistakes.

But the fact is, at some level the "try it"/"make it crudely" dogma runs smack-dab into frightened managements and huge legal staffs—and the U.S. legal system. When the CEO asks of a proposal, "What do the lawyers say?" that almost inevitably portends delay and, ultimately, a more tepid response.

This is not the place to debate business ethics, important as that topic is. Some CEOs, in desperate pursuit of another two pennies per share (literally) in next quarter's earnings, do put subtle, or not so subtle, pressure on managers to cut corners (on worker safety, product safety, etc.). Overall, though, the ardent pursuit of a "risk-free society" is converted into counterproductive overcaution in most (big) corporate settings.

The pursuit of "risk-free," within the corporation, means answering any and all questions with "no" or "it depends"—and something worse, creating "review processes" that assure the process creator will not be blamed if something goes awry. Consider the Americans with Disabilities Act, new legislation that I wholeheartedly applaud. I cannot tell you how many big-company personnel chiefs have written me to say, "Well, Tom, there goes your crusade against job descriptions [one small example of stultification]. The ADA *mandates* job descriptions."

My opinion of Congress is not high, but I still couldn't imagine that it would have demanded job descriptions. Well, it didn't, it turns out. Job descriptions are one way, after the fact, to cover your ass if you have an ADA claim brought against you. On the other hand, they are in no way required.

As usual, the *real* answer to "coping with" ADA is thinking through what the Act means, counseling and coaching people to do the right thing, and setting a progressive tone from the top boss's office. I confidently predict that those with enlightened top teams, short manuals, and small personnel and legal departments will comply more thoughtfully—and vigorously and imaginatively—than those with ponderous procedures, lengthy manuals, and a CYA mindset. So, too, with safety issues attendant on new-product development—and every other issue where the drive for risklessness contends with the need to just "do it." Oddly enough, relative to burgeoning legislation or developing new products, those that pursue "risk-free" by hiding behind regulations that delay action are doubtless putting themselves into the highest risk category.

38

Marketizing's Imperatives III: Renegades and Traitors, Passion, Arrogance

You almost have to be a true believer to be competitive . . . a true believer in your product, a true believer in your industry. Of the hundreds and hundreds of world-class companies from around the world that I studied, an enormous proportion were privately owned or were run by some maniac who had spent the last 20 years of his life on a crusade to produce the best product.

> MICHAEL PORTER
> *Across the Board*
> September 1990

Whether revered or reviled in their lifetimes, history's movers framed their questions in ways that were entirely disrespectful of conventional wisdom. Civilization has always advanced in the shimmering wake of its discontents.

> GARRY TRUDEAU, quoted in
> Richard Saul Wurman's *Follow the Yellow Brick Road*

Effectively managing any enterprise today, all of GE or a single Burger King franchise, demands perpetual discontent and a willingness to question everything. Then question it again. On the one hand, such constant questioning could be deadening, micromanagement by another name. On the other, it could lead to liberation: the slaying of all sacred cows. Ah, that's it. The slayers of sacred cows! We must—simply must—learn to welcome into every corporate cranny those with zest, with a touch (or more) of the zany in their blood. Those who will try anything—and induce others to try anything—are tomorrow's kings and queens.

Some such yeasty folks are the sisters and brothers of Mother Teresa. Others are rogues and even scalawags. ("He who fears corruption fears life"—radical organizer Saul Alinsky.) None countenances the status quo. Our problem: In the past, we've scorned these irreverent system-busters. Now we desperately need them, need them in large numbers, need them in accounting and purchasing as well as product design and marketing, and need to figure out how to create an environment which will attract them—and retain them. Only the thoroughly irreverent organization stands even a chance of navigating today's "permanently white water," as organization researcher Peter Vaill calls it.

THE ALL-NUT NINE: ZANY CHIEFS FOR ZANY TIMES

> Generally speaking, people in Britain [in early 1940] thought Churchill to be impulsive, erratic, wordy, unduly combative, a maverick, perhaps a publicity hound; in one word, unsteady.
>
> JOHN LUKACS
> *The Duel—10 May–31 July 1940:*
> *The Eighty-Day Struggle*
> *Between Churchill and Hitler*

> Every style that is not boring is a good one.
>
> VOLTAIRE

I was born in 1942 and reached semi-adult awareness during the Tasty Kake Eisenhower years. Young men about to enter the world were admonished "keep your nose clean," "don't make waves"—and collect your gold watch after 40 years of labor for reliable old XYZ Widgets.

Such advice was sound, then. (Maybe.) The '90s, however, are decidedly different! So I worry a lot about these words, uttered in 1990, by Ford chairman Red Poling: "The three most important things in business and golf are consistency, dependability, and predictability."

Maybe he's right about golf. But unless Mr. Poling's ready to quit and hang out on the links, I'd suggest he think again about business. In fact, I believe that (1) the two most important traits in business today are *in*consistency and *un*predictability; and (2) we desperately need more *traitors* inside the corporate moat.

When Poling spoke, Ford's spectacular gains in the '80s seemed to be wearing thin. Ford had reverted to dull product offerings. The spunk had skedaddled. So if Red Poling is to make a mark, he needs to be far less consistent and far more daring. Fortunately for America, the lackluster performance of a GM or Ford is far from the whole story. The U.S. was shaped by rule-breakers—Ben Franklin, Ethan Allen, Tom Paine, Thomas Jefferson and company. Subsequently saved by a master rule-breaker, Abe Lincoln. Vaulted to economic preeminence by rule-breakers—Carnegie, Ford, Rockefeller, Morgan. And we still produce an unfair share of rule-breakers. Jack Welch, of uppity $60-billion General Electric, is neither consistent nor predictable. "Change everything, then change it again"—that's his trademark. He's hardly alone. My "All-Nut Nine" features Welch, Ted Turner (Turner Broadcasting), Craig McCaw (McCaw Cellular), Roger Milliken (Milliken & Co.), Bob Crandall (American Airlines), Philip "Buck" Knight (Nike), Fred Smith (Federal Express), Les Wexner (The Limited), Mike Walsh (UPRR, now Tenneco), T. J. Rodgers (Cypress Semiconductor), Vaughn Beals (Harley Davidson), Bob Swanson (Genentech), Larry Ellison (Oracle), Hal Rosenbluth (Rosenbluth Travel), and Michael Dell (Dell Computer). Sure it's more than nine. But this *is* a treatise on unpredictability! (My international head table of disturbers of the peace includes Percy Barnevik of ABB, Lord Hanson of Hanson PLC, Anita Roddick of The Body Shop, Akio Morita of Sony, Richard Branson of the Virgin Group, Chung Se Yung of Hyundai, Stan Shih of Taiwan's Acer, Ricardo Semler of Semco, and Siegfried Meister of Rational.)

From textiles to TV, each of these characters ignored the rules, fought City Hall, absorbed arrows in the vitals—and invented or reinvented industries in the process.

The Fortune 500 bobs along, with islands of excellence amid oceans of mediocrity. Full-fledged renewals of the GE and Harley Davidson variety are rare indeed. In fact, the continuing failure to renew in the face of problems that have festered for decades has led me to a desperate measure: I renounce my oft-made plea for renegades, rogues, and scalawags in the corporate ranks. I demand instead traitors. A renegade simply disturbs the peace. But a traitor finds the current regime abhorrent, and is determined to do no less than topple it. I think our giants *do* need many more rogues—and more than a few traitors—in their consistently sleepy midsts. Only wholesale corporate makeovers will do.

In short, Chairman Poling, the Eisenhower years are gone. Put your golf clubs in mothballs. Swap your golf cart for a 1340-cc Harley. Dull times call for dull leaders. Zany times beg for zany leaders.

SOBs and Other Mostly Necessary Characters

[William Paley was] a genius, possessed of enough energy to propel a dozen brilliant careers, generous, thoughtful and, above all, charming.

> CHRISTOPHER BUCKLEY,
> reviewing Sally Bedell Smith's biography
> of Paley, *In All His Glory*,
> in *The New York Times*
> *Book Review*

[William Paley was] a toweringly small man: insecure, petty, jealous, ungrateful, snobbish . . . a philanderer . . . a tyrannical father, a pathological liar; abusive, resentful, cruel, neurotic, self-absorbed, tightfisted and greedy.

> CHRISTOPHER BUCKLEY,
> in the same review

By the end of the book one cannot help liking this appallingly ambitious and lonesome brat.

> *Financial Times* review of
> *Hard Drive—Bill Gates*
> *and the Making of the*
> *Microsoft Empire*
> June 9, 1992

Reflect on this passage from *Agent of Influence*, an acclaimed spy novel by former senior National Security Council staffer David Aaron: "The State Department representative was saying: 'We all want the same thing. An international system that encourages stable economic growth and—'

" 'All your talk about growth,' Bresson intruded from his end of the table, 'you gentlemen forget the most important thing—scoundrels. What room in your theories do you allow for scoundrels? They are the engines of progress. Krupp, Farben and Thyssen in Germany, Astor, Vanderbilt, Rockefeller, Ford in America. Rothschilds in France and England.' "

Denigrate the source if you will: The fictional Bresson is a global publishing mogul, who also turns out to be a KGB colonel. But my contention is that "Bresson" is mostly right. "The prevailing theory of capitalism suffers from one central and disabling flaw: a profound distrust and incomprehension of capitalists," George Gilder writes in *The Spirit of Enterprise*. "Modern economics . . . resembles a vast mathematical drama, on an elaborate stage of theory, without a protagonist to animate the play."

At 913 Emerson Street, a stone's throw from my office in Palo Alto, you'll find California Registered Historical Landmark No. 836. It commemorates the site of the Federal Telephone Co., where Lee De Forest and two colleagues worked on developing the modern vacuum tube in 1911–13. Their efforts were a significant step along the path to "modern radio communication, television and the electronics age," the bronze plaque tells us without ado. In *Risk & Other Four-Letter Words*, former Citicorp chairman Walter Wriston describes De Forest's recompense. The pioneer was soon "arrested for stock fraud [because he claimed] that his invention would be able to transmit the human voice across the Atlantic. . . . The jury acquitted De Forest, but the judge admonished him to forget his crackpot inventions and go 'get a common, garden-type job and stick to it.' "

More recently, Roy Disney's lawyer Stanley Gold is reported to have made a speech to the Disney board that was instrumental in getting superstar Michael Eisner appointed chairman in 1984. "Guys like Eisner [are] a little crazy . . . but every great studio has been run by crazies," John Taylor reported in *Storming the Magic Kingdom*. "[Walt Disney] was off the goddamned wall. This is a creative institution. It needs to be run by crazies again."

I was reminded of the above while contemplating the minor furor caused by *Confessions of an S.O.B.*, the best-selling 1989 autobiography of former Gannett chairman Al Neuharth. A former Gannett employee, assessing the book for *Fortune* magazine, titled his review: "Why It Works to Be a Jerk." I was hounded by the press for comments on the Neuharth book. I suspect the interviewers thought I'd dismiss it out of hand and come down squarely on the side of sweetness and light in the executive suite. They were dead wrong. I'm not sure I would want to work for Neuharth—but then, I'm not sure I'd want to work for a lot of our best-known innovators.

The fact is, if you're going to buck conventional wisdom in a big-league way, as Neuharth did with the creation of *USA Today*, a lot of people are going to be gunning for you. *Confessions of an S.O.B.* and the 1987 book *The Making of McPaper* by Peter Prichard describe some of the crude attacks on Neuharth, Gannett, and anyone associated therewith: The idea of a national daily, then its journalistic style, were denounced as sheer folly. Even the distinctive street-corner dispensers were subject to ridicule (and lawsuits). Moreover, the attacks went on year after year. (*USA Today*, though reaching the million circulation mark in just seven months, went five years before recording its first profitable month—which made it tough to silence critics.)

De Forest, Eisner, Neuharth—and all members of my All-Nut Nine— have been decried as lunatics, ogres, egomaniacs, or worse. Citicorp's Wriston himself was scorned for tenaciously championing global banking, national banking, and even automatic teller machines; yet his innovations (regardless of Citicorp's current major case of the hiccups) transformed the financial services sector worldwide.

The bold risk-taker, the sturdy venturer, the true visionary is despised by one and almost all. The establishment, for good reason, is invariably out to get him or her. One practical consequence: Only a person with a somewhat large (or larger) ego, unreasonable self-confidence, a streak of irrationality, a thick skin, and a touch of paranoia stands much of a chance of success.

It's not my intent to diminish the numerous accomplishments of managers and executives possessed of grace and a gentle touch. (I've devoted page after page of this book—and my earlier ones—to praising such folks, in fact.) But I do want to propose that being a persistent and demanding SOB, or a seemingly outright nut like De Forest, may almost be a requisite for crawling through fields of withering fire and creating a revolution. The times call for a more than normal share of Neuharths and De Forests. Agents of radical change rarely lurk behind a beatific smile, a calm demeanor, and a diminutive ego.

Arrogance!

Prime Minister Margaret Thatcher had the politician's great gift of being able to persuade masses of people that her policies were not merely the only possible ones, but simple common sense that only a fool couldn't accept. This persuasive arrogance was her great strength for years, but it finally became her fatal weakness.

CRAIG R. WHITNEY,
reporting in *The New York Times*, November 23, 1990, on Mrs. Thatcher's resignation

You get an idea while meeting with a customer, reading a novel, dousing yourself in the shower. Usually nothing comes of it. (After all, research shows that we have about 90 thoughts per minute.) But now and again, one clicks. You begin to study it, chat up a few friends, do a touch of library research. It usually dies at this juncture; but once in a while one slips through the gate; your interest is piqued.

Now your objectivity wanes. You start selectively "seeing things" associated with the idea. And your response to what psychologists call cognitive dissonance kicks in: The idea *must* be neat, or you wouldn't be spending so much time on it! Your attachment becomes an irrational obsession—which is a success prerequisite. So many land mines loom in the real world that only zealots have a prayer of creating the next CNN or *USA Today*. (George Bernard Shaw: "The reasonable man adapts himself to the world; the unreasonable one persists in trying to adapt the world to himself. . . . All progress depends on the unreasonable man." Peter Drucker: "Whenever anything is being accomplished, it is being done . . . by a monomaniac with a mission.")

Most smart, obsessed people are *not* Steve Jobs or Ted Turner. You never hear of them. Why? They fail. For any of a million loosely connected reasons—state of the technology, customer needs, competitor strengths, tight market for financing, alignment of the stars—their obsession is a mismatch with the environment at the time. Obsession, then, doesn't guarantee success. On the other hand, a lack of obsession *does* guarantee failure.

Okay, you turn out to be the one-in-a-million grabbed by the brass ring. Your wallet bulges. The press takes a shine to you. Customers applaud heartily. Employees made rich overnight adore you. Messages to your mind: (l) What a great product/service I invented! (2) What a fine human being I am! You continue to work like the devil, fueled by all the attention. You find an alter ego for your spurting firm's No. 2 slot, and prosperity surges thanks to her or his managerial talents.

Then a new, arrogant, obsessive upstart comes along—with a quirky restaurant on your block, a new flavor of software or personal computer in your niche. Now what? You make a superficial change here or there. But a quick review of your press clippings and personal assets statement convinces you that you alone know the turf. So you fight *fundamental* change tooth and nail. You fire your No. 2 for insisting that major overhauls are necessary, and seek out another and another (like sick folks pursuing doctors to find one, somewhere, to assure them that their fatal disease isn't).

But that clever new competitor fails in spite of himself, for some random set of reasons. Your faith in you is renewed. And then *another* upstart comes along. The cycle repeats itself for a while, maybe 10 years. But when the genuine article finally arrives, your basically unrefurbished gem is badly tarnished. You're history.

Such is the pathology of arrogance. Can't live without it. Can't live with it.

But hold on, you protest. At some point I *will* listen. Don't bet on it! History (political, commercial, etc.) says you won't listen until it's too late; in fact, the harder the evidence against you, the more complex and convincing the rationale you'll construct to explain it away; in the end only bankruptcy will silence you.

Of course, some firms do last—3M, Johnson & Johnson, General Electric. These three, not coincidentally, are and have been blessed with radically decentralized organization structures that support monomaniacs and occasional anarchists. (GE almost lost its way, but Jack Welch, an out-of-the-closet anarchist himself, returned it to its obstreperous roots.)

Lessons to be learned: (1) Over the long haul there's scant hope for corporate renewal unless numerous wild-eyed egomaniacs are running crazy on your premises—with performance agreements that keep you from canning them for reasons other than moral turpitude. (2) Figure out, if you can, how to exit gracefully (or ungracefully). But do exit. You could, for instance, consider the Thurgood Marshall stratagem. The Justice said he'd step down when his wife told him it was time. (Maybe she did.) Make such a deal with your wife or best friend. Or find a hobby, like racing cars at 170 mph, and try to shift your obsession. (Not likely.)

Proposing such lame antidotes to the founder's once useful arrogance is not my true objective. My real point is to insist that arrogance *is* the spice of life, no matter how obnoxious its manifestations at times and no matter how toxic it becomes to its carrier (person, organization). Not comprehending the essential role arrogance plays in creation and renewal is as dangerous as underestimating its dysfunctional side effects.

BODY, SOUL, PASSION, *AND* PROFIT

The passions are the only advocates that always persuade. The simplest man with passion will be more persuasive than the most eloquent without.

DESCARTES

Freud said that all the unimportant decisions you make logically, and all the important decisions illogically or emotionally.

I believe it. . . . In my own case, I trust my emotional decisions quite often more than the logical ones. Why? There is more power behind them to carry them out.

BILL CAUDILL, founder, CRSS
The TIBs (for This I Believe)

On March 27, 1976, the first Body Shop opened at 22 Kensington Gardens, Brighton, England. At the end of the day, Anita Roddick stuffed the first day's take, $225, into the pocket of her dungarees. In early 1992 the firm has a stock market value of about one billion dollars, with at least one securities analyst predicting 40 percent annual growth for the next five years.

"A great advantage I had when I started The Body Shop," Roddick writes in *Body and Soul*, "was that I had never been to business school." The lessons she provides are surely not taught at any business schools I know. To wit: "If I had to name a driving force in my life, I'd plump for passion every time." She adds that "the twin ideas of love and care touch everything we do."

Passion, love, care? Roddick hasn't found much of it among her competitors. "The world of retailing . . . taught me nothing," she insists; it's "populated by tired executives working tired systems. . . . Huge corporations [are] dying of boredom caused by the inertia of giantism."

The Body Shop prospers by following a decidedly more zesty regimen. "For us the business of business is to keep the company alive and breathlessly excited, to protect the workforce, to be a force for good in our society and then, after all that," Roddick claims, "to think of the [shareholders]." Alternatively, "If companies are in business solely to make money, you can't fully trust whatever else they do or say. . . . The whole sense of fun is lost, the whole sense of play, of derring-do, of 'Oh God we screwed that one up.' "

The Body Shop has made its mark by educating customers, a far cry from the hype that marks the rest of the cosmetics industry of which it's nominally a part. "The idea that everyone should walk out of our shops having bought something is anathema to me," Roddick insists. "We prefer to give staff information about the products, anecdotes about the history and derivation of the ingredients, and any funny stories about how they came [to be] on Body Shop shelves. We want to spark conversations with our customers, not browbeat them to buy."

Ban the Bland

Since The Body Shop does no advertising, such conversation with customers is paramount. "By creating conversation" instead of pursuing traditional branding through advertising, Roddick tells us, "we let our customers spread our message by word of mouth." Enthusiasm helps, too. The Body Shop "positively radiates passion," she adds. "I can't bear to be around people who are bland and bored and uninterested (or to employ them). The kind of brain-dead, gum-chewing assistants you find in so many shops drive me wild. I want everyone who works for us to feel the same excitement that I feel; to share my passion for education and customer care. . . . Every time I go into one of my stores I want to be thrilled by what I see and by the people I meet. I want to be delighted and surprised."

The Body Shop's various public-interest "campaigns," such as joint efforts with Greenpeace and Amnesty International, have attracted customer notice and gained media attention. But, "much more important," according to Roddick, "is the tremendous spinoff [from the program] for our staff. . . . You can be proud to work for The Body Shop—and, boy, does that have an effect on morale and motivation."

Before starting The Body Shop, Anita and husband Gordon Roddick blew their first retail venture, a restaurant. The disaster held important lessons: "We had done everything wrong. . . . What saved us . . . was our willingness to recognize that we were wrong and our ability to move swiftly to the next idea." That determination to try anything marks today's Body Shop and is reflected in a management style that Anita Roddick describes as "loosely structured, collaborative, imaginative and improvisatory, rather than by the book." She says she and Gordon have "fostered a kind of benevolent anarchy by encouraging everyone to question what they [are] doing and how they [are] doing it." The peripatetic Roddick herself is always in desperate pursuit of new ideas: "We believe that everything is subject to change and we have learned to love change. . . . I will go anywhere to talk to people who say they are doing things in a better way, in case we can adopt or adapt it."

Seek Out the Anarchists

With growth, The Body Shop has had to fight the normal tendency toward inertia that Anita Roddick dreads so much. Gordon, she reports, "is now talking about running the company without an office, just a chair which will move from department to department." And Anita has taken to making somewhat risky decisions just to prove that the firm still has spunk. Otherwise, she speculates, "We would have all our managers running around and getting incredibly excited about our profits, the annual report and forgetting that business is not just about performance but also about staying human."

The most important defense against entropy, Roddick suggests, is learning "to love the person who irritates you. Tap the energy of the anarchist and he will be the one to push your company ahead. I believe [such anarchists] will be the future custodians of the culture of this company." Unfortunately, she adds, "I don't think they're going to be found among the ranks of managers and executives—the [future] custodians of our culture will be found among the young kids who are joining us now."

Where's the Joy?

In the last 15 years, in an intensely competitive industry, Roddick saw her global empire grow to 709 shops, which in 1991 tallied $26 million in profits on $238 million in revenue. And make no mistake, she's done it her way. "For me there are no modern-day heroes in the business world," she flatly states in *Body and Soul.* "I have met no captains of industry who made my blood surge. I have met no corporate executive who values labor and who exhibits a sense of joy, magic or theater. . . . In the 15 years I have been involved in the world of business it has taught me nothing. There is so much ignorance in top management and boards of directors: All the big companies seem to be led by accountants and lawyers and become moribund carbon-copy versions of each other. If there is excitement and adventure in their lives, it is contained in the figures on the profit-and-loss sheet. What an indictment!"

Summarizing her unconventional values, Roddick is clear: "First, you have to have fun. Second, you have to put love where your labor is. Third, you have to go in the opposite direction to everyone else."

TOWARD PRODUCTIVE ANARCHY

Can you translate any of this into practical affairs? First and foremost, there's a mindset that's essential, a mindset that grasps the implications of uncalm times, that cherishes inconsistency and unpredictability, that respects passion and the need for anarchists. But beyond that:

• <u>Hire entrepreneurs and renegades</u>. You want entrepreneurs and renegades? Hire entrepreneurs and renegades. There's surprisingly high agreement among those who have done research on the wellsprings of entrepreneurship: The best—some would say only—half-decent predictor of entrepreneurship is entrepreneurship. The person who behaves in an entrepreneurial fashion today (independently, or on someone's payroll) is the person who was entrepreneurial at the age of seven, organizing the other kids on the block to support him or her in selling lemonade door-to-door. Entrepreneurship then begets entrepreneurship now.

So if you want obstreperous entrepreneurial sorts, look for those who have been obstreperous and entrepreneurial in the past—perhaps starting a business or club in high school or college, or leading a 2,000-person campus rally against the bomb. (This is especially important if you make bombs. Consider: P&G's top environmental officer was a co-organizer of the first Earth Day. Southern California Edison's chairman, John Bryson, was former head of the scrappy Natural Resources Defense Council.) Many years ago, I helped select people for a special program at the Stanford Graduate School of

Business. I pawed through hundreds of applications. I had mixed feelings about any number of candidates, but one popped out as a "must accept." I still call him "the one-ton cookie man." As an undergraduate he'd organized a bunch of classmates to bake—honest!—a one-ton cookie. As I recall, he ended up in one of the "world record" books.

Ever since, when counseling executives, I've said, "Hunt for the one-ton cookie men." (And women!) If you want to find people who are likely to do something intriguing, search for people who have done something intriguing—and, yes, it really is almost that simple.

● Protect entrepreneurs and renegades. Getting renegades on the payroll is not enough. Protecting them from the bureaucrats—and make no mistake, every firm with more than one employee has bureaucrats (even the ones profiled in this book)—becomes a prime job for managers at all levels. Renegades, especially those in pursuit of visionary new-product dreams, break *a lot* of china, irritate *a lot* of people.

I'm not contending that a few don't break too much china. They do, and run roughshod over others; at some point they may have to be dismissed. The separation of Steve Jobs from Apple, for example, was almost inevitable. His tirades and outbursts became increasingly dysfunctional in a multibillion-dollar firm, peopled with slightly older professionals than had been the case at the outset. On the other hand, I suspect that any major future success at Apple will likely come from finding a new, disruptive Steve Jobs clone. Have I described yet another Catch-22? You bet! Keep him and you're in hot water. Let him go and you're in hot water. But then that's the story of innovation, isn't it?

● Send entrepreneurs and renegades underground. One of the best reasons to open an office 5,000 miles from headquarters, even for a young company with 15 people on the payroll, is to implant a few loonies far enough away from "home" so that they can avoid the infection of "conventional head-office wisdom." If distant enough, the merry little band will (1) be influenced automatically by other ideas/cultures and (2) more likely develop a healthy disregard for company policy.

The idea is to invent devices that are largely "you-proof." That is, devices that up the odds of traitorous—and potentially company-saving—behavior far from your daily field of view. The chief who has the guts to carefully plant and fertilize the seeds of his or her own possible destruction is rare. That had best change.

● Hire passion/joie de vivre. Anita Roddick wants passion. So she hires passion. Case closed. Except most of us, even if we purport to want passion, fail to formally put it among our recruiting and hiring criteria.

You've seen it. I've seen it. Jack walks into a room and 5, 55, or 555 people tense up instantly. Gloom and doom follow in his wake. Then there's Maria. She walks in, under exactly the same conditions (good or bad), and people lighten up a bit, feel a little more energetic. Look for "Marias." Avoid "Jacks" like the plague. And have no doubt: Marias are recruitable. Once you start to think about it, you can develop as clear a view of Maria-ism (or Jack-ism) as you can about the educational credentials on a curriculum vitae. But to develop such judgment, you've got to decide to add "passion" to your list of hiring criteria in the first place. (Hint: In these turbulent times, I'd suggest that such joie de vivre *top* the list.)

• <u>Promote passion/joie de vivre</u>. Jack and Maria are candidates for promotion. Unless an ax murder shows up in her background, promote Maria. (Legendary adman David Ogilvy goes one step further. In his *Principles of Management*, he advises abruptly firing the merchants of gloom and doom. Sorry, Jack, old boy.)

What's the role of "vision" in perpetual innovation? Of a sound R&D "strategy"? Beats me. Recruit passion. Hire passion. Protect passion. Promote passion. I'll trade you an ounce of passion for a page of vision and a pound of plans any day. (And especially tomorrow.)

LAST (DISCOURAGING) WORD

It's impossible to overestimate the problems big-firm chiefs face in trying to induce even a little innovation. On the one hand, they'd best keep their mouths shut. When Yutaka Kume was appointed president of Nissan, his company's cars "were unpopular," Canon chairman Ryuzaburo Kaku said in a speech to the Second Global Conference on Management Innovation (London, December 1991). "[Kume] said that whenever he commented on a mock-up of a new model, a revised mock-up incorporating his comment would [soon] appear. In some cases, the revised version would be worse than the original version. So, he tried not to say a word on the mock-ups. And he even stopped mumbling about a mock-up when he found out that a staff member was taking notes. He refrained from even opening his mouth. Mr. Kume insists that thereafter, Nissan began to produce popular cars in the market."

On the other hand, perhaps those chiefs had better keep their mouths wide open, and their presence felt. That's what Anita Roddick seems to claim in *Body and Soul*:

One day I was having a conversation with a group of management staff and they were complaining about the red culottes that they had been given to wear for their current uniform. I said, "Do you like them?" and they said, "Oh no!" I said, "Do you feel like nerds wearing them?" and they said, "Yeah!" So I said, "Then why the fuck are you wearing them?" I told them to parcel all the culottes up and send them to me and I would find someone in the world that did want them, which I eventually did in Romania. Those situations always surprised me. There we were, banging the drum about empowering our staff, encouraging them to speak up whenever they were unhappy about anything, yet they waited until I was around before they said how much they hated those culottes.

There is no patented way out. Which may lead us back to the de facto "leadership" tactics embedded in our earlier discussion of violent market-injection strategies. If even the most zestful, vigilant, and antiestablishmentarian leader—and Roddick qualifies on all three counts—is, in the end, fighting a losing battle, then it almost seems that only willful self-dismantling of the ABB, IDG, and Thermo Electron varieties stands a chance of keeping the twin wolves of inertia and entropy from the door.

39

Marketizing's Imperatives IV: Loosening Up

What a distressing contrast there is between the radiant intelligence of the child and the feeble mentality of the average adult.

SIGMUND FREUD

Strategies are okayed in boardrooms that even a child would say are bound to fail. The problem is, there is never a child in the boardroom.

VICTOR PALMIERI
business turnaround expert
Fortune, February 24, 1992

The key to success for Sony, and to everything in business, science and technology . . . is never to follow the others.

MASARU IBUKA, Sony co-founder
Fortune, February 24, 1992

Recall that one observer declared, "Microsoft's only factory asset is the human imagination." Fine. And true, for all of us in fact, in this age of brain-based value-added. But what then? How do you "manage" ("corral"?) the human imagination? Obviously you don't. Instead, you "unleash," "create the context for the expression of," whatever.

In any event, unleashing the human imagination on a large scale, and in the purchasing office as well as the R&D shop, is a *big* idea. Not even the boldest proponents of "self-managed work teams" and "empowerment" have come close to dealing with this imposing concept.

The "problem" (and opportunity) is aptly captured by the epigraph from Freud, overstated or not. Corporate leaders in the '90s must seek nothing less than the application of childlike "radiant intelligence"—in any and all business settings.

If "managing" the human imagination is clearly wrongheaded, perhaps "loosening up" is at least a step along the right path. Hiring traitors and learning to love anarchists is part of it (see Chapter 38), but only part. Traitors and anarchists are foreign bodies, who aim to shake up "the feeble [corporate] mentality." Hiring them is important, but necessarily a reactive response.

Is there, then, a proactive approach to fending off the development of corporate feeblemindedness before it's too far advanced? Can one create a corporate context wherein the imagination (of dozens, thousands) is constantly—and productively—sparked? Perhaps.

TOWARD THE CURIOUS CORPORATION

If I don't do something like play music or work out or fly my airplane or ride a bike every day, I can't survive. I can be creative and excited at work only if I have a chance to think about something else.

Philippe Kahn
CEO, Borland
Computerworld, June 22, 1992

Is not curiosity the principal mark of Freud's "radiant intelligence of the child"? "Manage" curiosity? Again, never! Develop and maintain a "curious corporation"? Some, at least, are trying. And, arguably, few quests are more important.

Voice Lessons for Publishing International's Chief

Most companies operating out of the boss's living room don't attract clients like Walt Disney or Fujitsu. But 10-employee Publishing International is not like most companies. The Sunnyvale, California, computer-game producer is run by someone who knows the value of curiosity to the corporation. "Curiosity and creativity are a natural state," CEO Brad Fregger told us. "And our fear of getting stepped on dampens our curiosity, because we tend to want security first." Fregger is "very careful" not to squelch that natural state. After all, he said, "What makes people curious and creative is what makes them committed."

By and large, Publishing International's employees work at home. Then, a couple of times a month, a product-design team gathers at Fregger's house for an all-day project review. "We work on milestones," Fregger said. "There's no '8 to 5' around here. In fact, one of our programmers normally works from 10 P.M. to 5 A.M." Michael Sandige, PI's manager of programming/entertainment, told us that Fregger simply says to employees, "We've got to have something to show in a week and a half, and I don't care if you do it all the night before and go out of town for the rest of the time."

Although they're spread out and mostly on their own, Fregger pushes people to change their activities—radically. "In the middle of a hard job, I remind people to go do something else," he said. "Bosses often want folks to work on nothing but their project, but sometimes people need to work on something completely different to get their best ideas. You have to give your subconscious mind a chance to work." Fregger himself takes voice lessons and practices singing when he needs a work break. His 10 employees go for a bike ride, see a movie, play a game, walk, read, or run during the workday. "Curious people are not afraid of what they'll encounter," director of design and development Michael Feinberg said. "And successful business requires that. Curiosity is a willingness to suspend disbelief for two minutes, three times a day, to leave space for something unexpected."

Water-gun Fights at Accolade

Accolade, of San Jose, California, with $28 million in 1991 revenue, markets the software produced by Publishing International and others. On a typical workday, technical-support people play Ping-Pong in a spare conference room. Gumby figures, origami, comic strips, and Pez dispenser collections fill the workstations. A tropical-fish tank bubbles in one employee's cubicle.

The finance department has regular water-gun fights on premises. And there's an after-hours, off-site company poker game every other payday. Workers also play cribbage, board games, competitors' software and strategy games with other companies by fax and mail—in between playing and testing their own software.

How does all this contribute to curiosity, much less productivity? "People can't sit in front of video terminals all day and stay inquisitive," said Paul Doctorow, vice president of business development, when we talked with him in 1991. "It takes away the fun. And if you rivet the same rivet nine zillion times a day, quality goes down: You need to pay attention, so sometimes you need to structure a non-boring approach." Several times a year the company closes for a day of moviegoing, miniature golf, or bowling—"to keep people excited and interested in their fellow employees," said Doctorow.

Respect for people and their eccentricities motivates people at Accolade to work longer hours and contributes to an incredibly low 2 percent employee turnover rate. Two workers fly in by private plane from Sacramento; and one commutes from Reno, Nevada, spending a couple of days at the office, working at home the rest of the week.

"We try to do things differently," chairman and founder Alan Miller told us. "I play a lot myself. You get a break, get exercise, and people think better after clearing their minds. It's good for employees to have lots of broad interests." The payoff: "Curious people have an appetite for leaning new things and they realize the necessity for change," Miller said. "Furthermore, they'll encourage it [in others]."

Astrologers at Banamex

Voice lessons and water-gun fights too much for you? Just Silicon Valley "freakishness"? (But how you'd love to have the Valley's spunk without the water guns, eh?) My answer, no surprise by now, is that such apparent lunacy is close to requisite in "brain factories"—and we're all running brain factories these days. Suppose, though, I concede you the Silicon Valley point: Can you so readily explain away bankers heading off to archaeological digs?

In Mexico, where senior bank officials are still addressed by the equivalent of "Sir," the iconoclastic, curiosity-inspired goings-on at one division of Banamex, the country's largest financial institution, are opening employees' eyes to new ways of doing business. Director of innovation Bill Beazley told us that the information systems division has "used humor and injected external influences into the workplace to avoid the syndrome of not seeing the forest for the trees."

At a Friday taco-and-beer bash, for example, the division presented a theatrical farce about overbearing bosses. It was "extremely controversial," Beazley admitted. "[Mostly], we try to bring in things that have nothing to do with banking or technology," he added. "We've brought in astrologers, dream analyzers, and archaeologists." But such doings ultimately serve a strategic purpose. "There's an archaeologist who believes in a mystical significance to the pyramids, and we brought him into one group's planning session to [shake people up]," Beazley reported. "We also set the session in a town known for archaeological sites. It caused debates and provoked an environment for going against the tide."

Anybody Know a Good Sci-fi Author?

"Many U.S. companies would be better off hiring one good science fiction writer for a month than buying 1,000 PC spreadsheets. The future is no longer a simple extrapolation of the past; it's an incredibly rich array of stories waiting to be told. . . . The issue here isn't predicting the future; it's embracing uncertainty in new ways. Of course, if you really want provocative scenarios, go to a specialist: Hire a science fiction writer. Who's better positioned to extrapolate technological discontinuities and their social implications than a cyberpunk novelist?"

MICHAEL SCHRAGE
San Jose Mercury News
April 15, 1991

Time Off from Tandem

After 16 years of growth, $1.9-billion (1991 revenue) Tandem Computer maintains the pace of a start-up. Many employees work 60-hour weeks, leaving little personal time. So the company retains a powerful renewal tool from its earliest days: six-week paid sabbaticals for every employee, every four years. Most use the time off to travel. Employees can combine sabbatical leave with their vacation. Or, they can take an eight-week paid "public service sabbatical"—to teach in the inner city, for instance.

"It's a chance to just get away from everyday work and think about new things," vice president for human resources Sue Cook told us. "You come back refreshed and able to tackle problems in a new way." Software designer Bob Strand spent his first sabbatical at the Cordon Bleu School of Cooking in London. During sabbatical No. 2 he studied Spanish in Cuernavaca, Mexico. "I got to do things I never would have gotten to do otherwise and will remember the rest of my life," Strand said. "I came back recharged, with a new point of view." He also started bringing gourmet desserts to staff meetings— and found he had "150 percent" attendance. Strand has sabbatical No. 3 scheduled for 1993.

ORGANIZED (LEGAL) GRAND LARCENY

Where do policy ideas come from? . . . Policy is something you can steal from everybody.

GOVERNOR LAWTON CHILES
on turning Florida into a
"kleptocracy," quoted in
The New York Times
August 11, 1991

Loosening up to deal better with fast-changing circumstances surely includes tolerating (welcoming!) the ideas of others. Surely. But oh so few do it with a vengeance. It's theft I'm talking about, you know.

Actually, I've plumped for larceny in the past. (There was a discussion of "creative swiping" in *Thriving on Chaos*.) But Chiles's notion of kleptocracy takes the idea to a new level—organizing systematically to steal constantly, and from the best. Who knows, maybe Governor Chiles swiped that idea from masterful car dealer Carl Sewell or Sara Lee Direct.

In his book *Customers for Life* (written with Paul Brown), Carl Sewell claims that grand larceny is a business essential. In 1967 he began energizing his father's moribund Dallas dealership, using his Rolodex as prime change agent. "Who are the best car dealers in the country?" he'd ask colleagues. Sewell got names, called, visited, and then visited some more. He listened. And listened. Took notes. And more notes. Then he went home and followed his favorite "try it" strategy, quickly adapting the best of what he'd observed to his place. Sewell's operations today are museums of tribute to others. Take Sewell Village Cadillac: You'll see some of super-grocer Stew Leonard here (focus groups, for one thing), American Airlines there (a variation on the AAdvantage program), a bit of Marriott somewhere else, then a touch of Neiman-Marcus, a glimmer from The Mansion at Turtle Creek (an award-winning hotel in Dallas), and a sparkle or two from Walt Disney. Such studenthood-in-perpetuity, especially "borrowing" from businesses *outside* your own industry, is all too rare. ("It can't work *here*. 'They' don't understand the car business." Heard those sorts of lines before?)

Ripping Off Chuck E. Cheese

"One of the things I hate about car dealerships is that they always have loudspeakers blaring the name of someone somebody is trying to find. It's annoying and unprofessional, but I didn't know what to do about it until I wandered into a pizza place.

"I had taken my kids to Chuck E. Cheese—that's the pizza chain where they have singing and dancing animals, rides, and loads of Nintendo video games. If you want something to eat, you walk up to the counter and place your order. Then you go watch the show, or put the kids on the rides, until your food is ready.

"Given the noise in that place—the 'animatronic' animals, the games, the screaming kids—there is no way for somebody to yell, 'Sewell, your pizza's done.' You'd never hear them.

"Here's how they handle it. After you've placed your order, they give you a number—just as they do at the supermarket deli counter. Then, every time an order is done, a pleasant-sounding chime goes off. That's your signal to look at the TV monitors they've put all over the place. Every time an order is ready, the corresponding number comes up on the monitors.

"The system works just fine. Nobody has to yell, and the customers don't have to mill around the kitchen door, wasting time, waiting for their food.

"I thought that was a heck of an idea. So we borrowed it and modified it a bit.

"What used to happen at our dealerships was that you'd pay your bill and the cashier would pick up a microphone and say, 'Please bring up car number 473.' Upon hearing the announcement, one of the customer service reps was supposed to go search the lot, find your car, and bring it around front for you.

"The system never worked very well. First, the announcements blared all day long. Second, we were never sure if the reps heard the page. They might have been inside another car, with the windows rolled up, or on the phone, or somebody might have been talking to them. The only way we really knew that they got the message was if they brought the car around. If they didn't, the customer waited, and waited, and waited, and would eventually complain. When he did, we'd make the announcement again, and the whole process would start all over. . . .

"Today—thanks to Chuck E. Cheese—here's what happens when you pay your bill: The cashier enters that information into a computer, and it also shows up on a computer monitor on the service drive. When they see it, a service rep logs on and says he's going to get the car, and that information is relayed back to the cashier. If the service rep doesn't log on, we know something is wrong, and someone is sent to find out what the problem is.

"With the new system, there are no loudspeaker announcements, and we always know whether or not the car is on the way up. More important, the average time of delivering the car to the customer has been cut from six minutes to two. All of these improvements can be traced directly back to our visit to the local pizza place."

CARL SEWELL and PAUL BROWN
Customers for Life

Sara Lee Direct

"The challenge of leadership," said Fritz Morrison, director of retail support services at Sara Lee Direct (SLD) outlet stores, is to "recognize and reward the theft of great ideas so people are not afraid of swiping, but proud of it." That view reflects how SLD combats what Morrison called the "stupidity" of the "not invented here" syndrome. "Nothing has been created new in the world since the wheel," Morrison told us in 1991. "Everything gets swiped." Given this philosophy, SLD steals unabashedly from everywhere. It even had teams compete to find companies that had the most theft-worthy ideas! "We picked very disparate companies," he added, "and learned key traits for future competitiveness." The teams studied or visited 12 organizations, including American Express, Marriott, Prodigy (the Sears-IBM information service venture), steelmaker Nucor, and professional basketball's Charlotte Hornets. Morrison contended that the formal competition, complete with prizes, was a "symptom of the idea that the highest form of flattery is stealing."

Pam Smith, with the information services unit when we talked with her, believes in pirating ideas, but told us the trick is "making people think it's their idea." She stressed that without the creative sweat of your own team, "you won't get buy-in." So Smith's team blended its own expertise with ideas from such companies as Ernst & Young and Duke Power Co., and came up with a new systems development methodology. She told us it enjoys "more widespread use" within SLD than if a system had been borrowed wholesale, without alterations.

In fact, SLD brands all its swipes with its own mark, while giving credit to the source. Don Folger, information services VP, took the concept of account execs from the advertising industry and proposed creation of an "information systems exec." These new information account managers are charged with "helping internal customers to determine their needs," a role Folger claimed is "destroying a little bit of hierarchy" and bashing the "we versus you" mentality, since it encourages information systems experts to operate cross-functionally.

Folger splits SLD's swiping practices into two categories—strategic and tactical. "Managers do general kinds of probing for more strategic swiping," he said. One example involved Levi Strauss & Co. "We shamelessly stole a lot of ideas from them on developing overall quality/productivity plans," Folger reported. Other steals are more "tactical," he said. "To get a bead on data storage equipment, we visited USAir and Burlington Industries. . . . Such visits are constant."

SLD even snatched ideas from Winston-Salem's Carver High School, using the students' rap music in training videos for SLD's merchandisers. "Creative swiping provides energy to an organization," SLD CEO Chuck Chambers concluded. The key is "understanding that an idea that worked elsewhere must be personalized so that it's unique, different. There's power in that." (Not incidentally, SLD gives as good as it gets. It also shares actively with those from whom it borrows.)

During seminars, I routinely rank organized grand larceny (and "strategic visitation") as one of the top dozen strategies that companies bent upon renewal must follow. In short, if you're not casing candidates for a minimum of three or four major visits this year (company-sponsored or on your own), you have no business being in business today.

On the Other Hand (Sorta)

Borrowing, and then adapting, is great. Not enough firms do it. But recall the epigraph from Sony's Ibuka: "Never . . . follow the others." Mindless "benchmarking," one of the latest rages in industry, is just that: mindless. But even mindful benchmarking is no panacea, as one executive pointed out in a letter to *Across the Board* (June 1992):

> Regarding "The Benchmarking Bonanza" [April], yes, benchmarking can help companies improve their modus operandi, but it shouldn't be mistaken as a tool for achieving excellence. Excellence requires an element of creativity that surpasses that of the competition. Honda and Toyota didn't get where they are by benchmarking themselves against the then world leaders in Detroit; they drew upon their internal creative abilities to excel. In the global competitive scene, to focus too heavily on benchmarking is to perpetuate mediocrity, to guarantee that one will always be a follower.

> WILLIAM J. ALTIER
> President
> Princeton Associates
> Buckingham, Pennsylvania

CHEKHOV AND CREATIVE BUSINESS STRATEGY

I came across a personal computing column, discussing new laptop models. It included this advice: "A business trip can be much more profitable when the five-hour plane ride can be spent working on a presentation or bid instead of watching a lousy movie on a tiny screen." As I read, a wave of sadness swept over me.

Why? I fear that the writer states the trade-off—crunching numbers or watching grade-B flicks—accurately. I ride on planes more than most. I watch people, especially young men and women, churning the numbers, hour after hour, on the way from San Francisco to New York, Dallas to Atlanta, or Chicago to Denver. They take a break only to watch Eddie Murphy or Clint Eastwood romp across the screen—then back to the numbers, the CRTs, the spreadsheets.

And I wonder: What do they think? Are they thinking? Is anything even slightly original going on in their heads?

I'm a half-baked student of the history of science and innovation. One finding pops out. The most successful scientists, inventors, and entrepreneurs draw upon wildly disparate sources (art, sailing, flower arranging) to subconsciously help them see troublesome problems in a new light.

There's no evidence that traces inspiration—for a corporate vision, a breakthrough drug, or a new sundae topping—to "thinking harder about sundaes," for instance. Instead, a Charles Darwin is inspired at the right moment by a chance reading of Adam Smith. A progressive hospital chief I know gets ideas from a 30-year addiction to theatergoing.

When I get on a plane, I look to see who's reading Chekhov—I'd bet on his or her stock. Or, at least, who are the computer makers reading *Mother Jones, Interview, Progressive Grocer* (a grocery-trade magazine), or *Pit & Quarry* (journal of the rock-mining trade)?

I'm lucky to have had several mentors whose sense of exploration rubbed off on me. My consulting career started at Peat, Marwick (now KPMG). My first boss was an avid beekeeper who regularly contributed to the chief journal in the field. Many of his novel ideas about organic management processes, which he applied to client R&D problems, were by-products of his passion for the ways of bees.

Later, as a business student at Stanford, I was the charge of a professor with boundless intellectual curiosity. A discussion of any management topic was typically enlarged by analogues from 14th-century politics, arcane mathematical theorems, and the traits of 50-year-old Sauternes. I—and all those who came and still come under his sway—benefit in unexpected ways from these astonishing twists and turns.

My first boss at McKinsey held degrees in physics and law (and not in business). When confronting oil exploration issues, he brought both disciplines to bear, along with dabblings in Eastern mysticism and a passion for folk singing. I—and his clients—were rewarded time and again by original notions that were influenced by such catholic tastes.

Today, in my small firm, I am counseled by a chief financial officer who was trained as a merchant seaman as well as an accountant. His abiding passions are great fiction and the London and New York theater. He's a demon when it comes to financial controls—but his almost matchless feel for the human predicament is his real value-added.

Each of these close colleagues has taught me a great deal about business and life. Any success I've had in concocting occasionally interesting management formulations, I attribute mostly to *their* breadth.

Now back to the friendly skies. Over the years, I've frequently flown with my mentors. They've fallen prey to Eddie Murphy from time to time. So have I. (The fact is, I'm a Murphy fan.) But none carries a laptop computer, prepares presentations, or otherwise "uses" the hours in the air to crunch numbers. One reads Octavio Paz. Another devours Sherlock Holmes. Another ingests Robert Pirsig's *Zen and the Art of Motorcycle Maintenance* yet again.

These are crazy times, which therefore require crazy solutions. And it's my unshakable belief that crazy solutions and breadth of mind are Siamese twins. So when I'm in the air, I don't work on columns, prepare presentations, or fiddle with laptop computers. On a recent trip, from Amsterdam to San Francisco, I read a lengthy essay on leadership passed along by my Stanford mentor—most of the references were to works written before 1500. I also read Graham Greene's *The Captain and the Enemy*. The language was lovely, the ideas provocative. What did I learn? I haven't got a clue. But somehow or other, I'm certain that a muon or two of Greene has snuck, directly or indirectly, into these pages.

ASKED ANY GOOD QUESTIONS LATELY?

Physicist Isidor Isaac Rabi, who won a Nobel prize for inventing a technique that permitted scientists to probe the structure of atoms and molecules in the 1930s, attributed his success to the way his mother used to greet him when he came home from school each day. "Did you ask any good questions today, Isaac?" shé would say.

RICHARD SAUL WURMAN
Follow the Yellow Brick Road

Anthony Suchman, a professor of medicine at the University of Rochester, wanting to give his daughter's third-grade class a feel for the life of a doctor, had students conduct mock medical interviews with a "patient" (the teacher) who had hypothetical problems. The kids, Suchman observed in a column in the *Rochester Democrat and Chronicle*, were a lot like most medical students and doctors. They cut to the chase and immediately pursued pet hypotheses (to complaints of a stomachache, for example, a third-grader asked whether the "patient" was under stress); they invariably failed to ask the much more basic, "What happened?"

Suchman argued that the poverty of open-ended questioning among medical professionals comes from training regimens—starting in nursery school—that make it risky to "leave the safety of right answers and [learn to] relish the unknown and unexpected."

Remember principal Dennis Littky of Thayer High School in Winchester, New Hampshire (p. 455)? He encouraged one of his teachers to present a six-week special class "on questioning." The youngsters ate it up, Littky reported in *Harper's*—but he "got a huge amount of flak from parents. They didn't want their kids pestering them with questions. We thought our job was somehow forcing these kids to use their minds. The parents thought we should take care of their kids during the day and eventually reward them with a diploma."

Littky's questioning class, Rabi's mom, and Suchman's "What happened?" share an essential idea: When in doubt, respond to a query with a query and turn responsibility (for learning, understanding, growth) back to "them."

I've tried it at seminars with great success. A while back a senior sales executive asked what I thought about a new objective-setting program he'd developed, and how and when it ought to be evaluated. I responded by asking him (1) what *his salespeople* thought about it, (2) how *they* thought it should be evaluated, and (3) *when* they thought it should be evaluated. A plant manager posed an even thornier question: How, after a merger, should he deal with a yawning salary gap between two similar staffs from the merged firms? Why not ask *them* how to deal with the issue, I replied.

All of the above hovers near the essence of humanness, which transcends the world of business and even the classroom. In clinical psychology, "Rogerian therapy" (after the late Carl Rogers) has been quite effective. It works like this:

Patient: "I'm feeling blue."

Psychologist: "So you are feeling rather poorly."

Patient: "Yes, over the past few days, I've etc., etc."

Psychologist: "So recently you've etc., etc."

Though I've provided a mere caricature, it gets to the heart of the matter: Lead patients (students, workers) toward *self*-discovery. Get them, in effect, to ask themselves, "What happened?"

The expert, whether classroom teacher or chairman of a $1-billion company, wants to be efficient, to help (probably, unconsciously, to demonstrate her or his expertise). In most cases, doing so inhibits the very growth and curiosity she or he is attempting to promote. "To instruct calls for energy, and to remain almost silent, but watchful and helpful, while students instruct themselves, calls for even greater energy," Canadian novelist Robertson Davies writes in *The Rebel Angels*. "To see someone fall (which will teach him not to fall again), when a word from you would keep him on his feet but ignorant of an important danger, is one of the tasks of the teacher that calls for special energy, because holding in is more demanding than crying out."

Following Davies, among others, I've suggested to managers that they earn 75 percent of their pay for declining the opportunity to "solve" other people's problems: Ask yourself at the end of each day, "Have I merited that three-quarters of my pay that comes from keeping my trap shut and allowing 'them' to learn in their own fashion?" I'm only being half-facetious. So, *have you?*

The Pursuit of Luck

Innovation is a low-odds business—and luck sure helps. (It's jolly well helped me!) If you believe that success does owe a lot to luck, and that luck in turn owes a lot to getting in the way of unexpected opportunities, you need not throw up your hands in despair. There *are* strategies you can pursue to get a little nuttiness into your life, and perhaps, then, egg on good luck. (By contrast, if you believe that orderly plans and getting up an hour earlier are the answer, then by all means arise before the rooster and start planning.)

Want to get lucky? Try following these 50 (!) strategies:

1. At-bats. More times at the plate, more hits.

2. Try it. Cut the baloney and get on with *something*.

3. Ready. Fire. Aim. (Instead of Ready. Aim. Aim. Aim. . . .)

4. "If a thing is worth doing, it is worth doing badly."—G. K. Chesterton. You've gotta start somewhere.

5. Read odd stuff. Look anywhere for ideas.

6. Visit odd places. Want to "see" speed? Visit CNN.

7. Make odd friends.

8. Hire odd people. Boring folks, boring ideas.

9. Cultivate odd hobbies. Raise orchids. Race yaks.

10. Work with odd partners.

11. Ask dumb questions. "How come computer commands all come from keyboards?" *Somebody* asked that one first; hence, the mouse.

12. Empower. The more folks feel they're running their own show, the more at-bats, etc.

13. Train without limits. Pick up the tab for training unrelated to work—keep everyone engaged, period.

14. Don't back away from passion. "Dispassionate innovator" is an oxymoron.

15. Pursue failure. Failure is success's only launching pad. (The bigger the goof, the better!)

16. Take anti-NIH pills. Don't let "not invented here" keep you from ripping off nifty ideas.

17. Constantly reorganize. Mix, match, try different combinations to shake things up.

18. Listen to everyone. Ideas come from anywhere.

19. Don't listen to anyone. Trust your inner ear.

20.   Get fired. If you're not pushing hard enough to get fired, you're not pushing hard enough. (More than once is OK.)

21.   Nurture intuition. If you can find an interesting market idea that came from a rational plan, I'll eat *all* my hats. (I have a collection.)

22.   Don't hang out with "all the rest." Forget the same tired trade association meetings, talking with the same tired people about the same tired things.

23.   Decentralize. At bats are proportional to the amount of decentralization.

24.   Decentralize again.

25.   Smash all functional barriers. Unfettered contact among people from different disciplines is magic.

26.   Destroy hierarchies.

27.   Open the books. Make everyone a "businessperson," with access to all the financials.

28.   Start an information deluge. The more real-time, unedited information people close to the action have, the more that "neat stuff" happens.

29.   Take sabbaticals.

30.   "Repot" yourself every 10 years. (This was the advice of former Stanford Business School dean Arjay Miller—meaning change careers each decade.)

31.   Spend 50 percent of your time with "outsiders." Distributors and vendors will give you more ideas in five minutes than another five-hour committee meeting.

32.   Spend 50 percent of your "outsider time" with wacko outsiders.

33.   Pursue alternative rhythms. Spend a year on a farm, six months working in a factory or burger shop.

34.   Spread confusion in your wake. Keep people off balance, don't let the ruts get deeper than they already are.

35.   *Dis*organize. Bureaucracy takes care of itself. The boss should be "chief dis-organizer," Quad/Graphics CEO Harry Quadracci told us.

36.   "Dis-equilibrate. . . . Create instability, even chaos." Good advice to "real leaders" from Professor Warren Bennis.

37.   Stir curiosity. Igniting youthful, dormant curiosity in followers is the lead dog's top task, according to Sony chairman Akio Morita.

38.   Start a Corporate Traitors' Hall of Fame. "Renegades" are not enough. You need people who despise what you stand for.

39.   Give out "Culture Scud Awards." Your best friend is the person who attacks your corporate culture head-on. Wish her well.

40. Vary your pattern. Eat a different breakfast cereal. Take a different route to work.

41. Take off your coat.

42. Take off your tie.

43. Roll up your sleeves.

44. Take off your shoes.

45. Get out of your office. Tell me, honestly, the last time something inspiring or clever happened at that big table in your office?!

46. Get rid of your office.

47. Spend a workday each week at home.

48. Nurture peripheral vision. The interesting "stuff" usually is going on beyond the margins of the professional's ever-narrowing line of sight.

49. Don't "help." Let the people who work for you slip, trip, fall—and grow and learn on their own.

50. Avoid moderation in all things. "Anything worth doing is worth doing to excess," according to Edwin Land, Polaroid's founder.

Now write down the opposite of each of the 50. Which set comes closer to your profile?*

In short, loosen up!

---

*This list was stimulated by a friend who attended a several-day seminar I conducted in early 1991. The group, I thought, was vigorous. Her comment on the last day: "Are *all* those people dead?" It shook me and got me wondering about the narrowness of my own vision. (The friend was *not* Anita Roddick, though it could have been. The lack of zip in most enterprises is the bane of Roddick's existence—see p. 593.)

40

Own Up to the Great Paradox: Success Is the Product of Deep Grooves / Deep Grooves Destroy Adaptivity

Environmental changes often transform earlier adaptive specializations into cruel traps. As a changing environment passes beyond the range of a gene pool narrowed and made less versatile by specialization, it often forces the extinction of whole species.

E. S. Dunn, quoted in *The Social Psychology of Organizing* by Karl Weick

No nation has ever withstood the ravages of time or the corrosive decay of success.

Richard Lamm, former governor of Colorado

Create and destroy. It's one of the titles I considered for this book. The idea is to "specialize" (per E. S. Dunn's epigraph), to establish a first-class organization with first-class habits—to know what you're about, to be quality-conscious, to create superb relationships with customers and vendors, to constantly improve everything. Then next season comes. New fashions. New competitors. New economic conditions. Now all those "wonderful" habits turn into Dunn's "cruel traps," leaving us at the mercy of the latest and newest competitors. ("Adaptation precludes adaptability," says Karl Weick.) Our only defense, it would seem, is to destroy ourselves before a competitor does. But not so fast. Unfortunately, organizations that are perpetually destroying themselves have the devil's own time creating that focus, that top-drawer quality, those deep and consistent relationships, that ethos of constant improvement in the first place.

THE VISION AND VALUES TRAP

All good ideas eventually get oversold. The importance of a corporate vision and values is no exception. The "vision and value thing" in business took off in the late 1970s. To empower workers to focus on quality and service, the time had come to chuck the four-pound policy manual and instill a paperless, shared notion of "what's important around here" that left lots of room for individual initiative. The idea was—and is—right. But there are caveats. Over time, values-in-action get elaborated. Before you know it, a value set becomes more rigid than the rule book it replaced. It ends up stifling the very initiative it was designed to induce.

Weighty policy manuals, organization charts, and job descriptions are clearly out of step with our noisy times. Yet anarchy's hardly the whole answer—consistency of product quality and service, for example, has never been more important. So a widely shared vision and set of core values remain the best alternative to an overweening, paper-based control system.

But we must acknowledge how quickly values can age, becoming hopelessly narrow, ludicrously ramified—and at odds with a shifting marketplace. Ironically, the more virtuous the value (service, people), the greater the chance of long-term perversion. Why? Because the "better" the value, the more "the establishment" tries to make sure that you adhere to it *exactly*. (None of this should surprise us. After all, most mass killing has been in the service of rigid, virtuous values, as in religious wars.)

What's the answer? Surely not a return to those 1,000-page policy manuals. How about "review your values and update them regularly"? Sounds good, but experience suggests caution. Those who live calcified values are the last to see destructive elaboration growing in their midst. Most value-review processes, even involving "honest broker" outsiders, are a waste of time. Or worse: They frequently end up producing even *more* convolutions. Maybe there ought to be a "values sunset statute"—throw a third of the corporate values out every 5 years, or burn the lot and start afresh every 10 years. There's a certain attractiveness to the idea, but is it practical?

The only sensible solution I can conjure is to try and create a corporate confederation of business units independent enough to develop their own values. YSL Parfums' Véronique Vienne (the job-hopper, remember—p. 222) observed such a strategy during her stint at Condé Nast. "They really understand *personality*," she told us. "Condé Nast builds each magazine around a distinct personality, not just a niche defined by market research. You can buy Grace Mirabella [former editor of *Vogue*] or Anna Wintour [current editor of *Vogue*], or Tina Brown [former editor of *Vanity Fair*]. Other magazines don't get it. They're still selling niches." It's no coincidence that Condé Nast is part of the Newhouse group. The giant enterprise's most distinguishing trademark, recall, is phenomenal unit autonomy—and an IDG-like perform-or-else ethos. But if the confederation is that loose, then why bother to have it at all? Go back and read our several analyses of "soul" in the Beyond Hierarchy section. The answer is clear: It's not clear why. Or how. Or when. Or whether at all.

Values? Vision? Can't live without 'em in today's world, which won't tolerate those hefty manuals. Can't live with 'em, either.

ORGANIZATIONAL TRANSFORMATION: A GRIM PROGNOSIS

We were not the victims of ancestor worship. We had the benefits of a fresh start.

MATHEW MILLER,
quoted on why his firm,
General Instruments, is ahead
of the pack on digital HDTV
The New York Times
July 12, 1992

Understandably, Professor Herbert Kaufman's provocative *Time, Chance, and Organizations* isn't commonly found on the coffee tables in the offices of Fortune 500 chieftains. In a tightly argued book on organizational theory, he concludes, "The survival of some organizations for great lengths of time is largely a matter of luck. . . . Such longevity comes about through the workings of chance." Attempts to induce flexibility as a response to these hapless circumstances, Kaufman writes, are doomed to failure. The "ravages of time" that beset large organizations are irreversible. "Organizations by and large are not capable of more than marginal changes, while the environment is so volatile that marginal changes are frequently insufficient to assure survival."

For economies taken as wholes, the answer is unmistakable, per Kaufman: to welcome, rather than deplore, "organizational replacement" (e.g., cheer rather than jeer the corporate raiders when they succeed and bust up a firm, applaud the high business failure rate in Silicon Valley). If there's any hope for big firms, Kaufman contends that it lies in chartering wholly independent business units, but he's not very sanguine about that possibility either.

Kaufman is not alone in his pessimism about changing individual corporations. Cornell professors Michael Hannan and John Freeman summarize a 15-year research program in their 1989 book *Organizational Ecology*. "In the mid-1970s . . . theory and research treated . . . organizations as rational, flexible and speedy adapters to changing environmental circumstances," the renegade business theorists write; but "the organizations we knew . . . [were] anything but flexible and quick in collective response to changing opportunities and constraints in the environment."

The authors' fresh look at the corporate panorama ignores internal corporate doings and instead puts a spotlight on changes in "populations" of organizations over time, i.e., the rate of business births and deaths in an industry or industry segment. "Most of the variability in core structures of organizations [functional vs. divisional vs. matrix forms, for example] comes about through the creation of new organizations and . . . the demise of older ones," they write. "Existing organizations, especially the largest and most powerful, rarely change strategy and structure quickly enough to keep up with . . . uncertain, changing environments."

Hannan and Freeman's research involved sophisticated time series analyses of the birth and demise of unions over a hundred-year period; the ups and downs of organizational size and population in the semiconductor industry from World War II through the late '80s; the birth and death of newspapers in San Francisco over a hundred-year span; and changing populations of specialty (e.g., pizza, Mexican food) and generalist restaurants in various locales around the United States. The pair conclude that "laws" of population dynamics per se explain more about the arrival and disappearance of firms than does the study of managerial strategies.

Darwin on Management

Hannan and Freeman hold most research and theorizing on organizations and organizational strategies in contempt (including mine). Or worse: They consider it downright dangerous. Almost no one, they say, has studied "the actual time path of change in organizational populations"; instead, "most writing and research on organizations concentrates on [only] the largest and most successful [firms]. This is almost always a mistake if one wants to learn about the [underlying] processes which result in success and failure."

The authors' approach, adapted from ecological theory, will throw most managers for a loop: "Nothing in the structure of evolutionary arguments supports the assertion that the [organization] forms that proliferate are well adapted in an engineering sense. In no sense does the use of [natural] selection logic imply that this is the best of all possible worlds or that organizations that have thrived in some periods are somehow deserving of success. Selection models insist on the importance of randomness in success."

To wit: Wal-Mart is formed in Bentonville, Arkansas, in the mid-'60s. For a host of unfathomable reasons, it follows certain business practices from the start as a one-store operation. A decade passes and not much happens. Yet these early practices become the characteristic "Wal-Mart way of doing business." Then the retail environment changes, for another host of reasons that have little or nothing to do with Wal-Mart. Wal-Mart spurts. Suddenly Sears (et al.) has problems. Did Wal-Mart's chiefs foresee the future? Absurd, Hannan and Freeman would snap. The nature of Wal-Mart's original strategy simply ends up working very well in the very different environmental context that subsequently emerges. The gross inability of Sears (and 10,000 complacent small-town store owners) to adapt to that new context (and to Wal-Mart) leads to decline and death among old-school retailers.

"Part of the genius of Darwinian theory," Hannan and Freeman write, "concerns the way in which it links diversity and adaptation. . . . Selection processes can only work on available diversity." Hence, the Wal-Marts—or Apples or Genentechs or Cypress Semiconductors or Limiteds or Benettons—and their novel structures and practices have to "spontaneously appear" (per Hannan and Freeman) on the scene before they can grow or be copied. The successful upstarts become, for a while, major players with numerous followers—until the environment changes and the next wave of beyond-Apples and beyond-Wal-Marts emerges.

Of course, any one beyond-Apple or beyond-Wal-Mart—i.e., the *average* next-generation start-up—is likely to fail. Failure is the norm for newly created firms—and new organization forms. For each success such as Apple, there are thousands of Osborns. But *some* beyond-Apple, *some* beyond-AST, or *some* beyond-Dell, with lucky/appropriate characteristics for the altered times, will eventually leave old Apple and AST and Dell in the dust—probably at about the same time the ink dries on the definitive "Apple [AST, Dell]-the-great" Harvard case study.

Thanks for the Memories

Consider Visicorp, developer of Visicalc, the first widely sold spreadsheet. Visicorp was the talk of many towns. Microsoft, Lotus, and others are direct beneficiaries of its success. Next-generation attributes of Microsoft and Lotus (beyond Visicorps) were too much for Visicorp, which could not adapt. Visicorp R.I.P. And thanks for the memories. Today Visicorp lives only on the elaborate Silicon Valley genealogy charts.

Just Try and Change!

Hannan and Freeman go on to adduce that "the current character of populations of organizations reflects historical conditions at the time of founding rather than recent adaptations." That is, the core properties of 3M *today*—respect for autonomy, try it—are a direct reflection of 3M's core properties *and* the business environment 70 years ago at founding. (And, *luckily* for 3M, unlike so many others, they largely still work—in fact 3M, which grew only fitfully for years, has surged in recent times as its original and invariant strategy has coincidentally become more in tune with these times.) The core properties of today's Sears and IBM and Kodak and Du Pont also mostly represent original, decades-old characteristics. (And, *unluckily*, they aren't panning out as well in altered environments.)

"We reject the view that the diversity of organization structures at any time reflects only recent adaptations of [existing] organizations," Hannan and Freeman write, "in favor of the view that diversity reflects a long history of foundings and displacements of organizations with fairly unchanging structures." That is, the diversity of organizational forms in, say, the computer industry is largely a by-product of different epochs of firm foundings—the IBM age, the DEC age, the Apple age, the Sun Microsystems age. They are much less the result of conscious strategic shifts by those firms: for example, though an IBM reorganizes regularly, it is beneficiary or victim of habits formed more than seven decades ago when the firm emerged from the primordial ooze under T. J. Watson's leadership. Case in point: The pronounced difference in IBM's and Apple's approach to vertical integration (discussed on p. 308) is mostly a function of when and where the two firms got their start.

The authors are most persuasive—unfortunately—when making the case for the failure of sizable organizations to change their ways, regardless of the intensity of external pressures. "Organizations are at best recalcitrant tools," they begin. "Organizational histories generate constraints on fundamental change. Once standards and procedures [become established], the cost of change increases greatly." Moreover, they argue, "organizations become ends in themselves." Most of their resources get absorbed by overhead needed to maintain the status quo—i.e., elaborating those old values. Consider the sorry fate of GM's once pathbreaking "decentralized" organization, as reported by a GM exec quoted in Maryann Keller's *Rude Awakening*:

> When [the GM assistant general sales manager] would fly in from the Chevrolet Central Office in Kansas City, I was assigned to stand outside the door of the Muehlenbach Hotel in a snowstorm and I was not to move because whenever he showed up, I had to be there to open the door. We bought the elevator and blocked it off so he'd have an elevator to go to. We had somebody assigned to stand outside his room all day to take his

shirts to the laundry and perform other tasks. And—this is true—we had learned that he had to have his morning orange juice a certain temperature, so we had somebody in the kitchen every day who tested the orange juice with a thermometer!

Damned If You Do, Damned If You Don't, Just Plain Damned

Hannan and Freeman present what at first blush appears to be a bizarre idea. It turns out to be the unpleasant nub of the issue. "We argue that organizational selection processes favor organizations with relatively inertial structures, that cannot change strategy and structure as quickly as their environment can change," they write. Translation: Winners will be those who invent, like early IBM, early Sears, or early 3M, a *very* distinctive competence—a competence that happens to work year after year. Executing that initial (lucky in retrospect) strategy to a T is a direct result of regularizing behavior—via a clearcut "corporate culture" and widely shared values. But such regularity (the basis for *past* excellence), if times do change as they have done for IBM, for Sears, becomes a special burden of the entrenched outfit. (As we observed before, IBM's very "goodness" at dealing with one set of customers with one set of beliefs has turned against the firm in a different age with different customers with different beliefs.)

"Institutionalization is a two-edged sword," the authors conclude. "It greatly lowers the cost of collective action by giving an organization a taken-for-granted character such that members do not continually question organizational purposes [and] authority. . . . The other edge of the sword is inertia: The very factors that make a system reproducible make it resistant to change." I.e., the better you get at doing *something*, which is a must for initial success, the less the likelihood of getting really good at something *else* (or even realizing that you *need* to get good at something else).

Hannan and Freeman insist there's little to be done. "High levels of inertia may produce serious mismatches between organizational outcomes and the intention of members [i.e., efforts to change strategy] in a changing environment," they write. "On the other hand, organizations that try to [fight back and] reorganize frequently may produce very little and have slight chances of survival." In the latter case, the constant churning accompanying reorganizations costs the firm its original distinctiveness.

Take Wal-Mart again. It comes along, unheralded, and for reasons of luck succeeds brilliantly. Then, the elders (Sears et al.), thwarted by the lucky upstart, try to fight back. The result is usually disastrous. "The worst of all possible worlds," Hannan and Freeman declare, "is to change structure continually only to find each time upon reorganization that the environment has already shifted to some new configuration that demands yet a different structure."

This is precisely what is apparently happening to those great reorganizers,

IBM, GM, and Sears, among others. Huge amounts of organizational and psychic resources are absorbed by the latest "final" reorganization at Sears, but not much real change occurs. It takes forever, for one thing, because Sears is so big and still so subconsciously glued to its old, proud-if-tattered culture. Moreover, the "new" Sears organization that emerges is 10 days late and 10 dollars short compared, still, to Wal-Mart. (Sears attempts "everyday low prices," but can't beat Wal-Mart, which in cost structure and flexibility, even after the Sears reorganization, is miles ahead of the bumbling Goliath.) Moreover, sluggish Sears is further victimized by still newer organizational "forms"—specialists such as The Gap or Toys "Я" Us. (And Wal-Mart itself, new king by luck, is also fearful of the emergence of so many specialists that take on and conquer a given niche so rapidly. Whether any one or another of these specialists survives or not is of no consequence to Wal-Mart; but the fact is, *some* set of survivor specialists is very likely to topple Wal-Mart eventually. And in increasingly volatile marketplaces, "eventuallys" hover ever closer at hand.)

A Genuine Original, as If It Mattered

OK. OK. I can hear the teeth gnashing. Just what is this "Wal-Mart strategy," you ask, that has so befuddled its competitors? First of all, it ain't a strategy. It's an elusive admixture. I've spent lots of time with Wal-Mart execs and board members, including the late Sam Walton, and have been to several stores. I've read hundreds of thousands of words about Wal-Mart propounding one "answer" or another (picked off small towns at first, information technology pioneer, etc.). All explanations are a little right, and a lot wrong. For it's the one-of-a-kind mixture per se that's the key.

Wal-Mart is (a) a true discounter, with an invariant "lowest-price-in-town-or-we'll-meet-the-lowest-price" policy; (b) friendly (greeters at the door; signs in the Cameron, Missouri, store in 1990 that said, "Buy all the film you need for vacation, return what you don't use"); (c) service-oriented, with shorter checkout lines than competitors (which means big spending on labor for the checkouts—not conventional "discounter" wisdom); (d) an information technology pioneer (galaxy-class, low-cost distribution—plus timely information that keeps managers ahead of the curve); (e) a reflection of complicated Sam Walton (no frills, no excess, try anything, down home, in the store two days a week even after the firm had become a giant, populist decision-making rallies every Saturday at 7:00 a.m.—and tough as nails); (f) people-oriented (hey, this is a 390,000-person family—honest!); (g) from Bentonville, Arkansas (which is not Chicago); (h) etc. (i) etc.

On the one hand, Wal-Mart could only have come from Bentonville,

Arkansas—it's aw-shucks to the core. On the other hand, it's 21st-century to the core. Mostly it's both, in an oddball "formula" that I'd hate like hell to compete against. (Part of Sears's problem is that it has both (a) lost its old-fashioned, down-home closeness to employees and customers, and (b) failed to be thoroughly modern, not taking full advantage of information technology for either efficient distribution or fast executive decision making.)

The real point: Wal-Mart is a genuine, unanticipated/unanticipatable original. And, someday, its strengths will turn into "rules" which will turn into more elaborate "rules"—shades of GM's orange-juice temperature monitors. Calcium will accumulate. And new organizations/organization forms will appear. . . . And Wal-Mart will try to adapt and be a half-day late and 50 cents short . . . and try again and be a day late and a dollar short . . . and . . . (And, yes, eventually Harvard will drop it from the approved case study list.)

The Case for "r-Strategies"*

There are two fundamentally different biological propagation strategies. The first, or *r-strategy*, is what Hannan and Freeman call an "opportunistic strategy." There are many reproductive events (flies, mosquitoes); a smidgen of energy goes into each. The life chances of any one offspring are poor. Nonetheless, *populations* of r-strategy practitioners "grow rapidly under the right conditions." The r-strategy "maximizes . . . the speed of growth in open environments."

The *K-strategy*, Hannan and Freeman write, is the "polar opposite," featuring a small number of reproductive events, with a great deal of energy going into each (e.g., whales, humans). A single offspring has a good chance of living, and "[the] population can expand even in the face of dense competition."

R-strategies "exploit new and ephemeral opportunities quickly, but at the expense of the capacity [to deal with huge rivals]." The K-strategy has the ability to withstand rivals, but is slow at coping with or taking advantage of change. When environmental change is fast, r-strategies—which exploit an open field, remember—are favored. When environmental change is slow, K-strategies are favored.

An r-strategy firm lucks out (i.e., succeeds) because it is created quickly and exploits a fleeting opportunity quickly. A population of r-strategy firms ipso facto represents a flexible response to an "open" environment. But that doesn't mean that any single new r-strategy firm has the flexibility to subsequently adapt and become something else. "Populations of r-strategist organizations flourish under conditions of rapid . . . change, not because the

---

* Also see p. 575: The r vs. K difference described here is analogous to Gunnar Hedlund's H-mode (hunter-gatherer) vs. A-mode (agriculture) distinction.

member organizations have the capacity for flexible response to widely varying conditions; rather, they flourish because the speed with which organizations [per se] can be constructed allows a founding rate that is high enough to offset high mortality rates," Hannan and Freeman write. "Our proposition that easy-to-build organizations proliferate in modern society [is] an argument that the character of [modern society's] environmental variations . . . favors the [r-strategy]."

I can imagine sizable "r-strategy firms"—such as 3M, IDG, Random House, CCT, or Thermo Electron—which themselves encompass "populations" of small opportunistic "firms." Yet, returning to the earlier argument, Hannan and Freeman would assert that the capacity to be flexible carries a steep price—an inability to perform everyday tasks flawlessly. Back to 3M: It does regularly come up short when it takes on systems products that require cross-corporate coordination skills of the sort a Boeing exercises.

(Boeing is part of a K-strategy world, more or less—though increased volatility even in Boeing's world is pushing the monster firm to try and work with more r-strategy pygmies, in order to keep up with the blinding speed of technological change occurring in this or that part of the aircraft. It's also trying to fend off Airbus—which benefits much more from the luck of later founding than from its big government subsidies. For example, Airbus took to wholly computerized flight controls before Boeing. Some call it Airbus's first big jump past Boeing. While there may be several explanations, I'd put my money on the fact that Airbus was "lucky enough" to be born during the Computer Age. Computerized controls seemed natural to it, unnatural to Boeing.)

If the environment is especially volatile ("open"), the flexible firm which is a collection of pygmies may have an advantage over, say, an IBM, even if it never comes to execute a chosen strategy with the virtual perfection that marked IBM from 1960 to 1980. Per Hannan and Freeman: "Environments in which change is turbulent and uncertain . . . may favor organizational forms that can take quick advantage of new opportunities. The capacity to respond quickly . . . competes with the capacity to perform reliably."

(Of course, old Catch-21.9 rears its head again. Can you in fact have a single firm that executes an r-strategy? Recall our discussion of true decentralization and the auto-correlation effect. Is 3M really a collection of 100 more or less independent companies? Or is it a collection of 100 small units, with each one mostly doing things "the 3M way"? It's probably in between—but its *relatively* high "r-ness" may keep it going, even in these mad times.)

All this amounts to far more than idle theorizing. The emergence of new technologies and new competitors is speedily moving almost every industry toward "open" domains—where r-strategies are more likely to succeed. Consider the fate of Norton, a century-old abrasives company, headquartered in Worcester, Massachusetts. Core-product technologies date back decades. Yet, today, materials science is showing as much vigor—and volatility—as electronics or biotechnology. Arguably, r-strategies—for the increasingly "open environment" in materials—are now appropriate for Norton. In addition, Norton has been confronted with a host of new and emerging competitors from high- and low-wage nations alike— e.g., Japan and China.

In fact, Norton became the target of a hostile takeover attempt by Britain's BTR in 1990. It fended off the unwanted suitor by leaping into the arms of France's St. Gobain. Norton was the product of a classic K-strategy environment. When confronted with change, it tried to adopt quality circles and other empowerment techniques. These came too late, and had marginal impact at best. Not only could Norton not clean up its *old* act sufficiently, but it was also unwilling to try serious internal r-strategy tactics—e.g., placing big bets on new, promising technologies at the expense of old, cash-generating technologies.

None of this would surprise Hannan and Freeman. Born "K-strategy," if you will, Norton faced almost insurmountable odds against changing its character and "going r." The defenders of Norton's old, profitable technologies vigorously fought the most minuscule threats of cannibalization by new technologies. In the end, the market "stepped in" (BTR, St. Gobain) because (1) Norton's old businesses had become confused due to "culture change" efforts and (2) potentially new businesses were clearly not being exploited to the hilt. The market, in a sense, had gone from "K" to "r" (closed to open), and Norton tripped while trying to learn to dance a jig. Norton qua Norton R.I.P.

Hannan and Freeman's meticulous research is of singular importance. It should amount to a word to the wise for all executives, in big firms and small. Inertia rules. Most strategies to overcome it will fail. Success (regularity of behavior that's proved useful in one environment) breeds failure (late or confused reactions to changes in the environment). At least, their results should dampen our enthusiasm for megastrategies and megamergers, and heighten our enthusiasm for the creation of more truly autonomous units.

K-strategies are looking ever more problematic. It's hardly good news for the Fortune 500. Nonetheless, forewarned may be slightly forearmed. In an interview with Ralph Nader for *The Big Boys*, the late Bill McGowan halffacetiously proposed a corporate "sunset rule"—firms should be disestablished 15 years after their founding. Informed that MCI had actually been chartered over 15 years before, McGowan replied, "Maybe 20 years." Maybe he got it right the first time!

C'mon

It's a disturbing idea that depressed people see reality correctly while non-depressed people distort reality in a self-serving way. . . . There is considerable evidence that

depressed people, though sadder, are wiser. . . .
Nondepressed people . . . believe they have much more control
over things than they actually do.

MARTIN SELIGMAN
Learned Optimism

I cannot countenance the language I frequently hear from organization design/strategy experts: "What we need are *very* flexible, *very* adaptive, *very* fluid, *very* nimble, 'learning organizations' that change shape daily and deliver *world-class* quality and *world-class* service to their customers by *partnering* with all members of the value chain."

What a crock! If you're infinitely fluid and change shape daily, you can't become good/great at anything. That's a harsh, cold fact.

You've got to become great at *something* in order to be great in the first place. When you do become great at something, you almost certainly ensure that you will not be able to be great for long. You are quickly victimized by tunnel vision (tunnel vision and greatness are synonymous—look at any Olympian or Nobel laureate) and are uniquely susceptible to end runs—in a world where end runs have become the norm.

Lesson: There is no easy way out, maybe no way out at all. But to fail to acknowledge all this is the height of foolishness. I, too, admit that I am mesmerized by—and have written about in these pages—pictures painted in the clouds of "nimble, adaptive, flexible, fluid, constantly changing organizations providing world class . . ." C'mon.

THE INTERDEPENDENCE/INDEPENDENCE PARADOX

I've skimmed the surface before, discussing the pros and cons of strategic alliances. More and more work will be done in conjunction with partners. "Outsider" (vendor, customer, distributor) membership on everything, starting with the simplest work teams will be commonplace. Alliances among numerous companies will routinely be created to exploit a market niche. Much more investment in long-term relationships with subcontractors will occur. All of this connotes linking, wiring up, greater *dependence* upon one another.

On the other hand, you can bet the farm that the next effective attack on your market will come out of nowhere. (Bentonville, Arkansas, was a good operational definition of "nowhere" if you were sitting in the magisterial Sears Tower 15 years ago.) The very linkages required to compete in today's complex world amount to deep grooves—inertial traps—in their own right.

There is a glib "answer": Keep changing the form and shape of the network, à la EDS or MCI. But even EDS and MCI can be—and have been—blindsided. Simply signing up for "network fluidity" is no adequate defense against inertia. To the contrary: The "better" these new networks become, the more entrenched *they* become. (Damn!)

Large, complicated systems "break down not only under the force of a mighty blow, but also at the drop of a pin," Per Bak and Kan Chen wrote in *Scientific American* in early 1991. "Large interactive systems perpetually organize themselves to a critical state in which a minor event starts a chain reaction that can lead to a catastrophe. [In the past it was] assumed that the response of a large interactive system was proportional to the disturbance."

Yes, our networks are uniquely at risk, and not just AT&T's, with its escalating vulnerability to a nationwide breakdown caused by a single absent-minded backhoe operator. Intricate commercial alliances are also vulnerable to outsiders—outsiders whose rapid responses can cause tightly linked sets of firms to make increasingly delayed and inappropriate responses.

Thus the vaunted "spiderweb" has its own special set of vulnerabilities, to which autonomy (as usual) is a useful response. But, of course, not a sufficient one (as usual). For the highly autonomous unit may not be linked to *enough* resources in the first place to make an impact! That's the downside of r-strategies. There is, by definition, no way out of the box.

(I reiterate that the "simple" way out, to alternate forms, is not a viable choice. Sounds good—"r" today, "K" tomorrow. Fat chance. GM's legendary Alfred Sloan counseled perpetual shifts between centralization and decentralization; but it never really happened. The autocratic Sloan actually commanded a highly centralized operation, which became a tiny bit more, then less, then more centralized over time. GM in 1930, notwithstanding management writings to the contrary, was not decentralized. It sure as hell is not today.)

CHANGE

What is freedom in the last analysis other than the state of being totally instead of only partially subject to the tyranny of chance.

PAUL BOWLES
A Distant Episode

My objective in this final Markets and Innovation chapter is to confuse you, not help you sort things out. It's my belief, in these turbulent times, that anyone who's not thoroughly confused has no chance of success. In a mid-1991 address in London, I offered the following propositions:

- Change of even the simplest sort is hopelessly complex. Consider the "little" story of Ingersoll-Rand's development of the Cyclone Grinder. Look beneath the surface, and the ability to explain evaporates. Jim Stryker deciding to hold a barbecue at the critical moment was important. Bringing five pairs of eyes to bear on a front-line worker holding the old-generation grinder was crucial. What if there had been three pairs of eyes, or seven? Would three have been insufficient? Would seven have slowed things down?

- Even "making the case for change" is close to impossible. Research says that most of those on the brink of disaster have difficulty realizing it. (I worked next door to the Nixon White House. Days before the impeachment vote in the House of Representatives, we really couldn't imagine that Nixon was on his last legs—we who, in theory, were closest to the scene were about the last 500 people in the U.S. to figure out what was up!) An intense debate about Ingersoll-Rand's grinder took place at one of our seminars. An executive from Johnson & Johnson said *the* key to the project's success was the public promise IR made to distributors to get the new model out in a year. Baloney, I replied. IR had made more or less the same promise several times in the past. Why was it "real" this time and not before? Beats me!

- Change is easy! Recall the Union Pacific Railroad: The 30,000-person operations organization was turned upside down in 90 days. And don't forget the over-the-weekend revolution at Titeflex. That is, when *all* the stars are aligned (external environmental situation, internal frustration, "right" leader, etc., etc.—most of the et ceteras being unfathomable in advance), change can be pulled off, and pulled off quickly.

- "They" are ready. The one obstacle to change that does *not* seem to exist is "them." "They" are ready. Uh—if everything has been done right (trustworthy leadership, etc., etc.).

- "The answer" is radical decentralization and the "marketization" of everything. If there is a single "answer," it is atomizing the organization and allowing market winds to blow at gale or hurricane force inside the corporate tent. Yet if atomization is overdone, as Hannan and Freeman argue so cogently, the very regularized behavior necessary for initial success will never be established in the first place (i.e., you'll never even get the tent up).

- Success begets failure, and there's not much you can do about it. There is no doubt, statistically speaking, that success begets failure—period. You are always on the precipice in today's world. Recall that MCI's McGowan said that the chump-to-champ-to-chump cycle "used to be three generations," but now it's about "five years."

- "Leadership" is highly overrated—maybe. It's easy to wish for the great man or woman on the white horse, arriving just in time to save the day. More than a few rodeo masters have galloped across these pages. On the other hand, that leader, per Hannan and Freeman, is just a "blind variation"—and unless a thousand thousand chance events conspire, the "great" leader stays stuck in the paddock. Trace Churchill's career. A great leader? To be sure. *In retrospect.* Change any of those thousand thousand variables infinitesimally—and Churchill would have been sidelined for good (he had already been sidelined "for good" many times) long before he made his seminal contribution during World War II.

- It all depends. This is a sneaky way of restating the first proposition. After the fact, when we've observed a successful event, we single out a half-dozen variables, maybe 20 or 30 at most—and build an airtight explanation of why things worked out the way they did. (See *In Search of Excellence*—P variables.) We then proceed to apply our "learning" to new situations. Hey, what else are we gonna do? On the other hand, in singling out even 30 variables, or 30 times 30, we have grotesquely oversimplified. Strategy A is terrific in context A. Put strategy A into even the most slightly altered context, and it's a different story with a different ending. This is the "lesson" that Hayek, Weick, Kaufman, and Hannan and Freeman—and all too few others—offer.

- The "change agenda" is staggering, and we must take it on "all at once." Whether the topic is speeding everything up by orders of magnitude, radically decentralizing, rewiring everything, exploiting information technology to the hilt, going global, or whatever, there is a lot to do—an extraordinary, unprecedented amount to do. "Do it all at once" is hardly helpful advice. To suggest an alternative is, however, dangerous. All at once is doubtless impossible. But not to take it on all at once presents an equal threat.

- If you're not crazed, you're out of luck. Look, understanding is impossible. (You're only in control when you're out of control, remember.) That is: The time for measured responses is past. Period.

VI

Fashion!

PROLOGUE: TERMINALLY TASTELESS OR *SUR/PETITION*?

Home again. We began with "fashion." Its imperatives triggered our analysis of bold new organizational arrangements (Learning to Hustle, Beyond Hierarchy) and our examination of, among other things, violent market-injection strategies (Markets and Innovation). Fashion, we said, calls for buckyborgs and shifting networks and alliances, for hiring traitors and cheering anarchists in our midst, for turning everyone into a professional-service provider and unleashing the power of the human imagination. "Touch it" is important, "Try it" a must. Now, though, it's time to look at fashion qua fashion in some detail:

- Trend spotter Faith Popcorn, in *The Popcorn Report*, informs us that "In Stamford, Connecticut, you can buy professionally catered, microwave-ready, pre-packaged meals from a truck at the railway station. The name of the business: 'Hi Honey, I'm Home.' Fax Grande Cuisine in Elmsford, New York, accepts faxed-in menu orders that can be picked up by returning-home commuters at their suburban train station."

- "Customized Cookies," the headline read in the December 16, 1991, issue of *Fortune*. "Decorated Christmas cookies are an annual favorite, but who has time to bake them or round up the colored icings? Made 'em Myself cookies by Nabisco Foods give kids the fun without the fuss. The ready-made vanilla cookies come with nine Christmas designs, including a Santa, a star, and a reindeer, stenciled in red food coloring. Kids fill in or outline the designs using two 1.25-ounce tubes of red and green icing, or turn the cookies over and create their own. Made 'em Myselfs are available in limited quantities—Nabisco has made 'em all and plans to run out before January 1. A 13.5-ounce bag of 40 cookies costs $3.79."

- On October 21, 1991, the *San Jose Mercury News* put the following question to its readers: "What can a small firm do to stand out amid the 50 acres of glitz and mayhem at [Comdex,] the computer industry's annual Las Vegas extravaganza?

"For Silicon Valley's terminally tasteless, Marty McGreevy will supply a 20-foot oil derrick or a life-size fiberglass longhorn from his vast warehouse of trade-show paraphernalia. For the totally tacky, he'll provide a Polynesian village with grass huts, plastic palm trees, a waterfall and massive stone idols carved from solid polyurethane. . . .

"During the past 10 years, [McGreevy's] Exhibit Emporium . . . has become one of the country's largest suppliers of trade-show booths, display materials and related services. A large manufacturer putting together a sizable exhibit for a major trade show can easily spend $250,000 on design and construction of a custom booth."

"Terminally tasteless," "totally tacky," or not, how in the hell else are you going to sell a computer in an enormous "technology" market that's become more fad-prone than Rodeo Drive? When I started to write about "soft stuff," intangibles, and customer perception 10 years ago, it was considered pretty far out. The "quality movement" of the '80s didn't change things much, unless it was to push the needle over further to the "hard" end of the scale. Quality may *sound* soft, but when the engineers had finished with it, you could measure distinctions the size of a gnat's eyebrow. Or so they said.

After a decade of quality fanaticism (of the hard sort) in Detroit, Robert D. Knoll of *Consumer Reports* told *Newsweek* in March 1992, "The Americans are building nice average cars but few 'gee-whiz-look-at-this' cars." The Japanese, on the other hand, have "upped the ante in what the experts call the more subtle 'sensory' side of a car's quality," *Newsweek* added. Whether it's a car's "turn-signal lever that doesn't wobble [or] the feel of a climate-control knob" (nuances pointed out to *Newsweek* by an auto designer), "microwave-ready, pre-pack-aged meals from a truck at the railway station," or using "plastic palm trees" to peddle computers at a Las Vegas trade show, something is afoot.

Could I have imagined a few years ago that *Design Management Journal* would devote a special issue to "Design in Service Industries: Managing the Evidence of Intangible Products"? Could I have imagined I'd be reading *Design Management Journal* at all? No. No. I guess I can get at what *Design Management Journal* means by "managing the evidence of intangible prod-ucts" by reading creativity guru Edward de Bono's latest—*Sur/Petition: Creating Value Monopolies When Everyone Else Is Merely Competing.*

De Bono argues that there are three "stages of business." In the first, "attention is on the product and on production." That is, get it right. Stage two focuses on is on the product relative to competition: "How can we do better or at least keep up?" The third stage, sur/petition (beyond competition), emphasizes "integrating into the complex values of the customer."

I think that "the more subtle 'sensory' side of the car" (*Newsweek*), "managing the evidence of intangible products" (*Design Management Jour-nal*), and "integrating into the complex values of the customer" (de Bono) add up to this:

— Fashion is here to stay.

— Many of us, advisers and practitioners alike, are having the devil's own time trying to figure out how to think systematically about this world gone soft and fickle.

The Orderly Swiss Embrace Fashion

The Swiss watch industry invented the quartz movement, but did not use the invention because it felt that this invention would kill [its] existing market. Anyone could use the quartz movement, whereas only the Swiss had the skills to make little cogwheels and balance springs. They were right in their thinking, as it turned out, but wrong in their strategy. Watchmakers in Japan and Hong Kong eagerly grabbed the quartz movement, and in one year the sale of Swiss watches dropped by 25 percent.

What rescued the Swiss watch industry was the very unSwiss concept of the Swatch. The sales of the Swatch at most accounted for only 2 percent of a $4 billion market, but the Swatch provided two things. First, it provided a bulk market for quartz movement so that prices could be brought down. More important, the Swatch signaled that telling time was no longer the most important thing in a watch. A $5 watch tells time every bit as well as a $30,000 watch. The Swatch was not selling time so much as fun and costume jewelry. The Swiss watch industry recovered as soon as it realized that it was not selling watches, but jewelry. Indeed, wearing an expensive watch is sometimes the only legitimate way that a man can wear, enjoy, and flaunt jewelry. And that has become the nature of the watch business today. You only have to open an in-flight magazine to find that fully 30 percent of its advertising is for very expensive watches. Telling time is only the gateway value to selling jewelry to men.

EDWARD DE BONO
Sur/Petition

P.S. *The New York Times* added its two bits on Swatch mania in May 1992—among other things, quoting Swatch chairman Nicholas Hayek: "We were convinced that if each of us could add our fantasy and culture to an emotional product, we could beat anybody. Emotions are something that nobody can copy." (And if that's not a fashion statement, I don't know what is!)

41

The Transformation of Positively Everything

I don't think anyone appreciated how fast Intel was going to throw new [micro]processors into the hopper. You put out a product, and in six to nine months, it has to be replaced. It's hard for a company of any size to keep up.

> RICHARD MILLER, vice president, NEC
> Technologies, quoted in "The Invasion
> That Failed," an analysis of
> Japan's problems in the PC market
> *Forbes*, January 20, 1992

Each day of our lives, twelve billion display ads, two and one-half million radio commercials, and over three hundred thousand television commercials are dumped into the collective consciousness.

> RONALD COLLINS
> *Columbia Journalism Review*
> November/December 1991

It's getting ludicrous! One hundred and four new cereal products came our way in 1991, not to mention 574 new varieties of cookies, 316 fruit and vegetable juices, and 463 salty snacks. All in all, 16,143 new drug and grocery store consumer products joined us, up from 2,689 in 1980. The average supermarket now carries 30,000 items vs. 9,000 in 1976. And the Nonprescription Drug Manufacturers Association says there are now 200,000 brands, varieties, and sizes of over-the-counter drugs.

Between 1980 and 1990, the number of mutual funds grew from 568 to 3,347. We've got 70 cable *networks* in the U.S., up from 27 in 1980. Local systems can receive 150 channels. (Read Bill McKibben's *The Age of Missing Information* for a challenging take on Fairfax, Virginia's, 93-station system—he watched every hour of every channel for one day in 1991.) Three hundred channels are just around the corner. *And?* Each week brings a new religious denomination.

Random House jumped (hollering all the way) from two major selling seasons a year to three in 1991. The same year, the toymakers of Playmobil were pushed onto fashion's bandwagon (likewise hollering), and had to go from one to two annual catalogs—with new products required in each.

Almost 700 basic varieties of cars confront us these days, a number that's also soaring. And car introductions? Remember the old days, when we waited excitedly for the one-time release of the year's new models—when dealers papered over their showroom windows for a few weeks to tease us? Forget it! Introductions of new models are continuous now.

What's the life of a new TV serial? Despite an investment that may run to several million dollars, the networks pull it off the air in a month or so if it's doing poorly—even more quickly in some cases. And then there's a patent just issued for a special beeper for docs. To tell them a patient is gravely ill? That they need to call the office? Forget it. Try this: To alert them that some new treatment (relevant to their specialty) has been reported in one of a jillion medical journals. New clinical approaches are coming along so fast that such a beeper, the inventor says, is a must to keep up. (The non-beeperized would doubtless have one less defense in any malpractice suit.)

Patent protection? Methodical market research? Forget those too. Computer models and semiconductors will last a year, at most. The race is to see if *you* can destroy what you've just done by superseding it before a competitor does the honors.

"The Limited's mass merchandisers can take the newest trend from Paris or New York and place cheaper versions in its stores weeks before the original designs are produced," *The New York Times* reported in May 1990. Once they used fax machines, but that's *yesterday's* technology. "The fax," the paper informs us, "has now been replaced [by] high-resolution computer images integrated into private satellite transmission networks [that] send fashion sketches between Far Eastern manufacturing centers and home offices in the United States." Stephen Du Mont, executive vice president of The Limited's manufacturing subsidiary, Mast Industries, added that "within 60 minutes of [receiving an] order, we can send a visual representation of the style, shown on the store's favorite model, to Hong Kong. It comes out on ink-jet printers with a quality similar to a lithograph . . . and we can do it in about 16-million colors." Mast shoots for a turnaround time of 1,000 hours between recognizing a new style and delivering the merchandise to The Limited's stores. The company has also been working with Sony on an advanced high-definition TV experiment—to provide "a virtual three-dimensional image, which gives the merchant much more of a feeling for the product," Du Mont told *The New York Times*. (And at this writing The Limited is suffering from somewhat shaky financial results—because even it isn't keeping up.)

Changing Tastes (Literally)

Faith Popcorn (*The Popcorn Report*) makes it clear that tastes are changing:

—In 1990, according to a Harris Survey, 19 percent of those sampled bought organic products for the first time. The same survey reports that 30 percent of us have changed our eating habits measurably in the last year.

—A Gallup survey claims that one-half of the 86 percent of us who regularly eat dinner at home now sit around the table munching on take-out food or prepackaged menu items we pick up or have delivered. (Take-out is now 15 percent of our food budget overall—and is expected to continue to grow at three times the rate of total food spending.)

—Use of fennel seed has grown by 255 percent in the last 10 years, and the average number of fresh produce items carried by groceries has grown from 65 to 250 during the same period.

Despite the explosion in grocery products in general, Popcorn says more customization is on the way, including a raft of forthcoming "engineered-for-health" specialty foods. Any way you look at it—with jaundiced eye at take-out growth or pleasure at more healthful offerings (or vice versa)—it ain't what it used to be. And it is changing, changing, changing. Would you have predicted that the grocery store would be the site of a fashion revolution? Whoops, I almost forgot. Grocery store? Popcorn also claims that home delivery of groceries is going to change the overall consumer food distribution process. And Campbell Soup, according to a *Harper's Index* statistic, is doing its planning based on projections that one-quarter of all cars will have a microwave oven on board by the year 2000. Watch out, McDonald's!

SMART, SMARTER, SMARTEST

Products are, well, different. In fact, "What's a product?" is a heck of a good question. It's those customized cookies and much, much more:

- In May 1991, *Forbes* told its readers about smart shopping carts: "In two cases out of three, shoppers don't have a clue which brand they plan to buy until they're staring at the supermarket shelf. They make their decisions on the spot. Which is pretty alarming if you're one of those trying to manipulate brand choices through the $70 billion spent annually on consumer goods advertising, or showering newspaper readers with over 270 billion cents-off coupons a year—fewer than seven billion of which ever get cashed in.

"But if you're John Malec, that two-cases-out-of-three is one of your favorite statistics. For Malec is the inventor of the Videocart, a normal shopping cart with a small computer screen bolted to its front rail and a battery pack underneath. The odd-looking contraption, now being rolled out nationwide, brings brand advertising right into the supermarket. . . . Working off a series of up to 150 infrared 'triggers' strategically placed in the stores, the Videocart screen flashes, say, a Pepsi ad just when the customer is in front of the soda shelf. At other times, the screen displays a list of products with featured prices in whatever aisle the cart happens to be. Very direct marketing—precisely at the moment when the clueless two-thirds are making their choices.

"The company racked up just $5 million in 1990 revenues, but even at that small size, it's doing business with the likes of Procter & Gamble, PepsiCo, Nabisco and Ralston Purina." Those companies, *Forbes* reported, "pay roughly $4 to reach 1,000 users, compared with about $7 for a newspaper coupon insert and $10 to $12 for a night-time network commercial."

Early evidence suggests that Malec's machine is no gimmick. In one Midwestern chain, *Forbes* said, items promoted by Videocart "were running 5 percent to 60 percent ahead of normal levels. A Von's store recently ran its own promotion featuring a recipe and the hint that Robert Mondavi Cabernet Sauvignon might go well with the meal. The store sold as much of the wine in two days as it normally sells in three months."

- Still skittish about parallel parking? On March 28, 1991, Volkswagen demonstrated an only somewhat futuristic model that parks itself. The *San Jose Mercury News* explains: "At the point most drivers begin craning their necks and twisting their bodies into unnatural positions, [the VW engineer who was driving the prototype] simply got out. With a push of a button, the steering wheel turned, and the car moved backward, forward, backward and forward again until it was neatly parked at the curb. The automatic parking system works via a battery of laser sensors and ultrasonic distance sensors on the front and sides of the car." VW expects to offer the feature routinely within five years. Price tag: $5,000 to $10,000.

• And don't overlook wise material! *Business Week* recently examined "materials that think for themselves," "smart composites," and "smart skins." To wit: "Plastic composites with built-in computers and optical-fiber sensors . . . make it possible to engineer everything from golf clubs with extra snap for hitting the ball to buildings that counteract the destructive force of earthquakes. . . . Optical fibers can function as sensors for collecting all manner of data, including pressure, strain and temperature."

U.S. News & World Report adds its two bits: " 'Smart' materials . . . combine artificial senses and muscles to enable substances to react to their surroundings by changing shape or stiffness. . . . FlexMedics Corporation in Minneapolis has developed a 'smart' dental brace that gently pressures teeth into place. . . . Sensors in a 'smart' construction beam that has sustained a crack might signal other beams to readjust their loads to compensate, for instance, just as a smart airplane wing might change its overall shape to make the plane fly more efficiently under various flying conditions."

SOFT, SOFTER, SOFTEST

Smart, as in computers, information technology, software, and telecommunications is one form of *soft*. But you could fairly claim that that's the least of it. "Softening" of goods and services goes much further. It's barely an exaggeration to say that *everyone* is getting into the entertainment business these days. Remember Britain's Imagination? Its zany staffers design wild and wacky events. Who are Imagination's clients? Microsoft? No. Apple? No. Try: British Steel. British Telecom. The Ford Motor Company. British Airways. Hardly a lighthearted lot! As the marketplace gets increasingly crowded, and companies reach further and further to add value, entertainment, in a host of forms, becomes more and more important. (What choice does British Airways have? It's competing with Richard Branson's Virgin Atlantic Airways. Branson, *The Wall Street Journal* reports, sees, "business as recreation" and adds that, "The airline industry had forgotten that it could be fun to fly.")

Of course there's entertainment *per se*. At the end of 1990, *Fortune*'s cover declared: "Pop Culture: America's Hottest Export Goes Boom!" Our trade balance for movies, music, TV programming, home video, and the like was $8 billion in the black, and climbing. *Fortune* reported, for example, that revenues from overseas sales of Madonna's CDs and videos are running two and a half times the domestic totals. " 'Smoke and mirrors,' Carnegie and Ford might mutter," *Fortune* added, but in 1990 "Walt Disney Co. sold $1.5 billion worth of consumer products—hats, watches, comic books—in Japan, where Coca-Cola earns more money than it does in the U.S. [Our] $20 billion-a-year music business—basically rock and roll—collects 70 percent of its revenue outside the U.S." (At the end of 1991, the *Financial Times* reported that the U.S. boasts 6 of the 10 "media giants," starting with number-one Time Warner. No offense, Detroit, but in 1992 I'd rather lead the world in media than autos. Think about it.)

Incidentally, the story from the other side of the Pacific is the same: The Japanese, expecting their annual recreation budget to grow from about $30 billion in 1990 to $130 billion by 1995, have tagged entertainment as the 1990s' fastest-growing global industry! They call it, *Fortune* said, "omizu shobai, or the 'water business,' meaning in its most modern sense, tricky to get a hold on."

Entertainment? Harley Davidson knows it's in the entertainment business! Its bikes are selling well in Europe. But bike derivatives—hats, jackets, and mugs bearing Harley logos—are really going wild. "Harleys are just a kind of attitude," *USA Today* was told by Ward Richter, a lawyer from Madison, Wisconsin, who had just bought one. Indeed, the last time I saw Harley president Rich Teerlink, he was returning from a trip to Walt Disney's Orlando operations. And not for recreation. He'd been discussing entertainment and Harleys with Disney execs.

Or consider the changing scene of pro sports. The ball team and the score are almost secondary. In "Game? What Game? Arenas Emphasize Ambiance and Amenities to Entice Fans," *The Wall Street Journal* (March 20, 1991) reminds us that "there was a time when athletic arenas were Spartan caverns, where the menu consisted of hot dogs, the seats grew harder by the quarter and the scoreboard just gave the score." No more. Now there is "the new Madison Square Garden." It has 88 luxury suites "where the caterers wheel in caviar," 2,100 club seats "from which patrons summon waiters," and "one TV-filled sports bar for refuge when the live action flags. . . . 'You have to understand you're in the entertainment business now, and you have to offer a full package of amenities,' says Justin Perkins, Madison Square Garden executive. . . . Phoenix's new [auditorium] will have a health club, Tampa's . . . a secretarial pool, Philadelphia's . . . boutiques." These "extras," the *Journal* claims, have become the decisive factors behind decisions to build (or not to build) new sports palaces to the tune of several hundred million dollars a copy.

Remember autographs? I used to wait for ballplayers, in a dingy, poorly lit alleyway behind Griffith Stadium in Washington, D.C. You don't do such things these days. Of course there are the autograph shows, where the big-leaguers show up (usually) to charge an arm and a leg (always) for their John Hancocks. But you needn't go to the trouble. A midsummer 1991 Hammacher Schlemmer catalog leads with offers of autographed baseballs: $149.95 for item 47734R, Ted Williams's signature; $79.95 for Dwight Goodin (47721R). If you want a ball "individually autographed by every living player to hit 500 home runs or more during their major league careers," Hammacher Schlemmer will send you one, mounted, for $599. (And if you've really got money to burn, The J. Peterman catalog—see p. 686—offers the real thing, a mint-condition *Babe Ruth* signature at $7,500.)

And more: Suppose you're away at work or on vacation, but just have to keep up with the home team. Well, consider tuning in to TeamLine, an area-code 800 phone service. On November 10, 1990, for example, you could have dialed up the Ohio State–Iowa game. For Ohio Staters, 1–800–225–5340 did the trick. For Iowa Hawkeye faithful, it was 1–800–225–5214. There was a one-time service charge of 50 cents for each game called; ongoing charges started at a maximum of 50 cents a minute and went down to 20 cents a minute—TeamLine, of course, bills your credit card of choice.

In the summer of 1991, I popped into a Williams-Sonoma store at the Stanford Shopping Center in Palo Alto, California. (The high-end retailer mainly sells gourmet cooking equipment.) While checking out, I noticed a neat stack of papers next to the cash register. It was the shop's July 1991 calendar. Excepting Sundays and the Independence Day holiday, 25 of the 26 remaining days featured tastings, teaching, or demonstrations. On July 2, for example, there was a tasting of dried cranberries, tart cherries, and blueberries. The next day offered a sample of Virginia peanuts. After the holiday, on Friday the fifth, a Krups demonstration was scheduled from 11:00 a.m. to 3:00 p.m. That is, Williams-Sonoma has moved beyond cookware and attractive retail presentation. It's in the soft, softer, softest business: *teaching and explaining.* (Faith Popcorn calls the shift toward instruction *the* retailing trend for the '90s.)

Ah, even the hardest of the hard are going soft! In July 1991, the tough-as-nails, down-and-dirty technofreaks at Intel joined the parade, mounting a huge mass-media ad blitz (TV, general circulation magazines). Intel's micro-processors, its bread and butter, are inside others' machines, where you can't see them. But now the firm is pitching Intel Inside™ (see opposite), in an unvarnished attempt to brand the invisible products in everyone's mind. Intel, and the companies that use its devices in their machines, plan to spend $250 million on the campaign by the end of 1992.

CASES IN "PRODUCT" TRANSFORMATION I: THE HOME-CENTER INDUSTRY

When I was a kid, Saturday mornings often meant a 10-mile trip to Annapolis, Maryland, to pick up lumber for one of my dad's projects. We'd go to the J. F. Johnson Lumber Co. I still remember the pungent odor of fresh sawdust, which covered my clothes upon our return home, and watching the powerful saw blades rip through a sheet of plywood in seconds. The tough old fellows at the saws often had a finger missing, a stern warning to any youngster dreaming about a career in home carpentry.

Since J. F. Johnson is what "home-improvement project" had meant to

The Intel Inside™ logo is a trademark of Intel Corporation. Used with permission of Intel.

me for years, you can imagine my surprise when I walked into vast McCormick Place in Chicago to give the 1989 keynote speech for the home-center industry's annual trade show. The affair had become the fifth-biggest retail show in the country. The magnitude is direct testimony to the industry's growth, from less than $25 billion in 1975 to $115 billion in 1991.

From afar, nothing could appear more mundane than the home-center industry. Guess again. The turmoil (and concomitant opportunities and traps) that besets the industry reflects the "fashionizing" of every last nook and cranny of the economy. The buying and selling of home-center businesses are going on at a record clip. Outfits merge, consolidate into chains, sometimes collapse. On the other hand, thanks to new techniques and technologies installed by wholesalers, growth of independent stores has outpaced the industry average for the last several years. The home-improvement industry, like most others, is bigger (more concentrated), smaller (more independent), and more networked (wholesalers doing more for their member customers) all at once.

Consider one fast-growing chain, Handy Andy Home Improvement Centers. The $500-million (1991 revenue) outfit, headquartered in Schaumburg, Illinois, boasts 55 stores throughout the Great Lakes area. At about the time I gave my speech, Handy Andy was profiled in the industry journal, *Home Center Magazine*, because of its remarkably successful "X-tra" retailing concept—which is a long way from sawdust on the customer's clothes at J. F. Johnson Lumber in 1952. "Tomorrow's homes will need more than just repair," said a Handy Andy exec. "They'll need excitement." (Ah, entertainment again!) X-tra aimed to provide that excitement. Moving far beyond two-by-fours and paint, Handy Andy's new stores, per *Home Center Magazine*, "keep getting more colorful, brightly lit and stocked with lifestyle merchandise." The article describes boutique-like departments, or "modules," which feature silk flowers, storage containers, imported furniture, and ultramodern lighting fixtures. (Move over, Bloomingdale's.)

In fact, *Home Center Magazine* offers article after article touting this sort of marketing as the wave of the future. One cover story, "The Elusive Female Customer," reports on women's growing interest in do-it-yourself; an accompanying survey claims that "about two-thirds [of women respondents] say DIY gives them an opportunity to be creative or express themselves." "Tomorrow's stores will be more entertainment-oriented," says an article summarizing another survey. (The very *word* itself.) Still other pieces argue that "customization" is vital; counsel the merchant to go beyond the conventional provision of good service and sell "solutions" to customer needs; and describe "value-added" services provided by distributors, such as teaching *their* customers (the stores) how to market various categories of products—a companion piece to this last article touted "Just-in-Time and Quick Response inventory management systems" as musts for competitive distributors.

Just-in-time is certainly a message that Hardware Wholesalers, Inc., a billion-dollar, member-owned distributor, understands. Its service-added philosophy goes far beyond delivering goods at a reasonable price. HWI's Data Phone System is a state-of-the-art application of electronic data interchange, which automates and speeds up the order/reorder process—and minimizes the inventory of member stores along the way. At least as important, HWI offers a host of other value-adding features, such as next-day UPS shipment of out-of-stock items, instant order-status reports, and electronic mail. It also pushes "Video Store Meeting," a monthly video-based training package, to its owner-members. And still further along the soft, softer, softest path to fashion is HWI's "Do-it center" concept, an overall store renovation package/program that includes exterior signage and interior department graphics and arrangement schemes, designed to vault independents into the forefront of merchandising. (For more, see our analyses of Home Depot on page 703 and Ikea on page 750.)

CASES IN "PRODUCT" TRANSFORMATION II: SELLING COMPUTERS

The following is my response to a letter from a sales trainer at a major multinational computer company:

Dr. Jane Doe
Sales Training Consultant
XYZ Computer Company

Dear Dr. Doe,

You asked what "competencies, skills and training" salespeople will need to deal with the new world of what you call "consultative selling." As you said, the average XYZ salesperson must become a "business partner," "consultant," and "change agent," rather than an "order taker" who merely "flogs iron" ["iron" is computerese for hardware]. I can think of four areas in which the salesperson (and sales team) must achieve nothing less than mastery.

1. <u>Technology, XYZ and non-XYZ</u>. Obviously, the salesperson must be technically sophisticated. He or she must know XYZ's world cold and be far ahead of the game on new technology, especially applications areas. Also, as has never been the case before, your salesperson needs to be an expert on *competitor products* (and the solutions they provide), and in particular, the many attractive alternatives and/or supplements from the "lesser-known brands."

It's especially important that the salesperson reduce, in a sense, his or her obvious "XYZ bias." The best salesperson (you said it—"consultant") must willingly and aggressively incorporate "favorites" of the customer's, even when there's an XYZ offering that's nearly as good (your salesperson would say better). You're better off with a 60 percent XYZ sell than none at all. If your customer is in love with Sun Microsystems' workstations, then by all means encourage him or her to incorporate them *in an XYZ network* (if that's possible—which I presume it is). Being a consultant means being unbiased and, within reason, your salespeople must offer some substantial degree of "best," bias-free advice. (If they don't, you can be sure that the customer will go to a systems house, such as EDS, that doesn't peddle hardware.)

2. <u>Salesperson as entrepreneur</u>. You used the term "business partner." I'd suggest adding "entrepreneur" and "independent businessperson." Information technology incorporated products and managing processes is the future, from Mrs. Fields' Cookies to the Chrysler Motor Company. The salesperson and sales team are the point persons, in many cases, in *teaching* the customer (i.e., leading the customer to learn) this critical, strategic truth. Though representing XYZ, of course, the salespersons need to see themselves as semi-autonomous entrepreneurs: They are businesspeople out to create the very best future possible for each customer.

3. <u>Value-added strategists</u>. Your average salesperson needs to hold a Harvard MBA/DBA equivalent in "strategic management." Information technology is the strategic future for most firms, of modest or giant size, in low technology or high, though many don't get it yet. So the full-blown Michael Porter course in strategic management (or the closest approximation you can deliver) is essential. The salesperson needs to be able to look at the customer's company within the context of the industry—and the changes besetting that industry. He or she

needs to understand the value-added chain, the various sources of competitive advantage, and what the customer's competitors, small and large, local and global, are up to from an information technology standpoint and in general.

4. <u>Salesperson as expert in organizational development</u>. And now for the next Harvard MBA/DBA! This one must be in organizational development. As you know so much better than I, most Big Bang information technology installations have been outright failures—or at least they've missed their potential by a country mile. The reason is obvious: The effective installation of information technology is above all about the reordering (and often destruction) of hierarchy and the redistribution of raw power throughout the firm. Most customers don't understand this. Even fewer computer salespersons understand it.

This past weekend, I was up at my cabin on the Pacific, a hundred miles north of San Francisco. After a lot of deliberation, my wife and I decided to buy a wood stove. We approached implementing the decision with some trepidation, because, among other things, it means cutting a hole in the roof (which has taken several years and several contractors to make leak-proof); also, we're seldom around and it would be inconvenient to be up there when the lengthy installation process takes place. But it turns out that we only stopped at one place—and made our buying decision without a "multi-vendor survey." The reason: We ran into salespersons (the two shop owners, actually) who assumed the combined "business partner," "consultant," and "change agent" roles.

They knew the ins and outs of installation, and made us feel comfortable letting them hang out in our house when we're not here. The approach they described to our temperamental roof made it clear that we were in loving hands. Also, their expert answers to questions about flash fires, insulation, and the like quelled many subterranean fears. In addition, they'll take care of the annual chimney sweeping (for a fee). Best of all, we had a marvelous discussion about wood! Most of the wood we get now is damp, which can cause dangerous creosote buildup in a wood stove. But they said they'd direct us to reliable sources, and, for no charge, even oversee the continuing delivery of the right wood.

We went away happy as clams and comfortable as could be. To use your industry's terminology, it was a "system sale" or "solution sale" of the highest order—and exceeded our wildest expectations. To use a less narrow analog, they are "heating physicians and heat-maintenance instructors with a marvelous bedside manner." Oh yes, they do sell a great basic product: the Vermont Castings wood stove. But as important as that is (especially to part-time Vermonters like my wife and me), it was *very* secondary to their turnkey effort. In fact, as I sit here dictating this letter they are at work on the installation. . . .

Sincerely yours,
Tom Peters

CASES IN "PRODUCT" TRANSFORMATION III: AGING

Consultant Ken Dychtwald, with Joe Flower, wrote *Age Wave: The Challenges and Opportunities of an Aging America*, the bible on the wildest demographic trend of all: The emergence/delineation of an aging mega-sector in the economy, which affects virtually every company of every size. The phenomenon Dychtwald examines also encapsulates this section's theme—fashion, entertainment, soft, softer, softest, and then some. But that gets ahead of the story.

By the late 1980s, one variety of "old," Americans over 65, numbered more than 30 million. Representing 12 percent of the population, the 65-plus bunch is growing twice as fast as the population as a whole, adding 6 million "members" each decade. To the extent that we have thought about the "elderly" at all (other than older relatives we might be taking care of), we have thought incorrectly, the authors argue. They offer, for example, a series of myths: "People over 65 are 'old'; most older people are in poor health; older minds are not as bright as young minds; older people are unproductive; older people are unattractive and sexless; and all older people are pretty much the same." Then they go on at length—and persuasively—to demolish each one.

Ever so slowly, in light of the magnitude of the opportunity, the aging phenomenon is beginning to captivate corporate America. Consider, for example, the explosion in newspapers and magazines aimed at the mature reader. Dychtwald and Flower report: "There was one such publication available in 1973, eight in 1977, 60 in 1985, and nearly 200 by mid-1988." As well there should be! If there's one thing that's certain, it's the economic power of this burgeoning group. Dychtwald and Flower also inform us that over-50's, though only 25 percent of the population: own 77 percent of all financial assets in America, purchase 43 percent of all new domestic cars and 48 percent of all luxury cars, spend more money on travel and recreation than any other age group, purchase 80 percent of all luxury travel, spend more on health and personal-care products than any other age group, spend more in the drugstore than any other age group, spend more per capita in the grocery store than any other age group, eat out an average of three times a week, purchase 41 percent of all food processors and toaster ovens, gamble more than any other age group, join more auto clubs than any other age group, watch television more than any other age group, read newspapers more than any other age group, and spend more on quality children's clothing for their grandchildren than the children's parents do!

The tastes of the economically potent mature bunch are noticeably different from the tastes of their youthful counterparts. For example, Dychtwald and Flower claim that older consumers "are more interested in purchasing 'experiences' than things: Older men and women are drawn to purchasing products or services insofar as they create a desirable experience. . . . Having the money and time to travel, to learn, and to explore new areas of their lives, mature consumers have as their goals satisfaction, personal well-being, and self-fulfillment." (Entertainment . . . again!)

They also rate "being 'comfortable' " as a "key psychological need," the authors tell us. "Convenience and access may be just as important as the product itself. . . . The older market has a need to feel appreciated, to be treated as special. . . . Home deliveries of everything from pizza to furniture and health-care services will be making a comeback, as thoughtful merchants and service providers look for ways to attract and assist the older shopper." (Indeed, the home health-care market is growing like Topsy—racking up $11 billion in 1991 revenues.)

Some of the wildest ideas in this important treatise appear in a chapter titled "Redesigning America." The physical changes brought about by aging, the authors observe, "cause thousands of mismatches in the way we interact with the world around us, changes so subtle that we often don't notice them at first." They list 16 areas ripe for redesign: "opening medicine packages, reading product labels, reaching high things, fastening buttons, snaps or zippers, vacuuming and dusting, going up and down stairs, cleaning bathtubs and sinks, washing and waxing floors, putting on clothes over one's head, putting on socks, shoes, or stockings, carrying purchases home, using tools, [dealing with helplessness] if something happened at home, since no one would know, using the shower or bathtub, tying shoelaces, bows, and neckties, moving around the house without slipping or falling."

Corporations, slowly rubbing the sleep out of their eyes, are starting to offer new tools and services. Among them, per Dychtwald and Flower: "Comb and brush extenders, long-handled sponges and dusters for hard-to-reach spots, such as high shelves; long-handled, easy-grip zipper pulls for back zippers; 'footmops,' handy sponges that slip on over a foot or shoe to make it possible to clean up spills without bending over; easy-to-grab wall extension mirrors for shaving and grooming; large-faced clocks, kitchen timers and thermostats; talking clocks that announce the time when touched; . . . nonskid slippers and socks to help prevent falls; . . . attractively designed, larger contoured-handle eating utensils for people who have difficulty gripping small objects tightly; electronic-touch lamp converters that allow lights to be turned on and off simply by touching any part of the lamp, thereby eliminating the possibility of burning a finger by reaching up under the shade . . . ; lightweight motorized garden tools."

"PRODUCT"

In light of the above (which barely scratches the surface), just what *is* a product? To begin with, there is still something recognizable as a *lump*. That is, the automobile, the seat per se in the luxury box at the baseball game. But even this most basic element of the product has changed remarkably. E-mail, groupware, expert systems, computer-aided design, computer-aided engineering, computer-aided software engineering, just-in-time schemes, computer-aided manufacturing, computer-integrated manufacturing, electronic data interchange, and the like have all reshaped the basic process of product design, customization, and delivery. (See also the Information Technology section.)

Beyond this much "softer" lump is *Software I*, the lump's "embedded smarts"—that is, the built-in software now found in smart buildings, smart shopping carts, smart cars. (And Trumpf's machine tools and Rational's combi-cookers.) Next, *Software II*: Attending to industrial design is essential to tapping the enormous marketplace potential of our aging population; some go so far as to call design and its larger mate, user-friendliness, the foremost keys to future product and service differentiation in a crowded marketplace. Americans, at least, have underrated design's importance (see Chapter 46 for more).

Software III includes attempts to go far beyond "close to the customer" and achieve genuine market symbiosis. Recall Rational's merry band of staff chefs, for example—company boss Siegfried Meister calls them the "customers' lawyers." And don't forget the singular intensity with which Ingersoll-Rand sought to ferret out the needs of end users. It adds up to wholesale dismantling of the wall that has long separated "them" (purchasers) and "us" (providers). *Software IV* is the revolution in delivery and logistics. The rise of companies like Federal Express is one obvious by-product, as is the trend to home delivery noted by Faith Popcorn.

Software V is the reformulation of the idea of service. Otis elevators and Trumpf laser cutters have diagnostics embedded in them. Also included: the almost routine provision of teaching and consultation—at Trumpf, Rational, Williams-Sonoma, Handy Andy, and The Body Shop, for example.

Software VI is a nod to the idea of "entertainment" (the ultimate in "service"?). Remember Dychtwald and Flower's observation that the aging "market" is in hot pursuit of "experiences." (If you've got the nerve, you could examine Japan's exploding market for high-tech funerals—a cultural trend I'd bet will come winging our way.) In *Sur/Petition*, Edward de Bono lists "four powerful value drivers which will be more important in the future." He further claims that the four—convenience, quality of life, self-importance, distraction—are "the key to value economies that has replaced survival economics." Sounds like entertainment to me!

I don't suggest that this little taxonomy of what constitutes tomorrow's "product" is exhaustive. Nor is it "right." My sole purpose is to provide a rather imposing "list" which unmistakably suggests that the "softs" far surpass the "hard"—and that even the "hard" ("lump") has itself gone mostly soft. "Matter is not all that matters!" is the way consultant Stan Davis puts it, with an exclamation point, in *Future Perfect*. "Value-added will come increasingly from intangibles, 'things' whose importance does not lie in their material existence. Managers who constantly work with the no-matter of their businesses will begin to pull ahead of their matter-minded competitors."

THE IRON LAW OF FASHION

Say "fashion," what words come to mind? How about: fleeting, fast, flair, fickle, frill, frivolous, flaky. What's wrong with that? A lot, many of us would say. Forty-one brands of Tylenol is just too damn many. And will fuzzy logic in my cruise control's "brain" make my life *that* much better? How come the frames of my golly-gee Armani glasses, purchased in 1991, have been discontinued in 1992? (Though the difference between the two styles is so slight that I can barely perceive it; though it was difference enough to force me to buy a completely new pair of glasses, lenses and all, after I busted the frames.)

Hold on! In a sense, "fashion" has always been the engine of progress. Civilization is as complex as it is, and trade so productive overall, F. A. Hayek writes, "because the subjective worlds of individuals differ so much. Apparently paradoxically, diversity of individual purposes leads to a greater power to satisfy needs than does homogeneity." That is, the simple fact that I want any given object—purple lipstick, new Reeboks, maple granola, or a variable-rate mortgage loan—slightly or not-so-slightly more or less than you do is the basis for all trade and exchange, local to global.

The problem for rationalists, to this day: Such diversity of wants/tastes/values—which directly create relative scarcity and indirectly create the price mechanism per se—is completely subjective! In the creation of products, markets, and trade itself, we are simply "playing up to" marginally or wildly different tastes among different individuals. You just have to own a house! (Probably something to do with your granddad's recollection of the Great Depression.) I, on the other hand, can't imagine why you would, at age 26, spend 39 percent of your after-tax income on mortgage interest. "To serve [such] a constantly changing scale of values," Hayek acknowledges, "may seem indeed repulsive."

Find a product, any product, thought to be a "necessity" today, and it probably started out as a frivol. The great European explorers were motivated in part by the desires of the rich to do something about the bland fare served at their tables. Hence Marco Polo journeyed East to hunt for spices. In 1900, a Mercedes-Benz study predicted there'd never be a market for more than a million cars. Why? No one could imagine cars driven by "civilians"—the million was the estimated limit to the supply of chauffeurs. Hey, there was really no *need* for the first wheel. Society, such as it was, was "designed" for wheellessness, obviously, since there were no wheels. We didn't need Post-it Notes until we got Post-it Notes. We didn't need personal computers until we got personal computers. We didn't need railroads until we got railroads. Before that, we didn't need canals until we got canals. And so on.

The late Paul Sherlock, a peerless developer and marketer of very high-tech products at Raychem, contended that buyers of sophisticated products are the world's biggest suckers for what he called "glow" and "tingle." Translation: They buy stuff that turns them on! The lengthy, button-down rationales they later concoct amount to mere boilerplate to assuage stick-in-the-mud corporate controllers. What is Raychem's irradiated polymer cable connector with a memory, then? Fashion, in the end, Sherlock would have insisted.

In 1926, when Henry Ford finally gave in to competitive pressure from General Motors (which was successfully providing different models, different colors, personal financing) and offered the mass consumer a color other than black, he was heading down the path toward fashion, frivolity, intangibles. Do we really *need*, in 1992, more than one color of automobile? Of course not. But the fact is that 1992's auto marketers are differentially aiming colors at the sexes, various age groups, and geographic locations—with success. But still, think of the "efficiency" if we went back to one color worldwide. Right?

Wrong! For it is the pursuit of the new at the margin that engenders all technological and economic advance in the long haul—and creates all jobs. In a world with one-color cars (etc.), all progress in the likes of materials science (paints) and software (relational databases to allow marketers to figure out who'll buy what colors) grinds to a halt—as it mostly did in the big command economies under Soviet sway for so many years. (And: "Lexus engineers pasted on fake fingernails when testing window controls"—the *International Herald Tribune*, June 24, 1992, on carmakers' efforts to cater to women, who now "buy 50 percent of all new cars, an increase of 13 percentage points in a decade.")

All this is a way of saying that soft, frivolous, and fashion is nothing new. It's an age-old story. The only game in town then, now, tomorrow. So don't fight it, embrace it.

What's new is that the soft dimensions have taken over (customized cookies, the prospect of 300 cable channels). In days gone by, you could at least pretend you were dealing in "substance"/lumps—a washing machine, only recently a commodity, seems more "real" than a smart, lightweight home-movie camera. But now the jig is up. Mastering any aspect of commerce means seeking a Ph.D. in fashion—a Ph.D. with a half-life of months, or a couple of years at the most. To handle all this requires a high tolerance for fickleness and failure. It's no wonder that so many of our leading inventors and marketers are in their 20s—some even in their teens. They "get" this fashion stuff. Do you?

More than a High Standard of Living

"We do not want only to satisfy our needs for food, shelter, sex, and comfort; we much more powerfully wish to establish ourselves as people to be reckoned with. Achilles sulked in his tent while the Achaean army failed to make any headway against the Trojans, not because the slavegirl Briseis was important as an item of consumption, but because he had lost face surrendering her to Agamemnon. Mankind is much more powerfully driven by the desire for recognition than by desires for a high standard of living. The mastery of nature owes more to the spirit of conquest than to economic calculation. A society, like our own, in which economic calculation holds sway is the byproduct of a history driven by the demand for recognition."

ALAN RYAN, on Francis
Fukuyama's *The End of History
and the Last of Man
New York Review of Books*
March 26, 1992

FASHION AS FRAGMENTATION

The Economist calls this the "era of manic specialization." The current pace of specialization represents a clear break with the past. It adds up to a difference in degree that's become a marked difference in kind. I sat down a while back with executives at a large brewery. I'm from a reasonably well-off Northern California community. On our grocery shelves, I said, microbrewers' products appeared to be pushing mainstream brands toward the rear—or at least to the side. My knowledgeable brewer friends smirked.

Should they have? Beats me. But the table opposite does show the growth of microbrewer high-end market share in the high-price beer market from 1982 through 1991. Six percent in a modest-size niche does not a revolution make, nor is it a fair basis for predicting catastrophe in Saint Louis, home to Anheuser-Busch. On the other hand, that "little" incursion parallels, almost exactly, the rise of import share in the automobile market in the late '60s. Detroit didn't sneer. It didn't laugh. It didn't even notice. (And *Business Week*, July 13, 1992: Coke and Pepsi "have concentrated on each other for so long, they've opened the way for others to grab a piece of the business." Cola's share of soft-drink sales volume in grocery stores, the article goes on to say, dropped

Microbrewer Market Share Soars

Year	Number of Microbrewers	Microbrewer Share of Domestic High-Price Beer Market
1982	8	0.06%
1983	7	0.11%
1984	14	0.16%
1985	22	0.27%
1986	28	0.32%
1987	36	0.89%
1988	51	1.49%
1989	64	2.31%
1990	83	3.90%
1991	103	5.66%
Source: R.S. Weinberg & Associates		

from 64 percent to 60 percent between 1986 and 1991. "New age" juice drinks are taking up most of the slack.)

As desktop publishing tools have improved and entrepreneurial energy has soared, the publishing industry has been transformed. Introductions of new consumer magazines spurted from about 75 in 1983 to almost 600 in 1989. The concomitant has been an extraordinary decline in circulation for the 10 largest general-interest, mass-circulation magazines; they bagged about 93 million subscribers in 1983, but by 1989 could command only 81 million paying customers—another tip of the hat to fragmentation.

Global branding was quite the rage for a while. It's a lovely idea, no doubt. One size fits all. (Back to the Model T philosophy.) As Europe gets more or less organized for "1993"—i.e., a major leap in economic integration—many pundits predict the emergence of mass Euro-markets for Euro-brands. Some, however, disagree. "Lifestyles around Europe [are] converging, but tastes [are] not," Nicholas Colchester and David Buchan write in *Europe Relaunched*. "To the contrary. As lifestyles become more cosmopolitan, more value-added oriented, tastes in fact diverge. The Italians will become, arguably, more Italian, the French more French, as their incomes rise." Sir John Harvey Jones, former chairman of Britain's ICI, concurs. "Europe's strength is its diversity, not its uniformity," he claimed in a 1990 address to a bureau of the European Commission. (Incidentally, in Harvey Jones's autobiography, *Making It Happen*, he points out that big chemical companies, once bastions of commodity thinking, are dramatically shifting from "producers of products" to "providers of chemical services." Once more, à la 3M—more knowledge, less material.)

"Sox Appeal"

"Why did I nearly start crying the last time I went to buy socks? I'd stopped in a store called Sox Appeal, the perfect place, one might imagine, to spend a pleasant few minutes acquiring a pair of white athletic socks. After a brief visit to the men's dress sock department—dallying with more than 300 varieties, among them products embroidered with bikini-clad women, neckties, flowers, Rocky and Bullwinkle, and elegant logos such as 'The Gold Bullion Collection: Imported' and 'D'zin Pour l'Homme'—I finally made it into the athletics section. Here, the product option high was even headier. Past the 'Hypercolor' socks that change hue, combination 'sport-and-dress' white socks, and 'EarthCare' environmentally safe socks (which, unfortunately, boast of decomposing easily) was hosiery for every sport: racquetball, running, walking, cycling, hiking, basketball, and aerobics. I needed help.

" 'What if I play racquetball occasionally and run occasionally and walk sometimes, but don't want to get a different sock for each one?' I asked the saleswoman. She wrinkled her nose: 'It's really a matter of personal preference.' Did she have any standard-issue white tube socks? The nose-wrinkle again. 'Well, yeah, you *could* get those, but—.' I started reading the backs of the boxes, elaborately illustrated with architects' renderings of the stress points in the 'Cushion-Engineered (TM) Zone Defense.' After briefly contemplating the implications of the Cross-Training Sock—'Shock-Woven elastic arch brace contours to arch, providing additional support and normal articulation of the bones in the foot, while keeping sock migration minimal'—I spent another five minutes studying shapes (anklet, crew, or quarter) and manufacturers, and grabbed a Cross Trainer, two walkers, and, in an environmental guilt-spasm, one pair of the EarthCare."

STEVE WALDMAN
The New Republic
January 27, 1992

When Special Isn't So Special

Niche. Microtization. Specialization. Many have sung that tune (e.g., me). And it *is* the right tune. On the other hand, to tout special and to be special are two different things. That is, special must be SPECIAL—never more so than in today's bulging marketplaces. In the '80s, the world's chemical giants got roughly the same idea at roughly the same time, wrenching production from commodity products to low-volume, specialty chemicals. The predictable result: overcrowding and paper-thin margins. Special in theory often turned out to be not so special after all in practice. The Goliaths mostly stuck to a production-driven model—shifting from commodity lumps to specialized lumps. They didn't realize that the true meaning of "special" involves something like those six flavors of "product" software discussed above.

(Buckman Labs—p. 426—has long been a stellar performer in specialty chemicals. Chairman Bob Buckman knows "consultative selling" as well as any exec I know, in any industry. He also knows that such selling takes a lot of expensive, superbly supported manpower. I've heard him chuckle many times about the inability of the industry giants to "get it"—even if they decommoditize product offerings, they find it next to impossible to decommoditize their culture when it comes to sales and technical sales support.)

All the major players in the computer industry, including IBM, are promoting open-system (anyone's products can be connected to anyone else's), network-based, close-to-the-customer problem solving as their "special" vision. And feature stories appearing simultaneously in *Fortune* and *Business Week* in November 1989 described the implementation of identical strategies at Procter & Gamble and AT&T: Each is blasting out excessive layers of management, scrunching people together in multifunction teams (design, operations, finance, etc.), sidling up to the market to provide fast, specialized solutions to ever-smaller sets of customers' needs. Sound familiar? It's a big part of the message of the Learning to Hustle and Beyond Hierarchy sections of this book. But it begs an important question. When all the flattening out, multifunction grouping, speeding up, and customer cuddling is done, each company should worry about what will have made its approach *unique*. How will Du Pont's "specialty" chemicals binge be noticeably different from BASF's and Monsanto's (not to mention Buckman Labs')? How will AT&T's "open-systems, customized-solution" computer strategy be noticeably different from DEC's?

There are no easy answers. On the one hand, speedy new processes are called for. Even in pharmaceuticals, let alone computers, semiconductors, software, or chemicals, it's becoming next to impossible to maintain a proprietary edge for long; copycats with swift product development systems now cut the ground out from under almost any leader's "proprietary" position in a matter of months, and legally. On the other hand, everyone's mindless emulation of everyone else's organizational strategies is unlikely to get anyone far either.

I'm surely not suggesting that a Monsanto, which has slashed its bulk-chemical business from about 70 percent of sales to just a couple of percent in the last 10 years, should go back to commodity production. Nor am I urging IBM to revert to the arm-twisting arrogance that accompanied its proprietary schemes in the past. I am proposing that special must indeed be *special*, and that it requires redefining our old friend, soul—per the examples above, not just a shift from producing commodities to producing specialty chemicals, but a unique investment in, say, *The Monsanto Way* of responding to customer needs.

It is simply not enough (though it's certainly no mean feat) to trim new-product development cycles from three years to one year or less and install close-to-the-customer, multifunctional teams. Beyond that, you must be able to articulate clearly what it is about your process (for example, the way *you* listen to customers) that is the basis for a sustainable difference. Recall the architects at CRSS—their intensive client-listening protocols are originals; moreover, CRSS refines its "soul" with each passing month. Only this sort of "special" stands a chance of staying the course.

My worries about trendy but predictable strategies jelled in 1990 upon hearing a well-known consultant applaud Apple's time-based product development process. He claimed it would allow Apple to know exactly what products it would release through 1995. For Apple's sake, I hope he's wrong. Consider the birth of the Macintosh computer: Company co-founder Steve Jobs got restless, stripped most of the stars from his/Apple's incomplete, "bet the business" Lisa computer project, carted them off to a little building, hoisted the Jolly Roger (literally), and got down to work on the Mac. Make no mistake, the next PC/workstation/whatever breakthrough is likely to emerge in a similar unpredictable fashion. (The burning question: Will it emerge from a buttoned-down "time-based scheme" at IBM, Apple, Compaq, or Sun? Or from some cranny in IBM, Apple, Compaq, or Sun? Or, at least as likely, from some rogue outfit none of us has heard of? Yo, Bentonville?)

At a seminar in 1991, a consumer-goods exec put another twist on the "special must be SPECIAL" theme. "As the marketplace becomes more and more crowded, and more and more firms do more and more market research," he said, "market research becomes less and less important." I think he's on to something. Market researchers tend to follow the crowd; for instance, right now the crowd is caught up with values and life-styles research (so-called VALS). As a result, almost all market researchers "discover" the same things. (Just as industrial design is going through a bit of a crisis right now, because everyone seems to be using the same computer-aided design software—with the result that my car looks like my blender looks like my bathtub looks like my binoculars looks like my camera looks like my . . .) While I'm not denigrating the value of market research, nor denying that some market research firms will create special metrics which will set *them* apart from the crowd, I am suggesting there's another approach, which we discussed in the Markets and Innovation section. If everybody's moving fast, and everybody's referencing the same studies, then one strategy would seem especially apt—"don't just stand there, do something." That is, get something into the market fast, and if it works, push it; if it bombs, bomb it. (Incidentally, "Don't just stand there, do something," turns out to be very *special*—and virtually uncopyable. Just ask PepsiCo or IDG or Quad/Graphics. Talk about weird soul!)

FASHION AS INTANGIBLES

Philip Morris bought Kraft for $12.9 billion in 1988. When the accountants concluded their tallies, it turned out that Philip Morris had purchased $1.3 billion worth of "hard assets"—factories, inventory (prewrapped slices of Velveeta cheese), and so on. The "leftovers"—"intangibles," or "goodwill" as the accounting profession would have it—added up to $11.6 billion.

At the moment (October 1992), I'm 49. To some of you that seems ancient. But it's not that old! When I pursued business studies 20 years ago, goodwill was no big deal. "Book value"—that which you could count upon—was the melted-down, scrap value of the steel in the smokestacks, more or less. That was a big deal. Today, in our "fashion goods" world, the value increasingly is in the "intangibles" (goodwill, etc.) by old standards.

So what did Philip Morris buy? Brand equity. Kraft's marketing prowess. The ideas in the heads of 51,000 Kraft employees. What it didn't spend much on were those slices of Velveeta cheese, or even the offices and factories Kraft runs.

Flip-flopped Ratios

I urge execs to keep the fraction 116/129 in mind (116/129 is the ratio of the $11.6 billion Philip Morris paid for Kraft's "intangibles" like goodwill to the $12.9 billion total price). That is, to appreciate—and manage—the 89.9 percent "intangibles share" of Kraft that Philip Morris bought. In "The Computerless Computer Company" in the July–August 1991 issue of the *Harvard Business Review*, computer industry guru Andy Rappaport and his colleague Shmuel Halevi put it almost the same way—without the figures: "Microsoft's MS-DOS and Windows operating environment may be the world's two leading computer brands—eminently more valuable than brand names like Intel or Compaq. . . . The more than eight million lines of code that comprise [Mentor Graphics'] Concurrent Design Environment . . . and Mentor's deep immersion in the needs of its primacy customers . . . are a more enduring source of utility than [the] price/performance ratios of Hewlett-Packard's hardware." Consultant Stan Davis claims that "product" value is best measured by the Intangibles/Tangibles ratio, adding that the faster you increase your products' I/T ratios relative to competitors, the more sustainable your overall competitive position.

The second ratio that's flip-flopped on us has to do with a company's share of "softies." Consider, for example, 94/100. Though IBM continues to be classed by government record-keepers as a "manufacturer," Davis reports in *Future Perfect* that about 94 percent of its employees work outside the factory. The debate over the importance of manufacturing all but disappears once you realize that nobody (more or less) in "manufacturing" manufactures anymore. The point here, though, is how much attention does the 6 percent (in the factory) get? How much attention does the "other" 94 percent get? At times it seems that we still spend about 94 percent of our time worrying about the 6 percent, and let "other"—the producers of fashion and intangibles—take care of itself. Once more: Are you managing your 94/100?

Tobin's q

"The most important assets of a firm . . . (such as the people in the organization and the brand names) are intangible, in that they are not capitalized and thus do not appear on the balance sheet," Professor David Aaker writes in the preface to *Managing Brand Equity*. "Depreciation is not assessed on 'intangible assets,' and thus [the] maintenance [of intangibles] must come directly out of cash flow and short-term profits." The most important word in Aaker's title is "managing." These intangible factors, the soft and fashiony factors which are providing most of today's high-tech or low-tech value, often as not go *un*managed. To get a more encompassing handle on the numbers involved, beyond the single example of Philip Morris and Kraft, consider "Tobin's q," named after Yale's Nobel laureate in economics, James Tobin.

Tobin's q is the ratio of a company's stock market value to the replacement value of its *physical* assets. Several ratios calculated by *Fortune* in 1991 reveal varying degrees of softness: Microsoft, for example, has an almost 8-to-1 ratio of market value to physical assets value. More hardware-oriented Emerson Electric sports a much lesser ratio of 2-to-1. (It's useful to point out, however, that even in the latter example, the "soft value" is significantly more than the "hard value.") University of California professor David Teece told *Fortune* that Tobin's q "reflects something . . . that's not on the balance sheet, part of which is intellectual capital." That is, intangibles.

In *Intelligent Enterprise*, Dartmouth professor Brian Quinn takes another crack at this phenomenon (see the chart on the next page, adapted from the book). He calls intangibles "service competency value"—the difference between an acquired firm's book value (hard assets) and the transaction value (the price the acquirer paid for the company). Note, especially, the differences

Service-Competency Values vs. Asset Values of Companies

Manufacturing Companies Acquired	Transaction Value (× $1,000)	Book Value of Net Assets (× $1,000)	Surplus = Service-Competency Value (× $1,000)	Service-Competency Value as % of Book Value
Georgia-Pacific acquires Northern Nekoosa (1990)	$3,640,564	$1,802,259	$1,838,305	102%
British Petroleum acquires Standard Oil (1987)	$7,995,213	$3,160,163	$4,835,050	153%
Eastman Kodak acquires Sterling Drug (1988)	$5,093,072	$1,010,530	$4,082,542	404%
Philip Morris acquires Jacobs Suchard (1990)	$4,183,358	$813,885	$3,369,483	414%
Beecham Group and SmithKline Beckman form SmithKline Beecham (1989)	$8,253,000	$1,590,173	$6,662,827	419%
Bristol-Myers acquires Squibb (1989)	$12,656,271	$1,485,478	$11,170,793	752%
Service Companies Acquired	**Transaction Value (× $1000)**	**Book Value of Net Assets (× $1000)**	**Surplus = Service-Competency Value (× $1000)**	**Service-Competency Value as % of Book Value**
Time Inc. acquires 50.6% of Warner Communications (1989)	$7,000,000	$1,067,073	$5,932,927	556%
McCaw Cellular Communications acquires 42% of Lin	$3,800,000	$208,677	$3,591,323	1,721%

in "service value as a percent of book value": When a hard-asset (e.g., forest-products) company is acquired, the service competency value as a percent of book value is relatively low: Georgia Pacific buys Northern Nekoosa—102 percent. When a soft-asset (e.g., pharmaceuticals) firm is purchased, the service competency value is much higher: Bristol-Myers buys Squibb—752 percent. And when McCaw Cellular bought Lin Broadcasting, mostly for Lin's cellular-phone franchise rights, the figure shot through the roof: $3.8 billion paid for $209 million in tangible assets; service competency value was 1,721 percent of book value!

David Aaker meticulously reviews the still scant, but belatedly growing, body of research on the value of intangibles. His special concern is the "equity" that's enclosed by all that surrounds a brand name per se. "American Motors," he reports, "tested a car (then called the Renault Premier) by showing an 'unbadged' (unnamed) model of it to customers and asking them what they would pay for it. The same question was then asked with the car identified by various names. The price was around $10,000 with no name, and about $3,000 more with the Renault Premier name on it. When Chrysler bought American Motors the car became the Chrysler Eagle Premier, and it was sold for a price [premium] close to the level suggested by the study. . . .

"Considering the price premium earned by a brand may not be the best way to quantify brand equity, especially for product classes like cigarettes and air travel where prices are fairly similar. An alternative is to consider the impact of the brand name upon the customer evaluation of the brand as measured by preference, attitude, or intent to purchase. What does the brand name do to the evaluation? One study showed that the approval rating for Kellogg's Corn Flakes went from 47 percent to 59 percent when the consumers were told the identity of the brand name. And when Armstrong tested a line of tiles against comparable products, the Armstrong name resulted in the preference going from 50–50 to 90–10."

Aaker is clear that perceived quality is very different from satisfaction: "A customer can be 'satisfied' because he or she had *low* expectations about the performance level. High perceived quality is not consistent with low expectations. It also differs from attitude: A positive attitude could be generated because a product of inferior quality is very inexpensive. Conversely, a person could have a negative attitude toward a high-quality product that is overpriced. Perceived quality is an intangible, overall feeling about the brand." And that "overall feeling," as the Philip Morris example suggests, can add up to billions to the market value of the firm. (Wrong. Not "add up to." The "overall feeling" *is* the value—116/129!)

Are You Paying Attention to the Brand?

What, Aaker asks, are the practical "indicators of an underemphasis on brand building"?

— "Managers cannot identify with confidence the brand associations and the strength of those associations. Further, there is little knowledge about how those associations differ across segments and through time.

— "There is no systematic, reliable, sensitive, and valid measure of customer satisfaction and loyalty—nor any diagnostic model that guides an ongoing understanding of why such measures may be changing.

— "There are no indicators of the brand tied to long-term success of the business that are used to evaluate the brand's marketing effort.

— "There is no person in the firm who is really charged with protecting the brand equity. Those nominally in charge of the brand, perhaps termed brand managers or product marketing managers, are in fact evaluated on the basis of short-term measures.

— "The measures of performance associated with a brand and its managers are quarterly and yearly. There are no longer-term objectives that are meaningful. Further, the managers involved do not realistically expect to stay long enough to think strategically, nor does ultimate brand performance follow them."

So, how do you measure up on the Aaker scale?

Gillette Escapes the Commodity Trap

"Since the 19th century, Gillette had succeeded because its name was synonymous with quality. Sponsoring the World Series in the 1950s, the company proudly proclaimed Gillette was the:

'Only Way to Get a Decent Shave'

"But in the early 1970s, Gillette's strength was sapped by diversification into fields where it couldn't be the quality leader. And competitors attacked its heart: Disposable razors offered a 'decent shave' and were sold at less than $2 per half-dozen. Gillette fought back and took a good portion of the disposables market, but the trend cut sharply into sales of $3-and-up shaving systems, such as the Trac II and the Atra. And that threw the market for blades—the 'continuing tribute to the company' paid by users everywhere—into decline.

"Profit margins slid. The simple reason: The consumer was no longer perceiving quality differences among competitors in the shaving business. Many people, inside and outside Gillette, concluded that razors were inevitably becoming a commodity. They concluded the company should sharply cut overhead in its 'cash cow' shaving business [and look elsewhere for profits]. Four separate takeover attempts in the 1980s sought to force the company to do exactly that.

"But the critics didn't understand the real problem. It was that Gillette had lost sight of what its brand was. . . . The battle in marketing of disposables—a significant innovation that naturally would cost Gillette some profits—had caused the company to lose sight of the quality advantages it still possessed. The Trac II and Atra shavers still gave many men a better shave than any disposables. But the noise of promotion of Gillette's 'Good News' disposables obscured that fact.

"Eventually the company began to practice good brand stewardship again. In 1979, it began development of the new Sensor razor—a process that would take more than a decade. Next, starting in Europe, it refocused its marketing. Leaving its disposables to sell themselves, it began putting all its marketing money into shaving systems that used replaceable cartridges.

"Thus, the razor-and-blade business began to come back. And when the Sensor was introduced in 1990, men demonstrated emphatically that the availability of a 'decent shave' at a lower price didn't keep them from being willing to spend money for quality. The Sensor's blades float on tiny springs to conform better to the contours of the shaver's face. Protected by 17 patents, the manufacture of the Sensor blade cartridge demands a machine that can make 93 precise laser welds per second. Initial sales exceeded company projections by 30 percent and might have been even higher if the company had been able to meet the demand.

"While abandoning businesses where it couldn't become the quality leader, Gillette has scored similar successes with its Braun small appliances, Oral-B toothbrushes, and PaperMate Flexgrip pens. Its sales and profits are at record levels, and some analysts are forecasting 20 percent-a-year profit increases. Those are dramatic gains for a big company whose businesses are all more-or-less mature and easily dismissed as 'commodities.'

"The achievement of market-perceived quality seems to produce superior returns in any industry. Marketers can create brand power and superior returns almost anywhere—if they focus on becoming perceived quality leaders."

BRADLEY GALE, former
head of the Strategic
Planning Institute
"Power Brands: The Essentials"
unpublished paper, November 1991

FASHIONIZING STRATEGIES

To deal with the subjective, the perceived, the fashionable, brand equity, market fragmentation, and the wholesale emphasis on intangibles, three principal strategies are necessary. The first strategy, simple to say and hard to execute, is management of the intangibles in a direct, tangible fashion. Most of the rest of this section is aimed precisely at that point.

The second strategy for dealing with a fickle world, discussed at length in the section Marketing and Innovation, is simply at-bats, taking as many entrepreneurial swings at the elusive marketplace as possible. As we've said, the Japanese get the point. Professor Hajine Yamashina, former chairman of the Department of Precision Engineering at Kyoto University, told the *Financial Times* in April 1991 that we're in the "constantly launching new products epoch." From afar, the Japanese look methodical. From up close, wandering along the Ginza, they look like wild-eyed, try-anything competitors. "Japanese companies rarely spend time doing detailed market research studies to get a feel for what extra features might help a new product to sell well," *The Economist* reported in 1989. "Far better, they argue, to rush even half-baked ideas into the shop, then listen carefully to what the real customers say. . . . Japanese engineers are never allowed to forget that, in their fiercely competitive home market, a company that launches a clever new gadget has only three to six months before half a dozen rivals come piling in with similar products."

The third strategy—which turns out to be the organizational response to the first two (managing and attending to intangibles, getting in lots of licks)— is illustrated by any number of cases we have reviewed so far. In short, the strategy boils down to: (1) flattening the organization; (2) inducing fluidity; (3) projectizing; (4) joining in temporary networks with all sorts of partners to accomplish a limited goal in the marketplace; (5) getting very independent, modest-size business units to "own" a market by serving it better; and (6) getting "beyond" close to the customer—that is, achieving symbiosis with the customer—by a variety of organizational means. In the table on pages 664–66, I've summarized the "fashionizing strategies" followed by any number of "our" cases/companies.

Fashionizing Strategies of Selected *Liberation Management* Companies

EDS
New SBU structure aims to focus energy on untapped opportunities. Generic closeness to customer hastens hyperresponsiveness.

ABB
Emphasizes small-within-big for responsiveness. Functional support devolves to the front line or close to it. Rapid-learning mechanism induces systemwide learning.

CNN
At the top: fast, nonbureaucratic decision-making. At the front line: flexible, multiskilled people who "change shape" at the drop of a hat. Lives for speed!

Ingersoll-Rand
All key functions and vendors, distributors, customers are involved in product development—at once and from the start. Design-for-manufacture program. Factory is involved early with product development team to ease subsequent team-to-factory pass-off.

UPRR
Railroads within railroads. Decision-making close to the customer. Empowers conductors, teams at Harriman/St. Louis to work nonbureaucratically with the customer. Regular cross-functional problem solving, often directly involving the customer and vendor.

Titeflex
Creates autonomous teams, then turns teams into quasi-independent business units. Shop-floor people out selling as a matter of course.

McKinsey
Fluid project structure in general abets responsiveness. New strategy is value-added through systematic mechanisms for bringing learning/knowledge to bear, fast—from around the globe.

Imagination
Strategy is to teach clients that "fashion is everything." Fluid organization lives by creativity, responsiveness—won't take new business unless clients provides opportunity to try new things.

David Kelley Design
In every nook and cranny, lives for hustle and creativity.

Chiat/Day/Mojo	Pushes customers toward high-risk, high-value-added solutions by not backing down from bold initiatives. Structured for very fast decision-making—and structured so that creatives are not run over by conservative account managers.
"Doing Deals"	General shape of investment banking firms is driven by the necessity for instant makeover. Constant reorganization (usually bottom-up). Strategic initiatives bubble up. Ever-changing network *is* the firm.
"Dallas Organization"	Various formal (crew brokers) and informal (word-of-mouth) mechanisms support creation of an "instant [network] organization" to perform a one-time task.
Véronique Vienne	Career is a series of learning opportunities. Won't take a new job unless it can sharpen/broaden skills.
Random House	Small, autonomous imprints allow fast response. Each one has a distinct "personality."
IDG	Starts new ventures at the drop of a hat. Attracts opinionated entrepreneurs, and gives them their heads—but demanding performance standards.
Acordia	Flat, autonomous, focused businesses. Size limited to 200 people. Develops overwhelming expertise in narrow area. Willing to customize anything. Will takeon tricky, smallish accounts, since to do otherwise jeopardizes existence.
Chromalloy Compressor Technologies (CCT)	Keeps units small (less than 100), flat, totally focused. Objective is responsiveness and greatest possible knowledge relative to the one or two components any one unit repairs. Creates mechanisms aimed at bringing systemwide expertise to bear—and creating a global "image."
Rational	Limits total size to 400 people: subcontracts more and more and reserves for itself highest value-added tasks. Matchless contact with end user (chef). Powerful in-house chefs represent the customer. No walls between functions. "Identification with the target" on everyone's lips.

MCI	Not tied to manufacturing. Organization design: flat, opportunistic response to technology via fluid network of ever-changing partners.
Skonie, M^2 (et al.)	Increasing number of supersubs *are* raw material that can be fitted into *any* temporary network to get a job done/exploit fleeting opportunity.
CRSS	Dogmatic about a technique that ensures customer symbiosis.
Quad/Graphics	Purposeful strategy of "obsoleting ourselves." Learning/teaching ethos enhances innovation and readiness to change ("We eat change for breakfast"). Mini-businesses (press teams) respond to customers. Press team–customer contact is constant. Teaching customers is routine.
Thermo Electron	Spins off parts of many divisions to public shareholders to keep up performance pressure. New divisions also spin off divisions— which means they are eternally pressured to come up with new ideas themselves. (Even central R&D was spun off!)
Cypress Semiconductor	Spins off energetic, modest-size new units: new state; incorporated; board of directors; equity stake.
Playmobil	New $30-million headquarters aimed at speedy communication (designers and mold makers especially). Very low-impedance communication style. Forget the buyers (and even the parents): Do the right thing for the kids.
Trumpf	Customer contact/teaching/customizing are watchwords. Leibinger: "Innovation is everything." Very easy communication.
The Body Shop	"Conversations" with customers. Teaching model. No advertising. Customers engage with Body Shop feeling, causes.

42

Fashion, Diversity, the Globe

It is an illusion to believe that the French are becoming more and more alike. . . . The French are becoming less and less alike. . . . People are recombining themselves in ethnic, recreational, ideological minority groups: The age of the minority, asserting its right to be different, has arrived. So there is now a whole variety of types of French people.

THEODORE ZELDIN
The French

The message of this section is fashion. Translation: diversity. The globe is shrinking. But as it shrinks, oddly enough, it is becoming more diverse, not less—no matter where you look.

AMERICA THE MANY

Adman Clyde Burleson's *Interstate Commerce: Regional Styles of Doing Business* is a pleasure to read—and provides a warning:

Three executives from Los Angeles . . . went to Knoxville on a matter relating to the world exposition held in the city a few years ago. The purpose of the meeting was to finalize an agreement dealing with the manufacture and sale of a number of novelties (T-shirts, pennants, ashtrays, etc.) bearing pictures and theme slogans of the fair. . . .

Arriving at the meeting, the West Coast team was ushered into a conference room. After the normal "You all care for some coffee?" and everyone was settled, the Los Angeles group opened their presentation along these lines:

"Based on the attendance estimates you supplied and our past experience with the various items, you've got a gold mine. We call the profit a very cool million seven, and your group keeps half. With no responsibility for the unsold merchandise. What doesn't move, we take back! . . ." As he spoke, he wrote the figure $1,700,000 on a chalk board so everyone could see the magic number.

The effect on the room was not what was expected. The Knoxvillians looked pained, looked at each other, looked away, and looked embarrassed.

Seeing the reaction, and thinking the amount wasn't sufficient or was below their expectations, the Californian pressed on, telling them the million seven was only an estimate and the income might go as high as two million.

The more he talked, the more he could see his words were only making things worse. Following his instincts, he closed his mouth and motioned to his associate, who gave her part of the presentation focusing on the items, their uniqueness, and the quality of workmanship. The Knoxville group brightened considerably and followed her with growing enthusiasm.

The third member of the Los Angeles team also received interest and attention during his discussion of the system for defining optimum locations for sales outlets.

The leader, in his selling close, again focused on profits and, to his dismay, saw the audience again fidget and appear uncomfortable. Everyone was cordial at the end of the meeting and, after reasonable adjournment amenities, parted.

The Los Angeles group did not get the order. In trying to discover why, the second presenter talked to one of the female executives on the buyer's side. The response was straightforward, but mysterious.

"It was obvious to all of us you know your business," the woman said, "but it was also clear we'd never get along with your boss. He's way too rude and pushy for us down here." . . .

Discussion of profits to be taken from a deal is a matter of regional variance. In Los Angeles, it is good form to plunge in and plug away at the subject. In the South, profits are taken for granted, but never, repeat never, publicly discussed. Mentioned, fine. Alluded to, great. Shown in detail on an operating summary sheet, necessary. But discussed? No. Made the opening feature and main point of a presentation? Never, never, never.

To the Southerners, the Los Angeles team leader's performance was barbaric. It appeared to them profit was his sole motive—the only part of the transaction he cared about. This created an impassable barrier. Each member of the Knoxville group could imagine all future discussion tinged by the specter of money. Worse, they could foresee endless arguments and awkward confrontations over money, a subject they hesitated to discuss with good friends in the best of circumstances. . . .

I'm loath to admit that something like that happened to me a couple of years ago. (And I'll never tell which role I played.) Appreciation of the fact that regional differences in the U.S. are as important as income or age variations has *begun* to affect everything from product design to advertising strategy among leading companies, from Campbell's Soup, Procter & Gamble, and PepsiCo to Nissan Motor USA. Such concerns explode, of course, when national borders are crossed, whether Canada's or Japan's.

We'll examine a few firms that are creating a significant global presence. Though in very different sectors of the economy, the approach each takes is marked by a common denominator—patience. They've accepted the axioms laid down by "borderlessness" guru Kenichi Ohmae, McKinsey's Japanese office chief, in the March–April 1989 issue of the *Harvard Business Review*: *Don't* expect a quick payback when trying to gain a toehold in a new part of the world. *Do* expect "unequal [financial] returns from various markets at various times."

SUTTER HEALTH HANGS OUT IN JAPAN

In the summer of 1990, a Japanese visitor to California became the first international patient to seek treatment at one of Sutter Health's 12 Northern California hospitals. When he entered the emergency room, the hospital was ready—with a cross-culturally trained staff, translators on-call around the clock, and payment terms provided by Japan's largest bank card company. The program resulted from four years of relationship-building between nonprofit Sutter Health ($501 million in 1991 revenue), Japanese credit card company JCB, and a network of U.S. health-care providers assembled by Sutter. It allows nearly 16 million JCB card holders to charge their care at any of 66 hospitals located near key business and tourist destinations around the United States. Patients and physicians at the hospitals can converse during the examination via the AT&T Language Line, which provides instant, 24-hour telephone access to translators (in any of 143 languages).

Squeezed by reduced federal Medicare payments, Sutter in 1986 sought new markets to support its acute-care services. It turned to the Pacific Rim when hospital trustee and former California assemblyman Robert Monagan pointed out the state's changing demographics—California will probably have an Asian-and-Hispanic majority by the year 2000—and suggested that Sutter prepare to better serve those communities. With this generally in mind, Sutter president and CEO Patrick Hays traveled to Japan on a study tour.

"We saw that the world was getting smaller," Hays told us. "Our goal in going to Japan was equally to develop relationships that would lead to greater cultural understanding and to develop new business relationships." Hays returned to Japan twice in the next two years to attend trade shows and develop alliances. Sutter also retained Herman Smith Associates of Redwood City, California, to analyze opportunities and strategies in 12 Asian countries. To minimize the risk, Sutter tested the waters, did its homework, and stayed cool. "We set out deliberately slowly," said Bill Mason, Sutter's senior vice president for program development, who headed up the company's international efforts. "You can drop a ton of money and end up with nothing, unless you're patient about these things." Mason invested little capital but lavish amounts of time—about 25 percent of his calendar for two years was devoted to visiting, hosting, studying, and talking with the Japanese.

First Sutter developed a sister-hospital relationship with Central Medical System (CMS), a 56-hospital, family-owned Tokyo group. The two organizations exchanged medical and nursing contingents to study clinical and social protocols in each country. Subsequently, Japanese physicians, managers, and journalists regularly toured Sutter Health facilities, studying health-care technology and management practices. And Sutter's nursing and front-line patient service staff attended classes on Asian customs and beliefs—from the taboo against organ transplants among strict Buddhists to the importance of color choices in several countries where white signifies mourning. In addition, Sutter and CMS developed a referral program for Japanese patients seeking specialty care not widely available in their country, such as organ transplants and mental health services. In 1989, for example, a Japanese patient whose doctors recommended a kidney transplant flew to Sutter Health for an evaluation.

Though few of the 3 million Japanese who visit the U.S. each year pass through Sutter's service area, the JCB deal was an important door-opener, giving Sutter the experience and contacts to do business internationally. Dealing with JCB and CMS has "pushed Sutter to think beyond admitting patients and increasing revenues, and toward becoming a real [international] health-care system," said Martin Light of Herman Smith Associates. "You have to build relationships and spend the first year or two educating yourself and building trust."

The slow, deliberate Japanese decision-making process is "sometimes frustrating" to Americans, Sutter's Mason admitted. Since Hays's first trip to Japan, other American health-care companies have approached the Japanese with ideas for programs similar to Sutter's. Mason is not alarmed about competitors, though. "The Japanese are not going to jump into a relationship with you," he remarked. "They want to look, feel, smell, touch, taste, and visit, visit, visit—to see if it's a solid relationship." Asked how he remains patient, Hays said, "We take a long view of things. We try to resist making [negotiations] an ego trip." Lee Iacocca could learn a thing or two from these guys!

APPLIED MATERIALS FINDS "GOD"

By some measures, semiconductor equipment maker Applied Materials is America's most successful entrant into Japanese markets, which is especially noteworthy given Japan's exclusionary bent in semiconductor equipment. In 1991, over 40 percent of the company's $650 million in revenue came from Japan.

Applied Materials' saga is meticulously documented in Jim and Jeffrey Morgan's *Cracking the Japanese Market*. (Jim Morgan is Applied Materials' CEO, son Jeffrey runs a small software firm.) One story the authors recount gives a flavor of the world they encountered:

On a train ride back to Tokyo from Japan's northern regions, a long-time Japanese friend explained to us the Japanese approach to business. "In the United States," he observed, "you say the customer is always right. In Japan, we say, '*okyakasuma wa kamisama desu*'—the customer is God. There is a big difference."

To illustrate his point, he told us about an associate of his who had been a divisional president within a major Japanese conglomerate some years ago. His division made turbines for use in hydroelectric plants and, during one particularly brisk period of business, the division was running a month late in delivering a giant turbine to a regional power company. The company was building a dam and power station along Japan's northwest coast and the delivery delay was causing a major disruption.

When news of the delay reached the president's office, he was mortified. The next day he traveled hundreds of miles to the remote town where the dam was being constructed. He arrived late at night, but at daybreak he was at the home of the general manager in charge of the construction project. When the general manager left for work that day, he found the distinguished division president down on his knees in the driveway. The president asked for forgiveness for the terrible loss of face his company had experienced by not meeting its customers' expectations and expressed his sorrow for the problems the delays were causing. He went on to give his solemn promise that the delivery would be made by a certain date. With the president's reputation on the line, work was conducted around the clock until the turbine was delivered as promised.

Jim Morgan has not prostrated himself in any customer driveways so far. Not physically, at least. But he has learned an abiding sense of respect for things Japanese. The biggest difference between Jim Morgan and most others is that he took his Japanese friend's story to heart, rather than dismissing it as wretched, quirky excess.

Fashion. *Okyakasuma wa kamisama desu*. The customer is God. It's tough to get more fashionized than that! (Begged forgiveness from any good customers—at home or abroad—lately?)

When Yes Means Anything But

Do we need another "how to do business in Japan" list? Perhaps. The 10 points that follow, from consultant Bonnie Williams (born in Japan in 1955, of American missionary parents), appeared in *Industry Week* in April 1992. It is particularly thoughtful and succinct:

1. Find out everything you can about the people you plan to meet. Though you'd do this anywhere in the world, do it with extra thoroughness for Japan. . . .

2. Never expect a quick deal. Be prepared for many meetings during which relationships can build slowly. The Japanese will want to establish that you are trustworthy and can think long-term.

3. Be ready and willing to take part in the small talk that precedes any real discussion of business. When negotiations are underway don't feel that you have to fill silences during the discussion. In Japan silences are normal and should not be a cause of discomfort or embarrassment. . . .

4. Avoid confrontation. Confrontation is liable to lead to a loss of face for one side or the other and can bring negotiations to a polite but abrupt end. . . .

5. Don't be deceived by what you regard as a lack of emotion among the Japanese. Japanese are, in fact, both emotional and sensitive. However, Japanese don't show their emotions; they contain them.

6. The Japanese don't proffer opinions easily or straightforwardly. You should not, therefore, inquire whether the Japanese with whom you are dealing agree or disagree with your position. They won't give you their [true] opinion but rather the answer they think you expect.

7. A nod of the head in Japan does not mean "yes." Even less does it mean "it's a deal." A nod is likely to mean no more than "I hear you" or "I take your point." . . .

8. A call for more meetings is a good sign. To you it may mean more delay, another failure to reach a decision. Don't show your exasperation, still less your anger. An invitation to further meetings means the Japanese are beginning to trust you. Count your blessings.

9. Only rarely is there a single identifiable decision-maker in Japanese business. You may be dealing with one person in a series of meetings, but he will still want to go away to talk with his colleagues,

both junior and senior. Eventually, he'll be back, not with his decision but with a consensus.

10. Consensus should not be undervalued. When it has been reached things will move very fast because on the Japanese side, everyone will be on board. Everyone has been kept informed and has been able to contribute. With consensus, everyone is ready to move ahead.

A. T. CROSS: A NICKEL AT A TIME

A. T. Cross of Lincoln, Rhode Island, sold $217 million worth of pens and pencils in 1991—*in 125 countries*. Cross makes a superb product. How else could it sustain its ability to sell $20 ballpoint pens, when usable 50-cent alternatives are readily available? (Shades of Swatch.) As any good Mittelstander knows (and Cross is as Mittelstand as any German counterpart), if the product is a gem, there's nothing to stop any firm of any size from heading overseas.

In *The Silent War: Inside the Global Business Battles Shaping America's Future*, consultant Ira Magaziner and journalist Mark Patinkin dissect the A. T. Cross story to determine the imperatives of overseas success:

• Persistence. It took Cross forever, it seemed, to gain toeholds in France and Germany. (Cross pens initially were considered too slim by German men, who cotton to very thick, black fountain pens.) And Cross has been in and out of politically volatile markets such as Argentina. Furthermore, small orders gained at first are often unprofitable—in fact, Cross execs allow as how a decade may pass without much positive cash flow to show for a lot of nights away from home in very strange places (Mittelstand again).

• Small orders taken seriously. A letter from a Costa Rican businessman led to a tiny order—and a Cross beachhead. Another letter, from an Israeli colonel, led to the penetration of that country's market. Cross's international chief, John Lawler, told Magaziner and Patinkin that it's very easy to pursue only big markets with big potential. But 10 Burundis, he added, can equal 1 Canada.

• Pursuit and support of hungry, modest-size distributors. Go for a local distributor champing at the bit to work with you, not necessarily the biggest or even the best. Then support that distributor to the hilt; at one point, for example, Cross was spending 25 percent of local gross revenue on advertising to aid its German distributor.

• Local production. To vigorously embrace the European market, Cross decided in 1971 to make products in Ballinasloe, Ireland. Unlike many American firms heading offshore to manufacture, the decision was not driven by costs (they were the same in Ireland and the U.S.). Instead, Cross forthrightly aimed to become a European "insider."

● Customization. Magaziner and Patinkin are caustic: "If it's rare for American firms to export, it's rarer still for them to design or adapt products for foreign markets." Not Cross. For Thailand, it modified ballpoint pens to deal with high humidity, which can adversely affect ink flow. To cater to European tastes, Cross developed a fountain pen. In fact, the European-produced Cross fountain pen eventually became a hit in the U.S. This reverse product flow, Magaziner and Patinkin observe, is a common, though unexpected, side benefit experienced by premier exporters/customizers of any size.

The obvious price of failing to think globally is lost potential. "But there can be an even greater price," Magaziner and Patinkin say. "Let your rivals have the world to themselves, and . . . it's likely they'll one day invade your own backyard. . . . The best way for American companies to keep that from happening is to go overseas first."

IS THAT ALL THERE IS?

Wait 10 years for a return if you have to, A. T. Cross says. And tailor your product. And choose a hungry distributor. (And oh, by the way, have a good product to begin with.) Los Angeles is not Knoxville, Clyde Burleson warns. Different returns from different countries, McKinsey's Ohmae insists.

The customer is god, Applied Materials' Jim Morgan chimes in. And Sutter Health says that if you hang out long enough in Japan, you'll likely build relations that allow you to begin to begin to get a toe in some door or other.

Is that all there is to "going global"? Of course not. Of course. A hundred books, many quite useful, have been written on the subject. And yet, I contend, they mostly boil down to these simple messages:

—We're all different, so pay attention to that (when in Rome . . .).

—Hang out, hang out, hang out, work at relationships and don't even think about the big splash at first.

—Ten years to get the first five-cent order is okay.

—Good things happen to good (patient) people with good products.

—If you want to become an internationalist, start spending time beyond your borders.

Get these "right," and you just might do well in Osaka—*and* Knoxville.

To Err Is Glorious

"Of all the lessons that come with 'going global,' the one that is arguably the most important of all is still proving a difficult pill to swallow. That is the admission that 'you got it wrong.' So observes Ashridge Management College's Dr. Ariane Antal as she sets up IOC-Ashridge, a new French-based center devoted to helping organizations manage change. Dr. Antal cites two prime elements needed for international success: the ability to be fluid, and the ability to find the right balance between meeting local and global needs.

"But the ability to admit failure is what is really going to make for success in the future,' she says. This is so because the world is in such a flux of changing markets and capabilities that no single model will now ensure success. The whole culture of companies must be changed so that all learning experiences are shared—from top to bottom and from country to country. . . . Adds colleague Kevin Barham, 'Managers frequently say, We tend to bury mistakes here without discussing them. Yet the most successful managers are those who exploit the learning from them.' Not only must forums be created where employees will admit to problems, but even the chairman must learn to say 'I got it wrong.' Only then is it possible to get it right."

Management Today
June 1992

43

Glow! Tingle! Wow! (Yuck!)

Quality doesn't have to be defined. You understand it without definition. Quality is a direct experience independent of and prior to intellectual abstractions.

ROBERT PIRSIG
Lila

The world can accept pillage or disembowelment, but not cheating at cards.

TALLEYRAND

Annual sales of Marlboro cigarettes run about $10 billion. But what *is* Marlboro? It's a brand of cigarette, as good as any other, I suppose, if you can get over the fact that it ups the odds of an early death. The box is OK, too, though nothing special. And jeez, that cowboy's been around forever! Where do they get off, using the same hombre in Tokyo, Guangzhou, Frankfurt, and Los Angeles?

You can buy a used car that works pretty well for $1,500, OK running shoes for $16.99, a massive batch of timely information for 35 cents a day (it's called a newspaper), and a nutritionally acceptable diet for a couple of bucks a day. All the rest is fluff. Pure, unmitigated fluff. (And it's getting fluffier—at 3M as well as at Sox Appeal.)

THE SLIPPERY INTANGIBLES

My primary objective in this section—and I'm not very optimistic about achieving it—is to draw you a step away from the rational, the logical. There may have been a little bit of rationality and logic associated with buying, for 700 bucks, Henry Ford's black Model-T (not *much* logic, because most people lived within horse, foot, or bicycle distance of wherever they needed to go to work or shop or visit Grandma); there's not a shred of logic, however, in your selection of a low-end Acura instead of a high-end Mercury, or whatever. (Though, human that you are, you'll construct a logical explanation after the fact—e.g., to save American jobs if you bought the Merc, to send our automakers a message if you went for the Acura.)

In a world driven by fashion we must learn to deal with the irrational. No! Exactly wrong. We must learn to revel in the irrational, cotton to it, take it to our bosom, smile at it, grin at it. It's not enough to "cope with it" or "deal with it," though that's more than most of us, trained as administrators, engineers, or scientists, do. Welcoming, laughing at, enjoying: That's more like it!

I Know It When I See It!

Quality, finally on the minds of Americans, has quickly become the province of technofreaks. Every aspect of it is measured and boiled down to its quantitative essence. (That's not all bad, because [1] it puts quality solidly on the agenda, given our strong "what gets measured gets done" bias; and [2] seat-of-the-pants approaches have failed us too often in the past.) At a 1990 seminar on quality, I listened to one of the most famous technofreaks slam a pre-technofreak quality adage: "I know it when I see it."

I'm not knocking "fish-bone" cause-and-effect diagrams or statistical process control, but I am telling you—and if you don't buy it, stop reading now—that *my* definition of quality is: "*I know it when I see it.*" You better believe that I do!

The chief operating officer of Federal Express followed Dr. Technofreak to the podium. He said his firm's goal is to consistently "meet customer expectations." I followed him to the dais and said: "Baloney!" What's so special about FedEx, and in such marked contrast with top-rank competitor UPS, is that the upstart so frequently *exceeds* expectations. Or, to use high-tech product developer Paul Sherlock's words again, FedEx makes me—and lots of others—"glow" and "tingle." It's not just that my Vermont FedEx courier, Chris Goddard, chugs up the long, icy dirt road to our house day after endless winter day. That's more or less expected. (Though some delivery folks won't come up the road, especially during Vermont's infamous Mud Season.) Instead, it's the time he grabbed the coffee cup I'd left perilously on the roof of the car and brought it into the house (I've driven off and busted them before in similar circumstances). It took him no more than a second or two, of course. But it was a "little" act of caring—in marked contrast to the UPS driver, who persists in throwing any and all boxes at the porch like a nine-year-old newspaper boy with errant aim.

Glow and tingle too much for you? Grocer Stew Leonard's "wow" (as in, "We want customers to say 'wow' when they walk through our store") go too far? Carl Sewell a damn fool for putting $275-a-roll wallpaper in the bathrooms of his Cadillac-Lexus dealership (and talking a restaurant into opening a branch in his service department for customers waiting for quick car repairs)? And Anita Roddick's "delight," "thrill" (her minimum expectation for any one of The Body Shop's 700-plus outlets) out of bounds? Maybe you'll at least admit to whispering "neat" now and again. C'mon, a new laptop or spreadsheet is "neat." Or not. We don't *need* any of this stuff. So that makes it all like the movies, right? You don't perform Pareto analyses on flubbed lines while you watch Schwarzenegger or Madonna or Woody Allen, do you? You say "neat," "yuck," etc. So, also, to a $200-million proposal from EDS or CSC. Right? Confess!

The Joyless Economy

When it comes to ignoring glow and tingle, economists take the prize, even if they did invent "subjective marginal utilities." Stanford University emeritus economics professor Tibor Scitovsky tries to set things right in *The Joyless Economy*:

> [The two] main types of human satisfaction—comfort and stimulation—are to some extent mutually exclusive. One can get more of both up to a point; but beyond that point, more of one can only be gotten at the sacrifice of the other. . . . There is hardly a species of animal that has not been observed to engage in play and exploration for the sheer fun of it. . . .
>
> The usefulness of useless activity is a paradox. . . . The fact is that the most pleasant is on the borderline with the unpleasant. . . . What is not new enough and surprising enough is boring; what is too new is bewildering. . . .
>
> The traditional theory of the consumer's behavior fails to recognize his need for novelty and variety. . . . The discovery that man needs stimulation as well as comfort is not new. After all, the ancient Romans clamored for bread *and* circuses. . . .
>
> We have unwittingly fallen into the habit of identifying a high standard of living with a high level of comfort, neglecting stimulation or

pleasure as a source of satisfaction and assuming that the more comfort we have the better off we must be. . . . The novelty of this book lies in introducing novelty as an objective of desire and a source of satisfaction. . . . The stimulus of novelty is among the most fundamental of human needs.

It's Slippery Out

Let me be clear—we *are* dealing here with slippery ideas. In mid-1991, Total Research Corporation released EquiTrend, a report of "Quality Perceptions Americans Have" for some 190 brands in 55 product categories. At the top of the heap: Disneyland/DisneyWorld, Kodak, Mercedes-Benz, CNN, Hallmark. Also in the top 20: Levi, IBM, Arm & Hammer, Lego, Maytag, Rubbermaid, Hershey, Tylenol, and Sea World. Perceived product quality can be worth billions. (Don't take my word for it; watch the intensity with which Disney's horde of lawyers fights anyone who tries to make even the most innocent unauthorized use of the Disney name or a Disney "character." *They* know where their bread is buttered! *They* understand 116/129.)

Customer satisfaction? Good stuff. But it's not enough. In the EquiTrend study, for example, Little Tikes (owned by Rubbermaid) ranked highest among five toy brands measured in user satisfaction. Terrific! On the other hand, Little Tikes came in last among the ranked toy brands in customer perception of quality. That is, those who use Little Tikes toys take a shine to them—hence the high customer satisfaction. But they aren't very memorable overall. (TRC researchers suggest that this disparity between satisfaction and perceived quality presents a mind-boggling opportunity for Rubbermaid to leverage that satisfaction with Little Tikes into a memorable brand franchise.) Former Strategic Planning Institute chief Brad Gale, who provided us with the Gillette saga, might well have predicted it. He's been among the few who have had the nerve to suggest that customer satisfaction is a very limited idea. To be useful, the notion must be extended to enfold customers we don't have— those we've lost, or who've never bothered to consider us.

PERCEPTION I: HOW HOT *IS* THAT WATER?

● A classic perception experiment uses water as its homely subject. Social psychologist Bob Cialdini reports in *Influence: Science and Practice*: "A nice demonstration of perceptual contrast is sometimes employed in psychophysics laboratories to introduce students to the principle. Each student takes a turn sitting in front of three pails of water—one cold, one at room temperature, and one hot. After placing one hand in the cold water and one in the hot water, the student is told to place both hands in the room-temperature water simultaneously. The look of amused bewilderment that immediately registers tells the story: Even though both hands are in the same bucket, the hand that has been in the cold water feels as if it is now in hot water, while the one that was in the hot water feels as if it is now in cold water. The point is that the same thing—in this instance, room-temperature water—can be made to *seem* very different depending on the nature of the event that precedes it." Moral: Where you stand depends on where you sit—and which bucket of water your hand's been in.

• In another well-known social psychology experiment, kids from different economic backgrounds are asked to draw a quarter. Youngsters from the ghetto tend to draw quarters the size of oranges. Wealthy kids often as not represent the quarter with a dime-size circle. Moral: A quarter is not a quarter.

• In *Verdict Pending*, Fredonia French Jacques systematically traces the origins of malpractice suits, a multibillion-dollar addition to the American health-care tab. One hospital administrator's comment captures the spirit of the book: "It is patients who have been slighted or treated abruptly who unconsciously look for a way to get even . . . who have been depersonalized, whose feelings have been hurt, who will sue. . . . Patients seldom sue those who have cared for them with kindness." Moral: Patient satisfaction may bear little relation to the surgeon's credentials or deftness with a scalpel.

• In *Medicine & Culture: Varieties of Treatment in the United States, England, West Germany and France*, medical journalist Lynn Payer observes that "Often all one must do to acquire a disease is to enter a country where the disease is recognized—leaving the country will either cure the malady or turn it into something else." Life is the stomach for the French, hence twice as many drugs for digestive ailments line their pharmacists' shelves as ours. German romanticism, Payer concludes, leads to a prescription rate for heart drugs that's six times higher than in France or Britain. Britain's stiff upper lip leads to minimal medical intervention. And America? We test, dose, and slice with reckless abandon. "American medicine is aggressive," Payer says. "American doctors want to do something, preferably as much as possible." Moral: Medicine as scientific pursuit? Forget it (mostly). It's as much a product of national character as of chemistry. (Just for laughs, Payer observes that despite radical differences in disease classification and treatment regimens, citizens of the four nations have almost exactly the same life expectancies.)

And more: Researchers have discovered that hospital stays can be cut significantly if, prior to surgery, doctors and nurses fully inform patients of the course of postoperative symptoms. Domino's 30-minute delivery guarantee redefined the pizza industry. But did you realize that the average mom-and-pop pizza shop usually delivers in less than 30 minutes? Disney's secret of line management in sultry Orlando, Florida, is not short lines, but signs that proclaim how long the wait is going to be. People expect to hurt after surgery, to wait in line at Disney, and Domino's promise is nothing special. It's the telling that is.

PERCEPTION II: THE EYE OF THE BEHOLDER

Judgment Under Uncertainty, edited by professors Daniel Kahneman, Paul Slovic, and Amos Tversky, adds kerosene to the fire. In 555 dense, well-documented pages, they reveal the slithery nature of human perception (and the way it colors our invariably rotten judgment of almost anything). The slightest difference in the way "evidence" is presented to us—what we see first, last, etc.—can wildly alter the way we perceive a situation. The authors identify any number of "soft" factors which dramatically affect our judgment. Here's a sample:

• Anchoring. Experimental subjects were given a multiplication to perform. One set got $8 \times 7 \times 6 \times 5 \times 4 \times 3 \times 2 \times 1$; the other, $1 \times 2 \times 3 \times 4 \times 5 \times 6 \times 7 \times 8$. The two strings are clearly equivalent. The catch: You've got five seconds to make an estimate. The average answer from $8 \times 7 \times \ldots$ group members was 2,250; from the $1 \times 2 \times \ldots$ group, 512. (The correct response is 40,320.) Welcome to the world of "anchoring." Where you finish depends on where you start. If the 8 is on the left, where we normally begin, we lock on to it and offer an answer *four times* higher than those "anchored" on the left by the lesser numeral 1.

• Retrievability. Is it more likely that a word starts with "r," or that a word has "r" as a third letter? Subjects answering this and a similar class of questions vote sharply for "starts with"—and are wrong. The prejudice at work: It's easier to "retrieve" certain categories from memory, in this case words that begin with a given letter rather than those with the letter in the third slot. In general, the ability to readily call to mind a vivid example plays havoc with (statistical) reality.

• The illusion of control. "[People] behave as though chance events are subject to control," social psychologist Ellen Langer writes in a chapter contributed to the Kahneman, Slovic, and Tversky book. In a typical experiment aimed at demonstrating the point, members of adjacent offices were given an opportunity to buy tickets for a lottery. Participants in one group chose their ticket (a card emblazoned with a football player's name, team, and picture) from a box. Participants in the other group were simply handed a card (of the same type). Later, but prior to the drawing, participants were asked how much they'd want for selling their ticket back. Those who'd *chosen* their cards from the box wanted $8.67 on average; those who'd been *handed* a card asked for $1.96. The effect of self-selection—in this purely chance event—upped perceived ticket value by a factor of 4.4!

● <u>More like me</u>. Student subjects were asked by a researcher to participate in an experiment by wearing a sign that read "EAT AT JOE's" around campus for 30 minutes. Those who agreed to wear the sign (only slight pressure was exerted to do so—"you might learn something") predicted that 62 percent of their fellow students would wear it if asked. Those refusing to wear the sign assumed that 33 percent of their fellows would agree to wear it. As I go, so goes the world.

● <u>Multistage events</u>. Business life routinely involves betting on complex, multistep events. Suppose a project consists of 10 key steps; further imagine that the odds of making it through any one step are 70 percent. What are the odds of surviving all 10 steps? The correct probability is $.7 \times .7 \times .7 \times .7 \times .7 \times .7 \times .7 \times .7 \times .7 \times .7$—or 3 percent. If the odds of success at any one stage are 50 percent, the overall chance of success $(.5 \times .5 \ldots)$ plummets to 0.1 percent. Now the research: In an experiment involving two to eight stages of varying difficulty, subjects overestimated their chances of success by a factor of 2 (in the simplest case) to a factor of 900,000 (in the most complex case)—that's right, *nine hundred thousand*.

In sum, you and I are wildly optimistic, grotesquely egocentric, easily distracted and misled—i.e., wretched judges. Moreover, other research in this scholarly volume decisively shows that the "professional judgment" of doctors, psychologists, auto mechanics, and geophysicists (concerning their own specialty) is no more reliable than that of laypersons.

PERCEPTION III: THE *REAL* WORLD

Smoke started pouring into the cabin of the small private-charter aircraft I was on, heading from Toronto to Glens Falls, New York. My pilot made an emergency landing. The problem turned out to be relatively minor. After an all-night stay at a Holiday Inn in Buffalo, I went on to Glens Falls in another small plane the next morning.

So what do I think? After my knees stopped shaking, was I angry? Not at all. The problem, which might have killed me, may have been the fault of a sleepy mechanic. I never bothered to inquire. I do know (1) I'm not only not irritated by the event, but (2) I'm pleased by the pilot's good work, and (3) I only wonder that such things don't happen more often.

On the other hand, there *is* an old memory that still rankles. A few months before the smoke-in-the-cabin emergency, I paid full-fare first class, about 800 or 900 smackeroos, for an American Airlines flight from Chicago to San Francisco. Yet on this four-hour, late-evening flight the crew couldn't even find a second bag of peanuts to serve. I was furious. I did a little spot on national TV about it. I wrote the chairman. Today, more than two years later, my "no second bag of peanuts" memory is clear. Translation: I can readily countenance smoke in the cabin, a life-and-death issue. But I can't countenance what I see as unspeakable neglect—i.e., no extra peanuts after forking over close to $1,000.

The Best There Is

What a system! There's not much doubt about the most "excellent"—complex, well-functioning—system in the world, or at least my world. It is the scheduled commercial air carrier system in the U.S. It's remarkably safe—which is an absolute wonder, considering that the average pterodactyl in whose belly we fly has a million parts. Moreover, planes land on time, or close to it, with incredible regularity—given the acts of God that mar each day of the year (snow in Denver in February, thunderstorms in Chicago in July, fog in Los Angeles in April, and so on). Even the "little stuff" works. I'm astonished at the airlines' baggage-handling skill. You only have 10 minutes between connections, due to a delay on the front leg, for instance; nonetheless, virtually without fail, the bag is there, waiting, when you land in San Francisco at midnight.

Now the catch: Among my frequent-flying friends, it's hardly an exaggeration to say that I don't know a single one who isn't furious at all the airlines, almost all the time. What's going on here? A shockingly complex system, astonishingly effective—that regularly drives most of its most regular customers to the brink of despair or beyond. The answer, in short: The airlines do a superb job at the big stuff, then undo most of their effort by screwing up the "peanuts."

We expect all long-distance calls to go through in a snap. We expect even a $7,000 car to start in 20-below-zero weather in Vermont. And we don't expect the plane to crash! Our expectations about the raw, technical performance of almost everything are sky-high these days. So, fair or not, we take the hardest part for granted and focus on "other." "Other" drives—and dominates—our judgment of overall product/service performance. And in the case of the airlines, "other" is a long-running misadventure in being treated like a preschooler.

The effect is multiplied because the act of flying means buckling yourself into a tiny tube-prison, then hurtling through clouds at 610 miles per hour. (The psychologists could tell the airlines what that means: We have lost control. Perceptually speaking—and how else is there to speak?—we are in a dangerous mood.)

The fix? A couple of years ago, customers got on the airlines' case and were heard in the halls of Congress. (Most congressmen are very frequent flyers, the poor sods.) There were calls for reregulation. Among other things, the airlines tried to improve their "on-time record." I don't know the "truth," but I don't think that performance—as a scientist or engineer would measure it—improved much. What did happen, with remarkable impact, was the stretching out of schedules (in response to the widespread publication of on-time data). Suddenly my *Official Airline Guide* says I'll arrive in Chicago on Bubba Airways flight 962 at 3:15 p.m., rather than 2:55, as had been posted before. So we arrive at 3:25, and I'm deliriously happy. Before I would have been among those screaming bloody murder. (The fact is that 2:55 p.m. vs. 3:15 p.m. makes no "real" difference at all, 99.99 percent of the time. But 10 minutes late versus 30 is a dramatic *perceptual* difference—"not too shabby" vs. "crappy, as usual.")

An Ode to Clogged Freeways

A *San Jose Mercury News* writer described a two-day junket on Continental. None of the predicted horrors materialized (no canceled flights, no lost baggage, etc.). Yet he got home thoroughly dispirited. The little stuff did him in! (Questionable food. Jammed into the seat next to strangers sleeping on his shoulder.) At the end of his article, he remarked at the joy of returning home, getting into *his* car, being *in control* in *his* 20 square feet of space, with *his* tape in *his* tapedeck—even though he was stuck in the interminable, daily rush-hour traffic jam on Interstate 280 near San Jose.

The point is utterly, deadly (from a commercial standpoint) serious. Yes, he's stuck in a traffic jam. How awful. Breathing noxious fumes, to boot. Accomplishing absolutely nothing. Frittering another 50 minutes of his life away. But a ton of psychological "locus of control" research says, unmistakably, that as he perceives it, he's totally in control. *He* chose to be in that car. It's *his* car. *He* can open his door and step out (not a wise idea, but he can do it). And that, in the end, is precisely what perception is all about.

KEYS TO SUCCESS (AND FAILURE)

And then there was the beautiful hotel I stayed at in St. Louis a couple of years ago. My office discovered it thanks to a book on terrific small hotels. The owners spent a bundle on marble and brass fittings. Staff was fine. At some point I must have stuffed my key into my coat pocket. On the airplane home, I pulled it out. It was then that I saw a little red sticker—"PLEASE RETURN ROOM KEY TO FRONT DESK UPON CHECKOUT. FAILURE TO DO SO WILL INCUR A $10.00 CHARGE TO YOUR ACCOUNT." For the rest of my life, that little hotel in St. Louis will be the

10-buck, red-key hotel! I will never forgive them. (And if they've rescinded the policy? Who cares? Perceptions like this one are immune to mere facts or the passage of time.)

Squandering a Precious Resource

The resort hotel sits astride some of Florida's most expensive oceanfront real estate. The buildings reek of deep investor pockets. (Shades of the St. Louis hotel.) Yet my experience was an abomination. A host of "little sins" blew away all the impact of all the big bucks that had been invested—and left me with a very, very sour taste. Tragically, each sin could have been rectified—*without cost*—if the hotelier had been focused on my (customer) experience. *Okyakasuma wa kamisama desu!*

- No newspapers. After a 6:30 a.m. walk, I stopped at the front desk and inquired about newspapers. "Don't have any," I was informed. The two retail stores at the resort (not particularly close by) did have them. Were they open? Not sure. Huh? Even Motel 6 has newspapers in nearby dispensers! (*"And we'll leave the lights on."*)

- No bedside phone. There *was* a phone in my bedroom. But it was 15 feet away, on the dresser across the room—and there was only about 4 feet of play in the cord. I seldom stand next to the dresser when I return my interminable series of daily calls.

- "We-know-you-steal-the-hangers." If you charge me $200 a night for a room, why must you then assume that my vocation is stealing coat hangers? Or why do you care if I do, at that rate? (Actually, NSH's—no-steal hangers— are right up there with no peanuts on the rankle rating.)

- "Room service." I use quotation marks, because, well . . . First, I called to place my breakfast order. They asked for my room number. (Fair enough, if slightly irritating, since I've gotten used to hotels with computer systems that automatically ID the caller's room number.) Then they ask my name. Huh? Then they ask for my "account number"—whatever the hell that is. (Oops, I remember. They gave me some goddam card when I checked in. But I don't carry it in my underpants pocket when I call for room service.) To top it off, I'm informed that it will take 30 to 45 minutes to get my breakfast. Zounds! Well, they were close—43 minutes, to be precise. (I've never sent a meal or bottle of wine back at a restaurant, but the melon *was* inedible—and this was Florida. It tasted like a sickly product from the shelves of the Grand Union in Vermont in February.)

- The message light! When I checked in, I collected my faxes (several). When I got to my room, my message light was on—so I called and was told I had faxes. "I picked them up," I said. The message light stayed on. Hey, nobody's perfect, and besides, it's just an eye-level adult version of the kiddie night-light, right? The next morning, light still on, I called again. Faxes, they said. I assumed they meant the same ones. Now the light went out. When I got back from my walk, the light was on again. Called in again. Faxes. Okay, *must* be new ones. I put my sweats back on and trudged the hundred yards or so to the front desk. No faxes. Leftover from last night. Come on!

• Dirty ashtrays. There was an ashtray next to the elevator closest to my room. It was dirty when I checked in at 10:00 p.m. And dirty when I went out to walk at 6:30 a.m.—i.e., cigarette butts, papers, yuck. Maybe I wouldn't have noticed, but . . . a couple of months before I was at the Disneyland Marriott. I got up to walk at 4:45 a.m. Two young men were in the lobby, *washing the leaves of the plants.* And, of course, at 4:45 a.m. all the Marriott ashtrays were spotless (even though they'd been dirty from still-active revelers when I got in after midnight the night before).

My ire at this resort stems less from the "little" sins per se than from their inexcusability. Fixing all of them, as best I can figure, would not cost a red cent. As I see it, the owners have jeopardized a huge investment by blowing it on a dozen little oversights (which I saw in the course of just 10 hours). By the way, "jeopardize" is not too strong a word: Other guests I chatted with were irritated as well. The point is not that location (as in "location, location, location") is *un*important, and that service is *all*-important. Instead, it's a reminder of how easy it is to squander the most extraordinary advantage. (Perception really *is* nutty! I must admit they nearly won me over. It was so bad that I started to feel as if I'd stopped at Fawlty Towers, which made it almost fun. Was it John Cleese who was manipulating that message light?)

Why ask the reader to relive my petty little gripes? Because it's just such "petty little gripes" that *don't* get written about in B-I-G, sweeping books on competitiveness, or even in books on "the 117 basics of customer service." But in a world dominated by *fashion*, where the retail or commercial customer confronts an exploding array of choices of everything, the little things—*and especially the sum of the little things*—are *the* name of *the* new game.

BEWITCHED, BOTHERED, AND BEWILDERED ABOUT BALDRIGE

I knew my hope was futile—that the powers-that-be would reach out somehow and award the 1991 Malcolm Baldrige National Quality Award to The J. Peterman Company of Lexington, Kentucky. Oh, but I wish they had! Consider this description of J. Peterman, which appeared in *GQ* (November 1991):

The J. Peterman catalogue, all ninety or so unslick, understated pages of it, is mail order of a higher order—a catalogue even a tree spiker could love. No windswept, glistening-skinned models staring soulfully into the distance. No dreary salespeak. Instead, the copy is wry and rugged and clean as a dry martini—as if the ghosts of Cole Porter and Ernest Hemingway had set up shop on Madison Avenue, writing pint-size stories set in exotic locations and peopled with urbane characters who just happen to be trying to sell you something. An authentic navy peacoat, for instance. Or a tie like one Clark Gable once wore onscreen, available in both blue and maroon. "Gable wore one or the other. We'll never know which. The movie was black and white," pens the copywriter with an insouciant shrug of his invisible shoulders.

On the page titled, "New York Fireman's Coat," the text begins, "Stop thinking fires. Think white-water boating, going to auctions, looking at real estate, driving vintage race cars, or just driving your kids north at Christmastime in order to cut the best-looking tree anybody ever saw." Below it, a watercolor of the coat that's evoked rests regally against a plain white background.

No wonder Larry Hagman had to have one. Paul Newman, on the other hand, prefers the duster. And Oprah Winfrey is rumored to have one of everything. (In a range of sizes, presumably.) She even interrupted the continuous loop of crackheads and codependents to devote a segment of one show to the catalogue's founder, [John Peterman]. . . .

The seeds for the catalogue were planted five years ago, when [Peterman] stopped to consider how many times a stranger had chased him down the street to ask where he'd found his full-length canvas duster. . . . Explains Peterman, "I don't believe in focus groups, and I'm slightly jaded on 'experts.'" He does, however, believe in tracking down the perfectly realized item, which, before he discovered it, you never realized you couldn't live without—including a plain muslin "Thomas Jefferson" shirt and a set of bracelets that prevent motion sickness. . . .

"People want things that are hard to find. Things that have romance, but a factual romance, about them," [Peterman says.] Can a bracelet that fends off motion sickness be romantic? Read the catalogue. Ten bucks says you'll order a set.

I'm a J. Peterman fan, and a regular buyer (my long-billed Hemingway hat helped me survive Bangkok's scorching sun during a 1992 hot-season visit). Yet I'm all but certain the company will never will win a Baldrige. If you'd ever looked at the award's application, brought to you by engineers and statisticians from our very own National Institute of Standards and Technology at the U.S. Department of Commerce, you'd know why. With all due respect, I have a nagging feeling that standards and technology "types" might not get the same "buzz" from J. Peterman that I do. Uhm, how do you quantify "buzz," guys?

I'm a big supporter of the Baldrige, believe it or not. It's taken us a long,

long way toward putting quality on the American map in a short, short while ("long, long way in a short, short while"—whoops, sorry techies, another qualitative judgment). And, boy, did we/do we need that! So "A" grades for spirit, intent, and above all symbolism. Yet I'm troubled that the Baldrige celebrates a lifeless form of quality which, while better than nothing, misses by hours tomorrow's crowded competitive boat. ("Better to make good, statistically reliable products that customers don't want than crappy ones that customers don't want," says a friend trying to put a positive spin on it.)

An October 1990 *Business Week* cover story clinched my concerns. The feature overflows with the D-word: *dazzle*. (Glow, tingle, wow—and dazzle.) Chairman Kenichi Yamamoto of Mazda dismissively notes that "any manufacturer can produce according to statistics." (Sorry, Dr. Deming.) *Business Week* reports that Japan has turned its attention (obsession!) to "*miryokuteki hinshitsu*," or "things gone right." (A traditional Detroit measurement of quality has been TGW, things gone wrong, or defects.) This "second phase" of quality, as the Japanese see it, moves beyond "*atarimae hinshitsu*," or "taken for granted" (statistically up to snuff) quality. A Mitsubishi exec says the new idea is the "personality of the product."

Product developer Paul Sherlock put Ziploc bags and Velcro at the top of his favorite products list. Why? "Neat." Ziploc. Velcro. Lexus. Acura. Post-its. The United Colors of Benetton. . . . Apple Computer. Sony. Sun Microsystems. Microsoft. . . . The Body Shop. Olivetti. Nordstrom. . . . Ford in 1915. IBM in 1960. People Express in 1983. (Not to mention J. Peterman!) When I think of these products or firms I think mostly about those taboo words— "dazzle," "glow," "bewitch," "tingle," "personality," "delight," "wow."

Sure, statistically reliable output is a big part of the "quality" story. I don't deny that for a moment. And I certainly don't belittle the need, even in 1992, for 99 percent of American firms, tiny or tremendous, to measure quality, to do their SPC (statistical process control), and to get much more reliable. But let us not, for a nanosecond, think that's the whole quality picture.

Quality and competitiveness are synonymous. But first you've got to get your definition of quality "right." For a rousing start, send away today for your very own J. Peterman Company catalog. Reviewing it, whether you are a biochemist or burger maven, may do your economic welfare a lot more good than perusing a Baldrige application.

Firmness, Commodity, Delight

Microsoft's Bill Gates says good software should exhibit "firmness" (consistency), "commodity" (be "worthy of the user's time and effort in understanding it") and "delight" ("engagement," "fun"). You wanna tell Gates he's all wet and doesn't understand his business? I don't.

Nothing Wrong Equals Nothing Right, or, How to Lose the Quality Wars

Nary a TGW! That is, nothing went wrong yesterday, a lazy Sunday. I didn't fall off my horse, Frequent Flyer. I didn't smash a thumb with a three-pound hammer during home-improvement hour.

Nonetheless, something *was* wrong. I *did* go riding, but I didn't gallop or try any new twist on a familiar theme. My 10 thumbs *did* survive my household "project," but I didn't put much zing into it. So while nothing went really wrong on Sunday, nothing went especially right, either. The same might at times be said about America's quality wars.

Motorola was one of the first of those Baldrige winners, in 1988. And the firm is keeping the pressure on, pursuing "six-sigma quality." (The Greek letter sigma is used in statistical analysis to represent "standard deviations" from the mean. Six-sigma quality amounts to 3.4 defects per million units—better than doctors at prescription writing, nowhere near as good as airlines at safety.) In the July–August 1990 *Harvard Business Review*, Motorola training chief Bill Wiggenhorn wrote that "the Six Sigma process means changing the way people do things so that nothing can go wrong." He illustrated with the case of a Motorola *chef* (at the huge training facility, Motorola University, in Schaumburg, Illinois). The fellow already made a six-sigma chocolate-chip cookie, said Wiggenhorn; the goal was getting him to improve his muffins to the same standard of excellence. Wiggenhorn was using the mundane example of the chef to make a larger point. He succeeded: He set off alarm bells.

Stick with cookies. I've never gotten sick from one of Mrs. Fields' or David's chocolate-chip cookies. So I assume these cookie-makers have first-rate quality-control systems—I'm hardly knocking their (or Motorola's) devotion to such systems as a competitive weapon. Nonetheless, let's consider the origins of the Mrs. Fields' enterprise, which was launched just four blocks from my Palo Alto office.

I've visited that premier location more than once—many, many times more. Mrs. F. makes great, yummy, gooey, sinful, chocolatey chocolate-chip cookies. And I think I can picture young Debbi Fields at the stove in the early days, smeared with chocolate, smacking her lips, revising the recipe over and over again, trying to figure out how to jam even *more* chocolate into her little calorie bombs. Chocolate's splattered all over her and the kitchen, reminiscent of Julia Child on PBS. What I *cannot* imagine is Debbi F. turning to her husband and future business partner, Randy, at the end of another day of struggle, and saying, "I made great progress, hon, toward my six-sigma cookie goal." Can you?

Wiggenhorn explained, in part, how his chef became a six-sigma man. It turns out that the guy wasn't trusted with the key to the freezer, and had to make his dough the night before. Following the new approach, which aims to remove all impediments to perfection, the chef is now allowed access to the freezer. Great! (Do I like that? Of course! Reread the last several hundred pages of this book.)

Nonetheless, those alarm bells keep clanging. I cheer Motorola's goal, but I worry a lot about any system aimed at ensuring that "nothing can go wrong." Six-sigma quality means improving and changing, to be sure, not accepting the status quo; even the trivial case of the chef and the locked refrigerator makes that clear. Yet the pursuit of greatness—high tech or mouth-watering new cookies such as those by Mrs. Fields—is as much or more about flair, grotesque mistakes, eccentricity, and passion as it is about "fail-proof" systems.

In short, reduce to zero the odds of something going wrong and you'll also reduce to zero the odds of anything interesting happening. My Sunday was a fine, six-sigma day—error-free, that is. Another 1,500 Sundays like that and, actuarially speaking, I'll be perfectly dead.

Sweet Corn and Business Strategy

"Stew Leonard, Jr., tells a story about his father, whose name adorns a famous Norwalk, Connecticut, food store. Stew Jr., 36, runs the store now, under his father's watchful eye. A couple of years ago, Stew Jr. and his brother, Tom, and some other managers from the store were getting ready to meet with a high-powered, high-priced consultant. Stew Sr. couldn't attend the meeting, so Stew Jr. asked him on the phone if there was anything particularly important he wanted discussed.

" 'I bought some corn yesterday,' Stew Sr. replied, 'and had it for dinner last night, and it wasn't really sweet.'

"Stew Jr. gently remonstrated with his father: 'Dad, this isn't that kind of meeting. We're talking about strategy, we're talking about merchandising. Isn't there anything really important that you want me to mention?'

" 'Yeah. The corn isn't really, really sweet.'

"From there, Stew Jr. recalls, their conversation turned immediately to how to get corn into the store the day it was picked. . . .

"The lesson of the story is not that Stew Leonard is obsessed with details. He used to be, he admits—he would walk into the store, hand some employee a clipboard with a yellow legal pad on it, and say, 'You write 'em down as I go around. Look at the cracked eggs, look at the dirty windows.' But he doesn't do that anymore. Instead, he focuses intently on details that matter—like sweet corn."

Nation's Business
June 1991

Riding Perception to Transformation

The magic of Disney is its commitment to *excitement*. And a lot of that magic—remember our discussion of carnivals—comes courtesy of the well-oiled underpark that allows the excitement to take place. The magic of Stew Leonard's is Stew's favorite word—*Wow!* But wow only "works" because the underlying systems are in place. So don't read these last few pages as knocking quality's new basics. I do, however, suggest that we should not leave quality to the technocrats. We've got to get our SPC act together, come up to Disney's fabulous underpark standards. But we've also got to understand that that's half the story at best.

Take the great location away from that resort hotel in Florida, and nobody would have come in the first place. You can be sure of that. (And you can be sure that I'm sure of that.) But having spent a ton on location, the owners proceeded to risk the whole kitty by ignoring the access to the morning newspaper. Good location. Great underpark. Amen. Newspapers in the morning. Sweet corn that's sweet. Amen. You need it *all*—but unfortunately (those damnable flipping fractions) we normally put 90 percent of our effort into location, 10 percent into things like newspapers at breakfast. In this crowded, fickle, madcap world, it ought to be darn near the other way around.

In the end, it's simple, OK?

(1) "product" + intangibles > "product."

In nonmathematical terms, a "product" (basic technical product or service offering) plus intangibles adds up to more than the technical offering. Of course. But in fact, it's more than "just" more than—a lot more. Professors Gary Eppen, Ward Hanson, and Kipp Martin, writing in the Summer 1991 issue of the *Sloan Management Review*, claim that a product (baseball season tickets) plus "soft" add-ons (special parking privileges) equals a *new* product. The idea is fundamental, and mostly missed. Clean ashtrays and readily available newspapers make that Florida resort I maligned into a *new resort*. That is,

(2) "product" + intangibles = *new* product.

Sometimes the addition of intangibles creates even more—a whole new industry. Apple's "softening" of computers created a new industry. So, too, did Federal Express's new definition of reliable delivery.

The Wall Street Journal reported on an Australian study of 48 cancer patients. Immediately after a patient visit, Dr. M. H. N. Tattersall dictated a letter to 24 of the patients summarizing the visit. No letter was sent to the other 24. During follow-up interviews, those who had received the letters ranked their overall satisfaction with the physician higher—13 of the 24 who got letters were "completely satisfied," compared to 4 of the 24 who didn't.

Letter recipients were also more satisfied with the doctor's explanation, remembered more of what they were told, and felt that they'd had a better opportunity to ask questions. To top it off, the satisfaction scores of letter recipients and no-letter patients were higher among those who had received bad news than among those who'd had positive prognoses. In short, a technically sound consultation *with* a letter is an entirely different product/service offering than the same technically sound consultation without the correspondence.

Po Lo and the Baldrige

If I were running the Baldrige process, would-be "examiners" (who assess applications) would be required to declaim for 15 minutes on the following, from J. D. Salinger's *Raise High the Roof-Beam, Carpenters*:

> Duke Mu of Chin said to Po Lo: "You are now advanced in years. Is there any member of your family whom I could employ to look for horses in your stead?" Po Lo replied: "A good horse can be picked out by its general build and appearance. But the superlative horse—one that raises no dust and leaves no tracks—is something evanescent and fleeting, elusive as thin air. The talents of my sons lie on a lower plane altogether; they can tell a good horse when they see one, but they cannot tell a superlative horse. I have a friend, however, one Chiu-fang Kao, a hawker of fuel and vegetables, who in things appertaining to horses is nowise my inferior. Pray see him."
>
> Duke Mu did so, and subsequently dispatched him on the quest for a steed. Three months later, he returned with the news that he had found one. "It is now in Shach'iu," he added. "What kind of a horse is it? asked the Duke. "Oh, it is a dun-colored mare," was the reply. However, someone being sent to fetch it, the animal turned out to be a coal-black stallion! Much displeased, the Duke sent for Po Lo. "That friend of yours," he said, "whom I commissioned to look for a horse, has made a fine mess of it. Why, he cannot even distinguish a beast's color or sex! What on earth can he know about horses?" Po Lo heaved a sigh of satisfaction. "Has he really got as far as that?" he cried. "Ah, then he is worth ten thousand of me put together. There is no comparison between us. What Kao keeps in view is the spiritual mechanism. In making sure of the essential, he forgets the homely details; intent on the inward qualities, he loses sight of the external. He sees what he wants to see, and not what he does not want to see. He looks at the things he

ought to look at, and neglects those that need not be looked at. So clever a judge of horses is Kao, that he has it in him to judge something better than horses."

When the horse arrived, it turned out indeed to be a superlative animal.

44

Follow the Yellow Brick Road (to Better Instruction Manuals)

Intelligence-added, intangibles, a touch of Wow: They're an increasing share of any advanced economy's total added value. Differentiation gets harder and harder as the market gets ever more crowded. Has it ever occurred to you that customer instruction manuals could be a unique—and surprisingly sustainable—strategic advantage? (That's right: strategic *and* sustainable were the words I chose.) It has occurred to *ACCESSGuide* series creator Richard Saul Wurman. (Oh, how I "love" those guides!) His *Follow the Yellow Brick Road* is all about instruction. "No one seems to know who writes [instruction manuals] or even where they come from," Wurman claims. He set his colleague Loring Leifer the task of finding out. Her amazing saga is reprinted here in full:

> Most of the people I talked to had a different version of the spontaneous generation theory.
>
> - "Our manuals are developed by the individual manufacturers."
> - "They just come in a box. I don't know who writes them. We just distribute them."
> - "I have no idea. I suppose it's someone over in Korea. We just get them already written."
> - "Gee, I don't know. I'll see if I can find out for you." Fat chance.
>
> My first attempt was with Sears, Roebuck. I figured everyone has owned some piece of equipment from Sears at some point in his/her life. I was transferred six times, from a Sears store in the Bronx, to the Parts

Department in Mount Vernon, New York, to what I thought was the Sears executive office in the Sears Tower in Chicago, which turned out to be the real estate office.

In Mount Vernon, a parts representative said that they are on a computer system and the only way she could order manuals was by the model number. (Sears must have taken lessons from the U.S. Army.) I explained that I was doing research for a book and was trying to locate the department where the manuals were produced. The determined and rather single-minded representative kept asking for a model number; I kept explaining that I was working on a book. She said, "Doesn't your mother have a Sears refrigerator?" Apparently, she thought Sears equipment was even more ubiquitous than I did.

The Parts Department didn't seem to have any idea where the manuals came from or who wrote them, nor did it have a desire to know.

Finally, I got in touch with Manny Banayo, manager of public affairs in the Chicago headquarters. He told me to write Jim Podany, who was the person in his department who could help me. On February 3, 1989, I wrote a letter explaining what I wanted. I am a patient person, but when he didn't respond by September 18 of that year, I decided to call him. A secretary told me that John Summers, the marketing manager for Sears appliances, was the man to contact. Summers returned my call promptly and even commiserated with me, saying that he was always buying appliances with manuals that were written by someone in another language and then translated into English by someone who didn't seem to be able to understand it. When I asked him where Sears operating manuals were written, he said he didn't know, but that he thought they were written by "different people," sometimes in marketing, sometimes by the individual manufacturers.

I asked him to send manuals for electronic equipment, such as a VCR and assembly instructions for a bike, which he did. Now optimistic, I decided to explore further. In February 1990, I called him back to ask more about the process for developing the manuals. He said that he was moving on to a new job and I should call Jackie Bitowt after the first week in March after she got back from her vacation. She was the new marketing/communications manager for home products. After three days of calling her office, I got her on the phone March 8. She said that she couldn't help me without a letter. I explained that I had written to other people in her office already. She said she would need to see a letter and that John Summers was out of the office until Monday. Then she said, "Since the reorganization, we're just trying to get the job done. It is unlikely that Sears would participate in your book."

I didn't need the entire Sears organization to write the book. I just wanted to talk to one person who had something to do with the Sears manuals. I explained this to her.

She answered politely, "There hardly is a department."

I gave up on Sears and decided to try Panasonic.

Panasonic has a phone system that makes callers feel like they are trying to break into Fort Knox. Its multi-tiered recorded instructions offer so many options and buttons to press that even the most focused individual is likely to forget why he or she called the company in the first place. If you are calling for information regarding a piece of Panasonic equipment, if you are calling for service, if you are calling for directions to our Secaucus store, there's a number to press. My index finger started to ache. Finally, I pressed the right series of buttons and Michael Maggio in customer service suggested that I call Ron Tomcyk in public relations. He [Ron Tomcyk] said that he thought about 90 percent of the manuals were written in Japan and that a couple of engineers in the United States revised them for the U.S. market. For any more information, I would have to call Justin Camerlengo, the general manager of corporate communications, he said. I left three messages and [Camerlengo] didn't return any of them. Apparently people can be just as impenetrable as recorded phone messages. A few days later, Ann Ballas called in his behalf. She said that the manuals were written in Japan, where the equipment was manufactured. She suggested that I might try calling Jerry Surprise, who was the product manager at the facility in Chicago or Mike Collichio in consumer relations.

The trail seemed to be disappearing, so I decided to try Sony.

Several calls later, I found Lloyd Barningham in Kansas City. He is in charge of distributing the operating manuals for Sony products. He says they are written in Japan and get sent over in a box and that he just distributes them. He did send a few examples of operating instructions, but I decided such passive acceptance of life wasn't going to get answers to my questions.

I began to suspect that there must be a secret program to mask the identity of manual writers along the lines of the Federal Witness Protection Program. I imagined this Manual-Writers Protection Program was probably designed to protect the lives of writers and their families from irate consumers who can't figure out how to record *Cheers* on their VCRs.

Suspicious, but still determined, I went on to General Electric. I have a General Electric refrigerator and I always thought the manual for it was quite helpful. Not only did it include understandable information on the installation, use, and maintenance of the unit, but it had material on how long different animal products would last in the refrigerator or the freezer. There were even instructions on how to get the racks out of the unit if the door couldn't be opened all the way.

The manual had a phone number to call for more information. It was in large type and on the first page. I am always suspicious of product manuals that have no phone number and sometimes even no address so that you couldn't possibly track down the company to ask any questions about its products. General Electric went out of its way to broadcast its accessibility. I also thought the manual was particularly well written.

So at noon on Friday, June 30, 1989, I called the GE Answer Center number to try to find the person who wrote the manual to tell him or her what a fine job I thought he or she was doing. To my great surprise, a live human voice answered after the first ring and identified himself as Mr. Miller. Explaining that the manuals weren't written in his office, he suggested that I write to the Customer Relations office in Louisville, Kentucky. I decided to call instead. Directory Assistance didn't have the number for that department, but an operator connected me with Customer Relations, which was answered by a machine that informed me that someone would call me back if I left my name and number. One hour and nine minutes later, a woman named Tonie Sullivan returned my call and promised to try to locate the author of the manual. At 3:22 PM she called to tell me that a Jean Hopwood would be able to help me, but she would be on vacation until July 24.

Meanwhile, I called the GE Answer Center to get other examples of GE instructions. An operator politely told me that I would have to have a model number, but that she would be happy to send me two catalogs of GE products. She explained that Thomson Consumer Electronics, Inc., had purchased the GE line of TVs, stereos, VCRs, radios and telephones, but that GE retained the home appliance division. After receiving the catalogs, I called the Answer Center to order instructions, but they became suspicious when I wanted so many different model numbers and said that this service was for owners of GE appliances. The operator suggested that I call Thomson directly.

Someone in the Louisville office told me to call Edith Garrett in Customer Relations and gave me a telephone number that turned out to be that of TCE Technical Publications. An operator told me that for $3.50 apiece, I could order any manual that I wanted. I inquired if this was the department where the manuals were written; she said she had no idea where they were written, but I could call the RCA referral number. An operator, who identified herself as Rosemary, heard my questions and rather aggressively wanted to know "Who gave you this number?" I think she was trained by the CIA. She said, with Secret Service pride, "I don't have any information." I didn't exactly threaten her with bamboo splints under the fingernails. Only my polite determination was able to get her to give me the Consumer Relations number, which was answered by a machine that offered me several confusing options. Number 4 was for operating manuals, but when I pressed the button, I got the same number I'd called before in Louisville. I had to hang up and dial again. I pressed number 5 this time for customer service and got another recorded voice promising options for various appliances.

At a point of total discouragement, a sympathetic man in the TV division let me talk to Dan Romisher, who used to work in technical publications. Dan actually divulged the names of the two women who were responsible for RCA and GE electronic equipment manuals. Pay dirt at last.

I actually had an extended conversation with a real, live, articulate person who, while she didn't compose the manuals from scratch, was responsible for adapting them for American consumers. Suzanne Deem was an administrator for consumer publications at Thomson (which makes GE electronic equipment). "We are supplied with a draft of operation instructions. We have developed a format for manuals based on meetings with merchandising, marketing, engineering, and product-planning people. We also use our common sense. When you receive a product, what is the first thing you do? You would open the package and take out the paperwork and read it. We start with the safety instructions first, followed by a table of contents, then a product features page, and then the operating instructions.

"Common sense tells us that this is the order of importance. But our vendors tell us that people don't read the manuals.

"Our manuals come in pidgin English. They are supplied by the manufacturers, who are often Korean or Japanese. It is a real headache. Because of the scheduling and the fact that the manual has to be ready in time to be packed into the box, we have to write or rewrite a manual while they are still making changes in the product. Sometimes we don't even get a workable unit on which to write a manual. For example, we are working right now on instructions for a TV. The software is being developed in Germany; the parts for the TV are being manufactured in Singapore; and it is being assembled in Taiwan. Product modifications are possible at any of these points. We're pressed for time. This process depends on a high level of communication between all these points and that's not easy when you are dealing with different people in different parts of the world who all speak different languages. It's a lot of anxiety. We're ready to print the manuals and we find out that the software is incorrect. If the manual is wrong, it's my fault," she said.

"There are 14 people in the technical-publications department, but only two of us who produce the owner's manual. We do about 40 a year. The rest of the people work in technical training and service data. "I have a bachelor's degree in business education with a minor in library science. Many in the tech pub field come from an English major background. The supervisor here tries to get nontechnical people because they are more likely to be able to communicate with consumers than the engineers who talk like engineers.

"In the first 5,000 pieces of equipment, RCA puts a questionnaire into the owner's manual. We are always open to suggestions and we review and modify manuals based on consumer feedback."

When asked if she was good at understanding manuals, she said, "I never read them. I always have my husband do it. I'm learning though. My brother and his friends, most of whom have master's degrees, couldn't figure out how to program a VCR and I was able to do it, but it wasn't easy.

"Our warranty department did a survey and found that 92 percent of the people could understand our VCR manuals. TVs got a slightly higher rating."

It adds up to wonderful confirmation of the importance of the "mostly unmanaged 116/129 fraction," eh? What an extraordinary opportunity! (By the way, I think I'll send a copy of this chapter to all the Baldrige "examiners." I suspect they never went to the trouble Loring Leifer did. They would have, had they truly been interested in "quality.")

On the Missing #8096 Left Hinge and Other Items

A letter I received certifies, in frustrating detail, the concerns implicit in Loring Leifer's account:

June 8, 1992

Sunbeam Outdoor Products Group
P.O. Box J
Neosho MO 64850

Gentlemen:

I recently purchased the Sunbeam Model 8032P Smoker Grill. I am pleased with the unit, now that the assembly is behind me, but feel that you could make some improvements in your documentation. Incidentally, it took over two hours to put your grill together. This time could be shortened with better instructions and some slight changes to the product.

First, I found the illustrations to be confusing. In attempting to orient the front & back etc., my shell and hole-pattern did not match any of the diagrams. I think that you have changed the manufactured product without updating the instructions and the parts list.

1. I really puzzled over the "stiffener," until at the end I found this part left over. It would help if you pointed to the stiffener and identified it (Step #1).

2. It is very difficult to attach the midtray brackets to the legs. There is just not room to get a screwdriver alongside the bracket and

have enough grip to drive a self-threading screw. A thru hole with a bolt and nut would help this a great deal.

3. There are too many different length screws. I believe that with a little study, the size range could be reduced, making it less of a problem for the user to select the proper one.

4. Step 2 should give explicit instructions to leave the bolts out of the bottom holes for Step 5. I missed this (which is easy to do) and had to remove them later.

5. I did not have a #8096 Left Hinge as noted in Step 3. Instead I had two #8095 parts.

6. The manner in which the link brace, hinge, etc. fasten to the Top Shell is not clear in the diagram (Step 3, Step 5 & Step 9). This needs a lot of help in order to be easily understood.

7. Some of the acorn nuts are regular nuts while some have nylon locking inserts. The instructions do not indicate which ones are to be used for which attachments.

8. I have some parts left over, but I have no idea where they go. This is a little disconcerting, as you can imagine.

I hope you will find my comments useful. I would also like for you to ship the missing #8096 Left Hinge noted in Item #5 above, as soon as possible.

Sincerely,

Dick Freshley
Gig Harbor, WA

cc: Tom Peters
    Consumer Reports

45

Building "Wow Factories"

High time we operationalize this "stuff." "Operationalize 'Wow'?" you say. "I thought the point was to preserve the mystique." Yes and no. There are some practical steps we can take—for one, lavish love and attention on the authors of instruction manuals, I should think. And there are some ways to work on mindset—i.e., get "wow-stuff" on the corporate agenda. That's what follows. But it is true that any of the following ideas can become hopelessly elaborate, and end up stamping out rather than encouraging "wowdom" throughout the organization. So even as you read and nod your head in agreement, beware. . . .

DEFINITIONS: TOWARD SYMBIOSIS AND INTERTWINING

A cultural revolution is taking place at Boeing. . . . It has adopted a more open stance towards the outside world and is encouraging airlines, suppliers and subcontractors to participate actively in the design of its latest airliner, the 777 wide-body twin engine jet. In the past, Boeing felt it knew what was best for its airline customers. "But with the 777, Boeing has for the first time given us direct access to the process of designing an aircraft," says Mr. James O'Sullivan, British Airways' chief project engineer on the 777 program.

Financial Times
May 7, 1992

Listen to customers. It was a message that marked each of my first three books. And a useful one—to a point. The problem is that exhorting people to listen, or even "installing" a raft of listening techniques, doesn't get you very far if you've got much of a hierarchy in place. It's not much of an exaggeration to say that the whole Beyond Hierarchy section was about listening to customers, or, rather, how to make intense listening automatic—i.e., inescapable, as at Acordia, IDG, CCT, EDS, and McKinsey.

But there's still more. A lot more, in fact. Even "inescapable" listening implies a degree of passivity. Recall CRSS, David Kelly Design, Imagination, and Chiat/Day/Mojo. At first blush, they are four of the world's premier "listeners." Think harder, though, and you'll quickly realize that they've gone far beyond listening: Their special ways of "hanging out" consistently lead them to invent products and services jointly with clients that neither they nor the clients had ever dreamed of. Let's ponder, then, "beyond listening," even "beyond automatic inescapable listening." How about *symbiosis*? Or *intertwining*?

Message to managers: In a 116/129 (Wow!) world, symbiosis/intertwining is strategy.

PURSUING CUSTOMER *COMMITMENT*

Beyond *listening* to customers to *intertwining* with them. And, of a piece, beyond *satisfied* customers to *committed* customers. "*Satisfied* customers remain independent from the firm," University of Michigan professor Dave Ulrich wrote in the Summer 1989 issue of *Sloan Management Review*. "Committed customers become interdependent with the firm through shared resources and values." The chief lever for moving from mere customer satisfaction to more encompassing customer commitment ("unity with customers"), he says, is that most "internally" oriented of management processes—"human resource" activities. Ulrich enumerates five traditionally sacrosanct areas of personnel management that can be recast to induce customer engagement with the firm:

— Appointments and promotions. Ulrich cites an office products company that has customers offer criteria for the selection of candidates who will subsequently become their account representatives. Then those customers review the finalists' curricula vitae. Having been involved in the decision from start to finish, Ulrich observes, the customer has a higher stake in making the rep (and hence the relationship) successful. He also reports, for example, that GE human resource staffers routinely solicit and use customer feedback in promotion decisions and succession planning.

— Performance appraisal. At one computer company plant, Ulrich found that customers virtually determine criteria for performance appraisal of line workers and managers; they even help the plant's staffers design the appraisal forms. Customers subsequently provide much of the information that goes into the appraisal.

—Training and development. Ulrich provides numerous examples of firms that have customers directly involved in product or service providers' sales, service, and technical training programs. For instance, appliance-maker Whirlpool routinely asks Sears execs to make presentations in its training programs. Ulrich discovered customers engaged in course design, too. In several situations, company trainers visited customers to perform a "needs analysis," which helped them determine the overall training curriculum.

—Customer-commitment incentives. Consider the case of an international protective services company: Every quarter, 25 percent of each branch's customers fill out a 50-question survey that directly focuses on long-term customer commitment (beyond current satisfaction or dissatisfaction). Fifty percent of the branch manager's financial incentive, Ulrich reports, depends directly on the survey outcome.

—Corporate communications. Ulrich's research unearthed examples ranging from the regular inclusion of columns written by customers in company newsletters to major "how-you-are-doing" presentations by customers at annual employee meetings.

Add it up—which is the point—and you've got the outline of a comprehensive approach to bringing the customer all the way into the corporate fold. And another case for strong language: to wit, symbiosis.

CONVERSING WITH CUSTOMERS

Recall that Williams-Sonoma cookware stores feature demonstrations and training sessions for customers almost every day. And don't forget the thousands of customers Trumpf works with and trains at its munificent demonstration center. At The Body Shop, Anita Roddick has made "conversations" with customers a strategic obsession to the point that the huge firm feels no need to do any advertising—in one of the world's most advertising-intense industries. But few understand customer-training-and-product-knowledge-as-strategy better than $5.1-billion (1991 revenue) Home Depot, king of the do-it-yourselfers. (Yes, "as strategy." These ideas are pure soul, not "service tactics.")

Home Depot

My colleague David Graulich reported: It's 7:14 a.m. and the subject is fertilizer. Ron Whited, head of the nursery department for the Home Depot store in Sunnyvale, California, holds up a wedge of cheddar, a package of bologna, and three slices of white bread. (Whited and several others have taken on new assignments since our research was completed.) "Fertilizer is to plants as food is to people," he says, gesturing with the cheese. "But just like too much Vitamin A is bad for your liver, a lawn can overdose on, say, nitrogen. If a customer lays the nitrogen on too heavy, next thing you know he's going to have stripes on his lawn and he'll come back mad at us."

Whited's "students" are 26 Home Depot employees, including sales-people, cashiers, and "lot men," who help customers with packages in the parking lot. All attendees at this in-store Saturday-morning class, on which we're sitting in, are paid for their time. In a typical month, 15 "product-knowledge classes" will be taught at the store, on everything from fertilizer to garage-door openers. For Home Depot, which invented the warehouse do-it-yourself concept with its first three Atlanta stores in 1979, such classes are the key ("our secret weapon," per merchandising VP Jim Inglis) to staving off a swarm of big new competitors, such as Builders Square and Lowe's.

Scott Manning, Sunnyvale store manager, decides which products to emphasize. With the start of what he calls "the springtime redwood season" in Northern California, the Sunnyvale store is stressing garden products and lawn care. The fertilizer class, for example, is held an hour before the store's 8:00 a.m. opening and includes employees of the nursery as well as the adjoining lumber and building materials department (so that customers with gardening questions can be guided to the right place). Steve Noren, regional manager for the company's five Northern California sites, explains: "Cashiers may see a customer leaving with a can of paint and ask if she has a paintbrush. A lot man may be loading a door onto someone's truck and ask if he remembered to buy hinges." Cashiers periodically participate in "store walk-throughs," so they'll know how to direct customers through the cavernous stores, which range between 67,000 and 140,000 square feet and stock some 30,000 products (compared with a typical home center's 10,000).

Employees typically receive 20 hours of training a month, including product classes taught on-site by vendors. But Steve Noren insists that "the classes taught by fellow employees are more real-world, because they know the questions customers are asking." Sometimes, Noren says, "We'll ask one of the least-informed salespeople to teach the class and give him three weeks to prepare. We want everyone to be knowledgeable about the products." (Employees also teach fellow employees by remote control—via Home Depot's proprietary satellite television network.)

Founders Pat Farrah, Bernard Marcus, and Arthur Blank, the original trainers in the Atlanta stores, have made the training and product-knowledge credo an integral part of the corporate culture. The three still personally instruct new manager trainees—and all senior officers are expected to do likewise. "No one gets into management without getting into training," Jim Inglis says.

Home Depot also routinely offers customers free "project demonstrations" and "clinics." Typical topics are "how to install skylights" and "how to build glass-block walls." The most popular clinic in the Sunnyvale store, when we visited, was "how to install ceramic tile." On the Saturday morning David Graulich dropped in, 30 customers crowded around a demonstration table near Cash Register 15. Matthew Pegues, who runs the flooring department, showed how to lay patterns of tile and hand-mix batches of grout, while dispensing a steady patter of advice—and a low-key sales pitch. "Make sure you have a pair of knee-pads to do this," he said. "You should buy about ten percent more tile than you need to allow for breakage and replacement—if you buy new tile later the colors won't match." Customers craned their necks and peppered Pegues with questions.

After classes like these, Manning says, customers are likely to buy their materials at Home Depot. (Cynics might claim that would-be customers attend such sessions, then seek out the lowest-cost provider. True occasionally—but rarely.) "There are people who would not have bought tile from anybody because they're scared," says Manning. Chet Czysen, the personnel director, adds, "Our customer is Joe Blow up the street. He's a do-it-yourselfer, but it's the first time he's done it. The fear factor is the biggest thing we have to overcome. That's why we offer all the training."

Potatoes with Pedigrees

"When [retailer] Paul Hawken [Smith & Hawken] went tramping through farm fields, he was less in search of the perfect potato than the pedigree he could attach to the bag. He was after the farmer who could grow the crop by use of a prescribed organic process. The result looked the same as any other, but Hawken knew there was a market for *the information* that the product was created a certain way. As a result, he sold fruits and vegetables in a bag with a descriptive label providing such information as a farmer's name, the location of his farm, fertilizers used, date grown, or any other information he thought was important to the natural food buyer. He sold the growing method, more compelling to the ultimate purchaser than the product itself. Was Paul Hawken selling a product or providing an information service? Where was the value added? What was the substance of the value added?"

Charles Leinbach
"Purchasing the Design of Service"
Design Management Journal, Winter 1992

TRUST THROUGH GUARANTEES THAT "THRILL"

Orvis, Vermont's peerless fishing rod and tackle producer, lives by this explicit dogma: "The customer is always right, even if you damn well know he is wrong. Replace, repair or adjust his product according to his wishes." (And I can tell you from experience, they do, and with a smile.) Stave Puzzle of Norwich, Vermont, makes customized, mind-warping jigsaw puzzles—and goes even further. President Steve Richardson's written guarantee: "You must be completely satisfied (no, make that thrilled) with the quality, inventiveness, and experience of putting together your Stave Puzzle, or the purchase price will be refunded, together with the cost of a bottle of aspirin." Orvis, Stave, and all too few others live—*and prosper*—by such unconditional guarantees. Sure, they start with a very good product or service. But others do, too. Why do these few go the last mile and add the likes of "always" and "unconditional" to their customer-is-right creed? Al Burger knows.

Roasters & Toasters

Al Burger won fame for his commercial pest-elimination company by building it around the most sweeping guarantee in his industry. He later sold "Bugs" Burger Bug Killers to S. C. Johnson (Johnson Wax, etc.) at a handsome profit. Then, in 1989, Burger opened Roasters & Toasters, a cafe catering to connoisseurs of gourmet coffee and baked goods. Run by his son Andy, the shop carries on the service tradition. Burger's menus and wall posters guarantee "uniquely exceptional and outstanding food and service or it's on the house"; in addition to a freebie, if you ask, they'll toss in a bag of bagel balls or coffee beans, gratis. And it's the customer who defines "outstanding": While most patrons are served in five minutes, if you want to be served in three, you can invoke the guarantee, Al Burger insists.

"I'm not afraid of being taken advantage of," Al B. explained to us. "Whatever the problem is, I want to know every bit of it." He added that the guarantee is only invoked about a dozen times a year, and the café has achieved a 95 percent customer-retention rate. The service guarantee is "the backbone of our business," said Andy B. "We treat everybody special and we stand behind it in writing. If we messed up an order for a dozen of something, we'll give them two dozen of something else on the house. Nobody leaves unhappy." He added, "Everybody I know says my father's crazy. He puts his neck on the chopping block. But the majority of Americans are honest. People think others will take advantage, but if they're crooks, they're not going to bother with confronting you face to face to get something free."

The purpose of the guarantee, Andy said, is "to make us work harder. If you put enough pressure on yourself to do a perfect job, you will."

The proof: Roasters & Toasters quickly hit the $1-million mark in revenue, and plans to open two new outlets in 1993. To top it off, the cafe "hasn't had to do a bit of advertising," according to Andy Burger. "Approximately eighty to ninety percent of customers come from word-of-mouth."

Delta Dental

A Boston-area benefits manager put it best: "When it comes to customer service, most insurance companies are just a step above self-service gas stations." Bob Hunter, president of the Delta Dental Plan of Massachusetts, agrees. "We surveyed the market and confirmed what we already knew—slow and sloppy claims processing, skyrocketing rates and indifferent service are the industry norm," he told us when we interviewed him in 1991. This was actually *good* news for the $105-million (1991 revenue) nonprofit firm. Delta had spent two and a half years installing new phone and computer systems and creating a more agile organization. Its customers—employee benefits managers who buy group coverage for their companies—gave Delta high marks for service.

But to dramatize—and capitalize on—its edge, in 1990 the firm announced a sweeping seven-point Guarantee of Service Excellence. Customers have described it as the most comprehensive in the insurance industry. The seven: (1) Minimum 10 percent savings; if the client company doesn't realize a 10 percent annual savings in dentists' usual fees, Delta refunds the difference. (2) No-hassle customer service; if a customer's question cannot be answered on the spot (most are), Delta's service reps return the call within 24 hours, or the plan pays the client company $50. (3) Quick claims processing; 90 percent of a company's claims are accurately processed within 15 calendar days and all claims are accurately processed within 30 days, or Delta credits the firm one month's administrative fee—anywhere from $120 to $12,000 (this promise represents improvements over the original guarantee, which was simply 85 percent in 15 days). (4) Smooth transition for new accounts; when clients sign on, they set the terms of conversion to the new plan—when coverage should begin, how enrollment will be handled, and so on (if the process is not deemed "smooth," as defined by the customer, Delta credits the client one month's administrative fee). (5) No balance-billing of patients; patients will not be billed for the difference between their dentists' usual fees and the discounted fees negotiated by Delta, or Delta pays $50 for the error. (6) Quick and accurate turnaround of ID cards; Delta pays $25 for each patient's ID card that is not accurately delivered within 15 days. (7) Timely management reports; Delta delivers its client reports (detailing claims and service costs) by the 10th of the month—or pays the client $50.

"We were good before the guarantee, or we could never have offered it," said VP of operations Tom Raffio. Even so, Bob Hunter added, "There was tremendous fear when we started talking about guaranteeing our service. We just didn't know what to expect. Employees were fearful about what mistakes would mean to them and the company's future." As it turns out, 98 percent of claims are processed within 15 days, versus the promised 90 percent, and cost savings have averaged 15 percent, versus the guaranteed 10 percent.

Key customers were brought into the planning process to define the services most important to them, the way the guarantee should be structured, and the size of the payout for service failures. Delta's efforts to involve clients in such decision-making are "exceptional," said Alan Breitman, a principal with employee benefits consultants William M. Mercer.

When the plan was announced, Delta budgeted $125,000 to cover claims against the program during its first year of operation; in fact, only $16,000 was paid out; and many of the payouts were made proactively, when a Delta account manager, for instance, knew that a report was sent late—even if the client did not complain. "We want to heighten awareness of the program among our clients and their employees, so they know we take this seriously," Raffio told us. To "reenergize" the program, "every department develops overarching goals for itself," he added. For example, the enrollment department devised a 14-point, yearlong improvement plan, which calls for increased cross-training, a new procedures manual, and joint client presentations with the marketing department.

More important than the payouts, in Raffio's view, are several changes in procedures that Delta has implemented as a result of the program. Each month a cross-functional payout committee, headed by quality coordinator Alan Bruno, reviews every reported problem, analyzes the cause, and proposes corrective action. For example, the committee found that one customer's missing report was the result of an incorrect mailing address; service reps now confirm all addresses by phone rather than relying on computer data.

The impact of the program has been "impressive" to Bill Hubert, employee benefits manager for Polaroid Corp. "When I phone, I know exactly what to expect, and they know what's expected of them," he told us. "The program has led them to truly make some decisions about what kind of company they want to be, and what they have to do to deliver on service." Hubert believes the guarantee represents a significant risk for Delta. "It's not a question of just twenty-five or fifty bucks. If they had to pay on thousands of missed calls or ID cards, it could cost them real money."

Delta's effort to take the bare-bones idea of superior service to a much higher plane (toward symbiosis!) has helped it withstand the ravages of recession in New England. As of mid-1992, sales leads were up 50 percent, the number of completed sales was 66 percent above plan, and customer retention had inched up from 95 to 98 percent.

GETTING PERSONAL

Have the guts to get off your analytic, hyperrational high horse and translate "strategic" business decisions into mundane, "real-life" terms! The point: You see, Mr./Ms. High and Mighty, the "silly little reasons" (with that MBA in hand, you're ashamed to talk about them) that lead you to go back to this local restaurant and not that one, to frequent this dry cleaner in preference to that one that's much closer, to send your teenager to this orthodontist and not that one, are the very same reasons that will lead thousands of individual commercial and retail customers to decide whether or not to do business with your $6-billion (assets) bank.

I call it the "check your feelings at the office door" syndrome. We all have personal "glow," "tingle," and "wow" experiences—and have become irate at some version of the missing second bag of peanuts on the airplane. But when we cross the office threshold at 7:59 a.m., we forget "all that silly stuff." We consign it to another world. It has no place, we implicitly say, in business decision-making.

To spur on your symbiosis/intertwining dialogue, you might do some "research"—with your spouse, children, yourself, a good pal. Examine the reasoning behind 10 or 15 purchases, a half-dozen decisions to start going someplace, to stop going someplace. Look at the "pivotal" issues: I'll bet you'll be surprised at how "mundane" they are. In general, try to get into the habit of personalizing—of taking seriously the flavor of everyday experience.

BECOMING A "PROCESS FREAK"

"The way customers judge a service may depend as much or even more on the service process than on the service outcome," according to premier service researcher Len Berry. Most of us are trained to be "outcome freaks," which is not all bad—but it does miss the boat when it comes to managing 116/129.

Emphasizing 116/129 means figuring out how people (e.g., customers) piece together little clues to get a bead on us and our products or services, about how they experience "dealing with" an airline, a computer vendor, a bank's commercial lending department. Again: If you could put accurate calipers on your calendar, I bet you'll find that almost no time goes into analyzing, discussing, or acting on the unfolding "process" by which your service or product is experienced by the customer (or distributor, etc.).

Reconsider that last point, about relating big issues to personal experience. Take a half-dozen colleagues out on the town. Next day, dissect the experience—the calls to make reservations for dinner and a show. Parking at the restaurant. Being greeted, seated. Spend a *full* day reliving the event. Draw flowcharts. Construct timelines. Remember moments of fleeting discomfort, moments that made you smile. Then, perhaps, do the same thing a month later with a competitor's product/service process—dissecting the experience from first touch (e.g., responding to a cold-call, area-code-800 inquiry) through after-sale follow-up. Once you've got the hang of it, try it out on your own products and services.

The key is always in the details, the feelings. Add some other tricks along the way. Put bits of this into your standard questioning repertoire: "But what does it *feel like* to clients?" "What's 'happening' to customers at this precise point or that—what are they seeing/feeling/sensing (recall the power of the Disney line sign) that provides clues about how much we care/don't care/trust/mistrust them?"

Process and the Management of Trust

"Customers usually must buy [a] service to actually experience it. Thus, they must trust a service company to deliver on its promises and conduct itself honorably. The customers' trust is a service company's most precious asset and smart services marketers use evidence management to underscore trust.

"Wendy's International, the fast food chain, has recaptured a successful identity through an advertising program that features its senior chairman, R. David Thomas. The campaign, ranked in the 1991 top ten by *Adweek*, is credited for much of the company's recent success, which is decidely counter to industry trends.

"Advertising executive George Lois says of Thomas's homespun, old-fashioned approach: 'He is talking to the right audience: down-home people who don't go to the Four Seasons for lunch. When you say Wendy's, you get an image of the guy who owns the place, goes in there, and is a fast-food junkie.' Thomas's anti-glitz demeanor and sincere enthusiasm for his company's products instill trust.

"Randall's Food and Drug, a highly successful Texas supermarket chain, manages trust in its fresh-food departments by allowing customers 'behind the scenes.' Its newest superstores feature two centrally located, walk-around prep islands: a 20'x20' fruit and juice bar and a 30'x20' produce area. Both prep islands are lined with color-rich displays of citrus fruits, cut melons, leaf lettuces, imported peppers, etc. At any hour, four to five associates can be seen in each station, preparing salads and juices and prepping produce. Not only is the commitment to freshness apparent to customers, but the employees may always be seen 'working clean.' In an adjacent 60'x20' production and service bakery, a staff of 20 prepares European-style breads and pastries in full view of customers. Randall's adheres to the advice of Swedish Professor Evert Gummesson to move 'the line of visibility for the service to show the customer what really goes on to deliver it.' "

Leonard L. Berry and
Kathleen Seiders
"Managing the Evidence in
Service Businesses"
Design Management Journal
Winter 1992

The Special Process of Keeping People Informed

I'm inching along in traffic on a winding road, on a hot day, heading toward Half Moon Bay, California. I've got that hopeless feeling, though my gut tells me I'm a mile away at most. Then I spot a highway marker: 2.53 miles to go. Then another, 2.50. Then 2.42, 2.28 . . . 0.91. . . . Funny how dramatically my spirits lifted once I started seeing the little signs. *Fact*: When I saw the first sign, I was almost three times farther from my objective than I'd imagined. *Reality*: Though tracking the little signs with their accurate, diminishing numbers did nothing to untangle the traffic snarl, it gave me a real sense of control.

Translation into the world of organizations: Three hearty cheers for the Radiology Department team at San Francisco's St. Francis Memorial Hospital. Of course I don't have the technical ability to judge their clinical skills. Moreover, my wife, there for a CAT scan in 1991, was badly delayed. Yet, I repeat: Three cheers! Why? Simple: They swamped us with information. Each little delay was promptly explained—an emergency understandably upset the schedule; there was trouble getting a clear radiographic image of another patient. When I wandered off for a few minutes, then returned to the waiting room, someone popped out from behind the desk to let me know Kate was late and why. The radiologist was also informative, providing my wife with a running commentary about what he was up to, what he was seeing, helping her to see what he was seeing—and thus diffusing her incipient terror.

It's no exaggeration: The most powerful force on earth is man's need for a sense of control. It led Richard Nixon, with a yawning lead in the 1972 polls, to plant the poison seeds that led to the bugging of the Watergate offices of the Democratic National Committee. It led historically paranoid Russia to annex Eastern Europe after the war, to create a buffer between itself and the rest of us. And it leads you and me to suffer the tortures of the damned when radiologists and lab techs fail to keep us informed, especially in situations where the perception of self-control is automatically low—e.g., whenever we put on a hospital gown.

We've noted that keeping patients informed can substantially shorten hospital stays. And Walt Disney's signs, letting customers know how long a wait to expect, help us feel relatively OK waiting in lines that are seldom shorter than anybody else's. Such evidence, and hundreds of studies of "locus of control," all point to one conclusion: Process beats substance. (Again.) The rhythm of the unfolding relationship, the way you are handled (informed, misinformed, belatedly informed, not informed) explains more about how you react to a service or product than the so-called "result" itself. Engineers, accountants, and doctors will bridle at this. But I dare them to find contrary evidence.

I'm hardly suggesting that we accept sloppy radiology in return for smooth relationships and accurate, timely information. The point, once more, is to urge service-delivery managers to pay strategic attention to the relationship as it develops, the process of keeping people constantly in the know. Hey, it doesn't take a million bucks—or a Ph.D.—to tell someone you're going to be late and here's why.

Given all this, why is "keeping mum" the favorite "process" of all too many service providers? Pride? Fear? Most likely, ignorance. Technically or administratively trained execs simply don't grasp the power of shared information to ameliorate, and frequently eliminate, even the most grievous "real" problems.

In fact, perversely, the worse the story the better. Just ask Carl Sewell. The matchless auto dealer figures he loses 1 percent of would-be service customers by continually jacking up his service-cost quotes 10 percent to insure against unanticipated problems. But in doing so, and then invariably meeting or beating his estimates, he goes a long way toward turning the 99 percent who stick around into friends for life!

Is the Sewell example a case of "managing" customer expectations? Sure. Doesn't it even border on "manipulating" expectations? Uh-huh. But mostly it's testimony to the power of telling the often raggedy truth to important "stakeholders" (e.g., customers) who are in perpetual, desperate pursuit of even a modicum of perceived control over their wobbly destinies. It is, in the end, one more vital and underattended aspect of attending to the perceived attributes of our "products."

"You are my hostage. You must obey."

Doctor/Nurse	Patient
I am healthy.	I am not.
I wear a uniform.	I am not even wearing my underwear—just a hospital gown.

I am standing.	I am sitting in a wheelchair or lying down.
I know about medical treatment.	I don't know anything.
I am confident.	I am scared.
I can probably give you your health back.	I probably cannot get my health back without you.

Where you sit depends on where you stand. The characterization of hospitalization above comes courtesy (with minor modifications) of Erie Chapman, CEO of Riverside Methodist Hospital in Columbus, Ohio. The bottom line on the above list, Chapman reported to Ron Zemke and Dick Schaaf in *The Service Edge,* is that the patient hears, "You are my hostage. You must obey."

TOWARD AUTOMATIC SYMBIOSIS: OBSESSING ON "LIFETIME VALUE"

How customers perceive their relationship with your company determines whether or not you'll have a customer for life. That's almost obvious, if almost always ignored. To keep the "lifetime customer idea" before you, I urge you to: Forget unit product or service price and religiously substitute prospective lifetime value. Experience suggests that you would automatically turn your business practices upside down if primary emphasis were placed on the lifetime value concept.

A couple of years ago, I put on a seminar for 200 pragmatic business-people—independent booksellers. Seconds before the starting time, I strode into the seminar room, went to a flip chart, and wrote, "What am I worth?" (The mild dramatics were intentional.) I turned to the group and said, "Think of me as a book lover—which is a fact. Think of me as a person who runs a several-million-dollar business, which I am. When I walk into your store, how much am I 'worth' to you?" Answers ranged from $50 to $1,000. I judged the median to be $250.

"How about $540,000?" I said.

Here's how I got to *my* answer: My line of work forces me to buy a lot of outrageously priced technical books, I said. Assume, conservatively it turns out, that my book bill averages $75 a week. Give me two weeks off—so multiply 50 weeks times $75, and we get $3,750. Round it off to $4,000. Now, my business: We purchase books for our seminar customers. Conservatively again, we shell out $5,000 each year. Add the $5,000 and the $4,000—and you get $9,000 a year. If I take a shine to your shop, I'll keep buying from you, and the statistics say I'll hang around for ten years. Multiply the $9,000 by ten years, and we're up to $90,000.

We're not through. The most powerful force in marketing—for Boeing or The Body Shop—is word-of-mouth. In short, though there are wide variations among industries, if I think highly of you, I'll create several "lifetime" customers for you by word-of-mouth. Interpreting the research data conservatively, I'll end up touting you to enough people to generate five new customers like me. Multiply the $90,000 by five, and you get $450,000. Add in the original $90,000—and we get that whopping half-million dollars plus.

My point is simple to the point of condescension. As a merchant, if you think of me as "worth $250," you might feel free to treat me differently than if you thought of me as a half-million bucks walking in the door (or out the door). Suppose I've overstated (I don't think I have). Knock a little more than half off my number, taking it from $540,000 to $250,000. We're still left with a thousandfold difference ($250 vs. $250,000). Mightn't you do some things for me if you think of me as a "bionic, half- (or quarter-) million-dollar man" that you wouldn't do for a "$250 man"? If you really think of me as "worth" a half-million dollars, you can afford to tell me when interesting books are coming out, deliver them to my house, roll out a red carpet for me when I arrive at the store. (Or at least try to remember my name—and make sure all the staff does, too.)

There are two key points. First, most service/product providers woefully underestimate the value of "lifetime" customers, even without word-of-mouth power (in my example, the seminar participants were off, as I see it, by a factor of 360—$250 vs. $90,000—before I added in word-of-mouth). Hence, they fail to think about what services are "economic" relative to such customers. Second, we fail to understand that we can, with a fair degree of accuracy (you don't have to be very accurate to miss by less than a factor of 1,000!), quantify such elusive concepts.

MORE ON SYMBIOSIS AND QUANTIFICATION: WHY "THEY" SWITCH

The Forum Corporation has conducted some of the most extensive research on why customers switch their loyalty from one producer to another. It was summarized in *The Customer-Driven Company*, by Forum vice chairman Richard Whiteley. Consider, for example, surveys taken of former customers of 14 major companies. (The 14, from both the "manufacturing" and "service" sectors, are engaged in business-to-business transactions—e.g., commercial banking.) Fifteen percent had switched because they "found a better product" from someone else. Another 15 percent "found a cheaper product." Twenty percent were bugged by "too little contact and individual attention." A whopping 49 percent "switched because the attention they did receive was poor in quality." Add the last two categories, and over two-thirds of those who switched did so for reasons that can be categorized as "lousy relationship management"! Only 30 percent switched because of price or traditionally defined quality (e.g., measures such as mean time between failures).

Make no mistake about what I am and am not saying. I *am* saying that two-thirds of customer defections are attributable to how people feel about dealing with you. Some literalists will jump overboard and say, "That idiot Peters thinks quality and price are irrelevant." Hold on! I am *not* saying that. When purchasers search for an automobile or jet engine, they rarely if ever "shop the market." If you're hunting for an auto in the low-end range, you look at Hyundai, Toyota, Honda, Chevrolet. It's highly unlikely that you'll also drop by a Cadillac or Lexus or Mercedes dealership. Likewise, if you're on a high-end search, you won't follow up trips to the Infiniti and BMW showrooms with a stop at the Geo dealer on the way home. From half-billion-dollar war planes to 79-cent pens, any company's product is almost always being compared with *a half-dozen or fewer* competitors, who offer more or less equivalent products. Within such a "more or less equivalent" range, relationship factors of the sort that surfaced in the Forum analysis are the prime cause of long-haul victory—or defeat. "Quality" and price are not. One more time: Traditional "quality" gets you onto the field, not to the goal line.

Professor Len Berry, mentioned before, developed the analytic framework for the Forum research. He also took the analysis a step further. Consider the 69 percent who skedaddled to a competitor because of lousy perceived service. Berry used factor analysis to sort the causes into five categories (see detailed definitions in the chart on the next page): "Reliability" (doing what you've said you'll do); "assurance" (conveying trust); "empathy"; "responsiveness" (perceived helpfulness); "tangibles" (equipment, appearance). The importance of each one to customers' perceptions is also indicated (as percentages) on the chart.* Again: The starting point for assigning these issues to the strategic agenda is an understanding of just how important they are to long-term business success.

"Defections Management" (and More Quantification)

The average firm, according to Frederick Reichheld of Bain & Company, loses 10 to 30 percent of its customers each year—and isn't even aware of it! Programs aimed at customer retention per se can make a huge difference.

Consider MBNA, a Delaware-based credit card company. Reichheld and

* Adapted from "Understanding Customer Expectations of Service," A Parasuraman, L. Berry, and V. Zeithaml, *Sloan Management Review*, Spring 1991. (Percentages do not add up to 100 because of rounding.)

The Five Dimensions of Service

SERVICE DIMENSION (Weighting of service dimension in overall customer rating, derived from regression coefficients)	DEFINITION	FOCUS GROUP COMMENTS
Reliability (30 percent)	The ability to perform the promised service dependably and accurately	"Sometimes they take care of your problems too fast. They fix your truck and two days later you have to take it back for the same problem. Sometimes I think they could be a little more attentive and fix the problem permanently." —Truck leasing customer
Responsiveness (25 percent)	The willingness to help customers and provide prompt service	"When I want to put a new policy into effect I get a quick response. But when I have a problem . . . forget it." —Business insurance customer
Assurance (20 percent)	The knowledge and courtesy of employees and their ability to convey trust and confidence	"I need the feeling of security. When I receive information from a competing company I would like to talk it over with my agent for reassurance that I still have a good policy." —Auto insurance customer
Empathy (16 percent)	The caring, individualized attention provided to the customer	"I would like to be able to communicate with the insurance provider who understands that while their actuarial tables are in black and white, life is played in shades of gray. I don't want to talk to an insurance person who is reading out of a book." —Auto insurance customer
Tangibles (7 percent)	The appearance of physical facilities, equipment, personnel, and communication materials	"Do something to the service areas of dealerships. They are cold, stark, uninviting places." —Auto repair customer

Harvard professor Earl Sasser report in the September–October 1990 issue of the *Harvard Business Review* that the firm began systematically collecting feedback from defecting customers in 1982—and acting on what it learned. "Eight years later, MBNA's [annual] defection rate is . . . 5 percent . . . half the average rate for the rest of the industry," the authors write. "That may seem like a small difference, but . . . profits have increased sixteen-fold." In general, even modest reductions in "defections" lead to enormous profit increases. Reichheld and Sasser found profit boosts of 25 percent to 85 percent when defections were reduced by 5 percent: For example, an auto-service chain's profits shot up 30 percent when defections were pared by 5 percent; for a credit card company, the increase was 75 percent; for a credit insurance firm, 25 percent; for an insurance brokerage, 50 percent; for an industrial distributor, 45 percent; for an industrial laundry, 45 percent; for an office building management concern, 40 percent; for a software house, 35 percent; for one bank's branch system, 85 percent.

"Defections management," as the authors label it, is not easy. "Sometimes defining a 'defection' takes some work,"Reichheld and Sasser observe."In the railroad business, for instance, few customers stop using your service completely, but a customer that shifts 80 percent of its shipments to trucks should not be considered 'retained.' . . . Even restaurants can collect data. A crab house in Maryland, for instance, started entering into its PC information from the reservation list. Managers can now find out how often particular customers return and contact those who seem to be losing interest in the restaurant."

Creating a "zero defection culture [and] managing toward zero defections is revolutionary," Reichheld and Sasser add, and requires "careful definition of defection, information systems that can measure results over time in comparison with competitors, and a clear understanding of the microeconomics of defection. Ultimately, defection should be a key performance measure for senior management and a fundamental component of incentive systems. Managers should know the company's defection rate, what happens to profit when the rate moves up or down, and why defections occur."

ANOTHER TAKE ON INTERTWINING: BUILDING AND EXPLOITING DATABASES

In *MaxiMarketing*, database marketing gurus Stan Rapp and Tom Collins report on a pioneering application of databases by Kimberly-Clark. In the mid-'80s, the big firm tried a new selling strategy for its Huggies disposable diapers. It poured $10 million (part of a $35-million marketing budget) into direct mailings to new mothers. With the help of hospitals and doctors, a database was constructed that included 75 percent of a year's 3.5

million new mothers. During her pregnancy, the mother-to-be was bombarded with personalized letters and pamphlets on how to care for a new baby. That budding relationship between Huggies and Mom was iced with a discount coupon waiting in the mailbox when Mom got home from delivering Baby. "Furthermore," Rapp and Collins write, "Kimberly-Clark now had a priceless by-product, a huge and annually-growing database of . . . parents and children by name and address. This database is as much a company asset as factories and forests." Costly? No, Kimberly-Clark contends, basing its arithmetic on the fact that a family spends $1,300 on premium-quality disposable diapers in the first two years of the child's life. "By focusing on the *lifetime value* of a customer (total sales) rather than the value of a unit sale," Rapp and Collins add, "the company found that if the entire loyalty-building program increased the number of regular Huggies diaper users by just 1 percent, it would pay for itself."

Overall, Rapp and Collins claim that it may almost be time to replace "location, location, location" with "database, database, database":

> We are living through the shift from selling virtually everyone the same thing a generation ago to fulfilling individual needs and tastes . . . by supplying . . . customized products and services. The shift [is] from "get a sale *now* at any cost" to building and managing . . . databases that track the lifetime value of your relationship with each customer.

In 1990, three years after *MaxiMarketing,* Rapp and Collins produced a readable, nuts-and-bolts sequel, *The Great Marketing Turnaround: The Age of the Individual—and How to Profit from It.* Fashion is their unmistakable theme: "Darwinian pressure on products, services, stores . . . threats to brand loyalty . . . clutter, clutter everywhere." With market targets narrowing, figuring out—precisely!—whom you're selling to, and then getting on with meeting his or her distinctive needs, is essential. Rapp and Collins's challenging answer is utilizing information technology, the ultimate in "impersonal," for precisely the opposite purpose—personalization.

The authors' basic premise is this: "[Database marketing is a] very personal form of marketing that recognizes, acknowledges, appreciates and serves the interests and needs of selected groups of consumers whose individual identities and market profiles are or become known to the advertiser. . . . It uses the newly-affordable power of the computer to target-contact-persuade-sell-and-build a profitable relationship with individual prospects and customers known to the marketer by name, address and other characteristics stored in the database."

But go for it, or don't bother, the authors advise. "Building an interactive relationship with individual users of your product or service is not to be treated simply as an afterthought or an add-on to the advertising and promotion," they write. "In the new marketing, it takes priority over everything else you do.

. . . It requires integration of advertising, sales promotion, direct marketing, event marketing and public relations, all fed by an interactive customer database."

Going for it includes several strategies for identifying and building relationships with customers (or potential customers):

- "From unknown to identified prospects and customers." Identifying customers, Rapp and Collins observe, is beginning to be practiced by former mass marketers. American Airlines started the trend, but now the likes of Ford, Buick, Austin Rover, RJR Nabisco, General Foods, Quaker Oats, Bristol-Myers, Procter & Gamble, Waldenbooks, and Radio Shack (as well as a surprising number of small businesses) have gotten into the act. Seagram's, for example, began building a database in 1986, and by 1989 had 6 million records (with 20 percent annual database growth); it uses the database to generate direct marketing pieces promoting Crown Royal, Chivas Regal, and Glenlivet.

- "From ad impressions counted to new customers won." Rapp and Collins discuss a "new perspective on advertising expenditures" and propose that consumer-goods marketers maintain two distinct advertising budgets— "one budget for gaining new customers, another for keeping the old." It's our old friend-lifetime value! Campbell's "core soup buyers" spend $200 annually and contribute about $10 to the big firm's bottom line. In short, Rapp and Collins declare, the company can afford to spend money figuring out who these repeat slurpers are, and then can afford to spend more to give them personalized attention.

- "From bombarding the marketplace to building relationships." "Customer clubs" turn out to be a potent tool for building relationships with customers, the authors claim. Consider Hallmark's Keepsake Ornament Collector's Club, which roped in 76,000 members in its first year. The club informs members by newsletter about new trends in collecting—and new Hallmark products. The "collectors" are also given an opportunity to purchase special items available only to members. (Note: These special orders must be picked up at the nearest Hallmark outlet!)

- "From passive consumers to involved participants." The Buick Open, Rapp and Collins say, illustrates "the power of marrying an involving event to individualized marketing." In 1987, the Buick Open was a ho-hum, 23-year-old PR event. Not many Buick division or dealer employees knew much about it. Neither did customers. Then an aggressive GM marketer turned it around. Television broadcasts of the event carried 32 commercial spots for Buicks. On-course signs linked Buick to the event. Tournament programs were turned into souvenirs. Dealer kits built up enthusiasm before the fact and provided ideas for local dealer tie-ins with the event.

But the big story was a mammoth direct-mail campaign—a "golf sweepstakes," including a test-drive incentive and a purchase incentive. The "driving contest" section of each mailing package included a different "yardage" figure. Recipients could take the entry to a Buick dealer and would win a prize if their yardage number matched a prize number. The grand prize was $180,000, the same amount awarded to the golfer who won the Buick Open. (The salesman who signed the grand prize winner's form received a prize of $10,000.) Ten thousand videotapes of Ben Crenshaw on "The Art of Putting," with a retail value of $89.95 each, were also distributed to contestants. The test-drive incentive was a sleeve of Buick Open golf balls, similar to the ones used in the tournament. Rapp and Collins report that the mailing went to 3.8 million prospects, primarily Buick owners, selected owners of competitive cars, and demographically desirable golf fans selected from lists of golfers and subscribers to golf magazines. Measurable results included 565,000 sweepstakes entries and 900,000 showroom visits. Buick can trace 26,000 sales directly to the campaign. Moreover, Buick planned to track every respondent indefinitely.

In a chapter called "The Best and the Boldest," Rapp and Collins recount the stunning story of Nintendo, master of what the authors, given to biz-babble from time to time, call "the big double D of the turnaround era—Database and Dialogue." Nintendo started with a sweepstakes, triggered by entry forms enclosed with product warranty cards. That lassoed data on 7 to 10 percent of the firm's customers. A Nintendo Fun Club was launched the next year; those who signed up got a membership card and a free subscription to a bimonthly newsletter. Over time, the number of phone calls from kids having questions about games grew to 120,000 a week. (By 1990, the company had over 120 "game counselors" handling the phones. The service was initially toll-free, but later shifted to toll calls without denting customer enthusiasm.) In 1988, the newsletter was converted to a 110-page, $15-per-year subscription magazine. The magazine "is our secret weapon," Nintendo's advertising director told Rapp and Collins. "You can't put a value on what relationship marketing has done for Nintendo."

Forty-five-Seat Restaurants, Too

As an executive in the semiconductor industry, Steve Weich spent a lot of time in Europe. "When we stayed at the George V in Paris, everybody knew our names," he told us. "I was knocked out by that kind of personal attention." In 1989, Weich opened La Crème, a small French restaurant in a quiet San Francisco neighborhood, and made personal attention his sole marketing strategy. Weich personally greets every patron of his 45-seat restaurant, offers wine tastings with dinner, and reminds diners to leave their cards, which he enters in a weekly drawing for a free dinner. The next day he writes a thank-you note to each customer and records in his computer database the customer's food and wine choices, the number of times he or she has been to the restaurant, and whatever personal details he's gleaned. When repeat customers call for a reservation, he checks his files for their favorite dishes and offers to prepare any item they've ordered before, even if it's not on the menu that night. And when taking their order, Weich explained, "I can say, 'I know you like the '84 Silverado Cabernet, would you like that again?' "

Weich also communicates with all his customers through a monthly newsletter announcing menu changes, wine tastings, and special dinners marketed only to past customers. These premium-priced events draw turn-away crowds and, more important, build a loyal following. Other than his newsletter mailings, Weich does no advertising; he estimates that 90 percent of his business is with repeat customers.

Damned If You Don't, Damned If You Do (As Usual)

To underscore the obvious, "all this" is happening because it's getting easier and cheaper to do. For one thing, the cost of holding a customer's name, address, and purchase history in an on-line database has fallen by a factor of 1,000 since 1970. Moreover, advances in both the friendliness and the sophistication of relational database software are occurring continuoually. Of course, the increasing economy and friendliness of database storage and manipulation are also its Achilles' heel. The fact is, lots of people are getting in on the act—which means (1) you'd better if you haven't, and (2) staying ahead of others means staying ahead of the game. In fact, staying ahead of the game, given the rate of improvement in the technology, is tough. Just after you've finished investing gobs of time and money in building a database, a slowpoke competitor finally jumps in—and takes advantage of a revolutionary advance made in the 24 months since you started your project. As usual in a fashionized world with fashionized technologies: Damned if you do, damned if you don't.

THE "L-WORD": SYMBIOSIS AND THE *REALLY* "SOFT" SIDE OF RELATIONSHIPS

The biggest complaint I hear from women is that their partners don't talk or listen to them. Women are seeking that certain kind of conversation that they feel is the essence of closeness and intimacy; that kind where I tell you everything that's on my mind and discuss everything with you. Men don't have those kinds of conversations, so they don't know what women are trying to get at. They can't figure out what women want from them. They feel that women just go on and on about nothing. So we have the scenario where the woman's trying to talk, and the guy's got the newspaper in front of his face because he feels there's nothing to talk about.

DEBORAH TANNEN
"Can We Talk?," an interview
in *New Age Journal*
November/December 1990

All purchase decisions, all repurchase decisions, hinge, ultimately, on *conversations* (Anita Roddick) and *relationships*. As we saw, Californians have one heck of a time being understood by folks from Tennessee. The Japanese find it almost impossible to understand Americans. Americans find it almost impossible to understand the Japanese. Men can't communicate with women. Women can't communicate with men.

"It's a communication problem" is one time-honored statement that men, especially, use to write such "stuff" off. Implied: *mere* communication. And yet, in a sense, communication/conversation is all there is when it comes to us humans—in personal as well as commercial dealings.

In reality, of course, there is no difference between personal and commercial dealings: All dealings are personal dealings in the end. (Need more evidence? The biggest commercial dealings of all, takeovers, are also the most personal. Glance at *Barbarians at the Gate*, the story of the $25-billion leveraged buyout of RJR Nabisco, if you've got any lingering doubts.)

In his "Service Edge" newsletter, Ron Zemke reports on the work of University of Texas professor Robert A. Peterson. A meticulous scholar with over 100 academic articles to his credit, Peterson couldn't for the life of him find the expected strong, positive correlation between "current customer satisfaction" and "repeat business." He kept digging and finally came up with an explanation—the "L-word," says Zemke. That is, *love*. Customers with genuine affection for an institution are loyal customers—me and Federal Express are a case in point. Others may be quite "satisfied," but unless there's an emotional bond, Peterson concludes, such satisfaction doesn't necessarily translate into future sales. Peterson began tapping this vein when he started adding questions to his customer surveys about "love" and "hate," rather than "like" and "satisfaction." (Now he's gone so far as to construct a "love index." Incidentally, in overall terms, per Peterson, consumers "love" their microwave ovens more than any other product.)

Consider this vignette from *301 Great Management Ideas from America's Most Innovative Small Companies*:

When you're selling to a foreign prospect, the pomp and circumstance of formal meetings may get in the way of closing a deal. After 20 years of selling internationally, Wayne Cooper decided to balance the formality with an evening of casual entertaining. It began when Cooper, CEO of 13-year-old Arcon Manufacturing, Inc., in Charlotte, North Carolina, invited a delegation from China over to his ranch to cook its favorite dishes. "They had been on the road for a month and missed their native cuisine," explains Cooper, who then sold them a grain-storage system the next day, after a year and a half of meetings.

To keep things simple, the five-to-six-person delegations just cook for themselves, Cooper and his wife, Judy. Business is not discussed. "In meetings prior to the dinner, they feel like you're trying to pull one over on them and are suspicious; afterward they want my advice," claims Cooper, who now turns his kitchen over to visiting chefs once a month.

Sure it's a "technique." Call it a "trick of the trade" if you must. Yet I suspect it's not: You couldn't survive such monthly rituals unless your heart was in it. So I'm more than willing to give Cooper the benefit of the doubt (and his sales record suggests that I should). It's one more teeny tale about "conversation"—and relationship-building.

Most of our moms and dads taught us to be polite. And most of us are, most of the time. At least we are *outside* of business. Yet what sorts of words and phrases does "good business" elicit as synonyms? "Tough-minded." "Pragmatic." "Results-oriented." "No-nonsense." "Doesn't waste words." "Doesn't fart around with nonessentials." We (especially males) tend to ignore, downgrade, or dismiss the so-called "little touches"—even consider them "wasteful."

It's not so much giving out 50-yard-line tickets for the Michigan–Ohio State game or the case of booze at Christmas anymore. That was usually an unemotional ritual anyway. It's "simply" a matter of attending to relationships, perpetually thinking relationships, taking the extra few minutes to talk things through, working—every day!—at being a little less abrupt, a little more empathetic, a little more patient, even a little more loving.

Sure, product life cycles are shrinking, shrinking. And you'd best be a fast-paced innovator if you want to survive. That was the message of the Learning to Hustle and the Markets and Innovation section. The overall message of *this* section is consistent—and inconsistent—with that message. We're talking about fashion goods. Which means fickle, etc., etc. That is, don't waste time, move fast, don't look back—good advice. But "fashion" also means that we must more and more emphasize the importance of those little touches—intangibles that can sustainably differentiate us from the horde of other folks in an increasingly product-, service-, and competitor-crowded world.

Can you "systematically" pay attention to relationships, though? No and yes. No, in that part of relationship-consciousness is a reflection of your essential humanness. "Attending to relationships" probably comes more easily to The Body Shop's Anita Roddick and Quad/Graphics' Harry Quadracci than it did to former GM chief Roger Smith. Yes, in that our old friend, paying attention per se, does help. If *you* (chief) obviously spend time on relationship-building, à la Arcon's Cooper in the kitchen, then "they" (senior and junior colleagues) will, too. Or you can be more formal: Do you feature a specific course/courses on relationship-building and relationship management—and conversation—within, say, your sales and marketing training curriculum? (Roddick does at The Body Shop.)

All this takes on special urgency in the global marketplace, where more and more business, even for smaller firms (like Cooper's Arcon again), will be done with people from different cultures. Constant miscommunication is not a possibility, it's a dead certainty!

Once more, my only objective is to get the issue "on the agenda" (as part of the larger intangible/perception issue). Relationships, often as not, are taken for granted, ignored, or dismissed as "just part of life." Read more novels and fewer business books: Relationships really are all there is.

46

A Special Case of Wow: An Encompassing View of Design

The classic symptom [of poor design] in most American living rooms is the relentlessly flashing "12:00 a.m." on the front of the VCR, evidence that nobody in the house can figure out how to set the clock. Indeed, according to industry surveys, nearly 80 percent of Americans have never programmed their VCRs, an operation that can take up to 10 steps with a button-packed front panel.

Newsweek
January 7, 1991

Design is the key factor that is going to separate high-tech company survivors from losers in the next 20 years.

CHARLES OWEN, Illinois
Institute of Technology, quoted in
"The Low Side of High-Tech,"
Chicago Tribune Sunday Magazine
February 11, 1990

I planned to include this discussion of design and user-friendliness in the previous chapter. But it deserves more than second billing as just one tactic among many for becoming symbiotically involved with customers. The pursuit of sustainable bases for product distinction is more feverish with each passing week. Yet the odds of achieving such differentiation, given the explosion of competitors and products, get lower and lower. The bottom line, according to British management expert Christopher Lorenz in *The Design Dimension*: Design may offer the most significant opportunity for achieving fundamental differentiation. Overstatement? If so, not by much.

DESIGN AS A TOOL FOR CORPORATE TRANSFORMATION

At Braun, the design function follows the Bauhaus ideal of being integrated with every aspect of the organization. Ever since [chief designer Dieter] Rams joined in 1955 Braun has identified design as a critical competitive advantage . . . in the intensely competitive world of consumer electronics. Rams and his 20-strong design team work alongside engineers, chemists, marketing executives and production planners to develop and refine the company's product range. Rams sits on the main board of Braun . . . and reports directly to the chairman. . . . Braun has more products than any other company in the design collection of New York's Museum of Modern Art.

Financial Times
July 31, 1991

Christopher Lorenz, borrowing from the Netherlands' electronics giant, Philips, presents an overall model for product development. The "industrial design vision" (aesthetic knowledge, social and cultural backgrounds, ergonomic requirements), he asserts, should be given the same intellectual and organizational weight as the "engineering vision" (technical research, production methods) and the "marketing vision" (market research, market analyses, distribution systems). The normally cautious Lorenz adds that an effectively conceived corporate design activity can become coach, catalyst, orchestrator, and overall integrator for the product development process. At Sony, for example, design plays precisely that encompassing role in the consumer products sector. Lorenz also argues that design's formal position on the organization chart is vital to its impact. For example, Ford's stunning success with Taurus and Sable, a wake-up call for industrial design in America, followed a major reorganization—in which design joined the other major functions (e.g., product engineering) as an equal at the strategy-making table. Lorenz also uncovered other organizational paths to design preeminence. At Italy's design-conscious Olivetti, for instance, outside designers call the shots—but they are engaged in a constant, intense dialogue with the chief executive officer (who's historically been a design fanatic).

The TRIAD Design Project

The Design Management Institute's ambitious TRIAD Design Project reported in 1989 on 13 case studies from North America, Europe, and Asia. Their monograph, "Designing for Product Success," highlights design's role in shifting corporate focus. For instance:

Bahco Tools of Stockholm, Sweden. The company is one of Europe's oldest and largest hand-tool makers, with a dominant market position in Scandinavia and a matchless reputation for quality. But in the '70s, competition from low-cost hand-tool producers and others who had closed the quality gap challenged Bahco to step out in a conservative marketplace "that expected traditional forms in tools such as screwdrivers," the TRIAD team writes. Bahco teamed up with The Ergonomic Design Group to make a revolution. For example (shades of the Ingersoll-Rand Cyclone Grinder case), designers went out and talked with and worked with 20 master craftsmen who used screwdrivers. Are there still things to be learned about the ubiquitous screwdriver? Yes, amazingly. For example, the designers discovered that these craftsmen placed both hands on the tool 70 percent of the time. The new Bahco screwdriver-handle design, in a radical departure from tradition, offered space for two hands! Another innovation, the case team reports, "was a standard-size handle for both large and small screwdrivers, because the user's hand does not change in size."

Bahco's Ergo screwdriver, which includes such features, was released in late 1982. Its dramatic success triggered an entire new line of tools, including adjustable wrenches, chisels, slip-joint pliers, and knives. Moreover, the TRIAD team declares, Bahco developed an entirely "new marketing concept that emphasized a close relationship with the end user. Bahco tools, always considered to be of high quality, now embodied a new dimension of quality in the eyes of its customers." The upshot: The company won back its lost market share in surprisingly short order.

CKD Corporation of Nagoya, Japan. CKD, which makes valves and pneumatic system components, started out by manufacturing products as a licensee of another company. Then it decided to enter the global market with a proprietary line. "The challenge," the TRIAD team observes, "was to differentiate a common industrial product in a market that was not accustomed to dramatic change." Though the product is mundane, CKD's original name, Creative Knowledge for Development, gives away its aspirations. President Shigeru Yoshida, the case team writes, is a bone-deep believer in "design [as] an active agent of improvement that links all specialties together in a unified solution." His design consultant, Takuo Hirano, is directly involved in overall issues of corporate strategy.

The Selix FRL (for filter, regulator, lubricator) was the brainchild of a 20-person project team that intimately integrated design, engineering, and manufacturing. "The design concept that emerged was a truly modular, flexible system," the TRIAD authors report. "Connections were kept compatible with earlier models to allow interchangeability. Design innovations included the use of lighterweight yet durable aluminum; a simpler . . . gauge that was easier to read, less likely to be broken, and required fewer parts; simple product graphics to express strength and quality." Internal engineering, they add, "was substantially improved with patentable features such as a new filter element, which had a life-span four times that of the previous model. Through the use of better materials and fewer parts, production costs were lowered 31 percent, while the retail price, due to improved functionality, could be raised 17 percent. Defects fell from 2 percent to 0.5 percent. The weight of the system was cut by 56 percent." As at Bahco, the first success triggered development of a family of products.

Over the last 10 years, the product line has won 54 G-Mark design awards, Japan's premier industrial design prizes. CKD's Pneumatics Component Division, home to the new line, has grown from a regional Japanese firm to an international powerhouse in its niche, with $179 million in 1990 sales.

The other 11 TRIAD cases bracket well-known firms such as Germany's Braun (see the epigraph) and Japan's Sharp Corporation (which pepped up a stagnant, me-too calculator business with a "Fashion Calculator project" that positioned its products as "personal electronic accessories"), as well as relative unknowns like Germany's ERCO Leutchten (gantry lighting systems). Each story is about transformation—of the entire corporation and usually the industry segment in which the firm competes—driven by a new encompassing sense of design's strategic role.

Deere & Co. Puts a Passenger Seat in the Combine

Scott Payne told us he spends six months a year in the cab of a John Deere combine, helping farmers across the West and Midwest harvest their wheat and corn crops. But he's more than the owner-operator of a fleet of eight harvesters. He's also a codeveloper of the $100,000 machines. Five years before we talked with him in 1990, a team of designers, engineers, service staff, assembly workers, purchasing agents, and accountants from $8-billion Deere had asked Payne to test a prototype of a harvester then in development. "It ran great," he said, but to his dismay he once unloaded a tankful of grain before moving the chute into position—the switches for the two operations were side by side. Payne suggested improvements in the machines' exterior lighting, seat, air filter—and different placement of those switches. The team returned to the engineering shop to refine the product, piece by piece, incorporating Payne's feedback and their own impressions of how the machine should behave.

In times past, the custom at Deere had followed the clumsy sequential product development model. Design engineers "threw their plans over the wall to the manufacturing engineers, who went to production workers and said, 'Here, build this,'" Michael Wyffels, product engineering manager at John Deere Harvester Works, recalled. "'Keep Out' signs hung outside the designers' offices."

Now, after parts for each prototype are bought or milled, for example, the design engineers don their overalls and help build the axle, cab, or engine they designed. "We'll hear some quiet guys swearing loudly," Wyffels chuckled. "Nonetheless, ninety percent of them say that all engineers should be required to assemble their own products." Production-line workers also join "design-for-manufacture" advisory teams as the design starts to take shape. They spend up to a year and a half reviewing design specifications, visiting suppliers, selecting machine tools and fixtures, and designing their own workstations. (More than 100 workers, representing all the key disciplines, participated in the design of John Deere's latest harvester.) As changes are made in the product, the multidisciplinary teams return to the field to test each prototype—*and even its operating manual* (Amen!)—under real-world conditions. "If a prototype breaks down in the field, the team services it," Wyffels told us. "Very quickly, boundaries between the disciplines start blurring. Today, understanding the use of the product and the needs of the user is as important for the purchasing guys as for the designer."

A new line of harvesters introduced by Deere in 1990 incorporates dozens of changes, thanks to the revised design process.

• The design team completely altered the placement and layout of the control panel, now located to the right of the driver's seat, adjacent to the armrest. Also, customers suggested the addition of a passenger seat—a simple but unprecedented amenity in such machines, according to Wyffels.

• A team accountant with no technical training suggested changes in front axle assembly that reduced tooling costs by $150,000. "He wasn't trained as an engineer, so he didn't know it couldn't be done," explained Dick Mason, manager of product engineering.

• A safety team added a pull-down ladder for safer access to the engine compartment, which is located six feet off the ground. A service team added a panel to the bottom of the engine compartment, making it unnecessary to remove the engine for many repairs.

When Wyffels and Harvester Works general manager Dick Kleine organized the first multifunctional design teams, the outcome was uncertain—and resistance was high. "Engineers are probably the hardest people to change," said Kleine. "Non-design people who could bring broader experience to bear were selected to head certain [subprojects]. It created a new balance of power." Deere experimented with several approaches to design management before hitting on one that worked. Initially, for example, Wyffels required people from every discipline to sign off on all drawings. This attempt at functional integration created a hopeless bureaucratic snarl. Now, with autonomous teams, "We spend more time on the front end of the design process," said Wyffels, "but overall, the process is twenty-five percent shorter."

The new approach is ratification of Deere's long-standing concern with design. Its 52-year-old alliance with the pioneering design firm Henry Dreyfuss Associates helped Deere build a reputation for well-integrated machine attachments, easy-to-use controls, and comfortable cabs. And its stunning corporate headquarters, designed by Finnish architect Eero Saarinen and nestled in 1,200 landscaped acres in Moline, Illinois, suggests by itself that Deere is no ordinary provider of farm tools.

Love, Hate, and Skilled Amateurs

"In the clubby world of the auto industry, where many executives are said to have gasoline in their veins, Gerald P. Hirshberg seems driven by an alternative fuel.

"As the top American at Nissan's design studio in California, Mr. Hirshberg is responsible for the shapes of three models this year, including two sedans that buck the current popular 'wedge' theme of low-slung hoods and high trunk lids. . . .

"At Nissan, Mr. Hirshberg shed many traditional rules about designing cars that he had learned at the General Motors Corporation. At GM, for example, designers were encouraged to draw the cars unencumbered by technical specifications that were believed to inhibit creativity. . . . [At Nissan] Mr. Hirshberg asks for all the technical data of a new model ahead of time, believing that 'obstacles are the primary motivation for creativity.' The result? Nissan engineers need only make minor adjustments to manufacture Nissan Design International's designs. . . .

"Nissan's is the only design studio wholly owned by an auto maker that takes on outside work, which Mr. Hirshberg says enriches and freshens the perspective he and his 13 designers bring to car assignments. Nissan Design International's portfolio includes a 105-foot yacht, a computer, a vacuum cleaner and an intravenous pump for hospitals. 'It keeps us skilled amateurs, rather than pros,' [Hirshberg says]. . . .

"Industry analysts say Mr. Hirshberg is fulfilling the mission first handed him by Nissan in 1980: add some zest to Nissan's product line. 'Nissan is really breaking away from stodgy designs that it was once known for,' said

Christopher Cedergren, senior vice president of the consulting firm Autopacific Group. 'Its offerings in recent years are 'clearly very expressive, very innovative,' he added. . . .

"GM and the Chrysler Corporation say they are trying to turn out bold 'love it or hate it' designs to best reach the top of consumers' shopping lists. Ford is spreading the rounded, aerodynamic look of its Taurus sedan across many of its cars.

"Design is not the only reason people buy cars, of course, though analysts note that it will grow in importance as auto makers achieve greater parity in quality."

The New York Times
May 11, 1992

DESIGN AS "PERSONALITY"

The Deere and TRIAD team examples suggest that "design" can be an encompassing idea, moving far beyond aesthetics and even product friendliness. "Design is the company's strategic objective made buyable, made *real* in customer terms," American industrial design consultant Michael Shannon told me. "It is how the company looks, feels, tastes, wears, rides—what the company is that customers care about." At companies like Braun, Olivetti, Sony, Bahco, CKD, and Deere, design is nothing less than "personality." Rodney Fitch, chairman of Fitch RS, fleshed out this idea in "Success in Retailing Identities" (*Design Management Journal*, Winter 1991):

> It is a depressing fact that, in all too many aspects of our lives, good design is an also-ran! Look around you and see what bad design has created or no design has left undone. . . . Can we imagine The Limited, The Gap . . . in the U.S. or Boots, Dillons . . . in the U.K. without committed design programs to underpin the development and trading personalities made manifest in these stores? . . . Indeed, why bother with personality at all? Perhaps the most compelling reason is to establish meaningful differentiation. . . .
>
> Only one store can distinguish itself as the cheapest in town. The rest have to depend on and profile other attributes. . . . Body Shop . . . is one of the best contemporary examples. Based around environmental concerns, everything in the well-designed shops speaks with the same tone of voice—packaging, posters, materials, the entire store seeks to project the company's ethics and beliefs.

Thomas Moser (see next page) would smile at all this.

"Say 'Hello' to Mark, Mark or Mark"

> It's the idea of bringing soul and one-on-one value to our customers. There's nothing like spending hours finishing a piece of furniture and then turning it over to some trucking company to have it dumped on some lady's lawn in a rainstorm, with some burly tattooed guy saying, "Sorry, lady, sign here."
>
> THOMAS MOSER, founder
> Thos. Moser Cabinetmakers
> Interview with research team
> member Paul Cohen, April 1992

In 1991 I bought a superb table (I sat at it to write this) and chairs from Auburn, Maine's Thos. Moser Cabinetmakers. Everything about the transaction was classy. It began with the extraordinary catalog, which does much more than feature fine furniture. It entices me to become a member of the Moser family. For example, there are profiles of various people who work at Moser—their backgrounds, aspirations, projects they're at work on now. Even phone conversations stood out. Each one was to the point and was followed up immediately with a letter—need I say it, on peerless stationery that echoed Moser's furniture design style. But one touch, mentioned in a Moser brochure, really tickled me pink:

> Having built our business in Maine affords us many benefits, the most important being the resource of talented, hardworking people. One of the problems is that we are at the end of the transportation system.
>
> In our early years, our customers provided the transportation—we would carry the furniture out to the car and off they would go! But, as our business grew, it changed—customers were now calling from the Midwest, the Southeast, and nearly every other region of the country. Shipping furniture was to be our next challenge.
>
> Initially we relied on common carriers for delivery services, but frustrated customers, damaged furniture, and the lack of service options prompted us to launch our own operation in 1987. . . .
>
> We take pride in is being able to deliver to you at a time that is convenient for you. We all know how frustrating it is to wait half a day for the phone company to show up. We have even equipped our 28-foot truck with a cellular phone so that should an unforeseen event occur, we can be reached.
>
> In offering shipping, our goal is to provide an excellent service that

meets the quality standards that we set for our furniture. We owe you an explanation for the headline. ["Say 'Hello' to Mark, Mark or Mark"] Three of the five gents who ship for us are named "Mark." The fourth is Denny, the brother of one of the Marks, and the fifth, Russ, is the brother of our Sanding Room supervisor, Debbie Bell.

"Nice words," you'll grant me. "But talk is cheap." Fair enough. My own skepticism led me to ask my California colleague Paul Cohen to head Down East last winter. Cohen followed the two not-Marks around on an icy day in January 1992:

At 5:00 a.m. on a cold winter morning, Denny Labonte and Russ La-Chance leave the loading dock with $25,000 worth of tables, chairs, and cabinets for seven customers in and around Boston, 150 miles south.

This day, the drivers hit every stop no later than five minutes into their scheduled two-hour window. For their first customer, waiting to go to work, they unload and unpack a rocking chair and place it carefully in her den, all in about three minutes. Later, they spend 20 minutes moving a large chest up a customer's snowy front walk, position it in the living room, show him how to adjust the shelves, and discuss the natural aging process that will turn the cherry wood from a pale blond to a mellow red.

The drivers are trained in furniture maintenance and can sand and rewax a piece on the spot, if need be, to eliminate a surface scratch. LaChance also doubles as mechanic for Moser's three-truck fleet. But they have no special customer-service training, relying instead on their own common sense, respect for the product, and love of the job. "We're on our own," says Labonte. "We're the ones who see the customers are happy."

Moser's delivery service—which won a 1991 Blue Chip Enterprise award from *Nation's Business* magazine and the U.S. Chamber of Commerce—has quickly become a profit center for the $5-million (1991 revenue) company. It now also ships goods for designers and other small craft-furniture makers. More important, Moser's delivery service is matchless testimony to the idea of design as personality. Prize-winning designer Thomas Moser clearly understands that the Thos. Moser Cabinetmaker's story doesn't end with the aesthetics and ergonomics of his chairs and tables.

MAKING DESIGN A GUT ISSUE

So far this analysis has been a bit "corporate," mostly emphasizing the nuts and bolts organizational considerations involved in putting design at or near the head of a firm's priority list. The flavor of the design opportunity—the emotional heart of the matter—has been shortchanged. And make no mistake, design is about emotion. Changing the org chart, then, is not the first step toward design nirvana. Just as trust must precede structural alterations when it comes to implementing widespread self-management, tinkering with your own head—and heart—must precede shifts in organization when it comes to design.

Somehow you've got to immerse yourself in design, absorb its pervasiveness in everyday affairs (a pervasiveness, need I add, which makes it such a potent "tool" in the competitiveness chase). Design is all around us, though we're usually oblivious to it. To learn to think big about design, we first need to think small:

● Under the headline "Read It and Weep," in January 1991, *Newsweek* cited Sharp Electronics' manual for a home fax machine:

Text: "The Remote Transfer Passcode can be used in Extension Telephone Function. To transfer a fax call from an extension phone to the UX-170 for reception. This function, the call is transferred to the UX-170 by pressing the passcode number and * key at the extension telephone. The passcode is a one-digit number, selected from 0 to 9. To change the Passcode, redo the entry operation. To check the Passcode, print-out and refer to the Program List (see P. 76). If an incorrect number is entered during the procedure, press the * key and repeat the entire procedure.

Translation: If you can understand and remember this for more than 10 minutes, you're a candidate for either computer programmer or game-show contestant.

● I forgot my shampoo while on a recent stay in Winnipeg. The hotel's complimentary offering came in a little plastic packet. I took two into the shower. But I couldn't for the life of me find a corner that would tear, especially with my fingers wet and slippery from bath soap and water. Attempts to bite the bag open failed, too. So I climbed out of the shower, trailed a miniature Niagara all the way across the room, and grabbed my red Bic pen lying on the bedside table. It still wasn't easy, but I finally managed to puncture the bag and didn't quite lose all the shampoo on the way back to the bathroom. P.S.: The pen never worked right again.

I want to turn you into a product-design-and-usability fanatic, which is what I've become. But should I succeed, you'll rue the day you read this. You'll perpetually wander about irritated as hell at the inconsiderateness that designers and manufacturers exhibit toward us average humans.

My antennae shot up after laughing and weeping my way through Donald Norman's *The Psychology of Everyday Things*. "Over the years I have fumbled my way through life," engineer-turned-psychologist Norman writes, "walking into doors, failing to figure out water faucets, incompetent at working the simple things of everyday life. 'Just me,' I would mumble. . . . But as I studied psychology and watched the behavior of other people, I began to realize that I was not alone. . . . I am quite expert at computers and electronics, and complex laboratory equipment. Why do I have so much trouble with doors, light switches, and water faucets? How come I can work a multimillion-dollar computer installation, but not my home refrigerator? While we all blame ourselves, the real culprit—faulty design—goes undetected. . . . It is time for a change."

Norman delves into the innermost aspects of design. For example, the renowned cognitive psychologist shows how the mind tries to make sense of things. And how designers get in the way. "Well-designed objects are easy to interpret and understand," says Norman. "They contain visible clues to their operation. Poorly designed objects . . . provide no clues—or sometimes false clues. They trap the user and thwart the normal process of interpretation and understanding. Alas, poor design predominates. The result is a world filled with frustration, with objects that cannot be understood, with devices that lead to error." When design "works," the principles are almost obvious. For example, "natural mapping": Take the case of light switches for an auditorium; following natural mapping, the layout of the switch panel mimics the pattern of the lights themselves.

But getting to the obvious requires painstaking effort. Ponder one small aspect of telephone design: the ridge of plastic which protects the button that, if depressed, disconnects the call. "Ever knock the telephone off the table and onto the floor while you were talking?" Norman asks. "Wasn't it nice when you didn't get disconnected? . . . The . . . Bell System designers explicitly recognized this problem and designed it with this in mind. They . . . protected the critical button with a shield that prevents the switch hook from hitting the ground. . . . A small feature, but an important one."

Design Is Not Aesthetics

Most of the examples peppered through Norman's book are bad, even ludicrous. Consider Norman's car radio: "Twenty-five controls, many apparently arbitrary. All tiny (so that they will fit the limited space available). Imagine trying to use the radio while driving at high speed, at night. Or in winter when wearing gloves, so that the attempt to push one button succeeds in pushing two. . . . You should be able to use things in the dark. A car radio should be usable with a minimum of visual cues. But the radio designers probably designed it in a laboratory, with little or no thought about the car or the driver. For all I know the design won a prize for its visual aesthetics."

In fact, Norman saves his most pointed barbs for designers. " 'It probably won a prize' is a disparaging phrase in this book," Norman writes. "Why? Because prizes tend to be given for some aspects of a design, to the neglect of all others . . . including usability." He offers the example of office buildings in Seattle and Los Angeles designed for the Federal Aviation Administration. In the case of Seattle, "those who would work in the building had a major say in the planning." In the other instance, the architects called the shots. "Which design do the users prefer? Why the Seattle one, of course. Which one got the award? Why the Los Angeles one, of course." The American Institute of Architects jury justified its denial of an award to the Seattle building on the basis of its "residential quality" and "lack of discipline and control of the interiors," Norman reports—precisely what the users liked most about it. (Shades of the laments of CRSS founder Bill Caudill.)

Designers go astray, Norman concludes, because "the reward structure of the design community tends to put aesthetics first. Design collections feature prize-winning clocks that are unreadable, alarms that cannot easily be set, can openers that mystify." Moreover, Norman contends, designers "are not typical users. They become so expert in using the object that they have designed they cannot believe that anyone else might have problems."

But it's stickier than that. Even when designers do things right and get users involved, they are often thwarted by those users' natural embarrassment over their apparent clumsiness. Norman provides a telling example from a large computer company that asked him to help evaluate a new product:

> I spent a day learning to use it and trying it out on various problems. In using the keyboard to enter data, it was necessary to differentiate between the "return" key and the "enter" key. If the wrong key was typed, the last few minutes' work was irrevocably lost. I pointed this problem out to the designer, explaining that I myself had made the error frequently . . . . The designer's first response was: ". . . Didn't you read the manual?" . . . "Yes, yes," I explained, "I understand the two keys, I simply confused them. . . . Certainly others have had similar problems." "Nope," said the designer. He claimed that I was the only person who had ever complained, and the company's secretaries had been using the system for many months. . . .
>
> We went together to some of the secretaries and asked them whether they had ever hit the "return" key when they should have hit "enter." . . . "Oh, yes," said the secretaries, "we do that a lot." "Well, how come nobody ever said anything about it?" we asked the secretaries. . . . The reason was simple: When the system stopped working or did something strange, the secretaries dutifully reported it as a problem. But when they made the "return" versus "enter" error, they blamed themselves. After all, they had been told what to do.

Norman's concern with designers' biases is an important addendum to Christopher Lorenz's views on design primacy with which I launched this chapter. Norman would, of course, agree with Lorenz about design's enormous potential. But, like David Kelley, he'd quickly point out that usability is different from aesthetics. Which in turn means that elevating any old designer (including an award-winning one) to a position of corporate prominence is no surefire path to competitive Nirvana. Design prominence, yes. But design must be defined "right"—aesthetics, usability, manufacturability, financial viability, per Kelley; personality or signature, per Michael Shannon and Rodney Fitch. Then the "right" designers must be put in place—i.e., folks who embody "beyond aesthetics" as defined above.

Join the Crusade

My goal is modest. I simply want to entice you to join my design-consciousness crusade. I started a list of design sins upon closing the back cover on Norman's book. In 60 days I generated 73 entries (and overlooked or forgot another 73, I'm sure). Included was a Marriott hotel elevator's controls: The floor marked one is the basement. Floor two is the lobby. Then there's the metal floor-lamp switch that you can't turn off without burning your fingers. (One retailer solved the problem by buying plastic switch caps at a local hardware store to replace producers' metal ones.) Another high-tech lamp switch is activated by a touch anywhere on the lamp's outer skin; but it intermittently goes on without being touched, due to random forces in the ethers, I suppose. Or is it random? Mine always seems to come on just after I've finally dropped off to sleep. (I touted such switches, recall, in our discussion of products for aging customers. Goes to show you, the most terrific idea can be poorly executed.) And then there's the buckle tongue on my L. L. Bean watch strap. I'd guess it has snared, and rendered unwearable, no fewer than a half-dozen sweaters. (I've got the occasional "good" entry on the list, too. One is Fellowes Econo/ Store Legal Size Bankers Boxes. The two-part box—body, lid—at first blush looks rather complicated. But directions are clear as day. Any number of ingenious traits turn a flimsy piece of cardboard into a sturdy container in seconds. It's even better than that: Putting the box together makes me feel like a mechanical genius!)

I beg you to start a list like mine, to go berserk over floors labeled two that should be labeled one, shampoo containers that a pointy-toothed genius couldn't crack, and watch straps that snag sweaters. Don't be like that company secretary and assume it's your fault. (In the L. L. Bean watch-strap example, I honestly did start to feel bad about buying sweaters with sensitive fabric—yikes!) That is, I urge you to become aware. Allow design and usability of everyday objects to worm their way into your consciousness. Allow yourself to become irritated, even furious, at the designer instead of feeling frustrated at yourself. It should convince you of how much can be done better, how big a little difference can be, and how important the whole idea is.

The battle for competitive advantage is increasingly over nonobvious sources of value-added. Becoming a "design and usability fanatic" in your "everyday life" is a giant first step toward becoming a design and usability fanatic in your corporate life. Start your list today. Enlist others, too. It will disturb your sense of well-being, but it may well make you rich in the end. After you've taken that step, then worry about design's place at the corporate head table.

THE *BIG* IDEA

So what is design? Where does it come from? Here's a stab at a summary:

- Design *is* about <u>aesthetics</u>, visual pleasure. Donald Norman's skepticism is well founded, but it *is* a turn-on to look at a Braun coffeemaker or a Moser table. Aesthetics are essential. And, Professor Norman, I *do* tingle at the sight of the objects in the industrial design collection at the New York Museum of Modern Art—user-friendly or not.

- <u>Usability</u>. Apple scored with a magnificent combination of aesthetics and, especially, "user-friendliness"—a term I'd never heard before meeting my Apple II in 1982. Usability is Norman's passion—and as I lost (at a crucial moment) the Golden State Warriors basketball game I was listening to in the car the night before I wrote this, by inadvertently hitting the "seek" or "scan" or something button on my X!—!** radio, his point struck home anew.

- <u>Signature, personality, distinction</u>. It's that "look, feel, taste, smell . . ." that design consultant Michael Shannon referred to. Design-centeredness is, per se, a distinctive strategy/culture/part of the soul of the firm. Design is no side issue at Bahco, CKD, Trumpf, Rational, Deere, Braun, Thos. Moser, or Sony.

- <u>Attitude</u>. Design is a way of thought, a certain habit of mindfulness that permeates the firm from the loading dock to the executive suite.

- <u>Organization chart</u>. Where the chief designer (or whatever you call him or her) sits—literally—is of vital importance. Sony understands that. So do a few others. Alas, very few others.

- <u>Project structure</u>. Designers' involvement, from the start, on multifunction product development teams (and, later, product enhancement teams) is a must. That's become conventional wisdom these days—except damn few practice it, especially in the thoroughgoing fashion of, say, Rational or Deere.

- <u>Leadership</u>. Trumpf's Leibinger, Braun's Rams, Playmobil's Brandstätter and Beck, CKD's Yoshida, Apple's Jobs (now Sculley): If "design sense" is not at or near the top of the leader's everyday agenda, then the enormous, encompassing design opportunity I staked out will not materialize. You can smell Steve Jobs's design obsession from a mile, perhaps a light-year, away. Just ask David Kelley! Jobs gives new meaning to the term "design perfectionist."

The title of a *San Jose Mercury News* story about David Kelley's firm captures the essence of my fears—"By Design, Final Look Is No Longer a By-product." Design is decidedly *not* "final look." Aesthetics, even if that word had been chosen for the *Mercury News* headline, is *not* the point. (It's just *one* important point among many important points—see above.) Design is a thoroughgoing attitude that gets reflected, *in part*, in "final look." But as long as we think of design as final look, the boat will be off course by a continent or two. To be sure, if more companies put "final look"-centered thinking on their agenda, they'd probably be better off. But they'd never, like Bahco or CKD, end up transforming themselves and reinventing an industry segment in the process. They'd still be leaving 98 percent (or so!) of design's potential lying on the table.

47

"Customerizing": Produced by, Directed by . . . and Starring—Our Customers

Anshin is the Japanese word for . . . security and comfort. Increasing the comfort level of your associates and customers in Japan goes far beyond providing quality products delivered on time and at the right price. Japanese want to feel comfortable and "in touch" with their suppliers and business partners. There is a human dimension to this desire along with the business side. Japanese want to know you can be trusted and are as interested in their success as you are in your own. The first order of *anshin* is to understand the customer's needs: response to customer demands is an obligation. This takes time and close relations. Two-way obligations between customers and suppliers are built over many years, and go far beyond traditional American expectations.

JIM AND JEFFREY MORGAN
Cracking the Japanese Market

Look through clear eyes and you'll find that almost all enterprises—hospitals, manufacturers, banks—are organized around, and for the convenience of, the "production function." The hospital is chiefly concocted to support doctors, surgery, and lab work. Manufacturers are fashioned to maximize factory efficiency. The bank's scheme is largely the by-product of "best backroom [operations] practice." I'm not arguing there's no benefit to customers from these practices. The patient generally gets well, the car or zipper usually works, the bank account is serviced. And enterprises do reach out, sporadically, to customers—holding focus groups, providing toll-free numbers to enhance customer dialogue, offering "customer care" training to staff. But how many build the entire logic of the firm around the flow of the customer through the A to Z process of experiencing the organization? Answer: Darn few!

Disney is the most notable exception. Its business concept *is* the creation of superb customer episodes, starting in the parking lot. Or even sooner: Fly to Orlando on Delta, for example, and you'll become tangled in Disney's tentacles in the air, or at least at the Orlando airport. Disney obviously promotes fantasy, and makes no bones about it. "Not me," you say, "I make products, not fantasies. You've lived in California too long, Tom." Baloney, I say.

There is no reality! Everyday life is the perception-tinted product of our cockeyed imaginations—period. And the bottom line in commercial life is the sum total of conjured-up dramas created by our customers. Now suppose, as car or computer maker, restaurant or hospital maestro, you bought that notion, embraced the "imagineering" business, as Disney and our friends at Britain's Imagination (Chapter 11) call it, then designed and ran your outfit accordingly. You'd start down the new strategic path, which necessarily means "zero basing" your entire enterprise, by gluing yourself to customers, tagging around after them, developing a sense for the myriad ways they "get a handle" on your company, the ways they form first impressions of you (from ads, landscaping, angry ex-customers, rumors, vendors, etc.). That is, what "vibes"—exactly the right word—do you give off from up close, from afar?

From there the process of specifying the customer's dramaturgical interchange with you proceeds logically, and illogically. As to the latter, remember we're dealing with pure fantasy: What are the scenes, acts, rhythms, denouements, of Apple, Microsoft, Marriott, The Body Shop to a typical customer? Though fantasy is the animating idea, part of the answer can be mapped in a careful, linear fashion, with one important twist: Normally, any such maps are "inside-out" (we → them), rather than "outside-in" (they → us). The theatrical map, on the other hand, must always put the audience/purchaser at the center of the universe—where you and I as customers always *do* put ourselves, as we create a script with idiosyncratic us starring in "me and Marriott," "me and DEC," "me and The Johns Hopkins Hospital."

Such "outside-in" imagery clashes with the current "customer focus" craze. Customer focus still clutches the tired imagery of "us" deigning to attend to "them"; "us" as active (the actors); "they" as passive (audience); "us" as the sun around which "they," the customers, revolve. In an illusory world, semantics by definition are everything—and "outside-in," "script-and-direction-by-customer," or "customer-experience-created" are more appropriate phrases. "We" (producers) are a mere derivative, the bit players in "their" (customers') show, not the reverse!

I've come to call all this "customerizing." It's an ugly word. And in general I heartily dislike such concoctions. Yet it seems to taste about right. One reason for choosing it is to point up the difference from *customizing*. Customizing, a good idea, is still pre-Copernican in slant. "We" are still the center of the universe, presenting "them" with a carefully crafted menu of offerings. It misses that huge Disney-leap into their creating us. Customer-as-initiator is the point.

Or customer as potter. After I first publicized this customerizing idea, I got a letter from a strongly supportive seminar participant. It read, in part: "The ways in which we satisfy the ideal image for our customers is not set in stone, it is like clay used to make pottery. Each time it is thrown on the wheel it needs to be molded by creative and inspired hands. The clay (customer) and the potter (provider) are working in tandem to create something neither one could have accomplished alone." He's 90 percent right, and 100 percent wrong. The image of clay/malleability is right on. And "creates something neither one could have accomplished alone"—I couldn't have said it better. But he blew the big one: Aren't I really suggesting that we try and make the customer the potter and us the provider of the clay? The customer should perceive that she/he has "created the organization," a big-league version of Burger King's "have it your way" idea. (Notice I say "idea." Burger King, even under enlightened new management, still falls far short of allowing us customers to have it our way, though the firm is better than most of its take-it-or-leave-it competition in this regard.)

FIRST THINGS LAST

According to the new model, the factory, operating room, or restaurant kitchen, for example, gets invented last, not first. The production function, regardless of the type of enterprise, is the consequence of the fantasy you hope customers will weave. Yet such an approach may lead, surprisingly, to more emphasis on the "factory"—e.g., the way Carl Sewell invites prospective and current customers to experience the innards of his service department; the way Stew Leonard openly displays the workings of his milk-processing operation to grocery store customers; the way The Body Shop and Home Depot have turned their operations into customer schoolhouses; and the way smart manufacturers such as Quad/Graphics and Titeflex use their plants as showrooms and their plant workers as chief salespersons.

In "The Service Factory" (July–August 1989 *Harvard Business Review*), Richard Chase and David Garvin begin: "The factory of the future is *not* a place where computers, robots and flexible machines do the drudge work. That is the factory of the present, which . . . any manufacturing business can build. Of course, any competitor can build one too—which is why it is becoming harder and harder to compete on manufacturing excellence alone. . . . The manufacturers that thrive into the next generation . . . will make the factory itself the hub of their efforts to get and hold customers. . . . Production workers and factory managers will be able to forge and sustain new relationships with customers because they will be in direct and continuing contact with them." Such a factory, Chase and Garvin conclude, must become an experimental laboratory that fully engages customers and workers in perpetual innovation and problem solving; and an open showroom that proudly exhibits the firm's skills to customers.

This overall "customerizing" concept clearly ought to be repeated for each set of stakeholders. Consider prospective employees: How do they create their Quad/Graphics fantasy, starting with the style of help-wanted ads or word-of-mouth from employees or alumni? How do vendors "imagine" you? Regulators? Communities?

I'll be the first to acknowledge that what I'm suggesting will be very tough sledding. You'll doubtless need outside help, since seeing yourself through truly naïve eyes is essential. (Incidentally, I'd suggest dramatists, virtual-reality practitioners, and software-game creators, not management consultants—prior encomiums for McKinsey notwithstanding.) But above all, a no-nonsense dramaturgical/"customerizing" strategy requires clinging to words like "myth," "fantasy," and "illusion." For better or for worse, your outfit is not real: It is no more, and no less, than the sum total of fictionalized, elliptical images created by your customers, employees, vendors, distributors, and communities as they experience you on a day-by-day basis.

Carol Hickey Airlines

26 July 1991

Bob Crandall
Chairman
American Airlines

Dear Bob,

This is really two letters in one. The first is a simple thanks and hearty commendation. A few weeks ago, before departing San Francisco for New York, Carol Hickey, your local Special Services Manager, came on board the flight to ask me and one other passenger if all was well. It's the first time such a thing had happened to me, and I was very impressed. (Translation: blown away!) I flew back to San Francisco from New York the next day, and she was there again upon arrival, to ask once more if it had been an OK trip.

This week, after a long, unexpected stay in San Francisco to attend to some personal business, I headed back to Vermont (home half the time). I was carrying five boxes of book research material, and was in a dither about it being out of my sight. My office called Ms. Hickey, who told us about AA's escorted baggage service. But that was the least of it. She accompanied my wife and me through the ropes—and made miracles happen when our original flight was cancelled. (See, I'm not even mad about the cancellation!) She also arranged for us to be met and chaperoned in Chicago by Ginny Borowski, your Special Services Manager there, who was also exceedingly helpful (including issuing an instant ticket replacement, since in the midst of the San Francisco scramble your ticket agent had inadvertently kept my wife's ticket). All in all, it was a memorable experience, and my hat is off to Carol Hickey, Ginny Borowski, and their helpful colleagues.

That's "letter No. 1." The second part is to reflect on my experience in light of the intermittent dialogue you and I have had over the years. In short, as a *very, very* frequent flyer for 17 years (my horse is even named Frequent Flyer), as a regular American Airlines patron (experiencing downs and ups), this is the very first time I have ever felt genuine "affection" for the airline, or any airline for that matter.

The issues, to me, are obvious:

—Why did it take 17 years for the first magical act? (Especially for a major-revenue passenger, who most often flies main routes, and therefore usually has a choice of carriers.)

—Isn't there a way to create competitive advantage here? And not only for VFFs (very frequent flyers), but for many, many MFFs (Moderately Frequent Flyers) and SFFs (Sorta Frequent Flyers)?

As a crusty old fart, I am shocked at the emotional impact this single event has had on me; and will have, I expect—AA has become personalized for me as CHA (Carol Hickey Airlines), and I'd bet a pretty penny this has an effect that lasts a long time. (Stay tuned!)

Let me make it clear. I've had lots of good American Airlines experiences (and lots of good experiences with other airlines, of course) and been the beneficiary of lots of special effort by your employees—and of course I've taken advantage of such benefits as AAdvantage mileage credit. But that mystical barrier—called "genuinely memorable"—was crossed for the first time with my Carol Hickey Airlines experience. And I'm too stubborn to believe such experiences can't be more or less replicated for lots of us passengers.

Sincerely,
Tom Peters

Note: I faxed the above to Crandall, and some time later received a perfunctory response from some junior aide. Can't win 'em all!

A "CUSTOMERIZING" FANTASY

The mythical, personalized, have-it-your-way, totally "customerized" company might have these traits:

• Personalization. That is, Carol Hickey Airlines. And Mark, Mark, or Mark (and Denny and Russ!) at Thos. Moser Cabinetmakers. These people personalized a big company and a small company alike. I had it my way. That's a lot of the trick at Federal Express, whose delivery person is (or appears to be, which is what counts) less harried than her or his UPS counterpart, and takes the time (a few words now and again) to build a relationship with the customer. Information technology can be a potent tool in support of mass personalization (recall the discussion of database marketing—p. 717); but beware (as usual); the technology is only an aid to caring employees (see below).

• Customization. A small Acordia company will jump through any hoop to customize for a customer of almost any size. So, too, ABB's 5,000 profit centers. Of course, as I have said repeatedly, customization has long been the norm at professional service firms—which is a major reason I chose them as models. But another word of caution: CRSS and Chiat/Day/Mojo are abnormal, as we said. Though customizers in theory, a lot of professional service firms peddle arrogance of the "have it *our* way or else" sort—i.e., designers with a closer eye on peers and awards than on their customer.

• Responsiveness. The nub is Shoshana Zuboff's "informated" idea— e.g., conductors at the Union Pacific who can bring all the railroad's knowledge instantly to bear for their customers.

• Friendliness. The entire start-up logic, from logo to operating-system software, at Apple Computer was "friendly"—taking formerly unfriendly devices and translating them into comfy, useful tools for the masses. In short, some institutions are friendly to do business with, and provide friendly products. Some aren't, and don't.

• The perception of choice. This is the carnival concept, the notion that the customer can, in effect, "create my own company" ("my Disney," "my FedEx"). In the best cases, there's much more to it than a thick catalog of options—e.g., the *feeling* a dedicated Acordia company gives that it'll invent almost anything you the customer can conjure up.

• Insiderism. At Quad/Graphics, EDS, McKinsey, Chiat/Day/Mojo, Imagination or CRSS, for example, customers are really part and parcel of the service provider's team. No information is withheld from them. They're members of the family (at least for a while), and made to "feel" that way in a hundred tangible—and intangible—ways. My first boss at McKinsey modeled the power of using the simple word "we." Whenever he spoke with clients, and even with fellow McKinsey team members when clients weren't around, he always talked about "we"—meaning Skelly Oil (and us), Getty Oil (and us), Basalt Rock (and us). In an almost insidious way, it made a big difference. Pretty soon almost everyone started *feeling* "we." (As EDS's Barry Sullivan warned, however, the service providers can start acting "too we"—and lose the arm's-length perspective they were hired in part to provide. Ah, always cautions.)

- Clubbishness. A twist on the customer-as-insider idea. Stan Rapp and Tom Collins described the "clubs" created by Hallmark, and others. It's part of making customers members of the family. (Case in point: My company publishes an expensive newsletter sent to about 8,000 subscribers. But in early 1991 we decided to put out an irregular, much less formal, free "The Tom Peters Group Update" for our best customers. It has a few "substantive" articles, but in the main it's chatty. The object of "Update" is conversation— to create pals and family members.)

- Transparency. Open up the factory or operations area—visually, in part—to the customer. Titeflex, Quad/Graphics, Sewell Village Cadillac, and Stew Leonard's are masters here.

- In the know. A cost-obsessed distribution-company CEO prefers more expensive FedEx over less expensive UPS largely because of the real-time, easy-to-access, detailed information on a shipment's status the former provides. The CEO's customers depend upon him for the parts they don't buy directly from manufacturers; he fulfills only 10 percent of their requirements— but it's the crucial fraction needed to deal with unanticipated demand surges. His ability, courtesy of FedEx, to tell his customers exactly what's happening when something goes astray—or even when it doesn't, but they're in a dither anyway—is invaluable, he reports. It's a special case of insiderization and transparency: The distribution company is able to expose *its* customers to the innards of its vendor (FedEx in this case).

- "House calls." Remember the Bookmobile? The Good Humor Man? The fresh-vegetable truck in the summer? I do. A lot of people didn't have cars when I was a kid and house calls were common. Then cars—and malls— became universal. House calls disappeared. But things are changing, and house calls (for a profit) are making a comeback—motivated largely by the ever greater value people are putting on their time. And don't forget Ken Dychtwald's analysis of the high-growth aging market—a population willing to spend a fortune (literally) on convenience. Of course, "house calls" take on new significance in light of the outpouring of information technology applications—home banking, shopping, etc. Catalogs may be the most pervasive form of "house calls" these days—catalog quality and customization have gone berserk. (Thomas Moser's catalog is so elegant that he gets away with charging $9 for it!)

• <u>Design that suits *my* convenience</u>. The model operation at Lakeland Regional Medical Center was designed around the patient's needs. (And, along the way, it ended up making life easier for doctors, nurses, and technicians—and saved money, too. Such "incidental" benefits are popping up all over: Serving the customer/patient better leads to more involving, more rewarding work for service providers. Nice.)

Cleaning Up

Upon checking in at a Marriott a while back, I found a menu-like card on my bed (the sort that can be hung over the doorknob). But it wasn't offering breakfast goodies. This one gave you a choice of times to have your room cleaned the next day.

Wow! I bet you've been as miffed as I on occasion—you're trying to work in your room, but the housekeeper knocks every 10 minutes. (Not true, of course. "Just" perceived.)

Fact is, Marriott's little service is *literally* unimportant—but it sure *smells* sweet: "We care, this hotel is for *your* convenience, not ours." (At least it made that impression on me—and I didn't even use the service.)

What a great deal for Marriott. Any number of us are doubtless tickled pink by the gesture. But most people are out of their rooms during normal housekeeping hours, so housekeepers' schedules will be largely unaffected. The cost to Marriott, I wager, is zilch.

• <u>Human scale</u>. Lakeland Regional Medical Center, once more, is a nice illustration. So, too, Acordia and Chromalloy Compressor Technologies. The parent company may or may not be a giant. But the empowered unit the customer interacts with feels "down home"—*by design*.

• <u>An educational experience</u>. Williams-Sonoma, Home Depot, The Body Shop, Quad/Graphics, Rational, and Trumpf, among others we examined, spend a lot of time, energy, and money teaching customers. Associating with these companies, from low-price retailer to million-dollar machine maker, allows us to learn along the way. We get more than a nice shopping experience or nifty tool.

• <u>Reliability</u>. The guarantees by Orvis, Delta Dental, and others amount to a remarkable promise of reliability—to the point of allowing the customer total freedom to define service adequacy and invoke the guarantee at will.

(And *potentially* at great expense to the provider—which makes it "feel" even more real, which is the essence of "customerizing.")

- Fun. It's a pleasure to do business with Disney, of course. But also The Body Shop and Imagination. Pleasure is OK. But "fun" is even better. The "fun" ideal is rarely met, partially because it's a tough standard. But mostly, I suspect, because it's even tough to imagine. One reason: We steadfastly refuse to use the f-u-n word in the grim, practical world of traditional business. ("Running your business for 'glow,' 'tingle,' and 'wow' " is another way to put it.)

- Theater. Theater is fun plus. All the world—including the commercial world—*is* a stage (thanks, W.S.). Imagination humanizes and "marketizes" the stodgiest industrial-products companies via straight theater. Anita Roddick says she has "no modern-day heroes in the business world"; all the execs she's run across lack "a sense of joy, magic, or theater." Why not theater?

Acting Classes

Just 15 months after opening in March 1990, the Museum of the Moving Image in London has joined the top 20 of Britain's tourist attractions—thanks largely to training techniques taken straight from the theater. Museum director Leslie Hardcastle employed a former actress, Mo Heard, to implement the idea of turning guides into actors. Says Heard, "I used my drama background to design training courses in a business environment. It has proved very successful."

Heard brought in director Phil Young, known for staging improvised plays, as a trainer. He calls his three-week courses "rehearsals" and relies heavily on improvisation sessions. Young takes guides through factual material using a technique known as hot seating, used in the theater for ad-lib work. The guide sits in a chair and Young fires questions which the guide has to answer in character.

Market research shows the guides' dramatic skills are a key to the museum's popularity. Attendance to date has exceeded targets by 25 percent, and the training scheme itself won a national training award.

- Emphasis on beginnings and ends. Carl Sewell bought a street sweeper, because he didn't think the City of Dallas was doing a good enough job of keeping the road clean in front of his dealership. And, Sewell says, first impressions are everything. (He devotes a whole chapter of his book *Customers for Life* to this "obvious" idea!) Disney's obsession with the parking lot amounts to the same thing. So many events begin with a downer—parking along with 35,000 other people at a baseball game, or in a distant corner of a shopping center's lot. If you don't turn around and go home, you're at least in a ratty mood before you start. Last impressions also carry disproportionate weight. Sewell, once more, sets the pace: His management of the tiniest detail of the payment and car fetching process (p. 605) is nothing short of remarkable. What's more remarkable, though, is that so few pay careful attention to these all-important bookends to a transaction.

• Consistency. In a world gone inconsistent, consistency is more valued than ever! You're busier than yesterday, and the furniture delivery team that shows up on the dot is a godsend—which Thomas Moser understands and most others don't. (Consider this line from a letter of "apology" I got from the president of a pricey Taos furniture company: "As far as the shipping schedule is concerned . . . we had no control. Sometimes carriers take two days . . . and sometimes two weeks." Should I send him a copy of this book, COD?) Several Union Pacific service workers report that most "real" problems simply evaporate if you keep the customer constantly in the know, another form of consistency. Len Berry's research (p. 715) lent empirical punch to the idea of consistency's power. Despite the newfound emphasis on raw speed (which is essential), doing it a *little* slower and a *lot* surer is also an important consideration.

• Class. It's neat to associate with classy outfits. Thos. Moser Cabinetmakers charges two arms and two legs. The raw product alone is worth it. But every phase of your dealings with Moser makes you feel as if you're part of something special.

• Emphasis on process. Like it or lump it, process beats substance. Disney's substance, designed for an earlier generation (mine!), started sagging a few years ago—and Michael Eisner spent big bucks getting it back to state-of-the-art. So substance is important. Nonetheless, the Disney difference was/is process: The "guest" feels that each nanosecond of her or his interaction with Disney has been worked over with a fine-tooth comb. (Actually, the guest does not feel this in any overt way, but usually realizes it long after the fact.) Why oh why are there so few process fanatics? I guess the question encloses the answer: Fanaticism is the key.

• Caring—a must! I think each item on this list is important. In fact, I honestly think each item is a bare-bones necessity. On the other hand, if you don't get this one right, you'll scuttle the rest. We have "a feeling" that some institutions genuinely give a damn about us as customers. ("Love and care touch everything we do," says Body Shop founder Anita Roddick.) And others act as if they're doing us a favor by doing business with us. Of course, the commercial process *is* reciprocal: Both buyer and seller pursue advantage. On the other hand, the kinder, gentler institution that bends over backwards, in a host of ways, to smile and offer some consideration is probably the long-term victor. Remember Texas professor Bob Peterson's conclusion that high customer satisfaction only translates into repeat business when there is an "emotive element"—i.e., love.

I like this list. And dislike it. I like it because I think it points us in the right direction. I dislike it because it lacks a certain wholeness, and fails to capture the "feel" of customerizing. As I see it, customerizing is light-years beyond customer-focused and close-to-the-customer—and even somewhat beyond the symbiosis ideas offered in Chapter 45. It transforms the essential logic of the corporation. So it's new. But it's also old. It amounts to the genuine meaning of "at your service"—*anshin* in Japan (see the epigraph to this chapter). I (provider) stand ready to let you call the shots, have you (customer) make me (provider) better by challenging me to be more than I could imagine. Isn't that, in the end, what the little Acordia companies, for example, are asking their customers to do? "Push us. Make us invent something for you that neither of us could imagine. Here, customer, you be our potter. Sure, we've got some expert knowledge about financial services. But that knowledge is the clay. Lead us to form it in a new configuration."

Destination

Global retailer Ikea, based in Sweden, markets what it calls a "new brand of shopping experience." The 105-store, $3.8-billion (1991 sales) furniture empire has raised self-service to high concept, capturing customers for whom a trip to the store is part family entertainment, part value-hunting.

"We operate from large, out-of-town sites so we have to offer our customers a destination instead of just a store," Cynthia Neiman, marketing manager of Ikea U.S. West, told us in 1992. "A visit to Ikea is a day's outing for the family, and we know we have to take care of their needs." Customers typically spend three hours shopping at an Ikea outlet vs. just one hour at the competition, according to Neiman. The cavernous stores offer a range of amenities. The Ballroom, for example, allows parents to park their kids in a supervised, glass-walled play area, where toddlers can slide into a pit of soft plastic balls while Mom and Dad shop. Parents can also borrow a stroller for younger children, or make use of a baby-care room where free diapers are provided. An in-store cafe sells Swedish meatballs and other specialties (including baby food)—and Ikea's Burbank cafe has made it onto two reviewers' lists of best meals under $10 in Los Angeles.

As they enter the store, shoppers can pick up an Ikea catalog, paper tape measure, notepad, and pencil. This "customer tool kit" is no mere contrivance: Shoppers must rely largely on the catalog and the store's fully furnished, color-coordinated room displays to choose from among thousands of items. Virtually all furniture comes unassembled, in flat boxes, which customers usually pull from the shelves of an in-store warehouse, place on a cart, and push to their cars. The flat packing of unassembled furniture is key to the Ikea concept, saving money on shipping, storage, and assembly. "Shoppers become what Alvin Toffler calls 'prosumers,' part producer, part consumer," said Neiman. "By participating in the process, our customers know they're realizing significant savings."

While it mails out several million catalogs a year, Ikea U.S. still offers no phone- or mail-order service. "The catalog is our most effective marketing tool," said Neiman. "It gets people excited and lets them do a lot of preshopping. It fuels the fantasy of great rooms and unbelievable prices." Ikea also rolls out big-budget ad campaigns when it enters a new market. More creative, though, are some of the merchandising tools it uses to build store traffic. Each December, for example, all Ikea outlets promote a "Christmas tree rental" plan: For $20, customers can rent a five- to seven-foot Douglas fir. After Christmas, they can return the tree to the store, get back $10, and have the tree ground up for garden mulch. Some stores also offer coupons good for a free seedling later in the year. The result: up to three customer visits generated by a single clever promotion.

In addition, in Europe and Canada, the company touts its "Ikea Family"—a customer club that for $15 a year, or a one-time purchase of $150 or more, offers members special discounts on merchandise and on meals in the cafe, a newsletter with decorating tips, and travel packages. Ikea Family members can even trade homes worldwide, for use while on vacation!

Furniture-industry consultant Jerry Epperson of Mann Armistead and Epperson told us there's a lot to be learned from Ikea's approach: "They offer a breadth of merchandise and price you're unlikely to find elsewhere; then they take care of the kids and feed you so you don't have to leave the store. They capture consumers' imagination and invite them to join the family and buy into the concept."

Afterword

Liberation Management

Recall that at Lakeland Regional Medical Center, nurse-technologist "care pairs" are spending over 50 percent of their time with patients, up from 21 percent before the hospital reorganized in 1989. Titeflex Teamsters now handle orders from start to finish, and routinely call on customers and vendors. That's liberation.

Very independent chief executives of tiny Acordia companies are hopping through tiny hoops for their very demanding customers. And many Thermo Electron "division" bosses are facing beady-eyed securities analysts (instead of smug corporate staffers) to explain their last quarter's results. That's liberation, too.

So it must be. Each *day* brings another 30 software programs and another 40 grocery or drugstore products to the American marketplace. With frenzy like that, only people (bosses, front-line "professionals"/"businesspersons") who are free to take almost any initiative stand much of a chance of success. Liberation may well be a "nice" idea. I think it is. But that's beside the point. The times make it a *necessary* idea. Hence, necessary disorganization into free-standing units so as to achieve necessary liberation for all—the essence of this book's title.

It's scary. Freedom always is, for an 8-year-old or a 48-year-old, for Americans after 200 years of practice or Hungarians after 2. Yet we found that workers are making the transition with relative ease—among other things, life on the job is looking more like life off the job for a change. ("For a change"? For the first time in a couple of hundred years is more like it.) Oddly enough, it's managers who are having the toughest time making the shift. Well, it's not so odd, on second thought. Many of their jobs are disappearing. (I can picture an old World War II Uncle Sam poster, with the ominous pointing finger and "Liberation Means Your Job Goes" as the inscription. A dreary thought.) Worse still, the ladder that managers aspired to climb is being turned to kindling in the liberated, horizontal, beyond-hierarchy environment.

Some of us were dad-blamed lucky. My first boss in the Navy, in 1966, left his young officers alone—and then demanded results. From there it was on to a largely unsupervised policy job in Washington, and then to a professional service firm, McKinsey & Co., for seven years—and thence to my own company. I've worked for some traditional outfits (e.g., the Navy), but have rarely been burdened with bosses who were bent on oppression. (Luckier still, each of my bosses had absurdly high standards, and left it up to me to figure out how to meet them—I'll admit it hasn't made for a lot of sleep over the years.) That is, I've taken to this so-called newfangled stuff (projects, create-your-own-firm) because it's where I've been from the start.

Most managers haven't been so fortunate. And for them the shift is wrenching, though, I contend, liberating if they can shed the shackles of ladderish metaphors and learn to take pleasure in the task and the team. The "new dependence" is upon peers and extended-network family (new horizontal dependence?), instead of upon the boss and the corporation (old vertical dependence?).

Lead dogs don't have it easy, either. After all, they've slowly worked their way through the pack, sniffing a lot of rear ends along the way. When they emerge at the front of the line, instant transformation is rare. It's hardly surprising that a 48-year-old, just-appointed company president, who's emerged into the sun after 26 years of political elbowing, doesn't immediately take to my jolly "You're only in control when you're out of control." Those who do take to it often had the sort of luck I did, following an unconventional path (e.g., former Union Pacific Railroad chief Mike Walsh starting his managerial career in a U.S. Attorney's office).

Then there's the matter of the public sector. It's unprepared, from the classroom to the U.S. Departments of Commerce and Health and Human Services, for a post-hierarchical commercial order. Our education, training, health, and social security schemes are formed around the big corporate lifetime employment "model" which has dominated the U.S. for the last century (during which time almost all social support programs were invented).

Well, my friends, the genies are not going back into their lamps. The information technology "revolution" is just gathering steam. The biotechnology revolution and the materials revolution and the telecommunications revolution (each dependent, in large measure, upon the infernal computing machine) are/will be almost as profound. Protectionist blather notwithstanding, global interdependence is another escaped genie. Then there's the spread of capitalism in general. And . . . And . . . That is, don't expect the number of new software programs or grocery and drugstore products or entrepreneurs to go into retreat any time soon. Do expect to hear ever wilder stories from ever wilder places. Hey, I wouldn't bet against India as a global economic powerhouse by 2020 (when the current crop of 22-year-olds will be my age today).

What follows are hardly "Prescriptions for Society 2000" (there are so damn many around already, including a few of my own, I hate to think about 1999). They're more personal than that. As an eight-hour seminar winds down, on a gloomy February day in London (or Chicago or Stockholm), the real questions start to come. Middle manager: "I've tried this stuff. I believe in it. It works. But my boss thinks I'm crazy. Help?!" MBA student: "You're telling me to 'trundle off to Eastern Europe for a year, it'll do you good.' Well, how much damn good can I afford to do with a $65,000 student loan to pay back?" I don't know—that's the real answer. But maybe the following contains a few clues. I hope.

STUDENTS

Mostly remember that (1) education is the *only* ticket to success and (2) education doesn't stop with the last certificate you pick up. Studenthood for life is a necessity, by definition, in a knowledge-based society. This is not advice from Dad to "hit those books." It is, I pray, slightly more profound. It's a suggestion, if you're 15, that you quit laughing at the nerds in your class—you're gonna be working for them someday!

Americans, and people in most developed societies, have long seen education as *the* engine of economic progress. But "see" it though we might, "we" (Americans, at least) have often as not taken it for granted—a few visits to elementary-school classrooms does not an "education president" make!

Now why am I talking education policy to 15- or 21-year-olds? Simple. You need to take your education—and the education of all others—very seriously. Education is the "big game" in the globally interdependent economy. Period.

For those a little further along in the education process, there's an additional charge: Take networking seriously. I think back to my Stanford Business School days (20 years ago). There was a handful of people whose ways seemed mysterious. They were the instinctive networkers (the Marion McGoverns in-the-making, perhaps). They left school with fat Rolodexes and bushels of friendships—and a surprising share of them are running companies today. It may be tautological to declare that networking is important in a networked society, but that doesn't mean it's not worth saying. It must be said again and again.

I'd also urge all students, and especially MBA sorts, to get the heck out of the country (whichever your country is). A little global breadth goes a long way. And the absence of a global instinct will increasingly pinch in the years ahead. If you, as college senior or fresh-caught MBA grad, can scrounge up a job of any kind beyond your national borders, go for it.

Finally, get turned on. Or follow your bliss, or whatever. Vacuous advice? Perhaps. But the practical implication is this: In a knowledge-based economy, you must—to survive—add some special value, be distinctively good at something. And the truth is, we usually only get good at stuff we like. If you love skiing and you're a newly minted MBA, look to get a job in some sporting-related industry that lets you turn skiing to professional advantage. Ain't nobody gonna take care of you on the job in a big company anymore: It's not dog-eat-dog out there, it's skill-eat-skill. If you're not skilled/motivated/passionate about *something*, you're in trouble!

"WORKERS"

"Workers," like "organization," gets quotes. Why? All jobs (in developed countries at least) are fast becoming professional service firm jobs. Managers are disappearing. "Workers" are all becoming "managers." Work is the same for all of us: projects, networks, etc. *All* of us? Yes, all. Titeflex and the Union Pacific Railroad are professional service firms, whether they call themselves that or not. The implications for Teamsters and United Transportation Union members—and employees of Professional Parking Services, Inc.—are clear:

• Education. See my advice to full-time students. As parker, receptionist, auto-worker, or graduate engineer, you *must* retrain yourself—constantly and forever. If your company helps, great. If the government helps, great (see next page). If it doesn't, well, that's too bad, but it doesn't alter my advice an iota. You must, by hook or by crook, keep at it.

• Risk. The biggest risk is not taking risks and getting pigeonholed. So your company is still very "steep," with the oldfangled hierarchy mostly in place. Tough. Your only path to "employment security" (new style: network employment security) is to reach out beyond your cubbyhole. Make yourself into an "Oticon person" (remember them wheeling their carts to the day's project?), even if your company is still light-years away from the Oticon model.

• Job-hopping. In Silicon Valley, many would-be employers are wary if candidates *haven't* had a few different jobs. Talk about a break with tradition! Silicon Valley, though phenomenally successful, is hardly the norm. But it is the way the world is heading (even, a little bit, in Japan). Increasingly, a portfolio of experience is the only basis for security. It's a paradox, but it's life.

MIDDLE MANAGERS

Am I a middle-management basher? Yes. Are most of the people who attend my seminars middle managers? Yes. Why do they come? Beats me. Middle management, as we have known it since the railroads invented it right after the Civil War, is dead. Therefore, middle managers, as we have known them, are cooked geese. If that's not clear from the preceding pages, then one of us has a very big problem. So what to do if your answer to the unasked question is "I are one"?

Simple. I've said it in these pages: Act like a consultant. Make friends with the line, create projects. And that, I think, is the "right" prescription. But it's also wrong, because it's a pat answer—and an emotionless one. Whether you're 33 and on a fast track to nowhere, or 52 and on a slow track to the exit, my *real* advice is: Raise hell!

First of all, why not? Your job, salary, and esteem are all in mortal danger. (As of this writing, some sizable companies are coming back from the recession—but they are still trimming managerial fat, and most have no plans for hiring in the foreseeable future.) Why not at least go out with a bang? Funny thing is, I'm serious. Maybe your Percy Barnevik hasn't come along yet, but she or he surely will in the next 10 years. And like Barnevik in Sweden with Asea in 1981, she or he may give you just 100 days or so to "find a job" in some line activity. Are you ready? The only way to lose is not to try.

It's over, d'ya hear? Over. Over. Over. Not every big firm is a Wal-Mart or CNN or ABB. Not every firm will be by the year 2000. But the trend is unmistakable. Frankly, I don't know how to do much more than exhort. "Build your own firm," "create your own network," "raise hell"—it's that or bust.

CHIEFS

This book, like my others, is mostly aimed at you. Which means I've said about all I know to say. The message is clear: (1) trust, (2) "they" can handle "it" (*whatever* "it" is), (3) you're only in control when you're out of control ("head" of a flat, radically decentralized "organization"). Ben Lytle (Acordia) believes it in the financial service business. Pat McGovern (International Data Group) believes it in the information industry.

McGovern was more or less born to it. Lytle got religion along the way. Remember the famous elevator incident: He'd just "decentralized" into "independent" units, and asked a claims processor about the effects. The only thing that had changed for her was the floor she worked on! Thus, via a convoluted path, the Acordia concept was born—small, very independent companies in their own buildings, etc., etc. Almost all chiefs who read this are staunch supporters of decentralization. Almost all chiefs who read this have decentralized. Almost none of their decentralized companies are decentralized. Got that?

THE COMMANDER IN CHIEF (AND HIS 535 PALS AT THE OTHER END OF PENNSYLVANIA AVENUE)

As I write, *Reinventing Government* by David Osborne and Ted Gaebler is well up on the national best-seller lists. The book, endorsed by prominent Democrats and Republicans alike, touts a less bureaucratic, more customer-responsive government to match the post-bureaucratic age in general. Who's to say whether Osborne and Gaebler have it right (I think they mostly do). The point is that government—in America, Japan, or France—hasn't been reinvented, and the world of commerce mostly has (though the task is far from finished). *Liberation Management* is not a public policy book. But the ideas put forth in these pages could be buttressed immeasurably by changes in several policy arenas.

● Trade. The Japanese are no saints when it comes to trade, but at least they're moving toward more openness (though Americans would like them to scuttle 3,000 years' worth of habits overnight—e.g., forget their focus on relationships). The Americans ("us" to this author) never were the saints we thought we were (some polls rank even us among the worst, when it comes to untoward trade practices), and we are clearly moving toward more trade restrictions, fast. If you have any doubt about that at all, please rush to your bookstore and buy James Bovard's *The Fair Trade Fraud*. (It's actually a hilarious book: You won't believe some of the stunts we pull to keep the goods of others out, or the way we tax the bejesus out of them once they get here.)

Adjusting to new technologies and the emerging reality of globalism will not be easy—for anyone. And, as always, some will suffer "unfairly" from the shifts in the world economy's tectonic plates. Still, I have not a shred of doubt that America and the world will prosper to the extent that we all open doors to each other's goods and services, rather than shut them. (And let us pray that new "blocs"—e.g., the North American free trade pact, the post-1992 European Community—don't become the basis for neoprotectionism.) Should the U.S. Trade Representative urge others to open their doors wider? Of course. Should the President have trade weapons he can use as a last resort? Yes. Should Congress micromanage trade, as it's increasingly prone to do? No. No. No. Congress, after the protectionist Smoot-Hawley debacle in 1930, was smart enough to legislate itself out of micromanaging trade for 50 years. Now, under the guise of saving jobs, it's rushing back onto the field. (God save us from Michigan's congressional delegation! Etc.)

There's little glamour in helping firms, especially small ones (individually insignificant), get better at exporting. But that's the sort of job that embassies and the Commerce Department can do, much more than is the case today. Few realize that the Japanese buy almost as much from us as we buy from them on a per capita basis—and that an exceptional share of our exports to them is courtesy of unsung companies (e.g., Applied Materials and A. T. Cross, see Chapter 42).

Overall, our trade balance in 1991 would have been positive if services had been added in (bizarrely, the popular trade figures exclude services, $50 billion in the black for the U.S. in 1991), and our oil imports (still humongous) had been subtracted. We do need to "work on" trade, learn in a hundred ways to think more globally. But we don't need "managed trade," as some are calling it (or "fair" trade, per Bovard). It's a simple fact: Almost every well-intended trade restriction, and many are well-intended, backfires. (We restrict the supply of certain electronics components, and end up rabbit-punching our planet-leading computer industry. Terrific!)

- Training. Training and trade have more in common than starting with "T." As Harvard's Robert Reich says, all so-called factors of production (such as capital) have become portable—except labor. The only "immutable" competitive base a nation has, now that commercial operations can be shifted from here to there with ease, is the relative intelligence of its work force. Happily, our "top 10 percent" of students matches anybody's on any measure you can name. But from there it's downhill. Whether the number is 10 million or 40 million, we have a disgracefully high number of functional illiterates. The horror stories that personnel staffers swap about basic math and reading deficiencies among so-called high school grads border on the unbelievable.

The K-12 system needs fixing. The wonderful news: We have an exciting—and sizable—collection of role-model schools to show us how it can be done (revisit the Dennis Littky tale in Chapter 30 for a case in point). The wretched news: Breaking the back of the school bureaucracy (administrators and teachers' unions in equal measure) is proving to be nigh on impossible. But corporations need fixing, too: While most are doing more training these days, few have put systematic brain development at the top of their strategic priority list (à la Quad/Graphics' Harry Quadracci, Chapter 26). Government could help a lot with a corporate investment tax credit aimed at brain enhancement (rather than one aimed at brick enhancement, still our favorite in the tax-credit game). Furthermore, workers need lifetime-training tax incentives and/or low-interest education loans—whether or not they are on someone's payroll and whether or not they are trying to get better at today's job or trying something completely different. (In the unfolding, job-hopping world, we need to support job-hoppers. Simple, yet still a radical idea.) In moving toward the 21st century, we must, above all, become an "education nation"—and support public-sector leaders at all levels who will make training and education their unmistakable top priority (policy and $$$).

- Antitrust. The long knives came out in the Reagan years, attempting to carve craters in 1890's Sherman Antitrust Act. Support for big was the message. We need B-I-G to compete in a B-I-G world—I guess that was their point, I can't find any other logic. What a crock! Vigor, not bigger, is the answer (which I hope these pages have demonstrated). Harvard's Michael Porter, who is pro-competition and not especially pro-small-company, surprised many of us with his almost ringing endorsement of strong antitrust enforcement in *The Competitive Advantage of Nations*. (The point: spur "vigorous domestic rivalry," *the* competitiveness answer from Porter's extensive research.) Energetic antitrust enforcement does not mean turning America into a nation of mom-and-pop shops, though we're sort of heading in that direction anyway (along with everyone else in the developed world), as brain-work increasingly dominates the creation of economic value. It does mean something other than automatic government approval when clumsy giants look for safety through marriage. But more important, frankly (since most combined clumsy giants eventually commit suicide), wariness toward "strategic alliances" and "consortia" of any and all flavors is called for. In 9 cases out of 10, such relationships are semi-blatant attempts to restrict competition (see Chapter 23). It's true that big and small firms alike must "network" to survive—so the issue is thorny. But it is competition that stands a good chance of getting most of the thorns stuck in it, if the tie-up-everyone-with-alliances game continues at its current, feverish pace. I don't want Apple and IBM to go steady (one wag calls such linkages "virtual keiretsu"—nice); I want them to get back to insulting each other, and bringing out more exciting products as a result!

• <u>Social security</u>. I'm not talking about the sort you start claiming in the "sunset years," but about a bigger issue: a social benefits network consistent with a work force increasingly detached from giant firms, and moving regularly on and off payrolls. I'm a fan of energetic, smaller companies (I've hardly hidden my bias in these pages). But, sad to say, the average, smaller firm does a lousy job when it comes to benefits—especially health care. We need legislation that either forces smaller outfits to get on board, or social support for workers which is not tied to their employer. This is true for health care, child care, training, and pensions, among other things. Workers, not corporations, should be the primary "carriers" of adequate benefit packages. It's no small part of the whole liberation idea. (Models exist. TIAA-CREF, founded in 1918, is the world's largest pension program. Serving 1.4 million members as of 1991, it is a portable scheme offered at 4,500 education and research institutions.)

• <u>Research</u>. As brainware gains economic supremacy, so should research. A coherent, pro-research policy should include (1) healthy basic-research funding for corporations, national labs, and, especially, universities; (2) a pronounced research funding bias toward small projects and individual investigators, rather than "sexy" monster projects ("small science," which is increasingly shortchanged by government funders, still produces most breakthroughs, claims by advocates of space station and human genome projects notwithstanding); (3) guaranteed, sustained (to the best of Congress's meager ability to do so) research-and-development tax credits for companies, with special provisions to assist smaller businesses; and (4) support for programs that explicitly encourage university-corporate ties (again, with an eye on smaller business-university links, which are usually neglected).

Two messages emerge from all this: Keep the competitive juices flowing (trade, antitrust) and invest in brains (training, research, social security). It adds up, you might say, to liberation.

THE FREEDOM TO FAIL

"The great freedom in America is the freedom to fail—and to try again and again," Richard Reeves wrote in the *International Herald Tribune*. While I was in the midst of a long, desultory exchange with a trapped middle manager, circa 1991, someone in the back of the seminar room butted in. "But neither of you gets it," he almost shouted. "This is so, well, liberating." He went on to describe his newly developed start-a-project, do-something, devil-may-care attitude toward his own bureaucracy (in the public sector, actually)—and the phenomenal results he and his group had achieved, despite the wary eyes peering at him from innumerable corners (wary eyes of timorous peers more than bosses, he sadly admitted).

From that unknown (by name) seminar participant—and Tom Strange and Joe Tilli at Titeflex—this book's title was born. I'm afraid that all too often we forget that the freedom to fail and try again is the essence of liberation, in America or elsewhere. (And it sure doesn't hurt in a fashionized marketplace, I'd add one last time.)

Acknowledgments

It's fitting that the development of this book should model the process its pages extol. It is "brainware," and the product of a unique, global, and temporary network. Only one name is on the cover, but if ever there was a "network effort," this is it.

First, the research. My teammates came from both sides of the Atlantic and included Andrea Meyer, Kathy Dalle-Molle, Allan Mitchell, Deborah Hudson, Marcia Wilkof, and Xueling Lin. In any number of instances, they "discovered" the companies, did the basic research—and then wrote their work up so well that I kept their contributions almost unchanged.

Several of the short cases first appeared in our newsletter, *On Achieving Excellence.* They were researched—and written up—by Paul Cohen, Darlene Viggiano, Donna Hawley, David Graulich, and Stuart Crainer. Their efforts, edited ever so lightly, are credited to them in the notes.

Several major cases surfaced as part of our PBS television shows. Paul Loewenwarter, Maggie Loewenwarter, Ed Fouhy, Marty Feinberg, John Teegarden, Ingrid Terhorst, and Shirley Robson researched, directed, or produced those shows. Our long partnership with Video Publishing House has contributed enormously to the book—special thanks to Von Polk and Judy Rodgers. And thanks to Pat Perini and Don Boswell of KERA-TV of Dallas, which has sponsored our PBS work time and again. (And to Bruce Christensen, boss of the PBS planet, who has been a longtime supporter.)

The real "stars," of course, are the hundreds who agreed to be interviewed for this book. And the thousands more who attended seminars from Seoul to Beijing to San Jose to Munich, giving me pointed feedback (and occasional encouragement).

Many of these ideas took root in my weekly syndicated column. My thanks to Tribune Media Services for distributing it, 80 or so newspaper editors for running it, and Paul Cohen (et al.) for editing it—and thousands of readers for writing everything from "Shut up you jerk" to five-page commentaries on my musings.

The intellectual inspiration for this book includes the scholars and authors whom I depend on so much, part of my "extended university." In particular, the influence of Brian Quinn and Charles Handy resides, at least between the lines, on almost every page. And, as usual, the influence of Gene Webb is visible to all of us who know him well.

The team that shaped the book itself is headed by my silent coauthor and longtime friend, Corona Machemer at Knopf. For four years she stood by watchfully, nudging gently, and deflecting a fair amount of heat from "on high" for not pushing harder. In the last year she has for the third time become a full-scale partner in shaping and reshaping—and reshaping—both the basic thrust of the book and its every page. (How many editors have you heard of these days who spend 48 consecutive days working on a draft, as she did in early 1992? The great editors of "old publishing" would understand.) Authors usually say in acknowledgments, "Thanks for the help, any shortcomings are my own." I've always found this imperious. Any success the book has is largely due to Corona, and she also participated in its shortcomings. She is a partner, period!

Turning out the finished product was a bicoastal effort. In California, Susan Bright Winn, an independent contractor and pal, transcribed the manuscript some eight times (it once ran 1,962 pages), starting in March 1990. She was also, for a year, its only reader; in that role, she was chief cheerleader and commentator as much as technical contributor. Susan also shares leadership with Corona in "weekends lost" to THE BOOK.

At The Tom Peters Group, Chris Gage has assisted with everything from basic research to managing thousands of pages of manuscript logistically—and then checking every page, several times, for the tiniest errors. Chris's colleague Alison Peterson stars in these pages (see Chapter 24) and was also a participant in numerous aspects of the book's development, both grand and mundane. Many other colleagues at The Tom Peters Group, especially Ian Thomson, Jim Kouzes, and Lennart Arvedson, have been staunch supporters in what were at times trying circumstances.

The process of verifying the facts is an enormous one, which takes an obsession for detail and a deep understanding of the book's basic ideas. Kathy Dalle-Molle is such an obsessive. She spent months, literally, checking every fact in these pages, and added much to the substance by essentially re-interviewing a large share of the people mentioned in these pages. (She even roped family members in to check this or that—talk about a network!)

In New York, at Knopf, our mates, besides Corona, were many—all working at top speed in the face of a mercilessly compressed schedule devised by the devil himself. Mel Rosenthal was "production" editor, overseeing the shaping of the manuscript into its final form. He was supported by a number of outside contractors, including copy editor Barbara Perris and three proofreaders, Laura Starrett, Eleanor Mikucki, and Lynn Warshow. Andy Hughes and Claire Bradley managed the making of the book itself (dealing with paper suppliers, compositors, printers and binders, etc.—you'd be surprised at the depth of consideration that goes into paper-stock selection). The team of compositors at ComCom (liaisons Linda Friedman and Carol Vince; programmers Michael Detweiler and Connie Yothers; technicians Gayle Diehl, Alice Wimmer, Ray Snyder, and Brenda Flores) moved heaven and earth to accommodate, in record time and with exceptional care, our many last-minute changes, and rate a special word of thanks. Cassandra Pappas designed the book (she played two roles—the text's designer for Knopf and free-lancer for me in producing the charts and diagrams). Though free-lancers do most jacket design work for Knopf, ours was created by Knopf's Barbara de Wilde ("officially," assistant to the head of jacket design, Carol Devine Carson). Maro Riofrancos indexed the book; he could easily have been in our "super subcontractor" chapter (the all-pro outsider runs his own small indexing company— talk about master of a micro-niche). Corona Machemer's then assistant, Kristen Tropoli, "fended off" the outside world while Corona worked with me in Vermont, just as Chris Gage did for me in California. Alison Biggert, of Knopf's publicity group, was of special assistance in putting together the facts on Random House, Inc.

And don't forget the "chiefs," whom you've read about in these pages. Knopf publisher Sonny Mehta has been a champion and supporter for years, and was mercifully patient during this book's painful birthing. "Big Random" honcho Alberto Vitale, like his predecessor, Bob Bernstein, made me feel like family rather than commercial property.

On the author's private team, the other co-star (along with Corona Machemer) is my wife, Kate Abbe. Kate is a poet, as economical in her use of language as I am expansive. As a professional, she is a continuing source of inspiration (and managed to make it through every page of the manuscript at its bloated maximum). As a partner, she is just that—a full-time partner who all too frequently bears the brunt of my moodiness and, more than occasionally, despair. Esther Newberg at ICM has also been a partner in this not-so-lonely process. She was agent (and agent provocateur—kind when kindness was needed, tough when toughness was called for), playing an important role in the overall development and market presentation of this book.

Kate and I live in California and Vermont. Our close Vermont neighbor Phil Hayes deserves a bow: The wondrous writing loft he built was my sanctuary for a long year of very tough going. Ed and Barbara Morrow, also Vermont neighbors, are the proprietors of Northshire Bookstore, one of the country's top independent booksellers. Ed and Barbara's encouragement during the long, down days and months was ever so uplifting. They acted as if they really wanted to see a book on their shelves in the end!

Putting together a book is a monstrous project. I've always questioned acknowledgment statements that are brief: A book's eventual personality absorbs the personality and passion of every participant. Production editor Mel Rosenthal's passion is as essential as my own. (Hollywood understands this better—the credits, "down to" the assistant grip, sometimes seem to run half as long as the movie.) And, lengthy as these acknowledgments are, I'm all too well aware of the hundreds not mentioned here who played a part directly or indirectly in the book's creation. The best I can do is offer them my silent thanks.

Now it is done. Like the members of the Dallas Organization (Chapter 12), we'll never all be together in the same "organization" again. We will all move on. And yet, an organization (no quotes) we certainly have been, in the increasingly important sense described in these pages. To all my "network" partners, my heartfelt thanks.

T.P.

Notes

page   vii   "With the advent . . . 'permanently ephemeral' ": Michael Benedikt, *Cyberspace: First Steps* (Cambridge, MA: The MIT Press, 1991), p. 11.

"Recently I was talking . . . moving these days": Paul Volcker and Toyoo Gyohten, *Changing Fortunes: The World's Money and the Threat to American Leadership* (New York: Times Books, 1992), p. 161.

"The Fortune 500 is over": Brian Dumaine, "Is Big Still Good?" *Fortune,* April 20, 1992, p. 50.

Preface

xxxii   Some 300 new . . . each *week: New Product News,* Chicago, IL.

I. NECESSARY DISORGANIZATION: THE NEW EXEMPLARS

Chapter 1

3   "First came Nike's . . . $125 a pair": Joseph Pereira, "From Air to Pump to Puma's Disc System, Sneaker Gimmicks Bound to New Heights," *The Wall Street Journal,* October 31, 1991, p. B1.

"You in the West . . . not seek permanence": Charles Leadbeater, "Masters of the Interior Universe," *Financial Times,* September 3, 1991, p. 16.

4   "We are trying . . . less materials": "60,000 and counting," *The Economist,* November 30, 1991, p. 71.

"Microsoft's only factory . . . human imagination": Fred Moody, "Mr. Software," *The New York Times Magazine,* August 25, 1991, p. 56.

As McKinsey & Co's Bill Pade . . . "hardware businesses": John Huey, "Why Matsushita Bought MCA," *Fortune,* December 31, 1990, p. 52.

The headline in the . . . "Fall Line": Paul B. Carroll, "IBM to Start Announcing Its Fall Line," *The Wall Street Journal,* September 3, 1991, p. B4.

New food products . . . for the microwave": Eben Shapiro, "All About Fat Substitutes; the Long, Hard Quest for Foods That Fool the Palate," *The New York Times,* September 29, 1991, Section 3, p. 5.

page

4 Over the past 10 . . . "to over 130": Taichi Sakaiya, *The Knowledge-Value Revolution* (Tokyo: Kodansha International, 1991), p. 55.

5 An article in the . . . biotechnology revolution: Alex Barnum, "Designer Mice: Genetic Engineers Are Building Better Disease Models," *San Jose Mercury News,* October 1, 1991, p. 1C.

"new class of souped-up . . . contested high-tech fields." Thomas McCarroll, "Solid as Steel, Light as a Cushion," *Time,* November 26, 1990, p. 49.

About 90 percent of . . . cellular phone: Advertisement, *Mobile Office,* March 1992, p. 19.

Grid Systems . . . in New York": "Unit of Tandy Rolls Out First 'Wearable' Computer," *The Wall Street Journal,* March 20, 1991, p. B10.

"Beyond a certain point . . . fashionable accessories": Michael Schrage, "Ah, the Sartorial Splendor of the Givenchy PC," *San Jose Mercury News,* August 12, 1991, p. 9E.

5–6 When the government looks . . . software role," Roach says: Marc Levinson, "America's Edge," *Newsweek,* June 8, 1992, p. 41.

6 My local newspaper . . . the "event" of "Draegering": Janet McGovern, "Only the Food Tells You It's a Supermarket," *The Peninsula Times Tribune,* September 30, 1991, p. B1.

the same paper featured . . . to stay competitive: Carol C. Horn, "Bookstores Turn Over a New Leaf: From Tarot to Lectures, Bookstores Branch Out," *The Peninsula Times Tribune,* September 19, 1991, p. W3.

California's raisin crop . . . raisins, that is: California Raisin Advisory Board, Fresno, CA, November 1990.

On Sunday, October 6 . . . Los Angeles bureau chief: Jeff Wilson, "Liz Taylor Makes Vows for Eighth Time Sunday," *Rutland Daily Herald,* October 4, 1991, p. 3.

From *The Economist* of . . . "advisor to Coca-Cola." "Soda-pop Celebrity," *The Economist,* September 14, 1991, p. 75.

6–7 From *Time* . . . "into a [116-page] magazine supplement": Alex Prud'homme, "What's It All About Calvin?" *Time,* September 23, 1991, p. 44.

7 And *Time* . . . trend-setting L.A.": Kurt Anderson, "California Dreamin'," *Time,* September 23, 1991, p. 38.

consider the lead . . . "value in computing": Andrew S. Rappaport and Shmuel Halevi, "The Computerless Computer Company," *Harvard Business Review,* July–August 1991, p. 69.

". . . the significance of . . . knowledge-value . . .": Taichi Sakaiya, *The Knowledge-Value Revolution,* p. 60.

8 The fabled Dow Jones . . . Disney and J. P. Morgan: "Dow Jones Industrial Components Changed to Reflect Shift to Services," *The Wall Street Journal,* May 3, 1991, p. C13.

"Competition is now . . . of its behavior": George Stalk, Philip Evans, and Lawrence E. Shulman, "Competing on Capabilities: The New Rules of Corporate Strategy," *Harvard Business Review,* March–April 1992, p. 62.

8–9 "People think the . . . ever happen, either": Interview with Tom Peters, May 1989.

page 9 "Employees who try to . . . ongoing drama": Véronique Vienne, "Make It Right . . . Then Toss It Away: An Inside View of Corporate Culture at Condé Nast," *Columbia Journalism Review,* July–August 1991, p. 29.

Britain's successful BTR . . . headquarters staff of 47: David Owen, "A tight rein with acceptable costs," *Financial Times,* March 11, 1991, p. 10.

10 the "informated" individual . . .: Shoshana Zuboff, *In the Age of the Smart Machine: The Future of Work and Power* (New York: Basic Books, 1988), p. 10.

12 The all-purpose global . . . "$500 million on nothing": "Saatchi brothers grudge against Bell and Sorell," *Management Week,* October 16, 1991, p. 5.

"When a friend . . . build working alliances": Charles M. Savage, *Fifth Generation Management: Integrating Enterprises through Human Networking* (Maynard, MA: Digital Equipment Corp., 1990), p. 200.

13 "If you want a . . . hog, not halfway": Nathan Gardels, "Adam Smith Was Right," *New Perspectives Quarterly,* Summer 1992, p. 47.

14 Summarizing 30 years . . . "Nobody knows anything!": Steven Bach, *Final Cut: Dreams and Disaster in the Making of Heaven's Gate* (New York: New American Library, 1985), p. 71.

Oliver Cromwell . . . "whither he is going": *The Home Book of Quotations,* 10th ed. (New York: Greenwich House, 1984), p. 1929.

F. A. Hayek insisted . . . "are paramount": F. A. Hayek, *The Fatal Conceit: The Errors of Socialism,* ed. W. W. Bartley III (Chicago: University of Chicago Press, 1988), p. 142.

"Ignorance of . . . is unpardonable": Arthur Schlesinger, Jr., "War in the Gulf: Counsel of Ignorance," *The New York Times,* December 17, 1990, p. A17.

15 "Anything worth . . . doing poorly!": G. K. Chesterton was quoted as saying, "If a thing is worth doing, it is worth doing badly." *Oxford Dictionary of Quotations,* 3rd ed. (Oxford: Oxford University Press, 1979), p. 148.

"I always tell . . . two different locations": Rich Karlgaard, "Philippe Kahn: Still a Barbarian?," *Upside,* September 1991, p. 38.

18 "When the sea . . . in floating." William Shakespeare, *Coriolanus,* Act 4, Scene 1, Lines 6–7.

Chapter 2

20–30 Research on Electronic Data Systems was conducted in May 1991 by Tom Peters.

Chapter 3

31–41 Research on Cable News Network was conducted in October 1990 through January 1991 by Tom Peters, Ed Fouhy, Shirley Robson, and John Teegarden. Additional information on CNN was derived from *CNN: The Inside Story* by Hank Whittemore (Boston: Little, Brown and Company, 1990), pp. 2, 4, 37, 48, 51, 55, 56, 121, 129, 133, 134, 142–7, 156, 198.

page   31   Usually one of the . . . Western states": Thomas L. Friedman, "By Trip's End, Moscow Looks Good," *The New York Times,* February 20, 1992, p. A6.

"Our philosophy . . . and *more* live": *CNN: The Inside Story,* p. 56.

33   A reporter from *Home Video* magazine . . . "that was a yo-yo!": *CNN: The Inside Story,* p. 156.

42–43   CNN's zany ways of "decision making": Kathleen Eisenhardt, "Speed and Strategic Choice: How Managers Accelerate Decision-Making," *California Management Review,* Spring 1990, pp. 39, 40, 41, 43, 47, 48, 49, 50, 51–2.

Chapter 4

45–55   Research on ABB Asea Brown Boveri was conducted in October 1991 and February 1992 by Tom Peters and Lennart Arvedson.

45   "People are not . . . no job security": Carla Rapoport, "A Tough Swede Invades the U.S.," *Fortune,* June 29, 1992, p. 77.

49–50   "You can't postpone . . . wherever we go": Taylor, "The Logic of Global Business," pp. 101, 104.

50   Olson, Fortune reported . . . to ABB subsidiaries: Rapoport, "A Tough Swede Invades the U.S.," p. 80.

51–52   Consider the Power Transformers . . . "gets you 24 in return": William Taylor, "Power Transformers—The Dynamics of Global Coordination," *Harvard Business Review,* March–April 1991, pp. 96–7.

52   Take Finland's ABB . . . rest of the ABB family: Taylor, "The Logic of Global Business," 1991, p. 105.

II. LEARNING TO HUSTLE

Prologue: The Quick and the Dead

59   "Since 1979 . . . every three weeks": Steven Brull, "As the Profit Machine Slows Down, Japan Rethinks the Product Cycle," *International Herald Tribune,* March 26, 1992, p. F-1.

"Intel's R&D costs . . . more rapid rate": James J. Mitchell, "Better Fast than Dead," *San Jose Mercury News,* February 11, 1992, p. 7E.

"The nineties will be . . . and the dead": David Vice, quoted on the book jacket of *The Quick and the Dead: Brian Mulroney, Big Business and the Seduction of Canada* by Linda McQuaig (New York: Viking, 1991).

60   Stalk and Hout begin . . . "surrender" to Honda: George Stalk, Jr., and Thomas M. Hout, *Competing Against Time: How Time-Based Competition Is Reshaping Global Markets* (New York: Free Press, 1990), pp. 58–9.

Stalk and Hout coin . . . *On average!:* Stalk and Hout, *Competing Against Time,* p. 76.

page   61   Even the most timely . . . "you have an advantage": Paul Cohen, "Saving Time Creates New Opportunities," *On Achieving Excellence,* April 1991, p. 5.

Chapter 5

62–71   Research on Titeflex was conducted in October 1990 through January 1991 by Tom Peters, Ed Fouhy, Shirley Robson, and John Teegarden.

   62   "It is time to stop . . . and start over": Michael Hammer, "Reengineering Work: Don't Automate, Obliterate," *Harvard Business Review,* July–August 1990, p. 104.

          "The idea was . . . the customers?": "How Long Does It Take to Launch an Effective Team-based Operation?," *Total Employee Involvement Newsletter* (Boston: Productivity, Inc., September 1991), pp. 2–3.

   68   "We believed . . . run with them": "How Long Does It Take to Launch an Effective Team-based Operation?," *Total Employee Involvement Newsletter* (Boston: Productivity, Inc., September 1991), pp. 2–3.

Chapter 6

72–83   Research on Ingersoll-Rand was conducted from October 1990 through January 1991 by Tom Peters, Ed Fouhy, Shirley Robson, and John Teegarden.

81–82   "Now, from time to time . . . or decide things": David Bohm, "On Dialogue," David Bohm Seminars, Ojai, CA, 1990, p. 11.

83–84   MIT Professor Eric von Hippel . . . in the past. Eric von Hippel and Cornelius Herstatt, "An Implementation of the Lead User Market Research Method in a Low-Tech Product Area: Pipe Hangers," Working Paper No. 3249-91-BPS, Alfred P. Sloan School of Management, Massachusetts Institute of Technology, February 1991.

Chapter 7

86–102   Research on the Union Pacific Railroad was conducted in May 1989 and October 1990 through January 1991 by Tom Peters, Ed Fouhy, Shirley Robson, John Teegarden, and Marcia Wilkof. Additional information was derived from the transcript of "Conversations between Senior Officials of Stanford University and Union Pacific Railroad," July 7–8, 1989.

   86   "The information component . . . information-driven business": Alvin Toffler, *Power Shift: Knowledge, Wealth, and Violence at the Edge of the 21st Century* (New York: Bantam, 1990), p. 76.

   87   "We used to change . . . do the job": Interview with Tom Peters, November 1990.

97–98   "The essence of . . . external audit fees": Ronald Henkoff, "Make Your Office More Productive," *Fortune,* February 25, 1991, pp. 76, 78.

   101   In a 1990 . . . deftly avoided it: Mike Walsh, Speech to Security Analysts, March 23, 1990, Omaha, NE.

page 102–03   To wit, the case . . . he disappeared again: John Markoff, "Computer Oracle Breaks Silence," *The New York Times,* June 3, 1992, pp. D1, D7.

103   George Leonard, author of . . . practice his bliss: George Leonard, *Mastery: The Keys to Long-Term Success and Fulfillment* (New York: Dutton, 1991), p. 95.

III. INFORMATION TECHNOLOGY: MORE, AND LESS, THAN PROMISED

Chapter 8

107   "By 2020, 80 percent . . . info-businesses": Stan Davis and Bill Davidson, *2020 Vision: Transform Your Business Today to Succeed in Tomorrow's Economy* (New York: Simon & Schuster, 1991), p. 76.

107–08   "We're beginning to think . . . and highly efficient": Bill Birchard, "Building Strategy on Technology," *Enterprise,* Summer 1991, pp. 11–13.

109   Harvard political . . . "paper entrepreneurs": Robert B. Reich, *The Next American Frontier* (New York: Times Books, 1983), p. 75.

111   In 1980, computers . . . are the major combatants: Markoff, John, "Supercomputing's Speed Quest," *The New York Times,* May 31, 1991, p. D1.

In fact, NCube . . . on June 10, 1992: John Markoff, "It May be Faster than Anyone Wants," *The New York Times,* June 10, 1992, p. D3.

"No nation can . . . smokestack period": Toffler, *Power Shift,* p. 369.

112   Congress has been . . . "highways of the mind": Roger Karraker, "Highways of the Mind," *Whole Earth Review,* Spring 1991, pp. 4, 5, 6.

113   Consultant Stan Davis . . . "real profit lies": Davis and Davidson, *2020 Vision,* p. 105.

"In the future . . . adjustments are necessary": Emily T. Smith, "Sewing Machines That Eavesdrop on Their Own Problems," *Business Week,* October 21, 1991, p. 104.

"Cattle were sold . . . until they are sold." Davis and Davidson, *2020 Vision,* p. 98.

"Want to turn . . . way to the store": William D. Marbach, "From Putt-putt to Vroom! with the Turn of a Key," *Business Week,* July 8, 1991, p. 73.

113–14   *The Globe and Mail . . .* "valued in excess of $1 million": "Coors Confident Its Talking Cans Won't Burp," *The Globe and Mail,* May 26, 1992, p. B4.

114   "When one of . . . buy the third flavor": Brett Anderson, "Industry Focus: Consumer Packaged Goods," *Mobile Office,* August 1991, p. 39.

"Information processing . . . percent in 1970": Meghan O'Leary, "Mapping Out Global Networks," *CIO,* March 1992, p. 33.

page   115   PC industry (hardware/software) sales . . . $2 billion in 1981: "Jockeying for the PC Lead," *The Wall Street Journal,* April 19, 1991, p. B1.

"In a move . . . for the project": *The Nihon Keizai Shimbun,* "Boeing, Japan Partners to Link Up on Design," *The Nikkei Weekly,* October 26, 1991, p. 9.

116–17   "The ultimate vision . . . home in December 1989": Jacob M. Schlesinger, "Get Smart: Everyday Products Will Soon Come with Built-in Intelligence," *The Wall Street Journal,* October 21, 1991, p. R18.

117   "Japanese home buyers . . . opening cupboards": Schlesinger, p. R18.

117–18   "The success of . . . *three days":* Robert Hall and Lea Tonkin, (eds.), *Manufacturing 21 Report: The Future of Japanese Manufacturing* (Wheeling, IL, Association of Manufacturing Excellence, 1990), pp. 26–27. Toffler's coinage of the term "prosumers" can be found on p. 11 of *The Third Wave.*

119   "All banking products" . . . transactions were automated: Thomas D. Steiner and Digo B. Teixeira, *Technology in Banking: Creating Value and Destroying Profits* (Homewood, IL: Dow Jones–Irwin, 1990), pp. xi, xiv, 49, 58, 210, 211.

CIO magazine reported . . . "with such companies": Meghan O'Leary, "Networking's World Beaters," October 1990, p. 72.

120   "The Wizard . . . New Technology Division.: Jean S. Bozman, "Oracle Links to Wizard," *Computerworld,* February 17, 1992, p. 10.

Chapter 9

121   "The quality and quantity . . . or a war": Mel Phelps, "One Big Network," *Upside,* June 1991, p. 104.

123   "One day, the electronics industry . . . 'best' for them": Phelps, p. 104.

"The best gross indicator . . . to information infrastructure": Draft manuscript of *2020 Vision,* October 14, 1990, p. 5/31.

123–24   "Expert networks . . . with their peers": Chandler Harrison Stevens, "Electronic Organization and Expert Networks: Beyond Electronic Mail and Computer Conferencing," Sloan School of Management Working Paper No. 1794-86, Massachusetts Institute of Technology, Management in the 1990s Research Program, May 1986.

124   "Deere [& Co.] discovered, . . . heavy computerization": Savage, *Fifth Generation Management,* p. 103.

125   "Despite years of . . . net value": Gary Loveman, "Cash Drain, No Gain," *Computerworld,* November 25, 1991, p. 69.

Former Citicorp . . . courtesy of information technology: Walter B. Wriston, "Technology and Sovereignty," *Foreign Affairs,* Winter 1988/89, pp. 63–75; and George Gilder, "The Planetary Unit," Policy Review, Spring 1988, pp. 50–53.

When Ted Turner . . . for 1991: "Prince of the Global Village," *Time,* January 6, 1992, p. 20.

126   "high touch": John Naisbitt, *Megatrends: Ten New Directions Transforming Our Lives* (New York: Warner Books, 1982), p. 1.

IV. BEYOND HIERARCHY

Chapter 10

page 131 "Battleship I.B.M. Is . . . destroyers": John Markoff, "IBM Will Change in Effort to Keep Market Dominance," *The New York Times,* November 27, 1991, p. C3.

132 "To have created a product . . . think about it": Diane Kunde, "Corporate Surgeon: McKinsey Builds Top Reputation on Bottom Line," *The Dallas Morning News,* September 22, 1991, p. B1.

"No doubt there . . . substance supporting it": John Merwin, "We Don't Learn from Our Clients, We Learn from Each Other," *Forbes,* October 19, 1987, p. 23.

136 "[The] sense of dedication . . . go out on 'engagements' ": *Forbes,* October 19, 1987, p. 27.

141 "Like [then Managing Director] Daniel . . . away with a lot": John Merwin, "Guiding the Flock," *Forbes,* October 1987, p. 29.

144 "Human beings . . . cut off his head": A. J. Vogl, "Breaking with Bureaucracy," *Across the Board,* January–February 1991, p. 18.

146–47 "checkerboard . . . from time to time": Toffler, *Power Shift,* pp. 191, 192, 194.

147 "jazz combos": Savage, *Fifth Generation Management,* p. 45.

"improvisational theater . . . continuously reconstructed": Karl E. Weick, "Organizational Design as Improvisation," unpublished paper.

"In the knowledge economy . . . and quality circles": Richard Crawford, *In the Era of Human Capital: The Emergence of Talent, Intelligence, and Knowledge as the Worldwide Economic Force and What It Means to Managers and Investors* (New York: HarperBusiness, 1991), p. 115.

"We need a . . . most fully reflected": D. Quinn Mills, *Rebirth of the Corporation* (New York: John Wiley & Sons, 1991), pp. 27, 28.

148–49 "The traditional concept . . . mission or strategy": Peter Keen, "The 'Metabusiness' Evolution: Challenging the Status Quo," *Advance,* October 1988, pp. 1, 8.

149–50 "One example . . . and reassembled": Raymond E. Miles, "Adapting to Technology and Competition: A New Industrial Relations System for the 21st Century," *California Management Review,* Winter 1989, pp. 17, 19.

150–51 The chimney . . . "not wages": Charles Handy, *The Age of Unreason* (London: Business Books Limited, 1989), pp. 11, 71–7 *passim.*

151–52 "Infinitely Flat . . . have more meaning": From Quinn, James Brian, and Paquette, Penny C., "Technology in Services: Creating Organizational Revolutions," *Sloan Management Review,* Winter 1990, pp. 67–78; and James Brian Quinn, Penny C. Paquette, and Thomas Doorley, "Technology in Services: Rethinking Strategic Focus," *Sloan Management Review,* Winter 1990, pp. 79–87.

153 "[Silicon Valley] is no respecter . . . ideas keep bubbling up": Geoffrey Owen, and Louise Kehoe, "A Hotbed of High-Tech," *Financial Times,* June 28, 1992, p. 20.

page   156–57   Robert X. Cringely's . . . "manufacturing and distribution." Robert X. Cringely, *Accidental Empires: How the Boys of Silicon Valley Make Their Millions, Battle Foreign Competition, and Still Can't Get a Date* (Reading, MA: Addison-Wesley, 1992), pp. 313, 314, 315, 319.

158   "series of incremental . . . capability to compete": Richard Bettis, Stephen Bradley, and Gary Hamel, "Outsourcing and Industrial Decline," *Academy of Management Executive,* February 1992, p. 7.

Chapter 11

159   "Unlike Detroit . . . are working on": Doran P. Levin, "Adjusting to Japan's Car Culture," *The New York Times,* March 3, 1992, p. C13.

160–65   Research on Imagination conducted in April 1991 and June 1991 by Tom Peters, Allan Mitchell, and Lennart Arvedson.

160   "Nowhere else under . . . and production managers": Marion Cotter, "The Power of Imagination," *PR Week,* April 1990, p. 21.

161   "the way forward . . . sales soaring": Christina Lamb, "Stimulating Creativity," *Financial Times,* March 20, 1990, p. 13.

166   "The pressure is . . . as your last ad": Carla Marinucci, "Over the Edge: A Week in the Type-A life of a Hot San Francisco Ad Agency," *Image,* July 7, 1991, p. 24.

167–71   Research on David Kelley Design was conducted in April 1991 by Tom Peters.

167   "When we have . . . take care of it": Chee Pearlman, "David Kelley," *ID,* September–October 1987, p. 42.

"In June 1991 . . . to do just that": Examiner Staff and Wire Reports, "3 Bay Companies to Form Product Development Firm," *San Francisco Examiner,* June 11, 1991, p. B-10.

168   "For the same . . . really add significant value": Steve Kaufman, "By Design: Final Look Is No Longer a By-product," *San Jose Mercury News,* January 1, 1991, p. 9D.

169   "self-proclaimed 'horizontal engineer' . . . the whole project": Renee Simon, "Mind Over Matter," *America West Airlines Magazine,* October 1988, p. 26.

"Kelley learned that . . . fresh ideas circulate": Pearlman, "David Kelley," pp. 42–3.

"We get everyone . . . that with rubber": Michael Rogers, "Silicon Valley's Newest Wizards," *Newsweek,* January 5, 1987, p. 36.

172–76   Research on Chiat/Day/Mojo was conducted in March 1989 and July 1989 by Andrea Meyer.

173   "The Agency has . . . the client wants": Cleveland Horton, "Agency of the Decade: Chiat Proves Big Can Be Better," *Advertising Age,* January 1, 1990, p. 10.

175   "Chiat . . . helped introduce . . . New York office": Christy Marshall, "Smart Guy," *Business Month,* April 1988, p. 34.

178–83   Phil Purcell . . . "and internal ties": Robert G. Eccles and Dwight B. Crane, *Doing Deals: Investment Banks at Work* (Cambridge, MA: Harvard Business School Press, 1988), pp. 2, 3, 121–7 *passim,* 131–8 *passim,* 143, 156, 157, 163, 164, 166, 169, 186, 188, 191.

Chapter 12

page 189–200 Research on the Dallas Organization was conducted in January 1991 by Shirley Robson.

Chapter 13

201–06 Research on Oticon was conducted in December 1991 by Xueling Lin.

Chapter 14

210 Q: Name something that . . . A: Baseball: Richard Saul Wurman with Loring Leifer, *Follow the Yellow Brick Road: Learning to Give, Take, & Use Instructions* (New York: Bantam, 1992), p. 13.

214–15 Takahiro Fujimoto . . . "quality index scores": Takahiro Fujimoto, "Product Integrity and the Role of Designer-as-Integrator," *Design Management Journal,* Spring 1991, pp. 32, 33.

215–16 Suppose, for example . . . project-based organization: Peter B. B. Turney, *Common Cents: The ABC Performance Breakthrough* (Hillsboro, OR: Cost Technology, 1991), pp. 4, 37, 70, 381.

220 "You are asked . . . they are here": John Sculley with John A. Byrne, *Odyssey: Pepsi to Apple . . . A Journey of Adventure, Ideas, and the Future* (New York: Harper & Row, 1987), pp. 125, 126.

"Tomorrow's typical career . . . probability of success": Tom Horton, "Second Careers, and Third, and . . .", *Management Review,* September 1990, p. 4.

"changing" . . . different activities: Charles Handy, *The Age of Unreason,* pp. 138, 146–7.

Even *Business Week* . . . "an escape hatch": Bruce Nussbaum, "I'm Worried About My Job!" *Business Week,* October 7, 1991, pp. 94–104.

221–22 "the personal projects . . . achieve their projects": R. Edward Freeman and Daniel R. Gilbert, Jr., *Corporate Strategy and the Search for Ethics* (Englewood Cliffs, NJ: Prentice-Hall, 1980), pp. 158, 160, 164, 165, 175.

222–25 At first blush . . . "good human being": Paul Cohen, "Living on the Edge: Story of a Master Networker," *On Achieving Excellence,* February 1992, pp. 2–4.

Chapter 15

226 "We want . . . a businessperson": Leslie Brokaw and Curtis Hartman, "Managing the Journey," *Inc.,* November 1990, p. 46.

226–27 "The long, multi-step" . . . the old regime: Michael Hammer, "Reengineering Work: Don't Automate, Obliterate," *Harvard Business Review,* July–August 1990, pp. 106, 107.

227 "design limit" . . . "becomes a business": Davis and Davidson, *2020 Vision,* p. 134.

229 "three to four dollars . . . writing it down": David O. Weber, "Six Models of Patient-Focused Care," *Healthcare Forum Journal,* July–August 1991, p. 24.

page   229   "the patient-focused . . . people in attendance": J. Philip Lathrop, "The Patient-Focused Hospital," *Healthcare Forum Journal,* July–August 1991, p. 17.

"At Indianapolis's 1041-bed . . . single incumbent": Weber, "Six Models," p. 26.

230   "Caregivers are cross-trained . . . 20 percent are possible": Lathrop, "Patient-Focused Hospital," p. 18.

231   The clincher: A second . . . scratching the surface": "Lakeland Regional Medical Center," *Operational Restructuring: 19 Pioneering Models,* a compendium that appeared in *Healthcare Forum Journal,* July–August 1992, p. 5.

231–32   in January 1990 . . . Bain Farris told Weber: Weber, *Healthcare Forum Journal,* pp. 24, 25, 26, 27.

232–34   At most banks . . . "that's ownership": Paul Cohen, "Bet on Small Units, Personal Accountability," *On Achieving Excellence,* January 1992, pp. 7–8.

234   "The University of Pittsburgh . . . 'attend the operation' ": Michael Alexander, "Is There a Doctor in the Network," *Computerworld,* December 9, 1991, p. 18.

236   The conversion of . . . corporate performance": Davis and Davidson, Working Manuscript of *2020 Vision,* Spring 1991.

A sleepy Rochester . . . the AS/400 should aim for: Roy A. Bauer, Emilio Collar, and Victor Tang with Jerry Wind and Patrick Houston, *The Silverlake Project: Transformation at IBM* (New York: Oxford University Press, 1992).

Chapter 16

238   " 'How did you . . . divided it up' ": "Managing the Journey," *Inc.,* November 1990, p. 46.

238–42   Research on Johnsonville Foods was conducted in February 1988 by Tom Peters, Paul Loewenwarter, and Marty Feinberg.

242–43   "Every six months . . . the shipping department": Ralph Stayer, "How Johnsonville Shares Profits on the Basis of Performance," *Harvard Business Review,* November–December 1990, p. 74.

243–45   a useful examination . . . to 10 in one instance): Peter Lazes and Marty Falkenberg, "Workgroups in America Today," *Journal for Quality and Participation,* June 1991, pp. 59–66 *passim.*

245–48   "the cluster organization": . . . and British Petroleum: D. Quinn Mills, *Rebirth of the Corporation,* pp. 3, 7, 29–36 *passim,* 42, 53–65 *passim.*

Chapter 17

249–55   Research on Federal Correctional Institution McKean was conducted in July 1991 by Deborah Hudson and in June 1992 by Paul Cohen.

255–56   Research on Preston Trucking was conducted in March 1989 and July 1989 by Andrea Meyer.

Chapter 18

page 257 "The advantages of smaller . . . the right size": Peter F. Drucker, "Choose Your Company's Size," *Fortune,* December 31, 1991, pp. 58–9.

258 Research on Goldmann Produktion was conducted in July 1991 by Ingrid Terhorst.

259 "You can do . . . little money": John S. McClenahen, "Robert Krieble's Capitalist Crusade," *Industry Week,* April 6, 1992, p. 69.

In late 1991 . . . stuff from Radio Shack!: Wavetracer Corporate Press Materials.

(And then there's . . . unimaginable computational feats.): Richard Preston, "Mountains of Pi," *The New Yorker,* March 2, 1992, pp. 36–67.

259–60 "The more they discover . . . of unusual properties": Elizabeth Pennisi, "Buckyballs Still Charm," *Science News,* August 24, 1991, pp. 120, 122, 123.

261 "You said . . . structured environment": Personal Correspondence to Tom Peters from Dave Bonini, October 18, 1991.

262–67 Research on Random House, Inc., was conducted in June 1992 by Tom Peters.

262 "daunting maze . . . within imprints": David Streitfeld, "Life at Random: Reading Between the Lines at America's Hottest Publishing House," *New York,* August 5, 1991, p. 32.

265 "a man who . . . seller of books": Jack, Ian, "Publishing's New Raja," *Vanity Fair,* May 1987, p. 86.

267–73 Research on International Data Group was conducted in October 1991 by Andrea Meyer.

267 "We think small . . . emotional involvement": "Rich and titled," *The Economist,* March 30, 1991, p. 64.

"Knows startups . . . like that": Michael S. Hopkins, "Dream Team," *Inc.,* April 1989, p. 108.

268 "I'm convinced that . . . myriad of possibilities": Pat McGovern, "The Networked Corporation," *Chief Executive,* April 1990, pp. 47–8.

Fritz Landmann . . . "have taken six months": Echo Montgomery Garrett, "IDG divides and conquers," *Folio's Publishing News,* August 15, 1990, p. 35.

269 "When I am driving . . . is better": McGovern, "Networked Corporation," p. 47.

"IDG is able to . . . I have hired." IDG Press Materials.

270 Faxon into the . . . circulation proceeds alone: William Brandel, "Two Local Firms Tap Soviet Need to Know," *Boston Business Journal,* May 28, 1990, p. 3.

"The editors of . . . publishing think tank": Echo Montgomery Garrett, "One Thing Leads to Another," *Folio's Publishing News,* August 15, 1990, p. 36.

271 "When we started . . . majority of the opportunity": "Patrick McGovern: High tech's Town Crier," *Boston Business Journal,* September 24, 1990, p. 3.

page   272   "We set aside . . . of the equipment": Corey Sandler, "Down-to-Earth Talk," *Human Capital,* November–December 1990, p. 42.

           273   "I constantly fight . . . enhanced beyond measure": McGovern, "Networked Corporation," p. 48.

           274   "Cap Gemini Sogeti . . . is not enforced: "Building Flexible Companies: Strategies and Structures for Fast-Moving Markets," Report No. P601, Business International Limited, London, 1991.

   274–82   Research on Acordia was conducted in October 1991 by Andrea Meyer and Tom Peters.

           282   "If Rolf Hueppi is right . . . that's an investment,' he says": Charles Fleming, "Zurich Group Switches Focus to the Specific from the Generalized," *The Wall Street Journal Europe,* June 23, 1992, p. 1.

   282–86   Research on Chromalloy Compressor Technologies was conducted in July 1991 by Andrea Meyer.

   286–87   A little over a decade . . . "PC-based systems": Ricardo Semler, "Managing Without Managers," *Harvard Business Review,* September–October 1989, pp. 76, 77, 78.

           287   Semler won't let . . . "where you are": Speech by Ricardo Semler at Interlaken 1990, sponsored by The Foresight Group.

Chapter 19

   293–301   Research on Rational was conducted in April and May 1991 by Tom Peters, Paul Loewenwarter, Marty Feinberg, and Ingrid Terhorst.

           294   his successful convection oven line . . . over half: Some say the convection oven accounted for as little as a third of sales. But in May 1990, in on-camera interviews, Helmut Stempel told me 40–50 percent. Siegfried Meister said 60 percent.

Chapter 20

           302   "The supreme . . . to PC users": Jessica Lipnack and Jeffrey Stamps, "New Meaning for Worldwide Company: McDonnell Douglas Airlines Presents Formidable Management Challenge," *St. Louis Post-Dispatch,* December 22, 1991, p. D-3.

                 Almost every new . . . "company": James Brian Quinn, Manuscript of his forthcoming book, *Intelligent Enterprise: A Knowledge and Service Based Paradigm for Industry,* to be published by The Free Press in September 1992.

           303   "When an American . . . are foreign nationals": Robert B. Reich, "Brainpower, Bridges, and the Nomadic Corporation," *New Perspectives Quarterly,* Fall 1991, p. 67.

   303–04   reports on $77-million . . . "could buy one": "A car is born," *The Economist,* September 29, 1990, p. 86.

           304   "Ford has signed . . . turned to Japan": Kevin Done, "Ford signs engine deal with Yamaha," *Financial Times,* March 6, 1991, p. 5.

                 "Dramatically staking . . . estimated $3 billion": Clinton Wilder, "Giant Firms Join Outsourcing Parade," *Computerworld,* September 30, 1991, p. 1.

page   304   In late 1991, McDonnell . . . and flight testing. Rick Wartzman, Susan Carey, and Jeremy Mark, "A McDonnell Deal in Asia would Jolt the Airliner Industry," *The Wall Street Journal,* November 15, 1991, p. 1.

               "In the 1990s . . . to their service [offerings]": Leonard Berry and A. Parasuraman, *Marketing Services: Competing Through Quality* (New York: Free Press, 1991), p. 177.

   306–08   Research on MCI was conducted in January 1989 by Tom Peters, Paul Loewenwarter, and Marty Feinberg.

      308   "I have to keep . . . for good partners": Marlene C. Piturro, "Oo la la, Sasson!," *World Trade,* January–February 1992, p. 64.

   309–10   Kao Corporation . . . research and development as of 1988!: Kenichi Ohmae, "Getting Back to Strategy," *Harvard Business Review,* November–December 1988, p. 153; and conversation with Kathy Dalle-Molle, August 1992.

      312   "Organizations have to . . . from external sources": Michael Schrage, "Beware the Innovation Protectionists," *The Wall Street Journal,* January 14, 1991, p. 32A.

      314   MCI shows the . . . tiny piece of business: Interview with Tom Peters, January 1989.

   316–17   "Move over, publishing . . . and distribute it": Roger Cohen, "Book Notes," *The New York Times,* July 31, 1991, p. C16.

Chapter 21

   318–20   Research on Professional Parking Services was conducted in April 1990 by Donna Hawley.

               Based on the . . . and a first-class service: Information from "Commitment to Excellence," Ira A. Lipman, Second Alden Miller Lecture to the University of Maryland Institute of Criminal Justice and Criminology, April 20, 1988; 1991 Guardsmark Brochure and 1991 Annual Report; and conversation between Ira Lipman and Tom Peters in May 1991.

      322   "*Time* reported . . . Police Department": "A Man the Guard Firms Love to Hate," *Time,* March 9, 1992, p. 47.

   322–25   Research on Words at Work was conducted in May 1991 by Kathy Dalle-Molle.

   325–28   Research on The Skonie Corporation was conducted in May 1990 by Donna Hawley.

      328   "Our skill is finding . . . everyone to win": "Looking Ahead 10 Years Later," *Network* (The Skonie Corporation client newsletter), Spring 1990, p. 2.

      329   "I wouldn't join . . . member": From *Groucho & Me* (1959, Chapter 26), *The Oxford Dictionary of Modern Quotations* (Oxford: Oxford University Press, 1991), p. 147.

      330   On March 11 . . . building maintenance: Michael Cassell, "Contracted Business Services," *Financial Times,* March 11, 1991, pp. 1, 3.

      331   "Last October . . . on the American scene": Michael Selz, "Small Companies Thrive by Taking Over Some Specialized Tasks for Big Concerns," *The Wall Street Journal,* September 11, 1991, p. B1.

page 331 "Need a CFO . . . different companies' payrolls": Research conducted in August 1991 by Kathy Dalle-Molle.

334–35 "Firms are drifting . . . in-house for long": Charles Sabel, Horst Kern, and Gary Herrigal, "Collaborative Manufacturing: New Supplier Relations in the Automobile Industry and the Redefinition of the Industrial Corporation," Massachusetts Institute of Technology Working Paper, March 31, 1989, pp. 2, 8, 9, 10, 14, 15, 17.

Chapter 22

336 "Hard as it is . . . wins a contract": "Farewell HQ," *The Economist,* March 24, 1990, p. 14.

"The division managers . . . the [headquarters] job": Shawn Tully, "A Boom Ahead in Company Profits," *Fortune,* April 6, 1992, p. 77.

336–37 "serve the financial . . . "attributable to the [central] treasury": Simon Holberton, "ABB engineers its money," *Financial Times,* February 15, 1991, p. 18.

337 "Competitors include not just . . . services": T. Kiely, "Fee Enterprise," *CIO,* April 1991, p. 47.

The GM Automotive . . . plants are customers: Interview with Jerry Bishop of General Motors Public Affairs, March 1991.

337–39 In 1991 . . . along the way: Paul Cohen, "Publisher Prospers by Bringing Market Incentives Inside the Firm," *On Achieving Excellence,* May 1991, pp. 2, 3.

339–40 They call themselves . . . This may be it: John Partridge, "Bold Experiment Shatters Newspaper Stereotypes," *The Globe and Mail,* July 22, 1992, pp. A1, A8.

340 on November 1 . . . "keeps you straight": Darlene Viggiano, "HP's Circuit Group Becomes Self-Sustaining Profit Center," *On Achieving Excellence,* May 1991, p. 4.

341 Robert Boynton, Jr., . . . large or small: Darlene Viggiano, "Shop grows by handing employees freelance work," *On Achieving Excellence,* May 1991, p. 5.

342–45 Correspondence between Tom Peters (August 20, 1991) and Seth Steingrath (June 12, 1991).

345 "Money is made . . . de facto standards." Cringely, *Accidental Empires,* p. 53.

Chapter 23

347 "Several years ago . . . of this collaboration": Berry and Parasuraman, *Marketing Services,* p. 178.

"In a strategic . . . more for free love." Leslie Colitt, "Leading a German Crusade on Strategic Alliances," *Financial Times,* April 22, 1991, p. 3.

348 "Competition by collaboration . . . select few suppliers." Keith Alm, Speech on Strategic Marketing, March 29, 1990.

349 German Cartel Office . . . "voluntary renunciation of competition." David Marsh, "Multinationals' Links Criticized," *Financial Times,* June 19, 1990, p. 2 (European news section).

Chapter 24

page 350 "People who write . . . of the network": Michael Schrage, *Shared Minds: The New Technologies of Collaboration* (New York: Random House, 1990), p. 48.

350–53 Research on the National Restaurant Association was conducted in April 1991 by Tom Peters.

357–65 Research on Management Maximizers was conducted in July 1991 by Tom Peters and Kathy Dalle-Molle.

367 "All the early franchisees . . . in the bottom line": Anita Roddick with Russell Miller, *Body and Soul* (London: Ebury Press, 1991), pp. 94–5.

367–68 In *The Female Advantage* . . . are made to order: Sally Helgesen, *The Female Advantage: Women's Ways of Leadership* (New York: Doubleday, 1990), p. 247.

368–69 My colleagues and I . . . "enjoy it more": Darlene Viggiano, "Sally Helgesen Articulates 'The Female Advantage,' " *On Achieving Excellence,* July 1990, p. 8.

Chapter 25

370 "After, when they . . . completely not to know": Robert Graves, "The Thieves," in *Anthology of Poems* (New York: Greenwich House, 1984), p. 397.

"Most managers get . . . origins and terminations": Karl Weick, *The Social Psychology of Organizing* (Reading, MA: Addison-Wesley, 1979), p. 86.

371 "Anyone who is . . . not understood it": John Gribbin, *In Search of Schrödinger's Cat: Quantum Physics and Reality* (New York: Bantam, 1984), p. 5.

"Einstein said that . . . world is crazy": John Horgan, "Quantum Philosophy," *Scientific American,* July 1992, p. 74.

"I remember discussions . . . atomic experiments?": Werner Heisenberg, *Physics and Philosophy* (New York: Harper & Row, 1958), p. 41.

372 "So far, 60 years into . . . and to the environment": Danah Zohar, *The Quantum Self: A Revolutionary View of Human Nature and Consciousness Rooted in the New Physics* (London: Bloomsbury, 1990), pp. 5, 6, 80.

"Discovery of the . . . behavior of the parts": Fritjof Capra, *The Turning Point: Science, Society, and the Rising Culture* (New York: Bantam, 1983), pp. 80, 81, 86, 87.

373–74 "visualize the Songlines . . . each other's existence": Bruce Chatwin, *The Songlines* (New York: Penguin, 1988), pp. 13, 56, 57, 58, 60, 72, 73.

374–75 "It was once again . . . my daughter and I": Max Frisch, *Homo Faber* (New York: Harcourt Brace Jovanovich, 1959), p. 64.

375–76 "There were two travelers . . . I leave this country": K. Mark Stevens and George E. Wehrfritz, *Southwest China Off the Beaten Track* (Hong Kong: The Guidebook Company, Ltd, 1988), p. 67.

page 376–77 "The real problem . . . things, but interactions": Gary Zukav, *The Dancing Wu Li Masters: An Overview of the New Physics* (New York: Bantam, 1980), pp. 72, 82, 92, 93.

380 "if you really . . . take them seriously": Roger Penrose, "The Biggest Enigma," *New York Review of Books,* March 28, 1991, p. 37.

Chapter 26

382 Learning is the new . . . productive activity": Shoshana Zuboff, *In the Age of the Smart Machine,* p. 395.

384–97 Research on McKinsey & Company's Rapid Response Network was conducted in May and August 1991 by Tom Peters.

397–99 Research on FI Group was conducted in June 1991 by Tom Peters and Lennart Arvedson.

399–404 Research on CRSS was conducted in March 1989 by Tom Peters, Paul Loewenwarter, and Marty Feinberg.

399–400 CRSS founder Bill Caudill . . . and Friday night": William W. Caudill, *Architecture by Team: A New Concept for the Practice of Architecture* (New York: Van Nostrand Reinhold, 1971), pp. 311–12.

401 "Team action . . . the other 'designers' ": Caudill, *Architecture by Team,* pp. 25, 32, 39, 41, 69, 70, 71.

401–02 "If programming is . . . the client's problem": William Peña with Steven Parshall and Kevin Kelley, *Problem Seeking: An Architectural Primer* (Washington, DC: AIA Press, 1987), pp. 15, 16, 20, 21.

402–03 "Brown sheets graphically . . . Statement of the Problem": Peña with Parshall and Kelley, *Problem Seeking,* pp. 165, 167, 170–9.

404–05 Research on the Buick Reatta Craft Centre was conducted in May 1990 by Donna Hawley.

404 "[We] were working . . . that's the point": Drew Winter, "The Supplier as Extended Family," *Ward's Auto World,* July 1988, p. 28.

405 "We're a know-how company . . . kids really take off": George Gendron and B. Burlingham, "Printer Harry Quadracci," *Inc.,* December 1986, p. 28.

405–06 Research on Quad/Graphics was conducted in May 1989 by Tom Peters, Paul Loewenwarter, and Marty Feinberg.

Chapter 27

413 "By 1993, IBM's British division . . . along similar lines": "The eternal coffee break," *The Economist,* March 7, 1992, p. 71.

414 "Clusters need an . . . handle a circumstance": Mills, *Rebirth of the Corporation,* p. 280.

414–15 The seven-story . . . than the 'boss' ": Paul Cohen, "Steelcase uses the power of the Pyramid," *On Achieving Excellence,* March 1990, p. 5.

415–16 Over time as the company . . . information are short: Stalk and Hout, *Competing Against Time,* p. 128.

416–18 Martin Beck is president . . . "happen to be there": Donna Hawley, "Fitch Richardson Smith Makes Its Workplace an Office Design Lab," *On Achieving Excellence,* March 1990, pp. 2–3.

page 418 The high-tech . . . "in a canning plant": Stuart Crainer, "Bottlers Put Office Staff Close to the Action," *On Achieving Excellence,* March 1990, p. 7.

   419 Chris Bartlett and . . . for a particular line of business: Chris Bartlett and Sumantra Ghoshal, *Managing Across Borders: The Transnational Solution* (Boston: Harvard Business School Press, 1989).

   420 "We find little . . . it across Europe": "Chairman's Letter," CSC Europe 1991 Annual Review, p. 4.

     GM's European operations . . . emerged almost overnight: "America's New King of Europe's Roads," *The Economist,* March 9, 1991, p. 63.

     Moreover, then European boss . . . mean" philosophy.): Paul Ingrassia and Timothy Aeppel, "Worried by Japanese, Thriving GM Europe Vows to Get Leaner," *The Wall Street Journal,* July 27, 1992, p. A6.

   421 "When IBM introduced . . . from IBM Japan": David E. Sanger, "Selling Now in Tokyo: Tiniest IBM Portable," *The New York Times,* April 11, 1991, pp. D1, D5.

 421–23 describes brand-new forms . . . "and innovate reciprocally": AnnaLee Saxenian, "The Origins and Dynamics of Production Networks in Silicon Valley." Prepared for the International Workshop on Networks of Innovators, Center for Research on the Development of Industry and Technology, University of Quebec, Montreal, May 1–3, 1990.

Chapter 28

   426 "As we move toward . . . leverage of knowledge": Robert H. Buckman, letter to Tom Peters, November 22, 1989, and opening remarks at Buckman Laboratories Canadian Marketing Conference, May 1992.

   428 Easynet, Digital Equipment's . . . "been geographic kingpins": Thayer C. Taylor, "DEC Gets Its House in Order," *Sales and Marketing Management,* July 1990, pp. 60–1.

   429 FedEx's Business Logistics . . . Laura Ashley": Chuck Hawkins, "FedEx: Europe Nearly Killed the Messenger," *Business Week,* May 25, 1992, p. 126.

     Kennametal . . . "some customers": Barnaby J. Feder, "Kennametal Finds the Right Tools," *The New York Times,* May 6, 1992, p. D1.

 429–30 "Artificial intelligence" gurus . . . a significant opportunity: Edward Feigenbaum, Pamela McCorduck, and Penny H. Nii, *The Rise of the Expert Company: How Visionary Companies are Using Artificial Intelligence to Achieve Higher Productivity and Profits* (New York: Vintage, New York, 1989), pp. x, xi.

 430–32 Still, most CEOs . . . leading business indicator: Mary E. Boone, *Leadership and the Computer: Top Executives Reveal How They Personally Use Computers to Communicate, Coach, Convince and Compete* (Rocklin, CA: Prima Publishing, 1991), pp. 21, 27, 28, 74, 75, 124, 125, 126, 127, 131, 132, 133, 227.

page   432–33   "There is no . . . subsidize a local pub": Thomas Winship, "The New Curmudgeon," *Editor and Publisher,* August 3, 1991, p. 3.

          434–36   "Real value in the . . . draft and revision": Michael Schrage, *Shared Minds: The New Technologies of Collaboration,* pp. 31–9 *passim,* 44, 48, 59, 66, 70, 71, 80, 91, 93, 96, 101, 103, 108, 109, 111, 112, 131, 192.

             437   "In the age . . . with his constituents": Howard Rheingold, "The Great Equalizer," *Whole Earth Review,* Summer 1991, pp. 5, 8, 9.

             438   "The traditional equation . . . experiences and contacts": Michael Benedikt, ed., *Cyberspace: First Steps,* pp. 383, 403–4.

Chapter 29

             440   "Social workers are . . . them at all": Peter Wilby, "The Professionals Who Fear We Could Manage Without Them," *The Independent,* April 14, 1991, p. 22.

             443   At General Electric's . . . for a discipline: Research on General Electric operation in Salisbury, NC, conducted in May 1990 by Donna Hawley.

         445–47   "At the end of . . . be famous for?": David H. Maister, "How's Your Asset?" (Boston: Maister Associates, Inc., 1991), pp. 1, 2, 3, 9.

Chapter 30

             448   "The project at . . . in all fields": Marilyn Berlin Snell, "Beyond Being and Becoming," *New Perspectives Quarterly,* Spring 1992, p. 27.

                  "The traditional job . . . job was completed": "Workshop Report: Motorola/Prestolite, Arcade, NY—Common Vision, Uncommon Spirit," *Target,* Winter 1988, p. 22.

             452   ". . . intuitive, [having] an inner sense . . . as a totality": Stanley M. Davis, *Future Perfect* (Reading, MA: Addison-Wesley, 1987), p. 222.

             453   "The myth is . . . all effective learning": Frank Smith, *Insult to Intelligency: The Bureaucratic Invasion of Our Classrooms* (New York: Arbor House, 1986), pp. ix, x.

                  "The large high school . . . called a child": "How Not to Fix the Schools," *Harper's,* February 1987, p. 46.

             454   To engage students . . . high expectations: Theodore R. Sizer, *Horace's Compromise: The Dilemma of the American High School* (Boston, MA: Houghton Mifflin, 1984), pp. 34, 51, 89, 106, 131, 136, 150, 160, 195.

         454–55   Pioneering New York City . . . big-school facilities: Deborah Meier, "In Education, Small Is Sensible," *The New York Times,* September 8, 1989, p. A25.

             455   "The contrast between . . . wasteful, triviality": Sizer, *Horace's Compromise,* p. 136.

         455–58   Research on Dennis Littky and Julia B. Thayer High School was conducted in February 1988 by Tom Peters, Paul Loewenwarter, and Marty Feinberg.

Chapter 31

page   460   "The chief lesson . . . to trust him": From *The Bomb and the Opportunity,* March 1946, according to *Bartlett's Familiar Quotations,* 15th edition (Boston: Little, Brown and Company, 1980).

"One day, at a nursing . . . state of *mindlessness.* Ellen J. Langer, *Mindfulness* (Reading, MA: Addison-Wesley, 1989), p. 1.

460–61   "Men who experience . . . make accurate decisions": Karlene H. Roberts, Suzanne K. Stout, and Jennifer J. Halpern, "Decision Dynamics in Two High Reliability Military Organizations," unpublished paper, 1990.

461   "The picture emerging . . . action on quality": "Quality: Everyone's Job, Many Vacancies." Summary and Highlights of a Gallup Survey of Employees' Attitudes Toward Their Jobs and Quality Improvement Activities (Milwaukee: American Society for Quality Control, 1990), p. 1.

A 1991 *Harvard Business Review* . . . new-product-planning.): Rosabeth Moss Kanter, "Transcending Business Boundaries: 12,000 World Managers View Change," *Harvard Business Review,* May–June 1991, pp. 151–64.

In a 1991 . . . 6 or less.): ISL International Surveys Ltd., Toronto, Ontario, Canada, April 1991.

Britain's Joshua Tetley . . . recall over 2,000: Joshua Tetley Stuart Crainer, "Recognizing Staff for Recognizing Customers," *On Achieving Excellence,* November 1989, p. 6.

462   "Don't show any . . . management or Heath": Ken Brekke, "Theme at Ovation Marketing: 'You Make the Call,' " *La Crosse Tribune,* September 2, 1991, p. C-1.

463   (In Roberts's study . . . then demanded results.): John Pfeiffer, "The Secret of Life at the Limits: Cogs Become Big Wheels," *Smithsonian,* July 20, 1989, pp. 38–48.

464–65   *Louis Agassiz* . . . a bit more: Lane Cooper, *Louis Agassiz as a Teacher* (New York: Comstock, 1945), pp. 79, 80.

465   "Timid men . . . sea of liberty": Thomas Jefferson, from *The Home Book of Quotations,* 10th ed. (New York: Greenwich House, 1984), p. 283.

Chapter 32

468   "Modernism, which dates . . . personal responsibility": Michael Prowse, "Post-modern Test for Government," *Financial Times,* April 21, 1992, p. 48.

"As a scientist . . . within randomness' ": Ilya Prigogine, *New Perspectives Quarterly,* p. 24.

468–69   "While we teach . . . and shrunken souls": Harold Leavitt, "Educating Our MBAs: On Teaching What We Haven't Taught," *California Management Review,* Spring 1989, p. 39.

469   "Breaking Up IBM" . . . Cover, *Fortune,* July 27, 1992.

"Johnson & Johnson . . . they better produce": Cover, *Business Week,* May 4, 1992.

page 469–70 "Abolishing its planning . . . among their number": "The Planned and the Damned," *The Economist,* February 18, 1989, p. 72.

470 ("The size of General Motors . . . to the desirable size."): John Kenneth Galbraith, *The New Industrial State* (Boston: Houghton Mifflin, 1971), p. 76.

470–71 "As 'strategy' has blossomed . . . of potential competitors": Gary Hamel and C. K. Prahalad, "Strategic Intent," *Harvard Business Review* May–June 1989, p. 64.

471 "Ed Brennan . . . no minder in sight": Nikki Tait and Barbara Durr, "US Retailer All Over the Shop," *Financial Times,* May 12, 1992, p. 18.

471–72 "What happens when . . . around focused tasks": Savage, *Fifth Generation Management,* pp. 150–1.

V. MARKETS AND INNOVATION: THE CASE FOR DISORGANIZATION

Prologue: Deconstructing the Corporation

479 "Lenin once said . . . be your own": Peter Huber, "The Unbundling of America," *Forbes,* April 13, 1992, p. 118.

Imperial Chemical Industries . . . split itself in two: "Spinoff Plan Hides Gloom at Imperial," *The New York Times,* July 31, 1992, p. C4.

479–80 In January 1992 . . . a 279 percent jump: Carol J. Loomis, "What If They Had Broken Up IBM Like AT&T?," *Fortune,* July 27, 1992, p. 52.

Chapter 33

481 "The 2 . . . Time and Luck": Kurt Vonnegut, *Hocus Pocus* (New York: Putnam Publishing Group, 1990), p. 21.

"Do everything right . . . animals with rabies": Ann Beattie, *Picturing Will* (New York: Random House, 1989), p. 52.

482 "Elephants have a . . . outlive everything": Mark Skousen, "Roaches Outlive Elephants: An Interview with Peter Drucker," *Forbes,* August 19, 1991, p. 72.

"Like nearly every . . . turn the product down": Cringely, *Accidental Empires,* p. 253.

"The two scientists . . . now for IBM brass": Richard L. Hudson, "How Two IBM Physicists Triggered the Frenzy Over Superconductors," *The Wall Street Journal,* August 19, 1987, pp. 1, 10.

What finally did . . . solution on [its existing operating system]." Richard Rappaport, "It's All Right Now," *Upside,* May 1992, pp. 60, 61.

483 "The only true . . . to oversee them": Julian L. Simon, letter to Tom Peters, April 1991.

484 "The market economy . . . deliberate design": Hayek, *The Fatal Conceit,* p. 111.

page   485   "More than fifteen . . . "I kin read writin": Cynthia Monaco, "The Difficult Birth of the Typewriter," *American Heritage of Invention & Technology,* Spring/Summer 1988, pp. 13, 15, 18.

486   "Every day the Naskapi . . . of human beings": Weick, *The Social Psychology of Organizing,* p. 262.

487   "Life the Game Cartoon": by Cheney, *The New Yorker,* July 23, 1990, p. 24.

488   Tom Watson, Jr., quoted in . . . or *Blind Luck*: Johanna Abrosio, "Tom Watson," *Computerworld,* June 22, 1992, p. 45.

In 1989, Continental Bank . . . had no choice: Kate Ballen, "Continental Comes Back," *Fortune,* June 19, 1989, p. 147.

"Thanks for your . . . always materialize!": Thomas C. Theobald, letter to Tom Peters, June 12, 1989.

489   "let a hundred flowers bloom, a thousand schools contend": Mao Zedong, speech at Peking, February 27, 1957.

490   "Although we have . . . into our work": Karl Weick, *The Social Psychology of Organizing,* p. 467.

491   "The contest begins . . . consistently flip heads": Burton G. Malkiel, *A Random Walk Down Wall Street* (New York: W. W. Norton & Company, 1981), p. 169.

494   "Society has become . . . management run amok: Henry Mintzberg, *Mintzberg on Management: Inside Our Strange World of Organizations* (New York: Free Press, 1989), pp. 349, 352.

Chapter 34

495   "The thematic terms . . . failing to experiment": L. E. Birdzell, Jr., and Nathan Rosenberg, *How the West Grew Rich: The Economic Transformation of the Industrial World* (New York: Basic Books, 1986), p. 33.

496   "After two years . . . central planning": Martin Wolf, "Minister with a mission," *Financial Times,* November 7, 1991, p. 11.

"There is . . . state enterprises." Sheryl WuDunn, "As China's Economy Thrives, the Public Sector Flounders," *The New York Times,* December 18, 1991, p. A14.

497–501   "Only a few . . . stink of sorcery." Hayek, *The Fatal Conceit,* pp. 6, 8, 24, 26, 29, 30, 39, 41, 42, 43, 45, 53, 54, 68, 71, 74, 76, 77, 80, 86, 90, 91, 93, 94, 95, 96, 99, 111.

502–03   "The most competitive . . . or machine tools.): Michael Porter, "Europe's Companies After 1992: Don't Collaborate, Compete," *The Economist,* June 9, 1990, p. 18.

503–05   But that was before . . . copyright protection hobbles: Michael E. Porter, *The Competitive Advantage of Nations* (New York: Free Press, 1990), pp. xii, 6, 19, 29, 72, 73–86, 100, 101, 105, 107, 120, 122, 123, 131, 173, 200, 617, 618, 621, 628, 629, 630, 631, 632, 633, 634, 635, 662, 663, 666, 667.

509–17   Research on Thermo Electron Corporation was conducted in September 1991 by Andrea Meyer.

page   509   "perpetual idea machine": Robert Cassidy, "Corporation of the Year: A Perpetual Idea Machine," *Research & Development,* November 1989, p. 55.

517–18   "Supercomputer standout . . . in the marketplace": Esther Dyson, "Divided We Flourish," *Forbes,* July 10, 1989, p. 102.

518   "There is new . . . Intel 80486 microprocessor." T. J. Rodgers, "The inequity of Sematech," *Financial Times,* August 13, 1991, p. 10.

519–22   "When we hit . . . single wafer tab": Interview with Paul Cohen, September 1991.

522   Body Shop founder . . . to conserve cash: Roddick with Miller, *Body and Soul,* p. 86.

522–24   Formed in Berkeley . . . large firms alike: Harvey E. Wagner, "The Open Corporation," *California Management Review,* Summer 1991, pp. 46, 47, 50, 51, 53, 54, 55, 58, 60.

524–25   Quad/Graphics boss . . . up under himself: Interview with Tom Peters, May 1989.

525   Sun Microsystems practices . . . "by innovating faster": "Land of the licensing Sun," *The Economist,* June 3, 1989, p. 69.

"We wouldn't hesitate . . . money doing it": Stalk and Hout, *Competing Against Time,* p. 142.

526   "A key factor . . . the external wind": Kenichi Ohmae, "Getting Back to Strategy," *Harvard Business Review,* November–December 1988, p. 151.

Chapter 35

528   "The shift from the . . . more than a century": Peter F. Drucker, *For the Future: The 1990s and Beyond* (New York: Dutton, 1992), p. 262.

"Buried deep below . . . and midsize companies": Hermann Simon, "Lessons from Germany's Midsize Giants," *Harvard Business Review,* March–April 1992, pp. 115, 121.

529   The 1989 *Business Week* . . . Huh?: "The *Business Week* Global 1000," *Business Week,* July 17, 1989, pp. 145–76.

The world's No. 1 . . . share in the U.S.: William J. Hastein, "Think Small: The Export Lessons to Be Learned from Germany's Midsize Companies," *Business Week,* November 4, 1991, p. 58, 59, 60, 62.

530   It turns out . . . barely breaking even: Peter Fuhrman, "Papa Siemens," *Forbes,* May 28, 1990, p. 100.

"The one clear . . . to corporate success": Gunter Rommel, "The secret of German competitiveness," *The McKinsey Quarterly 1991,* No. 3, p. 40.

530–37   Research on Playmobil was conducted in April 1991 by Tom Peters, Paul Loewenwarter, Marty Feinberg, and Ingrid Terhorst.

536–37   "In the days of . . . for our company": Letter from Horst Brandstätter, May 5, 1991.

537–47   Research on Trumpf was conducted in April 1991 by Tom Peters, Paul Loewenwarter, Maggie Loewenwarter, Marty Feinberg, and Ingrid Terhorst.

page   538 "Trumpf Industrial . . . an on-site call": "Trumpf Industrial Lasers Add Telediagnostics to Service Capability": *Trumpf News,* March 1991, p. 2.

          552 "The Third Italy . . . looms in textiles": Jonathan Zeitlin, "Lessons for Enterprise Culture from the Third Italy," *Quarterly Enterprise Digest,* October 1989, pp. 7, 8.

Chapter 36

          553 "The most suspect . . . increase in bureaucracy": James O'Toole, "Big or Small," unpublished paper, 1991.

               "There are two . . . someone else does": Interview with Tom Peters, May 1989.

          554 "Hey, size . . . excellence": Rich Karlgaard, "Unstoppable Bill Gates," *Upside,* April 1992, p. 73.

               "Although Japan . . . going to survive": Gene Bylinsky, "Biotech Firms Tackle the Giants," *Fortune,* August 12, 1991, pp. 73, 78, 79.

               "Is it better . . . or small?": O'Toole, "Big or Small?," p. 14.

          555 "The Flow and Ebb of the Fortune 500": John Case, *From the Ground Up: The Resurgence of American Entrepreneurship* (New York: Simon & Schuster, 1992), p. 32.

          556 "The average bank . . . slightly less profitable": "Are Fewer Banks Better?," *Business Week,* August 17, 1992, p. 92.

               "Two-bit labs . . . megabuck materials": "Two-bit Labs Can't Make Megabucks Materials," *Business Week,* July 29, 1991, p. 88.

               The same issue . . . "also-ran globally": William Glasgall, "Ready, Set, Merge," *Business Week,* July 29, 1991, p. 24.

          557 "packed off . . . marketing and finance": Fuhrman, "Papa Siemens," p. 100.

               "Overall size is . . . competitive challenges ahead": Porter, "Europe's Companies After 1992," *The Economist,* p. 18.

               "On the whole . . . in the U.K.": Paul Geroski, "On Diversity and Scale—Extant Firms and Extinct Goods?" *Sloan Management Review,* Fall 1989, pp. 75, 81.

          558 "The era of mass production . . . 150 employees": Joel Kotkin, "Creators of the New Japan," *Inc.,* October 1990, p. 96.

       558–59 *"Question:* We keep . . . small business": Patricia Silverstein, "Small Businesses Expand Workforce, Help Boost Economy," *Rocky Mountain News,* February 2, 1992, p. 124.

          559 "As Big Banks . . . Are Hiring." *San Francisco Chronicle,* July 16, 1992, p. B1.

          561 A study by economist Robert Summers . . . tend to focus: Gary S. Becker, "Actually, Small-Fry Nations Can Do Just Fine," *Business Week,* October 1, 1990, p. 20.

               (see *American Steel*): Richard Preston, *American Steel: Hot Metal Men and the Resurrection of the Rust Belt* (Englewood Cliffs, NJ: Prentice-Hall, 1991).

               "The newest technologies . . . even further": "Think of the 1992 Company; Size Alone May Not Help Companies to Prosper in Europe's Single Market," *The Economist,* January 20, 1990, p. 16.

page   562   "Between 1975 . . . for hierarchies": "The Incredible Shrinking Company," *The Economist,* December 15, 1990, p. 65.

563–64   "vital to . . . in exports": William J. Holstein with Kevin Kelley, "Little Companies, Big Exports," *Business Week,* April 13, 1992, p. 70.

564–65   "American orchestras have . . . riotous Christopher Rouse": Mark Swed, "Sleeping Giants and Nimble Dwarfs," *Connoisseur,* November 1988, p. 49.

565   "The vertical and . . . between those civilizations": Mario Vargas Llosa, "Questions of Conquest: What Columbus Wrought, and What He Did Not," *Harper's,* December 1990, p. 49.

570–71   In 1989, A. T. Kearney . . . among the also-rans: "Study of Top-Performing Companies," A. T. Kearney, 1991.

571   Former Pepsi-Cola boss . . . Don Kendall: Brian Dumaine, "Those Highflying PepsiCo Managers," *Fortune,* April 10, 1989, p. 79.

571–72   "To help U.S. . . . to survive competitively": C. Gordon Bell, "The Fewer Engineers Per Project, the Better," *IEEE Spectrum,* February 1989, p. 22.

572–73   "product churning" . . . "CDs into tapes": "What Makes Yoshio Invent," *The Economist,* January 12, 1991, p. 61.

573   "Most large markets . . . made it happen": Regis McKenna, "Marketing in an Age of Diversity," *Harvard Business Review,* September–October 1988, pp. 91, 92, 93.

IBM has lost out . . . "The guerrillas are winning": Ron Wolf, "Q&A: The Fall of Big Blue," *San Jose Mercury News,* February 6, 1989, p. 6D.

574   "that simply ask . . . tomorrow's customers will": Gary Hamel and C. K. Prahalad, "Corporate Imagination and Expeditionary Marketing," *Harvard Business Review,* July–August 1991, p. 85.

575   business analyst David Rogers . . . "to retreat quickly": David J. Rogers, "Ride a Small Horse: The Business Wisdom of Genghis Khan," *Success,* June 1988, p. 16.

575–76   he contrasts an "A-mode" . . . "a decent continued life": Gunnar Hedlund, "Milking Cows Versus Going Hunting: Conceptions of Corporate Strategies," unpublished paper, December 9, 1987.

Chapter 37

577   "If you can make . . . fix it crudely": David Holzman, "Masterful Tinkering of Genius," *Insight,* June 25, 1990, p. 11.

"free the Thoreaus and Tom Paines": Ricardo Semler, "Managing Without Managers," *Harvard Business Review,* September–October 1989, p. 79.

578   "Dead ends are . . . went about it": Clifford Stoll, *The Cuckoo's Egg: Tracking a Spy Through the Maze of Computer Espionage* (New York: Doubleday, 1989), p. 87.

"I was helping . . . Keep it up": Richard Muller, *Nemesis: The Death Star* (New York: Weidenfeld & Nicolson, 1988), pp. 23–4.

page   579   "every one" of his subjects . . . 2,450 years to Plato": Michael Dixon, "Why Intellectual Skills May Not Be Enough," *Financial Times,* September 7, 1990, Recruitment Section, p. 1.

"Using plans . . . draws near [the target]": Harry V. Quadracci, "The Corporate Cruise Missile," *Success,* June 1988, p. 8.

579–80   All teach one . . . in the end: Michael Gershman, *Getting It Right the Second Time: How American Ingenuity Transformed Forty-nine Marketing Failures into Some of Our Most Successful Products* (Reading, MA: Addison-Wesley, 1990), pp. xiv, xv, 78, 79, 150.

580–81   When I got to . . . and push buttons!": Richard P. Feynman, *Surely You're Joking, Mr. Feynman!: Adventures of a Curious Character* (New York: W. W. Norton & Co., 1984), pp. 49–50.

581–82   "There is only one . . . grasping of the hand": Kimon Nicolaides, *The Natural Way to Draw: A Working Plan for Art Study* (Boston: Houghton Mifflin, 1969), pp. xiii, 2, 3, 9, 10, 11, 14, 15.

582–83   *"Hear* the sound . . . my increasing success": Bamberger, Michael, "Listening to the Good Sounds of Golf," *M inc.,* May 1992, p. 108.

583–84   "In January 1967 . . . need to 'do it' ": Henry Fairlie, "Fear of Living," *The New Republic,* January 23, 1989, p. 14.

Chapter 38

586   "You almost have . . . the best product": Michael Porter, "Have We Lost Our Faith in Competition?", *Across the Board,* September 1990, p. 38.

"Whether revered or . . . wake of its discontents": Wurman with Leifer, *Follow the Yellow Brick Road,* p. 202.

587   "Generally speaking, people . . . one word, unsteady": John Lukacs, *The Duel: 10 May–31 July 1940, The Eighty-Day Struggle Between Churchill and Hitler* (New York: Ticknor & Fields, 1991), p. 22.

"Every style . . . a good one": *L'Enfant Prodigue,* preface to the edition of 1738.

"The three most . . . dependability, and predictability": Deidre Fanning, Office or Golf Course, The Game Is the Same," *The New York Times,* October 14, 1990, Section 3, Part 2, p. 25.

589   "[William Paley] was . . . and greedy": Christopher Buckley, "Success Was Not Enough," *The New York Times Book Review,* November 4, 1990, p. 1.

"By the end . . . lonesome brat": Max Wilkinson, "From Cyberbrat to Superman," *Financial Times,* June 9, 1992, Section 111, p. 1.

"The State Department . . . in France and England' ": David Aaron, *Agent of Influence* (New York: G. P. Putnam's Sons, 1989), p. 235.

589–90   "The prevailing theory . . . animate the play." George Gilder, *The Spirit of Enterprise* (New York: Simon & Schuster, 1984), p. 15.

590   "arrested for stock fraud . . . and stick to it' ": Walter B. Wriston, *Risk & Other Four-Letter Words* (New York: Harper & Row, 1986), p. 226.

"Guys like Eisner . . . run by crazies again": John Taylor, *Storming the Magic Kingdom: Wall Street, the Raiders and the Battle for Disney* (New York: Alfred A. Knopf, 1987), pp. 220–1.

page   590   A former Gannett . . . titled his review: Aloysius Ehrbar, "Why It Works to Be a Jerk," *Fortune*, October 23, 1989, p. 201.

591   "Prime Minister Margaret . . . her fatal weakness": Craig R. Whitney, "Ungentle Persuader: How a Great Strength Became a Fatal Flaw," *The New York Times*, November 23, 1990, p. A1.

592   "The reasonable man . . . unreasonable man": From *Maxims for Revolutionists,* according to *The Home Book of Quotations,* 10th edition (New York: Greenwich House), 1984.

"Whenever anything is . . . with a mission": Peter F. Drucker, *Adventures of a Bystander* (New York: Harper & Row, Publishers, 1978), p. 225.

593   The passions are . . . most eloquent without": Roddick with Miller, *Body and Soul,* p. 145.

593–94   "Freud said that . . . carry them out": William Caudill, *The TIBS of Bill Caudill* (Dallas: CRSS, 1984), p. 25.

594–96   On March 27, 1976, . . . "direction to everyone else": Roddick with Miller, *Body and Soul,* pp. 7, 18–25 *passim,* 63, 77, 99, 115, 128, 141, 176, 215–28 *passim,* 235.

596   In the last 15 years . . . $238 million in revenue: Rahul Jacob, "What Selling Will Be Like in the 90s," *Fortune,* January 13, 1992, p. 63.

598   In his *Principles . . .* gloom and doom: David Ogilvy, *Principles of Management* (New York: Ogilvy & Mather, 1968).

When Yutaka Kume was . . . "popular cars in the market": Executive Summary of presentation by Ryuzaburo Kaku, Chairman and Representative Director, Canon, Inc., from Management Centre Europe's Second Global Conference on Management Innovation, December 2–4, 1991.

598–99   "One day I was having . . . hated those culottes": Roddick with Miller, *Body and Soul,* p. 149.

Chapter 39

600   "What a distressing . . . the average adult": Robert Bly, *Iron John: A Book About Men* (Reading, MA: Addison-Wesley, 1990), p. 7.

"Strategies are okayed . . . child in the boardroom": Victor Palmieri, "Now Hear This," *Fortune,* February 24, 1992, p. 18.

"The key to . . . follow the others": Brenton R. Schlender, "How Sony Keeps the Magic Going," *Fortune,* February 24, 1992, p. 77.

601   "If I don't do . . . about something else": Paul Gillin, "Philippe Kahn," *Computerworld,* June 22, 1992, p. 29.

601–03   Most companies operating out . . . "they'll encourage it in others": Darlene Viggiano, "Culture of Curiosity helps create successful companies," *On Achieving Excellence,* July 1991, pp. 2–3.

603   In Mexico . . . "against the tide": Darlene Viggiano, "Banamex challenges employees to challenge assumptions," *On Achieving Excellence,* July 1991, p. 6.

page   603–04   "Many U.S. companies . . . cyberpunk novelist?": Michael Schrage, "Spreadsheets Endanger Corporate Health," *San Jose Mercury News,* April 15, 1991, p. 4F.

604   After 16 years of . . . for their colleagues: Paul Cohen, "Time off promotes growth at Tandem Computer," *On Achieving Excellence,* July 1991, p. 4.

"Where do policy . . . steal from everybody": Tim Golden, "Florida Governor Aims to Reinvent Ailing State," *The New York Times,* August 11, 1991, p. 16.

605–06   "One of the things . . . local pizza place": Carl Sewell and Paul B. Brown, *Customers for Life: How to Turn That One-Time Buyer into a Lifetime Customer* (New York: Doubleday, 1990), pp. 143–4.

606–07   "The challenge of leadership . . . power in that": Darlene Viggiano, "Sara Lee Direct: Not Held Hostage to 'Not Invented Here,' " *On Achieving Excellence,* June 1991, p. 2.

608   "Regarding "The Benchmarking . . . always be a follower": William J. Altier, "Letter to the Editor," *Across the Board,* June 1992, p. 7.

610   "Physicist Isidor Isaac . . . she would say": Wurman with Leifer, *Follow the Yellow Brick Road,* p. 153.

Anthony Suchman, a professor . . . "unknown and unexpected": Anthony L. Suchman, "First Ask Patient What Happened," *Rochester Democrat and Chronicle,* October 17, 1990, p. 7A.

610–11   The youngsters ate . . . "reward them with a diploma": "How Not to Fix the Schools," *Harper's,* February 1987, p. 46.

611   "To instruct calls for energy . . . demanding than crying out": Robertson Davies, *The Rebel Angels* (New York: Viking Penguin, 1983), p. 92.

612   "If a thing . . . doing badly": G. K. Chesterton, *Oxford Dictionary of Quotations,* 3rd ed. (Oxford: Oxford University Press, 1979), p. 148.

613   "Dis-equilibrate . . . even chaos": Warren Bennis, *On Becoming a Leader* (Reading, MA: Addison-Wesley, 1989), p. 89.

614   "Anything worth doing . . . to excess": "The wisdom of Edwin Land," *The Boston Globe,* March 2, 1991, p. 8.

Chapter 40

615   "Environmental changes . . . entire species": Weick, *The Social Psychology of Organizing,* p. 7.

"No nation has . . . decay of success": Richard Lamm, "Challenge Facing America Is Great, Hour Growing Late," *Rocky Mountain News,* June 11, 1989, p. 65.

616   "Adaptation precludes adaptability . . .": Weick, *The Social Psychology of Organizing,* p. 7.

616–17   "They really understand . . . still selling niches": Interview with Paul Cohen, January 1992.

617   "We were not . . . a fresh start": Edmund L. Andrews, "And Now for Something Substantially Different: Digital TV," *The New York Times,* July 12, 1992, p. E22.

page 617 "The survival of some . . . to assure survival": Herbert Kaufman, *Time, Chance, and Organizations: Natural Selection in a Perilous Environment* (Chatham House, NJ: Chatham House Publishers, 1991), pp. 66–7.

618–25 "In the mid-1970s" . . . truly autonomous units: Michael T. Hannan and John Freeman, *Organizational Ecology* (Cambridge, MA: Harvard University Press, 1989), pp. xi, 11, 12, 19, 25, 26, 36, 70, 75, 77, 90, 118, 123.

620–21 "When the GM . . . with a thermometer": Maryann Keller, *Rude Awakening: The Rise, Fall, and Struggle for Recovery of General Motors* (New York: William Morrow and Co., 1989), p. 33.

625 In an interview . . . "maybe 20 years": Ralph Nader and William Taylor, *The Big Boys: Power and Position in Corporate America* (New York: Pantheon, 1986), p. 95.

625–26 "It's a disturbing idea . . . they actually do.": Martin E. P. Seligman, *Learned Optimism: How to Change Your Mind and Your Life* (New York: Pocket Books, 1990), pp. 108, 109.

627 "break down not . . . to the disturbance": Per Bak and Kan Chen, "Self-organized Criticality," *Scientific American,* January 1991, p. 46.

"What is freedom . . . tyranny of chance." Paul Bowles, *A Distant Episode: The Selected Stories* (New York: The Ecco Press, 1988), p. 221.

VI. FASHION!

Prologue: Terminally Tasteless or Sur/Petition?

633 "In Stamford, Connecticut . . . suburban train station": Faith Popcorn, *The Popcorn Report* (New York: Doubleday, 1991), p. 82.

"Decorated Christmas cookies . . . cookies costs $3.79": Alison L. Sprout, "Products to Watch, *Fortune,* December 16, 1991, p. 125.

633–34 "What can a small . . . of a custom booth": Ron Wolf, "Exhibit Emporium Caters Comdex Kitsch," *San Jose Mercury News,* October 21, 1991, p. 1D.

634 "The Americans are building . . . climate-control knob": Larry Reibstein, "The Hardest Sell," *Newsweek,* March 30, 1992, p. 45.

"Design in Service Industries: Managing the Evidence of Intangible Products": *Design Management Journal,* Winter 1992.

De Bono argues . . . "values of the customer": Edward de Bono, *Sur/Petition: Creating Value Monopolies When Everyone Else Is Merely Competing* (New York: HarperBusiness, 1992), p. 111.

635 "The Swiss watch . . . selling jewelry to men": De Bono, *Sur/Petition,* pp. 118–19.

The New York Times added . . . "nobody can copy": Patricia Leigh Brown, "What time is it? Time for another Swatch," *The New York Times,* May 11, 1992, p. B1.

Chapter 41

636 "I don't think . . . to keep up": Julie Pitta, "The Invasion That Failed," *Forbes,* January 20, 1992, p. 103.

page   636   "Each day of . . . collective consciousness": Ronald Collins, "Clutter," *Columbia Journalism Review*, November–December 1991, p. 49.

636–37   One hundred and four . . . receive 150 channels: Data from *New Product News* in Chicago, IL.

637   Read Bill McKibben's . . . one day in 1991: Bill McKibben, *The Age of Missing Information* (New York: Random House, 1992).

Almost 700 . . . also soaring": Data from *New Product News* in Chicago, IL.

a patent just . . . to keep up: "System Helps Doctors Keep Up to Date," *The New York Times*, July 13, 1991, p. 34.

637–38   "The Limited's mass . . . for the product": Woody Hochswender, "How Fashion Spreads Around the World at the Speed of Light," *The New York Times*, May 13, 1990, p. E5.

638   In *The Popcorn Report* . . . distribution process: Popcorn, *The Popcorn Report*, pp. 36, 147.

And Campbell Soup . . . by the year 2000: Harper's Index, *Harper's*, March 1991, p. 17.

639   "In two cases out of three . . . sells in three months": Joshua Levine, "The Ultimate Sell," *Forbes*, May 13, 1991, p. 108.

639–40   "At the point most drivers . . . sides of the car": Associated Press, "Far Beyond the Beetle: Concept Car Parks Itself," *San Jose Mercury News*, March 28, 1991, p. 1A.

640   "materials that think for themselves . . . strain and temperature": "These Materials Are Downright Precocious," *Business Week*, September 16, 1991, p. 112.

" 'Smart' materials . . . flying conditions": William F. Allman, "The Stuff of Dreams," *U.S. News & World Report*, November 26, 1990, p. 60.

"business as recreation . . . fun to fly": Ken Wells, "Adventure Capitalist Is Nipping at the Tail of Big British Airways," *The Wall Street Journal*, May 22, 1992, p. A1.

640–41   At the end of 1990 . . . "revenue outside the U.S.": John Huey, "America's Hottest Export: Pop Culture," *Fortune*, December 31, 1990, p. 50.

641   At the end of 1991 . . . number-one Time Warner. Bronwen Maddox, "Headline Makers," *Financial Times*, December 17, 1991, p. 16.

The Japanese . . . a hold on": "America's Hottest Export," *Fortune*, December 31, 1990, p. 50.

"Harleys are just" . . . just bought one: Jeffrey Potts, "Yuppies Help Fuel Demand," *USA Today*, July 22, 1991, p. 2B.

"there was a time . . . boutiques": John Helyar, "Game? What Game? Arenas Emphasize Ambiance and Amenities to Entice Fans," *The Wall Street Journal*, March 20, 1991, p. B1.

642   TeamLine . . . credit card of choice: Advertisement in *The National*, November 9–10, 1990, p. 32.

643–44   "keep getting more" . . . ultramodern lighting fixtures: Mark L. Johnson, "Creating a Masterpiece," *Home Center Magazine*, May 1988.

page   644   One cover story . . . or express themselves": Cori Dunn and Holly Jenks, "The Elusive Female Customer," *Home Center Magazine,* August 1988, pp. 59, 62.

"Tomorrow's stores . . . for competitive distributors": Robert Wilson, "Stores of the Future Revisited," *Home Center Magazine,* November 1988, p. 62.

647–48   By the late 1980s . . . motorized garden tools": Ken Dychtwald with Joe Flower, *Age Wave: The Challenges and Opportunities of an Aging America* (New York: Bantam, 1990), pp. 6, 30, 52, 73, 268, 269, 286, 287, 291, 299, 301, 312, 313, 318, 319.

649   "four powerful value drivers . . . in the future": De Bono, *Sur/Petition,* p. 134.

650   "Matter is not . . . matter-minded competitors": Stanley M. Davis, *Future Perfect,* pp. 92, 94.

"because the subjective worlds . . . homogeneity": Hayek, *The Fatal Conceit,* p. 95.

"To serve . . . seem repulsive": Hayek, *The Fatal Conceit,* p. 96.

In 1900 . . . a million cars: Stewart Brand, *The Media Lab: Inventing the Future at M.I.T.* (New York: Penguin Books, 1988), pp. 255–6.

651   The late Paul Sherlock . . . "glow" and "tingle": Paul Sherlock, *Rethinking Business to Business Marketing* (New York: The Free Press, 1991), p. 65.

"Lexus engineers pasted . . . in a decade": Arthur Higbee, "With Pink Paint Job Far Behind, Carmakers Tune Ads for Women," *International Herald Tribune,* June 24, 1992, p. 3.

652   "We do not want . . . demand for recognition": Alan Ryan, "Hegel Goes to Washington—The End of History and the Last Man," *New York Review of Books,* March 26, 1992, p. 7.

"era of manic specialization": "Winged Victory," *The Economist,* December 2, 1989, p. 83.

Microbrewer figures from R. S. Weinberg & Associates, St. Louis, Missouri, 1992.

652–53   (And *Business Week* . . . 1986 and 1991).: Walecia Konrad, "The Cola Kings are Feeling a Bit Jumpy," *Business Week,* July 13, 1992, p. 112.

653   Introductions of new consumer magazines . . . 78 million paying customers: Information from Samir A. Husni, Ph.D., University of Mississippi, Department of Journalism.

"Lifestyles around . . . in *Europe Relaunched:* Nicholas Colchester and David Buchan, *Europe Relaunched: Truths and Illusions on the Way to 1992* (London: Hutchinson Business Books Limited, 1990), p. 227.

"Europe's strength . . . its uniformity": John Harvey Jones, in a presentation at the European Economic Community Conference, September 1990, Nice, France.

654   "Why did I nearly . . . pair of the EarthCare": Steven Waldman, "The Tyranny of Choice," *The New Republic,* January 27, 1992, p. 22.

page 655 And feature stories appearing . . . customers' needs: Brian Dumaine, "P&G Rewrites the Marketing Rules," *Fortune,* November 6, 1989, pp. 34–48; and John J. Keller and Mark Maremont, "Bob Allen Is Turning AT&T into a Live Wire," *Business Week,* November 6, 1989, pp. 140–52.

657–58 "Microsoft's MS-DOS and . . . Hewlett-Packard's hardware": Andrew S. Rappaport and Shmuel Halevi, "The Computerless Computer Company," *Harvard Business Review,* July–August 1991, p. 71.

658 Though IBM continues . . . manufactures anymore: Stanley M. Davis, *Future Perfect,* p. 97.

"The most important . . . short-term profits": David A. Aaker, *Managing Brand Equity: Capitalizing on the Value of a Brand Name* (New York: Free Press, 1991), p. 14.

Tobin's q is the . . . "intellectual capital": Thomas A. Stewart, "Brainpower," *Fortune,* June 3, 1991, p. 50.

658–59 another crack at this phenomenon (see the chart): James Brian Quinn, from the manuscript of his forthcoming book, *Intelligent Enterprise.*

660–61 His special concern . . . "follow them": Aaker, *Managing Brand Equity,* pp. 9, 23, 24, 86.

661–62 "Since the 19th century . . . perceived quality leaders": Bradley Gale, "Power Brands: The Essentials," unpublished paper, November 1991. An adaptation of this paper, entitled "Quality Comes First When Hatching Power Brands," appears in the July–August 1992 issue of *Planning Review.*

663 Professor Hajine Yamashina . . . *Financial Times.* Simon Holberton, "A Japanese View of Competition," *Financial Times,* April 26, 1991, p. 20.

The Economist . . . late 1989: Nicholas Valery, "Thinking Ahead," *The Economist,* December 2, 1989, p. 45.

Chapter 42

667 "It is an illusion . . . types of French people: Theodore Zeldin, *The French* (New York: Pantheon, 1982), pp. 44, 45, 507.

667–69 Three executives from . . . best of circumstances": Clyde W. Burleson, *Interstate Commerce: Regional Styles of Doing Business* (New York: Franklin Watts, 1987), pp. 9–10.

669 "unequal [financial] returns . . . various times": Kenichi Ohmae, "The Global Logic of Strategic Alliances," *Harvard Business Review,* March–April 1989, p. 143.

669–70 In the summer of . . . from these guys!: Paul Cohen, "Thinking Globally: Healthcare Provider Looks to Japan," *On Achieving Excellence,* June 1990, pp. 2–3.

671 "On a train ride back . . . delivered as promised": James Morgan and J. Jeffrey Morgan, *Cracking the Japanese Market: Strategies for Success in the New Global Economy* (New York: Free Press, 1991), pp. 53, 54.

672–73 The 10 points that . . . to move ahead: James Bredin, "Japan Needs to Be Understood," *Industry Week,* April 20, 1992, pp. 24, 26.

page 673–74 A. T. Cross of Lincoln . . . "go overseas first": Ira Magaziner and Mark Patinkin, *The Silent War: Inside the Global Business Battles Shaping America's Future* (New York: Random House, 1989), pp. 171, 172, 174, 176, 181, 182, 185, 186, 188, 192, 198.

675 "Of all the . . . to get it right": "The Unpalatable Key to Global Success," *Management Today,* June 1992, p. 23.

676 "Quality doesn't have . . . to intellectual abstractions": Robert M. Pirsig, *Lila: An Inquiry into Morals* (New York: Bantam, 1991), p. 64.

678–79 "[The two] main types . . . of human needs": Tibor Scitovsky, *The Joyless Economy: An Inquiry into Human Satisfaction and Consumer Dissatisfaction* (New York: Oxford University Press, 1978), pp. viii, 32, 33, 34, 150, 152, 282.

679 In mid-1991, Total Research . . . can be worth billions: Horovitz, Bruce, "Disney Tops Poll of Best Brand Names," *The Los Angeles Times,* July 10, 1991, p. D2.

In the EquiTrend study . . . memorable brand franchise): "Domestic Brands Gain in Battle of Perceptions," *The Wall Street Journal,* July 9, 1991, p. B1.

679–80 "A nice demonstration . . . event that precedes it": Robert B. Cialdini, *Influence: Science and Practice* (New York: HarperCollins, 1988), p. 13.

680 "It is patients who . . . them with kindness": Fredonia French Jacques, *Verdict Pending: A Patient Representative's Intervention* (Garden Grove, CA: Capistrano Press, Ltd., 1983), p. 188.

"Often all one must . . . preferably as much as possible": Lynn Payer, *Medicine & Culture: Varieties of Treatment in the United States, England, West Germany and France* (New York: Henry Holt and Company, 1988), pp. 25, 124.

681–82 *Anchoring.* Experimental subjects . . . (in the most complex case): Daniel Kahneman, Paul Slovic, and Amos Tversky, *Judgment Under Uncertainty: Heuristics and Biases* (New York: Cambridge University Press, 1982), pp. 12, 15, 141, 231, 236, 237, 357.

684 A *San Jose Mercury* . . . is all about: Larry Slonaker, "Airplane 1988: A Disaster Story Wherein Our Intrepid Reporter Does the Unthinkable—Flies 4,600 Miles on (Gasp!) Continental," *West (San Jose Mercury News),* April 24, 1988, p. 6.

686–87 "The J. Peterman catalogue . . . you'll order a set": Hilary Sterne, "Please, Mr. Postman," *GQ,* November 1991, p. 78.

688 "any manufacturer can . . . of the product": David Woodruff, Karen Lowry Miller, Larry Armstrong, and Thane Peterson, "A New Era for Auto Quality: Just as Detroit Is Catching Up, the Very Concept Is Changing," *Business Week,* October 22, 1990, p. 84.

689 "the Six Sigma process" . . . standard of excellence: William Wiggenhorn, "The Language of Quality," *Harvard Business Review,* July–August 1990, p. 74.

690 "Stew Leonard, Jr., tells a story . . . like sweet corn": Michael Barrier, "A New Sense of Service," *Nation's Business,* June 1991, p. 16.

691 a product (baseball . . . equals a *new* product. Gary D. Eppen, Ward Hanson, and R. Kipp Martin, "Bundling—New Products, New Markets, Low Risk," *Sloan Management Review,* p. 82.

page   691–92   *The Wall Street Journal* reported . . . without the correspondence: Jerry E. Bishop, "Technology and Medicine: Doctors Get Results By Sending Letters After Treatments," *The Wall Street Journal,* October 11, 1991, p. B4.

692–93   "Duke Mu of Chin . . . a superlative animal": J. D. Salinger, *Raise High the Roof Beam, Carpenters* (Boston: Little, Brown and Company, 1963), pp. 4–5.

Chapter 44

694–99   "Most of the people I talked to . . . got a slightly higher rating": Wurman with Leifer, *Follow the Yellow Brick Road,* pp. 262–70 *passim.*

Chapter 45

701   "A cultural revolution . . . the 777 program": Paul Betts, "A Revolution on the Runway," *Financial Times,* May 7, 1992, p. 14.

702–03   *"Satisfied* customers remain" . . . at annual employee meetings: David Ulrich, "Tie the Corporate Knot: Gaining Complete Customer Commitment," *Sloan Management Review,* Summer 1989, pp. 19–25 *passim.*

703–05   It's 7:14 A.M. . . . "all the training": David Graulich, "At Home Depot Stores, Training Is by and for the People," *On Achieving Excellence,* June 1988, pp. 2–3.

705   "When [retailer] Paul Hawken . . . of the value added?": Charles Leinbach, "Purchasing the Design of Service," *Design Management Journal,* Winter 1992, p. 48.

706–07   Al Burger won fame . . . "from word of mouth": Darlene Viggiano, "Trust Your Customers, Says Service Star," *On Achieving Excellence,* August 1991, p. 5.

707–08   A Boston-area benefits . . . to 98 percent: Paul Cohen, "Change the Rules of Your Industry's Game with an Ironclad Guarantee," *On Achieving Excellence,* August 1991, pp. 2–3.

710–11   "Customers usually must . . . goes on to deliver it' ": Leonard L. Berry and Kathleen Seiders, "Managing the Evidence in Service Businesses," *Design Management Journal,* Winter 1992, p. 100.

712–13   "You are my hostage. You must obey": Adapted from Ron Zemke with Dick Schaaf, *The Service Edge: 101 Companies That Profit from Customer Care* (New York: New American Library, 1989), p. 145.

714–15   The Forum Corporation has . . . time between failures): Richard C. Whiteley, *The Customer Driven Company: Moving from Talk to Action* (Reading, MA: Addison-Wesley, 1991), pp. 9, 10.

715   Professor Len Berry . . . on the chart: Leonard Berry, A. Parasuranman, and V. Zeithaml, "Understanding Customer Expectations of Service," *Sloan Management Review,* Spring 1991, p. 92.

715–17   Consider MBNA . . . "why defections occur": Frederick F. Reichheld and W. Earl, Sasser, Jr., "Zero Defections: Quality Comes to Services," *Harvard Business Review,* September–October 1990, pp. 106, 107, 108.

page   717–18   database marketing gurus . . . "with each customer": Stan Rapp and Tom Collins, *MaxiMarketing: The New Direction in Advertising, Promotion and Marketing Strategy* (New York: McGraw-Hill, 1987), pp. vii, 50, 51.

718–20   "Darwinian pressure on products . . . done for Nintendo": Stan Rapp and Tom Collins, *The Great American Marketing Turnaround: The Age of the Individual—and How to Profit From It* (Englewood Cliffs, NJ: Prentice-Hall, 1990), pp. 52, 54, 117, 141, 142, 143, 144, 165, 166, 167, 169, 244, 246, 249.

720–21   As an executive . . . with repeat customers: Paul Cohen, "Restaurant's Marketing Plan: Personalized Service," *On Achieving Excellence,* April 1990, p. 5.

721–22   "The biggest complaint . . . nothing to talk about": Peggy Taylor, "Can We Talk?," *New Age Journal,* November–December 1990, p. 33.

722   Ron Zemke reports . . . "like" and "satisfaction": Ron Zemke, "What's Love Got to Do with It?," *Service Edge,* June 1991, p. 8.

Peterson concludes . . . other product.): Letter, dated June 15, 1991, from Robert A. Peterson to Tom Peters.

722–23   "When you're selling . . . chefs once a month": Sara Noble (ed.), *301 Great Management Ideas from America's Most Innovative Small Companies* (Boston: Inc., 1991), p. 144.

Chapter 46

725   "The classic symptom . . . button-packed front panel": Michael Rogers, "The Right Button: Why Machines Are Getting Harder and Harder to Use," *Newsweek,* January 7, 1991, p. 46.

"Design is the key . . . next 20 years": William Mullen, "The Low Side of High Tech," *Chicago Tribune Sunday Magazine,* February 11, 1990, p. 13.

726   Design may offer . . . a design fanatic): Christopher Lorenz, *The Design Dimension: The New Competitive Weapon for Business* (Oxford: Basil Blackwell, 1987).

"At Braun . . . Museum of Modern Art": Alice Rawsthorn, "No frills, no spills," *Financial Times,* July 31, 1991, p. 10.

727–28   The Design Management . . . design's strategic role: *Designing for Product Success: Essays and Cases from the TRIAD Design Exhibit* (Boston: Design Management Institute, 1989).

728–30   Scott Payne told us . . . provider of farm tools: Paul Cohen, "John Deere Runs with a New Design Program," *On Achieving Excellence,* October 1990, pp. 2–3.

730–31   "In the clubby world . . . parity in quality": Adam Bryant, "Breaking Molds for Nissan," *The New York Times,* May 11, 1992, pp. D1, D2.

731   "It is a depressing . . . into the personality": Fitch, Rodney, "Success in Retailing Identities," *Design Management Journal,* Winter 1991, pp. 58, 59, 60.

733   "Nice words . . . customers are happy": Paul Cohen, "Caring Drivers Deliver Prize-winning Customer Service," *On Achieving Excellence,* April 1992, p. 5.

page   734   "Text: 'The Remote Transfer . . . game-show contestant'": "Read It and Weep," *Newsweek,* January 7, 1991, p. 46.

734–36   "Over the years I have fumbled . . . told what to do": Donald A. Norman, *The Psychology of Everyday Things* (New York: Basic Books, Inc., 1988), pp. vii, viii, 2, 35, 94, 144, 145, 151, 152. The paperback edition was published under the title *The Design of Everyday Things* (New York: Doubleday, 1989).

Chapter 47

740   *"Anshin* is the Japanese word . . . and mutual friends": Morgan and Morgan, *Cracking the Japanese Market,* pp. 58–9.

742–43   "The factory of the future" . . . by competing in time: Richard B. Chase and David A. Garvin, "The Service Factory," *Harvard Business Review,* July–August 1989, pp. 61, 62.

748   Just 15 months . . . national training award: Stuart Crainer, "Theatrical Training Techniques Make Museum a Hit," *On Achieving Excellence,* June 1990, p. 6.

750–51   Global retailer Ikea . . . "buy into the concept": Paul Cohen, "Capture the Imagination: Create a Total Customer Experience," *On Achieving Excellence,* March 1992, pp. 6–7.

Afterword

763   "The great freedom . . . again and again": Richard Reeves, "As Times Keep Changing, Spring Still Follows Winter," *International Herald Tribune,* December 6, 1990, p. 5.

Index

Permissions Acknowledgments

Computer Espionage by Clifford Stoll. Copyright © 1989 by Clifford Stoll. Reprinted by permission of Doubleday.

Ebury Press: Excerpts from *Body and Soul* by Anita Roddick with Russell Miller. Copyright © 1991 by The Body Shop International plc and Russell Miller. Reprinted with permission of Ebury Press, London, England.

The Economist: Excerpt from "The Planned and the Damned," *The Economist,* February 18, 1989. Copyright © 1989 by *The Economist.* Reprinted with special permission.

Editor & Publisher: Excerpt from "The New Curmudgeon" by Thomas Winship, *Editor & Publisher,* August 3, 1991. Copyright © 1991 by *Editor & Publisher.*

Enterprise Magazine: Excerpt from "Building Strategy on Technology" by Bill Birchard. Reprinted from *Enterprise Magazine,* Summer 1991. Copyright © by 1991 Digital Equipment Corporation.

Financial Times: Excerpt from "U.S. Retailer All over the Shop," *Financial Times,* by Barbara Durr and Nikki Tait, May 12, 1992. Copyright © 1992 by *Financial Times.*

Forbes: Exerpt from "We Don't Learn from Our Clients, We Learn from Each Other" by John Merwin. Excerpted by permission of *Forbes* magazine, October 19, 1987. Copyright © 1987 by Forbes, Inc.

Fortune: Excerpt from "Make Your Office More Productive" by Ronald Henkoff. Reprinted by permission from *Fortune,* February 25, 1991. Copyright © 1991 by Time Inc.

Franklin Watts: Excerpts from *Interstate Commerce: Regional Styles of Doing Business* by Clyde W. Burleson. Copyright © 1987 by Clyde W. Burleson. Published by Franklin Watts, New York, New York. Reprinted with permission of the author.

The Free Press, a Division of Macmillan, Inc.: Excerpts from *Managing Brand Equity: Capitalizing on the Value of a Brand Name* by David A. Aaker, reprinted with the permission of The Free Press, a Division of Macmillan, Inc. Copyright © 1991 by David A. Aaker. Excerpts from *Competing Against Time: How Time-Based Competition Is Reshaping Global Markets* by George Stalk, Jr., and Thomas M. Holt. Reprinted with the permission of The Free Press, a Division of Macmillan, Inc. Copyright © 1990 by The Free Press. Excerpts from *Cracking the Japanese Market: Strategies for Success in the New Global Economy* by James C. Morgan and J. Jeffrey Morgan. Reprinted with the permission of The Free Press, a Division of Macmillan, Inc. Copyright © 1991 by James C. Morgan and J. Jeffrey Morgan.

GQ: Excerpt from "Please, Mr. Postman" by Hilary Sterne, *GQ,* November 1991. Copyright © 1991 by Gentleman's Quarterly.

The Guidebook Company, Ltd.: Excerpt from *Southwest China Off the Beaten Track* by K. Mark Stevens and George E. Wehrfritz. Copyright © 1988 The Guidebook Company, Ltd.

Harper's Magazine: Excerpts from "Questions of Conquest" by Mario Vargas Llosa. Copyright © 1990 by *Harper's Magazine.* All rights reserved. Reprinted from the December issue by special permission.

Harvard Business Review: Excerpts reprinted by permission of the *Harvard Business Review.* Excerpt from "How Johnsonville Shares Profits on the Basis of Performance" by Ralph Stayer (November–December 1990). Copyright © 1990 by the President and Fellows of Harvard College; all rights reserved. Excerpt from "Managing Without Managers" by Ricardo Semler (September–October 1989). Copyright © 1989 by the President and Fellows of Harvard College; all rights reserved. Excerpts from "Re-engineering Work: Don't Automate, Obliterate" by Michael Hammer (July–August 1990). Copyright © 1990 by the President and Fellows of Harvard College; all rights reserved. Excerpts from "Power Transformers—The Dynamics of Global Coordina-

A Note About the Author

Tom Peters is the co-author of *In Search of Excellence* (with Robert H. Waterman, Jr.) and *A Passion for Excellence* (with Nancy Austin), and the author of *Thriving on Chaos.* Though he is founder and chief (to the extent there is one) of The Tom Peters Group, located in Palo Alto, California, he and his family spend much of their time on a farm in Vermont, thanks to the information technology revolution (the Fax machine).

A Note on the Type

The text of this book was set in a type face called Times Roman, designed by Stanley Morison (1889–1967) for *The Times* (London) and first introduced by that newspaper in 1932.

Among typographers and designers of the twentieth century, Stanley Morison was a strong forming influence—as a typographical advisor to The Monotype Corporation, as a director of two distinguished English publishing houses, and as a writer of sensibility, erudition, and keen practical sense.

Composed, printed, and bound by the Haddon Craftsmen, Inc., Scranton, Pennsylvania

Designed by Cassandra Pappas